The Sampler Bible

Published by

onyourgates.com

6539 Noffke Dr.
Caledonia, Michigan 49316
Marie@onyourgates.com
(616) 893-4880
www.onyourgates.com

The Sampler Bible
By Steven Elzinga B.A.; M.Div and Benjamin Elzinga B.A.; PHD
Copyright 2013 by Onyourgates

All rights reserved. No portion of this publication my be reproduced by any means without prior permission from the publisher: Onyourgates, 6539 Noffke Dr. Caledonia, MI. 49316

The ESV® Bible (The Holy Bible, English Standard Version®) Copyright © 2001 by Crossway, a publishing ministry of Good News Publishers. ESV® Text Edition: 2011. The ESV® text has been reproduced in cooperation with and by permission of Good News Publishers. Unauthorized reproduction of this publication is prohibited. All rights reserved.

THE HOLY BIBLE, NEW INTERNATIONAL VERSION®, NIV® Copyright © 1973, 1978, 1984, 2011 by Biblica, Inc.™ Used by permission. All rights reserved worldwide.

Scripture quotations taken from the New American Standard Bible®, Copyright © 1960, 1962, 1963, 1968, 1971, 1972, 1973, 1975, 1977, 1995 by The Lockman Foundation Used by permission." (www.Lockman.org)

Scripture quotations marked (NLT) are taken from the Holy Bible, New Living Translation, copyright © 1996, 2004, 2007 by Tyndale House Foundation. Used by permission of Tyndale House Publishers, Inc., Carol Stream, Illinois 60188. All rights reserved.

New Revised Standard Version Bible, copyright 1989, Division of Christian Education of the National Council of the Churches of Christ in the United States of America. Use by permission. All rights reserved.

Scripture taken from the New King James Version®. Copyright © 1982 by Thomas Nelson, Inc. Used by permission. All rights reserved.

Scripture taken from the New Century Version®. Copyright © 2005 by Thomas Nelson, Inc. Used by permission. All rights reserved.

Scripture taken from The Expanded Bible. Copyright ©2011 by Thomas Nelson, Inc. Used by permission. All rights reserved.

Scripture taken from The Voice™. Copyright © 2008 by Ecclesia Bible Society. Used by permission. All rights reserved.

Taken from the HOLY BIBLE: EASY-TO-READ VERSION © 2001 by World Bible Translation Center, Inc. and used by permission.

Scripture quotations marked HCSB are taken from the Holman Christian Standard Bible®, Copyright © 1999, 2000, 2002, 2003, 2009 by Holman Bible Publishers. Used by permission.

Scripture taken from the Contemporary English Version © 1991, 1992, 1995 by American Bible Society. Used by Permission.

Scripture taken from GOD'S WORD®, © 1995 God's Word to the Nations. Used by permission of Baker Publishing Group.

Scripture taken from The Message. Copyright © 1993, 1994, 1995, 1996, 2000, 2001, 2002. Used by permission of NavPress Publishing Group.

Scriptures and additional materials quoted are from the Good News Bible © 1994 published by the Bible Societies/HarperCollins Publishers Ltd UK, Good News Bible© American Bible Society 1966, 1971, 1976, 1992. Used with permission.

Scripture taken from the Common English Bible®, CEB® Copyright © 2010, 2011 by Common English Bible.™ Used by permission. All rights reserved worldwide.

Scripture quoted by permission. All scripture quotations, unless otherwise indicated, are taken from the NET Bible® copyright ©1996-2006 by Biblical Studies Press, L.L.C.

Other personalized books in this Bible series:

The 6 Day Bible Tract

The John Bible
(Book of John)

The Luke Bible
(Book of Luke)

The 30 Second Bible

The Jesus Bible

The Sampler Bible

The New Testament Bible
(NIV, KJV, KJV+)

All of these Bibles can be printed with your cover, your info, and a unique message for your unique church or ministry.

What is the Sampler Bible and why should you bother reading it?

Although the Bible has been the best-selling book every year in a row since the invention of the printing press (a 500 year run), it often sits on shelves ... unread.

Why?

1. It is a big book. Actually, it is a compilation of 66 books. It would take the average reader about 100 hours to read the Bible from cover to cover.

2. It is a confusing book. It was written by more that 40 authors over a period of 1500 years in three different languages of events that took place in several different countries. No wonder it can leave you scratching your head.

3. It is an old book—often hard to relate to. The Bible times and modern times don't always match up.

4. It is boring, or it can be. So many names and places that you can't even pronounce let alone keep track of.

5. It is a complicated book. Where do you even begin reading it? The beginning? The Psalms? Proverbs? The Gospels? The book of Romans? Every Bible believing Christian seems to have a different opinion about it.

6. It is a disturbing book. War. Death. Miracles. Sacrifice. Betrayal. Eternity. Hell. Heaven. Love. Joy. Peace. Hope.

So how can the Sampler Bible help you overcome some of these stumbling blocks?

1. It is relatively small. At 1/4 the size of the full Bible, it only would take the average person 25 hours to read.

2. It is understandable. Care was exercised in choosing the main events for the Sampler Bible, and notes on the side help explain what might be difficult to figure out.

3. It is surprisingly relevant. Again, because the Sampler Bible is only the highlights of the full Bible, it contains events and issues of the Bible that are easy to relate to with your life.

4. It is interesting. Not only does the Sampler Bible give you the most interesting samples of each book of the Bible, but it also gives you samples of the most popular versions (translations) of the Bible (19 different versions were used in the Sampler Bible).

5. It is straightforward. Since the Sampler Bible is only the highlights of the full Bible, you can just start reading it from the beginning—just like any book you might read.

6. It could be life-changing. The words found in the Sampler Bible have influenced so much: architecture, philosophy, art, history, science, literature, and most importantly, lives.

This is the Sampler Bible!

Steve Elzinga is the Senior Pastor of Pathway Church in Grand Rapids, Michigan. He is the founder of Onyourgates—a ministry that provides personalized, Bible-based evangelism products so that churches and Christian organizations can reach out in a personalized way to their own communities.

Part 1: Old Testament

The 5 Books of Moses
Genesis	9	Numbers	72
Exodus	48	Deuteronomy	77
Leviticus	66		

The 12 Historical Books
Joshua	81	1,2 Chronicles	139
Judges	89	Ezra	140
Ruth	94	Nehemiah	144
1,2 Samuel	99	Esther	148
1,2 Kings	119		

The 5 Poetic Books
Job	156	Ecclesiastes	182
Psalms	166	Song of Songs	188
Proverbs	175		

The 5 Major Prophets
Isaiah	192	Ezekiel	208
Jeremiah	200	Daniel	213
Lamentations	206		

The 12 Minor Prophets
Hosea	219	Nahum	233
Joel	222	Habakkuk	234
Amos	224	Zephaniah	235
Obadiah	226	Haggai	236
Jonah	227	Zechariah	238
Micah	231	Malachi	241

The 4 Gospels - Matthew, Mark, Luke, John

Part 1: the Coming of Jesus	245
Part 2: The Teaching Ministry of Jesus	
Event Based	251
His Sayings	257
The 7 "I am" Sayings	262
Other Sayings	266
Parables	268
Part 3: The Miracles of Jesus	275
Part 4: The Plot to Kill Jesus	280
Part 5: The Death of Jesus	288
The 7 Words of the Cross	289
The Story Continues ...	290
Part 6: The Resurrection of Jesus	291
Part 7: The Great Commission of Jesus	296

The Book of Acts   297

The Letters

Romans	331	Titus	376
1,2 Corinthians	341	Philemon	378
Galatians	352	Hebrews	380
Ephesians	357	James	384
Philippians	362	1,2 Peter	386
Colossians	366	1,2,3 John	390
1, 2 Thessalonians	369	Jude	393
1,2 Timothy	372		

The Book of Revelation   394

Part One:
The Old Testament

the book of Genesis

Category: *The 5 Books of Moses*
Author: *Moses*
Theme: *Beginnings*
Location & Date: *Middle East*
Bible Version: *English Standard Version (ESV)*
Summary: *The book of Genesis is the story of how things "began" (that is what Genesis means). How the world began. How sin came into the world. How God responded with a plan of salvation that began through a couple—Abraham and Sarah. Genesis tells of the generations that follow: Isaac and Rebekah, Jacob and Rachel, Leah, Bilhah (Jacob had 4 wives). Then follows the dramatic story of Joseph and his brothers. The book unexpectedly ends with the 12 brothers and their families stuck in Egypt.*

The Creation of the World

Genesis 1:1 **In the beginning**, God created the heavens and the earth. 2 The earth was without form and void, and darkness was over the face of the deep. And the Spirit of God was hovering over the face of the waters.

See John 1, pg. 245.

3 And God said, "Let there be **light**," and there was light. 4 And God saw that the light was good. And God separated the light from the darkness. 5 God called the light Day, and the darkness he called Night. And there was evening and there was morning, the first day.

Day 1: Light

6 And God said, "Let there be an expanse in the midst of the waters, and let it separate the waters from the waters." 7 And God made the expanse and separated the waters that were under the expanse from the waters that were above the expanse. And it was so. 8 And God called the expanse **Heaven**. And there was evening and there was morning, the second day.

9 And God said, "Let the waters under the heavens be gathered together into one place, and let the dry land appear." And it was so. 10 God called the dry land Earth, and the waters that were gathered together he called **Seas**. And God saw that it was good.

Day 2: Sky and Sea

11 And God said, "Let the earth sprout **vegetation**, **plants** yielding seed, and fruit trees bearing fruit in which is their seed, each according to its kind, on the earth." And it was so. 12 The earth brought forth vegetation, plants yielding seed according to their own kinds, and trees bearing fruit in which is their seed, each according to its kind. And God saw that it was good. 13 And there was evening and there was morning, the third day.

Day 3: Plants and Vegetation

> Day 4: The sun and moon fill or rule over the light that was made on the 1st day.

14 And God said, "Let there be lights in the expanse of the heavens to separate the day from the night. And let them be for signs and for seasons, and for days and years, 15 and let them be lights in the expanse of the heavens to give light upon the earth." And it was so. 16 And God made the **two great lights**—the greater light to rule the day and the lesser light to rule the night—and the stars. 17 And God set them in the expanse of the heavens to give light on the earth, 18 to rule over the day and over the night, and to separate the light from the darkness. And God saw that it was good. 19 And there was evening and there was morning, the fourth day.

> Day 5: The birds and fish fill the sky and the sea that was made on the 2nd day.

20 And God said, "Let the waters swarm with swarms of living creatures, and let birds fly above the earth across the expanse of the heavens." 21 So God created the great **sea creatures** and every living creature that moves, with which the waters swarm, according to their kinds, and every winged bird according to its kind. And God saw that it was good. 22 And God blessed them, saying, "Be fruitful and multiply and fill the waters in the seas, and let **birds** multiply on the earth." 23 And there was evening and there was morning, the fifth day.

> Day 6: The animals fill or complete the land that was made on the 3rd day.

24 And God said, "Let the earth bring forth living creatures according to their kinds—**livestock** and **creeping things** and **beasts of the earth** according to their kinds." And it was so. 25 And God made the beasts of the earth according to their kinds and the livestock according to their kinds, and everything that creeps on the ground according to its kind. And God saw that it was good.

26 Then God said, "Let us make man in our image, after our likeness. And let them have dominion over the fish of the sea and over the birds of the heavens and over the livestock and over all the earth and over every creeping thing that creeps on the earth."

> The last to be created is humankind-filling, subduing, benefiting from all of creation. You, as a human being, are the crown of creation. Do you feel like that?

27 So **God created man in his own image, in the image of God he created him; male and female he created them.**

28 And God blessed them. And God said to them, **"Be fruitful and multiply and fill the earth and subdue it, and have dominion over the fish of the sea and over the birds of the heavens and over every living thing that moves on the earth."** 29 And God said, "Behold, I have given you every plant yielding seed that is on the face of all the earth, and every tree with seed in its fruit. You shall have them for food. 30 And to every beast of the earth and to every bird of the heavens and to everything that creeps on the earth, everything that has the breath of life, I have given every green plant for food." And it was so. 31 And God saw everything that he had made, and behold, it was very good. And there was evening and there was morning, the sixth day.

The Seventh Day, God Rests

2:2 Thus the heavens and the earth were finished, and all the host of them. 2 And on the seventh day God finished his work that he had done, and he rested on the seventh day from all his work that he had done. 3 So God blessed the seventh day and made it holy, because on it God rested from all his work that he had done in creation.

The Creation of Man and Woman

7 ... then the Lord God formed the man of dust from the ground and breathed into his nostrils the breath of life, and the man became a living creature. 8 And the Lord God planted a garden in Eden, in the east, and there he put the man whom he had formed. 9 And out of the ground the Lord God made to spring up every tree that is pleasant to the sight and good for food. The tree of life was in the **midst** of the garden, **and the tree of the knowledge of good and evil.**

15 The LORD God took the man and put him in the garden of Eden to work it and keep it. 16 And the LORD God commanded the man, saying, "You may surely eat of every tree of the garden, 17 but of the **tree of the knowledge of good and evil you shall not eat, for in the day that you eat of it you shall surely die.**"

18 Then the LORD God said, "It is **not good that the man should be alone**; I will make him a helper fit for him." 19 Now out of the ground the LORD God had formed every beast of the field and every bird of the heavens and brought them to the man to see what he would call them. And whatever the man called every living creature, that was its name. 20 The man gave names to all livestock and to the birds of the heavens and to every beast of the field. But for Adam there was not found a helper fit for him. 21 So the LORD God caused a deep sleep to fall upon the man, and while he slept took one of his ribs and closed up its place with flesh. 22 And the rib that the LORD God had taken from the man he made into a woman and brought her to the man. 23 Then the man said,

"This at last is bone of my bones and flesh of my flesh; she shall be called **Woman, because she was taken out of Man.**"

24 Therefore a man shall leave his father and his mother and hold fast to his wife, and they shall become one flesh. 25 And the man and his wife were both naked and were not ashamed.

The Fall

3:1 Now the **serpent** was more **crafty** than any other beast of the field that the LORD God had made.

He said to the woman, **"Did God actually say, 'You shall not eat of any tree in the garden'?"** 2 And the woman said to the serpent, "We may eat of the fruit of the trees in the garden, 3 but God said, 'You shall not eat of the fruit of the tree that is in the midst of the garden, neither shall you touch it, lest you die.'" 4 But the serpent said to the woman, **"You will not surely die.** 5 For God knows that when you eat of it your eyes will be opened, and you will be like God, knowing good and evil." 6 So when the woman saw that the tree was good for food, and that it was a delight to the eyes, and that the tree was to be desired to make one wise, she took of its fruit and ate, and she also gave some to her husband who was with her, and he ate. 7 **Then the eyes of both were opened, and they knew that they were naked. And they sewed fig leaves together and made themselves loincloths.**

8 And they heard the sound of the LORD God walking in the garden in the cool of the day, and the man and his wife hid them-

---

A "test" is placed in the middle of the garden... meaning Adam and Eve had to pass that way no matter where they went in the garden.

Each day of creation God declared good. But now it is "not good." It will take a woman to make creation good.

The first woman came from a man, but every man since has come from a woman.

The serpent/devil uses lies:
1. Bend the truth.
2. Break the truth.

Two things happen after Adam and Eve sin:
1. They hide from the each other in their nakedness.

The 5 Books of Moses

2. They hide from God when He comes around.

selves from the presence of the LORD God among the trees of the garden. 9 But the **LORD God called** to the man and said to him, "Where are you?" 10 And he said, "I heard the sound of you in the garden, and I was afraid, because I was naked, and **I hid** myself." 11 He said, "Who told you that you were naked? Have you eaten of the tree of which I commanded you not to eat?" 12 The man said, "The woman whom you gave to be with me, she gave me fruit of the tree, and I ate." 13 Then the LORD God said to the woman, "What is this that you have done?" The woman said, "The serpent deceived me, and I ate."

14 The LORD God said to the serpent, "Because you have done this, cursed are you above all livestock and above all beasts of the field; on your belly you shall go, and dust you shall eat all the days of your life. 15 I will put enmity between you (the Devil) and the woman (Eve), and between your offspring (the host of Hell) and her offspring (all of humankind); he (this is Jesus) shall bruise your (the Devils) head, and you (the Devil) shall bruise (the cross) his (Jesus) heel."

Pain is a result of the shame, insecurity, and fear we have as we hide from God and the people in our life.

16 To the woman he said, "I will surely multiply your **pain** in childbearing; in **pain** you shall bring forth children. Your desire shall be for your husband, and he shall rule over you."

17 And to Adam he said, "Because you have listened to the voice of your wife and have eaten of the tree of which I commanded you, 'You shall not eat of it,' cursed is the ground because of you; in **pain** you shall eat of it all the days of your life; 18 thorns and thistles it shall bring forth for you; and you shall eat the plants of the field. 19 By the sweat of your face you shall eat bread, till you return to the ground, for out of it you were taken; for you are dust, and to dust you shall return."

But God will not leave you alone in your fear, insecurity and nakedness.

We need to find a way to the tree of life. (Hint: Jesus)

20 The man called his wife's name Eve, because she was the mother of all living. 21 And the LORD **God made for Adam and for his wife garments of skins and clothed them.**

22 Then the LORD God said, "Behold, the man has become like one of us in knowing good and evil. Now, lest he reach out his hand and take also of the tree of life and eat, and live forever—" 23 therefore the LORD God sent him out from the garden of Eden to work the ground from which he was taken. 24 He drove out the man, and at the east of the garden of Eden he placed the cherubim and a flaming sword that turned every way to guard the way to the **tree of life.**

Cain and Abel

Apparently his offering was not given for the right reasons.

4:1 Now Adam knew Eve his wife, and she conceived and bore Cain. 2 And again, she bore his brother Abel. Now Abel was a keeper of sheep, and Cain a worker of the ground. 3 In the course of time Cain brought to the LORD an offering of the fruit of the ground, 4 and Abel also brought of the firstborn of his flock and of their fat portions. And the LORD had regard for Abel and his offering, 5 but **for Cain and his offering he had no regard.** So Cain was very angry, and his face fell. 6 The LORD said to Cain, "Why are you angry, and why has your face fallen? 7 If you do well, will you not be accepted? And if you do not do well, **sin is crouching at the door. Its desire is for you**, but you must rule over it."

8 Cain spoke to Abel his brother. And when they were in the field, Cain rose up against his brother Abel and killed him. 9 Then the LORD said to Cain, "Where is Abel your brother?" He said, "I do not know; **am I my brother's keeper?**" 10 And the LORD said, "What have you done? The voice of your brother's blood is crying to me from the ground. 11 And now you are cursed from the ground, which has opened its mouth to receive your brother's blood from your hand. 12 When you work the ground, it shall no longer yield to you its strength. You shall be a fugitive and a wanderer on the earth." 13 Cain said to the LORD, "My punishment is greater than I can bear. 14 Behold, you have driven me today away from the ground, and from your face I shall be hidden. I shall be a fugitive and a wanderer on the earth, and whoever finds me will kill me." 15 Then the LORD said to him, "Not so! If anyone kills Cain, vengeance shall be taken on him sevenfold." And the LORD put a mark on Cain, lest any who found him should attack him. 16 Then Cain went away from the presence of the LORD and settled in the land of Nod, east of Eden.

25 And Adam knew his wife again, and she bore a son and called his name Seth, for she said, "God has appointed for me another offspring instead of Abel, for Cain killed him." 26 To Seth also a son was born, and he called his name Enosh. At that time people began to call upon the name of the LORD.

Adam's Descendants to Noah

5:1 This is the book of the generations of Adam. When God created man, he made him in the likeness of God. 2 Male and female he created them, and he blessed them and named them Man when they were created. 3 When Adam had lived 130 years, he fathered a son in his own likeness, after his image, and named him Seth ...

Increasing Corruption on Earth

6:1 When man began to multiply on the face of the land and daughters were born to them ...

5 The LORD saw that the **wickedness of man** was great in the earth, and that every intention of the thoughts of his heart was only evil continually. 6 And the LORD regretted that he had made man on the earth, and it grieved him to his heart. 7 So the LORD said, "I will blot out man whom I have created from the face of the land, man and animals and creeping things and birds of the heavens, for I am sorry that I have made them." 8 But Noah found favor in the eyes of the LORD.

11 Now the earth was corrupt in God's sight, and the earth was filled with violence. 13 And God said to Noah, "I have determined to make an end of all flesh .... 14 Make yourself an ark ....

17 For behold, I will bring a flood of waters upon the earth to destroy all flesh in which is the breath of life under heaven. Ev-

---

An interesting description of sin.

Yes you are. Who is your brother or sister?

The first murder in recorded history is one brother killing another. Why do you think Cain killed his brother?

The rest of chapter 5 tells of the 7 generations that follow Adam and Eve leading up to Noah.

Things haven't changed much.

The 5 Books of Moses

A covenant is a promise agreement.

erything that is on the earth shall die. 18 But I will establish my **covenant** with you, and you shall come into the ark, you, your sons, your wife, and your sons' wives with you. 19 And of every living thing of all flesh, you shall bring two of every sort into the ark to keep them alive with you. They shall be male and female. 20 Of the birds according to their kinds, and of the animals according to their kinds, of every creeping thing of the ground, according to its kind, two of every sort shall come in to you to keep them alive.

22 Noah did this; he did all that God commanded him.

7:1 Then the LORD said to Noah, "Go into the ark, you and all your household, for I have seen that you are righteous before me in this generation.

Jesus was in the desert without food for 40 days and 40 nights. See Mark 1:13; pg. 244.

4 For in seven days I will send rain on the earth **forty days and forty nights**, and every living thing that I have made I will blot out from the face of the ground." 5 And Noah did all that the Lord had commanded him.

11 In the six hundredth year of Noah's life, in the second month, on the seventeenth day of the month, on that day all the fountains of the great deep burst forth, and the windows of the heavens were opened. 12 And rain fell upon the earth forty days and forty nights. 13 On the very same day Noah and his sons, Shem and Ham and Japheth, and Noah's wife and the three wives of his sons with them entered the ark, 14 they and every beast, according to its kind, and all the livestock according to their kinds, and every creeping thing that creeps on the earth, according to its kind, and every bird, according to its kind, every winged creature. 15 They went into the ark with Noah, two and two of all flesh in which there was the breath of life. 16 And those that entered, male and female of all flesh, went in as God had commanded him. And the LORD shut him in.

17 The flood continued forty days on the earth. The waters increased and bore up the ark, and it rose high above the earth. 18 The waters prevailed and increased greatly on the earth, and the ark floated on the face of the waters. 19 And the waters prevailed so mightily on the earth that all the high mountains under the whole heaven were covered.

23 He blotted out every living thing that was on the face of the ground, man and animals and creeping things and birds of the heavens. They were blotted out from the earth. Only Noah was left, and those who were with him in the ark. 24 And the waters prevailed on the earth 150 days.

The Flood Subsides

8:1 But God remembered Noah and all the beasts and all the livestock that were with him in the ark. And God made a wind blow over the earth, and the waters subsided. 2 The fountains of the deep and the windows of the heavens were closed, the rain from the heavens was restrained, 3 and the waters receded from the earth continually. At the end of 150 days the waters had abated, 4 and in the seventh month, on the seventeenth day of the month, the ark came to rest on the mountains of Ararat. 5 And the waters continued to abate until the tenth month; in the tenth month, on the first day of the month, the tops of the mountains were seen.

6 At the end of forty days Noah opened the window of the ark that he had made 7 and sent forth a **raven**. It went to and fro until the waters were dried up from the earth. 8 Then he sent forth a dove from him, to see if the waters had subsided from the face of the ground. 9 But the dove found no place to set her foot, and she returned to him to the ark, for the waters were still on the face of the whole earth. So he put out his hand and took her and brought her into the ark with him. 10 He waited another seven days, and again he sent forth the **dove** out of the ark. 11 And the dove came back to him in the evening, and behold, in her mouth was a freshly plucked olive leaf. So Noah knew that the waters had subsided from the earth. 12 Then he waited another seven days and sent forth the dove, and she did not return to him anymore.

13 In the six hundred and first year, in the first month, the first day of the month, the waters were dried from off the earth. And Noah removed the covering of the ark and looked, and behold, the face of the ground was dry.

15 Then God said to Noah, 16 "Go out from the ark, you and your wife, and your sons and your sons' wives with you. 17 Bring out with you every living thing that is with you of all flesh - birds and animals and every creeping thing that creeps on the earth - that they may swarm on the earth, and be fruitful and multiply on the earth."

God's Covenant with Noah

20 Then Noah built an altar to the LORD and took some of every clean animal and some of every clean bird and offered burnt offerings on the altar. 21 And when the LORD smelled the pleasing aroma, the LORD said in his heart, "I will never again curse the ground because of man, for the intention of man's heart is evil from his youth. Neither will I ever again strike down every living creature as I have done. 22 While the earth remains, seedtime and harvest, cold and heat, summer and winter, day and night, shall not cease."

9:1 And God blessed Noah and his sons and said to them, **"Be fruitful and multiply and fill the earth."**

8 Then God said to Noah and to his sons with him, 9 "Behold, I establish my covenant with you and your offspring after you, 10 and with every living creature that is with you, the birds, the livestock, and every beast of the earth with you, as many as came out of the **ark**; it is for every beast of the earth. 11 I establish my covenant with you, that never again shall all flesh be cut off by the waters of the flood, and never again shall there be a flood to destroy the earth." 12 And God said, "This is the sign of the covenant that I make between me and you and every living creature that is with you, for all future generations: 13 I have set my **bow** in the cloud, and it shall be a sign of the covenant between me and the earth. 14 When I bring clouds over the earth and the bow is seen in the clouds, 15 I will remember my covenant that

---

God used a raven to save the prophet Elijah many years later. Elijah becomes a symbol of the coming of the Messiah, Jesus. See 1 Kings 17:4; pg. 117.

When Jesus was baptized the Holy Spirit descended on Him ... in the form of a dove. See Mark 1:10; pg. 250.

This same command was given to Adam and Eve in Genesis 1:2.

God used an ark. In our day God uses the church. How is the church like an ark?

The sign of the rainbow- Did you ever

> take note which way the bow is pointed? Up. God is saying, "Cross my heart and hope to die if I am not telling the truth."

is between me and you and every living creature of all flesh. And the waters shall never again become a flood to destroy all flesh. 16 When the bow is in the clouds, I will see it and remember the everlasting covenant between God and every living creature of all flesh that is on the earth." 17 God said to Noah, "This is the sign of the covenant that I have established between me and all flesh that is on the earth."

28 After the flood Noah lived 350 years. 29 All the days of Noah were 950 years, and he died.

The Tower of Babel

11:1 Now the whole earth had one language and the same words. 2 And as people migrated from the east, they found a plain in the land of Shinar and settled there. 4 Then they said, "Come, let us build ourselves a city and a tower with its top in the heavens, and let us make a name for ourselves, lest we be dispersed over the face of the whole earth."

5 And the LORD came down to see the city and the tower, which the children of man had built. 6 And the LORD said, "Behold, they are one people, and they have all one language, and this is only the beginning of what they will do. And nothing that they propose to do will now be impossible for them. 7 Come, let us go down and there **confuse their language**, so that they may not understand one another's speech." 8 So the LORD dispersed them from there over the face of all the earth, and they left off building the city. 9 Therefore its name was called Babel, because there the LORD confused the language of all the earth. And from there the LORD dispersed them over the face of all the earth.

> This was reversed many years later with the coming of the Holy Spirit. See Acts 2, pg. 298.

Shem's Descendants

10 These are the **generations of Shem**. When Shem was 100 years old, he fathered Arpachshad two years after the flood...

26 When **Terah** had lived 70 years, he fathered Abram, Nahor, and Haran.

> Verses 11-26 list the ten generations of Shem ending with Terah who is the father of Abraham.

Terah's Descendants

27 Now these are the generations of **Terah**. Terah fathered Abram, Nahor, and Haran; and Haran fathered Lot. 28 Haran died in the presence of his father Terah in the land of his kindred, in Ur of the Chaldeans. 29 And Abram and Nahor took wives. The name of Abram's wife was Sarai, and the name of Nahor's wife, Milcah, the daughter of Haran the father of Milcah and Iscah. 30 Now Sarai was barren; she had no child.

> Lot is the nephew of Abram, both of whose story will now be told.

31 Terah took Abram his son and **Lot** the son of Haran, his grandson, and Sarai his daughter-in-law, his son Abram's wife, and they went forth together from Ur of the Chaldeans to go into the land of Canaan, but when they came to Haran, they settled there. 32 The days of Terah were 205 years, and Terah died in Haran.

The Call of Abram

12:1 Now the LORD said to Abram, "**Go from** your country and your kindred and your father's house to the land that I will show you. 2 And I will make of you a great nation, and I will bless you and make your name great, so that you will be a blessing. 3 I will bless those who bless you, and him who dishonors you I will curse, and in you all the families of the earth shall be blessed."

4 So Abram went, as the LORD had told him, and Lot went with him. Abram was seventy-five years old when he departed from Haran. 5 And Abram took Sarai his wife, and Lot his brother's son, and all their possessions that they had gathered, and the people that they had acquired in Haran, and they set out to go to the land of Canaan.

God's Covenant with Abram

15:1 After these things the word of the LORD came to Abram in a vision: "Fear not, Abram, I am your shield; your reward shall be very great." 2 But Abram said, "O Lord GOD, what will you give me, for I continue childless, and the heir of my house is Eliezer of Damascus?"

5 And he brought him outside and said, "Look toward heaven, and number the stars, if you are able to number them." Then he said to him, "So shall your offspring be." 6 And he believed the LORD, and he counted it to him as righteousness.

7 And he said to him, "I am the LORD who brought you out from Ur of the Chaldeans to give you this land to possess." 8 But he said, "O Lord GOD, **how am I to know that I shall possess it?**"

Sarai and Hagar

16:1 Now Sarai, Abram's wife, had borne him no children. She had a female Egyptian servant whose name was **Hagar**.

Abraham and the Covenant of Circumcision

17:1 When Abram was ninety-nine years old the LORD appeared to Abram and said to him, "I am God Almighty; walk before me, and be blameless, 2 that I may make my covenant between me and you, and may multiply you greatly." 3 Then Abram fell on his face. And God said to him, 4 "Behold, my covenant is with you, and you shall be the father of a multitude of nations. 5 No longer shall your name be called Abram, but your name shall be **Abraham**, for I have made you the father of a multitude of nations. 6 I will make you exceedingly fruitful, and I will make you into nations, and kings shall come from you. 7 And I will establish my covenant between me and you and your offspring after you throughout their generations for an everlasting covenant, to be God to you and to your offspring after you. 8 And I will give to you and to your offspring after you the land of your sojournings, all the land of Canaan, for an everlasting possession, and I will be their God."

9 And God said to Abraham, "As for you, you shall keep my covenant, you and your offspring after you throughout their gener-

---

It takes faith to step out from what you know to go to what you do not know. When have you exercised this kind of faith?

God answers His question with a sign that says, "Just trust me."

Sarai convinces Abram to have a son (Ishmael) with Hagar, but he is not the promised one.

This same Abraham became the patriarch of 3 different religions: Judaism, Islam, and Christianity.

> *A sign that Abraham and his future offspring belong to God.*

ations. 10 This is my covenant, which you shall keep, between me and you and your offspring after you: Every male among you shall be **circumcised**. 11 You shall be circumcised in the flesh of your foreskins, and it shall be a sign of the covenant between me and you. 12 He who is eight days old among you shall be circumcised.

Isaac's Birth Promised

15 And God said to Abraham, "As for Sarai your wife, you shall not call her name Sarai, but Sarah shall be her name. 16 I will bless her, and moreover, I will give you a son by her. I will bless her, and she shall become nations; kings of peoples shall come from her." 17 Then Abraham fell on his face and laughed and said to himself, "Shall a child be born to a man who is a hundred years old? Shall Sarah, who is ninety years old, bear a child?" 18 And Abraham said to God, "Oh that **Ishmael** might live before you!" 19 God said, "No, but Sarah your wife shall bear you a son, and you shall call his name Isaac. I will establish my covenant with him as an everlasting covenant for his offspring after him. 20 As for Ishmael, I have heard you; behold, I have blessed him and will make him fruitful and multiply him greatly. He shall father twelve princes, and I will make him into a great nation. 21 But I will establish my covenant with Isaac, whom Sarah shall bear to you at this time next year."

> *According to Islam, Ishmael becomes the chosen one, not Isaac.*

22 When he had finished talking with him, God went up from Abraham. 23 Then Abraham took Ishmael his son and all those born in his house or bought with his money, every male among the men of Abraham's house, and he circumcised the flesh of their foreskins that very day, as God had said to him. 24 Abraham was ninety-nine years old when he was circumcised in the flesh of his foreskin.

18:1 And the LORD appeared to him by the oaks of Mamre, as he sat at the door of his tent in the heat of the day. 2 He lifted up his eyes and looked, and behold, three men were standing in front of him. When he saw them, he ran from the tent door to meet them and bowed himself to the earth 3 and said, "O Lord, if I have found favor in your sight, do not pass by your servant. 4 Let a little water be brought, and wash your feet, and rest yourselves under the tree, 5 while I bring a morsel of bread, that you may refresh yourselves, and after that you may pass on—since you have come to your servant." So they said, "Do as you have said." 6 And Abraham went quickly into the tent to Sarah and said, "Quick! Three seahs of fine flour! Knead it, and make cakes." 7 And Abraham ran to the herd and took a calf, tender and good, and gave it to a young man, who prepared it quickly. 8 Then he took curds and milk and the calf that he had prepared, and set it before them. And he stood by them under the tree while they ate.

9 They said to him, "Where is Sarah your wife?" And he said, "She is in the tent." 10 The LORD said, "I will surely return to you about this time next year, and Sarah your wife shall have a son." And Sarah was listening at the tent door behind him. 11 Now Abraham and Sarah were old, advanced in years. The way of women had ceased to be with Sarah. 12 So Sarah laughed to

herself, saying, "After I am worn out, and my lord is old, shall I have pleasure?" 13 The LORD said to Abraham, "Why did Sarah laugh and say, 'Shall I indeed bear a child, now that I am old?' 14 **Is anything too hard for the LORD?** At the appointed time I will return to you, about this time next year, and Sarah shall have a son."

16 Then the men set out from there, and they looked down toward Sodom. And Abraham went with them to set them on their way. 17 The LORD said, "Shall I hide from Abraham what I am about to do, 18 seeing that Abraham shall surely become a great and mighty nation, and all the nations of the earth shall be blessed in him? 19 For I have chosen him, that he may command his children and his household after him to keep the way of the LORD by doing righteousness and justice, so that the LORD may bring to Abraham what he has promised him." 20 Then the LORD said, "Because the outcry against Sodom and Gomorrah is great and their sin is very grave, 21 I will go down to see whether they have done altogether according to the outcry that has come to me. And if not, I will know."

Abraham Intercedes for Sodom

22 So the men turned from there and went toward Sodom, but Abraham still stood before the LORD. 23 Then Abraham drew near and said, "Will you indeed sweep away the righteous with the wicked? 24 Suppose there are fifty righteous within the city. Will you then sweep away the place and not spare it for the fifty righteous who are in it? 25 Far be it from you to do such a thing, to put the righteous to death with the wicked, so that the righteous fare as the wicked! Far be that from you! **Shall not the Judge of all the earth do what is just?**" 26 And the LORD said, "If I find at Sodom fifty righteous in the city, I will spare the whole place for their sake."

27 Abraham answered and said, "Behold, I have undertaken to speak to the Lord, I who am but dust and ashes. 28 Suppose five of the fifty righteous are lacking. Will you destroy the whole city for lack of five?" And he said, "I will not destroy it if I find forty-five there." 29 Again he spoke to him and said, "Suppose forty are found there." He answered, "For the sake of forty I will not do it." 30 Then he said, "Oh let not the Lord be angry, and I will speak. Suppose thirty are found there." He answered, "I will not do it, if I find thirty there." 31 He said, "Behold, I have undertaken to speak to the Lord. Suppose twenty are found there." He answered, "For the sake of twenty I will not destroy it." 32 Then he said, "Oh let not the Lord be angry, and I will speak again but this once. Suppose ten are found there." He answered, **"For the sake of ten I will not destroy it."** 33 And the LORD went his way, when he had finished speaking to Abraham, and Abraham returned to his place.

God Rescues Lot

19:1 The two angels came to Sodom in the evening, and Lot was sitting in the gate of Sodom. When Lot saw them, he rose to meet them and bowed himself with his face to the earth 2 and said, "My lords, please turn aside to your servant's house and spend the night and wash your feet. Then you may rise up early

---

Mary the mother of Jesus had the same conversation with an angel in Luke 1:26-38, pg. 248.

What hard thing are you facing these days? Whatever it is, bring it to the Lord.

God plans on destroying Sodom. Abraham knows his nephew lives there, so he negotiates with God for Sodom.

The sad thing was that there weren't even 10 righteous.

and go on your way." They said, "No; we will spend the night in the town square." 3 But he pressed them strongly; so they turned aside to him and entered his house. And he made them a feast and baked unleavened bread, and they ate.

> *Why do we linger in doing the right thing?*

15 As morning dawned, the angels urged Lot, saying, "Up! Take your wife and your two daughters who are here, lest you be swept away in the punishment of the city." 16 **But he lingered.** So the men seized him and his wife and his two daughters by the hand, the LORD being merciful to him, and they brought him out and set him outside the city. 17 And as they brought them out, one said, "Escape for your life. Do not look back or stop anywhere in the valley. Escape to the hills, lest you be swept away." 18 And Lot said to them, "Oh, no, my lords. 19 Behold, your servant has found favor in your sight, and you have shown me great kindness in saving my life. But I cannot escape to the hills, lest the disaster overtake me and I die. 20 Behold, this city is near enough to flee to, and it is a little one. Let me escape there—is it not a little one?—and my life will be saved!" 21 He said to him, "Behold, I grant you this favor also, that I will not overthrow the city of which you have spoken. 22 Escape there quickly, for I can do nothing till you arrive there." Therefore the name of the city was called Zoar.

God Destroys Sodom

23 The sun had risen on the earth when Lot came to Zoar. 24 Then the LORD rained on Sodom and Gomorrah sulfur and fire from the LORD out of heaven. 25 And he overthrew those cities, and all the valley, and all the inhabitants of the cities, and what grew on the ground. 26 But Lot's wife, behind him, looked back, and she became a pillar of salt.

27 And Abraham went early in the morning to the place where he had stood before the LORD. 28 And he looked down toward Sodom and Gomorrah and toward all the land of the valley, and he looked and, behold, the smoke of the land went up like the smoke of a furnace.

29 So it was that, when God destroyed the cities of the valley, God remembered Abraham and sent Lot out of the midst of the overthrow when he overthrew the cities in which Lot had lived.

The Birth of Isaac

21:1 The LORD visited Sarah as he had said, and the LORD did to Sarah as he had promised. 2 And Sarah conceived and bore Abraham a son in his old age at the time of which God had spoken to him. 3 Abraham called the name of his son who was born to him, whom Sarah bore him, Isaac. 4 And Abraham circumcised his son Isaac when he was eight days old, as God had commanded him. 5 Abraham was a hundred years old when his son Isaac was born to him. 6 And Sarah said, "God has made laughter for me; everyone who hears will laugh over me." 7 And she said, "Who would have said to Abraham that Sarah would nurse children? Yet I have borne him a son in his old age." 8 And the child grew and was weaned. And Abraham made a great feast on the day that

Isaac was weaned.

The Sacrifice of Isaac

22:1 After these things God tested Abraham and said to him, "Abraham!" And he said, "Here I am." 2 He said, "Take your son, your **only son** Isaac, whom you love, and go to the land of Moriah, and offer him there as a burnt offering on one of the mountains of which I shall tell you." 3 So Abraham rose early in the morning, saddled his donkey, and took two of his young men with him, and his son Isaac. And he cut the wood for the burnt offering and arose and went to the place of which God had told him. 4 On the third day Abraham lifted up his eyes and saw the place from afar. 5 Then Abraham said to his young men, "Stay here with the donkey; I and the boy will go over there and worship and come again to you." 6 And Abraham took the wood of the burnt offering and laid it on Isaac his son. And he took in his hand the fire and the knife. So they went both of them together. 7 And Isaac said to his father Abraham, "My father!" And he said, "Here I am, my son." He said, "Behold, the fire and the wood, but where is the lamb for a burnt offering?" 8 Abraham said, "**God will provide for himself the lamb** for a burnt offering, my son." So they went both of them together.

9 When they came to the place of which God had told him, Abraham built the altar there and laid the wood in order and bound Isaac his son and laid him on the altar, on top of the wood. 10 Then Abraham reached out his hand and took the knife to slaughter his son. 11 But the angel of the LORD called to him from heaven and said, "Abraham, Abraham!" And he said, "Here I am." 12 He said, "Do not lay your hand on the boy or do anything to him, for now I know that you fear God, seeing you have not withheld your son, your only son, from me." 13 And Abraham lifted up his eyes and looked, and behold, behind him was a ram, caught in a thicket by his horns. And Abraham went and took the ram and offered it up as a burnt offering instead of his son. 14 So Abraham called the name of that **place**, "The LORD will provide"; as it is said to this day, "On the mount of the LORD it shall be provided."

Isaac and Rebekah

24:1 Now Abraham was old, well advanced in years. And the LORD had blessed Abraham in all things. 2 And Abraham said to his servant, the oldest of his household, who had charge of all that he had, "Put your hand under my thigh, 3 that I may make you swear by the LORD, the God of heaven and God of the earth, that you will not take a wife for my son from the daughters of the Canaanites, among whom I dwell, 4 but will go to my country and to my kindred, and take a wife for my son Isaac." 5 The servant said to him, "Perhaps the woman may not be willing to follow me to this land. Must I then take your son back to the land from which you came?" 6 Abraham said to him, "See to it that you do not take my son back there. 7 The LORD, the God of heaven, who took me from my father's house and from the land of my kindred, and who spoke to me and swore to me, 'To your offspring I will give this

---

Margin notes:

John 3:16: "God so loved the world that He gave His only son ...."

God ultimately did provide a lamb to be slain: Jesus. See John 1:29; pg. 250.

The "place" is called the Rock of the Dome located on the Temple Mount in Jerusalem.

land,' he will send his angel before you, and you shall take a wife for my son from there. 8 But if the woman is not willing to follow you, then you will be free from this oath of mine; only you must not take my son back there." 9 So the servant put his hand under the thigh of Abraham his master and swore to him concerning this matter.

10 Then the servant took ten of his master's camels and departed, taking all sorts of choice gifts from his master; and he arose and went to Mesopotamia to the city of **Nahor**. 11 And he made the camels kneel down outside the city by the well of water at the time of evening, the time when women go out to draw water. 12 And he said, "O LORD, God of my master Abraham, please grant me success today and show steadfast love to my master Abraham. 13 Behold, I am standing by the spring of water, and the daughters of the men of the city are coming out to draw water. 14 Let the young woman to whom I shall say, 'Please let down your jar that I may drink,' and who shall say, 'Drink, and I will water your camels'—let her be the one whom you have appointed for your servant Isaac. By this I shall know that you have shown steadfast love to my master."

Remember Nahor was the brother of Terah who is the father of Abraham. So this is Abraham's uncle.

15 Before he had finished speaking, behold, **Rebekah**, who was born to Bethuel the son of Milcah, the wife of Nahor, Abraham's brother, came out with her water jar on her shoulder. 16 The young woman was very attractive in appearance, a maiden whom no man had known. She went down to the spring and filled her jar and came up. 17 Then the servant ran to meet her and said, "Please give me a little water to drink from your jar." 18 She said, "Drink, my lord." And she quickly let down her jar upon her hand and gave him a drink. 19 When she had finished giving him a drink, she said, "I will draw water for your camels also, until they have finished drinking." 20 So she quickly emptied her jar into the trough and ran again to the well to draw water, and she drew for all his camels. 21 **The man gazed at her in silence** to learn whether the LORD had prospered his journey or not.

So Rebekah is the granddaughter of the brother of Abraham.

Can you imagine the anticipation?

22 When the camels had finished drinking, the man took a gold ring weighing a half shekel, and two bracelets for her arms weighing ten gold shekels, 23 and said, "Please tell me whose daughter you are. Is there room in your father's house for us to spend the night?" 24 She said to him, "I am the daughter of Bethuel the son of Milcah, whom she bore to Nahor." 25 She added, "We have plenty of both straw and fodder, and room to spend the night." 26 The man bowed his head and worshiped the LORD 27 and said, "Blessed be the LORD, the God of my master Abraham, who has not forsaken his steadfast love and his faithfulness toward my master. As for me, **the LORD has led me in the way to the house of my master's kinsmen**." 28 Then the young woman ran and told her mother's household about these things.

God often answers our prayers when we specifically ask for something. Try it and see what happens.

29 Rebekah had a brother whose name was Laban. Laban ran out toward the man, to the spring. 30 As soon as he saw the ring and the bracelets on his sister's arms, and heard the words of Rebekah his sister, "Thus the man spoke to me," he went to the man.

And behold, he was standing by the camels at the spring. 31 He said, "Come in, O blessed of the LORD. Why do you stand outside? For I have prepared the house and a place for the camels." 32 So the man came to the house and unharnessed the camels, and gave straw and fodder to the camels, and there was water to wash his feet and the feet of the men who were with him. 33 Then food was set before him to eat. But he said, "I will not eat until I have said what I have to say." He said, "Speak on."

34 So he said, "I am Abraham's servant. 35 **The LORD has greatly blessed my master, and he has become great.** He has given him flocks and herds, silver and gold, male servants and female servants, camels and donkeys. 36 And Sarah my master's wife bore a son to my master when she was old, and to him he has given all that he has. 37 My master made me swear, saying, 'You shall not take a wife for my son from the daughters of the Canaanites, in whose land I dwell, 38 but you shall go to my father's house and to my clan and take a wife for my son.' 39 I said to my master, 'Perhaps the woman will not follow me.' 40 But he said to me, 'The LORD, before whom I have walked, will send his angel with you and prosper your way. You shall take a wife for my son from my clan and from my father's house. 41 Then you will be free from my oath, when you come to my clan. And if they will not give her to you, you will be free from my oath.'

The marriage negotiations begin.

42 "I came today to the spring and said, 'O LORD, the God of my master Abraham, if now you are prospering the way that I go, 43 behold, I am standing by the spring of water. Let the virgin who comes out to draw water, to whom I shall say, "Please give me a little water from your jar to drink," 44 and who will say to me, "Drink, and I will draw for your camels also," let her be the woman whom the LORD has appointed for my master's son.'

He retells his story.

45 "Before I had finished speaking in my heart, behold, Rebekah came out with her water jar on her shoulder, and she went down to the spring and drew water. I said to her, 'Please let me drink.' 46 She quickly let down her jar from her shoulder and said, 'Drink, and I will give your camels drink also.' So I drank, and she gave the camels drink also. 47 Then I asked her, 'Whose daughter are you?' She said, 'The daughter of Bethuel, Nahor's son, whom Milcah bore to him.' So I put the ring on her nose and the bracelets on her arms. 48 Then I bowed my head and worshiped the LORD and blessed the LORD, the God of my master Abraham, who had led me by the right way to take the daughter of my master's kinsman for his son. 49 Now then, if you are going to show steadfast love and faithfulness to my master, tell me; and if not, tell me, that I may turn to the right hand or to the left."

God answers his prayer.

50 Then Laban and Bethuel answered and said, "The thing has come from the LORD; we cannot speak to you bad or good. 51 Behold, Rebekah is before you; **take her and go**, and let her be the wife of your master's son, as the LORD has spoken."

It is a done deal!

52 When Abraham's servant heard their words, he bowed himself to the earth before the LORD. 53 And the servant brought out jewelry of silver and of gold, and garments, and gave them to Re-

I guess it is not a done deal. Marriage between two families can be quite complicated.

Shows a lot of faith on Rebekah's part.

Now it is a done deal!

bekah. He also gave to her brother and to her mother costly ornaments. 54 And he and the men who were with him ate and drank, and they spent the night there. When they arose in the morning, he said, "Send me away to my master." 55 Her brother and her mother said, **"Let the young woman remain with us a while, at least ten days; after that she may go."** 56 But he said to them, "Do not delay me, since the LORD has prospered my way. Send me away that I may go to my master." 57 They said, "Let us call the young woman and ask her." 58 And they called Rebekah and said to her, "Will you go with this man?" She said, **"I will go."** 59 So they sent away Rebekah their sister and her nurse, and Abraham's servant and his men. 60 And they blessed Rebekah and said to her, "Our sister, may you become thousands of ten thousands, and may your offspring possess the gate of those who hate him!"

61 Then Rebekah and her young women arose and rode on the camels and followed the man. **Thus the servant took Rebekah and went his way.**

Why do you think this comment is included?

62 Now Isaac had returned from Beer-lahai-roi and was dwelling in the Negeb. 63 And Isaac went out to meditate in the field toward evening. And he lifted up his eyes and saw, and behold, there were camels coming. 64 And Rebekah lifted up her eyes, and when she saw Isaac, she dismounted from the camel 65 and said to the servant, "Who is that man, walking in the field to meet us?" The servant said, "It is my master." So she took her veil and covered herself. 66 And the servant told Isaac all the things that he had done. 67 Then Isaac brought her into the tent of Sarah his mother and took Rebekah, and she became his wife, and he loved her. **So Isaac was comforted after his mother's death.**

25:7 These are the days of the years of Abraham's life, 175 years. 8 Abraham breathed his last and died in a good old age, an old man and full of years, and was gathered to his people.

The Birth of Esau and Jacob

Her mother-in-law Sarah, Abraham's wife, was barren in the beginning of her marriage as well.

19 These are the generations of Isaac, Abraham's son: Abraham fathered Isaac, 20 and Isaac was forty years old when he took Rebekah, the daughter of Bethuel the Aramean of Paddan-aram, the sister of Laban the Aramean, to be his wife. 21 And Isaac prayed to the LORD for his wife, because she was **barren**. And the LORD granted his prayer, and Rebekah his wife conceived. 22 The children struggled together within her, and she said, "If it is thus, why is this happening to me?" So she went to inquire of the LORD. 23 And the LORD said to her, "Two nations are in your womb, and two peoples from within you shall be divided; the one shall be stronger than the other, the older shall serve the younger."

The name Jacob means "grabber" or "deceiver."

24 When her days to give birth were completed, behold, there were twins in her womb. 25 The first came out red, all his body like a hairy cloak, so they called his name Esau. 26 Afterward his brother came out with his hand holding Esau's heel, so his name was called **Jacob**. Isaac was sixty years old when she bore them.

27 When the boys grew up, Esau was a skillful hunter, a man of the field, while Jacob was a quiet man, dwelling in tents. 28 Isaac

loved Esau because he ate of his game, but Rebekah loved Jacob.

Esau Sells His Birthright

29 Once when Jacob was cooking stew, Esau came in from the field, and he was exhausted. 30 And Esau said to Jacob, "Let me eat some of that red stew, for I am exhausted!" (Therefore his name was called **Edom.**) 31 Jacob said, "Sell me your birthright now." 32 Esau said, "I am about to die; of what use is a birthright to me?" 33 Jacob said, "Swear to me now." So he swore to him and sold his birthright to Jacob. 34 Then Jacob gave Esau bread and lentil stew, and he ate and drank and rose and went his way. Thus Esau despised his birthright.

The descendants of Esau were called Edomites. They became enemies of Israel in later history.

Isaac Blesses Jacob

27:1 When Isaac was old and his eyes were dim so that he could not see, he called Esau his older son and said to him, "My son"; and he answered, "Here I am." 2 He said, "Behold, I am old; I do not know the day of my death. 3 Now then, take your weapons, your quiver and your bow, and go out to the field and hunt game for me, 4 and prepare for me delicious food, such as I love, and bring it to me so that I may eat, that my soul may bless you before I die."

5 Now Rebekah was listening when Isaac spoke to his son Esau. So when Esau went to the field to hunt for game and bring it, 6 Rebekah said to her son Jacob, "I heard your father speak to your brother Esau, 7 'Bring me game and prepare for me delicious food, that I may eat it and bless you before the LORD before I die.' 8 Now therefore, my son, obey my voice as I command you. 9 Go to the flock and bring me two good young goats, so that I may prepare from them delicious food for your father, such as he loves. 10 And you shall bring it to your father to eat, so that he may bless you before he dies." 11 But Jacob said to Rebekah his mother, "Behold, my brother Esau is a hairy man, and I am a smooth man. 12 Perhaps my father will feel me, and I shall seem to be mocking him and bring a curse upon myself and not a blessing." 13 His mother said to him, "Let your curse be on me, my son; only obey my voice, and go, bring them to me."

14 So he went and took them and brought them to his mother, and his mother prepared delicious food, such as his father loved. 15 Then Rebekah took the best garments of Esau her older son, which were with her in the house, and put them on Jacob her younger son. 16 And the skins of the young goats she put on his hands and on the smooth part of his neck. 17 And she put the delicious food and the bread, which she had prepared, into the hand of her son Jacob.

18 So he went in to his father and said, "My father." And he said, "Here I am. Who are you, my son?" 19 Jacob said to his father, "I am Esau your firstborn. I have done as you told me; now sit up and eat of my game, that your soul may bless me." 20 But Isaac said to his son, "How is it that you have found it so quickly, my son?" He answered, "Because the LORD your God granted me success."

21 Then Isaac said to Jacob, "Please come near, that I may feel you, my son, to know whether you are really my son Esau or not." 22 So Jacob went near to Isaac his father, who felt him and said, "The voice is Jacob's voice, but the hands are the hands of Esau." 23 And he did not recognize him, because his hands were hairy like his brother Esau's hands. So he blessed him. 24 He said, "Are you really my son Esau?" He answered, "I am." 25 Then he said, "Bring it near to me, that I may eat of my son's game and bless you." So he brought it near to him, and he ate; and he brought him wine, and he drank.

26 Then his father Isaac said to him, "Come near and kiss me, my son." 27 So he came near and kissed him. And Isaac smelled the smell of his garments and blessed him and said, "See, the smell of my son is as the smell of a field that the LORD has blessed! 28 May God give you of the dew of heaven and of the fatness of the earth and plenty of grain and wine. 29 Let peoples serve you, and nations bow down to you. Be lord over your brothers, and may your mother's sons bow down to you. Cursed be everyone who curses you, and blessed be everyone who blesses you!"

30 As soon as Isaac had finished blessing Jacob, when Jacob had scarcely gone out from the presence of Isaac his father, Esau his brother came in from his hunting. 31 He also prepared delicious food and brought it to his father. And he said to his father, "Let my father arise and eat of his son's game, that you may bless me." 32 His father Isaac said to him, "Who are you?" He answered, "I am your son, your firstborn, Esau." 33 Then Isaac trembled very violently and said, "Who was it then that hunted game and brought it to me, and I ate it all before you came, and I have blessed him? Yes, and he shall be blessed." 34 As soon as Esau heard the words of his father, he cried out with an exceedingly great and bitter cry and said to his father, "Bless me, even me also, O my father!" 35 But he said, "Your brother came **deceitfully**, and he has taken away your blessing." 36 Esau said, "Is he not **rightly named Jacob**? For he has cheated me these two times. He took away my birthright, and behold, now he has taken away my blessing." Then he said, "Have you not reserved a blessing for me?" 37 Isaac answered and said to Esau, "Behold, I have made him lord over you, and all his brothers I have given to him for servants, and with grain and wine I have sustained him. What then can I do for you, my son?" 38 Esau said to his father, "Have you but one blessing, my father? **Bless me, even me also**, O my father." And Esau lifted up his voice and wept.

39 Then Isaac his father answered and said to him: "Behold, away from the fatness of the earth shall your dwelling be, and away from the dew of heaven on high. 40 By your sword you shall live, and you shall serve your brother; but when you grow restless you shall break his yoke from your neck."

41 Now Esau hated Jacob because of the blessing with which his father had blessed him, and Esau said to himself, "The days of mourning for my father are approaching; then I will kill my brother Jacob." 42 But the words of Esau her older son were told to Re-

---

Margin notes:

Jacob lives up to his name, "grabber" or "deceiver," taking what is not his.

When have you felt like you have missed out on what should have been yours?

bekah. So she sent and called Jacob her younger son and said to him, "Behold, your brother Esau comforts himself about you by planning to kill you. 43 Now therefore, my son, obey my voice. Arise, flee to Laban my brother in Haran 44 and stay with him a while, until your brother's fury turns away—45 until your brother's anger turns away from you, and he forgets what you have done to him. Then I will send and bring you from there. Why should I be bereft of you both in one day?"

Jacob Sent to Laban

28:1 Then Isaac called Jacob and blessed him and directed him, "You must not take a wife from the Canaanite women. 2 Arise, go to Paddan-aram to the house of Bethuel your mother's father, and take as your wife from there one of the daughters of Laban your mother's brother. 3 God Almighty bless you and make you fruitful and multiply you, that you may become a company of peoples. 4 May he give the blessing of Abraham to you and to your offspring with you, that you may take possession of the land of your sojournings that God gave to Abraham!" 5 Thus Isaac sent Jacob away.

Jacob's Dream

10 Jacob left Beersheba and went toward Haran. 11 And he came to a certain place and stayed there that night, because the sun had set. Taking one of the stones of the place, he put it under his head and lay down in that place to sleep. 12 And he dreamed, and behold, there was a ladder set up on the earth, and the top of it reached to heaven. And behold, **the angels of God were ascending and descending** on it! 13 And behold, the LORD stood above it and said, "I am the LORD, the God of Abraham your father and the God of Isaac. The land on which you lie I will give to you and to your offspring. 14 Your offspring shall be like the dust of the earth, and you shall spread abroad to the west and to the east and to the north and to the south, and in you and your offspring shall all the families of the earth be blessed. 15 Behold, I am with you and will keep you wherever you go, and will bring you back to this land. For I will not leave you until I have done what I have promised you." 16 Then Jacob awoke from his sleep and said, "Surely the LORD is in this place, and I did not know it." 17 And he was afraid and said, "How awesome is this place! This is none other than the house of God, and this is the gate of heaven."

18 So early in the morning Jacob took the stone that he had put under his head and set it up for a pillar and poured oil on the top of it. 19 He called the name of that place Bethel, but the name of the city was Luz at the first. 20 Then Jacob made a vow, saying, "If God will be with me and will keep me in this way that I go, and will give me bread to eat and clothing to wear, 21 so that I come again to my father's house in peace, then **the LORD shall be my God**, 22 and this stone, which I have set up for a pillar, shall be God's house. And of all that you give me I will give a full tenth to you."

Jesus told a disciple that he would "see heaven opened, and the angels of God ascending and descending on the Son of Man." (John 1:51). Jesus is the bridge between heaven and earth.

Jacob finally accepts God as his God. At some point you have to accept or reject God on your own terms.

Jacob Marries Leah and Rachel

29:1 Then Jacob went on his journey and came to the land of the people of the east. 2 As he looked, he saw a well in the field, and behold, three flocks of sheep lying beside it, for out of that well the flocks were watered. The stone on the well's mouth was large, 3 and when all the flocks were gathered there, the shepherds would roll the stone from the mouth of the well and water the sheep, and put the stone back in its place over the mouth of the well.

4 Jacob said to them, "My brothers, where do you come from?" They said, "We are from Haran." 5 He said to them, "Do you know Laban the son of Nahor?" They said, "We know him." 6 He said to them, "Is it well with him?" They said, "It is well; and see, Rachel his daughter is coming with the sheep!" 7 He said, "Behold, it is still high day; it is not time for the livestock to be gathered together. Water the sheep and go, pasture them." 8 But they said, "We cannot until all the flocks are gathered together and the stone is rolled from the mouth of the well; then we water the sheep."

9 While he was still speaking with them, Rachel came with her father's sheep, for she was a shepherdess. 10 Now as soon as Jacob saw Rachel the daughter of Laban his mother's brother, and the sheep of Laban his mother's brother, Jacob came near and **rolled the stone from the well's mouth** and watered the flock of Laban his mother's brother. 11 Then Jacob kissed Rachel and wept aloud. 12 And Jacob told Rachel that he was her father's kinsman, and that he was Rebekah's son, and she ran and told her father.

13 As soon as Laban heard the news about Jacob, his sister's son, he ran to meet him and embraced him and kissed him and brought him to his house. Jacob told Laban all these things, 14 and Laban said to him, "Surely you are my bone and my flesh!" And he stayed with him a month.

15 Then Laban said to Jacob, "Because you are my kinsman, should you therefore serve me for nothing? Tell me, what shall your wages be?" 16 Now Laban had two daughters. The name of the older was Leah, and the name of the younger was Rachel.

18 Jacob loved Rachel. And he said, "I will serve you seven years for your younger daughter Rachel." 19 Laban said, "It is better that I give her to you than that I should give her to any other man; stay with me." 20 So Jacob served seven years for Rachel, and **they seemed to him but a few days because of the love he had for her**.

21 Then Jacob said to Laban, "Give me my wife that I may go in to her, for my time is completed." 22 So Laban gathered together all the people of the place and made a feast. 23 But in the evening he took his daughter Leah and brought her to Jacob, and he went in to her. 24 (Laban gave his female servant Zilpah to his daughter Leah to be her servant.) 25 **And in the morning, behold, it was Leah!** And Jacob said to Laban, "What is this you have done to me? Did I not serve with you for Rachel? Why then have you deceived me?" 26 Laban said, "It is not so done in our country, to give the younger before the firstborn. 27 Complete the week of this one, and we

---

Jacob got to do what all young men want to do - impress the girl he loves with his ability to take care of problems. He also got connected to the girl he eventually married, just like his father and mother years before.

Young love.

Can you imagine?

will give you the other also in return for serving me another seven years." 28 Jacob did so, and completed her week. Then Laban gave him his daughter Rachel to be his wife. 29 (Laban gave his female servant Bilhah to his daughter Rachel to be her servant.) 30 So Jacob went in to Rachel also, and **he loved Rachel more than Leah**, and served Laban for another seven years.

Jacob's Children

31 When the LORD saw that Leah was hated, he opened her womb, but **Rachel was barren**. 32 And Leah conceived and bore a son, and she called his name Reuben, for she said, "Because the LORD has looked upon my affliction; for now my husband will love me." 33 She conceived again and bore a son, and said, "Because the LORD has heard that I am hated, he has given me this son also." And she called his name **Simeon**. 34 Again she conceived and bore a son, and said, "Now this time my husband will be attached to me, because I have borne him three sons." Therefore his name was called Levi. 35 And she conceived again and bore a son, and said, "This time I will praise the LORD." Therefore she called his name **Judah**. Then she ceased bearing.

30:1 When Rachel saw that she bore Jacob no children, she envied her sister. She said to Jacob, "Give me children, or I shall die!" 2 Jacob's anger was kindled against Rachel, and he said, "Am I in the place of God, who has withheld from you the fruit of the womb?" 3 Then she said, "Here is my servant Bilhah; go in to her, so that she may give birth on my behalf, that even I may have children through her." 4 So she gave him her servant Bilhah as a wife, and Jacob went in to her. 5 And Bilhah conceived and bore Jacob a son. 6 Then Rachel said, "God has judged me, and has also heard my voice and given me a son." Therefore she called his name **Dan**. 7 Rachel's servant Bilhah conceived again and bore Jacob a second son. 8 Then Rachel said, "With mighty wrestlings I have wrestled with my sister and have prevailed." So she called his name **Naphtali**.

9 When Leah saw that she had ceased bearing children, she took her servant Zilpah and gave her to Jacob as a wife. 10 Then Leah's servant Zilpah bore Jacob a son. 11 And Leah said, "Good fortune has come!" so she called his name **Gad**. 12 Leah's servant Zilpah bore Jacob a second son. 13 And Leah said, "Happy am I! For women have called me happy." So she called his name **Asher**.

14 In the days of wheat harvest Reuben went and found mandrakes in the field and brought them to his mother Leah. Then Rachel said to Leah, "Please give me some of your son's mandrakes." 15 But she said to her, "Is it a small matter that you have taken away my husband? Would you take away my son's mandrakes also?" Rachel said, "Then he may lie with you tonight in exchange for your son's mandrakes." 16 When Jacob came from the field in the evening, Leah went out to meet him and said, "You must come in to me, for I have hired you with my son's mandrakes." So he lay with her that night. 17 And God listened to Leah, and she conceived and bore Jacob a fifth son. 18 Leah said, "God has given me my wages because I gave my servant to my husband."

One wonders how Leah felt through all this.

Just like grandmother Sarah and mother Rebekah.

Judah became the line from which King David and ultimately Jesus came from.

The 5 Books of Moses

So she called his name **Issachar**.

19 And Leah conceived again, and she bore Jacob a sixth son. 20 Then Leah said, "God has endowed me with a good endowment; now my husband will honor me, because I have borne him six sons." So she called his name **Zebulun**. 21 Afterward she bore a daughter and called her name Dinah.

22 Then God remembered Rachel, and God listened to her and opened her womb. 23 She conceived and bore a son and said, "God has taken away my reproach." 24 And she called his name **Joseph**, saying, "May the LORD add to me another son!"

[margin: The 12 sons of Jacob by 4 different mothers become the 12 tribes of Israel.]

Jacob's Prosperity

25 As soon as Rachel had borne Joseph, Jacob said to Laban, "Send me away, that I may go to my own home and country. 26 Give me my wives and my children for whom I have served you, that I may go, for you know the service that I have given you." 27 But Laban said to him, "the LORD has blessed me because of you. 28 Name your wages, and I will give it." 29 Jacob said to him, "You yourself know how I have served you, and how your livestock has fared with me. 30 For you had little before I came, and it has increased abundantly, and the LORD has blessed you wherever I turned. But now when shall I provide for my own household also?" 31 He said, "What shall I give you?" Jacob said, "You shall not give me anything. If you will do this for me, I will again pasture your flock and keep it: 32 let me pass through all your flock today, removing from it every speckled and spotted sheep and every black lamb, and the spotted and speckled among the goats, and they shall be my wages. 33 So my honesty will answer for me later, when you come to look into my wages with you. Every one that is not speckled and spotted among the goats and black among the lambs, if found with me, shall be counted stolen." 34 Laban said, "Good! Let it be as you have said." 35 But that day Laban removed the male goats that were striped and spotted, and all the female goats that were speckled and spotted, every one that had white on it, and every lamb that was black, and put them in the charge of his sons. 36 And he set a distance of three days' journey between himself and Jacob, and Jacob pastured the rest of Laban's flock.

37 Then Jacob took fresh sticks of poplar and almond and plane trees, and peeled white streaks in them, exposing the white of the sticks. 38 He set the sticks that he had peeled in front of the flocks in the troughs, that is, the watering places, where the flocks came to drink. And since they bred when they came to drink, 39 the flocks bred in front of the sticks and so the flocks brought forth striped, speckled, and spotted. 40 And Jacob separated the lambs and set the faces of the flocks toward the striped and all the black in the flock of Laban. He put his own droves apart and did not put them with Laban's flock. 41 Whenever the stronger of the flock were breeding, Jacob would lay the sticks in the troughs before the eyes of the flock, that they might breed among the sticks, 42 but for the feebler of the flock he would not lay them there. So the feebler would be Laban's, and the stronger Jacob's. 43 Thus the man increased greatly and had large flocks, female servants and male

[margin: Again Jacob was trying to gain advantage by deception.]

servants, and camels and donkeys.

Jacob Flees from Laban

31:1 Now Jacob heard that the sons of Laban were saying, "Jacob has taken all that was our father's, and from what was our father's he has gained all this wealth." 2 And Jacob saw that Laban did not regard him with favor as before. 3 Then the LORD said to Jacob, "Return to the land of your fathers and to your kindred, and I will be with you."

Jacob Fears Esau

32:3 And Jacob sent messengers before him to Esau his brother in the land of Seir, the country of Edom, 4 instructing them, "Thus you shall say to my lord Esau: Thus says your servant Jacob, 'I have sojourned with Laban and stayed until now. 5 I have oxen, donkeys, flocks, male servants, and female servants. I have sent to tell my lord, in order that I may find favor in your sight.'"

6 And the messengers returned to Jacob, saying, "We came to your brother Esau, and he is coming to meet you, and there are four hundred men with him." 7 Then Jacob was greatly afraid and distressed. He divided the people who were with him, and the flocks and herds and camels, into two camps, 8 thinking, "If Esau comes to the one camp and attacks it, then the camp that is left will escape."

9 And Jacob said, "O God of my father Abraham and God of my father Isaac, O LORD who said to me, 'Return to your country and to your kindred, that I may do you good,' 10 **I am not worthy of the least of all the deeds of steadfast love and all the faithfulness that you have shown to your servant, for with only my staff I crossed this Jordan, and now I have become two camps.** 11 Please deliver me from the hand of my brother, from the hand of Esau, for I fear him, that he may come and attack me, the mothers with the children. 12 But you said, 'I will surely do you good, and make your offspring as the sand of the sea, which cannot be numbered for multitude.'"

This is a good example of how to pray for something.

13 So he stayed there that night, and from what he had with him he took a **present** for his brother Esau, 14 two hundred female goats and twenty male goats, two hundred ewes and twenty rams, 15 thirty milking camels and their calves, forty cows and ten bulls, twenty female donkeys and ten male donkeys.

Jacob Wrestles with God

22 The same night he arose and took his two wives, his two female servants, and his eleven children, and crossed the ford of the Jabbok. 23 He took them and sent them across the stream, and everything else that he had. 24 And Jacob was left alone. And a man wrestled with him until the breaking of the day. 25 When the man saw that he did not prevail against Jacob, he touched his hip socket, and Jacob's hip was put out of joint as he wrestled with him. 26 Then he said, "Let me go, for the day has broken." But Jacob said, "I will not let you go unless you bless me." 27 And he said to him, "What is your name?" And he said, "Jacob." 28 Then

Jacob then sent all this livestock on ahead to Esau hoping to appease him (remember Esau wanted to kill Jacob years before for stealing his blessing).

[margin note: Israel means "striving with God."]

[margin note: Peniel means "face of God."]

he said, "Your name shall no longer be called Jacob, but **Israel**, for you have striven with God and with men, and have prevailed." 29 Then Jacob asked him, "Please tell me your name." But he said, "Why is it that you ask my name?" And there he blessed him. 30 So Jacob called the name of the place **Peniel**, saying, "For I have seen God face to face, and yet my life has been delivered." 31 The sun rose upon him as he passed Penuel, limping because of his hip. 32 Therefore to this day the people of Israel do not eat the sinew of the thigh that is on the hip socket, because he touched the socket of Jacob's hip on the sinew of the thigh.

Jacob Meets Esau

33:1 And Jacob lifted up his eyes and looked, and behold, Esau was coming, and four hundred men with him. So he divided the children among Leah and Rachel and the two female servants. 2 And he put the servants with their children in front, then Leah with her children, and Rachel and Joseph last of all. 3 He himself went on before them, bowing himself to the ground seven times, until he came near to his brother.

4 But Esau ran to meet him and embraced him and fell on his neck and kissed him, and they wept. 5 And when Esau lifted up his eyes and saw the women and children, he said, "Who are these with you?" Jacob said, "The children whom God has graciously given your servant." 6 Then the servants drew near, they and their children, and bowed down. 7 Leah likewise and her children drew near and bowed down. And last Joseph and Rachel drew near, and they bowed down. 8 Esau said, "What do you mean by all this company that I met?"

Jacob answered, "To find favor in the sight of my lord." 9 But Esau said, "I have enough, my brother; keep what you have for yourself."

[margin note: There is nothing like a family reunion. Do you need one?]

10 Jacob said, "No, please, if I have found favor in your sight, then accept my present from my hand. For I have seen your face, which is like seeing the face of God, and **you have accepted me.** 11 Please accept my blessing that is brought to you, because God has dealt graciously with me, and because I have enough." Thus he urged him, and he took it.

12 Then Esau said, "Let us journey on our way, and I will go ahead of you."

13 But Jacob said to him, "My lord knows that the children are frail, and that the nursing flocks and herds are a care to me. If they are driven hard for one day, all the flocks will die. 14 Let my lord pass on ahead of his servant, and I will lead on slowly, at the pace of the livestock that are ahead of me and at the pace of the children, until I come to my lord in Seir."

15 So Esau said, "Let me leave with you some of the people who are with me."

But he said, "What need is there? Let me find favor in the sight of my lord." 16 So Esau returned that day on his way to Seir. 17 But Jacob journeyed to Succoth, and built himself a house and made booths for his livestock.

God Blesses and Renames Jacob

35:1 God said to Jacob, "Arise, go up to **Bethel** and dwell there. Make an altar there to the God who appeared to you when you fled from your brother Esau."

2 So Jacob said to his household and to all who were with him, "Put away the foreign gods that are among you and purify yourselves and change your garments. 3 Then let us arise and go up to Bethel, so that I may make there an altar to the God who answers me in the day of my distress and has been with me wherever I have gone." 4 So they gave to Jacob all the foreign gods that they had, and the rings that were in their ears. Jacob hid them under the terebinth tree that was near Shechem.

9 God appeared to Jacob again, when he came from Paddan-aram, and blessed him. 10 And God said to him, "Your name is Jacob; no longer shall your name be called Jacob, but Israel shall be your name." So he called his name Israel. 11 And God said to him, "I am God Almighty: be **fruitful and multiply**. A nation and a company of nations shall come from you, and kings shall come from your own body. 12 The land that I gave to Abraham and Isaac I will give to you, and I will give the land to your offspring after you." 13 Then God went up from him in the place where he had spoken with him. 14 And Jacob set up a pillar in the place where he had spoken with him, a pillar of stone. He poured out a drink offering on it and poured oil on it. 15 So Jacob called the name of the place where God had spoken with him **Bethel**.

The Deaths of Rachel and Isaac

16 Then they journeyed from Bethel. When they were still some distance from Ephrath, Rachel went into labor, and she had hard labor. 17 And when her labor was at its hardest, the midwife said to her, "Do not fear, for you have another son." 18 And as her soul was departing (for she was dying), she called his name Ben-oni; but his father called him **Benjamin**. 19 So Rachel died, and she was buried on the way to Ephrath (that is, **Bethlehem**), 20 and Jacob set up a pillar over her tomb. It is the pillar of Rachel's tomb, which is there to this day. 21 Israel journeyed on and pitched his tent beyond the tower of Eder.

Now the sons of Jacob were **twelve**. 23 The sons of Leah: **Reuben** (Jacob's firstborn), **Simeon**, **Levi**, **Judah**, **Issachar**, and **Zebulun**. 24 The sons of Rachel: **Joseph** and **Benjamin**. 25 The sons of Bilhah, Rachel's servant: **Dan** and **Naphtali**. 26 The sons of Zilpah, Leah's servant: **Gad** and **Asher**. These were the sons of Jacob who were born to him in Paddan-aram.

28 Now the days of Isaac were 180 years. 29 And Isaac breathed his last, and he died and was gathered to his people, old and full of days. And his sons Esau and Jacob buried him.

Bethel was the place Jacob had the dream with the ladder to heaven. It seems to have been a place where Jacob gets serious about his relationship to God. Where is your Bethel?

The same command given by God in Genesis 1. The same place where he first made his commitment to God when he had nothing and was running for his life.

The birthplace of Jesus.

Benjamin was the last of the 12 children of Jacob to become the 12 tribes of Israel.

Joseph's Dreams

37:1 Jacob lived in the land of his father's sojournings, in the land of Canaan. 2 These are the generations of Jacob.

Joseph, being seventeen years old, was pasturing the flock with his brothers. And Joseph brought a bad report of them to their father. 3 Now Israel loved Joseph more than any other of his sons, because he was the son of his old age. And he made him a **robe of many colors**. 4 But when his brothers saw that their father loved him more than all his brothers, **they hated him** and could not speak peacefully to him.

5 Now Joseph had a dream, and when he told it to his brothers they hated him even more. 6 He said to them, "Hear this dream that I have dreamed: 7 Behold, we were binding sheaves in the field, and behold, my sheaf arose and stood upright. And behold, your sheaves gathered around it and bowed down to my sheaf." 8 His brothers said to him, "Are you indeed to reign over us?" So they hated him even more for his dreams and for his words.

9 Then he dreamed another dream and told it to his brothers and said, "Behold, I have dreamed another dream. Behold, the sun, the moon, and eleven stars were bowing down to me." 10 But when he told it to his father and to his brothers, his father rebuked him and said to him, "What is this dream that you have dreamed? Shall I and your mother and your brothers indeed come to bow ourselves to the ground before you?" 11 And his brothers were **jealous** of him, but his father kept the saying in mind.

Joseph Sold by His Brothers

12 Now his brothers went to pasture their father's flock near Shechem. 13 And Israel said to Joseph, "Are not your brothers pasturing the flock at Shechem? Come, I will send you to them." And he said to him, "Here I am." 14 So he said to him, "Go now, see if it is well with your brothers and with the flock, and bring me word." So he sent him from the Valley of Hebron, and he came to Shechem. 15 And a man found him wandering in the fields. And the man asked him, "What are you seeking?" 16 "I am seeking my brothers," he said. "Tell me, please, where they are pasturing the flock." 17 And the man said, "They have gone away, for I heard them say, 'Let us go to Dothan.'" So Joseph went after his brothers and found them at Dothan.

18 They saw him from afar, and before he came near to them they conspired against him to kill him. 19 They said to one another, "Here comes this dreamer. 20 Come now, let us kill him and throw him into one of the pits. Then we will say that a fierce animal has devoured him, and we will see what will become of his dreams." 21 But when Reuben heard it, he rescued him out of their hands, saying, "Let us not take his life." 22 And Reuben said to them, "Shed no blood; throw him into this pit here in the wilderness, but do not lay a hand on him"—that he might rescue him out of their hand to restore him to his father. 23 So when Joseph came to his brothers, they stripped him of his robe, the robe of many colors that he wore. 24 And they took him and threw him into a pit. The

---

Joseph, you are special!

It is hard not to sympathize with the brothers' attitude toward Joseph. But why is that? Why do we in our minds develop a pecking order of importance? We do it in school, at work, in church. The end result: jealousy.

pit was empty; there was no water in it.

25 Then they sat down to eat. And looking up they saw a caravan of Ishmaelites coming from Gilead, with their camels bearing gum, balm, and myrrh, on their way to carry it down to Egypt. 26 Then Judah said to his brothers, "What profit is it if we kill our brother and conceal his blood? 27 Come, let us sell him to the Ishmaelites, and let not our hand be upon him, for he is our brother, our own flesh." And his brothers listened to him. 28 Then Midianite traders passed by. And they drew Joseph up and lifted him out of the pit, and sold him to the Ishmaelites for **twenty shekels of silver**. They took Joseph to Egypt.

29 When Reuben returned to the pit and saw that Joseph was not in the pit, he tore his clothes 30 and returned to his brothers and said, "The boy is gone, and I, where shall I go?" 31 Then they took Joseph's robe and slaughtered a goat and dipped the robe in the blood. 32 **And they sent the robe of many colors and brought it to their father and said, "This we have found; please identify whether it is your son's robe or not."** 33 And he identified it and said, "It is my son's robe. A fierce animal has devoured him. Joseph is without doubt torn to pieces." 34 Then Jacob tore his garments and put sackcloth on his loins and mourned for his son many days. 35 All his sons and all his daughters rose up to comfort him, but he refused to be comforted and said, "No, I shall go down to Sheol to my son, mourning." Thus his father wept for him. 36 Meanwhile the Midianites had sold him in Egypt to Potiphar, an officer of Pharaoh, the captain of the guard.

Joseph and Potiphar's Wife

39:1 Now Joseph had been brought down to Egypt, and Potiphar, an officer of Pharaoh, the captain of the guard, an Egyptian, had bought him from the **Ishmaelites** who had brought him down there. 2 The LORD was with Joseph, and he became a successful man, and he was in the house of his Egyptian master. 3 His master saw that the LORD was with him and that the LORD caused all that he did to succeed in his hands. 4 So Joseph found favor in his sight and attended him, and he made him overseer of his house and put him in charge of all that he had. 5 From the time that he made him overseer in his house and over all that he had, **the LORD blessed the Egyptian's house for Joseph's sake**; the blessing of the LORD was on all that he had, in house and field. 6 So he left all that he had in Joseph's charge, and because of him he had no concern about anything but the food he ate.

Now Joseph was handsome in form and appearance. 7 And after a time his master's wife cast her eyes on Joseph and said, "Lie with me." 8 But **he refused** and said to his master's wife, "Behold, because of me my master has no concern about anything in the house, and he has put everything that he has in my charge. 9 He is not greater in this house than I am, nor has he kept back anything from me except you, because you are his wife. How then can I do this great wickedness and **sin against God**?" 10 And as she spoke to Joseph day after day, he would not listen to her, to lie beside her or to be with her.

Jesus was betrayed for 30 shekels of silver.

How is it that human beings can be so evil... especially to the people closest to them?

These are the descendants of Ishmael, the firstborn son of Abraham.

God blesses people through God's people.

Leadership is taking responsibility.

Interesting that Joseph says it is

a sin, not against his master, but against God.

11 But one day, when he went into the house to do his work and none of the men of the house was there in the house, 12 she caught him by his garment, saying, "Lie with me." But he left his garment in her hand and fled and got out of the house. 13 And as soon as she saw that he had left his garment in her hand and had fled out of the house, 14 she called to the men of her household and said to them, "See, he has brought among us a Hebrew to laugh at us. He came in to me to lie with me, and I cried out with a loud voice. 15 And as soon as he heard that I lifted up my voice and cried out, he left his garment beside me and fled and got out of the house." 16 Then she laid up his garment by her until his master came home, 17 and she told him the same story.

19 As soon as his master heard the words that his wife spoke to him, "This is the way your servant treated me," his anger was kindled. 20 And Joseph's master took him and put him into the prison. 21 But the LORD was with Joseph and showed him steadfast love and gave him favor in the sight of the keeper of the prison. 22 And the keeper of the prison put Joseph in charge of all the prisoners. Whatever was done there, he was the one who did it. 23 The keeper of the prison paid no attention to anything that was in Joseph's charge, because the LORD was with him. And whatever he did, the LORD made it **succeed**.

Success in your life is ultimately a God thing.

Joseph Interprets Two Prisoners' Dreams

40:1 Some time after this, the cupbearer of the king of Egypt and his baker committed an offense against their lord the king of Egypt. 2 And Pharaoh was angry with his two officers, the chief cupbearer and the chief baker, 3 and he put them in custody in the house of the captain of the guard, in the prison where Joseph was confined. 4 The captain of the guard appointed Joseph to be with them, and he attended them. They continued for some time in custody.

5 And one night they both dreamed—the cupbearer and the baker of the king of Egypt, who were confined in the prison—each his own dream, and each dream with its own interpretation. 6 When Joseph came to them in the morning, he saw that they were troubled. 7 So he asked Pharaoh's officers who were with him in custody in his master's house, "Why are your faces downcast today?" 8 They said to him, "We have had dreams, and there is no one to interpret them." And Joseph said to them, "Do not interpretations belong to God? Please tell them to me."

9 So the chief cupbearer told his dream to Joseph and said to him, "In my dream there was a vine before me, 10 and on the vine there were three branches. As soon as it budded, its blossoms shot forth, and the clusters ripened into grapes. 11 Pharaoh's cup was in my hand, and I took the grapes and pressed them into Pharaoh's cup and placed the cup in Pharaoh's hand." 12 Then Joseph said to him, "This is its interpretation: the three branches are three days. 13 In three days Pharaoh will lift up your head and restore you to your office, and you shall place Pharaoh's cup in his hand as formerly, when you were his cupbearer. 14 Only remember me, when it is well with you, and please do me the kindness to

mention me to Pharaoh, and so get me out of this house. 15 For I was indeed stolen out of the land of the Hebrews, and here also I have done nothing that they should put me into the pit."

16 When the chief baker saw that the interpretation was favorable, he said to Joseph, "I also had a dream: there were three cake baskets on my head, 17 and in the uppermost basket there were all sorts of baked food for Pharaoh, but the birds were eating it out of the basket on my head." 18 And Joseph answered and said, "This is its interpretation: the three baskets are three days. 19 **In three days Pharaoh will lift up your head—from you!—and hang you on a tree.** And the birds will eat the flesh from you."

20 On the third day, which was Pharaoh's birthday, he made a feast for all his servants and lifted up the head of the chief cupbearer and the head of the chief baker among his servants. 21 He restored the chief cupbearer to his position, and he placed the cup in Pharaoh's hand. 22 But he hanged the chief baker, as Joseph had interpreted to them. 23 **Yet the chief cupbearer did not remember Joseph, but forgot him.**

Joseph Interprets Pharaoh's Dreams

41:1 After two whole years, Pharaoh dreamed that he was standing by the Nile, 2 and behold, there came up out of the Nile seven cows attractive and plump, and they fed in the reed grass. 3 And behold, seven other cows, ugly and thin, came up out of the Nile after them, and stood by the other cows on the bank of the Nile. 4 And the ugly, thin cows ate up the seven attractive, plump cows. And Pharaoh awoke. 5 And he fell asleep and dreamed a second time. And behold, seven ears of grain, plump and good, were growing on one stalk. 6 And behold, after them sprouted seven ears, thin and blighted by the east wind. 7 And the thin ears swallowed up the seven plump, full ears. And Pharaoh awoke, and behold, it was a dream. 8 So in the morning his spirit was troubled, and he sent and called for all the magicians of Egypt and all its wise men. Pharaoh told them his dreams, but there was none who could interpret them to Pharaoh.

9 Then the chief cupbearer said to Pharaoh, "I remember my offenses today. 10 When Pharaoh was angry with his servants and put me and the chief baker in custody in the house of the captain of the guard, 11 we dreamed on the same night, he and I, each having a dream with its own interpretation. 12 A young Hebrew was there with us, a servant of the captain of the guard. When we told him, he interpreted our dreams to us, giving an interpretation to each man according to his dream.

14 Then Pharaoh sent and called Joseph, and they quickly brought him out of the pit. 15 And Pharaoh said to Joseph, "I have had a dream, and there is no one who can interpret it. I have heard it said of you that when you hear a dream you can interpret it." 16 Joseph answered Pharaoh, "**It is not in me; God** will give Pharaoh a favorable answer." 17 Then Pharaoh said to Joseph, "Behold, in my dream I was standing on the banks of the Nile. 18 Seven cows, plump and attractive, came up out of the Nile and fed in the reed

---

Not the interpretation he was hoping for.

Why is it so easy to forget those who have helped you get to where you are?

Try to use this phrase a few times today.

grass. 19 Seven other cows came up after them, poor and very ugly and thin, such as I had never seen in all the land of Egypt. 20 And the thin, ugly cows ate up the first seven plump cows, 21 but when they had eaten them no one would have known that they had eaten them, for they were still as ugly as at the beginning. Then I awoke. 22 I also saw in my dream seven ears growing on one stalk, full and good. 23 Seven ears, withered, thin, and blighted by the east wind, sprouted after them, 24 and the thin ears swallowed up the seven good ears. And I told it to the magicians, but there was no one who could explain it to me."

25 Then Joseph said to Pharaoh, "The dreams of Pharaoh are one; God has revealed to Pharaoh what he is about to do. 26 The seven good cows are seven years, and the seven good ears are seven years; the dreams are one. 27 The seven lean and ugly cows that came up after them are seven years, and the seven empty ears blighted by the east wind are also seven years of famine. 28 It is as I told Pharaoh; God has shown to Pharaoh what he is about to do. 29 There will come seven years of great plenty throughout all the land of Egypt, 30 but after them there will arise seven years of famine, and all the plenty will be forgotten in the land of Egypt. The famine will consume the land, 31 and the plenty will be unknown in the land by reason of the famine that will follow, for it will be very severe. 32 And the doubling of Pharaoh's dream means that the thing is fixed by God, and God will shortly bring it about. 33 Now therefore let Pharaoh select a discerning and wise man, and set him over the land of Egypt. 34 Let Pharaoh proceed to appoint overseers over the land and take one-fifth of the produce of the land of Egypt during the seven plentiful years. 35 And let them gather all the food of these good years that are coming and store up grain under the authority of Pharaoh for food in the cities, and let them keep it. 36 That food shall be a **reserve** for the land against the seven years of famine that are to occur in the land of Egypt, so that the land may not perish through the famine."

Not a bad strategy for one's own finances.

Joseph Rises to Power

37 This proposal pleased Pharaoh and all his servants. 38 And Pharaoh said to his servants, "Can we find a man like this, in whom is the Spirit of God?" 39 Then Pharaoh said to Joseph, "Since God has shown you all this, there is none so discerning and wise as you are. 40 You shall be over my house, and all my people shall order themselves as you command. Only as regards the throne will I be greater than you." 41 And Pharaoh said to Joseph, "See, I have set you over all the land of Egypt." 42 Then Pharaoh took his signet ring from his hand and put it on Joseph's hand, and clothed him in garments of fine linen and put a gold chain about his neck. 43 And he made him ride in his second chariot. And they called out before him, "Bow the knee!" Thus he set him over all the land of Egypt. 44 Moreover, Pharaoh said to Joseph, "I am Pharaoh, and without your consent no one shall lift up hand or foot in all the land of Egypt." 45 And Pharaoh called Joseph's name Zaphenath-paneah. And he gave him in marriage Asenath, the daughter of Potiphera priest of On. So Joseph went out over

the land of Egypt.

46 Joseph was **thirty years old** when he entered the service of Pharaoh king of Egypt. And Joseph went out from the presence of Pharaoh and went through all the land of Egypt. 47 During the seven plentiful years the earth produced abundantly, 48 and he gathered up all the food of these seven years, which occurred in the land of Egypt, and put the food in the cities.

50 Before the year of famine came, two sons were born to Joseph. Asenath, the daughter of Potiphera priest of On, bore them to him. 51 Joseph called the name of the firstborn **Manasseh**. "For," he said, "God has made me forget all my hardship and all my father's house." 52 The name of the second he called **Ephraim**, "For God has made me fruitful in the land of my affliction."

53 The seven years of plenty that occurred in the land of Egypt came to an end, 54 and the seven years of famine began to come, as Joseph had said. There was famine in all lands, but in all the land of Egypt there was bread. 55 When all the land of Egypt was famished, the people cried to Pharaoh for bread. Pharaoh said to all the Egyptians, "Go to Joseph. What he says to you, do."

56 So when the famine had spread over all the land, Joseph opened all the storehouses and sold to the Egyptians, for the famine was severe in the land of Egypt. 57 Moreover, all the earth came to Egypt to Joseph to buy grain, because the famine was severe over all the earth.

Joseph's Brothers Go to Egypt

42:1 When Jacob learned that there was grain for sale in Egypt, he said to his sons, **"Why do you look at one another?"** 2 And he said, "Behold, I have heard that there is grain for sale in Egypt. Go down and buy grain for us there, that we may live and not die." 3 So ten of Joseph's brothers went down to buy grain in Egypt. 4 But Jacob did not send Benjamin, Joseph's brother, with his brothers, for he feared that harm might happen to him. 5 Thus the sons of Israel came to buy among the others who came, for the famine was in the land of Canaan.

6 Now Joseph was governor over the land. He was the one who sold to all the people of the land. And Joseph's brothers came and bowed themselves before him with their faces to the ground. 7 Joseph saw his brothers and recognized them, but he treated them like strangers and spoke roughly to them. "Where do you come from?" he said.

They said, "From the land of Canaan, to buy food." 8 And Joseph recognized his brothers, but they did not recognize him. 9 And Joseph remembered the dreams that he had dreamed of them. And he said to them, "You are spies; you have come to see the nakedness of the land."

10 They said to him, "No, my lord, your servants have come to buy food. 11 We are all sons of one man. We are **honest** men. Your servants have never been spies."

Jesus was 30 years old when he started his ministry.

Manasseh = to forget

Ephraim = fruitful

Sounds just like an impatient father with his kids, doesn't it?

Really? You sold your brother into slavery and lied about it to your father!

12 He said to them, "No, it is the nakedness of the land that you have come to see."

13 And they said, "We, your servants, are twelve brothers, the sons of one man in the land of Canaan, and behold, the youngest is this day with our father, and one is no more."

14 But Joseph said to them, "It is as I said to you. You are spies. 15 By this you shall be tested: by the life of Pharaoh, you shall not go from this place unless your youngest brother comes here. 16 Send one of you, and let him bring your brother, while you remain confined, that your words may be tested, whether there is truth in you. Or else, by the life of Pharaoh, surely you are spies." 17 And he put them all together in custody for three days.

18 On the third day Joseph said to them, "Do this and you will live, for I fear God: 19 if you are honest men, let one of your brothers remain confined where you are in custody, and let the rest go and carry grain for the famine of your households, 20 and bring your youngest brother to me. So your words will be verified, and you shall not die." And they did so.

21 Then they said to one another, "In truth we are guilty concerning our brother, in that we saw the distress of his soul, when he begged us and we did not listen. That is why this distress has come upon us."

22 And Reuben answered them, "Did I not tell you not to sin against the boy? But you did not listen. So now there comes a reckoning for his blood." 23 They did not know that Joseph understood them, for there was an interpreter between them. 24 **Then he turned away from them and wept.** And he returned to them and spoke to them. And he took Simeon from them and bound him before their eyes. 25 And Joseph gave orders to fill their bags with grain, and to replace every man's money in his sack, and to give them provisions for the journey. This was done for them.

26 Then they loaded their donkeys with their grain and departed. 27 And as one of them opened his sack to give his donkey fodder at the lodging place, he saw his money in the mouth of his sack. 28 He said to his brothers, "My money has been put back; here it is in the mouth of my sack!" At this their hearts failed them, and they turned trembling to one another, saying, "What is this that God has done to us?"

29 When they came to Jacob their father in the land of Canaan, they told him all that had happened to them, saying, 30 "The man, the lord of the land, spoke roughly to us and took us to be spies of the land. 31 But we said to him, 'We are honest men; we have never been spies. 32 We are twelve brothers, sons of our father. One is no more, and the youngest is this day with our father in the land of Canaan.' 33 Then the man, the lord of the land, said to us, 'By this I shall know that you are honest men: leave one of your brothers with me, and take grain for the famine of your households, and go your way. 34 Bring your youngest brother to me. Then I shall know that you are not spies but honest men, and I will deliver your brother to you, and you shall trade in the land.'"

Can you imagine the emotions Joseph was dealing with? Anger, nostalgia, love, hate, regret. All these years Joseph could have gone back to his family, but he didn't. He put his painful past behind him. But our past has a way of coming back to us. What painful past are you ignoring?

35 As they emptied their sacks, behold, every man's bundle of money was in his sack. And when they and their father saw their bundles of money, they were afraid. 36 And Jacob their father said to them, "You have bereaved me of my children: Joseph is no more, and Simeon is no more, and now you would take Benjamin. All this has come against me." 37 Then Reuben said to his father, "Kill my two sons if I do not bring him back to you. Put him in my hands, and I will bring him back to you." 38 But he said, "**My son shall not go down with you**, for his brother is dead, and he is the only one left. If harm should happen to him on the journey that you are to make, you would bring down my gray hairs with sorrow to Sheol."

> So Jacob was willing to sacrifice his son Simeon rather than risk losing his son Benjamin.

Joseph's Brothers Return to Egypt

43:1 Now the famine was severe in the land. 2 And when they had eaten the grain that they had brought from Egypt, their father said to them, "Go again, buy us a little food."

3 But Judah said to him, "The man solemnly warned us, saying, 'You shall not see my face unless your brother is with you.' 4 If you will send our brother with us, we will go down and buy you food. 5 But if you will not send him, we will not go down, for the man said to us, 'You shall not see my face, unless your brother is with you.'"

6 Israel said, "Why did you treat me so badly as to tell the man that you had another brother?"

7 They replied, "The man questioned us carefully about ourselves and our kindred, saying, 'Is your father still alive? Do you have another brother?' What we told him was in answer to these questions. Could we in any way know that he would say, 'Bring your brother down'?"

8 And Judah said to Israel his father, "Send the boy with me, and we will arise and go, that we may live and not die, both we and you and also our little ones. 9 I will be a pledge of his safety. From my hand you shall require him. If I do not bring him back to you and set him before you, then let me bear the blame forever."

11 Then their father Israel said to them, "If it must be so, then do this: take some of the choice fruits of the land in your bags, and carry a present down to the man, a little balm and a little honey, gum, myrrh, pistachio nuts, and almonds. 12 Take double the money with you. Carry back with you the money that was returned in the mouth of your sacks. Perhaps it was an oversight. 13 Take also your brother, and arise, go again to the man. 14 May God Almighty grant you mercy before the man, and may he send back your other brother and Benjamin. And as for me, if I am bereaved of my children, I am bereaved."

15 So the men took this present, and they took double the money with them, and Benjamin. They arose and went down to Egypt and stood before Joseph.

16 When Joseph saw Benjamin with them, he said to the steward of his house, "Bring the men into the house, and slaughter

an animal and make ready, for the men are to dine with me at noon." 17 The man did as Joseph told him and brought the men to Joseph's house. 18 And the men were afraid because they were brought to Joseph's house, and they said, "It is because of the money, which was replaced in our sacks the first time, that we are brought in, so that he may assault us and fall upon us to make us servants and seize our donkeys." 19 So they went up to the steward of Joseph's house and spoke with him at the door of the house, 20 and said, "Oh, my lord, we came down the first time to buy food. 21 And when we came to the lodging place we opened our sacks, and there was each man's money in the mouth of his sack, our money in full weight. So we have brought it again with us, 22 and we have brought other money down with us to buy food. We do not know who put our money in our sacks."

23 He replied, "Peace to you, do not be afraid. Your God and the God of your father has put treasure in your sacks for you. I received your money." Then he brought Simeon out to them. 24 And when the man had brought the men into Joseph's house and given them water, and they had washed their feet, and when he had given their donkeys fodder, 25 they prepared the present for Joseph's coming at noon, for they heard that they should eat bread there.

26 When Joseph came home, they brought into the house to him the present that they had with them and bowed down to him to the ground. 27 And he inquired about their welfare and said, "Is your father well, the old man of whom you spoke? Is he still alive?"

28 They said, "Your servant our father is well; he is still alive." And they bowed their heads and prostrated themselves.

> When have you experienced this kind of emotion for someone?

29 And he lifted up his eyes and saw his brother Benjamin, his mother's son, and said, "Is this your youngest brother, of whom you spoke to me? God be gracious to you, my son!" 30 Then Joseph hurried out, for **his compassion grew warm for his brother**, and he sought a place to weep. And he entered his chamber and wept there. 31 Then he washed his face and came out. And controlling himself he said, "Serve the food." 32 They served him by himself, and them by themselves, and the Egyptians who ate with him by themselves, because **the Egyptians could not eat with the Hebrews**, for that is an abomination to the Egyptians. 33 And they sat before him, the firstborn according to his birthright and the youngest according to his youth. And the men looked at one another in amazement. 34 Portions were taken to them from Joseph's table, but Benjamin's portion was five times as much as any of theirs. And they drank and were merry with him.

> This is a hint that things would eventually go bad for the Israelites in Egypt.

Joseph Tests His Brothers

44:1 Then he commanded the steward of his house, "Fill the men's sacks with food, as much as they can carry, and put each man's money in the mouth of his sack, 2 and put my cup, the silver cup, in the mouth of the sack of the youngest, with his money for the grain." And he did as Joseph told him.

3 As soon as the morning was light, the men were sent away with their donkeys. 4 They had gone only a short distance from the

city. Now Joseph said to his steward, "Up, follow after the men, and when you overtake them, say to them, 'Why have you repaid evil for good?'"

6 When he overtook them, he spoke to them these words. 7 They said to him, "Why does my lord speak such words as these? Far be it from your servants to do such a thing! 8 Behold, the money that we found in the mouths of our sacks we brought back to you from the land of Canaan. How then could we steal silver or gold from your lord's house? 9 Whichever of your servants is found with it shall die, and we also will be my lord's servants." 10 He said, "Let it be as you say: he who is found with it shall be my servant, and the rest of you shall be innocent." 11 Then each man quickly lowered his sack to the ground, and each man opened his sack. 12 And he searched, beginning with the eldest and ending with the youngest. And the cup was found in Benjamin's sack. 13 Then they tore their clothes, and every man loaded his donkey, and they returned to the city.

14 When Judah and his brothers came to Joseph's house, he was still there. They fell before him to the ground. 15 Joseph said to them, "What deed is this that you have done? Do you not know that a man like me can indeed practice divination?" 16 And Judah said, "What shall we say to my lord? Or how can we clear ourselves? God has found out the guilt of your servants; behold, **we are my lord's servants, both we and he also in whose hand the cup has been found.**" 17 But he said, "Far be it from me that I should do so! Only the man in whose hand the cup was found shall be my servant. But as for you, go up in peace to your father."

18 Then Judah went up to him and said, "Oh, my lord, please let your servant speak a word in my lord's ears, and let not your anger burn against your servant, for you are like Pharaoh himself. 19 My lord asked his servants, saying, 'Have you a father, or a brother?' 20 And we said to my lord, 'We have a father, an old man, and a young brother, the child of his old age. His brother is dead, and he alone is left of his mother's children, and his father loves him.' 21 Then you said to your servants, 'Bring him down to me, that I may set my eyes on him.' 22 We said to my lord, 'The boy cannot leave his father, for if he should leave his father, his father would die.' 23 Then you said to your servants, 'Unless your youngest brother comes down with you, you shall not see my face again.'

24 "When we went back to your servant my father, we told him the words of my lord. 25 And when our father said, 'Go again, buy us a little food,' 26 we said, 'We cannot go down. If our youngest brother goes with us, then we will go down. For we cannot see the man's face unless our youngest brother is with us.' 27 Then your servant my father said to us, 'You know that my wife bore me two sons. 28 One left me, and I said, "Surely he has been torn to pieces," and I have never seen him since. 29 If you take this one also from me, and harm happens to him, you will bring down my gray hairs in evil to **Sheol**.'

30 "Now therefore, as soon as I come to your servant my father, and the boy is not with us, then, as his life is bound up in the boy's

---

It is interesting that the brothers who so willingly threw Joseph "under the bus" so many years ago are now willing to sacrifice themselves for the sake of their brother Benjamin.

The place of the dead.

life, 31 as soon as he sees that the boy is not with us, he will die, and your servants will bring down the gray hairs of your servant our father with sorrow to Sheol. 32 For your servant became a pledge of safety for the boy to my father, saying, 'If I do not bring him back to you, then I shall bear the blame before my father all my life.' 33 Now therefore, please **let your servant remain instead of the boy as a servant to my lord,** and let the boy go back with his brothers. 34 For how can I go back to my father if the boy is not with me? I fear to see the evil that would find my father."

Joseph Provides for His Brothers and Family

45:1 Then Joseph could not control himself before all those who stood by him. He cried, "Make everyone go out from me." So no one stayed with him when Joseph made himself known to his brothers. 2 And **he wept aloud**, so that the Egyptians heard it, and the household of Pharaoh heard it. 3 And Joseph said to his brothers, "I am Joseph! Is my father still alive?" But his brothers could not answer him, for they were dismayed at his presence.

4 So Joseph said to his brothers, "Come near to me, please." And they came near. And he said, "I am your brother, Joseph, whom you sold into Egypt. 5 And now do not be distressed or angry with yourselves because you sold me here, for **God sent me before you to preserve life**. 6 For the famine has been in the land these two years, and there are yet five years in which there will be neither plowing nor harvest. 7 And God sent me before you to preserve for you a remnant on earth, and to keep alive for you many survivors. 8 **So it was not you who sent me here, but God.** He has made me a father to Pharaoh, and lord of all his house and ruler over all the land of Egypt. 9 Hurry and go up to my father and say to him, 'Thus says your son Joseph, God has made me lord of all Egypt. Come down to me; do not tarry. 10 You shall dwell in the land of Goshen, and you shall be near me, you and your children and your children's children, and your flocks, your herds, and all that you have. 11 There I will provide for you, for there are yet five years of famine to come, so that you and your household, and all that you have, do not come to poverty.' 12 And now your eyes see, and the eyes of my brother Benjamin see, that it is my mouth that speaks to you. 13 You must tell my father of all my honor in Egypt, and of all that you have seen. Hurry and bring my father down here." 14 Then he fell upon his brother Benjamin's neck and wept, and Benjamin wept upon his neck. 15 And he kissed all his brothers and wept upon them. After that his brothers talked with him.

16 When the report was heard in Pharaoh's house, "Joseph's brothers have come," it pleased Pharaoh and his servants. 17 And Pharaoh said to Joseph, "Say to your brothers, 'Do this: load your beasts and go back to the land of Canaan, 18 and take your father and your households, and come to me, and I will give you the best of the land of Egypt, and you shall eat the fat of the land.' 19 And you, Joseph, are commanded to say, 'Do this: take wagons from the land of Egypt for your little ones and for your wives, and bring your father, and come. 20 Have no concern for your goods, for the best of all the land of Egypt is yours.'"

Sidebar notes:

Judah offered himself as the sacrifice for Benjamin. Judah was the line through which Jesus comes - the sacrifice for all of us.

The things of "family" are often the source of tears - good and bad.

Romans 8:28: "And we know that for those who love God all things work together for good, for those who are called according to his purpose."

This story illustrates how God's plan of salvation will go forward despite any and all odds against it. And you are part of that plan of salvation.

21 The sons of Israel did so: and Joseph gave them wagons, according to the command of Pharaoh, and gave them provisions for the journey. 22 To each and all of them he gave a change of clothes, but to Benjamin he gave three hundred shekels of silver and five changes of clothes. 23 To his father he sent as follows: ten donkeys loaded with the good things of Egypt, and ten female donkeys loaded with grain, bread, and provision for his father on the journey. 24 Then he sent his brothers away, and as they departed, he said to them, "**Do not quarrel on the way.**"

Why do you think Joseph said this to his brothers?

25 So they went up out of Egypt and came to the land of Canaan to their father Jacob. 26 And they told him, "Joseph is still alive, and he is ruler over all the land of Egypt." And his heart became numb, for **he did not believe them**. 27 But when they told him all the words of Joseph, which he had said to them, and when he saw the wagons that Joseph had sent to carry him, the spirit of their father Jacob revived.

Sometimes the grace of God is too hard to believe.

Joseph Brings His Family to Egypt

46:1 So Israel took his journey with all that he had and came to Beersheba, and offered sacrifices to the God of his father Isaac. 2 And God spoke to Israel in visions of the night and said, "Jacob, Jacob." And he said, "Here I am." 3 Then he said, "I am God, the God of your father. Do not be afraid to **go down to Egypt**, for there I will make you into a great nation. 4 I myself will go down with you to Egypt, and I will also bring you up again, and Joseph's hand shall close your eyes."

5 Then Jacob set out from Beersheba. The sons of Israel carried Jacob their father, their little ones, and their wives, in the wagons that Pharaoh had sent to carry him. 6 They also took their livestock and their goods, which they had gained in the land of Canaan, and came into Egypt, Jacob and all his offspring with him, 7 his sons, and his sons' sons with him, his daughters, and his sons' daughters. All his offspring he brought with him into Egypt.

Interesting. Mary and Joseph also escaped to Egypt for a time.

Jacob and Joseph Reunited

28 He had sent Judah ahead of him to Joseph to show the way before him in Goshen, and they came into the land of Goshen. 29 Then Joseph prepared his chariot and went up to meet Israel his father in Goshen. He presented himself to him and fell on his neck and wept on his neck a good while. 30 Israel said to Joseph, "Now let me die, since I have seen your face and know that you are still alive." 31 Joseph said to his brothers and to his father's household, "I will go up and tell Pharaoh and will say to him, 'My brothers and my father's household, who were in the land of Canaan, have come to me. 32 And the men are **shepherds**, for they have been keepers of livestock, and they have brought their flocks and their herds and all that they have.' 33 When Pharaoh calls you and says, 'What is your occupation?' 34 you shall say, 'Your servants have been keepers of livestock from our youth even until now, both we and our fathers,' in order that you may dwell in the land of Goshen, for every shepherd is an abomination to the Egyptians."

King David was a shepherd. The announcement of the birth of Jesus was first delivered to shepherds. In Psalm 23 (pg. 108), God refers to himself as our Shepherd.

47:13 Thus Israel settled in the land of Egypt, in the land of Goshen. And they gained possessions in it, and were fruitful and multiplied greatly. 28 And Jacob lived in the land of Egypt seventeen years. So the days of Jacob, the years of his life, were 147 years.

Jacob Blesses His Sons

49:28 All these are the twelve tribes of Israel. This is what their father said to them as he blessed them, blessing each with the blessing suitable to him. 29 Then he commanded them and said to them, "I am to be gathered to my people; bury me with my fathers in **the cave** that is in the field of Ephron the Hittite, 30 in the cave that is in the field at Machpelah, to the east of Mamre, in the land of Canaan, which Abraham bought with the field from Ephron the Hittite to possess as a burying place. 31 There they buried Abraham and Sarah his wife. There they buried Isaac and Rebekah his wife, and there I buried Leah—32 the field and the cave that is in it were bought from the Hittites." 33 When Jacob finished commanding his sons, he drew up his feet into the bed and breathed his last and was gathered to his people.

50:1 Then Joseph fell on his father's face and wept over him and kissed him. 2 And Joseph commanded his servants the physicians to embalm his father. So the physicians embalmed Israel. 3 Forty days were required for it, for that is how many are required for embalming. And the Egyptians wept for him seventy days.

4 And when the days of weeping for him were past, Joseph spoke to the household of Pharaoh, saying, "If now I have found favor in your eyes, please speak in the ears of Pharaoh, saying, 5 'My father made me swear, saying, "I am about to die: in my tomb that I hewed out for myself in the land of Canaan, there shall you bury me." Now therefore, let me please go up and bury my father. Then I will return.'" 6 And Pharaoh answered, "Go up, and bury your father, as he made you swear." 7 So Joseph went up to bury his father. With him went up all the servants of Pharaoh, the elders of his household, and all the elders of the land of Egypt, 8 as well as all the household of Joseph, his brothers, and his father's household. Only their children, their flocks, and their herds were left in the land of Goshen.

12 Thus his sons did for him as he had commanded them, 13 for his sons carried him to the land of Canaan and buried him in the cave of the field at Machpelah, to the east of Mamre, which Abraham bought with the field from Ephron the Hittite to possess as a burying place. 14 After he had buried his father, Joseph returned to Egypt with his brothers and all who had gone up with him to bury his father.

God's Good Purposes

15 When Joseph's brothers saw that their father was dead, they said, "It may be that Joseph will hate us and pay us back for all the evil that we did to him." 16 So they sent a message to Joseph, saying, "Your father gave this command before he died: 17 'Say to Joseph, "Please forgive the transgression of your brothers and

---

The cave was the only tangible evidence of the land promised to Abraham. Ironic... a burial cave representing the future, the hope of the people Israel—much like the cross of Jesus representing our future, our hope.

their sin, because they did evil to you."' And now, please forgive the transgression of the servants of the God of your father." Joseph wept when they spoke to him. 18 His brothers also came and fell down before him and said, "Behold, we are your servants." 19 But Joseph said to them, "Do not fear, for am I in the place of God? 20 **As for you, you meant evil against me, but God meant it for good, to bring it about that many people should be kept alive**, as they are today. 21 So do not fear; I will provide for you and your little ones." Thus he comforted them and spoke kindly to them.

The Death of Joseph

22 So Joseph remained in Egypt, he and his father's house. Joseph lived 110 years. 23 And Joseph saw Ephraim's children of the third generation. The children also of **Machir** the son of Manasseh were counted as Joseph's own. 24 And Joseph said to his brothers, "I am about to die, but God will visit you and bring you up out of this land to the land that he swore to Abraham, to Isaac, and to Jacob." 25 Then Joseph made the sons of Israel swear, saying, "God will surely visit you, and you shall **carry up my bones from here.**" 26 So Joseph died, being 110 years old. They embalmed him, and he was put in a coffin in Egypt.

The king of Egypt tried to put an end to God's plan of salvation by killing all the male children. Many years later, King Herod tried the same thing after the birth of Jesus in Bethlehem.

Nickname for Joseph's son Manasseh.

Bones representing hope and a future... ultimately resurrection.

the book of Exodus

Category: *The 5 Books of Moses*
Author: *Moses*
Theme: *Exit; Deliverance; Salvation*
Location & Date: *Egypt and the Sinai Desert; 1445-1405 B.C.*
Version of Bible: *Good News Translation (GNT)*
Summary: *In this book Moses tells his own story. A story of an unlikely hero who struggled with his identity. A story of a leader of a people not eager to be led. The story of the 12 sons of Jacob who became the 12 tribes of Israel living in bondage to Egypt. The story of the struggle to set them free. The story of the challenge to create a nation out of a people with no land, no knowledge of God, and no idea of His purpose for their lives. This book follows an important Biblical pattern: God saves; then He shows those He saves how to live (through the Law). Law follows salvation, not the other way around. We are saved and with the energy of that salvation we live as God shows the way.*

Exodus 1:6 In the course of time Joseph, his brothers, and all the rest of that generation died, 7 but their descendants, the Israelites, had many children and became so numerous and strong that Egypt was filled with them.

8 Then, a new king, who knew nothing about Joseph, came to power in Egypt. 9 He said to his people, "These Israelites are so numerous and strong that they are a threat to us. 10 In case of war they might join our enemies in order to fight against us, and might escape from the country. We must find some way to keep them from becoming even more numerous." 11 So the Egyptians put slave drivers over them to crush their spirits with hard labor. The Israelites built the cities of Pithom and Rameses to serve as supply centers for the king. 12 But the more the Egyptians oppressed the Israelites, the more they increased in number and the farther they spread through the land. The Egyptians came to fear the Israelites 13-14 and made their lives miserable by forcing them into cruel slavery. They made them work on their building projects and in their fields, and they had no pity on them.

15 Then the king of Egypt spoke to Shiphrah and Puah, the two midwives who helped the Hebrew women. 16 "When you help the Hebrew women give birth," he said to them, "**kill the baby if it is a boy**; but if it is a girl, let it live." 17 But the midwives were God-fearing and so did not obey the king; instead, they let the boys live. 18 So the king sent for the midwives and asked them, "Why are you doing this? Why are you letting the boys live?"

When Jesus was born, King Herod ordered that all male children be killed.

19 They answered, "The Hebrew women are not like Egyptian women; they give birth easily, and their babies are born before either of us gets there." 20-21 Because the midwives were God-fearing, God was good to them and gave them families of their own. And the Israelites continued to increase and become strong. 22 Finally the king issued a command to all his people: "Take every newborn Hebrew boy and throw him into the Nile, but let all the girls live."

Moses' Birth

2:1 During this time a man from the tribe of **Levi** married a woman of his own tribe, 2 and she bore him a son. When she saw what a fine baby he was, she hid him for three months. 3 But when she could not hide him any longer, she took a basket made of reeds and covered it with tar to make it watertight. She put the baby in it and then placed it in the tall grass at the edge of the river. 4 The baby's sister stood some distance away to see what would happen to him.

5 The king's daughter came down to the river to bathe, while her servants walked along the bank. Suddenly she noticed the basket in the tall grass and sent a slave woman to get it. 6 The princess opened it and saw a baby boy. He was crying, and she felt sorry for him. "This is one of the Hebrew babies," she said.

7 Then his sister asked her, "Shall I go and call a Hebrew woman to nurse the baby for you?"

8 "Please do," she answered. So the girl went and brought the baby's own mother. 9 The princess told the woman, "Take this baby and nurse him for me, and I will pay you." So she took the baby and nursed him. 10 Later, when the child was old enough, she took him to the king's daughter, who adopted him as her own son. She said to herself, "I pulled him out of the water, and so I name him **Moses**."

Moses Escapes to Midian

11 When Moses had grown up, he went out to visit **his people, the Hebrews**, and he saw how they were forced to do hard labor. He even saw an Egyptian kill a Hebrew, one of Moses' own people. 12 Moses looked all around, and when he saw that no one was watching, he killed the Egyptian and hid his body in the sand. 13 The next day he went back and saw two Hebrew men fighting. He said to the one who was in the wrong, "Why are you beating up a **fellow Hebrew**?"

14 The man answered, "Who made you our ruler and judge? Are you going to kill me just as you killed that Egyptian?" Then Moses was afraid and said to himself, "People have found out what I have done." 15-16 When the king heard about what had happened, he tried to have Moses killed, but Moses fled and went to live in the land of Midian.

One day, when Moses was sitting by a well, seven daughters of Jethro, the priest of Midian, came to **draw water** and fill the troughs

---

The tribe of Levi was the priestly tribe.

The name Moses means "drawn out."

Moses, like many of us, needed to deal with his past - his origins. But it didn't go well. Moses was not accepted by his own people nor the people that adopted him.

Moses' name.

> *The main character of the action met his wife at a well for shepherds, just like Isaac and Jacob.*
>
> *Moses didn't know who he was and didn't have a place to belong.*

for their father's sheep and goats. 17 But some shepherds drove Jethro's daughters away. Then Moses went to their rescue and watered their animals for them. 18 When they returned to their father, he asked, "Why have you come back so early today?"

19 "An Egyptian rescued us from the shepherds," they answered, "and he even **drew water for us and watered our animals.**"

20 "Where is he?" he asked his daughters. "Why did you leave the man out there? Go and invite him to eat with us."

21 So Moses decided to live there, and Jethro gave him his daughter Zipporah in marriage, 22 who bore him a son. Moses said to himself, "**I am a foreigner** in this land, and so I name him Gershom."

23 Years later the king of Egypt died, but the Israelites were still groaning under their slavery and cried out for help. Their cry went up to God, 24 who heard their groaning and remembered his covenant with Abraham, Isaac, and Jacob. 25 He saw the slavery of the Israelites and was concerned for them.

Moses at the Burning Bush

3:1 One day while Moses was taking care of the sheep and goats of his father-in-law Jethro, the priest of Midian, he led the flock across the desert and came to Sinai, the holy mountain. 2 There the angel of the Lord appeared to him as a flame coming from the middle of a bush. Moses saw that the bush was on fire but that it was not burning up. 3 "This is strange," he thought. "Why isn't the bush burning up? I will go closer and see."

4 When the Lord saw that Moses was coming closer, he called to him from the middle of the bush and said, "Moses! Moses!"

He answered, "Yes, here I am."

5 God said, "Do not come any closer. Take off your sandals, because you are standing on holy ground. 6 I am the God of your ancestors, the God of Abraham, Isaac, and Jacob." So Moses covered his face, because he was afraid to look at God.

7 Then the Lord said, "I have seen how cruelly my people are being treated in Egypt; I have heard them cry out to be rescued from their slave drivers. I know all about their sufferings, 8 and so I have come down to rescue them from the Egyptians and to bring them out of Egypt to a spacious land, one which is rich and fertile. 9 I have indeed heard the cry of my people, and I see how the Egyptians are oppressing them. 10 Now I am sending you to the king of Egypt so that you can lead my people out of his country."

11 But Moses said to God, "**I am nobody**. How can I go to the king and bring the Israelites out of Egypt?"

12 God answered, "I will be with you, and when you bring the people out of Egypt, you will worship me on this mountain. That will be the proof that I have sent you."

> *Ever feel unqualified for the task that God seems to be calling you to?*

God's Special Name

13 But Moses said to God, "If I now come to the Israelites and say to them, 'The God of your ancestors has sent me to you,' they are going to ask me, 'What's this God's name?' What am I supposed to say to them?"

14 God said to Moses, "**I Am Who I Am**. So say to the Israelites, 'I Am has sent me to you.'" 15 God continued, "Say to the Israelites, 'The LORD, the God of your ancestors, Abraham's God, Isaac's God, and Jacob's God, has sent me to you.' This is my name forever; this is how all generations will remember me.

Moses Goes Back to Egypt

4:29 So **Moses** and **Aaron** went to Egypt and gathered all the Israelite leaders together. 30 Aaron told them everything that the Lord had said to Moses, and then Moses performed all the miracles in front of the people. 31 They believed, and when they heard that the Lord had come to them and had seen how they were being treated cruelly, they bowed down and worshiped.

First Meeting with Pharaoh

5:1 Then Moses and Aaron went to the king of Egypt and said, "The Lord, the God of Israel, says, 'Let my people go, so that they can hold a festival in the desert to honor me.'"

2 "Who is the Lord?" the king demanded. "Why should I listen to him and let Israel go? I do not know the Lord; and I will not let Israel go."

3 Moses and Aaron replied, "The God of the Hebrews has revealed himself to us. Allow us to travel three days into the desert to offer sacrifices to the Lord our God. If we don't do so, he will kill us with disease or by war."

4 The king said to Moses and Aaron, "What do you mean by making the people neglect their work? Get those slaves back to work! 5 You people have become more numerous than the Egyptians. And now you want to stop working!"

6 That same day the king commanded the Egyptian slave drivers and the Israelite foremen: 7 "Stop giving the people **straw** for making bricks. Make them go and find it for themselves. 8 But still require them to make the same number of bricks as before, not one brick less. They don't have enough work to do, and that is why they keep asking me to let them go and offer sacrifices to their God! 9 Make them work harder and keep them busy, so that they won't have time to listen to a pack of lies."

10 The slave drivers and the Israelite foremen went out and said to the Israelites, "The king has said that he will not supply you with any more straw. 11 He says that you must go and get it for yourselves wherever you can find it, but you must still make the same number of bricks." 12 So the people went all over Egypt looking for straw. 13 The slave drivers kept trying to force them to make the same number of bricks every day as they had made when they

---

Ultimately we know who God is by how He walks with us.

Then Moses left his father-in-law Jethro, met up with his brother Aaron, and returned to Egypt to meet with the Israelite elders.

Straw was combined with clay to make strong bricks.

were given straw. 14 The Egyptian slave drivers beat the Israelite foremen, whom they had put in charge of the work. They demanded, "Why aren't you people making the same number of bricks that you made before?"

15 Then the foremen went to the king and complained, "Why do you do this to us, Your Majesty? 16 We are given no straw, but we are still ordered to make bricks! And now we are being beaten. It is your people that are at fault."

17 The king answered, "You are lazy and don't want to work, and that is why you ask me to let you go and offer sacrifices to the Lord. 18 Now get back to work! You will not be given any straw, but you must still make the same number of bricks." 19 The foremen realized that they were in trouble when they were told that they had to make the same number of bricks every day as they had made before.

20 As they were leaving, they met Moses and Aaron, who were waiting for them. 21 They said to Moses and Aaron, "The Lord has seen what you have done and will punish you for making the king and his officers hate us. You have given them an excuse to kill us."

Moses Complains to the Lord

22 Then Moses turned to the Lord again and said, "Lord, why do you mistreat your people? **Why did you send me here?** 23 Ever since I went to the king to speak for you, he has treated them cruelly. And you have done nothing to help them!"

God Reassures Moses

6:1 Then the Lord said to Moses, **"Now you are going to see what I will do** to the king. I will force him to let my people go. In fact, I will force him to drive them out of his land."

God Calls Moses

2 God spoke to Moses and said, "I am the Lord. 3 I appeared to Abraham, to Isaac, and to Jacob as Almighty God, but I did not make myself known to them by my holy name, the Lord. 4 I also made my **covenant** with them, promising to give them the land of Canaan, the land in which they had lived as foreigners. 5 Now I have heard the groaning of the Israelites, whom the Egyptians have enslaved, and I have remembered my covenant. 6 So tell the Israelites that I say to them, 'I am the Lord; I will rescue you and set you free from your slavery to the Egyptians. I will raise my mighty arm to bring terrible punishment upon them, and I will save you. 7 I will make you my own people, and I will be your God. You will know that I am the Lord your God when I set you free from slavery in Egypt. 8 I will bring you to the land that I solemnly promised to give to Abraham, Isaac, and Jacob; and I will give it to you as your own possession. I am the Lord.'"

9 Moses told this to the Israelites, but **they would not listen to him, because their spirit had been broken** by their cruel slavery.

10 Then the Lord said to Moses, 11 "Go and tell the king of

Margin notes:

When in your life have you asked God this question?

Be patient with God's plan for your life.

A covenant is a promise agreement.

Sometimes it is hard to hear God's voice when we are suffering.

Egypt that he must let the Israelites leave his land."

7:7 At the time when they spoke to the king, Moses was eighty years old, and Aaron was eighty-three.

Aaron's Walking Stick

8 The Lord said to Moses and Aaron, 9 "If the king demands that you prove yourselves by performing a miracle, tell Aaron to take his walking stick and throw it down in front of the king, and it will turn into a snake." 10 So Moses and Aaron went to the king and did as the Lord had commanded. Aaron threw his walking stick down in front of the king and his officers, and it turned into a snake. 11 Then the king called for his wise men and magicians, and by their magic they did the same thing. 12 They threw down their walking sticks, and the sticks turned into snakes. But Aaron's stick swallowed theirs. 13 The king, however, remained stubborn and, just as the Lord had said, the king would not listen to Moses and Aaron.

Disasters Strike Egypt: Blood

14 Then the Lord said to Moses, "The king is very stubborn and refuses to let the people go. 15 So go and meet him in the morning when he goes down to the Nile. Take with you the walking stick that was turned into a snake, and wait for him on the riverbank. 16 Then say to the king, 'The Lord, the God of the Hebrews, sent me to tell you to let his people go, so that they can worship him in the desert. But until now you have not listened. 17 Now, Your Majesty, the Lord says that you will find out who he is by what he is going to do. Look, I am going to strike the surface of the river with this stick, and the water will be turned into blood. 18 The fish will die, and the river will stink so much that the Egyptians will not be able to drink from it.'"

19 The Lord said to Moses, "Tell Aaron to take his stick and hold it out over all the rivers, canals, and pools in Egypt. The water will become blood, and all over the land there will be blood, even in the wooden tubs and stone jars."

20 Then Moses and Aaron did as the Lord commanded. In the presence of the king and his officers, Aaron raised his stick and struck the surface of the river, and all the water in it was turned into blood. 21 The fish in the river died, and it smelled so bad that the Egyptians could not drink from it. There was blood everywhere in Egypt. 22 Then the king's magicians did the same thing by means of their magic, and the king was as stubborn as ever. Just as the Lord had said, the **king refused to listen to Moses and Aaron**. 23 Instead, he turned and went back to his palace without paying any attention even to this. 24 All the Egyptians dug along the bank of the river for drinking water, because they were not able to drink water from the river. 25 Seven days passed after the Lord struck the river. '

Invasion of Frogs

8:1 Then the Lord said to Moses, "Go to the king and tell him

The plague of blood did not change Pharaoh's heart.

The 5 Books of Moses

The plague of frogs did not change Pharaoh's heart.

that the Lord says, 'Let my people go, so that they can worship me. 2 If you refuse, I will punish your country by covering it with frogs. 3 The Nile will be so full of **frogs** that they will leave it and go into your palace, your bedroom, your bed, the houses of your officials and your people, and even into your ovens and baking pans. 4 They will jump up on you, your people, and all your officials.'"

Gnats

The plague of gnats did not change Pharaoh's heart.

16 The Lord said to Moses, "Tell Aaron to strike the ground with his stick, and all over the land of Egypt the dust will change into **gnats**."

Flies

The plague of flies did not change Pharaoh's heart.

20 The Lord said to Moses, "Early tomorrow morning go and meet the king as he goes to the river, and tell him that the Lord says, 'Let my people go, so that they can worship me. 21 I warn you that if you refuse, I will punish you by sending **flies** on you, your officials, and your people. The houses of the Egyptians will be full of flies, and the ground will be covered with them. 22 But I will spare the region of Goshen, where my people live, so that there will be no flies there. I will do this so that you will know that I, the Lord, am at work in this land. 23 I will make a distinction between my people and your people. This miracle will take place tomorrow.'"

Death of Animals

The plague of a terrible disease did not change Pharaoh's heart.

9:1 The Lord said to Moses, "Go to the king and tell him that the Lord, the God of the Hebrews, says, 'Let my people go, so that they may worship me. 2 If you again refuse to let them go, 3 I will punish you by sending **a terrible disease on all your animals**—your horses, donkeys, camels, cattle, sheep, and goats. 4 I will make a distinction between the animals of the Israelites and those of the Egyptians, and no animal that belongs to the Israelites will die. 5 I, the Lord, have set tomorrow as the time when I will do this.'"

Boils

The plague of boils (rash on skin) did not change Pharaoh's heart.

8 Then the Lord said to Moses and Aaron, "Take a few handfuls of ashes from a furnace; Moses is to throw them into the air in front of the king. 9 They will spread out like fine dust over all the land of Egypt, and everywhere they will produce **boils** that become open sores on the people and the animals."

Hail and Thunder

13 The Lord then said to Moses, "Early tomorrow morning meet with the king and tell him that the Lord, the God of the Hebrews, says, 'Let my people go, so that they may worship me. 14 This time I will punish not only your officials and your people, but I will punish you as well, so that you may know that there is no one like me in all the world. 15 If I had raised my hand to strike you and your people with disease, you would have been completely destroyed. 16 But to show you my power I have let you live so that my fame might spread over the whole world. 17 Yet you are still

arrogant and refuse to let my people go. 18 This time tomorrow I will cause a heavy hailstorm, such as Egypt has never known in all its history. 19 Now give orders for your livestock and everything else you have in the open to be put under shelter. **Hail** will fall on the people and animals left outside unprotected, and they will all die.'" 20 Some of the king's officials were afraid because of what the Lord had said, and they brought their slaves and animals indoors for shelter.

The plague of hail did not change Pharaoh's heart.

Locusts

10:1 Then the Lord said to Moses, "Go and see the king. I have made him and his officials stubborn, in order that I may perform these miracles among them 2 and in order that you may be able to tell your children and grandchildren how I made fools of the Egyptians when I performed the miracles. All of you will know that I am the Lord."

3 So Moses and Aaron went to the king and said to him, "The Lord, the God of the Hebrews, says, 'How much longer will you refuse to submit to me? Let my people go, so that they may worship me. 4 If you keep on refusing, then I will bring **locusts** into your country tomorrow. 5 There will be so many that they will completely cover the ground. They will eat everything that the hail did not destroy, even the trees that are left. 6 They will fill your palaces and the houses of all your officials and all your people. They will be worse than anything your ancestors ever saw.'" Then Moses turned and left.

The plague of locusts did not change Pharaoh's heart.

Darkness Covers Egypt

21 The Lord then said to Moses, "Raise your hand toward the sky, and a **darkness** thick enough to be felt will cover the land of Egypt." 22 Moses raised his hand toward the sky, and there was total darkness throughout Egypt for three days. 23 The Egyptians could not see each other, and no one left his house during that time. But the Israelites had light where they were living.

The plague of darkness did not change Pharaoh's heart.

Moses Announces the Death of the First-Born

11:1 Then the Lord said to Moses, "I will send only one more punishment on the king of Egypt and his people. After that he will let you leave. In fact, he will drive all of you out of here. 2 Now speak to the people of Israel and tell all of them to ask their neighbors for gold and silver jewelry." 3 The Lord made the Egyptians respect the Israelites. Indeed, the officials and all the people considered Moses to be a very great man.

4 Moses then said to the king, "The Lord says, 'At about midnight I will go through Egypt, 5 and every first-born son in Egypt will die, from the king's son, who is heir to the throne, to the son of the slave woman who grinds grain. The first-born of all the cattle will die also. 6 There will be loud crying all over Egypt, such as there has never been before or ever will be again.

The Passover

12:1 The Lord spoke to Moses and Aaron in Egypt: 2 "This month is to be the first month of the year for you. 3 Give these instructions to the whole community of Israel: On the tenth day of this month each man must choose either a **lamb** or a young goat for his household. 4 If his family is too small to eat a whole animal, he and his next-door neighbor may share an animal, in proportion to the number of people and the amount that each person can eat. 5 You may choose either a sheep or a goat, but it must be a one-year-old male without any defects. 6 Then, on the evening of the fourteenth day of the month, the whole community of Israel will kill the animals. 7 The people are to take some of the blood and put it on the doorposts and above the doors of the houses in which the animals are to be eaten. 8 That night the meat is to be roasted, and eaten with bitter herbs and with **bread made without yeast**. 9 Do not eat any of it raw or boiled, but eat it roasted whole, including the head, the legs, and the internal organs. 10 You must not leave any of it until morning; if any is left over, it must be burned. 11 You are to eat it quickly, for you are to be dressed for travel, with your sandals on your feet and your walking stick in your hand. It is the Passover Festival to honor me, the Lord.

12 "On that night I will go through the land of Egypt, killing every first-born male, both human and animal, and punishing all the gods of Egypt. I am the Lord. 13 The blood on the doorposts will be a sign to mark the houses in which you live. When I see the blood, **I will pass over you** and will not harm you when I punish the Egyptians.

21 Moses called for all the leaders of Israel and said to them, "Each of you is to choose a lamb or a young goat and kill it, so that your families can celebrate Passover. 22 Take a sprig of **hyssop**, dip it in the bowl containing the animal's blood, and wipe the blood on the doorposts and the beam above the door of your house. Not one of you is to leave the house until morning. 23 When the Lord goes through Egypt to kill the Egyptians, he will see the blood on the beams and the doorposts and will not let the Angel of Death enter your houses and kill you. 24 You and your children must obey these rules forever. 25 When you enter the land that the Lord has promised to give you, you must perform this ritual. 26 When your children ask you, 'What does this ritual mean?' 27 you will answer, 'It is the sacrifice of Passover to honor the Lord, because he passed over the houses of the Israelites in Egypt. He killed the Egyptians, but spared us.'"

The Israelites knelt down and worshiped. 28 Then they went and did what the Lord had commanded Moses and Aaron.

The Death of the First-Born

29 At midnight the Lord killed all the first-born sons in Egypt, from the king's son, who was heir to the throne, to the son of the prisoner in the dungeon; all the first-born of the animals were also killed. 30 That night, the king, his officials, and all the other Egyptians were awakened. There was loud crying throughout Egypt, because there was not one home in which there was not a dead

---

Margin notes:

Jesus was called "the lamb of God" at His baptism. See John 1:29, pg. 250.

Bread without yeast-like a cracker.

Hence the name Passover.

Hundreds of years later with Jesus on a cross, a sponge was dipped in wine vinegar and lifted up on a stalk of hyssop - identifying Jesus as the Passover lamb. John 19:28-29, pg. 290.

son. 31 That same night the king sent for Moses and Aaron and said, "Get out, you and your Israelites! Leave my country; go and worship the Lord, as you asked. 32 Take your sheep, goats, and cattle, and leave. Also pray for a blessing on me."

13:1 The Lord said to Moses, 2 "Dedicate all the first-born males to me, for every first-born male Israelite and every first-born male animal belongs to me."

The First-Born

11 "The Lord will bring you into the land of the Canaanites, which he solemnly promised to you and your ancestors. When he gives it to you, 12 you must offer every first-born male to the Lord. Every first-born male of your animals belongs to the Lord, 13 but you must **buy back** from him every first-born male donkey by offering a lamb in its place. You must buy back every first-born male child of yours. 14 In the future, when your son asks what this observance means, you will answer him, 'By using great power the Lord brought us out of Egypt, the place where we were slaves. 15 When the king of Egypt was stubborn and refused to let us go, the Lord killed every first-born male in the land of Egypt, both human and animal. That is why we sacrifice every first-born male animal to the Lord, but buy back our first-born sons. 16 This observance will be a reminder, like something tied on our hands or on our foreheads; it will remind us that the Lord brought us out of Egypt by his great power.'"

> The Israelites had to give their firstborn to God and then buy them back with a sacrifice. God ultimately paid the price Himself with his first-born Jesus.

The Pillar of Cloud and the Pillar of Fire

17 When the king of Egypt let the people go, God did not take them by the road that goes up the coast to Philistia, although it was the shortest way. God thought, "I do not want the people to change their minds and return to Egypt when they see that they are going to have to fight." 18 Instead, he led them in a roundabout way through the desert toward the Red Sea. The Israelites were armed for battle.

19 Moses took the body of Joseph with him, as Joseph had made the Israelites solemnly promise to do. Joseph had said, "When God rescues you, you must **carry my body with you** from this place."

20 The Israelites left Sukkoth and camped at Etham on the edge of the desert. 21 During the day the Lord went in front of them in a pillar of cloud to show them the way, and during the night he went in front of them in a pillar of fire to give them light, so that they could travel night and day. 22 The pillar of cloud was always in front of the people during the day, and the pillar of fire at night.

> Only in Christianity is their hope in the face of death.

Crossing the Red Sea

14:1 Then the Lord said to Moses, 2 "Tell the Israelites to turn back and camp in front of Pi Hahiroth, between Migdol and the Red Sea, near Baal Zephon. 3 The king will think that the Israelites are wandering around in the country and are **closed in** by the desert. 4 I will make him stubborn, and he will pursue you, and my

> Do you ever feel closed in? Sometimes God lets us have our way all the way into some corner just so we will learn to trust Him.

victory over the king and his army will bring me honor. Then the Egyptians will know that I am the Lord." The Israelites did as they were told.

5 When the king of Egypt was told that the people had escaped, he and his officials changed their minds and said, "What have we done? We have let the Israelites escape, and we have lost them as our slaves!" 6 The king got his war chariot and his army ready. 7 He set out with all his chariots, including the six hundred finest, commanded by their officers. 8 The Lord made the king stubborn, and he pursued the Israelites, who were leaving triumphantly. 9 The Egyptian army, with all the horses, chariots, and drivers, pursued them and caught up with them where they were camped by the Red Sea near Pi Hahiroth and Baal Zephon.

10 When the Israelites saw the king and his army marching against them, they were terrified and cried out to the Lord for help. 11 They said to Moses, "Weren't there any graves in Egypt? **Did you have to bring us out here in the desert to die?** Look what you have done by bringing us out of Egypt! 12 Didn't we tell you before we left that this would happen? We told you to leave us alone and let us go on being slaves of the Egyptians. It would be better to be slaves there than to die here in the desert."

13 Moses answered, "Don't be afraid! Stand your ground, and you will see what the Lord will do to save you today; you will never see these Egyptians again. 14 **The Lord will fight for you**, and all you have to do is keep still."

15 The Lord said to Moses, "**Why are you crying out for help? Tell the people to move forward.** 16 Lift up your walking stick and hold it out over the sea. The water will divide, and the Israelites will be able to walk through the sea on dry ground. 17 I will make the Egyptians so stubborn that they will go in after them, and I will gain honor by my victory over the king, his army, his chariots, and his drivers. 18 When I defeat them, the Egyptians will know that I am the Lord."

19 The angel of God, who had been in front of the army of Israel, moved and went to the rear. The pillar of cloud also moved until it was 20 between the Egyptians and the Israelites. The cloud made it dark for the Egyptians, but gave light to the people of Israel, and so the armies could not come near each other all night.

21 Moses held out his hand over the sea, and the Lord drove the sea back with a strong east wind. It blew all night and turned the sea into dry land. The water was divided, 22 and the Israelites went through the sea on dry ground, with walls of water on both sides. 23 The Egyptians pursued them and went after them into the sea with all their horses, chariots, and drivers. 24 Just before dawn the Lord looked down from the pillar of fire and cloud at the Egyptian army and threw them into a panic. 25 He made the wheels of their chariots get stuck, so that they moved with great difficulty. The Egyptians said, "The Lord is fighting for the Israelites against us. Let's get out of here!"

26 The Lord said to Moses, "Hold out your hand over the sea,

After all the miracles the people had experienced, they still didn't believe.

When have you seen God fight for you in your life?

Sometimes we need to just walk.

and the water will come back over the Egyptians and their chariots and drivers." 27 So Moses held out his hand over the sea, and at daybreak the water returned to its normal level. The Egyptians tried to escape from the water, but the Lord threw them into the sea. 28 The water returned and covered the chariots, the drivers, and all the Egyptian army that had followed the Israelites into the sea; not one of them was left. 29 But the Israelites walked through the sea on dry ground, with walls of water on both sides.

30 On that day the Lord saved the people of Israel from the Egyptians, and the Israelites saw them lying dead on the seashore. 31 When the Israelites saw the great power with which the Lord had defeated the Egyptians, **they stood in awe of the Lord; and they had faith in the Lord and in his servant Moses.**

The Manna and the Quails

16:1 The whole Israelite community set out from Elim, and on the fifteenth day of the second month after they had left Egypt, they came to the desert of Sin, which is between Elim and Sinai. 2 There in the desert **they all complained to Moses** and Aaron 3 and said to them, "We wish that the Lord had killed us in Egypt. There we could at least sit down and eat meat and as much other food as we wanted. But you have brought us out into this desert to starve us all to death."

4 The Lord said to Moses, "Now I am going to cause food to rain down from the sky for all of you. The people must go out every day and gather enough for that day. In this way I can test them to find out if they will follow my instructions. 5 On the sixth day they are to bring in twice as much as usual and prepare it."

6 So Moses and Aaron said to all the Israelites, "This evening you will know that it was the Lord who brought you out of Egypt. 7 In the morning you will see the dazzling light of the Lord's presence. He has heard your complaints against him—yes, against him, because we are only carrying out his instructions." 8 Then Moses said, "It is the Lord who will give you meat to eat in the evening and as much bread as you want in the morning, because he has heard how much you have complained against him. When you complain against us, you are really complaining against the Lord."

13 In the evening a large flock of quails flew in, enough to cover the camp, and in the morning there was dew all around the camp. 14 When the dew evaporated, there was something thin and flaky on the surface of the desert. It was as delicate as frost. 15 When the Israelites saw it, they didn't know what it was and asked each other, "**What is it?**"

Moses said to them, "This is the food that the Lord has given you to eat. 16 The Lord has commanded that each of you is to gather as much of it as he needs, two quarts for each member of his household."

17 The Israelites did this, some gathering more, others less. 18 When they measured it, those who gathered much did not have too much, and those who gathered less did not have too little.

Margin notes:

The people's trust in God and Moses didn't last very long as you will soon see.

I told you their trust wouldn't last long.

The Hebrew word for "what is it?" is manna. See John 6:32 to see the Jesus connection (pg. 202).

Each had gathered just what he needed. 19 Moses said to them, "No one is to keep any of it for tomorrow."

31 The people of Israel called the food manna. It was like a small white seed, and tasted like thin cakes made with honey. 32 Moses said, "The Lord has commanded us to save some manna, to be kept for our descendants, so that they can see the food which he gave us to eat in the desert when he brought us out of Egypt."

Water from a Rock

17:1 The whole Israelite community left the desert of Sin, moving from one place to another at the command of the Lord. They camped at Rephidim, but there was no water there to drink. 2 They complained to Moses and said, "Give us water to drink."

Moses answered, "Why are you complaining? Why are you putting the Lord to the test?"

3 But the people were very thirsty and continued to complain to Moses. They said, "Why did you bring us out of Egypt? To kill us and our children and our livestock with thirst?"

4 Moses prayed earnestly to the Lord and said, "What can I do with these people? They are almost ready to stone me."

5 The Lord said to Moses, "Take some of the leaders of Israel with you, and go on ahead of the people. Take along the stick with which you struck the Nile. 6 I will stand before you on a rock at Mount Sinai. Strike the rock, and water will come out of it for the people to drink." Moses did so in the presence of the leaders of Israel.

Massah = test

Meribah = argument

7 The place was named **Massah** and **Meribah**, because the Israelites complained and put the Lord to the test when they asked, "Is the Lord with us or not?"

Jethro Visits Moses

18:6 Jethro came with Moses' wife and her two sons into the desert where Moses was camped at the holy mountain. 6 He had sent word to Moses that they were coming, 7 so Moses went out to meet him, bowed before him, and kissed him. They asked about each other's health and then went into Moses' tent. 8 Moses told Jethro everything that the Lord had done to the king and the people of Egypt in order to rescue the Israelites. He also told him about the hardships the people had faced on the way and how the Lord had saved them. 9 When Jethro heard all this, he was happy 10 and said, "Praise the Lord, who saved you from the king and the people of Egypt! Praise the Lord, who saved his people from slavery! 11 Now I know that the Lord is greater than all the gods, because he did this when the Egyptians treated the Israelites with such contempt." 12 Then Jethro brought an offering to be burned whole and other sacrifices to be offered to God; and Aaron and all the leaders of Israel went with him to eat the sacred meal as an act of worship.

The Appointment of Judges

13 The next day Moses was settling disputes among the people, and he was kept busy from morning till night. 14 When Jethro saw everything that Moses had to do, he asked, "What is all this that you are doing for the people? Why are you doing this all alone, with people standing here from morning till night to consult you?"

15 Moses answered, "I must do this because the people come to me to learn God's will. 16 When two people have a dispute, they come to me, and I decide which one of them is right, and I tell them God's commands and laws."

17 Then Jethro said, "You are not doing this right. 18 You will wear yourself out and these people as well. This is too much for you to do alone. 19 Now let me give you some good advice, and God will be with you. It is right for you to represent the people before God and bring their disputes to him. 20 You should teach them God's commands and explain to them how they should live and what they should do. 21 **But in addition, you should choose some capable men and appoint them as leaders of the people: leaders of thousands, hundreds, fifties, and tens.** They must be God-fearing men who can be trusted and who cannot be bribed. 22 Let them serve as judges for the people on a permanent basis. They can bring all the difficult cases to you, but they themselves can decide all the smaller disputes. That will make it easier for you, as they share your burden. 23 If you do this, as God commands, you will not wear yourself out, and all these people can go home with their disputes settled."

24 **Moses took Jethro's (his father-in-law) advice** 25 and chose capable men from among all the Israelites. He appointed them as leaders of thousands, hundreds, fifties, and tens. 26 They served as judges for the people on a permanent basis, bringing the difficult cases to Moses but deciding the smaller disputes themselves.

27 Then Moses said good-bye to Jethro, and Jethro went back home.

> Jethro's advice not only helped Moses but can help anyone that seeks to lead people.

> This is not something you read every day.

The Israelites at Mount Sinai

19:1-2 The people of Israel left Rephidim, and on the first day of the third month after they had left Egypt they came to the desert of Sinai. There they set up camp at the foot of Mount Sinai, 3 and **Moses went up the mountain to meet with God.**

The Ten Commandments

20:1 God spoke, and these were his words: 2 "I am the Lord your God who brought you out of Egypt, where you were slaves.

3 "Worship no god but me.

4 "Do not make for yourselves images of anything in heaven or on earth or in the water under the earth. 5 Do not bow down to any idol or worship it, because I am the Lord your God and I tolerate no rivals. I bring punishment on those who hate me and on their descendants down to the third and fourth generation. 6 But I show

> Moses went up the mountain and God gave him the commandments.

my love to thousands of generations of those who love me and obey my laws.

7 "Do not use my name for evil purposes, for I, the Lord your God, will punish anyone who misuses my name.

8 "Observe the Sabbath and keep it holy. 9 You have six days in which to do your work, 10 but the seventh day is a day of rest dedicated to me. On that day no one is to work—neither you, your children, your slaves, your animals, nor the foreigners who live in your country. 11 In six days I, the Lord, made the earth, the sky, the seas, and everything in them, but on the seventh day I rested. That is why I, the Lord, blessed the Sabbath and made it holy.

12 "Respect your father and your mother, so that you may live a long time in the land that I am giving you.

13 "Do not commit murder.

14 "Do not commit adultery.

15 "Do not steal.

16 "Do not accuse anyone falsely.

17 "Do not desire another man's house; do not desire his wife, his slaves, his cattle, his donkeys, or anything else that he owns."

The People's Fear

18 When the people heard the thunder and the trumpet blast and saw the lightning and the smoking mountain, they trembled with fear and stood a long way off. 19 They said to Moses, "If you speak to us, we will listen; but we are afraid that if God speaks to us, we will die."

20 Moses replied, "Don't be afraid; God has only come to test you and make you keep on obeying him, **so that you will not sin**." 21 But the people continued to stand a long way off, and only Moses went near the dark cloud where God was.

The Gold Bull-Calf

32:1 When the people saw that Moses had not come down from the mountain but was staying there a long time, they gathered around Aaron and said to him, "We do not know what has happened to this man Moses, who led us out of Egypt; so make us a god to lead us."

2 Aaron said to them, "Take off the gold earrings which your wives, your sons, and your daughters are wearing, and bring them to me." 3 So all the people took off their gold earrings and brought them to Aaron. 4 He took the earrings, melted them, poured the gold into a mold, and made a **gold bull-calf**.

The people said, "Israel, this is our god, who led us out of Egypt!"

5 Then Aaron built an altar in front of the gold bull-calf and announced, "Tomorrow there will be a festival to honor the Lord." 6 Early the next morning they brought some animals to burn as

God's desire with the law is not to hurt you but to keep you from sin. The goal of sin is to hurt you.

The calf was a symbol of fertility in that ancient culture.

sacrifices and others to eat as fellowship offerings. The people sat down to a feast, which turned into an orgy of drinking and sex.

7 The Lord said to Moses, "Hurry and go back down, because your people, whom you led out of Egypt, have sinned and rejected me. 8 They have already left the way that I commanded them to follow; they have made a bull-calf out of melted gold and have worshiped it and offered sacrifices to it. They are saying that this is their god, who led them out of Egypt. 9 I know how stubborn these people are. 10 Now, don't try to stop me. I am angry with them, and I am going to destroy them. Then I will make you and your descendants into a great nation."

11 But Moses pleaded with the Lord his God and said, "Lord, why should you be so angry with your people, whom you rescued from Egypt with great might and power? 12 Why should the Egyptians be able to say that you led your people out of Egypt, planning to kill them in the mountains and destroy them completely? Stop being angry; change your mind and do not bring this disaster on your people. 13 Remember your servants Abraham, Isaac, and Jacob. Remember the solemn promise you made to them to give them as many descendants as there are stars in the sky and to give their descendants all that land you promised would be their possession forever." 14 So the Lord changed his mind and did not bring on his people the disaster he had threatened.

15 Moses went back down the mountain, carrying the two stone tablets with the commandments written on both sides. 16 God himself had made the tablets and had engraved the commandments on them.

17 Joshua heard the people shouting and said to Moses, "I hear the sound of battle in the camp."

18 Moses said, "That doesn't sound like a shout of victory or a cry of defeat; it's the sound of singing."

19 When Moses came close enough to the camp to see the bull-calf and to see the people dancing, he became furious. There at the foot of the mountain, he threw down the tablets he was carrying and broke them. 20 He took the bull-calf which they had made, melted it, ground it into fine powder, and mixed it with water. Then he made the people of Israel drink it. 21 He said to Aaron, "What did these people do to you, that you have made them commit such a terrible sin?"

22 Aaron answered, "Don't be angry with me; you know how determined these people are to do evil. 23 They said to me, 'We don't know what has happened to this man Moses, who brought us out of Egypt; so make us a god to lead us.' 24 I asked them to bring me their gold ornaments, and those who had any took them off and gave them to me. **I threw the ornaments into the fire and out came this bull-calf!**"

30 The next day Moses said to the people, "You have committed a terrible sin. But now I will again go up the mountain to the Lord; perhaps I can obtain forgiveness for your sin." 31 Moses then returned to the Lord and said, "These people have commit-

> "Out came this calf." Really? Is it sometimes hard to take responsibility for you own mistakes?

ted a terrible sin. They have made a god out of gold and worshiped it. 32 Please forgive their sin; but if you won't, then remove my name from the book in which you have written the names of your people."

33 The Lord answered, "It is those who have sinned against me whose names I will remove from my book. 34 Now go, lead the people to the place I told you about. Remember that my angel will guide you, but the time is coming when I will punish these people for their sin."

35 So the Lord sent a disease on the people, because they had caused Aaron to make the gold bull-calf.

The Second Set of Stone Tablets

34:1 The Lord said to Moses, "Cut two stone tablets like the first ones, and I will write on them the words that were on the first tablets, which you broke. 2 Get ready tomorrow morning, and come up Mount Sinai to meet me there at the top. 3 No one is to come up with you; no one is to be seen on any part of the mountain; and no sheep or cattle are to graze at the foot of the mountain."

Moses Goes Down from Mount Sinai

29 When Moses went down from Mount Sinai carrying the Ten Commandments, his face was shining because he had been speaking with the Lord; but he did not know it. 30 Aaron and all the people looked at Moses and saw that his face was shining, and they were afraid to go near him. 31 But Moses called them, and Aaron and all the leaders of the community went to him, and Moses spoke with them. 32 After that, all the people of Israel gathered around him, and Moses gave them all the laws that the Lord had given him on Mount Sinai. 33 When Moses had finished speaking with them, he covered his face with a veil. 34 Whenever Moses went into the Tent of the Lord's presence to speak to the Lord, he would take the veil off. When he came out, he would tell the people of Israel everything that he had been commanded to say, 35 and they would see that **his face was shining**. Then he would put the veil back on until the next time he went to speak with the Lord.

See 2 Corinthians 3:7; pg. 348.

Offerings for the Sacred Tent

35:4 Moses said to all the people of Israel, "This is what the Lord has commanded: 5 Make an offering to the Lord. Everyone who wishes to do so is to bring an offering of gold, silver, or bronze ....

10 "All the skilled workers among you are to come and make everything that the Lord commanded: 11 the **Tent**, its covering and its outer covering, its hooks and its frames, its crossbars, its posts, and its bases; 12 the **Covenant Box**, its poles, its lid, and the curtain to screen it off; 13 the table, its poles, and all its equipment; the bread offered to God; 14 the lampstand for the light and its equipment; the lamps with their oil; 15 the altar for burning incense and its poles; the anointing oil; the sweet—smelling incense; the curtain for the entrance of the Tent; 16 the altar on which to burn

The people begin the building of the tabernacle - a movable tent temple.

The Covenant Box was also called the Ark.

offerings, with its bronze grating attached, its poles, and all its equipment; the washbasin and its base; 17 the curtains for the enclosure, its posts and bases; the curtain for the entrance of the enclosure; 18 the Tent pegs and ropes for the Tent and the enclosure; 19 and the magnificent garments the priests are to wear when they serve in the Holy Place—the sacred clothes for Aaron the priest and for his sons."

The People Bring Their Offerings

20 All the people of Israel left, 21 and everyone who wished to do so brought an offering to the Lord for making the Tent of the Lord's presence. They brought everything needed for use in worship and for making the priestly garments.

29 All the people of Israel who wanted to brought their offering to the Lord for the work which he had commanded Moses to do.

The People Bring Many Gifts

36:2 Moses called Bezalel, Oholiab, and all the other skilled men to whom the Lord had given ability and who were willing to help, and Moses told them to start working. 3 They received from him all the offerings which the Israelites had brought for constructing the sacred Tent. But the people of Israel continued to bring Moses their offerings every morning. 4 Then the skilled men who were doing the work went 5 and told Moses, **"The people are bringing more than is needed for the work which the Lord commanded to be done."**

Now that's giving!

6 So Moses sent a command throughout the camp that no one was to make any further contribution for the sacred Tent; so the people did not bring any more. 7 What had already been brought was more than enough to finish all the work.

Setting Up and Dedicating the Tent of the Lord's Presence

40:1 The Lord said to Moses, 2 "On the first day of the first month set up the Tent of the Lord's presence.

The Cloud Over the Tent of the Lord's Presence

34 Then the cloud covered the Tent and the dazzling light of the Lord's presence filled it. 35 Because of this, Moses could not go into the Tent. 36 The Israelites moved their camp to another place only when the cloud lifted from the Tent. 37 As long as the cloud stayed there, they did not move their camp. 38 During all their wanderings they could see the cloud of the Lord's presence over the Tent during the day and a fire burning above it during the night.

the book of Leviticus

Category: *The 5 Books of Moses*
Author: *Moses*
Theme: *Traditions, Festivals, and Laws.*
Location & Date: *The Sinai Desert; 1445-1405 B.C.*
Version of Bible: *New Living Translation (NLT)*

Summary: *The people of Israel didn't know who they were; they didn't know who God was; and they didn't know what their future held. Traditions, festivals, and laws formed and united people into a community, establishing and reinforcing shared values, expectations, and dreams for the future. As you read, ask yourself how we today might benefit from following some of the traditions found in the book of Leviticus.*

The Day of Atonement

Leviticus 16:2 The LORD said to Moses, "Warn your brother, Aaron, not to enter the **Most Holy Place** behind the inner curtain whenever he chooses; if he does, he will die. For the Ark's cover —the place of atonement—is there, and I myself am present in the cloud above the atonement cover.

3 "When Aaron enters the sanctuary area, he must follow these instructions fully. He must bring a young bull for a sin offering and a ram for a burnt offering. 4 He must put on his linen tunic and the linen undergarments worn next to his body. He must tie the linen sash around his waist and put the linen turban on his head. These are sacred garments, so he must bathe himself in water before he puts them on. 5 Aaron must take from the community of Israel two male goats for a sin offering and a ram for a burnt offering.

6 "Aaron will present his own bull as a sin offering to purify himself and his family, making them right with the LORD. 7 Then he must take the two male goats and present them to the LORD at the entrance of the Tabernacle. 8 He is to cast sacred lots to determine which goat will be reserved as an offering to the LORD and which will carry the sins of the people to the wilderness of Azazel. 9 Aaron will then present as a sin offering the goat chosen by lot for the LORD. 10 The other goat, the **scapegoat** chosen by lot to be sent away, will be kept alive, standing before the LORD. When it is sent away to Azazel in the wilderness, the people will be purified and made right with the LORD.

11 "Aaron will present his own bull as a sin offering to purify himself and his family, making them right with the LORD. After he has slaughtered the bull as a sin offering, 12 he will fill an incense

The Most Holy Place was in the Tabernacle.

Jesus was the scapegoat taking the blame for our sin. He was both the sacrifice and the one sent away. He was crucified outside the city.

burner with burning coals from the altar that stands before the LORD. Then he will take two handfuls of fragrant powdered incense and will carry the burner and the incense behind the inner curtain. 13 There in the LORD's presence he will put the incense on the burning coals so that a cloud of incense will rise over the Ark's cover—the place of atonement—that rests on the Ark of the Covenant. If he follows these instructions, he will not die. 14 Then he must take some of the blood of the bull, dip his finger in it, and sprinkle it on the east side of the atonement cover. He must sprinkle blood seven times with his finger in front of the atonement cover.

15 "Then Aaron must slaughter the first goat as a sin offering for the people and carry its blood **behind the inner curtain**. There he will sprinkle the goat's blood over the atonement cover and in front of it, just as he did with the bull's blood. 16 Through this process, he will purify the Most Holy Place, and he will do the same for the entire Tabernacle, because of the defiling sin and rebellion of the Israelites. 17 No one else is allowed inside the Tabernacle when Aaron enters it for the purification ceremony in the Most Holy Place. No one may enter until he comes out again after purifying himself, his family, and all the congregation of Israel, making them right with the LORD.

What is all this about? check it out: Hebrews 10:19-22, pg. 380.

18 "Then Aaron will come out to purify the altar that stands before the LORD. He will do this by taking some of the blood from the bull and the goat and putting it on each of the horns of the altar. 19 Then he must sprinkle the blood with his finger seven times over the altar. In this way, he will cleanse it from Israel's defilement and make it holy.

20 "When Aaron has finished purifying the Most Holy Place and the Tabernacle and the altar, he must present the live goat. 21 He will lay both of his hands on the goat's head and confess over it all the wickedness, rebellion, and sins of the people of Israel. In this way, he will transfer the people's sins to the head of the goat. Then a man specially chosen for the task will drive the goat into the wilderness. 22 As the goat goes into the wilderness, it will carry all the people's sins upon itself into a desolate land.

23 "When Aaron goes back into the Tabernacle, he must take off the linen garments he was wearing when he entered the Most Holy Place, and he must leave the garments there. 24 Then he must bathe himself with water in a sacred place, put on his regular garments, and go out to sacrifice a burnt offering for himself and a burnt offering for the people. Through this process, he will purify himself and the people, making them right with the LORD. 25 He must then burn all the fat of the sin offering on the altar.

26 "The man chosen to drive the scapegoat into the wilderness of Azazel must wash his clothes and bathe himself in water. Then he may return to the camp.

27 "The bull and the goat presented as sin offerings, whose blood Aaron takes into the Most Holy Place for the purification ceremony, will be **carried outside the camp**. The animals' hides, internal organs,

Jesus was crucified outside the camp (the garbage dump outside Jerusalem).

and dung are all to be burned. 28 The man who burns them must wash his clothes and bathe himself in water before returning to the camp.

29 "On the tenth day of the appointed month in early autumn, you must deny yourselves. Neither native-born Israelites nor foreigners living among you may do any kind of work. This is a permanent law for you. 30 On that day offerings of purification will be made for you, and you will be purified in the LORD's presence from all your sins. 31 It will be a Sabbath day of complete rest for you, and you must deny yourselves. This is a permanent law for you. 32 In future generations, the purification ceremony will be performed by the priest who has been anointed and ordained to serve as high priest in place of his ancestor Aaron. He will put on the holy linen garments 33 and purify the Most Holy Place, the Tabernacle, the altar, the priests, and the entire congregation. 34 This is a permanent law for you, to purify the people of Israel from their sins, making them right with the LORD once each year."

Moses followed all these instructions exactly as the LORD had commanded him.

The Appointed Festivals

23:1 The LORD said to Moses, 2 "Give the following instructions to the people of Israel. These are the LORD's appointed festivals, which you are to proclaim as official days for holy assembly.

3 "You have six days each week for your ordinary work, but the seventh day is a Sabbath day of complete rest, an official day for holy assembly. It is the LORD's Sabbath day, and it must be observed wherever you live.

4 "In addition to the Sabbath, these are the LORD's appointed festivals, the official days for holy assembly that are to be celebrated at their proper times each year.

Passover and the Festival of Unleavened Bread

5 "The LORD's **Passover** begins at sundown on the fourteenth day of the first month. 6 On the next day, the fifteenth day of the month, you must begin celebrating the Festival of Unleavened Bread. This festival to the LORD continues for seven days, and during that time the bread you eat must be made without yeast. 7 On the first day of the festival, all the people must stop their ordinary work and observe an official day for holy assembly. 8 For seven days you must present special gifts to the LORD. On the seventh day the people must again stop all their ordinary work to observe an official day for holy assembly."

Celebration of First Harvest

9 Then the LORD said to Moses, 10 "Give the following instructions to the people of Israel. When you enter the land I am giving you and you harvest its **first crops**, bring the priest a bundle of grain from the first cutting of your grain harvest. 11 On the day after the Sabbath, the priest will lift it up before the LORD so it may be

---

Appointed festivals were scheduled times where God's people celebrated God together. What appointed times do you have in your life to be with God and His people?

See Exodus 12, pg. 55.

This celebration is also called the Feast of the Firstfruits...

accepted on your behalf. 12 On that same day you must sacrifice a one-year-old male lamb with no defects as a burnt offering to the LORD. 13 With it you must present a grain offering consisting of four quarts of choice flour moistened with olive oil. It will be a special gift, a pleasing aroma to the LORD. You must also offer one quart of wine as a liquid offering. 14 Do not eat any bread or roasted grain or fresh kernels on that day until you bring this offering to your God. This is a permanent law for you, and it must be observed from generation to generation wherever you live.

when the first of the barley crop was given as an offering in support of the priests. Jesus rose from the dead on this day.

The Festival of Harvest

15 "From the day after the Sabbath—the day you bring the bundle of grain to be lifted up as a special offering—count off seven full weeks. 16 Keep counting until the day after the seventh Sabbath, **fifty days later**. Then present an offering of new grain to the LORD. 17 From wherever you live, bring two loaves of bread to be lifted up before the LORD as a special offering. Make these loaves from four quarts of choice flour, and bake them with yeast. They will be an offering to the LORD from the first of your crops. 18 Along with the bread, present seven one-year-old male lambs with no defects, one young bull, and two rams as burnt offerings to the LORD. These burnt offerings, together with the grain offerings and liquid offerings, will be a special gift, a pleasing aroma to the LORD. 19 Then you must offer one male goat as a sin offering and two one-year-old male lambs as a peace offering.

This festival is called the Feast of Weeks in Jewish circles. It is called Pentecost (meaning 50) in Christian circles. See Acts 2, pg. 298.

20 "The priest will lift up the two lambs as a special offering to the LORD, together with the loaves representing the first of your crops. These offerings, which are holy to the LORD, belong to the priests. 21 That same day will be proclaimed an official day for holy assembly, a day on which you do no ordinary work. This is a permanent law for you, and it must be observed from generation to generation wherever you live.

22 "When you harvest the crops of your land, do not harvest the grain along the edges of your fields, and do not pick up what the harvesters drop. Leave it for the poor and the foreigners living among you. I am the LORD your God."

The Festival of Trumpets

23 The LORD said to Moses, 24 "Give the following instructions to the people of Israel. On the first day of the appointed month in early autumn, you are to observe a day of complete rest. It will be an official day for holy assembly, a day commemorated with loud blasts of a trumpet. 25 You must do no ordinary work on that day. Instead, you are to present special gifts to the LORD."

This was a festival looking forward to the day the trumpet will blow signaling the end of the world as we know it.

The Day of Atonement

26 Then the LORD said to Moses, 27 "Be careful to celebrate the **Day of Atonement** on the tenth day of that same month - nine days after the Festival of Trumpets. You must observe it as an official day for holy assembly, a day to deny yourselves and present special gifts to the LORD. 28 Do no work during that entire day be-

Perhaps you have heard of this as Yom

cause it is the Day of Atonement, when offerings of purification are made for you, making you right with the LORD your God. 29 All who do not deny themselves that day will be cut off from God's people. 30 **And I will destroy anyone among you who does any work on that day.** 31 You must not do any work at all! This is a permanent law for you, and it must be observed from generation to generation wherever you live. 32 This will be a Sabbath day of complete rest for you, and on that day you must deny yourselves. This day of rest will begin at sundown on the ninth day of the month and extend until sundown on the tenth day."

> Kippur. See Leviticus 16. It is interesting that God has to threaten us to get us to take a day off.

The Festival of Shelters

33 And the LORD said to Moses, 34 "Give the following instructions to the people of Israel. Begin celebrating the Festival of Shelters on the fifteenth day of the appointed month—five days after the Day of Atonement. This festival to the LORD will last for seven days. 35 On the first day of the festival you must proclaim an official day for holy assembly, when you do no ordinary work. 36 For seven days you must present special gifts to the LORD. The eighth day is another holy day on which you present your special gifts to the LORD. This will be a solemn occasion, and no ordinary work may be done that day.

40 On the first day gather branches from magnificent trees— palm fronds, boughs from leafy trees, and willows that grow by the streams. Then celebrate with joy before the LORD your God for seven days. 41 You must observe this festival to the LORD for seven days every year. This is a permanent law for you, and it must be observed in the appointed month from generation to generation. 42 **For seven days you must live outside in little shelters.** All native-born Israelites must live in shelters. 43 This will remind each new generation of Israelites that I made their ancestors live in shelters when I rescued them from the land of Egypt. I am the LORD your God."

> This was like an annual church camp. Can you imagine the memories that would build on top of each other year after year?

44 So Moses gave the Israelites these instructions regarding the annual festivals of the LORD.

The Sabbath Year

25:1 While Moses was on Mount Sinai, the LORD said to him, 2 "Give the following instructions to the people of Israel. When you have entered the land I am giving you, the land itself must observe a Sabbath rest before the LORD every seventh year. 3 For six years you may plant your fields and prune your vineyards and harvest your crops, 4 but during the **seventh year the land must have a Sabbath year of complete rest.** It is the LORD's Sabbath. Do not plant your fields or prune your vineyards during that year. 5 And don't store away the crops that grow on their own or gather the grapes from your unpruned vines. The land must have a year of complete rest. 6 But you may eat whatever the land produces on its own during its Sabbath.

> The Israelites were way ahead in terms of land management and rotating crops.

The Year of Jubilee

8 "In addition, you must count off seven Sabbath years, seven sets of seven years, adding up to forty-nine years in all. 9 Then on the Day of Atonement in the fiftieth year, blow the ram's horn loud and long throughout the land. 10 Set this year apart as holy, a time to proclaim freedom throughout the land for all who live there. It will be a jubilee year for you, when each of you may return to the land that belonged to your ancestors and return to your own clan. 11 This fiftieth year will be a jubilee for you. During that year you must not plant your fields or store away any of the crops that grow on their own, and don't gather the grapes from your unpruned vines. 12 It will be a jubilee year for you, and you must keep it holy. But you may eat whatever the land produces on its own. 13 **In the Year of Jubilee each of you may return to the land that belonged to your ancestors.**

14 "When you make an agreement with your neighbor to buy or sell property, you must not take advantage of each other. 15 When you buy land from your neighbor, the price you pay must be based on the number of years since the last jubilee. The seller must set the price by taking into account the number of years remaining until the next Year of Jubilee. 16 The more years until the next jubilee, the higher the price; the fewer years, the lower the price. After all, the person selling the land is actually selling you a certain number of harvests. 17 Show your fear of God by not taking advantage of each other. I am the LORD your God.

> You could not lose your land. It would always come back to your family every 50 years. So in effect, you could only rent out your land.

the book of Numbers

Category: The 5 Books of Moses
Author: Moses.
Theme: Not trusting in God
Location & Date: The Sinai Desert; 1445-1405 B.C.
Version of Bible: Expanded Bible (EXB)
Summary: The people were counted (thus the name Numbers), and then organized into camps surrounding the tabernacle (the symbol of God's presence). As they journeyed to the Promised Land, the travelers lost faith that they would be able to enter it. So God made them wander about in the desert until that unbelieving generation died.

The People of Israel Are Counted

Numbers 1:1 The LORD spoke to Moses in the Meeting Tent (the Tabernacle) in the Desert (Wilderness) of Sinai. This was on the first day of the second month in the second year after the Israelites left Egypt [Ex. 12:50–51]. He said to Moses: 2 "You and Aaron must count [take a census of] all the people of Israel [community/congregation/assembly of the sons] by families [clans] and family groups, listing the name of each man [male].

21 The tribe of Reuben totaled 46,500 men. 23 The tribe of Simeon totaled 59,300 men. 25 The tribe of Gad totaled 45,650 men. 27 The tribe of Judah totaled 74,600 men. 29 The tribe of Issachar totaled 54,400 men. 31 The tribe of Zebulun totaled 57,400 men. 33 The tribe of Ephraim totaled 40,500 men. 35 The tribe of Manasseh totaled 32,200 men. 37 The tribe of Benjamin totaled 35,400 men. 39 The tribe of Dan totaled 62,700 men. 41 The tribe of Asher totaled 41,500 men. 43 The tribe of Naphtali totaled 53,400 men. 45 Every man of Israel twenty years old or older who was able to serve in the army was counted and listed with his family group. 46 The total number of men was 603,550. 47 The families groups from the tribe of Levi were not listed [counted] with the others, because 48 the Lord had told Moses: 49 "Do not count the tribe of Levi or include [take a census of; lift the head of] them with the other Israelites. 50 Instead put the Levites in charge of the Holy Tent [Tabernacle] of the Agreement [Treaty; Covenant; Testimony] and everything that is with it.

The Camp Arrangement

Why this camping arrangement?

2:1 The LORD said to Moses and Aaron: 2 "The Israelites should make their **camps** around the Meeting Tent, but they should not camp too close to it. They should camp under their family flag [standard] and banners [ensign]."

3 The camp of Judah will be [camp] on the east side, where the sun rises, and they will camp by divisions there under their flag [banner]. The leader of the people (sons; descendants) of Judah is Nahshon son of Amminadab.

5 Next to them the tribe of Issachar will camp. The leader of the people of Issachar is Nethanel son of Zuar.

10 The divisions of the camp of Reuben will be on the south side, where they will camp under their flag (banner). The leader of the people of Reuben is Elizur son of Shedeur.

12 Next to them the tribe of Simeon will camp. The leader of the people of Simeon is Shelumiel son of Zurishaddai.

14 Next is the tribe of Gad. The leader of the people of Gad is Eliasaph son of Deuel.

17 When the camp of the Levites march out with the Meeting Tent, they will be in the middle of the other camps. The tribes will march out in the same order as they camp, each in its place under its flag.

18 The divisions of the camp of Ephraim will be on the west side, where they will camp under their flag. The leader of the people of Ephraim is Elishama son of Ammihud.

20 Next to them the tribe of Manasseh will camp. The leader of the people of Manasseh is Gamaliel son of Pedahzur.

25 The divisions of the camp of Dan will be on the north side, where they will camp under their flag. The leader of the people of Dan is Ahiezer son of Ammishaddai.

27 Next to them the tribe of Asher will camp. The leader of the people of Asher is Pagiel son of Ocran.

29 Next is the tribe of Naphtali. The leader of the people of Naphtali is Ahira son of Enan.

32 These are the Israelites who were counted by families groups. The total number in the camps, counted by divisions, is 603,550. 33 Moses obeyed the LORD and did not count the Levites among the other people of Israel.

34 So the Israelites obeyed everything the LORD commanded Moses. They camped under their flags [banners] and marched out by and family groups.

The Spies Explore Canaan

13:1 The LORD said to Moses, 2 "Send men to explore [spy on] the land of Canaan, which I will give to the Israelites. Send one leader from each tribe [Deut. 1:19–46]."

17 Moses sent them to explore [spy on] Canaan and said, "Go through southern Canaan [the Negev] and then into the mountains. 18 See what the land looks like. Are the people who live there strong or weak? Are there a few or many? 19 What kind of land do they live in? Is it good or bad? What about the towns

---

The Israelites were newly freed from slavery. They had no idea who they were. They had no land to call their own. Everything was new, unstable, and threatening. They were constantly on the move.

But no matter where the Israelites roamed, each family tent was in the exact spot relative to the other families in their tribe and other tribes as well.

And the most amazing thing: God's tent was right there with them—right in the middle.

they live in—are they open like camps [unwalled], or do they have walls? 20 What about the soil? Is it fertile [rich] or poor? Are there trees there? Try to [or Be courageous and] bring back some of the fruit from that land." (It was the season for the first grapes.)

21 So they went up and explored [spied on] the land. 23 In the Valley of Eshcol, they cut off a branch of a grapevine that had one bunch of grapes on it and carried that branch on a pole between two of them. They also got some pomegranates and figs. 25 After forty days of exploring [spying on] the land, the men returned to the camp.

26 They came back to Moses and Aaron and all the Israelites. The men reported to them and showed everybody [all the community/congregation/assembly] the fruit from the land. 27 They told [reported to] Moses, "We went to the land where you sent us, and it is a fertile land [land flowing with milk and honey]! Here is some of its fruit. 28 But the people who live there are strong. Their cities are walled and very large.

30 Then Caleb told the people near Moses to be quiet, and he said, "We should certainly go up and take the land for ourselves. **We can certainly do it.**"

31 But the men who had gone with him said, "We can't attack those people; they are stronger than we are." 32 And those men gave the Israelites a bad report about the land they explored, saying, "The land that we explored [spied on] is too large to conquer [devours its inhabitants]. All the people we saw are very tall. 33 We saw the Nephilim people there [perhaps named for the pre-flood people mentioned in Gen. 6:4]. (The Anakites come from the Nephilim people.) We felt like grasshoppers, and we looked like **grasshoppers** to them."

The People Complain Again

14:1 That night all the people in the camp began crying loudly. 2 All the Israelites complained [grumbled] against Moses and Aaron, and all the people said to them, "We wish we had died in Egypt or in this desert [wilderness]. 3 Why is the LORD bringing us to this land to be killed with (make us fall by swords?) Our wives and children will be taken away [war plunder]. We would be better off **going back** to Egypt." 4 They said to each other, "Let's choose a leader and go back to Egypt."

5 Then Moses and Aaron bowed [fell] facedown in front of all the Israelites gathered there. 6 Joshua son of Nun and Caleb son of Jephunneh, who had explored [spied on] the land, tore their clothes [ritual of grief]. 7 They said to all of the Israelites, "The land we explored [spied on] is very good. 8 If the LORD is pleased with us, he will lead us into that land and give us that fertile land [land flowing with milk and honey]. 9 Don't turn [rebel] against the LORD! Don't be afraid of the people in that land! We will chew them up. They have no protection, but **the LORD is with us**. So don't be afraid of them."

10 Then all the people talked about killing them with stones.

"We can certainly do it." Do you feel this way about the challenges you face?

Problems can seem so big; we end up feeling small.

So often we want to go back to whatever has enslaved us rather than face the challenges of a new and better life. Why is that?

If you were certain the Lord was with you, what challenge would you take on?

But the glory of the LORD [representing his manifest presence] appeared at the Meeting Tent to all the Israelites. 11 The LORD said to Moses, "How long will these people ignore [despise] me? How long will they not believe me in spite of the miracles [signs] I have done among them? 12 I will give them a terrible sickness [strike them with disease/pestilence] and get rid of [disinherit; dispossess] them. But I will make you into a great nation that will be stronger than they are."

13 Then Moses said to the LORD, "The Egyptians will hear about it! You brought these people from there by your great power, 14 and the Egyptians will tell this to those who live in this land [Canaan]. They have already heard about you, LORD. They know that you are with your people and that you were seen face to face. They know that your cloud [representing God's presence] stays over your people and that you lead your people with that cloud during the day and with fire at night. 15 If you put these people to death all at once, the nations who have heard about your power will say, 16 'The LORD was not able to bring them into the land he promised [swore to] them. So he killed [slaughtered] them in the desert [wilderness].'

17 "So show your strength now, Lord. Do what you said: 18 'The LORD doesn't become angry quickly [is slow to anger], but he has great love [covenant love; loyalty]. He forgives sin and law breaking. 19 **By your great love, forgive these people's sin**, just as you have forgiven them from the time they left Egypt until now.'"

20 The LORD answered, "I have forgiven them as you asked. 21 But, as surely as I live and as surely as my glory fills the whole earth, I make this promise: 22 All these people saw my glory and the miracles [signs] I did in Egypt and in the desert [wilderness], but they disobeyed me [did not listen to my voice] and tested me ten times [symbolic for many times]. 23 So not one of them will see the land I promised [swore to give] to their ancestors. No one who rejected [despised] me will see that land. 24 But my servant Caleb **thinks differently** [has a different spirit] and follows me completely. So I will bring him into the land he has already seen, and his children [seed] will own [possess] that land.

The Lord Punishes the People

26 The LORD said to Moses and Aaron, 27 "How long will these evil people complain [grumble] about me? I have heard the complaining [grumbling] of these Israelites. 28 So tell them, 'This is what the LORD says. I heard what you said, and as surely as I live, I will do those very things to you: 29 You will die [your dead bodies will fall] in this desert. Every one of you who is twenty years old or older [of military age] and who was counted with the people—all of you who complained [grumbled] against me—will die. 30 Not one of you will enter the land where I promised [lifted my hand as when swearing an oath] you would live; only Caleb son of Jephunneh and Joshua son of Nun will go in. 31 You said that your children would be taken away [war plunder], but I will bring them into the land to enjoy what you refused. 32 As for you, you will die [your bodies will fall] in this desert. 33 Your children will be shepherds

Moses fulfilled the role of mediator between God and his people - pointing to the perfect mediator - Jesus.

In what ways do Christians think differently?

here for forty years. Because you were not loyal [unfaithful; the term suggests sexual unfaithfulness as a metaphor of spiritual unfaithfulness], they will suffer until you lie dead [the last of your bodies lie] in the desert. 34 For forty years you will suffer for your sins—a year for each of the forty days you explored [spied on] the land. You will know me as your enemy.'

Moses Disobeys God

20:2 There was no water for the people, so they came together [assembled] against Moses and Aaron. 3 They argued with [contended with; brought a case against] Moses and said, "We should have died in front of the LORD as our brothers did. 4 Why did you? Are we and our animals to die here? 5 Why did you bring us from Egypt to this terrible place? It has no grain, figs, grapevines, or pomegranates, and there's no water to drink!"

6 So Moses and Aaron left the people and went to the entrance of the Meeting Tent. There they bowed facedown [fell on their faces], and the glory of the LORD [his manifest presence] appeared to them. 7 The LORD said to Moses, 8 "Take your walking stick [staff], and you and your brother Aaron should gather the people. Speak to that rock in front of them so that its water will flow from it. When you bring the water out from that rock, give it to the people and their animals."

9 So Moses took the stick [staff] from in front of the LORD, as he had said. 10 Moses and Aaron gathered [assembled] the people in front of the rock, and Moses said, "Now listen to me, you who turn against God [rebels]! Do you want us [rather than God] to bring water out of this rock?" 11 **Then Moses lifted his hand and hit the rock twice with his stick** [staff; he was supposed to speak to it]. Water began pouring out, and the people and their animals drank it.

12 But the LORD said to Moses and Aaron, "Because you did not believe [trust] me, and because you did not honor me as holy [show my holiness] before the people, you will not lead them into the land I will give them."

21:4 The Israelites left Mount Hor and went on the road toward the Red [or Reed] Sea, in order to go around the country of Edom. But the people became impatient on the way 5 and grumbled at [spoke against] God and Moses. They said, "Why did you bring us out of Egypt to die in this desert? There is no bread and no water, and we hate this terrible food!"

6 So the LORD sent them poisonous [burning] snakes; they bit the people, and many of the Israelites died. 7 The people came to Moses and said, "We sinned when we grumbled at [spoke against] you and the LORD. Pray that the LORD will take away these snakes." So Moses prayed for the people.

8 The LORD said to Moses, "Make a bronze snake, and put it on a pole. When anyone who is bitten looks at it, that person will live." 9 So Moses made a bronze snake and put it on a pole. Then when a snake bit anyone, that person looked at the bronze snake and lived [2 Kin. 18:4; John 3:14]."

Why did Moses hit the rock?

Moses' life story: He was rejected by his family (that's how it may have felt to him) and raised in a foreign home (among the Egyptians). When he was a young man he tried to reconnect with his people - only to be rejected. He then ran away into the desert and started a family with people not his own. Then God called him to lead a people that constantly didn't appreciate him. So he hit the rock. What may be causing you to hit the rock in your own life?

the book of Deuteronomy

Category: *The 5 Books of Moses*
Author: *Moses*
Theme: *Moses' last will and testament*
Location & Date: *The Sinai Desert; 1405 B.C.*
Version of Bible: *Contemporary English Bible (CEB)*
Summary: *Moses was about to die. He wouldn't be leading the people into the Promised Land. So he, like a grandfather on his deathbed, spoke his last words, reminding the people of everything that had happened, all that God had done for them, and all that God would do for them—if they followed His ways.*

The Most Important Commandment

Deuteronomy 6:1 Moses said to Israel: The LORD told me to give you these **laws** and teachings, so you can obey them in the land he is giving you. Soon you will cross the Jordan River and take that land. 3 Pay attention, Israel! Our ancestors worshiped the LORD, and he promised to give us this land that is rich with milk and honey. Be careful to obey him, and you will become a successful and powerful nation.

4 Listen, Israel! The LORD our God is the only true God! 5 So love the LORD your God with all your heart, soul, and strength. 6 Memorize his laws 7 and tell them to your children over and over again. **Talk about them** all the time, whether you're at home or walking along the road or going to bed at night, or getting up in the morning. 8 Write down copies and tie them to your wrists and foreheads to help you obey them. 9 Write these laws on the door frames of your homes and on your town gates.

The ten commandments.

Worship Only the LORD

Moses said to Israel: 10 The LORD promised your ancestors Abraham, Isaac, and Jacob that he would give you this land. Now he will take you there and give you large towns, with good buildings that you didn't build, 11 and houses full of good things that you didn't put there. The LORD will give you wells that you didn't have to dig, and vineyards and olive orchards that you didn't have to plant. But when you have eaten so much that you can't eat any more, 12 don't forget it was the LORD who set you free from slavery and brought you out of Egypt.

If you want God in your life, if you want God in your relationships you must create a culture of listening to His voice (the Bible).

The LORD Takes Care of You

Moses said: 8:2 Don't forget how the LORD your God has led

you through the desert for the past forty years. He wanted to find out if you were truly willing to obey him and depend on him, 3 so he made you go hungry. Then he gave you manna, a kind of food that you and your ancestors had never even heard about. The LORD was teaching you that people need more than food to live— they need every word that the LORD has spoken.

4 Over the past forty years, your clothing hasn't worn out, and your feet haven't swollen. 5 So keep in mind that the LORD has been correcting you, just as parents correct their children. 6 Obey the commands the LORD your God has given you and worship him with fear and trembling.

7 The LORD your God is bringing you into a good land with streams that flow from springs in the valleys and hills. 8-9 You can dig for copper in those hills, and the stones are made of iron ore. And you won't go hungry. Wheat and barley fields are everywhere, and so are vineyards and orchards full of fig, pomegranate, and olive trees, and there is plenty of honey.

Don't Forget the LORD

Moses said to Israel: 10 After you eat and are full, give praise to the LORD your God for the good land he gave you. 11 Make sure that you never forget the LORD or disobey his laws and teachings that I am giving you today. If you always obey them, 12 you will have plenty to eat, and you will build good houses to live in. 13 You will get more and more cattle, sheep, silver, gold, and other possessions.

14 But when all this happens, don't be proud! Don't forget that you were once slaves in Egypt and that it was the LORD who set you free. 15 Remember how he led you in that huge and frightening desert where poisonous snakes and scorpions live. There was no water, but the LORD split open a rock, and water poured out so you could drink. 16 He also gave you manna, a kind of food your ancestors had never even heard about. The LORD was testing you to make you trust him, so that later on he could be good to you.

17 When you become successful, don't say, "I'm rich, and I've earned it all myself." 18 Instead, remember that **the LORD your God gives you the strength to make a living**. That's how he keeps the promise he made to your ancestors

Your ability to succeed is a gift to you from God.

Choose Life, Not Death

Moses said to Israel:

30:11 You know God's laws, and it isn't impossible to obey them. 12 His commands aren't in heaven, so you can't excuse yourselves by saying, "How can we obey the LORD's commands? They are in heaven, and no one can go up to get them, then bring them down and explain them to us." 13 And you can't say, "How can we obey the LORD's commands? They are across the sea, and someone must go across, then bring them back and explain them to us." 14 No, these commands are nearby and you know them by heart. All you have to do is obey!

15 Today I am giving you a choice. **You can choose life and success or death and disaster.** 16-18 I am commanding you to be loyal to the LORD, to live the way he has told you, and to obey his laws and teachings. You are about to cross the Jordan River and take the land that he is giving you. If you obey him, you will live and become successful and powerful.

On the other hand, you might choose to disobey the LORD and reject him. So I'm warning you that if you bow down and worship other gods, you won't have long to live.

19 Right now I call the sky and the earth to be witnesses that I am offering you this choice. Will you choose for the LORD to make you prosperous and give you a long life? Or will he put you under a curse and kill you? Choose life! 20 Be completely faithful to the LORD your God, love him, and do whatever he tells you. The LORD is the only one who can give life, and he will let you live a long time in the land that he promised to your ancestors Abraham, Isaac, and Jacob.

We all face this same choice, don't we?

Joshua Is Appointed the Leader of Israel

31:1 Moses again spoke to the whole nation of Israel: 2 I am a hundred twenty years old, and I am no longer able to be your leader. And besides that, the LORD your God has told me that he won't let me cross the Jordan River. 3-5 But he has promised that he and Joshua will lead you across the Jordan to attack the nations that live on the other side. The LORD will destroy those nations just as he destroyed Sihon and Og, those two Amorite kings. Just remember—whenever you capture a place, kill everyone who lives there.

6 **Be brave and strong!** Don't be afraid of the nations on the other side of the Jordan. The LORD your God will always be at your side, and he will never abandon you.

7 Then Moses called Joshua up in front of the crowd and said: Joshua, be brave and strong as you lead these people into their land. The LORD made a promise long ago to Israel's ancestors that this land would someday belong to Israel. That time has now come, and you must divide up the land among the people. 8 The LORD will lead you into the land. He will always be with you and help you, so don't ever be afraid of your enemies.

Are these words you need to hear for what you are facing today?

The Death of Moses

34:1 Sometime later, Moses left the lowlands of Moab. He went up Mount Pisgah to the peak of Mount Nebo, which is across the Jordan River from Jericho. The LORD showed him all the land as far north as Gilead and the town of Dan. 2 He let Moses see the territories that would soon belong to the tribes of Naphtali, Ephraim, Manasseh, and Judah, as far west as the Mediterranean Sea. 3 The LORD also showed him the land in the south, from the valley near the town of Jericho, known as The City of Palm Trees, down to the town of Zoar.

4 The LORD said, "Moses, this is the land I was talking about

A sad scene.

when I solemnly promised Abraham, Isaac, and Jacob that I would give land to their descendants. **I have let you see it, but you will not cross the Jordan and go in."**

5 And so, Moses the LORD's servant died there in Moab, just as the LORD had said. 6 The LORD buried him in a valley near the town of Beth-Peor, but even today no one knows exactly where. 7 Moses was a hundred twenty years old when he died, yet his eyesight was still good, and his body was strong.

8 The people of Israel stayed in the lowlands of Moab, where they mourned and grieved thirty days for Moses, as was their custom.

Joshua Becomes the Leader of Israel

9 Before Moses died, he had placed his hands on Joshua, and the LORD had given Joshua wisdom. The Israelites paid attention to what Joshua said and obeyed the commands that the LORD had given Moses.

Moses Was a Great Prophet

Moses is a "type" of Jesus.

10 **There has never again been a prophet in Israel like Moses.** The LORD spoke face to face with him 11 and sent him to perform powerful miracles in the presence of the king of Egypt and his entire nation. 12 No one else has ever had the power to do such great things as Moses did for everyone to see.

the book of Joshua

Category: *The 12 Historical Books*
Author: *Joshua*
Theme: *Conquest*
Location & Date: *Israel (Canaan); 1405-1385 B.C.*
Version of Bible: *Contemporary English Bible (CEV)*
Summary: *Joshua, who was Moses' right hand man for the 40 years in the desert, modeled well how one follows a leader. In this book, Joshua leads the people of Israel as they battle for the Promised Land. At the end of his life, Joshua put the question to the people of whom, ultimately, they would follow. Would they follow God or the gods of the land of their conquest?*

Joshua Becomes the Leader of Israel

Joshua 1:1 Moses, the LORD's servant, was dead. So the LORD spoke to Joshua son of Nun, who had been the assistant of Moses. The LORD said:

2 My servant Moses is dead. Now you must lead Israel across the Jordan River into the land I'm giving to all of you. 3 Wherever you go, I'll give you that land, as I promised Moses. 4 It will reach from the Southern Desert to the Lebanon Mountains in the north, and to the northeast as far as the great Euphrates River. It will include the land of the Hittites, and the land from here at the Jordan River to the Mediterranean Sea on the west. 5 Joshua, I will always be with you and help you as I helped Moses, and no one will ever be able to defeat you.

6-8 Long ago I promised the ancestors of Israel that I would give this land to their descendants. So be strong and brave! Be careful to do everything my servant Moses taught you. Never stop reading The Book of the Law he gave you. Day and night you must think about what it says. If you obey it completely, you and Israel will be able to take this land.

9 I've commanded you to be strong and brave. **Don't ever be afraid or discouraged! I am the LORD your God, and I will be there to help you wherever you go.**

Rahab Helps the Israelite Spies

2:1 Joshua chose two men as spies and sent them from their camp at Acacia with these instructions: "Go across the river and find out as much as you can about the whole region, especially about the town of Jericho."

Afraid? Discouraged? Face your fears. God will be with you.

The two spies left the Israelite camp at Acacia and went to Jericho, where they decided to spend the night at the house of a prostitute named Rahab.

2 But someone found out about them and told the king of Jericho, "Some Israelite men came here tonight, and they are spies." 3-7 So the king sent soldiers to Rahab's house to arrest the spies.

Meanwhile, Rahab had taken the men up to the flat roof of her house and had hidden them under some piles of flax plants that she had put there to dry. The soldiers came to her door and demanded, "Let us have the men who are staying at your house. They are spies."

She answered, "Some men did come to my house, but I didn't know where they had come from. They left about sunset, just before it was time to close the town gate. I don't know where they were going, but if you hurry, maybe you can catch them."

8 Rahab went back up to her roof. The spies were still awake, so she told them: 9 I know that the LORD has given Israel this land. Everyone shakes with fear because of you. 10 We heard how the LORD dried up the Red Sea so you could leave Egypt. 11 We know that the LORD your God rules heaven and earth, and we've lost our courage and our will to fight. 12 Please promise me in the LORD's name that you will be as kind to my family as I have been to you. Do something to show 13 that you won't let your people kill my father and mother and my brothers and sisters and their families.

14 "Rahab," the spies answered, "if you keep quiet about what we're doing, we promise to be kind to you when the LORD gives us this land. We pray that the LORD will kill us if we don't keep our promise!"

15 Rahab's house was built into the town wall, and one of the windows in her house faced outside the wall. She gave the spies a rope, showed them the window, and said, "Use this rope to let yourselves down to the ground outside the wall. 16 Then hide in the hills. The men who are looking for you won't be able to find you there. They'll give up and come back after a few days, and you can be on your way."

17-20 The spies said: You made us promise to let you and your family live. We will keep our promise, but you can't tell anyone why we were here. You must tie this **red rope** on your window when we attack, and your father and mother, your brothers, and everyone else in your family must be here with you. We'll take the blame if anyone who stays in this house gets hurt. But anyone who leaves your house will be killed, and it won't be our fault.

21 "I'll do exactly what you said," Rahab promised. Then she sent them on their way and tied the red rope to the window.

22 The spies hid in the hills for three days while the king's soldiers looked for them along the roads. As soon as the soldiers gave up and returned to Jericho, 23 the two spies went down into the Jordan valley and crossed the river. They reported to Joshua

---

The "red rope" saved Rahab. Some scholars believe that the red rope is symbolic of the blood of Jesus - the one who saves all of us.

It is also interesting to note that Rahab was mentioned in the great hall of fame in Hebrews 11:31, pg. 382.

and told him everything that had happened. 24 "We're sure the LORD has given us the whole country," they said. "The people there shake with fear every time they think of us."

Israel Crosses the Jordan River

3:1 Early the next morning, Joshua and the Israelites packed up and left Acacia. They went to the Jordan River and camped there that night. 2 Two days later their leaders went through the camp, 3-4 shouting, "When you see some of the priests carrying the **sacred chest**, you'll know it is time to cross to the other side. You've never been there before, and you won't know the way, unless you follow the chest. But don't get too close! Stay about half a mile back."

5 Joshua told the people, "Make yourselves acceptable to worship the LORD, because he is going to do some **amazing things** for us."

7 The LORD told Joshua, "Beginning today I will show the people that you are their leader, and they will know that I am helping you as I helped Moses. 8 Now, tell the priests who are carrying the chest to go a little way into the river and stand there."

9 Joshua spoke to the people: Come here and listen to what the LORD our God said he will do! 10 The Canaanites, the Hittites, the Hivites, the Perizzites, the Girgashites, the Amorites, and the Jebusites control the land on the other side of the river. But the living God will be with you and will force them out of the land when you attack. And now, God is going to prove that he's powerful enough to force them out. 11-13 Just watch the sacred chest that belongs to the LORD, the ruler of the whole earth. **As soon as the priests carrying the chest step into the Jordan, the water will stop flowing** and pile up as if someone had built a dam across the river.

The LORD has also said that each of the twelve tribes should choose one man to represent it.

14 The Israelites packed up and left camp. The priests carrying the chest walked in front, 15 until they came to the Jordan River. The water in the river had risen over its banks, as it often does in springtime. But as soon as the feet of the priests touched the water, 16-17 the river stopped flowing, and the water started piling up at the town of Adam near Zarethan. No water flowed toward the Dead Sea, and the priests stood in the middle of the dry riverbed near Jericho while everyone else crossed over.

The People Set Up a Monument

4:1 After Israel had crossed the Jordan, the LORD said to Joshua: 2-3 Tell one man from each of the twelve tribes to pick up a large rock from where the priests are standing. Then have the men set up those rocks as a monument at the place where you camp tonight.

4 Joshua chose twelve men; he called them together, 5 and told them: Go to the middle of the riverbed where the sacred chest is, and pick up a large rock. Carry it on your shoulder to our camp.

The Ark.

What amazing things has God done for you?

You pray that God would make something happen in your life and nothing happens. Maybe God is waiting for you to step out in faith and then He will make things happen.

The 12 Historical Books

What reminders (rocks) do you have of God's provision in your life?

There are twelve of you, so there will be one rock for each tribe. **6-7 Someday your children will ask, "Why are these rocks here?"** Then you can tell them how the water stopped flowing when the chest was being carried across the river. These rocks will always remind our people of what happened here today.

The People of Israel Set Up Camp at Gilgal

10-13 The army got ready for battle and crossed the Jordan. They marched quickly past the sacred chest and into the desert near Jericho. Forty thousand soldiers from the tribes of Reuben, Gad, and East Manasseh led the way, as Moses had ordered.

The priests stayed right where they were until the army had followed the orders that the LORD had given Moses and Joshua. Then the army watched as the priests carried the chest the rest of the way across.

14-18 "Joshua," the LORD said, "have the priests come up from the Jordan and bring the chest with them." So Joshua went over to the priests and told them what the LORD had said. And as soon as the priests carried the chest past the highest place that the floodwaters of the Jordan had reached, the river flooded its banks again.

That's how the LORD showed the Israelites that Joshua was their leader. For the rest of Joshua's life, they respected him as they had respected Moses.

19 It was the tenth day of the first month of the year when Israel crossed the Jordan River. They set up camp at Gilgal, which was east of the land controlled by Jericho. 20 The men who had carried the twelve rocks from the Jordan brought them to Joshua, and they made them into a monument. 21 Then Joshua told the people:

What is the most significant event in your life that you would tell your children many years from now?

Years from now your children will ask you why these rocks are here. 22-23 Tell them, "The LORD our God dried up the Jordan River so we could walk across. He did the same thing here for us that he did for our people at the Red Sea, 24 because he wants everyone on earth to know how powerful he is. And he wants us to worship only him."

Israel Captures Jericho

5:13 One day, Joshua was near Jericho when he saw a man standing some distance in front of him. The man was holding a sword, so Joshua walked up to him and asked, "Are you on our side or on our enemies' side?"

Many think this is Jesus.

14 "Neither," he answered. "I am here because **I am the commander of the LORD's army.**"

Joshua fell to his knees and bowed down to the ground. "I am your servant," he said. "Tell me what to do."

The same exact words that were said to Moses at the burning bush (Exodus 3:5, pg. 50).

15 **"Take off your sandals,"** the commander answered. **"This is a holy place."** So Joshua took off his sandals.

6:1 Meanwhile, the people of Jericho had been locking the

gates in their town wall because they were afraid of the Israelites. No one could go out or come in. 2-3 The LORD said to Joshua: With my help, you and your army will defeat the king of Jericho and his army, and you will capture the town. Here is how to do it: March slowly around Jericho once a day for six days. 4 Take along the sacred chest and have seven priests walk in front of it, carrying trumpets.

But on the seventh day, march slowly around the town seven times while the priests blow their trumpets. 5 Then the priests will blast on their trumpets, and everyone else will shout. The wall will fall down, and your soldiers can go straight in from every side.

6 Joshua called the priests together and said, "Take the chest and have seven priests carry trumpets and march ahead of it."

7-10 Next, he gave the army their orders: "March slowly around Jericho. A few of you will go ahead of the chest to guard it, but most of you will follow it. Don't shout the battle cry or yell or even talk until the day I tell you to. Then let out a shout!"

As soon as Joshua finished giving the orders, the army started marching. One group of soldiers led the way, with seven priests marching behind them and blowing trumpets. Then came the priests carrying the chest, followed by the rest of the soldiers. 11 They obeyed Joshua's orders and carried the chest once around the town before returning to camp for the night.

12-14 Early the next morning, Joshua and everyone else started marching around Jericho in the same order as the day before. One group of soldiers was in front, followed by the seven priests with trumpets and the priests who carried the chest. The rest of the army came next. The seven priests blew their trumpets while everyone marched slowly around Jericho and back to camp. They did this once a day for six days.

15 On the seventh day, the army got up at daybreak. They marched slowly around Jericho the same as they had done for the past six days, except on this day they went around seven times. 16 Then the priests blew the trumpets, and Joshua yelled:

Get ready to shout! The LORD will let you capture this town. 17 But you must destroy it and everything in it, to show that it now belongs to the LORD. The woman Rahab helped the spies we sent, so protect her and the others who are inside her house.

20 The priests blew their trumpets again, and the soldiers shouted as loud as they could. The walls of Jericho fell flat. Then the soldiers rushed up the hill, went straight into the town, and captured it. 27 The LORD helped Joshua in everything he did, and Joshua was famous everywhere in Canaan.

{The next chapters deal with many battles and lands awarded to the different tribes of Israel. One memorable battle is found here in chapter 10.}

The Sun Stops

10:8 "Joshua," the LORD said, "don't be afraid of the Amorites.

They will run away when you attack, and I will help you defeat them."

9 Joshua marched all night from Gilgal to Gibeon and made a surprise attack on the Amorite camp. 10 The LORD made the enemy panic, and the Israelites started killing them right and left. They chased the Amorite troops up the road to Beth-Horon, until they reached the towns of Azekah and Makkedah. 11 And while these troops were going down through Beth-Horon Pass, the LORD made huge hailstones fall on them all the way to Azekah. More of the enemy soldiers died from the hail than from the Israelite weapons.

12-13 The LORD was helping the Israelites defeat the Amorites that day. So about noon, Joshua prayed to the LORD loud enough for the Israelites to hear: "Our LORD, make the sun stop in the sky over Gibeon, and the moon stand still over Aijalon Valley."

So the sun and the moon stopped and stood still until Israel defeated its enemies.

This poem can be found in The Book of Jashar. The sun stood still and didn't go down for about a whole day. 14 Never before and never since has the LORD done anything like that for someone who prayed. The LORD was really fighting for Israel.

Joshua's Farewell Speech

23:1 The LORD let Israel live in peace with its neighbors for a long time, and Joshua lived to a ripe old age. 2 One day he called a meeting of the leaders of the tribes of Israel, including the old men, the judges, and the officials. Then he told them:

I am now very old. 3 You have seen how the LORD your God fought for you and helped you defeat the nations who lived in this land. 4-5 There are still some nations left, but the LORD has promised you their land. So when you attack them, he will make them run away. I have already divided their land among your tribes, as I did with the land of the nations I defeated between the Jordan River and the Mediterranean Sea.

6 Be sure that you carefully obey everything written in The Book of the Law of Moses and do exactly what it says.

7 Don't have anything to do with the nations that live around you. Don't worship their gods or pray to their idols or make promises in the names of their gods. 8 Be as faithful to the LORD as you have always been.

9 When you attacked powerful nations, the LORD made them run away, and no one has ever been able to stand up to you. 10 Any one of you can defeat a thousand enemy soldiers, because the LORD God fights for you, just as he promised. 11 Be sure to always love the LORD your God.

14 I will soon die, as everyone must. **But deep in your hearts you know that the LORD has kept every promise he ever made to you.** Not one of them has been broken. 15-16 Yes, when the LORD makes a promise, he does what he has promised. But when he makes a

Has this been true for you?

threat, he will also do what he has threatened. The LORD is our God. He gave us this wonderful land and made an agreement with us that we would worship only him.

We Will Worship and Obey the LORD

24:1 Joshua called the tribes of Israel together for a meeting at Shechem. 2 Then Joshua told everyone to listen to this message from the LORD, the God of Israel: Long ago your ancestors lived on the other side of the Euphrates River, and they worshiped other gods. This continued until the time of your ancestor Terah and his two sons, Abraham and Nahor. 3 But I brought Abraham across the Euphrates River and led him through the land of Canaan. I blessed him by giving him Isaac, the first in a line of many descendants. 4 Then I gave Isaac two sons, Jacob and Esau. I had Esau live in the hill country of Mount Seir, but your ancestor Jacob and his children went to live in Egypt.

5-6 Later I sent Moses and his brother Aaron to help your people, and I made all those horrible things happen to the Egyptians. I brought your ancestors out of Egypt, but the Egyptians got in their chariots and on their horses and chased your ancestors, catching up with them at the Red Sea. 7 Your people cried to me for help, so I put a dark cloud between them and the Egyptians. Then I opened up the sea and let your people walk across on dry ground. But when the Egyptians tried to follow, I commanded the sea to swallow them, and they drowned while you watched.

You lived in the desert for a long time, 8 then I brought you into the land east of the Jordan River.

11 You crossed the Jordan River and came to Jericho. The rulers of Jericho fought you, and so did the Amorites, the Perizzites, the Canaanites, the Hittites, the Girgashites, the Hivites, and the Jebusites. I helped you defeat them all. 12 Your enemies ran from you, but not because you had swords and bows and arrows. I made your enemies panic and run away, as I had done with the two Amorite kings east of the Jordan River.

13 You didn't have to work for this land—I gave it to you. Now you live in towns you didn't build, and you eat grapes and olives from vineyards and trees you didn't plant.

14 Then Joshua told the people: Worship the LORD, obey him, and always be faithful. Get rid of the idols your ancestors worshiped when they lived on the other side of the Euphrates River and in Egypt. 15 But if you don't want to worship the LORD, then choose right now! Will you worship the same idols your ancestors did? Or since you're living on land that once belonged to the Amorites, maybe you'll worship their gods. I won't. **My family and I are going to worship and obey the LORD!**

16 The people answered: We could never worship other gods or stop worshiping the LORD. 17 The LORD is our God. We were slaves in Egypt as our ancestors had been, but we saw the LORD work miracles to set our people free and to bring us out of Egypt. Even though other nations were all around us, the LORD protect-

What about your family? Who will you worship?

ed us wherever we went. 18 And when we fought the Amorites and the other nations that lived in this land, the LORD made them run away. Yes, we will worship and obey the LORD, because the LORD is our God.

19 Joshua said: The LORD is fearsome; he is the one true God, and I don't think you are able to worship and obey him in the ways he demands. You would have to be completely faithful, and if you sin or rebel, he won't let you get away with it. 20 If you turn your backs on the LORD and worship the gods of other nations, the LORD will turn against you. He will make terrible things happen to you and wipe you out, even though he had been good to you before.

21 But the people shouted, "We won't worship any other gods. We will worship and obey only the LORD!"

22 Joshua said, "You have heard yourselves say that you will worship and obey the LORD. Isn't that true?"

"Yes, it's true," they answered.

> *It is easy to say you will follow God and his ways and yet hold on to things that are unGodly and go your own way.*

23 Joshua said, "But you still have some idols, like those the other nations worship. Get rid of your idols! **You must decide once and for all that you really want to obey the LORD God of Israel."**

24 The people said, "The LORD is our God, and we will worship and obey only him."

25 Joshua helped Israel make an agreement with the LORD that day at Shechem. Joshua made laws for Israel 26 and wrote them down in The Book of the Law of God. Then he set up a large stone under the oak tree at the place of worship in Shechem 27 and told the people, "Look at this stone. It has heard everything that the LORD has said to us. Our God can call this stone as a witness if we ever reject him."

28 Joshua sent everyone back to their homes.

The Bones of Joseph Are Buried

31 As long as Joshua lived, Israel worshiped and obeyed the LORD. There were other leaders old enough to remember everything that the LORD had done for Israel. And for as long as these men lived, Israel continued to worship and obey the LORD.

> *Hope in the face of death.*

32 When the people of Israel left Egypt, they brought the **bones of Joseph** along with them. They took the bones to the town of Shechem and buried them in the field that Jacob had bought for one hundred pieces of silver ...

the book of Judges

Category: The 12 Historical Books
Author: Samuel
Theme: On a treadmill to nowhere
Location & Date: Israel (Canaan); 1043 B.C.
Version of Bible: New American Standard Bible (NASB)
Summary: This book is summarized best in Judges 16:6: "In those days there was no king in Israel; every man did what was right in his own eyes." The people of Israel walked away from God, and trouble came their way. They called to God for help and he sent a Judge to save them. They followed God for a short time and then started the cycle all over again.

The Generation of Joshua Dies

Judges 2:6 When Joshua had dismissed the people, the sons of Israel went each to his inheritance to possess the land. 7 The people served the LORD all the days of Joshua, and all the days of the elders who survived Joshua, who had seen all the great work of the LORD which He had done for Israel.

10 All that generation also were gathered to their fathers; and there arose another generation after them who did not know the LORD, nor yet the work which He had done for Israel.

Israel Serves Baals

11 Then the sons of Israel did evil in the sight of the LORD and served the **Baals**, 12 and they forsook the LORD, the God of their fathers, who had brought them out of the land of Egypt, and followed other gods from among the gods of the peoples who were around them, and bowed themselves down to them; thus they provoked the LORD to anger. 13 So they forsook the LORD and served Baal and the Ashtaroth. 14 The anger of the LORD burned against Israel, and He gave them into the hands of plunderers who plundered them; and He sold them into the hands of their enemies around them, so that they could no longer stand before their enemies.

16 Then the LORD raised up judges who delivered them from the hands of those who plundered them. 17 Yet they did not listen to their judges, for they played the harlot after other gods and bowed themselves down to them... 18 When the LORD raised up judges for them, the LORD was with the judge and delivered them from the hand of their enemies all the days of the judge; for the LORD was moved to pity by their groaning because of those

Baal was the local god of the Canaanites: a fertility god that one had to pay homage to (sometimes with human sacrifice) for his or her own crops, livestock and offspring.

This paragraph is a good summary of

The 12 Historical Books

the book of Judges.

who oppressed and afflicted them. 19 But it came about when the judge died, that they would turn back and act more corruptly than their fathers, in following other gods to serve them and bow down to them; they did not abandon their practices or their stubborn ways.

Israel Oppressed by Midian

6:1 Then the sons of Israel did what was evil in the sight of the LORD; and the LORD gave them into the hands of Midian seven years.

{The Midianites waited until it was harvest time and then raided the Israelites, taking and/or destroying their crops.}

7 Now it came about when the sons of Israel cried to the LORD on account of Midian ....

Gideon Is Visited

11 Then the angel of the LORD came and sat under the oak that was in Ophrah, which belonged to Joash the Abiezrite as his son Gideon was beating out wheat in the wine press in order to save it from the Midianites. 12 The angel of the LORD appeared to him and said to him, "The LORD is with you, O valiant warrior." 13 Then Gideon said to him, "O my lord, if the LORD is with us, why then has all this happened to us? And where are all His miracles which our fathers told us about, saying, 'Did not the LORD bring us up from Egypt?' But now the LORD has abandoned us and given us into the hand of Midian." 14 The LORD looked at him and said, "Go in this your strength and deliver Israel from the hand of Midian. **Have I not sent you?**" 15 He said to Him, "O Lord, how shall I deliver Israel? **Behold, my family is the least in Manasseh, and I am the youngest in my father's house.**" 16 But the LORD said to him, "Surely I will be with you, and you shall defeat Midian as one man." 17 So Gideon said to Him, "If now I have found favor in Your sight, then show me a sign that it is You who speak with me.

Gideon was arrogant until the angel told him he had been chosen.

Manasseh was the smallest and weakest of the 12 tribes of Israel, so in a sense Gideon was saying that he was the least in the whole nation of Israel. Nevertheless, God called him to save Israel. What is your excuse when God calls?

Sign of the Fleece

36 Then Gideon said to God, "If You will deliver Israel through me, as You have spoken, 37 behold, I will put a fleece of wool on the threshing floor. If there is dew on the fleece only, and it is dry on all the ground, then I will know that You will deliver Israel through me, as You have spoken." 38 And it was so. When he arose early the next morning and squeezed the fleece, he drained the dew from the fleece, a bowl full of water. 39 Then Gideon said to God, "Do not let Your anger burn against me that I may speak once more; please let me make a test once more with the fleece, let it now be dry only on the fleece, and let there be dew on all the ground." 40 God did so that night; for it was dry only on the fleece, and dew was on all the ground.

After Gideon received the sign of the fleece, he stepped up to a leadership position.

Gideon's 300 Chosen Men

7:1 Then Jerubbaal (that is, Gideon) and all the people who were with him, rose early and camped beside the spring of Harod; and the camp of Midian was on the north side of them by the hill of Moreh in the valley.

2 The LORD said to Gideon, "The people who are with you are too many for Me to give Midian into their hands, for Israel would become boastful, saying, 'My own power has delivered me.' 3 Now therefore come, proclaim in the hearing of the people, saying, 'Whoever is afraid and trembling, let him return and depart from Mount Gilead.'" So 22,000 people returned, but 10,000 remained.

4 Then the LORD said to Gideon, "The people are still too many; bring them down to the water and I will test them for you there. Therefore it shall be that he of whom I say to you, 'This one shall go with you,' he shall go with you; but everyone of whom I say to you, 'This one shall not go with you,' he shall not go." 5 So he brought the people down to the water. And the LORD said to Gideon, "You shall separate everyone who laps the water with his tongue as a dog laps, as well as everyone who kneels to drink." 6 Now the number of those who lapped, putting their hand to their mouth, was 300 men; but all the rest of the people kneeled to drink water. 7 The LORD said to Gideon, "I will deliver you with the 300 men who lapped and will give the Midianites into your hands; so let all the other people go, each man to his home." 8 So the **300 men** took the people's provisions and their trumpets into their hands. And Gideon sent all the other men of Israel, each to his tent, but retained the 300 men ...

16 He divided the 300 men into three companies, and he put trumpets and empty pitchers into the hands of all of them, with torches inside the pitchers. 17 He said to them, "Look at me and do likewise. And behold, when I come to the outskirts of the camp, do as I do. 18 When I and all who are with me blow the trumpet, then you also blow the trumpets all around the camp and say, 'For the LORD and for Gideon.'"

Confusion of the Enemy

19 So Gideon and the hundred men who were with him came to the outskirts of the camp at the beginning of the middle watch, when they had just posted the watch; and they blew the trumpets and smashed the pitchers that were in their hands. 20 When the three companies blew the trumpets and broke the pitchers, they held the torches in their left hands and the trumpets in their right hands for blowing, and cried, "A sword for the LORD and for Gideon!" 21 Each stood in his place around the camp; and all the army ran, crying out as they fled. 22 When they blew 300 trumpets, the LORD set the sword of one against another even throughout the whole army; and the army fled as far as Beth-shittah toward Zererah, as far as the edge of Abel-meholah, by Tabbath.

{They were routed and defeated.}

Philistines Oppress Again

13:1 Now the sons of Israel again did evil in the sight of the LORD, so that the LORD gave them into the hands of the Philis-

The odds were so far against Gideon and his men that if they succeeded, it would be because God made it happen.

The 12 Historical Books

Like so many mothers of mainline Biblical characters.

tines forty years.

2 There was a certain man of Zorah, of the family of the Danites, whose name was Manoah; and his wife was **barren** and had borne no children. 3 Then the angel of the LORD appeared to the woman and said to her, "Behold now, you are barren and have borne no children, but you shall conceive and give birth to a son. 4 You shall conceive and give birth to a son, and no razor shall come upon his head, for the boy shall be a Nazirite to God from the womb; and he shall begin to deliver Israel from the hands of the Philistines."

24 Then the woman gave birth to a son and named him Samson; and the child grew up and the LORD blessed him.

Samson's Weakness

16:4 ... it came about that he loved a woman in the valley of Sorek, whose name was Delilah. 5 The lords of the Philistines came up to her and said to her, "Entice him, and see where his great strength lies and how we may overpower him that we may bind him to afflict him. Then we will each give you eleven hundred pieces of silver." 6 So Delilah said to Samson, "Please tell me where your great strength is and how you may be bound to afflict you." 7 Samson said to her, "If they bind me with seven fresh cords that have not been dried, then I will become weak and be like any other man." 8 Then the lords of the Philistines brought up to her seven fresh cords that had not been dried, and she bound him with them. 9 Now she had men lying in wait in an inner room. And she said to him, "The Philistines are upon you, Samson!" But he snapped the cords as a string of tow snaps when it touches fire. So his strength was not discovered.

10 Then Delilah said to Samson, "Behold, you have deceived me and told me lies; now please tell me how you may be bound." 11 He said to her, "If they bind me tightly with new ropes which have not been used, then I will become weak and be like any other man." 12 So Delilah took new ropes and bound him with them and said to him, "The Philistines are upon you, Samson!" For the men were lying in wait in the inner room. But he snapped the ropes from his arms like a thread.

13 Then Delilah said to Samson, "Up to now you have deceived me and told me lies; tell me how you may be bound." And he said to her, "If you weave the seven locks of my hair with the web and fasten it with a pin, then I will become weak and be like any other man." 14 So while he slept, Delilah took the seven locks of his [hair and wove them into the web]. And she fastened it with the pin and said to him, "The Philistines are upon you, Samson!" But he awoke from his sleep and pulled out the pin of the loom and the web.

Delilah Extracts His Secret

"Okay but you are trying to have me killed." Love is blind.

15 Then she said to him, "How can you say, 'I love you,' when your heart is not with me? **You have deceived me these three times and have not told me where your great strength is.**" 16 It came about when she pressed him daily with her words and urged him, that his soul was annoyed to death. 17 So he told her all that was in his heart

and said to her, "A razor has never come on my head, for I have been a Nazirite to God from my mother's womb. If I am shaved, then my strength will leave me and I will become weak and be like any other man."

18 When Delilah saw that he had told her all that was in his heart, she sent and called the lords of the Philistines, saying, "Come up once more, for he has told me all that is in his heart." Then the lords of the Philistines came up to her and brought the money in their hands. 19 She made him sleep on her knees, and called for a man and had him shave off the seven locks of his hair. Then she began to afflict him, and his strength left him. 20 She said, "The Philistines are upon you, Samson!" And he awoke from his sleep and said, "I will go out as at other times and shake myself free." But he did not know that the LORD had departed from him. 21 Then the Philistines seized him and gouged out his eyes; and they brought him down to Gaza and bound him with bronze chains, and he was a grinder in the prison. 22 However, the hair of his head began to grow again after it was shaved off.

23 Now the lords of the Philistines assembled to offer a great sacrifice to Dagon their god, and to rejoice, for they said, "Our god has given Samson our enemy into our hands."

24 When the people saw him, they praised their god, for they said, "Our god has given our enemy into our hands, Even the destroyer of our country, Who has slain many of us."

25 It so happened when they were in high spirits, that they said, "Call for Samson, that he may amuse us." So they called for Samson from the prison, and he entertained them. And they made him stand between the pillars. 26 Then Samson said to the boy who was holding his hand, "Let me feel the pillars on which the house rests, that I may lean against them." 27 Now the house was full of men and women, and all the lords of the Philistines were there. And about 3,000 men and women were on the roof looking on while Samson was amusing them.

Samson Is Avenged

28 Then Samson called to the LORD and said, "O Lord GOD, please remember me and please strengthen me just this time, O God, that I may at once be avenged of the Philistines for my two eyes." 29 Samson grasped the two middle pillars on which the house rested, and braced himself against them, the one with his right hand and the other with his left. 30 And Samson said, "Let me die with the Philistines!" And he bent with all his might so that the house fell on the lords and all the people who were in it. So the dead whom he killed at his death were more than those whom he killed in his life. 31 Then his brothers and all his father's household came down, took him, brought him up and buried him between Zorah and Eshtaol in the tomb of Manoah his father. Thus he had judged Israel twenty years.

the book of Ruth

Category: The 12 Historical Books
Author: Unknown
Theme: Redemption
Location & Date: Moab & Bethlehem; 1030-1010 B.C.
Version of Bible: The Message (MSG)
Summary: This book is a beautiful story of lost and found—a story of redemption—a story of someone paying a price to restore and save someone else.

They left Bethlehem (the birth town of Jesus) and went to Moab (a foreign country).

Ruth 1:1-2 Once upon a time—it was back in the days when judges led Israel—there was a famine in the land. A man from **Bethlehem** in Judah left home to live in the country of Moab, he and his wife and his two sons. The man's name was Elimelech; his wife's name was Naomi; his sons were named Mahlon and Kilion-all Ephrathites from Bethlehem in Judah. They all went to the country of Moab and settled there.

3-5 Elimelech died and Naomi was left, she and her two sons. The sons took Moabite wives; the name of the first was Orpah, the second Ruth. They lived there in Moab for the next ten years. But then the two brothers, Mahlon and Kilion, died. Now the woman was left without either her young men or her husband.

6-7 One day she got herself together, she and her two daughters-in-law, to leave the country of Moab and set out for home; she had heard that GOD had been pleased to visit his people and give them food. And so she started out from the place she had been living, she and her two daughters-in-law with her, on the road back to the land of Judah.

8-9 After a short while on the road, Naomi told her two daughters-in-law, "Go back. Go home and live with your mothers. And may GOD treat you as graciously as you treated your deceased husbands and me. May GOD give each of you a new home and a new husband!" She kissed them and they cried openly.

10 They said, "No, we're going on with you to your people."

11-13 But Naomi was firm: "Go back, my dear daughters. Why would you come with me? Do you suppose I still have sons in my womb who can become your future husbands? Go back, dear daughters—on your way, please! No, dear daughters; this is a bitter pill for me to swallow—more bitter for me than for you. GOD has dealt me a hard blow."

14 Again they cried openly. Orpah kissed her mother-in-law

good-bye; but Ruth embraced her and held on.

15 Naomi said, "Look, your sister-in-law is going back home to live with her own people and gods; go with her."

16-17 But Ruth said, "Don't force me to leave you; don't make me go home. **Where you go, I go**; and where you live, I'll live. Your people are my people, your God is my god; where you die, I'll die, and that's where I'll be buried, so help me GOD—not even death itself is going to come between us!"

18-19 When Naomi saw that Ruth had her heart set on going with her, she gave in. And so the two of them traveled on together to Bethlehem.

When they arrived in Bethlehem the whole town was soon buzzing: "Is this really our Naomi? And after all this time!"

20-21 But she said, "Don't call me Naomi; call me **Bitter**. The Strong One has dealt me a bitter blow. I left here full of life, and GOD has brought me back with nothing but the clothes on my back. Why would you call me Naomi? God certainly doesn't. The Strong One ruined me."

22 And so Naomi was back, and Ruth the foreigner with her, back from the country of Moab. They arrived in Bethlehem at the beginning of the barley harvest.

2:1 It so happened that Naomi had a relative by marriage, a man prominent and rich, connected with Elimelech's family. His name was Boaz.

2 One day Ruth, the Moabite foreigner, said to Naomi, "I'm going to work; I'm going out to glean among the sheaves, following after some harvester who will treat me kindly."

Naomi said, "Go ahead, dear daughter."

3-4 And so she set out. She went and started **gleaning** in a field, following in the wake of the harvesters. Eventually she ended up in the part of the field owned by Boaz, her father-in-law Elimelech's relative. A little later Boaz came out from Bethlehem, greeting his harvesters, "GOD be with you!" They replied, "And GOD bless you!"

5 Boaz asked his young servant who was foreman over the farm hands, "Who is this young woman? Where did she come from?"

6-7 The foreman said, "Why, that's the Moabite girl, the one who came with Naomi from the country of Moab. She asked permission. 'Let me glean,' she said, 'and gather among the sheaves following after your harvesters.' She's been at it steady ever since, from early morning until now, without so much as a break."

8-9 Then Boaz spoke to Ruth: "Listen, my daughter. From now on don't go to any other field to glean—stay right here in this one. And stay close to my young women. Watch where they are harvesting and follow them. And don't worry about a thing; I've given orders to my servants not to harass you. When you get thirsty, feel free to go and drink from the water buckets that the servants

---

Sidebar notes:

This is a great example of commitment - of friendship, marriage, and our relationship to God.

There is bitterness toward God. Have you been there?

God commanded harvesters to leave a little of the harvest for the poor, thus helping the poor help themselves (the poor still had to motivate themselves and work hard for the food). How might we do that today?

have filled."

10 She dropped to her knees, then bowed her face to the ground. "How does this happen that you should pick me out and treat me so kindly—me, a foreigner?"

11-12 Boaz answered her, "**I've heard all about you**—heard about the way you treated your mother-in-law after the death of her husband, and how you left your father and mother and the land of your birth and have come to live among a bunch of total strangers. GOD reward you well for what you've done—and with a generous bonus besides from GOD, to whom you've come seeking protection under his wings."

13 She said, "Oh sir, such grace, such kindness—I don't deserve it. You've touched my heart, treated me like one of your own. And I don't even belong here!"

14 At the lunch break, Boaz said to her, "Come over here; eat some bread. Dip it in the wine."

So she joined the harvesters. Boaz passed the roasted grain to her. She ate her fill and even had some left over.

15-16 When she got up to go back to work, Boaz ordered his servants: "Let her glean where there's still plenty of grain on the ground—make it easy for her. Better yet, pull some of the good stuff out and leave it for her to glean. Give her special treatment."

17-18 Ruth gleaned in the field until evening. When she threshed out what she had gathered, she ended up with nearly a full sack of barley! She gathered up her gleanings, went back to town, and showed her mother-in-law the results of her day's work; she also gave her the leftovers from her lunch.

19 Naomi asked her, "So where did you glean today? Whose field? GOD bless whoever it was who took such good care of you!"

Ruth told her mother-in-law, "The man with whom I worked today? His name is Boaz."

20 Naomi said to her daughter-in-law, "Why, GOD bless that man! GOD hasn't quite walked out on us after all! He still loves us, in bad times as well as good!"

Naomi went on, "That man, Ruth, is one of our circle of **covenant redeemers, a close relative of ours!**"

3:1-2 One day her mother-in-law Naomi said to Ruth, "My dear daughter, isn't it about time I arranged a good home for you so you can have a happy life? And isn't Boaz our close relative, the one with whose young women you've been working? Maybe it's time to make our move. Tonight is the night of Boaz's barley harvest at the threshing floor.

3-4 "Take a bath. Put on some perfume. Get all dressed up and go to the threshing floor. But don't let him know you're there until the party is well under way and he's had plenty of food and drink. When you see him slipping off to sleep, watch where he lies down and then go there. Lie at his feet to let him know that you are avail-

---

A reputation of integrity gets around.

When each family within each tribe of Israel inherited their land (in the Promised Land), there were rules and laws to help families keep it. One of those laws allowed a widow to keep her husband's land if a close relative were to "buy" it. Boaz is a close relative.

able to him for marriage. Then wait and see what he says. He'll tell you what to do."

5 Ruth said, "If you say so, I'll do it, just as you've told me."

6 She went down to the threshing floor and put her mother-in-law's plan into action.

7 Boaz had a good time, eating and drinking his fill—he felt great. Then he went off to get some sleep, lying down at the end of a stack of barley. Ruth quietly followed; she lay down to signal her availability for marriage.

8 In the middle of the night the man was suddenly startled and sat up. Surprise! This woman asleep at his feet!

9 He said, "And who are you?"

She said, "I am Ruth, your maiden; take me under your protecting wing. You're my close relative, you know, in the circle of covenant redeemers—you do have the right to marry me."

10-13 He said, "GOD bless you, my dear daughter! What a splendid expression of love! And when you could have had your pick of any of the young men around. And now, my dear daughter, don't you worry about a thing; I'll do all you could want or ask. Everybody in town knows what a courageous woman you are—a real prize! You're right, I am a close relative to you, but there is one even closer than I am. So stay the rest of the night. In the morning, if he wants to exercise his customary rights and responsibilities as the closest covenant redeemer, he'll have his chance; but if he isn't interested, as GOD lives, I'll do it. Now go back to sleep until morning."

14 Ruth slept at his feet until dawn, but she got up while it was still dark and wouldn't be recognized. Then Boaz said to himself, "No one must know that Ruth came to the threshing floor."

15 Boaz said, "Bring the shawl you're wearing and spread it out."

She spread it out and he poured it full of barley, six measures, and put it on her shoulders. Then she went back to town.

16-17 When she came to her mother-in-law, Naomi asked, "And how did things go, my dear daughter?"

Ruth told her everything that the man had done for her, adding, "And he gave me all this barley besides—six quarts! He told me, 'You can't go back empty-handed to your mother-in-law!'"

18 Naomi said, "Sit back and relax, my dear daughter, until we find out how things turn out; that man isn't going to fool around. Mark my words, he's going to get everything wrapped up today."

4:1 Boaz went straight to the public square and took his place there. Before long the "closer relative," the one mentioned earlier by Boaz, strolled by.

"Step aside, old friend," said Boaz. "Take a seat." The man sat down.

2 Boaz then gathered ten of the town elders together and said,

"Sit down here with us; we've got some business to take care of." And they sat down.

3-4 Boaz then said to his relative, "The piece of property that belonged to our relative Elimelech is being sold by his widow Naomi, who has just returned from the country of Moab. I thought you ought to know about it. Buy it back if you want it—you can make it official in the presence of those sitting here and before the town elders. You have first redeemer rights. If you don't want it, tell me so I'll know where I stand. You're first in line to do this and I'm next after you."

He said, "I'll buy it."

5 Then Boaz added, "You realize, don't you, that when you buy the field from Naomi, you also get Ruth the Moabite, the widow of our dead relative, along with the redeemer responsibility to have children with her to carry on the family inheritance."

6 Then the relative said, "Oh, I can't do that—I'd jeopardize my own family's inheritance. You go ahead and buy it—you can have my rights—I can't do it."

8 So when Boaz's "redeemer" relative said, "Go ahead and buy it," he signed the deal by **pulling off his shoe**.

> *A way of sealing an agreement.*

9-10 Boaz then addressed the elders and all the people in the town square that day: "You are witnesses today that I have bought from Naomi everything that belonged to Elimelech and Kilion and Mahlon, including responsibility for Ruth the foreigner, the widow of Mahlon—I'll take her as my wife and keep the name of the deceased alive along with his inheritance. The memory and reputation of the deceased is not going to disappear out of this family or from his hometown. To all this you are witnesses this very day."

11-12 All the people in the town square that day, backing up the elders, said, "Yes, we are witnesses. May GOD make this woman who is coming into your household like Rachel and Leah, the two women who built the family of Israel. May GOD make you a pillar in Ephrathah and famous in Bethlehem! With the children GOD gives you from this young woman, may your family rival the family of Perez, the son Tamar bore to Judah."

13 Boaz married Ruth. She became his wife. Boaz slept with her. By GOD's gracious gift she conceived and had a son.

14-15 The town women said to Naomi, "Blessed be GOD! He didn't leave you without family to carry on your life. May this baby grow up to be famous in Israel! He'll make you young again! He'll take care of you in old age. And this daughter-in-law who has brought him into the world and loves you so much, why, she's worth more to you than seven sons!"

16 Naomi took the baby and held him in her arms, cuddling him, cooing over him, waiting on him hand and foot.

17 The neighborhood women started calling him "Naomi's baby boy!" But his real name was Obed. Obed was the father of Jesse, and Jesse **the father of David.**

> *The book of Ruth is a story of redemption. Ruth was lost - a foreigner and a widow - but miraculously she was redeemed by Boaz into a family. They had a baby boy who became the grandfather of the great King David. David became the great, great, great ... great grandfather of Jesus - the one who redeems. The one who bought us back from our lostness.*

the books of 1 & 2 Samuel

Category: *The 12 Historical Books*
Author: *Samuel*
Theme: *The people want a king*
Location & Date: *Israel (Canaan); 930-722 B.C.*
Version of Bible: *God's Word (GW)*

Summary: *These two books are about three main characters—Samuel, the Lord's prophet, King Saul, and King David. The people wanted a king like all the other nations and thereby rejected God as their king. God gave them a king; it didn't go well. He gave them another king; it went better, but not great.*

Samuel's Birth

1 Samuel 1:1 There was a man named Elkanah from Ramathaim Zophim in the mountains of Ephraim. 2 Elkanah had two wives, one named Hannah, the other Peninnah. Peninnah had children, but **Hannah had none.** 3 Every year this man would go from his own city to worship and sacrifice to the LORD of Armies at Shiloh.

4 Whenever Elkanah offered a sacrifice, he would give portions of it to his wife Peninnah and all her sons and daughters. 5 He would also give one portion to Hannah because he loved her, even though the LORD had kept her from having children. 6 Because the LORD had made her unable to have children, her rival Peninnah tormented her endlessly in order to make her miserable. 7 This happened year after year. Whenever Hannah went to the LORD's house, Peninnah would make her miserable, and Hannah would cry and not eat.

9 One day, after Hannah had something to eat and drink in Shiloh, she got up. (The priest Eli was sitting on a chair by the door of the Lord's temple.) 10 Though she was resentful, she prayed to the LORD while she cried. 11 She made this vow, "**LORD of Armies, if you will look at my misery, remember me, and give me a boy, then I will give him to you for as long as he lives.** A razor will never be used on his head." 12 While Hannah was praying a long time in front of the LORD, Eli was watching her mouth. 13 She was praying silently. Her voice couldn't be heard; only her lips were moving. Eli thought she was drunk.

14 "How long are you going to stay drunk?" Eli asked her. "Get rid of your wine."

15 Hannah responded, "No sir. I'm not drunk. I'm depressed. I'm pouring out my heart to the LORD. 16 Don't take me to be

Here's another barren woman who was promised a child of prominence.

Hannah showed her faith in the Lord by praying for a son. When the Lord granted her one, she showed her devotion by offering her son's services to the Lord. Samuel then

became a means by which God brought salvation to Israel, in contrast to the tumultuous time of the Judges.

a good-for-nothing woman. I was praying like this because I've been troubled and tormented."

17 Eli replied, "Go in peace, and may the God of Israel grant your request."

18 "May you continue to be kind to me," she said. Then the woman went her way and ate. She was no longer sad.

19 Early in the morning Elkanah and his family got up and worshiped in front of the LORD. Then they returned home to Ramah. Elkanah made love to his wife Hannah, and the LORD remembered her. 20 Hannah became pregnant and gave birth to a son. She named him Samuel [God Hears], because she said, "I asked the LORD for him."

Samuel's Childhood

24 She brought him to the LORD's house at Shiloh while the boy was still a child.

25 Then the parents ... brought the child to Eli. 26 "Sir," Hannah said, "as sure as you live, I'm the woman who stood here next to you and prayed to the LORD. 27 I prayed for this child, and the LORD granted my request. 28 In return, I am giving him to the LORD. He will be dedicated to the LORD for his whole life."

The LORD Calls Samuel

3:1 The boy Samuel was serving the LORD under Eli. In those days a prophecy from the LORD was rare; visions were infrequent. 2 One night Eli was lying down in his room. His eyesight had begun to fail so that he couldn't see well. 3 The lamp in God's temple hadn't gone out yet, and Samuel was asleep in the temple of the LORD where the ark of God was kept.

4 Then the LORD called Samuel. "Here I am," Samuel responded. 5 He ran to Eli and said, "Here I am. You called me."

"I didn't call you," Eli replied. "Go back to bed." So Samuel went back and lay down.

6 The LORD called Samuel again. Samuel got up, went to Eli, and said, "Here I am. You called me."

"I didn't call you, son," he responded. "Go back to bed." 7 Samuel had no experience with the LORD, because the word of the LORD had not yet been revealed to him.

8 The LORD called Samuel a third time. Samuel got up, went to Eli, and said, "Here I am. You called me."

Then Eli realized that the LORD was calling the boy. 9 "Go, lie down," Eli told Samuel. "When he calls you, say, 'Speak, LORD. I'm listening.'" So Samuel went and lay down in his room.

10 The LORD came and stood there. He called as he had called the other times: "Samuel! Samuel!" And Samuel replied, "Speak. I'm listening."

11 Then the LORD said to Samuel, "I am going to do something

in Israel that will make the ears of everyone who hears it ring. 12 On that day I am going to do to Eli and his family everything I said from beginning to end. 13 I told him that I would hand down a permanent judgment against his household because he knew about his sons' sin—that they were cursing God—but he didn't try to stop them. 14 That is why I have taken an oath concerning Eli's family line: No offering or sacrifice will ever be able to make peace for the sins that Eli's family committed."

15 Samuel remained in bed until morning. Then he opened the doors of the LORD's house. But Samuel was afraid to tell Eli about the vision.

16 Then Eli called Samuel. "Samuel, my son!" he said.

"Here I am," he responded.

17 "What did the LORD tell you?" he asked. "Please don't hide anything from me. May God strike you dead if you hide anything he told you from me."

18 So Samuel told Eli everything.

Eli replied, "He is the LORD. May he do what he thinks is right."

19 Samuel grew up. The LORD was with him and didn't let any of his words go unfulfilled. 20 All Israel from Dan to Beersheba knew Samuel was the LORD's appointed prophet. 21 The LORD continued to appear in Shiloh, since the LORD revealed himself to Samuel in Shiloh through the word of the LORD. And Samuel spoke to all Israel.

The Ark Captured

4:10 The Philistines fought and defeated Israel. Every Israelite soldier fled to his tent. It was a major defeat in which 30,000 Israelite foot soldiers died. 11 **The ark of God was captured.** Both of Eli's sons, Hophni and Phinehas, died.

12 A man from the tribe of Benjamin ran from the front line of the battle. He went to Shiloh that day with his clothes torn and dirt on his head. 13 When he arrived, Eli was sitting on a chair beside the road, watching. He was worried about the ark of God. The man went into the city to tell the news. The whole city cried out. 14 Hearing the cry, Eli asked, "What is this commotion?" So the man went quickly to tell Eli the news. 15 (Eli was 98 years old, and his eyesight had failed so that he couldn't see.)

16 The man told Eli, "I'm the one who came from the battle. I fled from the front line today."

"What happened, son?" Eli asked.

17 "Israel fled from the Philistines," the messenger answered. "Our troops suffered heavy casualties. Your two sons, Hophni and Phinehas, also are dead, and the ark of God has been captured."

18 When the messenger mentioned the ark of God, Eli fell from his chair backwards toward the gate. He broke his neck, and he died.

> The Israelites were at war with the Philistines. They used the Ark of the Covenant as a sort of magic charm - it didn't work.

{After the Philistines captured the Ark, they brought it to a temple in Ashdod and placed it next to a statue of their god Dagon.}

5:3 Early the next day the people of Ashdod saw that Dagon had fallen forward on the ground in front of the LORD's ark. So they took Dagon and put him back in his place. 4 But the next morning they saw that Dagon had again fallen forward on the ground in front of the LORD's ark. Dagon's head and his two hands were cut off and were lying on the temple's threshold. The rest of Dagon's body was intact.

{God continued to wreak havoc on the Philistines by sending an outbreak of tumors. The Philistines singled out the Ark as the cause of this epidemic and sent it to other cities. But no matter where the Ark ended up, the Lord's hand was heavy on those people. The Philistines ultimately decided to send the Ark back to the Israelites.}

Israel Rejects the LORD as King

8:1 When Samuel was old, he made his sons judges over Israel. 2 The name of his firstborn son was Joel; the name of his second son was Abijah. They were judges in Beersheba. 3 The sons didn't follow their father's example but turned to dishonest ways of making money. They took bribes and denied people justice.

4 Then all the leaders of Israel gathered together and came to Samuel at Ramah. 5 They told him, "You're old, and your sons aren't following your example. Now appoint a king to judge us so that we will be like all the other nations."

6 But Samuel considered it wrong for them to request a king to judge them. So Samuel prayed to the LORD. 7 The LORD told Samuel, "Listen to everything the people are saying to you. They haven't rejected you; they've rejected me. 8 They're doing just what they've done since I took them out of Egypt—leaving me and serving other gods. 9 Listen to them now, but be sure to warn them and tell them about the rights of a king."

10 Then Samuel told the people who had asked him for a king everything the LORD had said. 11 Samuel said, "These are the rights of a king: He will draft your sons, make them serve on his chariots and horses, and make them run ahead of his chariots. 12 He will appoint them to be his officers over 1,000 or over 50 soldiers, to plow his ground and harvest his crops, and to make weapons and equipment for his chariots. 13 He will take your daughters and have them make perfumes, cook, and bake. 14 He will take the best of your fields, vineyards, and olive orchards and give them to his officials. 15 He will take a tenth of your grain and wine and give it to his aids and officials. 16 He will take your male and female slaves, your best cattle, and your donkeys for his own use. 17 He will take a tenth of your flocks.

In addition, you will be his servants. 18 "When that day comes, you will cry out because of the king whom you have chosen for yourselves. The LORD will not answer you when that day comes."

19 But the people refused to listen to Samuel. They said, "No, we want a king! 20 Then **we, too, will be like all the other nations**. Our

Peer pressure. Where in

king will judge us, lead us out to war, and fight our battles."

21 When Samuel heard everything the people had to say, he reported it privately to the LORD. 22 The LORD told him, "Listen to them, and give them a king."

Saul Searches for His Father's Donkeys

9:1 There was a man from the tribe of Benjamin whose name was Kish. 2 He had a son named Saul, a handsome, young man. No man in Israel was more handsome than Saul. He stood a head taller than everyone else.

3 When some donkeys belonging to Saul's father Kish were lost, Kish told Saul, "Take one of the servants with you, and go look for the donkeys."

4 They went through the mountains of Ephraim and the region of Shalisha without finding the donkeys.... 5 When they came to the territory of Zuph, Saul told his servant who was with him, "Let's go back, or my father will stop worrying about the donkeys and worry about us instead."

Saul Seeks Samuel's Advice

6 The servant responded, "There's a man of God in this city, a highly respected man. Everything he says is sure to happen. Let's go there. Maybe he'll tell us which way we should go."

10 Saul told his servant, "That's a good idea! Come on, let's go." They went to the city where the man of God was.

14 So Saul and his servant went to the city. As they entered it, Samuel was coming toward them on his way to the worship site. 15 Now, the LORD had revealed the following message to Samuel one day before Saul came: 16 "About this time tomorrow I will send you a man from the territory of Benjamin. Anoint him to be ruler of my people Israel. He will save my people from the Philistines because I've seen my people's suffering and their cry has come to me." 17 When Samuel noticed Saul, the LORD told him, "There's the man I told you about. This man will govern my people."

18 Saul approached Samuel inside the gateway and said, "Please tell me where the seer's house is."

19 Samuel replied, "I'm the **seer**. Go ahead of me to the worship site. You will eat with me today. In the morning I'll let you go after I tell you all that's on your mind. 20 Don't trouble yourself about the donkeys that were lost three days ago because they've been found. Who will have all that is desirable in Israel? Won't it be you and your father's family?"

21 **Saul replied, "I am a man from the tribe of Benjamin, the smallest tribe of Israel. My family is the most insignificant of all the families of the tribe of Benjamin. So why are you saying such things to me?"**

Saul Anointed by Samuel

10:1 Samuel took a flask of olive oil, poured it on Saul's head,

your life are you falling for it?

A prophet, a visionary, a fortune teller.

God often chooses the most insignificant to carry out his will.

kissed him, and said, "The LORD has anointed you to be ruler of his people Israel. You will rule his people and save them from all their enemies. This will be the sign that the LORD has anointed you to be ruler of his people. 2 When you leave me today, two men will be at Rachel's grave on the border of Benjamin at Zelzah. They'll tell you, 'We've found the donkeys you went looking for. Your father no longer cares about them. Instead, he's worried about you. He keeps asking, "What can I do to find my son?"' 3 Keep going until you come to the oak tree at Tabor. There you will find three men on their way to worship God at Bethel: One will be carrying three young goats, one will be carrying three loaves of bread, and one will be carrying a full wineskin. 4 They will greet you and give you two loaves of bread, which you should accept from them. 5 After that, you will come to the hill of God, where the Philistines have a military post. When you arrive at the city, you will meet a group of prophets prophesying as they come from the worship site. They will be led by men playing a harp, a tambourine, a flute, and a lyre. 6 Then the LORD's Spirit will come over you. You will be a different person while you prophesy with them. 7 When these signs happen to you, do what you must, because God is with you.

Saul's Anointing Confirmed by Signs

> *This is what happens when a person becomes a Christian. Has it happened to you?*

9 When Saul turned around to leave Samuel, **God changed Saul's attitude.** That day all these signs happened. 10 When Saul came to the hill, a group of prophets came to meet him, and God's Spirit came over him. He prophesied with them. 11 When all who had known him before saw how he prophesied with the prophets, the people asked one another, "What has happened to the son of Kish? Is Saul one of the prophets?" 12 But a man from that place asked, "But who's the chief prophet?" So it became a proverb: "Is Saul one of the prophets?" 13 And when he had finished prophesying, he came to the worship site.

The LORD Chooses Saul

17 Samuel called the people to come into the presence of the LORD at Mizpah. 18 He said to the Israelites, "This is what the LORD God of Israel says: I brought Israel out of Egypt and rescued you from the power of the Egyptians and all the kings who were oppressing you. 19 But now you have rejected your God, who saves you from all your troubles and distresses. You said, 'No! Place a king over us.' Now then, stand in front of the LORD by your tribes and family groups."

20 When Samuel had all the tribes of Israel come forward, the tribe of Benjamin was chosen. 21 When he had the tribe of Benjamin come forward by families, the family of Matri was chosen. Then Saul, the son of Kish, was chosen. They looked for him but couldn't find him. 22 They asked the LORD again, "Has he arrived here yet?"

> *God is calling you for some special task. What baggage are you hiding behind?*

The LORD answered, **"He's hiding among the baggage."**

23 They ran and got him from there. As he stood among the people, he was a head taller than everyone else. 24 Samuel asked

the people, "Do you see whom the LORD has chosen? There is no one like him among all the people."

Then all the people shouted, "Long live the king!"

25 Samuel explained the laws concerning kingship to the people. He wrote the laws on a scroll, which he placed in front of the LORD. Then Samuel sent the people back to their homes. 26 Saul also went home to Gibeah. With him went some soldiers whose hearts God had touched.

The First Battle for Saul Does Not Go Well

13:7 Some Hebrews crossed the Jordan River into the territory of Gad and Gilead. But Saul remained in Gilgal, and all the people who followed him trembled in fear.

8 He waited seven days, the time set by Samuel. But Samuel had not come to Gilgal, and the troops began to scatter. 9 Then Saul said, "Bring me the animals for the burnt offering and the fellowship offerings." So **he sacrificed the burnt offering**. 10 As he finished sacrificing the burnt offering, Samuel came, and Saul went to greet him.

11 Samuel asked, "What have you done?"

Saul replied, "I saw the troops were scattering. You didn't come when you said you would, and the Philistines were assembling at Michmash. 12 So I thought, 'Now, the Philistines will come against me at Gilgal, but I haven't sought the LORD's favor.' I felt pressured into sacrificing the burnt offering."

13 "**You did a foolish thing**," Samuel told Saul. "You didn't follow the command of the LORD your God. If you had, the LORD would have established your kingdom over Israel permanently. 14 But now your kingdom will not last. The LORD has searched for a man after his own heart. The LORD has appointed him as ruler of his people, because you didn't follow the command of the LORD."

{The Israelites would eventually route the Philistine armies (1 Samuel 14), but Saul was already showing his true colors as king.}

Saul Disobeys the LORD

15:1 Samuel told Saul, "The LORD sent me to anoint you king of his people Israel. Now listen to the LORD's words. 2 This is what the LORD of Armies says: I will punish Amalek for what they did to Israel. They blocked Israel's way after the Israelites came from Egypt. 3 Now go and attack Amalek. Claim everything they have for God by destroying it."

{Saul didn't carry out the Lord's instructions.}

The LORD Rejects Saul

10 Then the LORD spoke to Samuel: 11 "I regret that I made Saul king. He turned away from me and did not carry out my instructions." Samuel was angry, and he prayed to the LORD all night. 12 Early in the morning he got up to meet Saul. Samuel was told, "Saul went to Carmel to set up a monument in his honor.

> Saul was not supposed to do the sacrifice.

Then he left there and went to Gilgal."

13 Samuel came to Saul, who said, "The LORD bless you. I carried out the LORD's instructions."

22 Then Samuel said, "Is the LORD as delighted with burnt offerings and sacrifices as he would be with your obedience? To follow instructions is better than to sacrifice. To obey is better than sacrificing the fat of rams. 23 Because you rejected the word of the LORD, he rejects you as king."

24 Then Saul told Samuel, "I have sinned by not following the LORD's command or your instructions. I was afraid of the people and listened to them. 25 Now please forgive my sin and come back with me so that I may worship the LORD."

26 Samuel told Saul, "I will not go back with you because you rejected what the LORD told you. So the LORD rejects you as king of Israel." 27 When Samuel turned to leave, Saul grabbed the hem of his robe, and it tore. 28 Samuel told him, "The LORD has torn the kingdom of Israel from you today. He has given it to your neighbor who is better than you.

David Chosen to Be King

16:1 The LORD asked Samuel, "How long are you going to mourn for Saul now that I have rejected him as king of Israel? Fill a flask with olive oil and go. I'm sending you to Jesse in Bethlehem because I've selected one of his sons to be king."

2 "How can I go?" Samuel asked. "When Saul hears about it, he'll kill me."

The LORD said, "Take a heifer with you and say, 'I've come to sacrifice to the LORD.' 3 Invite Jesse to the sacrifice. I will reveal to you what you should do, and you will anoint for me the one I point out to you."

4 Samuel did what the LORD told him. When he came to Bethlehem, the leaders of the city, trembling with fear, greeted him and said, "May peace be with you."

5 "Greetings," he replied, "I have come to sacrifice to the LORD. Perform the ceremonies to make yourselves holy, and come with me to the sacrifice." He performed the ceremonies for Jesse and his sons and invited them to the sacrifice. 6 When they came, he saw Eliab and thought, "Certainly, here in the LORD's presence is his anointed king."

7 But the LORD told Samuel, "Don't look at his appearance or how tall he is, because I have rejected him. God does not see as humans see. **Humans look at outward appearances, but the LORD looks into the heart.**"

8 Then Jesse called Abinadab and brought him to Samuel. But Samuel said, "The LORD has not chosen this one either."

9 Then Jesse had Shammah come to Samuel. "The LORD has not chosen this one either," Samuel said. 10 So Jesse brought seven more of his sons to Samuel, but Samuel told Jesse, "The

Why is it not wise to judge a book by its cover?

LORD has not chosen any of these. 11 Are these all the sons you have?"

"There's still the youngest one," Jesse answered. **"He's tending the sheep."**

Samuel told Jesse, "Send someone to get him. We won't continue until he gets here."

12 So Jesse sent for him. He had a healthy complexion, attractive eyes, and a handsome appearance. The LORD said, "Go ahead, anoint him. He is the one." 13 Samuel took the flask of olive oil and anointed David in the presence of his brothers. The LORD's Spirit came over David and stayed with him from that day on. Then Samuel left for Ramah.

> Again the main character chosen by God for some dramatic role was unexpected and unassuming.

David Plays the Lyre for Saul

14 Now, the LORD's Spirit had left Saul, and an evil spirit from the LORD tormented him. 15 Saul's officials told him, "An evil spirit from God is tormenting you. 16 Your Majesty, why don't you command us to look for a man who can play the lyre well? When the evil spirit from God comes to you, he'll strum a tune, and you'll feel better."

17 Saul told his officials, "Please find me a man who can play well and bring him to me."

18 One of the officials said, "I know one of Jesse's sons from Bethlehem who can play well. He's a courageous man and a warrior. He has a way with words, he is handsome, and the LORD is with him."

19 Saul sent messengers to Jesse to say, "Send me your son David, who is with the sheep."

20 Jesse took six bushels of bread, a full wineskin, and a young goat and sent them with his son David to Saul. 21 David came to Saul and served him. Saul loved him very much and made David his armorbearer. 22 Saul sent this message to Jesse, "Please let David stay with me because I have grown fond of him."

23 Whenever God's spirit came to Saul, David took the lyre and strummed a tune. Saul got relief from his terror and felt better, and the evil spirit left him.

David and Goliath

17:1 The Philistines assembled their armies for war. They assembled at Socoh, which is in Judah, and camped between Socoh and Azekah at Ephes Dammim. 2 So Saul and the army of Israel assembled and camped in the Elah Valley. They formed a battle line to fight the Philistines. 3 The Philistines were stationed on a hill on one side, and the Israelites were stationed on a hill on the other side. There was a ravine between the two of them.

4 The Philistine army's champion came out of their camp. His name was Goliath from Gath. He was ten feet tall. 5 He had a bronze helmet on his head, and he wore a bronze coat of armor scales weighing 125 pounds. 6 On his legs he had bronze shin

guards and on his back a bronze javelin. 7 The shaft of his spear was like the beam used by weavers. The head of his spear was made of 15 pounds of iron. The man who carried his shield walked ahead of him.

8 Goliath stood and called to the Israelites, "Why do you form a battle line? Am I not a Philistine, and aren't you Saul's servants? Choose a man, and let him come down to fight me. 9 If he can fight me and kill me, then we will be your slaves. But if I overpower him and kill him, then you will be our slaves and serve us." 10 The Philistine added, "I challenge the Israelite battle line today. Send out a man so that we can fight each other." 11 When Saul and all the Israelites heard what this Philistine said, they were gripped with fear.

12 David was a son of a man named Jesse from the region of Ephrath and the city of Bethlehem in Judah. Jesse had eight sons, and in Saul's day he was an old man.

14 and David was the youngest. The three oldest joined Saul's army. 15 David went back and forth from Saul's camp to Bethlehem, where he tended his father's flock.

16 Each morning and evening for 40 days, the Philistine came forward and made his challenge.

17 Jesse told his son David, "Take this half-bushel of roasted grain and these ten loaves of bread to your brothers. Take them to your brothers in the camp right away. 18 And take these ten cheeses to the captain of the regiment. See how your brothers are doing, and bring back some news about them. 19 They, along with Saul and all the soldiers of Israel, are in the Elah Valley fighting the Philistines."

20 David got up early in the morning and had someone else watch the sheep. He took the food and went, as Jesse ordered him. He went to the camp as the army was going out to the battle line shouting their war cry. 21 Israel and the Philistines formed their battle lines facing each other. 22 David left the supplies behind in the hands of the quartermaster, ran to the battle line, and greeted his brothers. 23 While he was talking to them, the Philistine champion, Goliath from Gath, came from the battle lines of the Philistines. He repeated his words, and David heard them. 24 When all the men of Israel saw Goliath, they fled from him because they were terrified. 25 The men of Israel said, "Did you see that man coming from the Philistine lines? He keeps coming to challenge Israel. The king will make the man who kills this Philistine very rich. He will give his daughter to that man to marry and elevate the social status of his family."

26 David asked the men who were standing near him, "What will be done for the man who kills this Philistine and gets rid of Israel's disgrace? Who is this uncircumcised Philistine that he should challenge the army of the living God?"

27 The soldiers repeated to David how the man who kills Goliath would be treated.

28 Eliab, David's oldest brother, heard David talking to the men. Then Eliab became angry with David. "Why did you come here," he asked him, "and with whom did you leave those few sheep in the wilderness? I know how overconfident and headstrong you are. You came here just to see the battle."

29 "What have I done now?" David snapped at him. "Didn't I merely ask a question?" 30 He turned to face another man and asked the same question, and the other soldiers gave him the same answer.

31 What David said was overheard and reported to Saul, who then sent for him. 32 David told Saul, "No one should be discouraged because of this. I will go and fight this Philistine."

33 Saul responded to David, "You can't fight this Philistine. You're just a boy, but he's been a warrior since he was your age."

34 David replied to Saul, "I am a shepherd for my father's sheep. Whenever a lion or a bear came and carried off a sheep from the flock, 35 I went after it, struck it, and rescued the sheep from its mouth. If it attacked me, I took hold of its mane, struck it, and killed it. 36 I have killed lions and bears, and this uncircumcised Philistine will be like one of them because he has challenged the army of the living God." 37 David added, **"The LORD, who saved me from the lion and the bear, will save me from this Philistine."**

"Go," Saul told David, "and may the LORD be with you."

38 Saul put his battle tunic on David; he put a bronze helmet on David's head and dressed him in armor. 39 David fastened Saul's sword over his clothes and tried to walk, but he had never practiced doing this. "I can't walk in these things," David told Saul. "I've never had any practice doing this." So David took all those things off.

40 He took his stick with him, picked out five smooth stones from the riverbed, and put them in his shepherd's bag. With a sling in his hand, he approached the Philistine. 41 The Philistine, preceded by the man carrying his shield, was coming closer and closer to David. 42 When the Philistine got a good look at David, he despised him.

43 The Philistine asked David, "Am I a dog that you come to attack me with sticks?" So the Philistine called on his gods to curse David. 44 "Come on," the Philistine told David, "and I'll give your body to the birds."

45 David told the Philistine, "You come to me with sword and spear and javelin, but I come to you in the name of the LORD of Armies, the God of the army of Israel, whom you have insulted. 46 Today the LORD will hand you over to me. I will strike you down and cut off your head. And this day I will give the dead bodies of the Philistine army to the birds and the wild animals. The whole world will know that Israel has a God. 47 Then everyone gathered here will know that the LORD can save without sword or spear, because the LORD determines every battle's outcome. He will hand all of you over to us."

> *To be so young and so confident! What "giants" are you facing in your life these days?*

48 When the Philistine moved closer in order to attack, David quickly ran toward the opposing battle line to attack the Philistine. 49 Then David reached into his bag, took out a stone, hurled it from his sling, and struck the Philistine in the forehead. The stone sank into Goliath's forehead, and he fell to the ground on his face.

51 David ran and stood over the Philistine. He took Goliath's sword, pulled it out of its sheath, and made certain the Philistine was dead by cutting off his head.

When the Philistines saw their hero had been killed, they fled. 55 As Saul watched David going out against the Philistine, he asked Abner, the commander of the army, "Abner, whose son is this young man?"

Abner answered, "I solemnly swear, as you live, Your Majesty, I don't know."

56 The king said, "Find out whose son this young man is."

57 When David returned from killing the Philistine, Abner brought him to Saul. David had the Philistine's head in his hand. 58 Saul asked him, "Whose son are you, young man?"

"The son of your servant Jesse of Bethlehem," David answered.

David's Love for Jonathan

Jonathan was the son of Saul.

18:1 David finished talking to Saul. After that, **Jonathan** became David's closest friend. He loved David as much as he loved himself. 2 (From that day on Saul kept David as his servant and didn't let him go back to his family.) 3 So Jonathan made a pledge of mutual loyalty with David because he loved him as much as he loved himself.

5 David was successful wherever Saul sent him. Saul put him in charge of the fighting men. This pleased all the people, including Saul's officials.

David's Success Makes Saul Jealous

6 As they arrived, David was returning from a campaign against the Philistines. Women from all of Israel's cities came to meet King Saul. They sang and danced, accompanied by tambourines, joyful music, and triangles. 7 The women who were celebrating sang, "Saul has defeated thousands but David tens of thousands!"

8 Saul became very angry because he considered this saying to be insulting. "To David they credit tens of thousands," he said, "but to me they credit only a few thousand. The only thing left for David is my kingdom." 9 From that day on Saul kept an eye on David.

10 The next day an evil spirit from God seized Saul. He began to prophesy in his house while David strummed a tune on the lyre as he did every day. Now, Saul had a spear in his hand. 11 He raised the spear and thought, "I'll nail David to the wall." But David got away from him twice.

12 Saul was afraid of David, because the LORD was with Da-

vid but had left Saul. 13 So he kept David away. He made David captain of a regiment. David led the troops out to battle and back again. 14 He was successful in everything he undertook because the LORD was with him. 15 Saul noticed how very successful he was and became even more afraid of him. 16 Everyone in Israel and Judah loved David, because he led them in and out of battle.

David Spares Saul's Life

24:1 When Saul came back from fighting the Philistines, he was told "Now David is in the desert near En Gedi." 2 Then Saul took 3,000 of the best-trained men from all Israel and went to search for David and his men on the Rocks of the Wild Goats. 3 He came to some sheep pens along the road where there was a cave. Saul went into it to relieve himself while David and his men were sitting further back in the cave.

4 David's men told him, "Today is the day the LORD referred to when he said, 'I'm going to hand your enemy over to you. You will do to him whatever you think is right.'"

David quietly got up and cut off the border of Saul's robe. 5 But afterward, David's conscience bothered him because he had cut off the border of Saul's robe. 6 He said to his men, "It would be unthinkable for me to raise my hand against His Majesty, the LORD's anointed king, since he is the LORD's anointed."

7 Saul left the cave and went out onto the road. 8 Later, David got up, left the cave, and called to Saul, "Your Majesty!" When Saul looked back, David knelt down with his face touching the ground. 9 David asked Saul, "Why do you listen to rumors that I am trying to harm you? 10 Today you saw how the LORD handed you over to me in the cave. Although I was told to kill you, I spared you, saying, 'I will not raise my hand against Your Majesty because you are the LORD's anointed.' 11 My master, look at this! The border of your robe is in my hand! Since I cut off the border of your robe and didn't kill you, you should know and be able to see I mean no harm or rebellion. I haven't sinned against you, but you are trying to ambush me in order to take my life. 12 May the LORD decide between you and me. May the LORD take revenge on you for what you did to me. However, I will not lay a hand on you. 15 So the LORD must be the judge. He will decide between you and me. He will watch and take my side in this matter and set me free from you."

16 When David finished saying this, Saul asked, "Is that you speaking, my servant David?" and Saul cried loudly. 17 He told David, "**You are more righteous than I.** You treated me well while I treated you badly. 18 Today you have proved how good you've been to me. When the LORD handed me over to you, you didn't kill me. 19 When a person finds an enemy, does he send him away unharmed? The LORD will repay you completely for what you did for me today. 20 Now I know that you certainly will rule as king, and under your guidance the kingdom of Israel will prosper. 21 Swear an oath to the LORD for me that you will not wipe out my descendants or destroy my name in my father's family."

The relationship between Saul and David keeps getting worse.

22 So David swore to Saul. Then Saul went home, and David and his men went to their fortified camp.

Samuel Predicts Saul's Downfall

28:16 Samuel said, 17 The LORD has done to you (King Saul) exactly what he spoke through me: The LORD has torn the kingship out of your hands and given it to your fellow Israelite David. 18 The LORD is doing this to you today because you didn't listen to him or unleash his burning anger on Amalek. 19 For the same reasons the LORD will hand you and Israel over to the Philistines. Tomorrow you and your sons will be with me. **And then the LORD will hand Israel's army over to the Philistines."**

20 Immediately, Saul fell flat on the ground. He was frightened by Samuel's words. He also had no strength left, because he hadn't eaten anything all day or all night.

Despite Saul's apparent change of heart after David spared him, he continued to pursue David as fervently as he had before. But God rejected Saul. The prophet Samuel put it to him plainly.

The Death of Saul

31:1 When the Philistines were fighting against Israel, the men of Israel fled from the Philistines and were killed in battle on Mount Gilboa. 2 The Philistines caught up to Saul and his sons. They killed Jonathan, Abinadab, and Malchishua, Saul's sons. 3 The heaviest fighting was against Saul. When the archers got him in their range, he was badly wounded by them.

4 Saul told his armorbearer, "Draw your sword! Stab me, or these godless men will come, stab me, and make fun of me." But his armorbearer refused because he was terrified. So Saul took the sword and fell on it. 5 When the armorbearer saw that Saul was dead, he also fell on his sword and died with him. 6 So Saul, his three sons, his armorbearer, and all his men died together that day.

8 The next day, when the Philistines came to strip the dead, they found Saul and his three sons lying on Mount Gilboa. 9 They cut off his head and stripped off his armor... 10 They put his armor in the temple of their goddesses—the Asherahs—and fastened his corpse to the wall of Beth Shan.

11 When the people living in Jabesh Gilead heard what the Philistines had done to Saul, 12 all the fighting men marched all night and took the dead bodies of Saul and his sons from the wall of Beth Shan. They came back to Jabesh and burned the bodies there. 13 They took the bones and buried them under the tamarisk tree in Jabesh. Then they fasted seven days.

David Anointed King of Israel

2 Samuel 5:1 All the tribes of Israel came to David at Hebron. "We are your own flesh and blood," they said. 2 "Even in the past when Saul ruled us, you were the one who led Israel in battle. The LORD has said to you, 'You will be shepherd of my people Israel, the leader of Israel.'"

3 All the leaders of Israel had come to Hebron. King David made an agreement with them at Hebron in front of the LORD. So they

anointed David king of Israel.

{The first thing David did as king was establish his capital in Jerusalem. He then brought the Ark to Jerusalem.}

David Brings the Ark to Jerusalem

6:2 He and all the people with him left Baalah in Judah to bring God's ark to Jerusalem. (The ark is called by the name of the LORD of Armies, who is enthroned over the angels.) 12 David joyfully went to get the ark of God .... 13 When those who carried the ark of the LORD had gone six steps, David sacrificed a bull and a fattened calf.

14 Wearing a linen ephod, David danced in the LORD's presence with all his might. 15 He and the entire nation of Israel brought the ark of the LORD with shouts of joy and the sounding of rams' horns. 16 When the ark of the LORD came to the City of David, Saul's daughter Michal looked out of a window and saw King David leaping and dancing in the LORD's presence, so she despised him.

20 When David returned to bless his family, Saul's daughter Michal came out to meet him. "How dignified Israel's king was today! He was exposing himself before the eyes of the slave girls of his palace staff—like a mindless fool might expose himself!"

21 David answered Michal, "I didn't dance in front of the slave girls but in front of the LORD. He chose me rather than your father or anyone in your father's house, and he appointed me leader of Israel, the LORD's people. I will celebrate in the LORD's presence, 22 and I will degrade myself even more than this. Even if I am humiliated in your eyes, I will be honored by these slave girls you speak about."

David's Wish to Build a House for God

7:1 While King David was living in his house, the LORD gave him peace with all his enemies around him. 2 So the king said to the prophet Nathan, "Look, I'm living in a house made of cedar, while the ark of God remains in the tent."

3 Nathan told the king, "Do everything you have in mind, because the LORD is with you."

4 But that same night the LORD spoke his word to Nathan: 5 "Say to my servant David, 'This is what the LORD says: Are you the one who will build me a house to live in? 6 I haven't lived in a house from the day I took Israel out of Egypt to this day. Instead, I moved around in a tent, the tent of meeting. 7 In all the places I've moved with all the Israelites, did I ever ask any of the judges of Israel whom I ordered to be shepherds of my people Israel why they didn't build me a house of cedar?' 8 "Now this is what you will say to my servant David: 'This is what the LORD of Armies says: I took you from the pasture where you followed sheep so that you could be the leader of my people Israel. 9 I was with you wherever you went, and I destroyed all your enemies in front of you. I will make your name famous like the names of the greatest people on earth.

10 I will make a place for my people Israel and plant them there. They will live in their own place and not be troubled anymore. The wicked will no longer oppress them as they used to do 11 ever since I appointed judges to rule my people Israel. So I will give you peace with all your enemies. I, the LORD, tell you that I will make a house for you.

12 "'When the time comes for you to lie down in death with your ancestors, I will send one of your descendants, one who will come from you. I will establish his kingdom. 13 He will build a house for my name, and I will establish the throne of his kingdom forever. 14 I will be his Father, and he will be my Son. If he sins, I will punish him with a rod and with blows inflicted by people. 15 But I will never stop showing him my love as I did to Saul, whom I took out of your way. 16 Your royal house will remain in my presence forever. Your throne will be established forever.'"

17 Nathan told David all these words and everything he had seen.

18 King David went into the tent and sat in front of the LORD. "**Who am I**, Almighty LORD," he asked, "and why is my house so important that you have brought me this far? 19 And even this you consider to be a small act, Almighty LORD. You've also spoken about the distant future of my house. Almighty LORD, this is the teaching about the man.

20 "What more can I, David, say to you, Almighty LORD, since you know me so well! 21 You've done this great thing because of your promise and your own desire. You made it known to me.

22 "That is why you are great, LORD God. There is no one like you, and there is no other god except you, as we have heard with our own ears. 23 Who is like your people Israel? It is the one nation on earth that God came to free in order to make its people his own, to make his name known, and to do great and wonderful things for them. You forced nations and their gods out of the way of your people, whom you freed from Egypt to be your own. 24 You created the people of Israel to be your people forever. And you, LORD, became their God.

25 "Now, LORD God, keep the promise you made to me and my house forever. Do as you promised. 26 Your name will be respected forever when people say, 'The LORD of Armies is God over Israel.' And the house of your servant David will be established in your presence. 27 You, LORD of Armies, God of Israel, have revealed it especially to me, saying, 'I will build a house for you.' That is why I have found the courage to offer this prayer to you.

28 "Almighty LORD, you are God, and your words are trustworthy. You promised me this good thing. 29 Now, please bless my house so that it may continue in your presence forever. Indeed, you, Almighty LORD, have promised it. With your blessing my house will be blessed forever."

{After establishing his kingdom in Jerusalem, David continued to serve the Lord and the nation of Israel well. He led numerous campaigns and had great military success.}

> This is a really good question when you stand before the Lord. When have you felt less than adequate for the task?

David Takes Bathsheba

11:1 In the spring, the time when kings go out to battle, David sent Joab, his mercenaries, and Israel's army to war. They destroyed the Ammonites and attacked Rabbah, while David stayed in Jerusalem.

2 Now, when evening came, David got up from his bed and walked around on the roof of the royal palace. From the roof he saw a woman bathing, and she was very pretty. 3 David sent someone to ask about the woman. The man said, "She's Bathsheba, daughter of Eliam and wife of Uriah the Hittite." 4 So David sent messengers and took her. She came to him, and he went to bed with her. Then she went home. 5 The woman had become pregnant. So she sent someone to tell David that she was pregnant.

6 Then David sent a messenger to **Joab**, saying, "Send me **Uriah the Hittite**." So Joab sent Uriah to David. 7 When Uriah arrived, David asked him how Joab and the troops were and how the war was going.

8 "Go home," David said to Uriah, "and wash your feet." Uriah left the royal palace, and the king sent a present to him. 9 But Uriah slept at the entrance of the royal palace among his superior's mercenaries. He didn't go home.

10 When they told David, "Uriah didn't go home," David asked Uriah, "Didn't you just come from a journey? Why didn't you go home?"

11 Uriah answered David, "The ark and the army of Israel and Judah are in temporary shelters, and my commander Joab and Your Majesty's mercenaries are living in the field. Should I then go to my house to eat and drink and go to bed with my wife? I solemnly swear, as sure as you're living, I won't do this!"

12 David said to Uriah, "Then stay here today, and tomorrow I'll send you back." So Uriah stayed in Jerusalem that day and the next. 13 **David summoned him, ate and drank with him, and got him drunk**. But that evening Uriah went to lie down on his bed among his superior's mercenaries. He didn't go home.

14 In the morning David wrote a letter to Joab and sent it with Uriah. 15 In the letter he wrote, "Put Uriah on the front line where the fighting is heaviest. Then abandon him so that he'll be struck down and die."

16 Since Joab had kept the city under observation, he put Uriah at the place where he knew the experienced warriors were. 17 The men of the city came out and fought Joab. Some of the people, namely, some of David's mercenaries, fell and died—including Uriah the Hittite.

26 When Uriah's wife heard that her husband Uriah was dead, she mourned for him. 27 When her mourning was over, David sent for her and brought her to his home, and she became his wife. Then she gave birth to a son. But the LORD considered David's actions evil.

Joab was the commander of the army and Uriah the Hittite was one of his fighting men.

You can guess what David was trying to do, can't you? Often it is more work and more trouble when you try to cover up your sin than just admitting it.

Nathan Confronts David

The prophet of God.

12:1 So the LORD sent **Nathan** to David. Nathan came to him and said, "There were two men in a certain city. One was rich, and the other was poor. 2 The rich man had a very large number of sheep and cows, 3 but the poor man had only one little female lamb that he had bought. He raised her, and she grew up in his home with his children. She would eat his food and drink from his cup. She rested in his arms and was like a daughter.

4 "Now, a visitor came to the rich man. The rich man thought it would be a pity to take one of his own sheep or cattle to prepare a meal for the traveler. So he took the poor man's lamb and prepared her for the traveler."

5 David burned with anger against the man. "I solemnly swear, as the LORD lives," he said to Nathan, "the man who did this certainly deserves to die! 6 And he must pay back four times the price of the lamb because he did this and had no pity."

It is easy to see the guilt in others. Where in your life do you need to come clean?

7 "**You are the man!**" Nathan told David. "This is what the LORD God of Israel says: I anointed you king over Israel and rescued you from Saul. 8 I gave you your master Saul's house and his wives. I gave you the house of Israel and Judah. And if this weren't enough, I would have given you even more. 9 Why did you despise my word by doing what I considered evil? You had Uriah the Hittite killed in battle. You took his wife as your wife. You used the Ammonites to kill him. 10 So warfare will never leave your house because you despised me and took the wife of Uriah the Hittite to be your wife.

11 "This is what the LORD says: I will stir up trouble against you within your own household, and before your own eyes I will take your wives and give them to someone close to you. He will go to bed with your wives in broad daylight. 12 You did this secretly, but I will make this happen in broad daylight in front of all Israel."

David took responsibility for his sin. What sin in your life do you need to take responsibility for?

13 **Then David said to Nathan, "I have sinned against the LORD."**

Nathan replied, "The LORD has taken away your sin; you will not die. 14 But since you have shown total contempt for the LORD by this affair, the son that is born to you must die." 15 Then Nathan went home.

The LORD struck the child that Uriah's wife had given birth to for David so that the child became sick. 16 David pleaded with God for the child; he fasted and lay on the ground all night. 17 The older leaders in his palace stood beside him to raise him up from the ground, but he was unwilling. And he wouldn't eat with them.

18 On the seventh day the child died. But David's officials were afraid to tell him that the child was dead. They thought, "While the child was alive, we talked to him, and he wouldn't listen to us. How can we tell him the child is dead? He may harm himself."

19 But when David saw that his officials were whispering to one another, he realized that the child was dead. "Is the child dead?" David asked them.

"Yes, he is dead," they answered.

20 So David got up from the ground, bathed, anointed himself, and changed his clothes. He went into the LORD's house and worshiped. Then he went home and asked for food. They placed food in front of him, and he ate.

21 His officials asked him, "Why are you acting this way? You fasted and cried over the child when he was alive. But as soon as the child died, you got up and ate."

22 David answered, "As long as the child was alive, I fasted and cried. I thought, 'Who knows? The LORD may be gracious to me and let the child live.' 23 But why should I fast now that he's dead? Can I bring him back? Someday I'll go to him, but he won't come back to me."

24 Then David comforted his wife Bathsheba. He went to bed with her, and she later gave birth to a son. David named him Solomon. The LORD loved the child 25 and sent a message through the prophet Nathan to name the baby **Jedidiah**.

Jedidiah means "The Lord's Beloved."

Trouble Continues in David's Household

{Amnon, one of David's sons, fell in love with his (half) sister, Tamar. Amnon eventually lured her into his home and raped her. Absalom, another of David's sons, killed Amnon for raping his sister and then fled out of fear for the wrath of David. After two years, Absalom was able to return home. But soon after this, Absalom began plotting to seize his father's throne.}

David Overthrown

15:1 Absalom acquired a chariot, horses, and 50 men to run ahead of him. 2 Absalom used to get up early and stand by the road leading to the city gate. When anyone had a case to be tried by King David, Absalom would ask, "Which city are you from?"

After the person had told him which tribe in Israel he was from, 3 Absalom would say, "Your case is good and proper, but the king hasn't appointed anyone to hear it." 4 He would add, "I wish someone would make me judge in the land. Then anyone who had a case to be tried could come to me, and I would make sure that he got justice." 5 When anyone approached him and bowed down, Absalom would reach out, take hold of him, and kiss him. 6 This is what he did for all Israelites who came to the king to have him try their case. So Absalom stole the hearts of the people of Israel.

13 Someone came to tell David, "The hearts of the people of Israel are with Absalom."

David Flees Jerusalem

14 David told all his men who were with him in Jerusalem, "Let's flee immediately, or none of us will escape from Absalom.."

{As David fled Jerusalem, his son Absalom entered and tried to establish himself as king by sleeping with his father's concubines

and killing those who remained loyal to David. But the father still loved his wayward son.}

18:5 The king ordered **Joab**, Abishai, and Ittai, "Treat the young man Absalom gently for my sake." All the troops heard him give all the commanders this order regarding Absalom.

> *The general of David's army.*

6 So the troops went out to the country to fight Israel in the forest of Ephraim. 7 There David's men defeated Israel's army.

9 Absalom happened to come face to face with some of David's men. He was riding on a mule, and the mule went under the tangled branches of a large tree. Absalom's head became caught in the tree. So he was left hanging in midair when the mule that was under him ran away. 10 A man who saw this told Joab, "I saw Absalom hanging in a tree."

11 "What! You saw that!" Joab said to the man who told him. "Why didn't you strike him to the ground? Then I would have felt obligated to give you four ounces of silver and a belt."

12 But the man told Joab, "Even if I felt the weight of 25 pounds of silver in my hand, I wouldn't raise my hand against the king's son. We heard the order the king gave you, Abishai, and Ittai: 'Protect the young man Absalom for my sake.' 13 If I had done something treacherous to him, would you have stood by me? Like everything else, it wouldn't stay hidden from the king."

14 Then Joab said, "I shouldn't waste time with you like this." He took three sharp sticks and plunged them into Absalom's heart while he was still alive in the tree. 15 Then ten of Joab's armor-bearers surrounded Absalom, attacked him, and killed him.

21 Then Joab said to a man from Sudan, "Go, tell the king what you saw." The messenger bowed down with his face touching the ground in front of Joab and then ran off.

31 Then the Sudanese messenger came (to King David). "Good news for Your Majesty!" he said. "Today the LORD has freed you from all who turned against you."

32 "Is the young man Absalom alright?" the king asked.

The Sudanese messenger answered, "May your enemies and all who turned against you be like that young man!"

33 The king was shaken by the news. He went to the room above the gate and cried. "My son Absalom!" he said as he went. "My son, my son Absalom! I wish I had died in your place! Absalom, my son, my son!"

{After the Death of Absalom, David was able to enter Jerusalem.}

the books of 1 & 2 Kings

Category: *The 12 Historical Books*
Author: *Unknown*
Theme: *The bad kings of Israel*
Location & Date: *Israel (Canaan); 561-538 B.C.*
Version of Bible: *New Century Version (NCV) - 1 Kings*
   Holman Christian Standard Version (HCSV) - 2 Kings
Summary: *These two books are about the division of Israel into two separate countries or kingdoms—Judah in the south and Israel in the north. Jerusalem was the capital of Judah and Samaria was the capital of Israel. Both countries had 19 kings before they were conquered: Israel by Assyria in 721 B.C. and Judah by Babylon in 586 B.C. It was a difficult time in the history of God's people. On the positive side there were a few good kings. And some of the prophets saw a gleamer of hope in the future.*

1 Kings 1:1 (NCV) At this time King David was very old ... 15 So Bathsheba went in to see the aged king in his bedroom ... 16 Bathsheba bowed and knelt before the king. He asked, "What do you want?"

17 She answered, "My master, you made a promise to me in the name of the LORD your God. You said, 'Your son Solomon will become king after me, and he will rule on my throne.'

29 Then the king made this promise, "The LORD has saved me from all trouble. As surely as he lives, 30 I will do today what I have promised you in the name of the LORD, the God of Israel. I promised that your son Solomon would be king after me and rule on my throne in my place."

The Death of David

2:1 Since it was almost time for David to die, he gave his son Solomon his last commands. 2 David said, "My time to die is near. **Be a good and strong leader.** 3 Obey the LORD your God. Follow him by obeying his demands, his commands, his laws, and his rules that are written in the teachings of Moses. If you do these things, you will be successful in all you do and wherever you go. 4 And if you obey the LORD, he will keep the promise he made to me. He said: 'If your descendants live as I tell them and have complete faith in me, a man from your family will always be king over the people of Israel.'

10 Then David died and was buried with his ancestors in Jerusalem. 11 He had ruled over Israel forty years ....

> Good words from father to son. Did you hear words like that from your parent(s)? Have you given words like this to someone?

Solomon Takes Control as King

12 Solomon became king after David, his father, and he was in firm control of his kingdom.

Solomon Asks for Wisdom

3:4 King Solomon went to Gibeon to offer a sacrifice, because it was the most important place of worship.... 5 While he was at Gibeon, the LORD appeared to him in a dream during the night. God said, "Ask for whatever you want me to give you."

7 LORD my God, now you have made me, your servant, king in my father's place. But I am like a little child; I don't know how to do what must be done. 8 I, your servant, am here among your chosen people, and there are too many of them to count. 9 I ask that you give me a heart that understands, so I can rule the people in the right way and will know the difference between right and wrong. Otherwise, it is impossible to rule this great people of yours."

10 The Lord was pleased that Solomon had asked this. 11 So God said to him, "You did not ask for a long life, or riches for yourself, or the death of your enemies. Since you asked for wisdom to make the right decisions, 12 I will do what you asked. I will give you wisdom and understanding that is greater than anyone has had in the past or will have in the future. 13 I will also give you what you did not ask for: riches and honor. During your life no other king will be as great as you. 14 If you follow me and obey my laws and commands, as your father David did, I will also give you a long life."

Solomon Makes a Wise Decision

16 One day two women who were prostitutes came to Solomon. As they stood before him, 17 one of the women said, "My master, this woman and I live in the same house. I gave birth to a baby while she was there with me. 18 Three days later this woman also gave birth to a baby. No one else was in the house with us; it was just the two of us. 19 One night this woman rolled over on her baby, and he died. 20 So she took my son from my bed during the night while I was asleep, and she carried him to her bed. Then she put the dead baby in my bed. 21 The next morning when I got up to feed my baby, I saw that he was dead! When I looked at him more closely, I realized he was not my son."

22 "No!" the other woman cried. "The living baby is my son, and the dead baby is yours!"

But the first woman said, "No! The dead baby is yours, and the living one is mine!" So the two women argued before the king.

23 Then King Solomon said, "One of you says, 'My son is alive and your son is dead.' Then the other one says, 'No! Your son is dead and my son is alive.'"

24 The king sent his servants to get a sword. When they brought it to him, 25 he said, "Cut the living baby into two pieces, and give each woman half."

26 The real mother of the living child was full of love for her son. So she said to the king, "Please, my master, don't kill him! Give the baby to her!"

But the other woman said, "Neither of us will have him. Cut him into two pieces!"

27 Then King Solomon said, "Don't kill him. Give the baby to the first woman, because she is the real mother."

28 When the people of Israel heard about King Solomon's decision, they respected him very much. They saw he had wisdom from God to make the right decisions.

Solomon's Wisdom

4:29 God gave Solomon great wisdom so he could understand many things. 30 His wisdom was greater than any wisdom of the East, or any wisdom in Egypt. 31 He was wiser than anyone on earth. 32 During his life he spoke three thousand wise sayings and also wrote one thousand five songs. 33 He taught about many kinds of plants—everything from the great cedar trees of Lebanon to the weeds that grow out of the walls. He also taught about animals, birds, crawling things, and fish. 34 People from all nations came to listen to King Solomon's wisdom. The kings of all nations sent them to him, because they had heard of Solomon's wisdom.

{Israel was in a golden age. The people were led by a wise king who brought wealth and peace to Israel. The time was now ripe for Solomon to build a temple to the Lord and thus fulfill one of the promises God made to David. Solomon spared no expense in constructing and furnishing the temple using all of the wealth he had acquired, as well as the conscripted labor of the people.}

Solomon Builds the Temple

6:1 Solomon began to build the Temple four hundred eighty years after the people of Israel had left Egypt. 11 The LORD said to Solomon: 12 "If you obey all my laws and commands, I will do for you what I promised your father David. 13 I will live among the Israelites in this Temple, and I will never leave my people Israel."

Solomon Addresses the People

8:12 Then Solomon said, "The LORD said he would live in a dark cloud. 13 LORD, I have truly built a wonderful Temple for you—a place for you to live forever."

14 While all the Israelites were standing there, King Solomon turned to them and blessed them. Then King Solomon and the priests (and the people) continued to praise the Lord by offering sacrifices, singing songs and praying.

The Lord Appears to Solomon Again

9:1 Solomon finished building the **Temple** of the LORD and his **royal palace** and everything he wanted to build. 2 Then the LORD appeared to him again just as he had done before, in Gibeon. 3 The LORD said to him: "I have heard your prayer and what you

It took 2 years to build the temple. It took 13 years to build Solomon's palace. What is wrong with this picture?

How do you do the same thing in your own life?

have asked me to do. You built this Temple, and I have made it a holy place. I will be worshiped there forever and will watch over it and protect it always.

4 "But you must serve me as your father David did; he was fair and sincere. You must obey all I have commanded and keep my laws and rules. 5 If you do, I will make your kingdom strong. This is the promise I made to your father David—that someone from his family would always rule Israel.

6 "But you and your children must follow me and obey the laws and commands I have given you. You must not serve or worship other gods. 7 If you do, I will force Israel to leave the land I have given them, and I will leave this Temple that I have made holy. All the nations will make fun of Israel and speak evil about them. 8 If the Temple is destroyed, everyone who passes by will be shocked. They will make fun of you and ask, 'Why did the LORD do this terrible thing to this land and this Temple?' 9 People will answer, 'This happened because they left the LORD their God. This was the God who brought their ancestors out of Egypt, but they decided to follow other gods. They worshiped and served those gods, so the LORD brought all this disaster on them.'"

The Queen of Sheba Visits Solomon

10:1 When the queen of Sheba heard about Solomon, she came to test him with hard questions. 2 She traveled to Jerusalem with a large group of servants and camels carrying spices, jewels, and much gold. When she came to Solomon, she talked with him about all she had in mind, 3 and Solomon answered all her questions. Nothing was too hard for him to explain to her. 4 The queen of Sheba learned that Solomon was very wise. She saw the palace he had built, 5 the food on his table, his many officers, the palace servants, and their good clothes. She saw the servants who served him at feasts and the whole burnt offerings he made in the Temple of the LORD. All these things amazed her.

6 So she said to King Solomon, "What I heard in my own country about your achievements and wisdom is true. 7 I could not believe it then, but now I have come and seen it with my own eyes. I was not told even half of it! Your wisdom and wealth are much greater than I had heard. 8 Your men and officers are very lucky, because in always serving you, they are able to hear your wisdom. 9 Praise the LORD your God, who was pleased to make you king of Israel. The LORD has constant love for Israel, so he made you king to keep justice and to rule fairly."

{Solomon's reputation rose with his wealth—"the whole world sought audience with Solomon to hear the wisdom God had put in his heart." (1 Kings 10:24) But all was not perfect. Solomon used forced labor to construct the temple, which planted seeds of unrest in the people. He also did evil in the eyes of the Lord by taking foreign wives and building high places for their gods and making sacrifices to them. Soon, a prophet would come to one of Solomon's officials, who was called Jeroboam, and predict the unraveling of Solomon's kingdom.}

11:29 One day as Jeroboam was leaving Jerusalem, Ahijah, the prophet from Shiloh, who was wearing a new coat, met him on the road. The two men were alone out in the country. 30 Ahijah took his new coat and tore it into twelve pieces. 31 Then he said to Jeroboam, "Take ten pieces of this coat for yourself. The LORD, the God of Israel, says: 'I will tear the kingdom away from Solomon and give you ten tribes. 32 But I will allow him to control one tribe. I will do this for the sake of my servant David and for Jerusalem, the city I have chosen from all the tribes of Israel. 33 I will do this because Solomon has stopped following me and has worshiped the Sidonian god Ashtoreth, the Moabite god Chemosh, and the Ammonite god Molech. Solomon has not obeyed me by doing what I said is right and obeying my laws and commands, as his father David did.

34 "'But I will not take all the kingdom away from Solomon. I will let him rule all his life because of my servant David, whom I chose, who obeyed all my commands and laws. 35 But I will take the kingdom away from his son, and I will allow you to rule over the ten tribes. 36 I will allow Solomon's son to continue to rule over one tribe so that there will always be a descendant of David, my servant, in Jerusalem, the city where I chose to be worshiped. 37 But I will make you rule over everything you want. You will rule over all of Israel,

Solomon's Death

40 Solomon tried to kill Jeroboam, but he ran away to Egypt, to Shishak king of Egypt, where he stayed until Solomon died.

42 Solomon ruled in Jerusalem over all Israel for forty years. 43 Then he died and was buried in Jerusalem, the city of David, his father. And his son Rehoboam became king in his place.

{After Solomon's death, his son, Rehoboam, was in position to become the next king. The people, along with Jeroboam, who came out of Egypt following Solomon's death, asked Rehoboam if he would lighten the heavy yoke that his father placed on the people. This was a reference to Solomon's heavy taxation and conscripted labor and military force. Rehoboam consulted the elders who served his father, and they advised him to lighten the yoke. He then consulted the friends he had grown up with...}

12:10 The young men who had grown up with him answered, "Those people said to you, 'Your father forced us to work very hard. Now make our work easier.' You should tell them, 'My little finger is bigger than my father's legs. 11 He forced you to work hard, but I will make you work even harder. My father beat you with whips, but I will beat you with whips that have sharp points.'"

When it came time for Rehoboam to give his answer, he went along with his friends' advice and promised an even harsher ruling than his father's. Because of this, Rehoboam lost the favor of the people. The tribe of Judah remained loyal to **Rehoboam**, but the rest of Israel sided with **Jeraboam**—just as the prophet had predicted.

{The kingdom was split in two, the north and south, and what

It's hard to keep these two apart. Rehoboam was one of Solomon's sons. He became King of Judah in the south. Jeraboam, the man promoted by Solomon in 1 Kings 11 and was invited to become king of the 10 northern tribes of Israel.

proceeded was a hard fall from the golden age of King Solomon for both kingdoms. Both Jeraboam in the north, the kingdom of Israel, and Rehoboam in the south, the kingdom of Judah, did evil in the eyes of the Lord. A prophet told Jeraboam of God's condemnation of his rule.}

14:9 But you have done more evil than anyone who ruled before you. You have quit following me and have made other gods and idols of metal. This has made me very angry, 10 so I will soon bring disaster to your family. I will kill all the men in your family, both slaves and free men. I will destroy your family as completely as fire burns up manure.

{Rehoboam did similar evil in the eyes of the Lord.}

23 The people built stone pillars and places to worship gods and Asherah idols on every high hill and under every green tree. 24 There were even male prostitutes in the land. They acted like the people who had lived in the land before the Israelites. They had done many evil things, and God had taken the land away from them.

{What followed from this less-than-promising start to these two nations was a series of kings who, with some exceptions, did evil in the Lord's sight and brought about the decline of both Israel and Judah. The worst example of a bad king was Ahab. He was continually challenged by the prophet Elijah.}

Ahab King of Israel

16:29 Ahab son of Omri became king of Israel during Asa's thirty-eighth year as king of Judah, and Ahab ruled Israel in the city of Samaria for twenty-two years. 30 More than any king before him, Ahab son of Omri did many things the LORD said were wrong. 31 He sinned in the same ways as Jeroboam son of Nebat, but he did even worse things. He married Jezebel daughter of Ethbaal, the king of Sidon. Then Ahab began to serve **Baal** and worship him. 32 He built a temple in Samaria for worshiping Baal and put an altar there for Baal. 33 Ahab also made an idol for worshiping Asherah. He did more things to make the LORD, the God of Israel, angry than all the other kings before him.

The god of the native people of that area.

Elijah Stops the Rain

17:1 Now Elijah the Tishbite was a prophet from the settlers in Gilead. "I serve the LORD, the God of Israel," Elijah said to Ahab. "As surely as the LORD lives, no rain or dew will fall during the next few years unless I command it."

2 Then the LORD spoke his word to Elijah: 3 "Leave this place and go east and hide near Kerith Ravine east of the Jordan River. 4 You may drink from the stream, and I have commanded **ravens to bring you food there**." 5 So Elijah did what the LORD said; he went to Kerith Ravine, east of the Jordan, and lived there. 6 The birds brought Elijah bread and meat every morning and evening, and he drank water from the stream.

See Genesis 8:8, pg. 15.

7 After a while the stream dried up because there was no rain.

8 Then the LORD spoke his word to Elijah, 9 "Go to Zarephath in Sidon and live there. I have commanded a widow there to take care of you."

10 So Elijah went to Zarephath. When he reached the town gate, he saw a widow gathering wood for a fire. Elijah asked her, "Would you bring me a little water in a cup so I may have a drink?" 11 As she was going to get his water, Elijah said, "Please bring me a piece of bread, too."

12 The woman answered, "As surely as the LORD your God lives, I have no bread. I have only a handful of flour in a jar and only a little olive oil in a jug. I came here to gather some wood so I could go home and cook our last meal. My son and I will eat it and then die from hunger."

13 "Don't worry," Elijah said to her. "Go home and cook your food as you have said. But first make a small loaf of bread from the flour you have, and bring it to me. Then cook something for yourself and your son. 14 The LORD, the God of Israel, says, 'That jar of flour will never be empty, and the jug will always have oil in it, until the day the LORD sends rain to the land.'"

15 So the woman went home and did what Elijah told her to do. And the woman and her son and Elijah had enough food every day. 16 The jar of flour and the jug of oil were never empty, just as the LORD, through Elijah, had promised.

Elijah Brings a Boy Back to Life

17 Some time later the son of the woman who owned the house became sick. He grew worse and worse and finally stopped breathing. 18 The woman said to Elijah, "Man of God, what have you done to me? Did you come here to remind me of my sin and to kill my son?"

19 Elijah said to her, "Give me your son." Elijah took the boy from her, carried him upstairs, and laid him on the bed in the room where he was staying. 20 Then he prayed to the LORD: "LORD my God, this widow is letting me stay in her house. Why have you done this terrible thing to her and caused her son to die?" 21 Then Elijah lay on top of the boy three times. He prayed to the LORD, "LORD my God, let this boy live again!"

22 The LORD answered Elijah's prayer; the boy began breathing again and was alive. 23 Elijah carried the boy downstairs and gave him to his mother and said, "See! Your son is alive!"

24 "Now I know you really are a man from God," the woman said to Elijah. "I know that the LORD truly speaks through you!"

Elijah Kills the Prophets of Baal

18:1 During the third year without rain, the LORD spoke his word to Elijah: "Go and meet King Ahab, and I will soon send rain." 2 So Elijah went to meet Ahab. By this time there was no food in Samaria.

16 So Obadiah went to Ahab and told him where Elijah was.

Then Ahab went to meet Elijah.

17 When he saw Elijah, he asked, "Is it you—the biggest troublemaker in Israel?"

18 Elijah answered, "I have not made trouble in Israel. You and your father's family have made all this trouble by not obeying the LORD's commands. You have gone after the Baals. 19 Now tell all Israel to meet me at Mount Carmel. Also bring the four hundred fifty prophets of Baal and the four hundred prophets of Asherah, who eat at Jezebel's table."

20 So Ahab called all the Israelites and those prophets to Mount Carmel. 21 Elijah approached the people and said, "**How long will you not decide between two choices?** If the LORD is the true God, follow him, but if Baal is the true God, follow him!" But the people said nothing.

22 Elijah said, "**I am the only prophet of the LORD here, but there are four hundred fifty prophets of Baal.** 23 Bring two bulls. Let the prophets of Baal choose one bull and kill it and cut it into pieces. Then let them put the meat on the wood, but they are not to set fire to it. I will prepare the other bull, putting the meat on the wood but not setting fire to it. 24 You prophets of Baal, pray to your god, and I will pray to the LORD. The god who answers by setting fire to his wood is the true God."

All the people agreed that this was a good idea.

25 Then Elijah said to the prophets of Baal, "There are many of you, so you go first. Choose a bull and prepare it. Pray to your god, but don't start the fire."

26 So they took the bull that was given to them and prepared it. They prayed to Baal from morning until noon, shouting "Baal, answer us!" But there was no sound, and no one answered. They danced around the altar they had built.

27 At noon Elijah began to make fun of them. "Pray louder!" he said. "If Baal really is a god, maybe he is thinking, or busy, or traveling! Maybe he is sleeping so you will have to wake him!" 28 The prophets prayed louder, cutting themselves with swords and spears until their blood flowed, which was the way they worshiped. 29 The afternoon passed, and the prophets continued to act like this until it was time for the evening sacrifice. But no voice was heard; Baal did not answer, and no one paid attention.

30 Then Elijah said to all the people, "Now come to me." So they gathered around him, and Elijah rebuilt the altar of the LORD, which had been torn down. 31 He took twelve stones, one stone for each of the twelve tribes, the number of Jacob's sons. (The LORD changed Jacob's name to Israel.) 32 Elijah used these stones to rebuild the altar in honor of the LORD. Then he dug a ditch around the altar that was big enough to hold about thirteen quarts of seed. 33 Elijah put the wood on the altar, cut the bull into pieces, and laid the pieces on the wood. 34 Then he said, "Fill four jars with water, and pour it on the meat and on the wood." Then Elijah said, "Do it again," and they did it again. Then he said, "Do it

---

What choices are you wavering between?

The great contest begins! The odds: 450 to 1.

a third time," and they did it the third time. 35 So the water ran off the altar and filled the ditch.

36 At the time for the evening sacrifice, the prophet Elijah went near the altar. "LORD, you are the God of Abraham, Isaac, and Israel," he prayed. "**Prove that you are the God of Israel** and that I am your servant. Show these people that you commanded me to do all these things. 37 LORD, answer my prayer so these people will know that you, LORD, are God and that you will change their minds."

38 Then fire from the LORD came down and burned the sacrifice, the wood, the stones, and the ground around the altar. It also dried up the water in the ditch. 39 When all the people saw this, they fell down to the ground, crying, "The LORD is God! The LORD is God!"

40 Then Elijah said, "Capture the prophets of Baal! Don't let any of them run away!" The people captured all the prophets.

The Rain Comes Again

45 After a short time the sky was covered with dark clouds. The wind began to blow, and soon a heavy rain began to fall. Ahab got in his chariot and started back to Jezreel. 46 The LORD gave his power to Elijah, who tightened his clothes around him and ran ahead of King Ahab all the way to Jezreel.

Elijah Runs Away

19:1 King Ahab told Jezebel every thing Elijah had done and how Elijah had killed all the prophets with a sword. 2 So Jezebel sent a messenger to Elijah, saying, "May the gods punish me terribly if by this time tomorrow I don't kill you just as you killed those prophets."

3 When Elijah heard this, he was afraid and ran for his life, taking his servant with him. When they came to Beersheba in Judah, Elijah left his servant there. 4 Then Elijah walked for a whole day into the desert. He sat down under a bush and asked to die. "I have had enough, LORD," he prayed. "Let me die. I am no better than my ancestors." 5 Then he lay down under the tree and slept.

Suddenly an angel came to him and touched him. "Get up and eat," the angel said. 6 Elijah saw near his head a loaf baked over coals and a jar of water, so he ate and drank. Then he went back to sleep.

7 Later the LORD's angel came to him a second time. The angel touched him and said, "Get up and eat. If you don't, the journey will be too hard for you." 8 So Elijah got up and ate and drank. The food made him strong enough to walk for **forty days and nights to Mount Sinai**, the mountain of God. 9 There Elijah went into a cave and stayed all night.

Then the LORD spoke his word to him: "Elijah! Why are you here?"

10 He answered, "LORD God All-Powerful, I have always served

When was there a time in your life that your really wanted God to prove to you that He is real?

The people of Israel, under Moses, traveled 40 years in the desert after receiving the Law of God on Mount Sinai.

you as well as I could. But the people of Israel have broken their agreement with you, destroyed your altars, and killed your prophets with swords. I am the only prophet left, and now they are trying to kill me, too."

11 The LORD said to Elijah, "Go, stand in front of me on the mountain, and I will pass by you." Then a very strong wind blew until it caused the mountains to fall apart and large rocks to break in front of the LORD . But the LORD was not in the wind. After the wind, there was an earthquake, but the LORD was not in the earthquake. 12 After the earthquake, there was a fire, but the LORD was not in the fire. After the fire, there was a quiet, gentle sound. 13 When Elijah heard it, he covered his face with his coat and went out and stood at the entrance to the cave.

Then a voice said to him, "Elijah! Why are you here?"

14 He answered, "LORD God All-Powerful, I have always served you as well as I could. But the people of Israel have broken their agreement with you, destroyed your altars, and killed your prophets with swords. I am the only prophet left, and now they are trying to kill me, too."

"Quit feeling sorry for yourself; I have things for you to do. Oh, and by the way, you are not the only one left."

15 The LORD said to him, "**Go back** on the road that leads to the desert around Damascus. Enter that city, and pour olive oil on Hazael to make him king over Aram. 16 Then pour oil on Jehu son of Nimshi to make him king over Israel. Next, pour oil on Elisha son of Shaphat from Abel Meholah to make him a prophet in your place. 17 Jehu will kill anyone who escapes from Hazael's sword, and Elisha will kill anyone who escapes from Jehu's sword. 18 I have seven thousand people left in Israel who have never bowed down before Baal and whose mouths have never kissed his idol."

Ahab Takes Naboth's Vineyard

21:1 After these things had happened, this is what followed. A man named Naboth owned a vineyard in Jezreel, near the palace of Ahab king of Israel. 2 One day Ahab said to Naboth, "Give me your vineyard. It is near my palace, and I want to make it into a vegetable garden. I will give you a better vineyard in its place, or, if you prefer, I will pay you what it is worth."

Part of the inheritance given to each family in Israel when the tribes first came to the Promised Land.

3 Naboth answered, "May the LORD keep me from ever giving my land to you. **It belongs to my family.**"

4 Ahab went home angry and upset, because he did not like what Naboth from Jezreel had said. Ahab lay down on his bed, turned his face to the wall, and refused to eat.

5 His wife, Jezebel, came in and asked him, "Why are you so upset that you refuse to eat?"

6 Ahab answered, "I talked to Naboth, the man from Jezreel. I said, 'Sell me your vineyard, or, if you prefer, I will give you another vineyard for it.' But Naboth refused."

7 Jezebel answered, "Is this how you rule as king over Israel? Get up, eat something, and cheer up. I will get Naboth's vineyard for you."

8 So Jezebel wrote some letters, signed Ahab's name to them, and used his own seal to seal them. Then she sent them to the elders and important men who lived in Naboth's town. 9 The letter she wrote said: "Declare a day during which the people are to fast. Call the people together, and give Naboth a place of honor among them. 10 Seat two troublemakers across from him, and have them say they heard Naboth speak against God and the king. Then take Naboth out of the city and kill him with stones."

{That's exactly what happened.}

15 When Jezebel heard that Naboth had been killed, she told Ahab, "Naboth of Jezreel is dead. Now you may go and take for yourself the vineyard he would not sell to you."

17 At this time the LORD spoke his word to the prophet Elijah the Tishbite. The LORD said, 18 "Go to Ahab king of Israel in Samaria. He is at Naboth's vineyard, where he has gone to take it as his own. 19 Tell Ahab that I, the LORD, say to him, 'You have murdered Naboth and taken his land. So I tell you this: In the same place the dogs licked up Naboth's blood, they will also lick up your blood!'"

20 When Ahab saw Elijah, he said, "So you have found me, my enemy!"

Elijah answered, "Yes, I have found you. You have always chosen to do what the LORD says is wrong. 21 So the LORD says to you, 'I will soon destroy you. I will kill you and every male in your family, both slave and free. 22 Your family will be like the family of King Jeroboam son of Nebat and like the family of King Baasha son of Ahijah. I will destroy you, because you have made me angry and have led the people of Israel to sin.'

23 "And the LORD also says, 'Dogs will eat the body of Jezebel in the city of Jezreel.'

24 "Anyone in your family who dies in the city will be eaten by dogs, and anyone who dies in the fields will be eaten by birds."

25 There was no one like Ahab who had chosen so often to do what the LORD said was wrong, because his wife Jezebel influenced him to do evil. 26 Ahab sinned terribly by worshiping idols, just as the Amorite people did. And the LORD had taken away their land and given it to the people of Israel.

27 After Elijah finished speaking, Ahab tore his clothes. He put on rough cloth, fasted, and even slept in the rough cloth to show how sad and upset he was.

28 The LORD spoke his word to Elijah the Tishbite: 29 "I see that Ahab is now sorry for what he has done. So I will not cause the trouble to come to him during his life, but I will wait until his son is king. Then I will bring this trouble to Ahab's family."

{Some time later, King Ahab met with King Jehoshaphat, who was then king of Judah, and they plotted to retake the land of Ramoth Gilead which was held by the king of Aram.}

22:29 So Ahab king of Israel and Jehoshaphat king of Judah

went to Ramoth in Gilead. 30 King Ahab said to Jehoshaphat, "I will go into battle, but I will wear other clothes so no one will recognize me. But you wear your royal clothes." So Ahab wore other clothes and went into battle.

31 The king of Aram had ordered his thirty-two chariot commanders, "Don't fight with anyone—important or unimportant—except the king of Israel." 32 When these commanders saw Jehoshaphat, they thought he was certainly the king of Israel, so they turned to attack him. But Jehoshaphat began shouting. 33 When they saw he was not King Ahab, they stopped chasing him.

34 By chance, a soldier shot an arrow, but he hit Ahab king of Israel between the pieces of his armor. King Ahab said to his chariot driver, "Turn around and get me out of the battle, because I am hurt!" 35 The battle continued all day. King Ahab was held up in his chariot and faced the Arameans. His blood flowed down to the bottom of the chariot. That evening he died. 36 Near sunset a cry went out through the army of Israel: "Each man go back to his own city and land."

37 In that way King Ahab died. His body was carried to Samaria and buried there. 38 The men cleaned Ahab's chariot at a pool in Samaria where prostitutes bathed, and the dogs licked his blood from the chariot. These things happened as the LORD had said they would.

{After the death of Ahab, the nation of Israel continued to decline, and the kings of Judah in the south continued to do evil in the eyes of the Lord. Both kingdoms were caught in a downward political and spiritual spiral and faced immanent destruction by their own wicked doing. During this time, however, there were still prophets who served the Lord and did His work. Elijah continued to do the Lord's work by contesting the wicked son of Ahab, but Elijah's time was coming to an end. It was time for his successor, Elisha, to take his place as the Lord had commanded.}

Elijah in the Whirlwind

2 Kings 2:1 (HCSB) The time had come for the LORD to take Elijah up to heaven in a whirlwind. Elijah and Elisha were traveling from Gilgal, 2 and Elijah said to Elisha, "Stay here; the LORD is sending me on to Bethel."

But Elisha replied, "As the LORD lives and as you yourself live, I will not leave you." So they went down to Bethel.

3 Then the sons of the prophets who were at Bethel came out to Elisha and said, "Do you know that the LORD will take your master away from you today?"

He said, "Yes, I know. Be quiet."

4 Elijah said to him, "Elisha, stay here; the LORD is sending me to Jericho."

But Elisha said, "As the LORD lives and as you yourself live, I will not leave you." So they went to Jericho.

5 Then the sons of the prophets who were in Jericho came up to Elisha and said, "Do you know that the LORD will take your master away from you today?"

He said, "Yes, I know. Be quiet."

6 Elijah said to him, "Stay here; the LORD is sending me to the Jordan."

But Elisha said, "As the LORD lives and as you yourself live, I will not leave you." So the two of them went on.

7 Fifty men from the sons of the prophets came and stood facing them from a distance while the two of them stood by the Jordan. 8 Elijah took his mantle, rolled it up, and struck the waters, which parted to the right and left. Then the two of them crossed over on dry ground. 9 After they had crossed over, Elijah said to Elisha, "Tell me what I can do for you before I am taken from you."

So Elisha answered, "Please, let me inherit two shares of your spirit."

10 Elijah replied, "You have asked for something difficult. If you see me being taken from you, you will have it. If not, you won't."

11 As they continued walking and talking, a chariot of fire with horses of fire suddenly appeared and separated the two of them. Then Elijah went up into heaven in the whirlwind. 12 As Elisha watched, he kept crying out, "My father, my father, the chariots and horsemen of Israel!" Then he never saw Elijah again. He took hold of his own clothes and tore them into two pieces.

Elisha Succeeds Elijah

13 Elisha picked up the mantle that had fallen off Elijah and went back and stood on the bank of the Jordan. 14 Then he took the mantle Elijah had dropped and struck the waters. "Where is the LORD God of Elijah?" he asked. He struck the waters himself, and they parted to the right and the left, and Elisha crossed over.

15 When the sons of the prophets from Jericho who were facing him saw him, they said, "The spirit of Elijah rests on Elisha." They came to meet him and bowed down to the ground in front of him.

{After Elijah was taken up into heaven, his successor continued in his footsteps, serving the Lord wherever he went. He performed miracles in the Lord's name and was a persistent thorn in the side of corrupt leaders.}

The Shunammite Woman's Hospitality

4:8 One day **Elisha** went to Shunem. A prominent woman who lived there persuaded him to eat some food. So whenever he passed by, he stopped there to eat. 9 Then she said to her husband, "I know that the one who often passes by here is a holy man of God, 10 so let's make a small room upstairs and put a bed, a table, a chair, and a lamp there for him. Whenever he comes, he can stay there."

Try to keep the characters straight. There is Elisha the prophet; Gehazi the prophet's servant;

finally the Shunammite woman.

The Shunammite Woman's Son

11 One day he came there and stopped and went to the room upstairs to lie down. 12 He ordered his attendant **Gehazi**, "Call this **Shunammite woman**." So he called her and she stood before him.

13 Then he said to Gehazi, "Say to her, 'Look, you've gone to all this trouble for us. What can we do for you? Can we speak on your behalf to the king or to the commander of the army?'"

She answered, "I am living among my own people."

14 So he asked, "Then what should be done for her?"

Gehazi answered, "Well, she has no son, and her husband is old."

15 "Call her," Elisha said. So Gehazi called her, and she stood in the doorway. 16 Elisha said, "At this time next year you will have a son in your arms."

Then she said, "No, my lord. Man of God, do not deceive your servant."

17 The woman conceived and gave birth to a son at the same time the following year, as Elisha had promised her.

The Shunammite's Son Raised

18 The child grew and one day went out to his father and the harvesters. 19 Suddenly he complained to his father, "My head! My head!"

His father told his servant, "Carry him to his mother." 20 So he picked him up and took him to his mother. The child sat on her lap until noon and then died. 21 Then she went up and laid him on the bed of the man of God, shut him in, and left.

22 She summoned her husband and said, "Please send me one of the servants and one of the donkeys, so I can hurry to the man of God and then come back."

24 Then she saddled the donkey and said to her servant, "Hurry, don't slow the pace for me unless I tell you." 25 So she set out and went to the man of God at Mount Carmel.

When the man of God saw her at a distance, he said to his attendant Gehazi, "Look, there's the Shunammite woman. 26 Run out to meet her and ask, 'Are you all right? Is your husband all right? Is your son all right?'"

And she answered, "Everything's all right."

27 When she came up to the man of God at the mountain, she clung to his feet. Gehazi came to push her away, but the man of God said, "Leave her alone—she is in severe anguish, and the LORD has hidden it from me. He hasn't told me."

28 Then she said, "Did I ask my lord for a son? Didn't I say, 'Do not deceive me?'"

29 So Elisha said to Gehazi, "Tuck your mantle under your belt, take my staff with you, and go. If you meet anyone, don't stop to

greet him, and if a man greets you, don't answer him. Then place my staff on the boy's face."

30 The boy's mother said to Elisha, "As the LORD lives and as you yourself live, I will not leave you." So he got up and followed her.

31 Gehazi went ahead of them and placed the staff on the boy's face, but there was no sound or sign of life, so he went back to meet Elisha and told him, "The boy didn't wake up."

32 When Elisha got to the house, he discovered **the boy lying dead** on his bed. 33 So he went in, closed the door behind the two of them, and prayed to the LORD. 34 Then he went up and lay on the boy: he put mouth to mouth, eye to eye, hand to hand. While he bent down over him, the boy's flesh became warm. 35 Elisha got up, went into the house, and paced back and forth. Then he went up and bent down over him again. The boy sneezed seven times and opened his eyes.

Jesus faced the same situation many years later.

The Multiplied Bread

42 A man from Baal-shalishah came to the man of God with his sack full of 20 loaves of barley bread from the first bread of the harvest. Elisha said, "Give it to the people to eat."

43 But Elisha's attendant asked, "What? **Am I to set 20 loaves before 100 men?**"

Naaman's Disease Healed

5:1 Naaman, commander of the army for the king of Aram, was a great man in his master's sight and highly regarded because through him, the Lord had given victory to Aram. The man was a brave warrior, but he had a skin disease.

2 Aram had gone on raids and brought back from the land of Israel a young girl who served Naaman's wife. 3 She said to her mistress, "If only my master would go to the prophet who is in Samaria, he would cure him of his skin disease."

4 So Naaman went and told his master what the girl from the land of Israel had said. 5 Therefore, the king of Aram said, "Go and I will send a letter with you to the king of Israel."

So he went and took with him 750 pounds of silver, 150 pounds of gold, and 10 changes of clothes. 6 He brought the letter to the king of Israel, and it read: When this letter comes to you, note that I have sent you my servant Naaman for you to cure him of his skin disease.

7 When the king of Israel read the letter, he tore his clothes and asked, "Am I God, killing and giving life that this man expects me to cure a man of his skin disease? Think it over and you will see that he is only picking a fight with me."

8 When Elisha the man of God heard that the king of Israel tore his clothes, he sent a message to the king, "Why have you torn your clothes? Have him come to me, and he will know there is a

This same thing happened to Jesus when He fed the 5,000 with 5 loaves and 2 fish (Luke 9:12-17; pg. 278).

prophet in Israel." 9 So Naaman came with his horses and chariots and stood at the door of Elisha's house.

10 Then Elisha sent him a messenger, who said, "Go wash seven times in the Jordan and your flesh will be restored and you will be clean."

11 But Naaman got angry and left, saying, "I was telling myself: He will surely come out, stand and call on the name of Yahweh his God, and will wave his hand over the spot and cure the skin disease. 12 Aren't Abana and Pharpar, the rivers of Damascus, better than all the waters of Israel? Could I not wash in them and be clean?" So he turned and left in a rage.

13 But his servants approached and said to him, "My father, if the prophet had told you to do some great thing, would you not have done it? How much more should you do it when he tells you, 'Wash and be clean'?" 14 So Naaman went down and dipped himself in the Jordan seven times, according to the command of the man of God. Then his skin was restored and became like the skin of a small boy, and he was clean.

15 Then Naaman and his whole company went back to the man of God, stood before him, and declared, "I know there's no God in the whole world except in Israel. Therefore, please accept a gift from your servant."

16 But Elisha said, "As the Lord lives, I stand before Him. I will not accept it." Naaman urged him to accept it, but he refused.

17 Naaman responded, "If not, please let your servant be given as much soil as a pair of mules can carry, for your servant will no longer offer a burnt offering or a sacrifice to any other god but Yahweh. 18 However, in a particular matter may the Lord pardon your servant: When my master, the king of Aram, goes into the temple of Rimmon to worship and I, as his right-hand man, bow in the temple of Rimmon—when I bow in the temple of Rimmon, may the Lord pardon your servant in this matter."

19 So he said to him, "Go in peace."

Gehazi's Greed Punished

After Naaman had traveled a short distance from Elisha, 20 Gehazi, the attendant of Elisha the man of God, thought: My master has let this Aramean Naaman off lightly by not accepting from him what he brought. As the Lord lives, I will run after him and get something from him.

{Gehazi pursued Naaman and told him that Elisha did, on second thought, want his reward. Naaman gave it to Elisha's servant Gehazi. Upon his arrival back home, Elisha asked Gehazi where he had been. Gehazi said ...}

"Your servant didn't go anywhere," he replied.

26 But Elisha questioned him, "Wasn't my spirit there when the man got down from his chariot to meet you? Is it a time to accept money and clothes, olive orchards and vineyards, sheep and

oxen, and male and female slaves? 27 Therefore, Naaman's skin disease will cling to you and your descendants forever." So **Gehazi went out from his presence diseased—white as snow.**

The Aramean War

{The king of Aram was at war with Israel. But the prophet Elisha, who received intel from God, exposed the enemies position. So the king of Aram sent "horses, chariots, and a massive army" to find and kill him. They went at night and surrounded the city.}

6:15 When the servant of the man of God got up early and went out, he discovered an army with horses and chariots surrounding the city. So he asked Elisha, "Oh, my master, what are we to do?"

16 Elisha said, "**Don't be afraid, for those who are with us outnumber those who are with them.**"

17 Then Elisha prayed, "Lord, please open his eyes and let him see." So the Lord opened the servant's eyes. He looked and saw that the mountain was covered with horses and chariots of fire all around Elisha.

18 When the Arameans came against him, Elisha prayed to the Lord, "Please strike this nation with blindness." So He struck them with blindness, according to Elisha's word. 19 Then Elisha said to them, "This is not the way, and this is not the city. Follow me, and I will take you to the man you're looking for." And he led them to Samaria. 20 When they entered Samaria, Elisha said, "Lord, open these men's eyes and let them see." So the Lord opened their eyes. They looked and discovered they were in Samaria.

21 When the king of Israel saw them, he said to Elisha, "My father, should I kill them? I will kill them."

22 Elisha replied, "Don't kill them. Do you kill those you have captured with your sword or your bow? Set food and water in front of them so they can eat and drink and go to their master."

23 So he prepared a great feast for them. When they had eaten and drunk, he sent them away, and they went to their master. The Aramean raiders did not come into Israel's land again.

{Elisha then continued to perform more miracles in service to the Lord. Despite these displays of the true God's power, the people of Israel and their leaders continued to do evil in the eyes of the Lord which ultimately led to the decline of Israel. During the reign of king Hoshea of Israel, after many successive kings who did evil in the eyes of the Lord, the city of Samaria was captured by the king of Assyria.}

The Fall of Samaria

17:6 In the ninth year of Hoshea, the king of Assyria captured Samaria. He deported the Israelites to Assyria and settled them in Halah and by the Habor, Gozan's river, and in the cities of the Medes.

Naaman started out with leprosy but humbled himself at Gehazi's suggestion and was healed. Gehazi, full of pride and greed, ended up with leprosy.

Sometimes "believing is seeing" instead of the other way around.

Why Israel Fell

7 This disaster happened because the people of Israel had sinned against the LORD their God who had brought them out of the land of Egypt from the power of Pharaoh king of Egypt and because they had worshipped other gods.

13 Still, the LORD warned Israel and Judah through every prophet and every seer, saying, "Turn from your evil ways and keep My commands and statutes according to all the law I commanded your ancestors and sent to you through My servants the prophets."

14 But they would not listen. Instead they became obstinate like their ancestors who did not believe the LORD their God. 15 They rejected His statutes and His covenant He had made with their ancestors and the decrees He had given them. They pursued worthless idols and became worthless themselves, following the surrounding nations the LORD had commanded them not to imitate.

16 They abandoned all the commands of the LORD their God. They made cast images for themselves, two calves, and an Asherah pole. They worshiped the whole heavenly host and served Baal. 17 They made their sons and daughters pass through the fire and practiced divination and interpreted omens. They devoted themselves to do what was evil in the LORD's sight and provoked Him.

18 Therefore, the LORD was very angry with Israel, and He removed them from His presence. Only the tribe of Judah remained. 19 Even Judah did not keep the commands of the LORD their God but lived according to the customs Israel had introduced. 20 So the LORD rejected all the descendants of Israel, afflicted them, and handed them over to plunderers until He had banished them from His presence.

{God warned the people of Israel time and time again since the days of Joshua that if they did not follow him, they would be punished. This warning was now coming true with the exile of the Israelites from the Promised Land. The northern kingdom had fallen, but the southern kingdom of Judah resisted Assyrian captivity under the leadership of King Hezekiah who did good in the eyes of the Lord.}

8:7 The LORD was with him, and wherever he went he prospered. He rebelled against the king of Assyria and did not serve him.

{It appeared, however, that Judah was beyond saving. While Hezekiah was still king, a prophet foretold the capture of Judah by the Babylonians and the deportation of the people to that nation. After the death of King Hezekiah, his son Manasseh succeeded him. Manasseh did such evil in the eyes of the Lord that he sealed the fate of Judah.}

12:10 The LORD spoke through His servants the prophets, saying, 11 "Since Manasseh king of Judah has committed all these detestable things—greater evil than the Amorites who preceded him had done—and by means of his idols has also caused Judah to sin, 12 this is what the LORD God of Israel says: 'I am about to bring such disaster on Jerusalem and Judah that everyone who hears about it will shudder. 13 I will stretch over Jerusalem the measuring line used on Samaria and the mason's level used on the house of Ahab, and I will wipe Jerusalem clean as one wipes a bowl—wiping it and turning it upside down. 14 I will abandon the remnant of My inheritance and hand them over to their enemies. They will become plunder and spoil to all their enemies, 15 because they have done what is evil in My sight and have provoked Me from the day their ancestors came out of Egypt until today.'"

16 Manasseh also shed so much innocent blood that he filled Jerusalem with it from one end to another. This was in addition to his sin that he caused Judah to commit. Consequently, they did what was evil in the LORD's sight.

{Following the reign of King Manasseh, the people were in such a spiritual drought that the Book of the Law was lost in the temple. When it was found and read to the current king, Josiah, he tore his robes and sought out means to make right the wrongs his forefathers had done to the Lord.}

23:1 So the king sent messengers, and they gathered all the elders of Jerusalem and Judah to him. 2 Then the king went to the Lord's temple with all the men of Judah—all the people from the youngest to the oldest. As they listened, he read all the words of the book of the covenant (the Bible of that time) that had been found in the Lord's temple. 3 Next, the king stood by the pillar and made a **covenant** in the presence of the Lord to follow the Lord and to keep His commands with all his mind and with all his heart, and to carry out the words of this covenant that were written in this book; all the people agreed to the covenant.

An agreement

21 The king commanded all the people, "Keep the Passover of the Lord your God as written in the book of the covenant." 22 No such Passover had ever been kept from the time of the judges who judged Israel through the entire time of the kings of Israel and Judah. 23 But in the eighteenth year of King Josiah, this Passover was observed to the Lord in Jerusalem.

26 In spite of all that, the LORD did not turn from the fury of His great burning anger, which burned against Judah because of all that Manasseh had provoked Him with. 27 For the LORD had said, "I will also remove Judah from My sight just as I have removed Israel. I will reject this city Jerusalem, that I have chosen, and the temple about which I said, 'My name will be there.'"

{And indeed, after a series of more kings, who again did evil in the eyes of the Lord, Jerusalem fell to the Babylonians during the reign of King Zedekiah.}

Nebuchadnezzar's Siege of Jerusalem

25:1 In the ninth year of Zedekiah's reign, on the tenth day of the tenth month, King Nebuchadnezzar of Babylon advanced against Jerusalem with his entire army. They laid siege to the city and built a siege wall against it all around. 2 The city was under siege until

King Zedekiah's eleventh year.

3 By the ninth day of the fourth month the famine was so severe in the city that the people of the land had no food. 4 Then the city was broken into, and all the warriors fled by night by way of the gate between the two walls near the king's garden, even though the Chaldeans surrounded the city. As the king made his way along the route to the Arabah, 5 the Chaldean army pursued him and overtook him in the plains of Jericho. Zedekiah's entire army was scattered from him. 6 The Chaldeans seized the king and brought him up to the king of Babylon at Riblah, and they passed sentence on him. 7 They slaughtered Zedekiah's sons before his eyes. Finally, the king of Babylon blinded Zedekiah, bound him in bronze chains, and took him to Babylon.

Jerusalem Destroyed

8 On the seventh day of the fifth month, which was the nineteenth year of Nebuchadnezzar king of Babylon, Nebuzaradan, the commander of the guards, a servant of the king of Babylon, entered Jerusalem. 9 He burned the LORD's temple, the king's palace, and all the houses of Jerusalem; he burned down all the great houses. 10 The whole Chaldean army with the commander of the guards tore down the walls surrounding Jerusalem. 11 Nebuzaradan, the commander of the guards, deported the rest of the people who were left in the city, the deserters who had defected to the king of Babylon, and the rest of the population. 12 But the commander of the guards left some of the poorest of the land to be vinedressers and farmers.

13 Now the Chaldeans broke into pieces the bronze pillars of the LORD's temple, the water carts, and the bronze reservoir, which were in the LORD's temple, and carried the bronze to Babylon. 14 They also took the pots, the shovels, the wick trimmers, the dishes, and all the bronze articles used in temple service. 15 The commander of the guards took away the firepans and the sprinkling basins—whatever was gold or silver.

16 As for the two pillars, the one reservoir, and the water carts that Solomon had made for the LORD's temple, the weight of the bronze of all these articles was beyond measure. 17 One pillar was 27 feet tall and had a bronze capital on top of it. The capital, encircled by a grating and pomegranates of bronze, stood five feet high. The second pillar was the same, with its own grating.

{*Some of the prominent people of Israel were killed and others were taken in exile to Babylon.*}

21 So Judah went into exile from its land.

the books of 1 & 2 Chronicles

Category: The 12 Historical Books
Author: Ezra
Theme: A retelling of Israel for a people in exile
Location & Date: Israel (Canaan); 450-430 B.C.
Version of Bible: New International Version (NIV)

Summary: At the end of 2 Kings, the people of God were at one of the lowest points in their history. The Kingdom of Israel was lost and Judah was in exile. The people had been rejected by God. The books of Chronicles were thought to have been written following an edict of King Cyrus the Great, which occurred 50 years after the exile and allowed the Israelites to return to Jerusalem and rebuild the temple. The people were in captivity for so long that they became detached from their history. Chronicles were written to reconnect the people with their history, their God, and their purpose. To this end, 1 Chronicles opens with a genealogy starting with David and going down to the present day. Not only did this record serve practical matters, it also served to give the Israelites a sense of continuity with their past. The rest of Chronicles retells the histories of David and Solomon which were already covered in Samuel and Kings. The focus of Chronicles is different however. More emphasis is put on religious institutions—especially the rebuilding of the temple—rather than political events.

Highlight verses:

1 Chronicles 28:9 And you, my son Solomon, acknowledge the God of your father, and serve him with wholehearted devotion and with a willing mind, for the Lord searches every heart and understands every desire and every thought. If you seek him, he will be found by you; but if you forsake him, he will reject you forever.

29:11 Yours, Lord, is the greatness and the power and the glory and the majesty and the splendor for everything in heaven and earth is yours. Yours, Lord, is the kingdom; you are exalted as head over all. 12 Wealth and honor come from you; you are the ruler of all things. In your hands are strength and power to exalt and give strength to all.

2 Chronicles 7:14 ... if my people, who are called by my name, will humble themselves and pray and seek my face and turn from their wicked ways, then I will hear from heaven, and I will forgive their sin and will heal their land.

16:8 Yet when you relied on the Lord, he delivered them into your hand. 9 For the eyes of the Lord range throughout the earth to strengthen those whose hearts are fully committed to him.

the book of Ezra

Category: *The 12 Historical Books*
Author: *Ezra*
Theme: *Rebuilding the temple*
Location & Date: *Jerusalem; 457-444 B.C.*
Version of Bible: *Common English Bible (CEB)*
Summary: *After 70 years of captivity, Ezra, with permission and the blessing from Cyrus King of Persia, led a group of Jews back to the Promised Land, back to Jerusalem. They rebuilt the temple and began to celebrate the festivals that were established in the book of Leviticus.*

Permission to Return to Jerusalem

Ezra 1:1 In the first year of King Cyrus of Persia's rule, to fulfill the Lord's word spoken by Jeremiah, the Lord stirred up the spirit of Persia's King Cyrus. The king issued a proclamation throughout his kingdom (it was also in writing) that stated: 2 Persia's King Cyrus says: The Lord, the God of heaven, has given me all the kingdoms of the earth. He has commanded me to build him a house at Jerusalem in Judah. 3 If there are any of you who are from his people, may their God be with them! They may go up to Jerusalem in Judah and build the house of the Lord, the God of Israel—he is the God who is in Jerusalem. 4 And as for all those who remain in the various places where they are living, let the people of those places supply them with silver and gold, and with goods and livestock, together with spontaneous gifts for God's house in Jerusalem.

Preparing to Return

5 Then the heads of the families of Judah and Benjamin, and the priests and the Levites—everyone whose spirit God had stirred up—got ready to go up and build God's house in Jerusalem. 6 All their neighbors assisted them with silver equipment, with gold, with goods, livestock, and valuable gifts, in addition to all that was freely offered.

Rebuilding the Alter

3:1 When the seventh month came and the Israelites were in their towns, the people gathered together as one in Jerusalem. 2 Then Jeshua, Jozadak's son along with his fellow priests, and Zerubbabel, Shealtiel's son along with his kin, started to rebuild the altar of Israel's God so that they might offer entirely burned offerings upon it as prescribed in the Instruction from Moses the man of God. 3 They set up the altar on its foundations, because they were afraid of the neighboring peoples, and they offered entirely burned offerings upon it to the Lord, both the morning and the evening offerings.

4 They celebrated the Festival of Booths, as prescribed. Every day they presented the number of entirely burned offerings required by ordinance for that day. 5 After this, they presented the continual burned offerings, the offerings at the new moons, and at all the sacred feasts of the Lord, and the offerings of everyone who brought a spontaneous gift to the Lord. 6 From the first day of the seventh month, they began to present entirely burned offerings to the Lord.

The Israelites had not celebrated these festivals (Leviticus 23, pg. 68) for many years.

Facing Opposition

4:1 When the enemies of Judah and Benjamin heard that the returned exiles were building a temple for the Lord, the God of Israel, 2 they came to Zerubbabel and the heads of the families and said to them, "Let's build with you, for we worship your God as you do, and we've been sacrificing to him ever since the days of Assyria's King Esarhaddon, who brought us here."

3 But Zerubbabel, Jeshua, and the rest of the heads of the families in Israel replied, "You'll have no part with us in building a house for our God. We alone will build because the Lord, the God of Israel, and Persia's King Cyrus commanded us."

4 The neighboring peoples discouraged the people of Judah, made them afraid to build, 5 and bribed officials to frustrate their plan. They did this throughout the rule of Persia's King Cyrus until the rule of Persia's King Darius.

{The efforts of the returning Israelites continued to be frustrated during the reign of Xerxes. Finally, during the reign of Artaxerxes, an edict was made that halted production of the temple.}

The Building Resumed: Help the Leaders in the Rebuilding

5:1 Then the prophet **Haggai** and the prophet **Zechariah**, Iddo's son, prophesied to the Jews who were in Judah and Jerusalem in the name of Israel's God who was over them. 2 Subsequently, Zerubbabel, Shealtiel's son, and Jeshua, Jozadak's son, began to rebuild God's house in Jerusalem. God's prophets were with them, helping them.

3 At the same time, Tattenai, the governor of the province Beyond the River, and Shethar-bozenai and their colleagues came to them and spoke to them, asking, "Who authorized you to build this house and finish preparing this building material?" 5 But their God looked after the elders of the Jews, and they didn't stop them until a report reached Darius and a letter with his response had arrived.

{King Darius, however, did not side with those who opposed the building of the temple. He searched his archives and found a scroll from the reign of King Cyrus containing this decree.}

See the book of Haggai (pg. 236) and the book of Zechariah (pg. 238).

A memorandum—6:3 In the first year of his rule, King Cyrus made a decree: Concerning God's house in Jerusalem: Let the house at the place where they offered sacrifices be rebuilt and let its foundations be retained. Its height will be ninety feet and its width ninety feet, 4 with three layers of dressed stones and one layer of timber. The cost will be paid from the royal treasury. 5 In addition, the gold and silver equipment from God's house, which Nebuchadnezzar took out of the temple in Jerusalem and brought to Babylon, is to be restored, that is, brought back to Jerusalem and put in their proper place in God's house.

{In light of this, Darius made his own decree that the construction of the temple should go on without opposition. He, in fact, commanded those who opposed the construction of the temple to finance it.}

The Building Completed: Exuberantly Celebrated the Dedication

14 So the elders of the Jews built and prospered because of the prophesying of the prophet Haggai and Zechariah, Iddo's son. They finished building by the command of Israel's God and of Cyrus, Darius, and King Artaxerxes of Persia. 15 This house was completed on the third day of the month of Adar, in the sixth year of the rule of King Darius.

16 Then the Israelites, the priests and the Levites, and the rest of the returned exiles joyfully celebrated the dedication of this house of God. 17 At the dedication of this house of God, they offered one hundred bulls, two hundred rams, four hundred lambs, and as a purification offering for all Israel, twelve male goats, according to the number of the tribes of Israel. 18 They set the priests in their divisions and the Levites in their sections for the service of God in Jerusalem, as it is written in the scroll from Moses.

Ezra Arrives

7:6 this Ezra came up from Babylon. He was a scribe skilled in the Instruction from Moses, which the Lord, the God of Israel, had given. Moreover, the king gave him everything he requested because the Lord his God's power was with him.

7 Some of the Israelites and some of the priests and the Levites, the singers and gatekeepers and the temple servants also came up to Jerusalem in the seventh year of King Artaxerxes. 8 They reached Jerusalem in the fifth month, in the seventh year of the king. 9 The journey from Babylon began on the first day of the first month, and they came to Jerusalem on the first day of the fifth month, for the gracious hand of his God was upon him. 10 Ezra had determined to study and perform the Lord's Instruction, and to teach law and justice in Israel.

11 This is a copy of the letter that Artaxerxes gave to Ezra the priest and scribe, a scholar of the text of the Lord's commandments and his requirements for Israel:

12 Artaxerxes, king of kings, to Ezra the priest, the scribe of the Instruction from the God of heaven. Peace!

And now 13 I decree that any of the people of Israel or their priests or Levites in my kingdom who volunteer to go to Jerusalem with you may go. 14 You are sent by the king and his seven counselors to investigate Judah and Jerusalem according to the Instruction from your God, which is in your hand.

15 You should bring the silver and gold that the king and his counselors have freely offered to the God of Israel, whose dwelling is in Jerusalem, 16 together with any of the silver and gold that you find in the entire province of Babylonia. You should also bring the spontaneous gifts of the people and the priests, given freely for God's house in Jerusalem. 17 With this money you will be careful to buy bulls, rams, and lambs, as well as their grain offerings and their drink offerings. And you will offer them on the altar of God's house in Jerusalem. 18 As long as it is God's will, you and your colleagues may do what you think best with the rest of the silver and gold.

21 I, King Artaxerxes, decree to all of the treasurers in the province Beyond the River: Whatever Ezra the priest and scribe of the Instruction from the God of heaven requires of you, it must be provided precisely, 22 even up to one hundred kikkars of silver, one hundred kors of wheat, one hundred baths of wine, one hundred baths of oil, and unlimited salt. 23 Whatever the God of heaven commands will be done carefully for the house of the God of heaven, or wrath will come upon the realm of the king and his heirs.

27 Bless the Lord, the God of our ancestors, who has moved the king to glorify the Lord's house in Jerusalem, 28 and who has demonstrated his graciousness for me before the king and his counselors and all the king's mighty officers. I took courage because the Lord my God's power was with me. I gathered leaders from Israel to go up with me.

{Thus, along with the supplies and gifts the king granted them, Ezra and several thousand other Israelites set forth to return to Jerusalem. After Ezra arrived, he learned that many of the exiles were engaging in intermarriage with the neighboring peoples. This was detestable because the people were supposed to be a separate and godly people. But in the end Ezra and the people repented.}

Ezra Prays

9:5 ... I fell upon my knees, spread out my hands to the Lord my God, 6 and said, "My God, I'm too ashamed to lift up my face to you. Our iniquities have risen higher than our heads, and our guilt has grown to the heavens."

{Ezra then confessed the sin of his people to the Lord and prayed for forgiveness. When the Israelites saw this, they too started to weep at the realization of their sin and thus hoped to become a separate and holy people once again.}

the book of Nehemiah

Category: The 12 Historical Books
Author: Nehemiah
Theme: Rebuilding the wall of Jerusalem
Location & Date: Jerusalem; 424-400 B.C.
Version of Bible: Common English Bible (CEB)
Summary: Nehemiah, like Ezra, led a group of Jews back to the Promised Land after 70 years of captivity in Babylon. The book tells of the struggle to rebuild the walls of Jerusalem in a hostile environment.

Nehemiah 1:1 These are the words of Nehemiah, Hacaliah's son.

In the month of Kislev, in the twentieth year, while I was in the fortress city of Susa, 2 Hanani, one of my brothers, came with some other men from Judah. I asked them about the Jews who had escaped and survived the captivity, and about Jerusalem.

3 They told me, "Those in the province who survived the captivity are in great trouble and shame! The wall around Jerusalem is broken down, and its gates have been destroyed by fire!"

4 When I heard this news, I sat down and wept. I mourned for days, fasting and praying before the God of heaven.

2:1 In the month of Nisan, in the twentieth year of King Artaxerxes, the king was about to be **served wine**. I took the wine and gave it to the king. Since I had never seemed sad in his presence, 2 the king asked me, "Why do you seem sad? Since you aren't sick, you must have a broken heart!"

I was very afraid 3 and replied, "May the king live forever! Why shouldn't I seem sad when the city, the place of my family's graves, is in ruins and its gates destroyed by fire?"

4 The king asked, "What is it that you need?"

I prayed to the God of heaven 5 and replied, "If it pleases the king, and if your servant has found favor with you, please send me to Judah, to the city of my family's graves so that I may rebuild it."

6 With the queen sitting beside him, the king asked me, "How long will you be away and when will you return?" So it pleased the king to send me, and I told him how long I would be gone.

7 I also said to him, "If it pleases the king, may letters be given me addressed to the governors of the province Beyond the River to allow me to travel to Judah. 8 May the king also issue a letter to

Nehemiah was a wine taster for King Artaxerxes.

Asaph the keeper of the king's forest, directing him to supply me with timber for the beams of the temple fortress gates, for the city wall, and for the house in which I will live."

9 So I went to the governors of the province Beyond the River and gave them the king's letters. The king had sent officers of the army and cavalry with me.

11 When I reached Jerusalem and had been there for three days, 12 I set out at night, taking only a few people with me. I didn't tell anyone what my God was prompting me to do for Jerusalem, and the only animal I took was the one I rode.

17 So I said to them, "You see the trouble that we're in: Jerusalem is in ruins, and its gates are destroyed by fire! Come, let's rebuild the wall of Jerusalem so that we won't continue to be in disgrace." 18 I told them that my God had taken care of me, and also told them what the king had said to me.

{Just when the Israelites began rebuilding the temple, there was opposition to rebuild the walls from outside forces.}

Opposition Mounts

4:1-2 When **Sanballat** heard that we were building the wall, he became angry and raged. He mocked the Jews, 2 saying in the presence of his associates and the army of Samaria: "What are those feeble Jews doing? Will they restore things themselves? Will they offer sacrifices? Will they finish it in a day? Will they revive the stones from the piles of rubble, even though they are burned?"

3 Tobiah the Ammonite, who was beside him, added: "If even a fox climbs on whatever they build, their wall of stones will crumble."

6 **We** continued to build the wall. All of it was joined together, and **it reached half** of its intended height because the people were eager to work.

7 But when Sanballat, Tobiah, the Arabs, the Ammonites, and the people of Ashdod heard that the work on the walls was progressing and the gaps were being closed, they were very angry. 8 They plotted together to come and fight against Jerusalem and to create a disturbance in it. 9 So we prayed to our God and set a guard as protection against them day and night.

13 So I took up a position in the lowest parts of the space behind the wall in an open area. Then I stationed the people by **families**, and they had their swords, spears, and bows. 14 After reviewing this, I stood up and said to the officials, the officers, and the rest of the people, "Don't be afraid of them! Remember that the Lord is great and awesome! **Fight for your families, your sons, your daughters, your wives, and your houses!**"

15 Then our enemies heard that we had found out and that God had spoiled their plans. So we all returned to doing our own work on the wall. 16 But from that day on, only half of my workers continued in the construction, while the other half held the spears, shields, bows, and body armor. Meanwhile, the leaders positioned

---

Margin notes:

The leader of a neighboring people group opposed the rebuilding of Jerusalem.

Nehemiah and his fellow Jews. Projects get about half way and then trouble begins. Why is that?

Why by families?

Oh, this is why.

themselves behind the whole house of Judah, 17 who were building the wall. The carriers did their work with a load in one hand and a weapon in the other. 18 The builders built with swords fastened in their belts, and the trumpeter stayed by my side.

6:15 So the wall was finished on the twenty-fifth day of the month of Elul. It took fifty-two days. 16 When our enemies heard about this, all of the nations around us were afraid and their confidence was greatly shaken. **They knew that this work was completed with the help of our God.**

{In the face of opposition by force and opposition by deception, Nehemiah remained steadfast. He continuously prayed to the Lord for guidance and the Lord gave him success. Now the temple and the wall were rebuilt and Israel was further on its way to becoming their own people again, spiritually and politically.}

Ezra and the Revelation

8:1 When the seventh month came and the people of Israel were settled in their towns, all the people gathered together in the area in front of the Water Gate. They asked Ezra the scribe to bring out the Instruction scroll from Moses, according to which the Lord had instructed Israel.

2 So on the first day of the seventh month, Ezra the priest brought the Instruction before the assembly. This assembly was made up of both men and women and anyone who could understand what they heard. 3 Facing the area in front of the Water Gate, he read it aloud, from early morning until the middle of the day. He read it in the presence of the men and the women and those who could understand, and everyone listened attentively to the Instruction scroll.

4 Ezra the scribe stood on a wooden platform that had been made for this purpose...

5 Standing above all of the people, Ezra the scribe opened the scroll in the sight of all of the people. And **as he opened it, all of the people stood up.** 6 Then Ezra blessed the Lord, the great God, and all of the people answered, "Amen! Amen!" while raising their hands. Then they bowed down and worshipped the Lord with their faces to the ground.

7 The Levites ... helped the people to understand the Instruction while the people remained in their places. 8 They read aloud from the scroll, the Instruction from God, **explaining and interpreting it so the people could understand what they heard.**

10 "Go, eat rich food, and drink something sweet," he said to them, "and send portions of this to any who have nothing ready! This day is holy to our Lord. Don't be sad, because the joy from the Lord is your strength!"

12 Then all of the people went to eat and to drink, to send portions, and to have a great celebration, because they understood what had been said to them.

18 He read from God's Instruction scroll every day, from the first

---

Why did the enemy lose their nerve. Not because of the wall, but because they knew God was behind it. You perhaps face some walls of your own today. Start with one brick- one thing. Trust that God will take care of you.

What honor they gave to this book, the Bible, at that time.

This is what a sermon is today.

until the last day of the festival. They kept the festival for seven days and held a solemn assembly on the eighth day, just as the Instruction required.

9:1-3 On the twenty-fourth day of this month, the people of Israel were assembled. They fasted, wore funeral clothing, and had dirt on their heads. 2 After the Israelites separated themselves from all of the foreigners, they stood to confess their sins and the terrible behavior of their ancestors. 3 They stood in their place and read the Instruction scroll from the Lord their God for a **quarter of the day**. For another quarter of the day, they confessed and worshipped the Lord their God.

5 Stand up and bless the Lord your God. From everlasting to everlasting bless your glorious name which is high above all blessing and praise. 6 You alone are the Lord. You alone made heaven, even the heaven of heavens, with all their forces. You made the earth and all that is on it, and the seas and all that is in them.

{After recounting the history of the Israelites from Abraham to the present day, and reminding themselves of the faithfulness of God, the people made a binding agreement to be a holy and separate people. They promised not to intermarry with neighboring peoples, to observe the Sabbath, and to maintain God's temple.}

Dedication of the Wall

12:27 When it was time for the dedication of Jerusalem's wall, they sought out the Levites in all the places where they lived in order to bring them to Jerusalem to celebrate the dedication with joy, with thanks and singing, and with cymbals, harps, and lyres. 28 The singers also gathered together both from the region around Jerusalem and from the villages of the Netophathites, 29 also from Beth-hagilgal and from the region of Geba and Azmaveth, because **the singers had built themselves villages** around Jerusalem.

31 Then I brought the leaders of Judah up onto the wall and organized two large groups to give thanks... 36 They brought the musical instruments of David the man of God. Ezra the scribe went in front of them. Some of the young priests had trumpets. Next, playing the musical instruments of David the man of God ...

37 When they reached the Fountain Gate they went straight up by the stairs of David's City, on the ascent to the wall, past the house of David to the Water Gate on the east. 38 The second group went in procession to the left...

40 Then both groups of those who gave thanks stood in God's house. I was there too along with the half of the officials who were with me.

43 They offered great sacrifices on that day and rejoiced, for God had made them rejoice with great joy. The women and children also rejoiced, and the sound of the joy in Jerusalem could be heard from far away.

> We think a church service is too long if it goes more than an hour.

> All you music lovers are thinking about this one, aren't you?

the book of Esther

Category: *The 12 Historical Books*
Author: *Unknown*
Theme: *Salvation*
Location & Date: *The court of Persia; 450-431 B.C.*
Version of Bible: *New English Translation (NET)*
Summary: *This is an amazing spine-chilling story of intrigue, betrayal, irony, loyalty, and ultimately of a God saving His people. Though Ezra and Nehemiah led a small group of Jews out of captivity (after the 70 years in Babylon), the vast majority of the people stayed behind in the land of their captivity. The book of Esther is about those who stayed behind.*

The King Throws a Lavish Party

Esther 1:1 The following events happened in the days of Ahasuerus... 2 In those days, as King Ahasuerus sat on his royal throne in Susa the citadel, 3 in the third year of his reign he provided a banquet for all his officials and his servants. The army of Persia and Media was present, as well as the nobles and the officials of the provinces.

4 He displayed the riches of his royal glory and the splendor of his majestic greatness for a lengthy period of time—a hundred and eighty days, to be exact! 5 When those days were completed, the king then provided a seven-day banquet for all the people who were present in Susa the citadel, for those of highest standing to the most lowly. It was held in the court located in the garden of the royal palace. 6 The furnishings included linen and purple curtains hung by cords of the finest linen and purple wool on silver rings, alabaster columns, gold and silver couches displayed on a floor made of valuable stones of alabaster, mother-of-pearl, and mineral stone. 7 Drinks were served in golden containers, all of which differed from one another. Royal wine was available in abundance at the king's expense. 8 There were no restrictions on the drinking, for the king had instructed all of his supervisors that they should do as everyone so desired. 9 Queen Vashti also gave a banquet for the women in King Ahasuerus' royal palace.

Queen Vashti Is Removed from Her Royal Position

10 On the seventh day, as King Ahasuerus was feeling the effects of the wine, he ordered ... the seven eunuchs who attended him, 11 to bring Queen Vashti into the king's presence wearing her royal high turban. He wanted to show the people and the officials her beauty, for she was very attractive. 12 But Queen Vashti

refused to come at the king's bidding conveyed through the eunuchs. Then the king became extremely angry, and his rage consumed him.

13 The king then inquired of the wise men who were discerners of the times—for it was the royal custom to confer with all those who were proficient in laws and legalities. 14 ... These men were the seven officials of Persia and Media who saw the king on a regular basis and had the most prominent offices in the kingdom. 15 The king asked, "By law, what should be done to Queen Vashti in light of the fact that she has not obeyed the instructions of King Ahasuerus conveyed through the eunuchs?"

16 Memucan then replied to the king and the officials, "The wrong of Queen Vashti is not against the king alone, but against all the officials and all the people who are throughout all the provinces of King Ahasuerus. 17 For the matter concerning the queen will spread to all the women, leading them to treat their husbands with contempt, saying, 'When King Ahasuerus gave orders to bring Queen Vashti into his presence, she would not come.' 18 And this very day the noble ladies of Persia and Media who have heard the matter concerning the queen will respond in the same way to all the royal officials, and there will be more than enough contempt and anger! 19 If the king is so inclined, let a royal edict go forth from him, and let it be written in the laws of Persia and Media that cannot be repealed, that Vashti may not come into the presence of King Ahasuerus, and let the king convey her royalty to another who is more deserving than she. 20 And let the king's decision which he will enact be disseminated throughout all his kingdom, vast though it is. Then all the women will give honor to their husbands, from the most prominent to the lowly." 21 The matter seemed appropriate to the king and the officials. So the king acted on the advice of Memucan.

It is amazing the trouble that comes into our lives and the whole world because husbands and wives can't get along.

Esther Becomes Queen in Vashti's Place

2:1 When these things had been accomplished and the rage of King Ahasuerus had diminished, he remembered Vashti and what she had done and what had been decided against her. 2 The king's servants who attended him said, "Let a search be conducted in the king's behalf for attractive young women. 3 And let the king appoint officers throughout all the provinces of his kingdom to gather all the attractive young women to Susa the citadel, to the harem under the authority of Hegai, the king's eunuch who oversees the women, and let him provide whatever cosmetics they desire. 4 Let the young woman whom the king finds most attractive become queen in place of Vashti." This seemed like a good idea to the king, so he acted accordingly.

5 Now there happened to be a Jewish man in Susa the citadel whose name was Mordecai. He was the son of Jair, the son of Shimei, the son of Kish, a Benjaminite, 6 who had been taken into exile from Jerusalem with the captives who had been carried into exile with Jeconiah king of Judah, whom Nebuchadnezzar king of Babylon had taken into exile. 7 Now he was acting as the guardian of Hadassah (that is, Esther), the daughter of his uncle, for neither

her father nor her mother was alive. This young woman was very attractive and had a beautiful figure. When her father and mother died, Mordecai had raised her as if she were his own daughter.

8 It so happened that when the king's edict and his law became known many young women were taken to Susa the citadel to be placed under the authority of Hegai. Esther also was taken to the royal palace to be under the authority of Hegai, who was overseeing the women. 9 This young woman pleased him, and she found favor with him. He quickly provided her with her cosmetics and her rations; he also provided her with the seven specially chosen young women who were from the palace. He then transferred her and her young women to the best quarters in the harem.

> *She was a Jew of the tribe of Benjamin living in foreign land.*

10 Now Esther had not disclosed her people or **her lineage**, for Mordecai had instructed her not to do so. 11 And day after day Mordecai used to walk back and forth in front of the court of the harem in order to learn how Esther was doing and what might happen to her.

> *Talk about a spa treatment.*

12 At the end of the **twelve months** that were required for the women, when the turn of each young woman arrived to go to King Ahasuerus—for in this way they had to fulfill their time of **cosmetic treatment: six months with oil of myrrh, and six months with perfume** and various ointments used by women—13 the woman would go to the king in the following way: Whatever she asked for would be provided for her to take with her from the harem to the royal palace. 14 In the evening she went, and in the morning she returned to a separate part of the harem, to the authority of Shaashgaz the king's eunuch who was overseeing the concubines. She would not go back to the king unless the king was pleased with her and she was requested by name.

15 When it became the turn of Esther daughter of Abihail the uncle of Mordecai (who had raised her as if she were his own daughter) to go to the king, she did not request anything except what Hegai the king's eunuch, who was overseer of the women, had recommended. Yet Esther met with the approval of all who saw her. 16 Then Esther was taken to King Ahasuerus at his royal residence ... 17 And the king loved Esther more than all the other women, and she met with his loving approval more than all the other young women. So he placed the royal high turban on her head and appointed her queen in place of Vashti. 18 Then the king prepared a large banquet for all his officials and his servants—it was actually Esther's banquet. He also set aside a holiday for the provinces, and he provided for offerings at the king's expense.

Mordecai Learns of a Plot Against the King

19 Now when the young women were being gathered again, Mordecai was sitting at the king's gate. 20 Esther was still not divulging her lineage or her people, just as Mordecai had instructed her. Esther continued to do whatever Mordecai said, just as she had done when he was raising her.

21 In those days while Mordecai was sitting at the king's gate, Bigthan and Teresh, two of the king's eunuchs who protected the

entrance, became angry and plotted to assassinate King Ahasuerus. 22 When Mordecai learned of the conspiracy, he informed Queen Esther, and Esther told the king in Mordecai's behalf. 23 The king then had the matter investigated and, finding it to be so, had the two conspirators hanged on a gallows. **It was then recorded in the daily chronicles in the king's presence.**

3:1 Some time later King Ahasuerus promoted Haman the son of Hammedatha, the Agagite, exalting him and setting his position above that of all the officials who were with him. 2 As a result, all the king's servants who were at the king's gate were bowing and paying homage to Haman, for the king had so commanded. However, Mordecai did not bow, nor did he pay him homage.

3 Then the servants of the king who were at the king's gate asked Mordecai, "Why are you violating the king's commandment?" 4 And after they had spoken to him day after day without his paying any attention to them, they informed **Haman** to see whether this attitude on Mordecai's part would be permitted. Furthermore, he had disclosed to them that he was a Jew.

5 When Haman saw that Mordecai was not bowing or paying homage to him, he was filled with rage. 6 But the thought of striking out against Mordecai alone was repugnant to him, for he had been informed of the identity of Mordecai's people. So Haman sought to destroy all the Jews (that is, the people of Mordecai) who were in all the kingdom of Ahasuerus. 7 In the first month ... in the twelfth year of King Ahasuerus' reign, **pur** (that is, the lot) was cast before Haman in order to determine a day and a month. It turned out to be the twelfth month (that is, the month of Adar).

8 Then Haman said to King Ahasuerus, "There is a particular people that is dispersed and spread among the inhabitants throughout all the provinces of your kingdom whose laws differ from those of all other peoples. Furthermore, they do not observe the king's laws. It is not appropriate for the king to provide a haven for them. 9 If the king is so inclined, let an edict be issued to destroy them. I will pay 10,000 talents of silver to be conveyed to the king's treasuries for the officials who carry out this business."

10 So the king removed his signet ring from his hand and gave it to Haman the son of Hammedatha, the Agagite, who was hostile toward the Jews. 11 The king replied to Haman, "Keep your money, and do with those people whatever you wish."

13 Letters were sent by the runners to all the king's provinces stating that they should destroy, kill, and annihilate all the Jews.

4:1 Now when Mordecai became aware of all that had been done, he tore his garments and put on sackcloth and ashes. He went out into the city, crying out in a loud and bitter voice. 2 But he went no further than the king's gate, for no one was permitted to enter the king's gate clothed in sackcloth. 3 Throughout each and every province where the king's edict and law were announced there was considerable mourning among the Jews, along with fasting, weeping, and sorrow... 4 When Esther's female attendants and her eunuchs came and informed her about Mordecai's behav-

---

Okay, you have to remember this event because it comes back later in the story.

A new character in the story.

It is from this word that the Jews celebrate something called Purim. More on that later.

ior, the queen was overcome with anguish. Although she sent garments for Mordecai to put on so that he could remove his sackcloth, he would not accept them. 5 So Esther called for Hathach, one of the king's eunuchs who had been placed at her service, and instructed him to find out the cause and reason for Mordecai's behavior. 6 So Hathach went to Mordecai at the plaza of the city in front of the king's gate. 7 Then Mordecai related to him everything that had happened to him, even the specific amount of money that Haman had offered to pay to the king's treasuries for the Jews to be destroyed. 8 He also gave him a written copy of the law that had been disseminated in Susa for their destruction so that he could show it to Esther and talk to her about it. He also gave instructions that she should go to the king to implore him and petition him on behalf of her people. 9 So Hathach returned and related Mordecai's instructions to Esther.

10 Then Esther replied to Hathach with instructions for Mordecai: 11 "All the servants of the king and the people of the king's provinces know that there is only one law applicable to any man or woman who comes uninvited to the king in the inner court—that person will be put to death, unless the king extends to him the gold scepter, permitting him to be spared. Now I have not been invited to come to the king for some thirty days!"

12 When Esther's reply was conveyed to Mordecai, 13 he said to take back this answer to Esther: "Don't imagine that because you are part of the king's household you will be the one Jew who will escape. 14 If you keep quiet at this time, liberation and protection for the Jews will appear from another source, while you and your father's household perish. **It may very well be that you have achieved royal status for such a time as this!**"

This is the most famous line in the book of Esther. Why do you think that is?

She becomes a picture of what Jesus was willing to do to save us.

15 Then Esther sent this reply to Mordecai: 16 "Go, assemble all the Jews who are found in Susa and fast in my behalf. Don't eat and don't drink for three days, night or day. My female attendants and I will also fast in the same way. Afterward I will go to the king, even though it violates the law. **If I perish, I perish!**"

5:1-3 It so happened that on the third day Esther put on her royal attire and stood in the inner court of the palace, opposite the king's quarters. The king was sitting on his royal throne in the palace, opposite the entrance. 2 When the king saw Queen Esther standing in the court, she met with his approval. The king extended to Esther the gold scepter that was in his hand, and Esther approached and touched the end of the scepter.

3 The king said to her, "What is on your mind, Queen Esther? What is your request? Even as much as half the kingdom will be given to you!"

4 Esther replied, "If the king is so inclined, let the king and Haman come today to the banquet that I have prepared for him." 5 The king replied, "Find Haman quickly so that we can do as Esther requests."

So the king and Haman went to the banquet that Esther had prepared. 6 While at the banquet of wine, the king said to Esther,

"What is your request? It shall be given to you. What is your petition? Ask for as much as half the kingdom, and it shall be done!"

7 Esther responded, "My request and my petition is this: 8 If I have found favor in the king's sight and if the king is inclined to grant my request and perform my petition, let the king and Haman come tomorrow to the banquet that I will prepare for them. At that time I will do as the king wishes.

9 Now Haman went forth that day pleased and very much encouraged. But when Haman saw Mordecai at the king's gate, and he did not rise nor tremble in his presence, Haman was filled with rage toward Mordecai. 10 But Haman restrained himself and went on to his home.

He then sent for his friends to join him, along with his wife Zeresh. 11 Haman then recounted to them his fabulous wealth, his many sons, and how the king had magnified him and exalted him over the king's other officials and servants. 12 Haman said, "Furthermore, Queen Esther invited only me to accompany the king to the banquet that she prepared! And also tomorrow I am invited along with the king. 13 Yet all of this fails to satisfy me so long as I have to see Mordecai the Jew sitting at the king's gate."

14 Haman's wife Zeresh and all his friends said to him, "Have a gallows seventy-five feet high built, and in the morning tell the king that Mordecai should be hanged on it. Then go with the king to the banquet contented."

6:1-2 Throughout that night the king was unable to sleep, so he asked for the **book containing the historical records** to be brought. As the records were being read in the king's presence, 2 it was found written that Mordecai had disclosed that Bigthana and Teresh, two of the king's eunuchs who guarded the entrance, had plotted to assassinate King Ahasuerus.

Remember, I told you this story would come back.

3 The king asked, "What great honor was bestowed on Mordecai because of this?" The king's attendants who served him responded, "Not a thing was done for him."

4 Then the king said, "Who is that in the courtyard?" Now Haman had come to the outer courtyard of the palace to suggest that the king hang Mordecai on the gallows that he had constructed for him. 5 The king's attendants said to him, "It is Haman who is standing in the courtyard." The king said, "Let him enter."

6 So Haman came in, and the king said to him, "What should be done for the man whom the king wishes to honor?" Haman thought to himself, "Who is it that the king would want to honor more than me?" 7 So Haman said to the king, "For the man whom the king wishes to honor, 8 let them bring royal attire which the king himself has worn and a horse on which the king himself has ridden—one bearing the royal insignia! 9 Then let this clothing and this horse be given to one of the king's noble officials. Let him then clothe the man whom the king wishes to honor, and let him lead him about through the plaza of the city on the horse, calling before him, 'So shall it be done to the man whom the king wishes to honor!'"

The 12 Historical Books

> *This is too good!*

10 The king then said to Haman, "Go quickly! Take the clothing and the horse, just as you have described, and do as you just indicated to Mordecai the Jew who sits at the king's gate. Don't neglect a single thing of all that you have said."

> *Oh, that must have hurt.*

11 So Haman took the clothing and the horse, and he clothed Mordecai. He led him about on the horse throughout the plaza of the city, calling before him, "So shall it be done to the man whom the king wishes to honor!"

12 Then Mordecai again sat at the king's gate, while Haman hurried away to his home, mournful and with a veil over his head. 13 Haman then related to his wife Zeresh and to all his friends everything that had happened to him...

14 While they were still speaking with him, the king's eunuchs arrived. They quickly brought Haman to the banquet that Esther had prepared.

7:1 So the king and Haman came to dine with Queen Esther. 2 On the second day of the banquet of wine the king asked Esther, "What is your request, Queen Esther? It shall be granted to you. And what is your petition? Ask up to half the kingdom, and it shall be done!"

3 Queen Esther replied, "If I have met with your approval, O king, and if the king is so inclined, grant me my life as my request, and my people as my petition. 4 For we have been sold—both I and my people—to destruction and to slaughter and to annihilation ...

5 Then King Ahasuerus responded to Queen Esther, "Who is this individual? Where is this person to be found who is presumptuous enough to act in this way?"

6 Esther replied, "The oppressor and enemy is this evil Haman!"

Then Haman became terrified in the presence of the king and queen. 7 In rage the king arose from the banquet of wine and withdrew to the palace garden. Meanwhile, Haman stood to beg Queen Esther for his life, for he realized that the king had now determined a catastrophic end for him.

8 When the king returned from the palace garden to the banquet of wine, Haman was throwing himself down on the couch where Esther was lying. The king exclaimed, "Will he also attempt to rape the queen while I am still in the building!"

As these words left the king's mouth, they covered Haman's face. 9 Harbona, one of the king's eunuchs, said, "Indeed, there is the gallows that Haman made for Mordecai, who spoke out in the king's behalf. It stands near Haman's home and is seventy-five feet high."

> *This is what one would call "irony."*

The king said, "Hang him on it!" 10 **So they hanged Haman on the very gallows that he had prepared for Mordecai.** The king's rage then abated.

8:1 On that same day King Ahasuerus gave the estate of Haman, that adversary of the Jews, to Queen Esther. Now Mordecai had come before the king, for Esther had revealed how he was related to her. 2 The king then removed his signet ring (the very one he had taken back from Haman) and gave it to Mordecai. And Esther designated Mordecai to be in charge of Haman's estate.

3 Then Esther again spoke with the king, falling at his feet. She wept and begged him for mercy, that he might nullify the evil of Haman the Agagite which he had intended against the Jews. 4 When the king extended to Esther the gold scepter, she arose and stood before the king.

5 She said, "If the king is so inclined and if I have met with his approval and if the matter is agreeable to the king and if I am attractive to him, let an edict be written rescinding those recorded intentions of Haman the son of Hammedatha, the Agagite, which he wrote in order to destroy the Jews who are throughout all the king's provinces. 6 For how can I watch the calamity that will befall my people, and how can I watch the destruction of my relatives?"

7 King Ahasuerus replied to Queen Esther and to Mordecai the Jew, "Look, I have already given Haman's estate to Esther, and he has been hanged on the gallows because he took hostile action against the Jews. 8 Now you write in the king's name whatever in your opinion is appropriate concerning the Jews and seal it with the king's signet ring. Any decree that is written in the king's name and sealed with the king's signet ring cannot be rescinded.

9 The king's scribes were quickly summoned—in the third month (that is, the month of Sivan), on the twenty-third day. They wrote out everything that Mordecai instructed to the Jews and to the satraps and the governors and the officials of the provinces all the way from India to Ethiopia—a hundred and twenty-seven provinces in all—to each province in its own script and to each people in their own language, and to the Jews according to their own script and their own language. 10 Mordecai wrote in the name of King Ahasuerus and sealed it with the king's signet ring. He then sent letters by couriers on horses, who rode royal horses that were very swift.

14 The couriers who were riding the royal horses went forth with the king's edict without delay. And the law was presented in Susa the citadel as well.

15 Now Mordecai went out from the king's presence in purple and white royal attire, with a large golden crown and a purple linen mantle. The city of Susa shouted with joy. 16 For the Jews there was radiant happiness and joyous honor. 17 Throughout every province and throughout every city where the king's edict and his law arrived, the Jews experienced happiness and joy, **banquets and holidays.**

> Today this celebration is called Purim. The story of Esther is read on this day. Whenever Hamon's name is mentioned everyone boo's. Whenever Mordecai's name is mentioned everyone cheers.

the book of Job

Category: *The 5 Poetic Books*
Author: *Unknown*
Theme: *Why do good people still suffer?*
Location & Date: *The land of Uz; Date unknown*
Version of Bible: *The Voice*
Summary: *Many believe this book was written in the time of Abraham, Isaac, and Jacob. The stage for this book is heaven and earth. God and Satan meet in the heavenly realm and end up making a wager, a bet if you will. The purpose of the bet is to answer this question: Does Job only serve God because God is good to him? To test Job's motivation, Satan brings great suffering to Job's life. Most of the book is about Job and his three friends trying to figure out why Job has to suffer. In the end, Job is restored but he never finds out why he had to suffer (this is often the case in our lives as well). Only we the readers know about the wager behind the scenes.*

Job 1:1 Once there was a man from Uz by the name of Job. He was a very good man—his character spotless, his integrity unquestioned. In fact, he so believed in God that he sought to honor Him in all things. He deliberately avoided evil in all of his affairs. 2 He had 7 sons and 3 daughters; 3 he owned 7,000 sheep, 3,000 camels, 500 teams of oxen, 500 female donkeys, and a large number of servants. Among Easterners, he was the most powerful and influential man. 4 His sons, who were all wealthy landowners, too, all used to gather together on each others' birthdays and special occasions. The brothers would take turns hosting the others in their homes, and they would invite their three sisters to eat and drink with them. 5 When these days of feasting were through, Job would call all of his family to his own house and purify them, rising up early in the morning to offer burnt sacrifices for each one.

Job: God, forgive my children for any secret sins or grudges they have against You deep in their hearts

Job did this again and again.

6 **Now one day**, it came time for the sons of God, God's heavenly messengers, to present themselves to the Eternal One to give reports and receive instructions. The Accuser was with them there.

Eternal One (to the Accuser): 7 Where have you been?

The Accuser: Oh, roaming here and there, running about the earth and observing its inhabitants.

Eternal One: 8 Well, have you looked into the man, Job, My servant? He is unlike any other person on the whole earth—a very

The scene shifts to heaven where the accuser (Satan) talks with God.

good man—his character spotless, his integrity unquestioned. In fact, he so believes in Me that he seeks, in all things, to honor Me and deliberately avoids evil in all of his affairs.

The Accuser: 9 I won't argue with You that he is pious, but is all of this believing in You and honoring You for no reason? 10 Haven't You encircled him with Your very own protection, and not only him but his entire household and all that he has? Not only this, but Your blessing accompanies whatever his hand touches, and see how his possessions have grown. **It is easy to be so pious in the face of such prosperity.** 11 So now extend Your hand! Destroy all of these possessions of his, and he will certainly curse You, right to Your face.

Eternal One: 12 I delegate this task to you. His possessions are now in your hand. One thing, though: you are not to lay a finger on the man himself. Job must not be touched.

With that, the Accuser left the court and the Eternal's presence.

13 **Now one day**, all of Job's children were gathered together under the roof of Job's firstborn for their usual celebration—feasting and drinking wine—14 when a messenger came to Job.

Messenger: We were in the field. The oxen were plowing, the donkeys were grazing nearby, 15 and out of nowhere, the Sabeans attacked. They stole your animals, all 1,000 oxen and donkeys, and as for your servants, they put their swords to us, and everyone is dead—every last one, except me. I am the only one who got away from the fields to tell you.

16 And while the words were still leaving the messenger's mouth, another messenger arrived.

Second Messenger: Lightning has struck! The fire of God fell from the sky and burned the 7,000 sheep alive ... alive! Shepherds, too - all of them burned; everyone is dead—every last one, except me. I am the only one who got away from the pastures to tell you.

17 And while the words were still leaving that messenger's mouth, a third messenger arrived.

Third Messenger: Chaldeans! Three groups of them attacked us. They converged on the camels and stole your 3,000 animals, and as for your servants, they put their swords to us, and everyone is dead—every last one, except me. I am the only one who got away to tell you.

18 And while the words were still leaving that messenger's mouth, yet a fourth messenger arrived.

Fourth Messenger: All of your children were gathered together today under the roof of your firstborn to celebrate—eating a feast and drinking wine—19 and then a powerful wind rose up from the other side of the desert, and it struck all four corners of the house. It collapsed! Everyone is dead—all of those young people—every last one, except me. I am the only one who got away from your son's house to tell you.

20 Then Job stood up, tore his robe, shaved his head, and fell

Is this true? Often we forget about God when things are good.

The scene is now back on earth.

to the ground. Face down, Job sprawled in the dirt to worship.

21 Job: **I was naked, with nothing, when I came from my mother's womb; and naked, with nothing, I will return to the earth.** The Eternal has given, and He has taken away. May the name of the Eternal One be blessed.

22 In all of this Job neither sinned nor did he make foolish charges against God.

2:1 **Now one day**, it was time for the sons of God, God's heavenly messengers, to present themselves to the Eternal One to give reports and receive instructions. The Accuser was with them there again, also ready to present himself to Him.

Eternal One (to the Accuser): 2 Where have you been?

The Accuser: Oh, roaming here and there, running about the earth and observing its inhabitants.

Eternal One: 3 Well, have you looked into the man, Job, My servant? He is unlike any other person on the whole earth—a very good man—his character spotless, his integrity unquestioned. In fact, he so believes in Me that he seeks, in all things, to honor Me and deliberately avoids evil in all of his affairs. And I have found him to be unswervingly committed, despite the fact that you provoked Me to wreck him **for no particular reason**, to take away My protection and his prosperity.

The Accuser: 4 Well, as they say, "Skin for skin!" It is easy to be so pious in the face of such health. Surely a man will give what he has for the sake of his own life, 5 so now extend Your hand! Afflict him, both bone and body, and he will curse You, right to Your face.

Eternal One: 6 Well then, this is how it will be: he is now in your hand. One thing, though: you will not take his life. Job must not be killed.

7 With that, the Accuser left the court and the Eternal's presence, and he infected Job with a painful skin disease. From the soles of his feet to the crown of his head, his body was covered with boils. 8 Job took a broken piece of pottery to scrape his wounds, and while he sat in the ashes just outside of town, 9 his wife found him.

Job's Wife: Will you still not swerve in your commitments? Curse God and die!

Job: 10 You're speaking nonsense like some depraved woman. **Are we to accept the good that comes from God, but not accept the bad?**

Throughout all of this, Job did not sin with his mouth; he would not curse God as the Accuser predicted.

11 Now Job had three friends: Eliphaz from Teman, Bildad from Shuah, and Zophar from Naamath. When these three received word of the horror that had befallen Job, they left their homes, and agreed to meet together to mourn with and comfort their friend.

12 They approached the town ash-heap, but they were still far off when they caught sight of Job. His sores were so severe

---

Margin notes:

These words are often said at funerals. Notice Job still blessed God's name in spite of all the losses.

The scene is back to heaven.

Ever feel like this has happened to you?

A good question.

and his appearance so changed by his condition that they almost didn't recognize him. Upon seeing him and apprehending the extent of his suffering, they cried out, burst into tears, tore their robes, reached down into the dust and ashes at their feet, and threw ash into the air and onto their heads. 13 Then, they sat with him on the ground and stayed there with him for seven days and seven nights, mourning as if he were already dead. All the while **no one spoke a single word** because they saw his profound agony and grief.

{The rest of the book of Job recounts the conversation held between Job and his friends in which they attempted to explain the recent events of Jobs life. It begins with a mournful monologue by Job in which he bemoaned his current state of affairs and cursed the day of his birth.}

3:1-2 After all of this, Job opened his mouth and broke the silence. He spoke a curse, not upon God but upon his day of birth.

3 Job: **May the day die on which I was born,** along with the night that spoke the words, "a boy is conceived." 4 May that day of birth become darkness, and when it has disappeared, may God above neither seek it out nor light find a way to shine on it... 6 As to that night of my conception—may it be snatched by the thick darkness of death's realm, Never to be released again for any year or any month—so my conception and life could never have happened... 9 And may the early—morning stars be extinguished.

{After this speech, a dialogue opened up between Job and his friends. First Eliphaz chastised Job, saying that surely there must have been some wickedness in Job's life that provoked God to punish him. He reasoned that because God is just and does not punish those who are blameless, Job must be guilty.}

4:1 Standing with Job and his other two friends in the trash heap, Eliphaz the Temanite tried to convince Job his suffering was temporary.

Eliphaz: 3 Look back, and think on the many you have taught; you have strengthened the weak hands of the suffering. 4 Your words propped up the tottering; you have strengthened mourners' wobbly knees. 5 May my words help you in that way, now that trouble arrives and you despair. It extends its hand, crushes you, and you are overwhelmed. 6 Isn't your fear of God true confidence and your unswerving commitment genuine hope? 7 Take pause; scan your memory: Who ever died among the innocent? And when have the righteous ever met with destruction? 8 The way I see it, those who pull the pernicious plow, Who sow sorrow's seeds, reap the same at harvest. 9 By God's breath, they meet destruction; when His anger explodes, they meet their end.

17 "Can a mortal stand innocent before God? Can a man or even a hero be pure before his Creator?"

{Eliphaz argued that since every mortal is by his own nature a sinner, any punishment received is just. Bildad echoed these sentiments, saying that Job must have brought this upon himself. He added that Job's children must have deserved the punishment

---

When someone is hurting, just being there is sometimes words enough.

Wow. You can't get more negative about your own birth than this.

they received as well.}

8:1 Then the second of Job's three friends, Bildad the Shuhite, addressed Job. 2 Bildad: How long will you say these things, your words whipping through air like a powerful wind? 3 Does God corrupt justice, or does the Highest One corrupt the good? 4 If your children sinned against Him, He merely administered the punishment due them for those sins. 5 But if you search for God and make your appeal to the Highest One, 6 If you are pure and righteous, I have no doubt He will arise for you and restore you to your righteous place. 7 From your modest beginnings, the future will be bright before you.

11:1 Finally, Job's third friend, Zophar the Naamathite, spoke to Job.

2 Zophar: Shall such a great volume of words remain unanswered and a long-winded man be so easily acquitted? 3 Shall your empty prattle silence people, and when you mock, shall no one shame you? 4 You've told us, "I have a clear understanding of things, and I am innocent in Your eyes, O Lord." 5 Ah, but I wish God would speak, that He would address you openly, so I will argue for Him. 6 I wish He would show you the secrets of great wisdom—for the two sides of sound wisdom are both found in His mercy and justice. Know this: God forgets some of your guilt.

7 Can you see to the unseen side of God, or explore the limits of the Highest One's knowledge? 8 Higher than the heavens—what can you do to reach it? Deeper than the realm of the dead—what can you know of it? 9 Its farthest reaches exceed the ends of the earth; its breadth spans far beyond the sea. 10 If He passes by, as is His routine, and throws you into prison, and calls you to testify about what you've done, who can challenge Him? 11 He recognizes worthless people without integrity, so do you really think when He sees wrongdoing He doesn't examine it?

{Job then challenged his friends to point out any blameworthy facet of his life. He argued that merely being a human is not reason enough to be punished. In the second round of speeches, his friends accused in the same fashion, posing many of the same arguments in slightly different ways—the main point being that Job must be blameworthy. In the third round, only Eliphaz and Bildad offered their opinions and Job again countered them forcefully. In all of this, Job did not curse God. In the middle of all this discouragement, gloom, and despair there was hope. Job longed for a mediator, a savior.}

12:4 As for me—the one who called upon God and whom God answered—now, I am pitiful, laughable, a just and upright joke.

14:1 Job: Humankind, born of woman, has a few brief years with much suffering. 2 Like a short-lived bloom, he springs up only to wither; like the brief shade gained by a fast-moving cloud, he passes swiftly.

5 Since a person's life is fixed, and You are the One who determines the number of his months, And You set a limit on the length of her life, and since they are incapable of exceeding Your decree,

6 The least You can do is turn Your gaze away from him until they pass, so that he can enjoy his day like a hired worker. 7 You know, at least there is a kind of hope for a tree: if it gets cut down, it may yet sprout again out of the roots. And very likely then, its tender shoots will not die. 8 Its roots may age deep under the ground, and the stump appear dead in the dry earth, 9 But even then it needs only the merest whiff of water to bud again and put forth shoots like a newly planted sapling. 10 But not so with humankind. The noblest of human beings dies and lies flat. Humans die, and where do they go? 11 Just as water evaporates from the sea, And riverbeds go parched and dry, 12 so humankind lies down and does not rise again. Until the day when the skies are done away with, humankind will neither awaken nor rouse from slumber. 13 O that You would merely hide me in the land of the dead and keep me in secret till Your wrath is gone, until a time You decide when You might think upon me. 14 **If one dies, can he live again?** Through these days of toil and struggle, I will patiently wait until my situation changes.

17:11 Even now my days have passed me by; My plans lie broken at my feet; the secret wishes of my heart grow cold. 12 And yet my friends say, this loss of hope is for good, turning my dark night into what appears to them as day. In the pitch darkness, these broken plans and secret wishes speak to me. They say, "There is light nearby."

13 If I hope only to live in the land of the dead, if I prepare for myself a bed in the darkness, 14 If I speak to my burial pit, calling it "Father," and to the worms in the earth, calling them "Mother" and "Sister," 15 Then **where will I find my hope?** And who will see it? 16 Will hope go with me to the place of death? Will hope accompany me into the ground?

19:7 Look! I cry out, "Violence!" but no response comes. I shout for help, but justice eludes me.

17 My breath is strange; even my wife avoids me; I'm loathsome to my relatives; they can't stand to be around me. 18 Even young children taunt me, and when I seek to rise, they mock me. 19 My closest friends can no longer bear me, and anyone I have ever loved has turned against me.

25 I know my **Redeemer** lives, and in the end He will rise and take His stand on the earth. 26 And though my skin has been stripped off, still, in my flesh, I will see God. 27 I, myself, will see Him: not some stranger, but actually me, with these eyes.

21:7 Why do the wicked live on an ever-upward path to long life and riches? 8 Their children become well-established in front of them; their offspring are guaranteed to grow up before their very eyes. 9 Their houses are immune to approaching terrors; the rod of God is not on their backs punishing them. 10 Their bulls are consistent breeders; their cows deliver healthy calves without miscarrying. 11 They produce flocks of children and send them all out into the world; their young ones dance around free of care. 12 They still participate in celebration, raising their voic-

> *This is the most important question that a human being can ask. To spend your whole life trying to find the answer would not be a waste.*

> *The second most important question.*

> *Jesus!*

...es to the song of the tambourine and the harp; delighting in the sound of the flute. 13 They pass their time in the lap of abundance, and they are even permitted to pass quickly to the land of the dead, instead of lingering with chronic pain.

23 One person dies when he is fit and strong, completely secure and totally at peace; 24 His body is vigorous and well fed; his bones are strong and moist. 25 Another person dies with a bitter soul, having never even tasted goodness. 26 But they lie down together in the same dust, covered by the same blanket of worms.

27:2 By God—who lives and has deprived me of justice, the Highest One who has also embittered my soul—3 I make this proclamation: that, while there is life in me, While the breath of that selfsame God is in my nostrils, 4 My lips will not let lies escape them, and my tongue will not form deceit. 5 So I will never concede that you three (Job's 3 friends) are right. Until the day I die, I will not abandon my integrity just to appease you. 6 On the contrary, I'll assert my innocence and never let it go; my heart will not mock my past or my future.

The great wisdom of the ages begins with fearing God. It is the evil of the world that clouds our understanding and leads us into foolishness.

29:2 Ah, that I were as I once was, months ago during the time when God oversaw me, 3 When His lamp shone above my head, and by His light, I walked through the darkness. 4 Ah, to be in the ripest time of life once more—when the intimacies of friendship with God enfolded my tent, 5 When the Highest One was with me and my children encircled me, 6 When my steps were bathed in milk and the rock poured out rivers of olive oil, showering my body, 7 When I went up to the gate of the city, when I took my seat in the town square where the elders meet. 8 There the young saw me and made room for me, in deference to elders. The old rose and stood out of respect. 9 The leaders stopped talking with their hands over their mouths. 10 The voices of nobles fell to a hush; their tongues stuck to the roofs of their mouths. 11 Every ear that heard me blessed me, and every eye that saw me testified to my greatness. 12 After all, I rescued the poor when they cried out for help and assisted the orphans when they had no one else. Great virtue has always begun with the treatment of the poor. Can Job be accused of having a hard heart? 13 The dying spoke their blessings over me, and the widows sang their joyful songs honoring what I did. 14 I adorned myself in righteousness, and it covered me; my justice fit me like a cloak and turban—conveying both my dignity and my authority. 15 I was the eyes for the blind, the feet for the lame, 16 A father for the needy, and I sought for the cause of whom I did not know. 17 I broke out the fangs of the wicked and wrested prey from their jaws.

18 Then I said, "I will pass from this earth in the comfort of my nest. My days will be more numerous than a beach's grains of sand. 19 My roots will grow deep, spreading out to the water's edge, and in the night, the dew will come to rest on my branches. 20 Respect will be accorded me every day, my skill with the bow

always new in my hand."

21 People used to listen to me, the sense of expectation visible on their faces; they waited in silence for my advice. 22 And when I finished, they did not hurry to speak again. They waited while my words dropped like dew upon them. 23 Indeed, they waited for me as one waits for a good rain, and they opened their mouths as if to catch spring showers on their tongues. 24 I smiled upon them when their confidence flagged, and they took comfort in my beaming face. 25 I led them in their way. I sat as their leader. I lived like a king among his troops. I was as a happy man spreading comfort among the mourners.

30:1 Job: But now they mock me, these young men whose fathers I hold in such contempt. I wouldn't trust them with my herds as I do my dogs.

16 And now my own soul is drawn out, poured over me. The days of misery have taken hold of me; I am firmly in their grasp. 17 By night, my pain is at work, boring holes in my bones; it gnaws at me and never lies down to rest. 18 With great force, God wraps around me like my clothing. He binds tightly about my neck as if He were the collar of my tunic. 19 He has pushed me off into the mud, and I am reduced from man to dust and ashes. 20 I call out to You, God, but You refuse to answer me. When I arise, You merely examine me.

26 And yet when I longed for the good, evil came; when I awaited the light, thick darkness arrived instead.

{In the final monologue, Elihu, a younger man who was holding his tongue out of respect, finally spoke. Elihu argued that God communicates to us through physical inflictions and that perhaps the pain Job received is a warning against sin. Job did not respond to Elihu because the Lord interjected after Elihu's speech and questioned Job himself. God asked Job a series of rhetorical questions which illustrated the vast incomprehensible wisdom of God compared to that of any man.}

38:1 Out of the raging storm, the Eternal One answered Job.

2 Eternal One: Who is this that darkens counsel, who covers over sound instruction with empty words void of knowledge? 3 Now, prepare yourself and gather your courage like a warrior. Prepare yourself for the task at hand. I'll be asking the questions, now—you will supply the answers. 4 Where were you when I dug and laid the foundation of the earth? Explain it to me, if you are acquainted with understanding. 5 Who decided on the measurements? Surely you know that! Who stretched out a line to measure the dimensions? 6 Upon what base was the foundation set? Or who laid the cornerstone 7 On the day when the stars of the morning broke out in song and God's heavenly throng, elated, shouted along?

40:1 The Eternal continued speaking to Job.

2 Eternal One: Have you heard enough? Will the one who finds fault with the Highest One now make his case? Let God's accuser

answer Him!

3 Job answered the Eternal.

4 Job: Oh, I am so small. How can I reply to You? I'll cover my mouth with my hand, for I've already said too much. 5 One time I have spoken, and I have no answer to give—two times, and I have nothing more to add.

6 The Eternal spoke to Job from the raging storm.

Eternal One: 7 Now, prepare yourself and gather your courage like a warrior. Prepare yourself for the task at hand. I'll be asking the questions, now—you will supply the answers. 8 Let Me ask you a new question: Would you go so far as to call into question My judgment? Would you imagine Me guilty merely in order to justify yourself? 9 Do you have an arm just as powerful as God's and does your voice thunder as His does? 10 Then dress yourself up in majesty and dignity. Deck yourself out in honor and splendor 11 And indulge your anger. Unleash your wrath! Look down on each and every proud soul, and cut him low. 12 Look down on all who are proud, and humiliate them. Raise your mighty foot, and stomp the wicked where they stand. 13 Bury them all together in the dirt, and shroud their frozen faces in the secret recesses of the grave. 14 If you can execute all this, then I—yes, even I—will praise you, for your great and mighty right hand earned you the victory!

42:1 Job answered the Eternal One.

2 Job: I know You can do everything; nothing You do can be foiled or frustrated. 3 You asked, "Who is this that conceals counsel with empty words void of knowledge?" And now I see that I spoke of—but did not comprehend—great wonders that are beyond me. I didn't know. 4 You said, "Hear Me now, and I will speak. I'll be asking the questions, and you will supply the answers." 5 Before I knew only what I had heard of You, but now I have seen You. 6 Therefore I realize the truth: I disavow and mourn all I have said and repent in dust and ash. 7 After the Eternal had spoken these words to Job, He turned and spoke to Eliphaz from Teman.

Eternal One: My anger is burning against you and your two friends because you have not spoken rightly of Me, as My servant Job has. 8 So now, gather your friends and bring seven bulls and seven rams. Then go to My servant Job, make a burnt offering for yourselves, and he will pray for you. I will accept his prayer. Despite the fact that you have not spoken rightly of Me, as My servant Job did, I will not deal with you according to your foolish ways.

9 So Eliphaz from Teman, Bildad from Shuhah, and Zophar from Naamath went and did as the Eternal commanded, and He accepted Job's prayer for them.

10 The Eternal restored the fortunes of Job after he prayed for his friends; He even doubled the wealth he had before. 11 All of his brothers and sisters, along with those he had known earlier, came and shared meals with him at his house. They sympathized with him and consoled him regarding the great distress the Eternal had

brought on him. Each guest gave him a sum of money and each, a golden ring. 12 The Eternal One blessed the last part of Job's life even more than the first part... 13 He also fathered 7 more sons and 3 more daughters. 15 Nowhere in all the land could one find women as captivatingly beautiful as Job's daughters, or as independently wealthy: their father gave them each a share of the family inheritance along with their brothers. 16 After all this, Job lived 140 years. He lived to see his children and their children and so on, to the fourth generation. 17 Then Job died, old, and satisfied with his days.

the book of **Psalms**

Category: The 5 Poetic Books
Author: King David and others
Theme: Songs of the heart
Location & Date: Israel (Canaan); 1410-450 B.C.
Version of Bible: Various versions
Summary: This book is a book of songs. Many were written by King David but some were written by authors unknown. Of course we do not have the music today, only the words. There is a great variety of songs that touch on a lot of issues of life. Though written thousands of years ago, the Psalms seem very relevant for our lives today.

> People say they want to be happy. Here is how.

Psalm 1 (EXB) 1 **Happy** [Blessed] are those who don't listen to [walk in the counsel of] the wicked, who don't go where sinners go [stand in the way of sinners], who don't do what evil people do [sit in the seat of mockers]. 2 They love [delight in] the Lord's teachings [laws; instructions], and they think about [meditate on] those teachings [laws; instructions] day and night. 3 They are like a tree planted by a river [streams of water; full of life, strong, vibrant]. The tree produces fruit in season, and its leaves don't die [wither]. Everything they do will succeed [prosper].

> chaff is what's left of the grain seed when the meat is taken out. It is the waste product of grain.

4 But wicked people are not like that. They are like **chaff** that the wind blows away [dead, unstable]. 5 So the wicked will not escape God's punishment [stand in the judgment]. Sinners will not worship with God's people [be in the assembly of the righteous].

6 This is because the Lord takes care of his people [knows the way of the righteous], but the way of the wicked will be destroyed.

> Have you done this?

> Ever wonder this?

Psalm 8 (ERV) 1 Lord our Lord, your name is the most wonderful in all the earth! It brings you praise everywhere in heaven. 2 From the mouths of children and babies come songs of praise to you. They sing of your power to silence your enemies who were seeking revenge. 3 **I look at the heavens** you made with your hands. I see the moon and the stars you created. 4 And I wonder, "**Why are people so important to you?** Why do you even think about them? Why do you care so much about humans? Why do you even notice them?"

5 But you made them almost like gods and crowned them with glory and honor. 6 You put them in charge of everything you made. You put everything under their control. 7 People rule over the sheep and cattle and all the wild animals. 8 They rule over the birds in the sky and the fish that swim in the sea. 9 Lord our Lord,

your name is the most wonderful name in all the earth!

Psalm 19 (NLT) 1 The heavens proclaim the glory of God. The skies display his craftsmanship. 2 Day after day they continue to speak; night after night they make him known. 3 They speak without a sound or word; their voice is never heard. 4 Yet their message has gone throughout the earth, and their words to all the world. God has made a home in the heavens for the sun. 5 It bursts forth like a radiant bridegroom after his wedding. It rejoices like a great athlete eager to run the race. 6 The sun rises at one end of the heavens and follows its course to the other end. Nothing can hide from its heat.

7 The instructions of the Lord are perfect, reviving the soul. The decrees of the Lord are trustworthy, making wise the simple. 8 The commandments of the Lord are right, bringing joy to the heart. The commands of the Lord are clear, giving insight for living.

9 Reverence for the Lord is pure, lasting forever. The laws of the Lord are true; each one is fair. 10 They are more desirable than gold, even the finest gold. They are sweeter than honey, even honey dripping from the comb. 11 They are a warning to your servant, a great reward for those who obey them.

12 How can I know all the sins lurking in my heart? Cleanse me from these hidden faults. 13 Keep your servant from deliberate sins! **Don't let them control me.** Then I will be free of guilt and innocent of great sin. 14 May the words of my mouth and the meditation of my heart be pleasing to you, O Lord, my rock and my redeemer.

> This is what sin wants to do.

Psalm 22 (KJV) 1 **My God, my God, why hast thou forsaken me?** Why art thou so far from helping me, and from the words of my roaring? 2 O my God, I cry in the daytime, but thou hearest not; and in the night season, and am not silent.

3 But thou art holy, O thou that inhabitest the praises of Israel. 4 Our fathers trusted in thee: they trusted, and thou didst deliver them. 5 They cried unto thee, and were delivered: they trusted in thee, and were not confounded. 6 But I am a worm, and no man; a reproach of men, and despised of the people. 7 All they that see me laugh me to scorn: they shoot out the lip, they shake the head, saying, 8 He trusted on the LORD that he would deliver him: let him deliver him, seeing he delighted in him.

9 But thou art he that took me out of the womb: thou didst make me hope when I was upon my mother's breasts. 10 I was cast upon thee from the womb: thou art my God from my mother's belly.

11 Be not far from me; for trouble is near; for there is none to help. 12 Many bulls have compassed me: strong bulls of Bashan have beset me round. 13 They gaped upon me with their mouths, as a ravening and a roaring lion.

> Jesus' words on the cross (Mark 15:34; pg. 290). When have you felt like saying these words?

14 I am poured out like water, and all my bones are out of joint: my heart is like wax; it is melted in the midst of my bowels. 15 My strength is dried up like a potsherd; and my tongue cleaveth to my jaws; and thou hast brought me into the dust of death. 16 For dogs have compassed me: the assembly of the wicked have inclosed me: they pierced my hands and my feet. 17 I may tell all my bones: they look and stare upon me. 18 They part my garments among them, and cast lots upon my vesture.

19 But be not thou far from me, O LORD: O my strength, haste thee to help me. 20 Deliver my soul from the sword; my darling from the power of the dog. 21 Save me from the lion's mouth: for thou hast heard me from the horns of the unicorns.

22 I will declare thy name unto my brethren: in the midst of the congregation will I praise thee. 23 Ye that fear the LORD, praise him; all ye the seed of Jacob, glorify him; and fear him, all ye the seed of Israel. 24 For he hath not despised nor abhorred the affliction of the afflicted; neither hath he hid his face from him; but when he cried unto him, he heard.

25 My praise shall be of thee in the great congregation: I will pay my vows before them that fear him. 26 The meek shall eat and be satisfied: they shall praise the LORD that seek him: your heart shall live for ever. 27 All the ends of the world shall remember and turn unto the LORD: and all the kindreds of the nations shall worship before thee. 28 For the kingdom is the LORD'S: and he is the governor among the nations. 29 All they that be fat upon earth shall eat and worship: all they that go down to the dust shall bow before him: and none can keep alive his own soul. 30 A seed shall serve him; it shall be accounted to the Lord for a generation. 31 They shall come, and shall declare his righteousness unto a people that shall be born, that he hath done this.

This Psalm has been used at more funerals to comfort more people than any other words written in human history.

Psalm 23 (KJV) 1 **The LORD is my shepherd**; I shall not want. 2 He maketh me to lie down in green pastures: he leadeth me beside the still waters. 3 He restoreth my soul: he leadeth me in the paths of righteousness for his name's sake. 4 Yea, though I walk through the valley of the shadow of death, I will fear no evil: for thou art with me; thy rod and thy staff they comfort me. 5 Thou preparest a table before me in the presence of mine enemies: thou anointest my head with oil; my cup runneth over. 6 Surely goodness and mercy shall follow me all the days of my life: and I will dwell in the house of the LORD for ever.

Psalm 24 (NKJV) 1 The earth is the Lord's, and all its fullness, The world and those who dwell therein. 2 For He has founded it upon the seas, And established it upon the waters.

3 Who may ascend into the hill of the Lord? Or who may stand in His holy place? 4 He who has clean hands and a pure heart, Who has not lifted up his soul to an idol, Nor sworn deceitfully.

5 He shall receive blessing from the Lord, And righteousness

from the God of his salvation. 6 This is Jacob, the generation of those who seek Him, Who seek Your face.

7 Lift up your heads, O you gates! And be lifted up, you everlasting doors! And the King of glory shall come in. 8 Who is this King of glory? The Lord strong and mighty, The Lord mighty in battle.

9 Lift up your heads, O you gates! Lift up, you everlasting doors! And the King of glory shall come in. 10 Who is this King of glory? The Lord of hosts, He is the King of glory.

Psalm 27 (NIV) 1 The LORD is my light and my salvation; whom shall I fear? The LORD is the strength of my life; of whom shall I be afraid?

Psalm 32 (NIV) 1 Blessed is the one whose transgressions are forgiven, whose sins are covered. 2 Blessed is the one whose sin the Lord does not count against them and in whose spirit is no deceit.

3 **When I kept silent**, my bones wasted away through my groaning all day long. 4 For day and night your hand was heavy on me; my strength was sapped as in the heat of summer.

5 Then I acknowledged my sin to you and did not cover up my iniquity. I said, "I will confess my transgressions to the Lord." And you forgave the guilt of my sin.

Maybe there is something wrong in your life that is taking the life right out of you. What is it? Bring it to the Lord.

Psalm 34 (EXB) 8 Examine and see how good the Lord is. Happy is the person who trusts him.

Psalm 40 (NKJV) I waited patiently for the Lord; And He inclined to me, And heard my cry. 2 He also brought me up out of a horrible pit, Out of the miry clay, And set my feet upon a rock, And established my steps. 3 He has put a new song in my mouth - Praise to our God; Many will see it and fear, And will trust in the Lord.

Psalm 42 (NKJV) 1 As the deer pants for the water brooks, So pants my soul for You, O God. 2 My soul thirsts for God, for the living God. When shall I come and appear before God? 3 My tears have been my food day and night, While they continually say to me, "Where is your God?" 4 When I remember these things, I pour out my soul within me. For I used to go with the multitude; I went with them to the house of God, With the voice of joy and praise, With a multitude that kept a pilgrim feast.

5 **Why are you cast down, O my soul?** And why are you disquieted within me? Hope in God, for I shall yet praise Him For the help of His countenance.

What things in your life cause you to be down?

6 O my God, my soul is cast down within me; Therefore I will remember You from the land of the Jordan, And from the heights of

Hermon, From the Hill Mizar. 7 Deep calls unto deep at the noise of Your waterfalls; All Your waves and billows have gone over me.

8 The Lord will command His lovingkindness in the daytime, And in the night His song shall be with me—A prayer to the God of my life.

9 I will say to God my Rock, "Why have You forgotten me? Why do I go mourning because of the oppression of the enemy?" 10 As with a breaking of my bones, My enemies reproach me, While they say to me all day long, "Where is your God?"

11 Why are you cast down, O my soul? And why are you disquieted within me? Hope in God; For I shall yet praise Him, The help of my countenance and my God.

Psalm 43 (KJV) 1 Judge me, O God, and plead my cause against an ungodly nation: O deliver me from the deceitful and unjust man. 2 For thou art the God of my strength: why dost thou cast me off? Why go I mourning because of the oppression of the enemy? 3 O send out thy light and thy truth: let them lead me; let them bring me unto thy holy hill, and to thy tabernacles. 4 Then will I go unto the altar of God, unto God my exceeding joy: yea, upon the harp will I praise thee, O God my God.

5 Why art thou cast down, O my soul? And why art thou disquieted within me? Hope in God: for I shall yet praise him, who is the health of my countenance, and my God.

Psalm 46 (NIV) 1 God is our refuge and strength, an ever-present help in trouble. 2 Therefore we will not fear, though the earth give way and the mountains fall into the heart of the sea, 3 though its waters roar and foam and the mountains quake with their surging. 10 He says, "Be still, and know that I am God; I will be exalted among the nations, I will be exalted in the earth."

Psalm 49 (CEV) 1 Everyone on this earth, now listen to what I say! 2 Listen, no matter who you are, rich or poor. 3 I speak words of wisdom, and my thoughts make sense. 4 I have in mind a mystery that I will explain while playing my harp. 5 Why should I be afraid in times of trouble, when I am surrounded by vicious enemies? 6 They trust in their riches and brag about all of their wealth. 7 You cannot buy back your life or pay off God!

8 It costs far too much to buy back your life. You can never pay God enough 9 to stay alive forever and safe from death. 10 We see that wise people die, and so do stupid fools. Then their money is left for someone else. 11 The grave will be their home forever and ever, although they once had land of their own. 12 Our human glory disappears, and, like animals, we die. 13 Here is what happens to fools and to those who trust the words of fools: 14 They are like sheep with death as their shepherd, leading them to the grave. In the morning God's people will walk all over them, as their bodies

lie rotting in their home, the grave. 15 But God will rescue me from the power of death.

Psalm 51 (NKJV) 10 Create in me a clean heart, O God, And renew a steadfast spirit within me. 11 Do not cast me away from Your presence, And do not take Your Holy Spirit from me. 12 Restore to me the joy of Your salvation, And uphold me by Your generous Spirit.

Psalm 55 (NIV) 22 Cast your cares on the Lord and he will sustain you.

Psalm 90 (NLT) 1 Lord, through all the generations you have been our home! 2 Before the mountains were born, before you gave birth to the earth and the world, from beginning to end, you are God.

3 You turn people back to dust, saying, "Return to dust, you mortals!" 4 For you, a thousand years are as a passing day, as brief as a few night hours. 5 You sweep people away like dreams that disappear. They are like grass that springs up in the morning. 6 In the morning it blooms and flourishes, but by evening it is dry and withered.

Psalm 91 (NKJV) 1 He who dwells in the secret place of the Most High Shall abide under the shadow of the Almighty. 2 I will say of the Lord, "He is my refuge and my fortress; My God, in Him I will trust."

3 Surely He shall deliver you from the snare of the fowler And from the perilous pestilence. 4 He shall cover you with His feathers, And under His wings you shall take refuge; His truth shall be your shield and buckler. 5 You shall not be afraid of the terror by night, Nor of the arrow that flies by day, 6 Nor of the pestilence that walks in darkness, Nor of the destruction that lays waste at noonday. 7 A thousand may fall at your side, And ten thousand at your right hand; But it shall not come near you. 8 Only with your eyes shall you look, And see the reward of the wicked.

9 Because you have made the Lord, who is my refuge, Even the Most High, your dwelling place, 10 No evil shall befall you, Nor shall any plague come near your dwelling; 11 For He shall give His angels charge over you, To keep you in all your ways. 12 In their hands they shall bear you up, Lest you dash your foot against a stone. 13 You shall tread upon the lion and the cobra, The young lion and the serpent you shall trample underfoot.

Psalm 92 (KJV) 1 It is a good thing to give thanks unto the LORD, and to sing praises unto thy name, O Most High: 2 To shew forth thy lovingkindness in the morning, and thy faithfulness every night.

Psalm 100 (KJV) 1 Make a joyful noise unto the LORD, all ye lands. 2 Serve the LORD with gladness: come before his presence with singing. 3 Know ye that the LORD he is God: it is he that hath made us, and not we ourselves; we are his people, and the sheep of his pasture.

4 Enter into his gates with thanksgiving, and into his courts with praise: be thankful unto him, and bless his name. 5 For the LORD is good; his mercy is everlasting; and his truth endureth to all generations.

Psalm 102 (NIV) 1 Hear my prayer, Lord; let my cry for help come to you. 2 Do not hide your face from me when I am in distress. Turn your ear to me; when I call, answer me quickly.

Psalm 103 (KJV) 1 Bless the LORD, O my soul: and all that is within me, bless his holy name. 2 Bless the LORD, O my soul, and forget not all his benefits: 3 Who forgiveth all thine iniquities; who healeth all thy diseases; 4 Who redeemeth thy life from destruction; who crowneth thee with lovingkindness and tender mercies; 5 Who satisfieth thy mouth with good things; so that thy youth is renewed like the eagle's.

Psalm 115 (KJV) 1 Not unto us, O LORD, not unto us, but unto thy name give glory, for thy mercy, and for thy truth's sake.

Psalm 117 (KJV) 1 O praise the LORD, all ye nations: praise him, all ye people. 2 For his merciful kindness is great toward us: and the truth of the LORD endureth for ever.

Psalm 119 (HCSB) 9 How can a young man keep his way pure? By keeping Your word. 11 I have treasured Your word in my heart so that I may not sin against You. 105 Your word is a lamp for my feet and a light on my path.

Psalm 121 (NKJV) 1 I will lift up my eyes to the hills—From whence comes my help? 2 My help comes from the Lord, Who made heaven and earth. 3 He will not allow your foot to be moved; He who keeps you will not slumber. 4 Behold, He who keeps Israel Shall neither slumber nor sleep. 5 The Lord is your keeper; The Lord is your shade at your right hand. 6 The sun shall not strike you by day, Nor the moon by night. 7 The Lord shall preserve you from all evil; He shall preserve your soul. 8 The Lord shall preserve your going out and your coming in From this time forth, and even forevermore.

Psalm 122 (NIV) 1 I was glad when they said unto me, Let us go into the house of the LORD.

Psalm 130 (MSG) 1-2 Help, God—the bottom has fallen out of my life! Master, hear my cry for help! Listen hard! Open your ears! Listen to my cries for mercy.

3-4 If you, God, kept records on wrongdoings, who would stand a chance? As it turns out, forgiveness is your habit, and that's why you're worshiped.

5-6 I pray to God—my life a prayer—and wait for what he'll say and do. My life's on the line before God, my Lord, waiting and watching till morning, waiting and watching till morning.

7-8 O Israel, wait and watch for God—with God's arrival comes love, with God's arrival comes generous redemption. No doubt about it—he'll redeem Israel, buy back Israel from captivity to sin.

Psalm 133 (NRSV) 1 How very good and pleasant it is when kindred live together in unity!

2 It is like the precious oil on the head, running down upon the beard, on the beard of Aaron, running down over the collar of his robes. 3 It is like the dew of Hermon, which falls on the mountains of Zion. For there the Lord ordained his blessing, life forevermore.

Psalm 139 (GW) 1 O Lord, you have examined me, and you know me. 2 You alone know when I sit down and when I get up. You read my thoughts from far away. 3 You watch me when I travel and when I rest. You are familiar with all my ways. 4 Even before there is a single word on my tongue, you know all about it, Lord. 5 You are all around me—in front of me and in back of me. You lay your hand on me. 6 Such knowledge is beyond my grasp. It is so high I cannot reach it.

7 Where can I go to get away from your Spirit? Where can I run to get away from you? 8 If I go up to heaven, you are there. If I make my bed in hell, you are there. 9 If I climb upward on the rays of the morning sun or land on the most distant shore of the sea where the sun sets, 10 even there your hand would guide me and your right hand would hold on to me. 11 If I say, "Let the darkness hide me and let the light around me turn into night," 12 even the darkness is not too dark for you. Night is as bright as day. Darkness and light are the same to you.

13 You alone created my inner being. You knitted me together inside my mother. 14 I will give thanks to you because I have been so amazingly and miraculously made. Your works are miraculous, and my soul is fully aware of this. 15 My bones were not hidden from you when I was being made in secret, when I was being skillfully woven in an underground workshop. 16 Your eyes saw me when I was only a fetus. Every day of my life was recorded in your book before one of them had taken place. 17 How precious are your thoughts concerning me, O God! How vast in number they are! 18 If I try to count them, there would be more of them than there are grains of sand. When I wake up, I am still with you.

23 Examine me, O God, and know my mind. Test me, and know my thoughts. 24 See whether I am on an evil path. Then lead me on the everlasting path.

Psalm 142 (ERV) 1 I cry out to the Lord. I beg the Lord to help me. 2 I tell him my problems; I tell him about my troubles.

3 I am ready to give up. But you, Lord, know the path I am on, and you know that my enemies have set a trap for me. 4 I look around, and I don't see anyone I know. I have no place to run. There is no one to save me.

5 Lord, I cry out to you for help: "You are my place of safety. You are all I need in life."

6 Listen to my prayer. I am so weak. Save me from those who are chasing me. They are stronger than I am. 7 Help me escape this trap, so that I can praise your name. Then good people will celebrate with me, because you took care of me.

Psalm 150 (KJV) 1 Praise ye the LORD. Praise God in his sanctuary: praise him in the firmament of his power. 2 Praise him for his mighty acts: praise him according to his excellent greatness. 3 Praise him with the sound of the trumpet: praise him with the psaltery and harp. 4 Praise him with the timbrel and dance: praise him with stringed instruments and organs. 5 Praise him upon the loud cymbals: praise him upon the high sounding cymbals. 6 Let every thing that hath breath praise the LORD. Praise ye the LORD.

the book of Proverbs

Category: *The 5 Poetic Books*
Author: *King Solomon and others*
Theme: *Wise sayings*
Date: *971-686 B.C.*
Version of Bible: *Easy-to-Read Version (ERV)*
Summary: *A proverb is a short, practical observation about how life works. Comparison and contrast, analogy and metaphor are figures of speech commonly employed by the authors of this book, making it a very interesting read.*

Introduction

Proverbs 1:1 These are the proverbs of Solomon, the son of David and king of Israel. 2 They will help you learn to be wise, to accept correction, and to understand wise sayings. 3 They will teach you to develop your mind in the right way. You will learn to do what is right and to be honest and fair. 4 These proverbs will make even those without education smart. **They will teach young people what they need to know and how to use what they have learned.** 5 Even the wise could become wiser by listening to these proverbs. They will gain understanding and learn to solve difficult problems. 6 These sayings will help you understand proverbs, stories with hidden meanings, words of the wise, and other difficult sayings.

This is quite a promise!

7 **Knowledge begins with fear and respect for the LORD**, but stubborn fools hate wisdom and refuse to learn.

The Blessing of Wisdom

3:5 Trust the LORD completely, and don't depend on your own knowledge. 6 With every step you take, think about what he wants, and he will help you go the right way. 7 Don't trust in your own wisdom, but fear and respect the LORD and stay away from evil. 8 If you do this, it will be like a refreshing drink and medicine for your body.

Without God in your life what do you really know?

9 Honor the LORD with your wealth and the first part of your harvest. 10 Then your barns will be full of grain, and your barrels will be overflowing with wine.

11 My son, don't reject the LORD's discipline, and don't be angry when he corrects you. 12 The LORD corrects the one he loves, just as a father corrects a child he cares about.

The Dangers of Being Lazy

6:6 You lazy people, you should **watch what the ants** do and learn

If you don't want to work for someone you better be a self motivated, self-starter ... like an ant.

from them. 7 Ants have no ruler, no boss, and no leader. 8 But in the summer, ants gather all of their food and save it. So when winter comes, there is plenty to eat.

9 You lazy people, how long are you going to lie there? When will you get up? 10 You say, "I need a rest. I think I'll take a short nap." 11 But then you sleep and sleep and become poorer and poorer. Soon you will have nothing. It will be as if a thief came and stole everything you owned.

Warning Against Adultery

20 My son, remember your father's command, and don't forget your mother's teaching. 21 **Remember their words always. Tie them around your neck and keep them over your heart.** 22 **Let this teaching lead you wherever you go.** It will watch over you while you sleep. And when you wake up, it will give you good advice.

23 Your parents give you commands and teachings that are like lights to show you the right way. This teaching corrects you and trains you to follow the path to life.

27 If you drop a hot coal in your lap, your clothes will be burned. 28 If you step on one, your feet will be burned. 29 If you sleep with another man's wife, you will be punished.

The Value of Wisdom

8:22 "The LORD made me in the beginning, long before he did anything else. 23 I was formed a long time ago, before the world was made. 24 I was born before there was an ocean, before the springs began to flow. 25 I was born before the mountains and hills were set into place, 26 before the earth and fields were made, before the dust of this world was formed."

Solomon's Proverbs

10:1 These are the proverbs of Solomon: A wise son makes his father happy; a foolish one makes his mother sad.

4 Lazy hands will make you poor; hard-working hands will make you rich.

12 Hatred causes arguments, but love overlooks all wrongs.

14 **Wise people are quiet and learn new things, but fools talk and bring trouble on themselves.**

16 What good people do brings life, but wicked people produce only sin.

32 Good people know the right things to say, but the wicked say things to make trouble.

11:2 Proud and boastful people will be shamed, but wisdom stays with those who are modest and humble.

3 Good people are guided by their honesty, but crooks who lie and cheat will ruin themselves.

13 People who tell secrets about others cannot be trusted.

How can you know what God wants from you if you never read, study, and memorize His Word? How can you take the Word of God with you wherever you go?

Are a talker or a listener? Which do you need to work on?

Those who can be trusted keep quiet.

22 A beautiful woman without good sense is like a gold ring in a pig's nose.

24 Some people give freely and gain more; others refuse to give and end up with less.

25 Give freely, and you will profit. Help others, and you will gain more for yourself.

27 People are pleased with those who try to do good. Those who look for trouble will find it.

28 Those who trust in their riches will fall like dead leaves, but good people will blossom.

29 Those who cause trouble for their families will inherit nothing but the wind. A foolish person will end up as a servant to one who is wise.

12:1 Whoever loves discipline loves to learn; whoever hates to be corrected is stupid.

4 A good wife is like a crown to her husband, but a shameful wife is like a cancer.

15 Fools always think their own way is best, but wise people listen to what others tell them.

16 Fools are easily upset, but wise people avoid insulting others.

22 The LORD hates people who tell lies, but he is pleased with those who tell the truth.

23 Smart people don't tell everything they know, but fools tell everything and show they are fools.

25 Worry takes away your joy, but a kind word makes you happy.

13:3 People who are careful about what they say will save their lives, but those who speak without thinking will be destroyed.

4 Lazy people always want things but never get them. Those who work hard get plenty.

11 Money gained by cheating others will soon be gone. Money earned through hard work will grow and grow.

12 Hope that is delayed makes you sad, but a wish that comes true fills you with joy.

20 Be friends with those who are wise, and you will become wise. Choose fools to be your friends, and you will have trouble.

24 If you don't correct your children, you don't love them. If you love them, you will be quick to discipline them.

14:23 **If you work hard**, you will have plenty. If you do nothing but talk, you will not have enough.

29 A patient person is very smart. A quick-tempered person makes stupid mistakes.

This has been mentioned a few times now. Why do you think that is?

30 Peace of mind makes the body healthy, but jealousy is like a cancer.

15:1 A gentle answer makes anger disappear, but a rough answer makes it grow.

5 Fools refuse to listen to their father's advice, but those who accept discipline are smart.

13 If you are happy, your face shows it. If you are sad, your spirit feels defeated.

15 Life is always hard for the poor, but the right attitude can turn it into a party.

18 A quick temper causes fights, but patience brings peace and calm.

23 People are happy when they give a good answer. And there is nothing better than the right word at the right time.

16:8 It is better to be poor and do right than to be rich and do wrong.

18 Pride is the first step toward destruction. Proud thoughts will lead you to defeat.

19 It is better to be a humble person living among the poor than to share the wealth among the proud.

31 Gray hair is a crown of glory on people who have lived good lives. It is earned by living right.

32 It is better to be patient than to be a strong soldier. It is better to control your anger than to capture a city.

17:1 It is better to have nothing but a dry piece of bread to eat in peace than a whole house full of food with everyone arguing.

6 Grandchildren are the pride and joy of old age, and children take great pride in their parents.

9 Forgive someone, and you will strengthen your friendship. Keep reminding them, and you will destroy it.

17 A friend loves you all the time, but a brother was born to help in times of trouble.

19 A troublemaker loves to start arguments. Anyone who likes to brag is asking for trouble.

22 Happiness is good medicine, but sorrow is a disease.

18:2 **Fools don't want to learn from others. They only want to tell their own ideas.**

So true.

7 Fools hurt themselves when they speak. Their own words trap them.

19 An insulted brother is harder to win back than a city with strong walls. Arguments separate people like the strong bars of a palace gate.

21 The tongue can speak words that bring life or death. Those who love to talk must be ready to accept what it brings.

22 If you find a wife, you have found something good. She shows that the LORD is happy with you.

24 Some **friends** are fun to be with, but a true friend can be better than a brother.

Do you have a friend like this?

19:13 A foolish son brings a flood of troubles to his father, and a complaining wife is like the constant dripping of water.

20:1 Wine and beer make people lose control; they get loud and stumble around. And that is foolish.

13 If you love to sleep, you will become poor. Use your time working and you will have plenty to eat.

19 You cannot trust someone who would talk about things told in private. So don't be friends with someone who talks too much.

22 Don't ever say, "I'll pay them back for what they did to me!" Wait for the LORD. He will make things right.

29 We admire a young man for his strength, but we respect an old man for his gray hair.

21:6 Wealth that comes from telling lies disappears quickly and leads to death.

13 Those who refuse to help the poor will not receive help when they need it themselves.

19 It is better to live alone in the desert than with a quick-tempered wife who loves to argue.

30 There is no one wise enough to make a plan that can succeed if the LORD is against it.

22:6 Teach children in a way that fits their needs, and even when they are old, they will not leave the right path.

24 Don't be friends with people who become angry easily. Don't stay around quick-tempered people. 25 If you do, you may learn to be like them. Then you will have the same problems they do.

26 Don't promise to pay someone else's debt. 27 If you cannot pay, you will lose everything you have. So why should you lose the bed you sleep on?

23:4 Don't ruin your health trying to get rich. If you are smart, you will give it up. 5 In the blink of an eye, money can disappear, as if it grew wings and flew away like a bird.

19 So listen, my son, and be wise. Always be careful to follow the right path. 20 Don't make friends with people who drink too much wine and eat too much food. 21 Those who eat and drink too much become poor. They sleep too much and end up wearing rags.

33 Wine will cause you to see strange things and to say things that make no sense. 34 When you lie down, you will think you are on a rough sea and feel like you are at the top of the mast.

25:14 People who promise to give gifts but never give them are like clouds and wind that bring no rain.

The 5 Poetic Books

Too much of a good thing.

16 Honey is good, but don't eat too much of it, or you will be sick.

17 And don't visit your neighbors' homes too often, or they will begin to hate you.

24 It is better to live in a small corner of the roof than to share the house with a woman who is always arguing.

A sad fact.

26:11 Like a dog that returns to its vomit, a fool does the same foolish things again and again.

Memorize this one.

20 Without wood, a fire goes out. Without gossip, arguments stop.

22 People love to hear gossip. It is like tasty food on its way to the stomach.

27:1 Never brag about what you will do in the future; you have no idea what tomorrow will bring.

2 Never praise yourself. Let others do it.

17 As one piece of iron sharpens another, so friends keep each other sharp.

8 A man away from home is like a bird away from its nest.

29:11 Fools are quick to express their anger, but wise people are patient and control themselves.

17 Correct your children whenever they are wrong. Then you will always be proud of them. They will never make you ashamed.

30:7 God, I ask you to do two things for me before I die. **8** Don't let me tell lies. And don't make me too rich or too poor—give me only enough food for each day. **9** If I have too much, I might deny that I need you, LORD. But if I am too poor, I might steal and bring shame to the name of my God.

18 There are three things that are hard for me to understand—really, four things that I don't understand: **19** an eagle flying in the sky, a snake moving on a rock, a ship moving across the ocean, and a man in love with a woman.

31:8 Speak up for people who cannot speak for themselves. Help people who are in trouble. **9** Stand up for what you know is right, and judge all people fairly. Protect the rights of the poor and those who need help.

The Perfect Wife

10 How hard it is to find the perfect wife. She is worth far more than jewels.

11 Her husband depends on her. He will never be poor.

12 She does good for her husband all her life. She never causes him trouble.

13 She is always gathering wool and flax and enjoys making things with her hands.

14 She is like a ship from a faraway place. She brings home food from everywhere.

15 She wakes up early in the morning, cooks food for her family, and gives the servants their share.

16 She looks at land and buys it. She uses the money she has earned and plants a vineyard.

17 She works very hard. She is strong and able to do all her work.

18 She works late into the night to make sure her business earns a profit.

19 She makes her own thread and weaves her own cloth.

20 She always gives to the poor and helps those who need it.

21 She does not worry about her family when it snows. She has given them all good, warm clothes.

22 She makes sheets and spreads for the beds, and she wears clothes of fine linen.

23 Her husband is a respected member of the city council, where he meets with the other leaders.

24 She makes clothes and belts and sells them to the merchants.

25 She is a strong person, and people respect her. She looks to the future with confidence.

26 She speaks with wisdom and teaches others to be loving and kind.

27 She oversees the care of her house. She is never lazy.

28 Her children say good things about her. Her husband brags about her and says,

29 **"There are many good women, but you are the best."**

30 Grace and beauty can fool you, but a woman who respects the LORD should be praised.

31 Give her the reward she deserves. Praise her in public for what she has done.

I think I'll write these words on a card and give it to my wife as a surprise.

the book of Ecclesiastes

Category: The 5 Poetic Books
Author: King Solomon
Theme: No satisfaction
Date: 940-931 B.C.
Version of Bible: Easy-to-Read Version (ERV)
Summary: Writing this book at the end of his life, Solomon reflected on the meaninglessness of the busyness of most of our lives. He sometimes writes from the point of view of a human trying to find meaning in a world without God. This book can be very sobering but it illustrates our need for God to bring purpose and meaning into our lives.

Nothing Makes Sense

Ecclesiastes 1:1 When the son of David was king in Jerusalem, he was known to be very wise, and he said: 2 Nothing makes sense! Everything is nonsense. I have seen it all—nothing makes sense!

3 What is there to show for all of our hard work here on this earth? 4 People come, and people go, but still the world never changes.

5 The sun comes up, the sun goes down; it hurries right back to where it started from. 6 The wind blows south the wind blows north; round and round it blows over and over again.

7 All rivers empty into the sea, but it never spills over; one by one the rivers return to their source.

8 All of life is far more boring than words could ever say. Our eyes and our ears are never satisfied with what we see and hear 9 Everything that happens has happened before; nothing is new, nothing under the sun. 10 Someone might say, "Here is something new!" But it happened before, long before we were born. 11 **No one who lived in the past is remembered anymore**, and everyone yet to be born will be forgotten too.

It Is Senseless to Be Wise

12 I said these things when I lived in Jerusalem as king of Israel. 13 With all my wisdom I tried to understand everything that happens here on earth. And God has made this so hard for us humans to do. 14 I have seen it all, and everything is just as senseless as chasing the wind.

15 If something is crooked, it can't be made straight; if something isn't there, it can't be counted.

"The time therefore that any man doth live, is but a little, and the place where he liveth, is but a very little corner of the earth, and the greatest fame that can remain of a man after his death, even that is but little, and that too, such as it is whilst it is, is by the succession of silly mortal men preserved, who likewise shall shortly die."
- Marcus Aurelius, the last great Emperor of Rome

16 I said to myself, "You are by far the wisest person who has ever lived in Jerusalem. You are eager to learn, and you have learned a lot." 17 Then I decided to find out all I could about wisdom and foolishness. Soon I realized that this too was as senseless as chasing the wind.

18 The more you know, the more you hurt; the more you understand, the more you suffer.

It Is Senseless to Be Selfish

2:1 I said to myself, "**Have fun and enjoy yourself!**" But this didn't make sense. 2 Laughing and having fun is crazy. What good does it do? 3 I wanted to find out what was best for us during the short time we have on this earth. So I decided to make myself happy with wine and find out what it means to be foolish, without really being foolish myself.

4 I did some great things. I built houses and planted vineyards. 5 I had flower gardens and orchards full of fruit trees. 6 And I had pools where I could get water for the trees. 7 I owned slaves, and their sons and daughters became my slaves. I had more sheep and goats than anyone who had ever lived in Jerusalem. 8 Foreign rulers brought me silver, gold, and precious treasures. Men and women sang for me, and I had many wives who gave me great pleasure.

9 I was the most famous person who had ever lived in Jerusalem, and I was very wise. 10 I got whatever I wanted and did whatever made me happy. But most of all, I enjoyed my work. 11 Then I thought about everything I had done, including the hard work, and it was simply chasing the wind. **Nothing on earth is worth the trouble.**

Wisdom Makes Sense

12 I asked myself, "What can the next king do that I haven't done?" Then I decided to compare wisdom with foolishness and stupidity. 13 And I discovered that wisdom is better than foolishness, just as light is better than darkness. 14 Wisdom is like having two good eyes; foolishness leaves you in the dark. But wise or foolish, we all end up the same.

15 Finally, I said to myself, "Being wise got me nowhere! The same thing will happen to me that happens to fools. Nothing makes sense. 16 **Wise or foolish, we all die and are soon forgotten.**" 17 This made me hate life. Everything we do is painful; it's just as senseless as chasing the wind.

18 Suddenly I realized that others would someday get everything I had worked for so hard, then I started hating it all. 19 Who knows if those people will be sensible or stupid? Either way, they will own everything I have earned by hard work and wisdom. It doesn't make sense.

20 I thought about all my hard work, and I felt depressed. 21 When we use our wisdom, knowledge, and skill to get what we own, why do we have to leave it to someone who didn't work for it? This is senseless and wrong. 22 What do we really gain from all

Solomon had wine, woman, fame, fortune, and all the stuff he could ever want. But what did it all mean?

"I can't get no satisfaction."

Back to the Marcus Aurelius quote, pg. 182.

of our hard work? 23 Our bodies ache during the day, and work is torture. Then at night our thoughts are troubled. It just doesn't make sense.

24 The best thing we can do is to enjoy eating, drinking, and working. I believe these are God's gifts to us, 25 and no one enjoys eating and living more than I do. 26 If we please God, he will make us wise, understanding, and happy. But if we sin, God will make us struggle for a living, then he will give all we own to someone who pleases him. This makes no more sense than chasing the wind.

Everything Has Its Time

3 Everything on earth has its own time and its own season. 2 There is a time for birth and death, planting and reaping, 3 for killing and healing, destroying and building, 4 for crying and laughing, weeping and dancing, 5 for throwing stones and gathering stones, embracing and parting.

6 There is a time for finding and losing, keeping and giving, 7 for tearing and sewing, listening and speaking.

8 There is also a time for love and hate, for war and peace.

What God Has Given Us to Do

9 What do we gain by all of our hard work? 10 I have seen what difficult things God demands of us. 11 God makes everything happen at the right time. Yet none of us can ever fully understand all he has done, and he puts questions in our minds about the past and the future. 12 I know the best thing we can do is to always **enjoy life**, 13 because God's gift to us is the happiness we get from our food and drink and from the work we do. 14 Everything God has done will last forever; nothing he does can ever be changed. God has done all this, so that we will worship him.

15 Everything that happens has happened before, and all that will be has already been—God does everything over and over again.

The Future Is Known Only to God

16 Everywhere on earth I saw violence and injustice instead of fairness and justice. 17 So I told myself that God has set a time and a place for everything. He will judge everyone, both the wicked and the good. 18 I know that God is testing us to show us that we are merely animals. 19 Like animals we breathe and die, and we are no better off than they are. It just doesn't make sense. 20 All living creatures go to the same place. We are made from earth, and we return to the earth. 21 **Who really knows if our spirits go up** and the spirits of animals go down into the earth? 22 We were meant to enjoy our work, and that's the best thing we can do. We can never know the future.

4:1 I looked again and saw people being mistreated everywhere on earth. They were crying, but no one was there to offer comfort, and those who mistreated them were powerful. 2 I said to myself, "The dead are better off than the living. 3 But those who have nev-

What about your life do you enjoy these days?

Have you ever thought this thought: What if there is no resurrection of the dead? Then when you die, that is it. Scary thought, isn't it? So scary it might just motivate you to give God a try.

er been born are better off than anyone else, because they have never seen the terrible things that happen on this earth."

7 Once again I saw that nothing on earth makes sense. 8 For example, some people don't have friends or family. But they are never satisfied with what they own, and they never stop working to get more. They should ask themselves, "Why am I always working to have more? Who will get what I leave behind?" What a senseless and miserable life!

It Is Better to Have a Friend

9 You are better off to have a friend than to be all alone, because then you will get more enjoyment out of what you earn. 10 **If you fall, your friend can help you up.** But if you fall without having a friend nearby, you are really in trouble. 11 If you sleep alone, you won't have anyone to keep you warm on a cold night. 12 Someone might be able to beat up one of you, but not both of you. As the saying goes, "A rope made from **three strands** of cord is hard to break."

Be Careful How You Worship

5:8 Don't be surprised if the poor of your country are abused, and injustice takes the place of justice. After all, the lower officials must do what the higher ones order them to do. 9 And since the king is the highest official, he benefits most from the taxes paid on the land.

10 If you love money and wealth, you will never be satisfied with what you have. This doesn't make sense either. 11 The more you have, the more everyone expects from you. Your money won't do you any good—others will just spend it for you. 12 If you have to work hard for a living, you can rest well at night, even if you don't have much to eat. But if you are rich, you can't even sleep.

Don't Depend on Wealth

6:1 There is something else terribly unfair, and it troubles everyone on earth. 2 God may give you everything you want—money, property, and wealth. Then God doesn't let you enjoy it, and someone you don't even know gets it all. That's senseless and terribly unfair!

3 You may live a long time and have a hundred children. But a child born dead is better off than you, unless you enjoy life and have a decent burial. 4-5 That child will never live to see the sun or to have a name, and it will go straight to the world of darkness. But it will still find more rest than you, 6 even if you live two thousand years and don't enjoy life. As you know, we all end up in the same place.

Some of Life's Questions

7:15 I have seen everything during this senseless life of mine. I have seen good citizens die for doing the right thing, and I have seen criminals live to a ripe old age. 16 So don't destroy yourself by being too good or acting too smart! 17 Don't die before your

When have you needed a friend to help you out?

Many couples use this verse at their wedding signifying the wife, the husband, and God.

time by being too evil or acting like a fool. 18 Keep to the middle of the road. You can do this if you truly respect God.

23 I told myself that I would be smart and try to understand all of this, but it was too much for me. 24 The truth is beyond us. It's far too deep.

One Day at a Time

9:1 I thought about these things. Then I understood that God has power over everyone, even those of us who are wise and live right. Anything can happen to any of us, and so we never know if life will be good or bad. 2 But exactly the same thing will finally happen to all of us, whether we live right and respect God or sin and don't respect God. Yes, the same thing will happen if we offer sacrifices to God or if we don't, if we keep our promises or break them.

3 It's terribly unfair for the same thing to happen to each of us. We are mean and foolish while we live, and then we die. 4 As long as we are alive, we still have hope, just as a live dog is better off than a dead lion. 5 We know that we will die, but the dead don't know a thing. Nothing good will happen to them—they are gone and forgotten. 6 Their loves, their hates, and their jealous feelings have all disappeared with them. They will never again take part in anything that happens on this earth.

It Pays to Work Hard

11 Be generous, and someday you will be rewarded. 2 Share what you have with seven or eight others, because you never know when disaster may strike. 3 Rain clouds always bring rain; trees always stay wherever they fall 4 If you worry about the weather and don't plant seeds, you won't harvest a crop.

5 No one can explain how a baby breathes before it is born. So how can anyone explain what God does? After all, he created everything. 6 **Plant your seeds early in the morning and keep working in the field until dark. Who knows? Your work might pay off, and your seeds might produce.**

Youth and Old Age

7 Nothing on earth is more beautiful than the morning sun. 8 Even if you live to a ripe old age, you should try to enjoy each day, because darkness will come and will last a long time. Nothing makes sense.

9 Be cheerful and enjoy life while you are young! Do what you want and find pleasure in what you see. But don't forget that God will judge you for everything you do.

10 Rid yourself of all worry and pain, because the wonderful moments of youth quickly disappear.

12:1 Keep your Creator in mind while you are young! In years to come, you will be burdened down with troubles and say, "I don't enjoy life anymore."

This day is the beginning of the rest of your life. Go for it! Try something new. Stretch yourself. Who knows, it may work. If not, what is the worse that could happen?

2 **Someday the light of the sun and the moon and the stars will all seem dim to you.** Rain clouds will remain over your head. 3 Your body will grow feeble, your teeth will decay, and your eyesight fail. 4 The noisy grinding of grain will be shut out by your deaf ears, but even the song of a bird will keep you awake. 5 You will be afraid to climb up a hill or walk down a road. Your hair will turn as white as almond blossoms. You will feel lifeless and drag along like an old grasshopper.

We each go to our eternal home, and the streets are filled with those who mourn. 6 The silver cord snaps, the golden bowl breaks; the water pitcher is smashed, and the pulley at the well is shattered. 7 So our bodies return to the earth, and the life-giving breath returns to God. 8 Nothing makes sense.

I have seen it all—nothing makes sense.

Respect and Obey God

9 I was a wise teacher with much understanding, and I collected a number of proverbs that I had carefully studied. 10 Then I tried to explain these things in the best and most accurate way.

11 Words of wisdom are like the stick a farmer uses to make animals move. These sayings come from God, our only shepherd, and they are like nails that fasten things together. 12 My child, I warn you to stay away from any teachings except these.

There is no end to books, and **too much study will wear you out.** 13 Everything you were taught can be put into a few words:

Respect and obey God! This is what life is all about.

Getting old with grace takes a lot of courage and faith. Do you have good examples in your life of those who got old with a lot of grace and faith?

Are you a student? Sick of school? Here is a verse for you.

the book of Song of Songs

Category: The 5 Poetic Books
Author: King Solomon
Theme: A love poem
Date: 971-965 B.C.
Version of Bible: The Message (MSG)
Summary: Solomon wrote this book as a poem, a song about two people falling in love. It is incredibly moving and explicit. This is definitely a PG (parental guidance suggested) book.

Song of Solomon

1 The Song—best of all songs—Solomon's song!

The Woman

2-3 Kiss me—full on the mouth! Yes! For your love is better than wine, headier than your aromatic oils. The syllables of your name murmur like a meadow brook. No wonder everyone loves to say your name!

The Man

15 **Oh, my dear friend! You're so beautiful!** And your eyes so beautiful—like doves!

The Woman

16-17 And you, my dear lover—**you're so handsome!** And the bed we share is like a forest glen. We enjoy a canopy of cedars enclosed by cypresses, fragrant and green.

The Man

2:2 A lotus blossoming in a swamp of weeds—that's my dear friend among the girls in the village.

The Woman

3-4 As an apricot tree stands out in the forest, my lover stands **above the young men in town**. All **I want is to sit in his shade**, to taste and savor his delicious love. He took me home with him for a festive meal, but his eyes feasted on me!

5-6 Oh! Give me something refreshing to eat—and quickly! Apricots, raisins—anything. I'm about to faint with love! His left hand cradles my head, and his right arm encircles my waist!

8-10 Look! Listen! There's my lover! Do you see him coming?

Now that is a good beginning to a love letter.

A woman likes to be told she's beautiful.

A man will never admit it but he likes being told he's handsome.

A man is competitive and needs his girl to see the best in him. A woman want to be protected.

Vaulting the mountains, leaping the hills. My lover is like a gazelle, graceful; like a young stag, **virile**. Look at him there, on tiptoe at the gate, all ears, all eyes—ready! My lover has arrived and he's speaking to me!

The Man

10-14 Get up, my dear friend, fair and beautiful lover—come to me! Look around you: Winter is over; the winter rains are over, gone! Spring flowers are in blossom all over. The whole world's a choir and singing! Spring warblers are filling the forest with sweet arpeggios. Lilacs are exuberantly purple and perfumed, and cherry trees fragrant with blossoms. Oh, get up, dear friend, my fair and beautiful lover—come to me! Come, my shy and modest dove—leave your seclusion, come out in the open. **Let me see your face**, let me hear your voice. For your voice is soothing and your face is ravishing.

The Woman

15 Then you must **protect me** from the foxes, foxes on the prowl. Foxes who would like nothing better than to get into our flowering garden.

16-17 **My lover is mine, and I am his.** Nightly he strolls in our garden, delighting in the flowers until dawn breathes its light and night slips away. Turn to me, dear lover. Come like a gazelle. Leap like a wild stag on delectable mountains!

3:1-4 Restless in bed and sleepless through the night, I longed for my lover. I wanted him desperately. His absence was painful. So I got up, went out and roved the city, hunting through streets and down alleys. I wanted my lover in the worst way! I looked high and low, and didn't find him. And then the night watchmen found me as they patrolled the darkened city. "Have you seen my dear **lost** love?" I asked. No sooner had I left them than I **found** him, found my dear lost love. I threw my arms around him and held him tight, wouldn't let him go until I had him home again, safe at home beside the fire.

The Man

4:1-5 **You're so beautiful**, my darling, so beautiful, and your dove eyes are veiled by your hair as it flows and shimmers, like a flock of goats in the distance streaming down a hillside in the sunshine. Your smile is generous and full-expressive and strong and clean. Your lips are jewel red, your mouth elegant and inviting, your veiled cheeks soft and radiant. The smooth, lithe lines of your neck command notice—all heads turn in awe and admiration! Your breasts are like fawns, twins of a gazelle, grazing among the first spring flowers.

6-7 The sweet, fragrant curves of your body, the soft, spiced contours of your flesh invite me, and I come. I stay until dawn breathes its light and night slips away. You're beautiful from head to toe, my dear love, beautiful beyond compare, absolutely flawless.

That is what a man wants to hear.

Men are visual. They want to see the woman they love.

A woman wants to be protected and ultimately to possess and be possessed by someone she trusts.

Love can seem like a game of lost and found, over and over again.

A woman not only appreciates her man noticing every bit of her, she also wants him to put it all in words.

The Woman

16 Wake up, North Wind, get moving, South Wind! Breathe on my garden, fill the air with spice fragrance. Oh, let my lover enter his garden! Yes, let him eat the fine, ripe fruits.

The Woman

5:10-16 My dear lover glows with health—red-blooded, radiant! **He's one in a million.** There's no one quite like him! My golden one, pure and untarnished, with raven black curls tumbling across his shoulders. His eyes are like doves, soft and bright, but deep-set, brimming with meaning, like wells of water. His face is rugged, his beard smells like sage, his voice, his words, warm and reassuring. **Fine muscles ripple beneath his skin**, quiet and beautiful. His torso is the work of a sculptor, hard and smooth as ivory. He stands tall, like a cedar, strong and deep-rooted, a rugged mountain of a man, aromatic with wood and stone. His words are kisses, his kisses words. Everything about him delights me, thrills me through and through! That's my lover, that's my man, dear Jerusalem sisters.

The Man

6:4-7 Dear, dear friend and lover, you're as beautiful as Tirzah, city of delights, lovely as Jerusalem, city of dreams, the ravishing visions of my ecstasy. Your beauty is too much for me—I'm in over my head. I'm not used to this! I can't take it in. Your hair flows and shimmers like a **flock of goats** in the distance streaming down a hillside in the sunshine. Your smile is generous and full-expressive and strong and clean. Your veiled cheeks are soft and radiant.

8-9 There's no one like her on earth, never has been, never will be. She's a woman beyond compare. My dove is perfection, Pure and innocent as the day she was born, and cradled in joy by her mother. Everyone who came by to see her exclaimed and admired her—All the fathers and mothers, the neighbors and friends, blessed and praised her:

7:1-9 Shapely and graceful your sandaled feet, and queenly your movement—your limbs are lithe and elegant, the work of a master artist. Your body is a chalice, wine-filled. Your skin is silken and tawny like a field of wheat touched by the breeze. Your breasts are like fawns, twins of a gazelle. Your neck is carved ivory, curved and slender. Your eyes are wells of light, deep with mystery. Quintessentially feminine! **Your profile turns all heads, commanding attention.** The feelings I get when I see the high mountain ranges—stirrings of desire, longings for the heights—remind me of you, and I'm spoiled for anyone else! Your beauty, within and without, is absolute, dear lover, close companion. You are tall and supple, like the palm tree, and your full breasts are like sweet clusters of dates. I say, "I'm going to climb that palm tree! I'm going to caress its fruit!" Oh yes! Your breasts will be clusters of sweet fruit to me, your breath clean and cool like fresh mint, your tongue and lips like the best wine.

A man needs his woman to believe in him and to tell him so.

A man wants to be strong for his woman.

A woman appreciates a man's attempt at being romantic even if he is not very good at it.

Most women want to be noticed.

The Woman

9-12 Yes, and yours are, too—my love's kisses flow from his lips to mine. **I am my lover's. I'm all he wants.** I'm all the world to him! Come, dear lover—let's tramp through the countryside. Let's sleep at some wayside inn, then rise early and listen to bird-song. Let's look for wildflowers in bloom, blackberry bushes blossoming white, Fruit trees festooned with cascading flowers. And there I'll give myself to you, my love to your love!

13 Love-apples drench us with fragrance, fertility surrounds, suffuses us, fruits fresh and preserved that I've kept and saved just for you, my love.

A woman wants a life commitment from a man. No looking at others.

The Woman

8:6-8 Hang my locket around your neck, **wear my ring on your finger. Love is invincible facing danger and death.** Passion laughs at the terrors of hell. The fire of love stops at nothing—it sweeps everything before it. Flood waters can't drown love, torrents of rain can't put it out. Love can't be bought, love can't be sold—it's not to be found in the marketplace. My brothers used to worry about me:

You are mine and together we can face life's challenges.

The Woman

14 Run to me, dear lover. Come like a gazelle. **Leap like a wild stag** on the spice mountains.

This is what a woman wants in a man.

the book of Isaiah

Category: *The 5 Major Prophets*
Author: *Isaiah*
Theme: *Salvation*
Location & Date: *Judah; 971-965 B.C.*
Version of Bible: *Easy-to-Read Version (ERV)*

Summary: *The prophet Isaiah lived in Judah during the time of its decline. He witnessed the fall of the northern tribes and foretold of a similar fate for Judah and its capital, Jerusalem (events recounted in 2 Kings). Since he lived in such a climate where the anger of God burned against His people, much of the book is focused on the destruction of Judah, the exile of its people, and punishment for those who oppose God. But there is much hope in the book of Isaiah as well.*

God Calls Isaiah to Be a Prophet

Isaiah 6:1 In the year that King Uzziah died, I saw the Lord sitting on a very high and wonderful throne. His long robe filled the Temple. 2 Seraph angels stood around him. Each angel had six wings. They used two wings to cover their faces, two wings to cover their bodies, and two wings to fly. 3 The angels were calling to each other, "Holy, holy, holy is the LORD All-Powerful. His Glory fills the whole earth." 4 The sound was so loud that it caused the frame around the door to shake, and the Temple was filled with smoke.

5 I was frightened and said, "Oh, no! I will be destroyed. I am not pure enough to speak to God, and I live among people who are not pure enough to speak to him. But I have seen the King, the LORD All-Powerful."

6 There was a fire on the altar. One of the Seraph angels used a pair of tongs to take a hot coal from the fire. Then the angel flew to me with it in his hand. 7 Then he touched my mouth with the hot coal and said, "When this hot coal touched your lips, your guilt was taken away, and your sins were erased."

8 Then I heard the Lord's voice, saying, "Who can I send? Who will go for us?"

So I said, **"Here I am. Send me!"**

12 The LORD will make the people go far away, and there will be large areas of empty land in the country. 13 A tenth of the people will be allowed to stay in the land, but it will be destroyed again. They will be like an oak tree. When the tree is chopped down, a stump is left. This stump will be a very special seed that will grow again.

Isaiah has the "can do" attitude. How about you?

{The times in which Isaiah lived shaped the content of his prophecy. Since he lived during a time of sinfulness, his prophecy invoked God's judgment. About 200 years before his time, the northern tribes of Israel split from Judah, and the southern Jews took on the name of Judah, the dominate tribe there. For 200 years, the northern tribes lived in sin. They worshiped idols and false gods, executed true prophets, followed corrupt leaders like King Ahab and Queen Jezebel, ignored true prophets like Elijah and disowned the true God. Isaiah would live to see them fall. God was going to uphold His covenant. He promised that he would bless his people for obedience, but punish them when they went astray.

From the very beginning of the book, much of Isaiah's prophecy focuses on the sins of the people of his homeland—Judah.}

1:1 This is the vision of Isaiah son of Amoz. God showed Isaiah what would happen to Judah and Jerusalem. Isaiah saw this during the time when Uzziah, Jotham, Ahaz, and Hezekiah were kings of Judah.

God's Case Against Israel

2 Heaven and earth, listen! This is what the LORD says:

"I raised my children and helped them grow up, but they have turned against me. 3 A bull knows its master, and a donkey knows where its owner feeds it. But Israel does not know me. My people do not understand."

4 Oh, what a sinful nation! Their guilt is like a heavy weight that they must carry. They are evil, destructive children. They left the LORD and insulted the Holy One of Israel. They turned away and treated him like a stranger.

5 What good will it do to keep punishing you? You will continue to rebel. Your whole head and heart are already sick and aching. 6 From the bottom of your feet to the top of your head, every part of your body has wounds, cuts, and open sores. You have not taken care of them. Your wounds have not been cleaned and bandaged.

7 Your land is in ruins, and your cities are in flames. Your enemies have taken your land, and foreigners are taking what it produces. It looks like some foreigners destroyed it.

Warnings for Jerusalem

16 "Wash yourselves and make yourselves clean. Stop doing the evil things I see you do. Stop doing wrong. 17 Learn to do good. Treat people fairly. Punish those who hurt others. Speak up for the widows and orphans. Argue their cases for them in court.

18 "I, the LORD, am the one speaking to you. Come, let's discuss this. **Even if your sins are as dark as red dye, that stain can be removed and you will be as pure as wool that is as white as snow.**

19 **"If you listen to what I say, you will get the good things from this land. 20 But if you refuse to listen and rebel against me, your enemies will destroy you."** The LORD himself said this.

Hope!

Simple. Why is it so hard to follow?

God Will Punish Israel

24:1 Look, the LORD is destroying this land. He will clean out the land completely and force all the people to go far away. 2 At that time whatever happens to the common people will also happen to the priests. Slaves and masters will be the same. Women slaves and their women masters will be the same. Buyers and sellers will be the same. Those who borrow and those who lend will be the same. Bankers and those who owe the bank will be the same. 3 Everyone will be forced out of the land. All the wealth will be taken. This will happen because the LORD commanded it. 4 The country will be empty and sad. The world will be empty and weak. The great leaders of the people in this land will become weak.

5 The people have ruined the land. They did what God said was wrong. They did not obey God's laws. They made an agreement with God a long time ago, but they broke their agreement with God. 6 The people living in this land are guilty of doing wrong, so God promised to destroy the land. The people will be punished, and only a few of them will survive.

{But the prophecy of Isaiah was not all doom a gloom.}

Israel's Punishment Will End

40:1 Your God says, "Comfort, comfort my people. 2 Speak kindly to Jerusalem and tell her, 'Your time of service is finished. You have paid the price for your sins.' I, the LORD, have punished you twice for every sin you committed."

3 Listen, there is someone shouting: "**Prepare a way** in the desert for the LORD. Make a straight road there for our God. 4 Every valley must be filled. Every mountain and hill should be made flat. The crooked roads should be made straight, and the rough ground made smooth. 5 Then the Glory of the LORD will be shown to everyone. Together, all people will see it. Yes, this is what the LORD himself said!"

6 A voice said, "Speak!" So the man said, "What should I say?"

The voice said, "People are like grass. Any glory they enjoy is like a wildflower. 7 When a wind from the LORD blows on them, the grass dies and the flower falls. Yes, all people are like grass. 8 Grass dies and flowers fall, but the word of our God lasts forever."

This verse became a prophecy about John the Baptist who prepared the way for Jesus.

People Cannot Imagine What God Is Like

21 Surely you know the truth, don't you? Surely you have heard. Surely someone told you long ago. Surely you understand who made the earth. 22 It is the Lord who sits above the circle of the earth. And compared to him, people are like grasshoppers. He rolled open the skies like a piece of cloth. He stretched out the skies like a tent to sit under. 23 He takes away the power of rulers. He makes the world's leaders completely worthless. 24 They are like plants that are planted in the ground. But before they can send their roots into the ground, God blows on the "plants"; they

become dead and dry, and the wind blows them away like straw.

30 Young men get tired and need to rest. Even young boys stumble and fall. 31 But those who trust in the LORD will become strong again. They will be like eagles that grow new feathers. They will run and not get weak. They will walk and not get tired.

{Isaiah prophesied that Jerusalem would be conquered and it's people exiled, but that one day the people would return and Jerusalem would be rebuilt to even greater glory. The good news didn't stop there. Isaiah spoke of a great Messianic King, a descendant of the line of David, who would lead the people during a new golden age.}

Immanuel—God Is with Us

7:10 Then the Lord spoke to Ahaz again 11 and said, "Ask for a sign from the Lord your God to prove to yourself that this is true. You can ask for any sign you want. The sign can come from a place as deep as Sheol or as high as the skies."

12 But Ahaz said, "I will not ask for a sign as proof. I will not test the Lord."

13 Then Isaiah said, "Family of David, listen very carefully! Is it not enough that you would test the patience of humans? Will you now test the patience of my God? 14 But the Lord will still show you this sign: **The young woman is pregnant and will give birth to a son. She will name him Immanuel.**

> Isaiah is talking about Jesus. Immanuel means "God with us."

A New Day Is Coming

9:1 But there will be an end to the gloom those people suffered. 2 Those people lived in darkness, but they will see a great light. They lived in a place as dark as death, but **a great light will shine** on them.

> Jesus again.

3 God, you will make the nation grow, and you will make the people happy. They will rejoice in your presence as they do at harvest time. It will be like the joy when people take their share of things they have won in war. 4 That will happen because you will lift the heavy yoke off their shoulders and take away their heavy burden. You will take away the rod that the enemy used to punish your people, as you did when you defeated Midian.

5 Every boot that marched in battle and every uniform stained with blood will be destroyed and thrown into the fire. 6 This will happen when the **special child is born**. God will give us a son who will be responsible for leading the people. His name will be "Wonderful Counselor, Powerful God, Father Who Lives Forever, Prince of Peace." 7 His power will continue to grow, and there will be peace without end. This will establish him as the king sitting on David's throne and ruling his kingdom. He will rule with goodness and justice forever and ever. The strong love that the LORD All-Powerful has for his people will make this happen!

> Jesus again.

The King of Peace Is Coming

11:1 **A small tree will begin to grow from the stump of Jesse.** That

> Have you ever seen a tree grow out

of a stump? Jesus is the new king (the tree) that will come from the line of Jesses (the father of King David).

branch will grow from Jesse's roots. 2 The LORD's Spirit will always be with that new king to give him wisdom, understanding, guidance, and power. The Spirit will help him know and respect the LORD. 3 He will find joy in obeying the LORD.

This king will not judge people by the way things look. He will not judge by listening to rumors. 4-5 He will judge the poor fairly and honestly. He will be fair when he decides what to do for the poor of the land ... Goodness and fairness will be like a belt he wears around his waist.

6 Then wolves will live at peace with lambs, and leopards will lie down in peace with young goats. Calves, lions, and bulls will all live together in peace. A little child will lead them. 7 Bears and cattle will eat together in peace, and all their young will lie down together and will not hurt each other. Lions will eat hay like cattle. 8 Even snakes will not hurt people. Babies will be able to play near a cobra's hole and put their hands into the nest of a poisonous snake. 9 People will stop hurting each other. People on my holy mountain will not want to destroy things because they will know the LORD. The world will be full of knowledge about him, like the sea is full of water.

Glorious as this new King will be, the Lord refers to him as "my servant". He will bring justice to the earth and be a light to not only God's people, but also to the gentiles. The Lord will be with him and he will be a redeemer to all nations of the earth.

The Lord's Special Servant

42:1 "Here is my servant, the one I support. He is the one I have chosen, and I am very pleased with him. I have filled him with my Spirit, and he will bring justice to the nations. 2 He will not cry out or shout or try to make himself heard in the streets. 3 He will not break even a crushed reed. He will not put out even the weakest flame. He will bring true justice. 4 He will not grow weak or give up until he has brought justice to the world. And people in faraway places will hope to receive his teachings."

The Lord Is Ruler and Maker of the World

5 The LORD, the true God, said these things. (He created the sky and spread it out over the earth. He formed the earth and everything it produced. He breathes life into all the people on earth. He gives a spirit to everyone who walks on the earth.) 6 "I, the LORD, was right to call you. I will hold your hand and protect you. You will be the sign of my agreement with the people. You will be a light for the other nations. 7 You will make the blind able to see. You will free those who are held as captives. You will lead those who live in darkness out of their prison.

8 "I am YAHWEH. That is my name. I will not give my glory to another. I will not let statues take the praise that should be mine. 9 In the past, I told you what would happen, and it happened! Now I am telling you something new, and I am telling you now, before it happens."

God Is Always With His People

43:1 Jacob, the LORD created you. Israel, he made you, and now he says, "Don't be afraid. I saved you. I named you. You are mine. 2 When you have troubles, I am with you. When you cross rivers, you will not be hurt. When you walk through fire, you will not be burned; the flames will not hurt you. 3 That's because I, the LORD, am your God. I, the Holy One of Israel, am your Savior. I gave Egypt to pay for you. I gave Ethiopia and Seba to make you mine.

God Calls His Special Servant

49:1 Hear me, people by the sea. Listen to me, you faraway nations. The LORD called me before I was born. He called my name while I was still in my mother's womb. 2 He used me to speak for him. He used me like a sharp sword, but he also held me in his hand to protect me. He used me like a sharp arrow, but he also kept me safe in his arrow bag. 3 He told me, "Israel, you are my servant. I will do wonderful things with you." 4 I said, "I worked hard for nothing. I wore myself out, but I did nothing useful. I used all my power, but I did not really do anything. So the LORD must decide what to do with me. He must decide my reward."

5 The LORD is the one who made me in my mother's womb, so that I could be his servant. He wanted me to lead Jacob and Israel back to him. The LORD gives me honor. I get my strength from my God. 6 And now he says, "You are a very important servant to me. You must bring back to me the tribes of Jacob. You must bring back the people of Israel who are still alive. But I have something else for you to do that is even more important: I will make you a light for the other nations. You will show people all over the world the way to be saved."

The Day of Salvation

8 This is what the LORD says: "There will be a special time when I show my kindness. Then I will answer your prayers. There will be a special day when I will save you. Then I will help you and protect you. And you will be the proof of my agreement with the people. The country is destroyed now, but you will give the land back to the people who own it. 9 You will tell the prisoners, 'Come out of your prison!' You will tell those who are in darkness, Come out of the dark!'

The people will eat along the road, and they will have food even on empty hills. 10 They will not be hungry or thirsty. The hot sun and wind will not hurt them. Their **Comforter** will lead them. He will lead them by springs of water. 11 I will make a road for my people. The mountains will be made flat, and the low roads will be raised. 12 "Look! People are coming to me from faraway places. They are coming to me from the north and from the west. They are coming to me from Aswan in Egypt."

13 Heavens and earth, be happy! Mountains, shout with joy! The LORD comforts his people. He is good to his poor people.

The Holy Spirit.

Isaiah was talking about the suffering of Jesus on the cross, that ultimately saved His people - people like you and me.

All these things happened to Jesus when He was put on the cross.

Although the servant is to be a great King, redeemer to the lost and chosen one of God, he only achieves these things through suffering. Indeed he is despised and persecuted by his own people. But he remains steadfast to the Lord and carries out His will unflinchingly, and the Lord stays by his side.

God's Suffering Servant

52:13 The Lord says, "Look, my servant will succeed in what he has to do, and he will be raised to a position of high honor. 14 It is true that many were shocked when they saw him. **He was beaten so badly that he no longer looked like a man.** 15 But it is also true that many nations will be amazed at him. Kings will look at him and be unable to speak. They will see what they had never been told. They will understand what they had never heard."

53:1 Who really believed what we heard? Who saw in it the LORD's great power?

2 He was always close to the Lord. He grew up like a young plant, like a root growing in dry ground. There was nothing special or impressive about the way he looked, nothing we could see that would cause us to like him. 3 **People made fun of him, and even his friends left him.** He was a man who suffered a lot of pain and sickness. We treated him like someone of no importance, like someone people will not even look at but turn away from in disgust.

Jesus took our place on the cross. He bore the punishment that we deserved.

4 **The fact is, it was our suffering he took on himself**; he bore our pain. But we thought that God was punishing him, that God was beating him for something he did. 5 But he was being punished for what we did. He was crushed because of our guilt. **He took the punishment we deserved**, and this brought us peace. We were healed because of his pain. 6 We had all wandered away like sheep. We had gone our own way. And yet the LORD put all our guilt on him.

See Mark 14:61; pg. 280.

7 He was treated badly, but he never protested. He said nothing, like a lamb being led away to be killed. He was like a sheep that makes no sound as its wool is being cut off. **He never opened his mouth to defend himself.** 8 He was taken away by force and judged unfairly. The people of his time did not even notice that he was killed. **But he was put to death for the sins of his people.** 9 He had done no wrong to anyone. He had never even told a lie. But he was buried among the wicked. His tomb was with the rich.

10 But the LORD was pleased with this humble servant who suffered such pain. Even after giving himself as an offering for sin, he will see his descendants and enjoy a long life. He will succeed in doing what the LORD wanted. 11 After his suffering he will see the light, and he will be satisfied with what he experienced.

God Gives "Food" That Really Satisfies

How have you wasted your time and money on things that do not really satisfy the deep desires of your soul?

55:1 "All you people who are thirsty, come! Here is water for you to drink. Don't worry if you have no money. Come, eat and drink until you are full! You don't need money. The milk and wine are free. 2 **Why waste your money on something that is not real food?** Why should you work for something that does not really satisfy you?

Listen closely to me and you will eat what is good. You will enjoy the food that satisfies your soul.

6 So you should look for the LORD before it is too late. You should call to him now, while he is near. 7 Evil people should stop living evil lives. They should stop thinking bad thoughts. They should come to the LORD again, and he will comfort them. They should come to our God because he will freely forgive them.

People Cannot Understand God

8 The LORD says, "My thoughts are not like yours. Your ways are not like mine. 9 Just as the heavens are higher than the earth, so my ways are higher than your ways, and my thoughts are higher than your thoughts.

10 "Rain and snow fall from the sky and don't return until they have watered the ground. Then the ground causes the plants to sprout and grow, and they produce seeds for the farmer and food for people to eat. 11 In the same way, my words leave my mouth, and they don't come back without results. **My words make the things happen that I want to happen.** They succeed in doing what I send them to do."

12 "So you will go out from there with joy. You will be led out in peace. When you come to the mountains and hills, they will begin singing. All the trees in the fields will clap their hands. 13 Large cypress trees will grow where there were thornbushes. Myrtle trees will grow where there were weeds. All this will happen to make the LORD known, to be a permanent reminder of his goodness and power."

The Lord's Message of Freedom

61:1 The Spirit of the Lord GOD is on me. The LORD has chosen me **to tell good news** to the poor and to comfort those who are sad. He sent me to tell the captives and prisoners that they have been set free. 2 He sent me to announce that the time has come for the LORD to show his kindness, when our God will also punish evil people. He has sent me to comfort those who are sad.

Be careful as you read this Sampler Bible - God's Words will accomplish what He desires.

Jesus quoted these words. See Luke 4:18; pg. 254.

the book of Jeremiah

Category: *The 5 Major Prophets*
Author: *Jeremiah*
Theme: *Bad things are going to happen*
Location & Date: *Jerusalem; 627-586 B.C.*
Version of Bible: *Easy-to-Read Version (ERV)*
Summary: *This book recounts the prophecy of Jeremiah, who lived in Judah during the time after the fall of the northern tribes of Israel. Jeremiah, through the revelations of God, predicted a similar fate for Judah and its capital, Jerusalem—an event he would witness firsthand. He was just a child when he was commissioned by the Lord to take on the burden of being a prophet during a stormy time in Jewish history. Jeremiah is often referred to as the "weeping prophet."*

God Calls Jeremiah

Jeremiah 1:4 The LORD's message came to me: 5 "Before I made you in your mother's womb, I knew you. **Before you were born, I chose you for a special work.** I chose you to be a prophet to the nations."

It may be hard to believe sometimes but this is true of you as well.

6 Then I said, "But, Lord GOD, I don't know how to speak. I am only a boy."

7 But the LORD said to me, "Don't say, 'I am only a boy.' You must go everywhere I send you and say everything I tell you to say. 8 Don't be afraid of anyone. **I am with you**, and I will protect you."

This one is for you too.

This Message Is from the LORD

9 Then the LORD reached out with his hand and touched my mouth. He said to me, "Jeremiah, I am putting my words in your mouth. 10 Today I have put you in charge of nations and kingdoms. You will pull up and tear down. You will destroy and overthrow. You will build up and plant."

Two Visions

11 The LORD's message came to me: "Jeremiah, what do you see?"

I answered, "I see a pot of boiling water. That pot is tipping over from the north."

14 The LORD said to me, "Something terrible will come from the north. It will happen to all the people who live in this country. 15 In a short time I will call all the people in the northern kingdoms."

This is what the LORD said. "The kings of those countries will come and set up their thrones near the gates of Jerusalem. They will attack the city walls of Jerusalem. They will attack all the cities in Judah. 16 And I will announce judgment against my people, because they are evil and have turned away from me. They offered sacrifices to other gods and worshiped idols they made with their own hands.

17 "As for you, Jeremiah, get ready. **Stand up and speak to the people.** Tell them everything that I tell you to say. Don't be afraid of the people. 18 As for me, today I will make you like a strong city, an iron column, a bronze wall. You will be able to stand against everyone in the land, against the kings of the land of Judah, the leaders of Judah, the priests of Judah, and against the people of the land of Judah. 19 All those people will fight against you, but they will not defeat you, because I am with you, and I will save you."

It would not be easy for Jeremiah as the bearer of bad news. But God promised to protect him.

This Message Is from the LORD

2:5 This is what the LORD says: "Do you think that I was not fair to your ancestors? Is that why they turned away from me? Your ancestors worshiped worthless idols, and they became worthless themselves.

7 **"I brought you into a good land, a land filled with many good things. I did this so that you could eat the fruit and crops that grow there. But you only made my land 'dirty.' I gave that land to you, but you made it a bad place.**

These words can often be said about you and me.

9 The LORD says, "So now I will accuse you again, and I will also accuse your grandchildren. 10 Go across the sea to the Islands of Kittim. Send someone to the land of Kedar. Look very carefully. See if anyone has ever done anything like this. 11 Has any nation ever stopped worshiping their old gods so that they could worship new gods? No! And their gods are not really gods at all! But my people stopped worshiping their glorious God and started worshiping idols that are worth nothing.

13 "My people have done two evil things. They turned away from me, and they dug their own water cisterns. I am the source of living water; those cisterns are broken and cannot hold water.

{Although Jeremiah warned the people of God's anger and advised them to repent and turn to the Lord, God made it clear that the destruction of Judah was inevitable.}

4:27 This is what the LORD says: "The whole country will be ruined, but I will not completely destroy the land. 28 So the people in the land will cry for the dead. The sky will grow dark. I have spoken and will not change. I have made a decision, and I will not change my mind."

{In fact, God was so determined to punish the people of Judah for their sins that he even dissuaded Jeremiah from praying for them: "So do not pray for this people nor offer any plea or petition for them; do not plead with me, for I will not listen to you..." (7:16). Jeremiah knew what was waiting for Judah and there was nothing he could do to stop it. Since he couldn't help the people, he simply

cried out to the Lord in frustration and sorrow.}

Jeremiah's Cry

This helpless situation pained Jeremiah deeply and added to his burden so much so that he cursed his own birth.

4:19 **My sadness and worry** is making my stomach hurt. I am bent over in pain. I am so afraid. My heart is pounding inside me. I cannot keep quiet, because I have heard the trumpet blow. The trumpet is calling the army to war. 20 Disaster follows disaster. The whole country is destroyed. Suddenly my tents are destroyed. My curtains are torn down! 21 How long must I see the war flags? How long must I hear the war trumpets?

20:14 **Curse the day that I was born!** Don't bless the day my mother had me. 15 Curse the man who told my father the news that I was born. "It's a boy!" he said. "You have a son." He made my father very happy when he told him the news. 16 Let that man be like the cities the LORD destroyed. He had no pity on them. Let him hear shouts of war in the morning; let him hear battle cries at noontime, 17 because he did not kill me while I was in my mother's womb. If he had killed me then, my mother would have been my grave, and I would not have been born. 18 Why did I have to come out of her body? All I have seen is trouble and sorrow, and my life will end in shame.

{But Jeremiah still actively spread God's Word, rebuked the people for their sins, and warned them of God's judgment. He did this in novel and even peculiar ways. A number of times he resorted to acting out God's word through elaborate and dramatic spectacles.}

The Broken Jar

19:1 The LORD said to me, "Jeremiah, go and buy a clay jar from a potter. Take some of the elders of the people and some priests with you. 2 Go out to the Valley of Ben Hinnom, near the front of the Potsherd Gate. I have a message I want you to announce there. 3 Say to those who are with you, 'King of Judah and people of Jerusalem, listen to this message from the LORD! This is what the LORD All-Powerful, the God of the people of Israel, says: I will soon make a terrible thing happen to this place! Everyone who hears about it will be amazed and full of fear. 4 I will do these things because the people of Judah have stopped following me. They have made this a place for foreign gods. The people of Judah have burned sacrifices in this place to other gods. The people long ago did not worship those gods. Their ancestors did not worship them. These are new gods from other countries. The kings of Judah filled this place with the blood of innocent children. 5 The kings of Judah built high places for the god Baal. They use those places to burn their sons in the fire. They burned their sons as burnt offerings to the god Baal. I did not tell them to do that. I did not ask them to offer their sons as sacrifices. I never even thought of such a thing. 6 Now people call this place Topheth and the Valley of Hinnom. But I give you this warning. This message is from the LORD: The days are coming, when people will call this place the Valley of Slaughter. 7 At this place, I will ruin the plans of the people of Judah and Jerusalem. The enemy will chase them, and I will let the people of Judah be killed with swords in this place. I will make their dead bodies food for the birds and wild animals. 8 I will completely destroy this city. People will whistle and shake their heads when they pass by Jerusalem. They will be shocked when they see how the city was destroyed. 9 The enemy will bring its army around the city. That army will not let people go out to get food, so the people in the city will begin to starve. They will become so hungry that they will eat the bodies of their own sons and daughters, and then they will begin to eat each other.'

10 "Jeremiah, tell this to the people, and while they are watching, break the jar. 11 Then say this: 'The LORD All-Powerful says, I will break the nation of Judah and the city of Jerusalem, just as someone breaks a clay jar! And like a broken jar, the nation of Judah cannot be put together again. It will be the same for the nation of Judah."

14 Then Jeremiah left Topheth where the LORD had told him to speak. Jeremiah went to the LORD's Temple and stood in the courtyard of the Temple. Jeremiah said to all the people: 15 "This is what the LORD All-Powerful, the God of Israel says: 'I said I would bring many disasters to Jerusalem and the villages around it. I will soon make this happen because the people are very stubborn. They refuse to listen and obey me.'"

{Jeremiah did not only prophesy doom, he also brought news of restoration: "'The days are coming,' declares the LORD, 'when I will bring my people Israel and Judah back from captivity and restore them to the land I gave their ancestors to possess,' says the LORD." (30:3). The Lord even set a date for the return to Jerusalem and promised that Judah's captors will be punished: "'But when the seventy years are fulfilled, I will punish the king of Babylon and his nation, the land of the Babylonians, for their guilt,' declares the LORD, 'and will make it desolate forever.'" (25:12).}

The New Israel

31:4 Israel, my bride, I will rebuild you. You will be a country again. You will pick up your tambourines again.

27 "The days are coming," says the LORD, "when I will help the family of Israel and Judah to grow. I will help their children and animals to grow too. It will be like planting and caring for a plant. 28 In the past I watched over Israel and Judah, but I watched for the time to pull them up. I tore them down. I destroyed them. I gave many troubles to them. But now I will watch over them to build them up and make them strong." This message is from the LORD.

The New Agreement

31 This is what the LORD said, "The time is coming when I will make a new agreement with the family of Israel and with the family of Judah. 32 It will not be like the agreement I made with their ancestors. I made that agreement when I took them by the hand and brought them out of Egypt. I was their master, but they broke that agreement." This message is from the LORD.

The 5 Major Prophets

33 "In the future I will make this agreement with the people of Israel." This message is from the LORD. "I will put my teachings in their minds, and I will write them on their hearts. I will be their God, and they will be my people."

The Potter and the Clay

18:1 This is the message that came to Jeremiah from the LORD: 2 "Jeremiah, go down to the potter's house. I will give you my message there."

3 So I went down to the potter's house and saw him working with clay at the wheel. 4 He was making a pot from clay. But there was something wrong with the pot. So the potter used that clay to make another pot. With his hands he shaped the pot the way he wanted it to be.

5 Then this message from the LORD came to me: 6 "Family of Israel, you know that I can do the same thing with you. **You are like the clay in the potter's hands, and I am the potter.**" This message is from the LORD. 7 "There may come a time when I will speak about a nation or a kingdom that I will pull up by its roots or tear down and destroy it. 8 But if the people of that nation change their hearts and lives and stop doing evil things, I will change my mind and not bring on them the disaster I planned. 9 There may come another time when I speak about a nation that I will build up or plant. 10 But if I see that nation doing evil things and not obeying me, I will think again about the good I had planned to do for them.

{Jeremiah witnessed the fall Jerusalem. The Babylonians were dominant for some time. They had already forced a tax from Jerusalem. And when King Zedekiah declared independence and stopped paying the tax, the Babylonian King Nebuchadnezzar became fed up and invaded Jerusalem.}

The Fall of Jerusalem

39:1 This is how Jerusalem was captured: During the tenth month of the ninth year that Zedekiah was king of Judah, King Nebuchadnezzar of Babylon marched against Jerusalem with his whole army. He surrounded the city to defeat it. 2 And on the ninth day of the fourth month in Zedekiah's eleventh year, the wall of Jerusalem was broken through.

4 King Zedekiah of Judah saw the officials from Babylon, so he and the soldiers with him ran away. They left Jerusalem at night. They went out through the king's garden and out through the gate that was between the two walls. Then they went toward the desert. 5 The Babylonian army chased Zedekiah and the soldiers with him. They caught up with Zedekiah in the plains of Jericho. They captured Zedekiah and took him to King Nebuchadnezzar of Babylon... At that place Nebuchadnezzar decided what to do to Zedekiah. 6 There ... the king of Babylon killed Zedekiah's sons and he killed all the royal officials of Judah while Zedekiah watched. 7 Then Nebuchadnezzar tore out Zedekiah's eyes. He put bronze chains on Zedekiah and took him to Babylon.

> God is the potter; your life is the clay. What good thing is God making out of you?

8 The army of Babylon set fire to the king's palace and the houses of the people of Jerusalem. And they broke down the walls of Jerusalem. 9 Nebuzaradan was the commander of the king of Babylon's special guards. He took all the people who had surrendered to him and all the people still in Jerusalem and made them captives. He carried them away to Babylon.

{Because Jeremiah advised King Zedekiah to surrender, King Nebuchadnezzar was lenient toward him and granted him his freedom. Jeremiah chose to stay in Judah. Nebuchadnezzar appointed a ruler over the area, but he was assassinated by rebellious Jews. Those responsible asked for Jeremiah's advice on whether to flee to Egypt for fear of retribution for the assassination. Jeremiah warned them that if they fled, the Lord would punish them and if they stayed they would one day flourish again. But they did not believe him. So they fled and forced Jeremiah to go with them.}

The Enemy Surrounds Jerusalem

6:16 This is what the LORD says: "Stand at the crossroads and look. Ask where the old road is. **Ask where the good road is, and walk on that road.** If you do, you will find rest for yourselves. But you people have said, 'We will not walk on the good road.'

A Letter to the Captives in Babylon

29:10 This is what the LORD says: "Babylon will be powerful for 70 years. After that time, I will come to you people who are living in Babylon. I will keep my good promise to bring you back to Jerusalem. 11 I say this because I know the plans that I have for you." This message is from the LORD. **"I have good plans for you. I don't plan to hurt you. I plan to give you hope and a good future.** 12 Then you will call my name. You will come to me and pray to me, and I will listen to you. 13 You will search for me, and when you search for me with all your heart, you will find me. 14 I will let you find me." This message is from the LORD. "And I will bring you back from your captivity. I forced you to leave this place. But I will gather you from all the nations and places where I have sent you," says the LORD, "and I will bring you back to this place."

When you come to a crossroad in your life, pray, read your Bible, and talk to others on the good road.

Maybe things have not been going well for you lately. God has a good plan for you. Believe.

the book of Lamentations

Category: *The 5 Major Prophets*
Author: *Jeremiah*
Theme: *Lament, sorrow*
Location & Date: *Jerusalem; 586 B.C.*
Version of Bible: *Easy-to-Read Version (ERV)*
Summary: *Jeremiah, in this book, described the fall of Jerusalem, the suffering of the people, and the exile. He said all of this with a profound sense of loss and despair. But he also wrote of hope.*

Jerusalem Cries Over Her Destruction

Lamentations 1:1 Jerusalem once was a city full of people, but now the city is so empty. She was one of the greatest cities in the world, but now she is like a poor widow. She was once a princess among cities, but now she has been made a slave.

2 She cries bitterly in the night. Her tears are on her cheeks. She has no one to comfort her. Many nations were friendly to her, but not one of them comforts her now. All her friends have turned their backs on her and have become her enemies.

3 Judah suffered very much, and then she was taken into captivity. She lives among other nations but has found no rest. The people who chased her caught her where there was no way out.

4 The roads to Zion are very sad, because **no one comes to Zion for the festivals anymore.** All of Zion's gates have been destroyed; all her priests groan in sorrow. Zion's young women have been taken away, and all this made Zion sad.

5 Jerusalem's enemies have won. Her enemies have been successful. This happened because the LORD punished her. He punished Jerusalem for her many sins. Her children have gone away. Their enemies captured them and took them away.

6 The beauty of Daughter Zion has gone away. Her princes were like deer that cannot find a meadow to feed in. They walk away without strength from those who chased them.

7 Jerusalem thinks back. She remembers the time when she was hurt and when she lost her home. She remembers all the nice things that she had in the past. She remembers those nice things that she had in the old days. She remembers when her people were captured by the enemy. She remembers when there was no one to help her. When her enemies saw her, they laughed, because she was destroyed.

Many of the festivals described in Leviticus 23 were yearly family pilgrimages filled with singing, campfires, storytelling, and good memories piled on top of each other. All gone.

10 **The enemy stretched out his hand. He took all her nice things. In fact, she saw the foreign nations go inside her Temple.** And you said those people could not join in our assembly!

11 All the people of Jerusalem are groaning. All of her people are looking for food. They are giving away all their nice things for food to stay alive. Jerusalem says, "Look, LORD. Look at me! See how people hate me."

12 All you who pass by on the road, you don't seem to care. But look at me and see. Is there any pain like my pain? Is there any pain like the pain that has come to me? Is there any pain like the pain that the LORD has punished me with? He has punished me on the day of his great anger.

16 "I cry about all these things. Tears are flowing down my cheeks. There is no one near to comfort me. There is no one who can make me feel better. **My children are like a wasteland, because the enemy won."**

The Lord Destroyed Jerusalem

2:11 My eyes are worn out with tears, and my insides are upset. My heart feels like it has been poured on the ground; I feel this way because of the destruction of my people. **Children and babies are fainting in the public squares of the city.**

12 **They ask their mothers, "Where is the bread and wine?" as they pour out their life in their mother's laps.**

20 Look at us, LORD! Have you ever treated anyone else so badly? Is it right for women to eat their own babies, the children they have cared for? Should priests and prophets be killed in the Temple of the Lord?

The Meaning of Suffering

3:21 But then I think about this, and I have hope: 22 **We are still alive because the LORD's faithful love never ends. 23 Every morning he shows it in new ways!** You are so very true and loyal! 24 I say to myself, "The LORD is my God, and I trust him." 25 The LORD is good to those who wait for him. He is good to those who look for him. 26 It is good to wait quietly for the LORD to save them.

A Prayer to the Lord

5:19 But you rule forever, LORD. Your kingly chair lasts forever and ever. 20 You seem to have forgotten us forever. You seem to have left us alone for such a long time. 21 **Bring us back to you, LORD. We will gladly come back to you.** Make our lives as they were before. 22 You were very angry with us. Have you completely rejected us?

The temple of God was destroyed and all the treasures used in the worship of God were melted down.

All the family histories and traditions: gone.

The conditions of the siege of Jerusalem were horrible.

How has God showed you His faithful love today in your life?

Nothing like a disaster in our lives to help us realize how we need God.

the book of Ezekiel

Category: *The 5 Major Prophets*
Author: *Ezekiel*
Theme: *Judgment and hope*
Location & Date: *Babylon; 590-570 B.C.*
Version of Bible: *Easy-to-Read Version (ERV)*
Summary: *The book of Ezekiel describes what took place after the exile of certain Jews to Babylon, but before the nation of Judah was completely dissolved. It focuses on the life and prophecy of Ezekiel, a priest, whose main message was of the destruction of the Jewish nation. But like other prophets, he also spoke of God's future plans to restore His people.*

The Chariot of the Lord — God's Throne

Ezekiel 1:4 I was watching a big storm come in from the north. It was a big cloud with a strong wind, and there was fire flashing from it. Light was shining out all around it. It looked like hot metal glowing in a fire. 5 Inside the cloud, there were four living beings that looked like people. 6 But each one of them had four faces and four wings. 7 Their legs were straight. Their feet looked like calves' feet, and they sparkled like polished brass.

10 Each living being had four faces. In the front they each had a man's face. There was a lion's face on the right side and a bull's face on the left side. There was an eagle's face on the back.

13 That is what the living beings looked like. Inside the area between the living beings, there was something that looked like burning coals of fire. This fire was like small torches that kept moving around among the living beings. The fire glowed brightly and lightning flashed from it. 14 The living beings ran back and forth — as fast as lightning.

15-16 I was looking at the living beings when I noticed four wheels that touched the ground. There was one wheel by each living being. All the wheels looked the same. The wheels looked as if they were made from a clear, yellow jewel. They looked like there was a wheel inside a wheel.

20 They went wherever the spirit wanted them to go, and the wheels went with them, because the power that moved the living being was in the wheels.

22 There was an amazing thing over the heads of the living beings. It was like a bowl turned upside down, and the bowl was clear like crystal.

25 The living beings stopped moving and lowered their wings. Then there was another loud sound that came from above the bowl over their heads. 26 There was something that looked like a throne on top of the bowl. It was blue like sapphire. There was also something that looked like a man sitting on the throne. 27 I looked at him from his waist up. He looked like hot metal with fire all around him. I looked at him from his waist down. It looked like fire with a glow that was shining all around him. 28 The light shining around him was like a rainbow in a cloud. It was the Glory of the LORD. As soon as I saw that, I fell to the ground. I bowed with my face to the ground, and then I heard a voice speaking to me.

The Lord Speaks to Ezekiel

2:1 The voice said, "Son of man, stand up and I will speak with you."

2 Then the Spirit came into me and lifted me up on my feet, and I listened to the one who spoke to me. 3 He said, "Son of man, I am sending you to speak to the family of Israel. Those people and their ancestors turned against me many times. They have sinned against me many times—and they are still sinning against me today. 4 I am sending you to speak to them, but they are very stubborn. They are very hardheaded, but you must speak to them. You must say, 'This is what the Lord GOD says.' 5 They are people who refuse to obey, so they may not listen to you. But even if they don't stop sinning, at least they will know that there is a prophet living among them.

6 "Son of man, don't be afraid of the people or what they say. It is true: they will turn against you and try to hurt you. Their words will be sharp like thorns and will sting like scorpions. But don't be afraid of what they say. They are people who refuse to obey, but don't be afraid of them. 7 You must tell them what I say, whether they listen or not. They are people who usually refuse to listen!

9 Then I saw an arm reach out toward me. It was holding a scroll with words written on it. 10 It rolled the scroll open in front of me. Words were on the front and on the back of the scroll. There were all kinds of sad songs, sad stories, and warnings.

3:1 Then God said, "Son of man, I am giving you this scroll. Swallow it! Let that scroll fill your body." So **I ate the scroll. It was as sweet as honey in my mouth.**

{By prompting Ezekiel to eat the scroll, God established, symbolically, that the prophet would be speak His word.}

Warnings About the Attack of Jerusalem

4:1 "Son of man, take a brick and scratch a picture on it. Draw a picture of a city—the city of Jerusalem. 2 And then pretend you are an army surrounding the city. Build a dirt wall around the city to help you attack it. Build a dirt road leading up to the city wall. Bring battering rams and set up army camps around the city. 3 And then take an iron pan and put it between you and the city. It will be like an iron wall separating you and the city. In this way you will show

We too are to "eat" the Word of God. That is what you are doing as you try read it and live it.

that you are against it. You will surround the city and attack it. This is an example for the family of Israel to show that I will destroy Jerusalem.

4 "Then you must lie down on your left side. You must do this thing that shows that you are taking the sins of the people of Israel on yourself. You will carry the guilt for as many days as you lie on your left side. 5 **You must bear the guilt of Israel** for 390 days. In this way I am telling you how long Israel will be punished; one day equals one year.

Jesus ultimately bore the guilt of our sin.

6 "After that time, you will lie on your right side for 40 days. This time you will bear the guilt of Judah for 40 days. One day equals one year. I am telling you how long Judah must be punished.

7 "Now, roll up your sleeve and raise your arm over the brick. Act like you are attacking the city of Jerusalem. Do this to show that you are speaking as my messenger to the people. 8 Now look, I am tying ropes on you. You will not be able to roll over from one side to the other until your attack against the city is finished.

9 "You must get some grain to make bread. Get some wheat, barley, beans, lentils, millet, and spelt. Mix all these things together in one bowl and grind them to make flour. You will use this flour to make bread. You will eat only this bread during the 390 days that you lie on your side. 10 You will be allowed to use only 1 cup of that flour each day to make bread. You will eat that bread from time to time throughout the day. 11 You can drink only 3 cups of water each day. You can drink it from time to time throughout the day. 12 You must make your bread each day...

16 Then God said to me, "Son of man, I am destroying Jerusalem's supply of bread. People will have only a little bread to eat. They will be very worried about their food supply, and they will have only a little water to drink. Every time they take a drink, they will feel more afraid. 17 That is because there will not be enough food and water for everyone. They will be terrified as they watch each other wasting away because of their sins.

People of Jerusalem Scattered

5:1 "Son of man, after your famine you must do this: Take a sharp sword and use it like a barber's razor. Shave off your hair and beard. Put the hair on a scale and weigh it. Separate it into three equal parts. Put a third of your hair on the brick that has the picture of the city on it. Burn that hair in that 'city.' Then use the sword and cut a third of your hair into small pieces all around the outside of the 'city.' Next, throw a third of your hair into the air and let the wind blow it away. This will show that I will pull out my sword and chase some of the people into faraway countries. 3 But then you must get a few of those hairs and wrap them up in your robe. 4 Take some of those hairs and throw them into the fire. This will show that a fire will start there and burn throughout the whole house of Israel."

5 Then the Lord GOD said to me, "The brick is a picture of Jerusalem. I put Jerusalem in the middle of other nations with coun-

tries all around her. 6 The people rebelled against my commands. They were worse than any of the other nations! They broke more of my laws than any of the people in the countries around them. They refused to listen to my commands. They did not obey my laws."

Shake With Fear

12:18 "Son of man, you must act as if you are very frightened. You must shake when you eat your food. You must act worried and afraid when you drink your water. 19 You must say this to the common people: 'This is what the Lord GOD says to the people living in Jerusalem and in the other parts of Israel. You will be very worried while you eat your food. You will be terrified while you drink your water, because everything in your country will be destroyed! Then you will know that I am the LORD.'"

The Lord Will Protect His Name

36:23 I will show the nations how holy my great name really is. You ruined my good name in those nations! But I will show you that I am holy. I will make you respect my name, and then those nations will know that I am the LORD.'" This is what the Lord GOD said.

24 "I will take you out of those nations, gather you together, and bring you back to your own land. 25 Then I will sprinkle pure water on you and make you pure. I will wash away all your filth, the filth from those nasty idols, and I will make you pure. 26 I will also put a new spirit in you to change your way of thinking. I will take out the heart of stone from your body and give you a tender, human heart. 27 I will put my Spirit inside you and change you so that you will obey my laws. You will carefully obey my commands. 28 Then you will live in the land that I gave to your ancestors. **You will be my people, and I will be your God.** 29 Also, I will save you and keep you from becoming unclean. I will command the grain to grow. I will not bring a famine against you. 30 I will give you large crops of fruit from your trees and the harvest from your fields so that you will never again feel the shame of being hungry in a foreign country..."

32 The Lord GOD says, "I want you to remember this: I am not doing these things for your good! I am doing them for my good name. Family of Israel, you should be ashamed and embarrassed about the way you lived!"

33 This is what the Lord GOD says: "On the day that I wash away your sins, I will bring people back to your cities. The ruined cities will be rebuilt. 34 People will begin again to work the land so when other people pass by they will not see ruins anymore. 35 They will say, 'In the past, this land was ruined, but now it is like the Garden of Eden. The cities were destroyed. They were ruined and empty, but now they are protected, and there are people living in them.'

36 "Then the nations that are still around you will know I am the LORD and that I rebuilt those places. I planted things in this land that was empty. I am the LORD. I said this, and I will make them

> Isn't this what we really want in life?

happen!"

37 This is what the Lord GOD says: "I will also let the family of Israel come to me and ask me to do these things for them. I will make them grow and become many people. They will be like flocks of sheep. 38 During the special festivals, Jerusalem was filled with flocks of sheep and goats that had been made holy. In the same way the cities and ruined places will be filled with flocks of people. Then they will know that I am the LORD."

The Vision of the Dry Bones

37:1 The LORD's power came on me. The Spirit of the LORD carried me out of the city and put me down in the middle of the valley. The valley was full of dead men's bones. 2 There were many bones lying on the ground in the valley. The Lord made me walk all around among the bones. I saw the bones were very dry.

3 Then the Lord said to me, "**Son of man, can these bones come to life?**" I answered, "Lord GOD, only you know the answer to that question."

> *This is every human beings ultimate question. Can bones come to life? Is there life after death and if there is how does one get it?*

4 Then he said to me, "Speak to these bones for me. Tell them, 'Dry bones, listen to the word of the LORD! 5 This is what the Lord GOD says to you: I will cause breath to come into you, and you will come to life! 6 I will put sinew and muscles on you, and I will cover you with skin. Then I will put breath in you, and you will come back to life! Then you will know that I am the LORD.'"

7 So I spoke to the bones for the LORD, as he said. I was still speaking, when I heard the loud noise. The bones began to rattle, and bone joined together with bone! 8 There before my eyes, I saw sinew and muscles begin to cover the bones. Skin began to cover them, but there was no breath in them.

9 Then the Lord said to me, "Speak to the wind for me. Son of man, speak to the wind for me. Tell the wind that this is what the Lord GOD says: 'Wind, come from every direction and breathe air into these dead bodies! Breathe into them and they will come to life again!'"

10 So I spoke to the wind for the LORD, as he said, and the breath came into the dead bodies. They came to life and stood up. There were many men—a very large army!

> *Maybe you feel this way about your own life.*

11 Then he said to me, "Son of man, these bones are like the whole family of Israel. The people of Israel say, '**Our bones have dried up; our hope is gone**. We have been completely destroyed!' 12 So speak to them for me. Tell them this is what the Lord GOD says: 'My people, I will open your graves and bring you up out of them! Then I will bring you to the land of Israel. 13 My people, I will open your graves and bring you up out of your graves, and then you will know that I am the LORD. 14 **I will put my Spirit in you, and you will come to life again**. Then I will lead you back to your own land. Then you will know that I am the LORD. You will know that I said this and that I made it happen.'" This is what the LORD said.

> *This is the Christian hope.*

the book of Daniel

Category: The 5 Major Prophets
Author: Daniel
Theme: God's sovereignty (He is in control)
Location & Date: Babylon; 530 B.C.
Version of Bible: Easy-to-Read Version (ERV)
Summary: The book of Daniel was written to the Jewish exiles in Babylon, not only to remind them of who they were (God's people), but also who God was (the God who is bigger than even the king of Babylon). This book ends with a lot of prophetic imagery about the future—much like the last book of the Bible—Revelation.

Daniel Taken to Babylon

Daniel 1:1 Nebuchadnezzar king of Babylon came to Jerusalem and surrounded it with his army. This happened during the third year that Jehoiakim was king of Judah. 2 The Lord allowed Nebuchadnezzar to defeat Jehoiakim king of Judah. Nebuchadnezzar took all the **dishes** and other things from God's Temple and carried them to Babylon. He put those things in the temple of his gods.

3 Then King Nebuchadnezzar ordered Ashpenaz, the man in charge of his officials, to bring some of the boys into the palace to train them. He was to include boys from among the Israelites, from important Judean families, and from the royal family of Judah. 4 King Nebuchadnezzar wanted only healthy boys who did not have any bruises, scars, or anything wrong with their bodies. He wanted handsome, **smart young men who were able to learn things quickly** and easily to serve in his palace. He told Ashpenaz to teach these young men the language and writings of the Chaldeans.

5 King Nebuchadnezzar gave the young men a certain amount of food and wine every day. This was the same kind of food that he ate. He wanted them to be trained for three years. After that **they would become servants of the king of Babylon**. 6 Among those young men were Daniel, Hananiah, Mishael, and Azariah from the tribe of Judah. 7 Ashpenaz gave them Babylonian names. Daniel's new name was Belteshazzar, Hananiah's was Shadrach, Mishael's was Meshach, and Azariah's was Abednego.

8 Daniel did not want to eat the king's rich food and wine because it would make him unclean. So he asked Ashpenaz for permission not to make himself unclean in this way.

9 God caused Ashpenaz, the man in charge of the officials, to be kind and loyal to Daniel. 10 But Ashpenaz told Daniel, "I am afraid of my master, the king. He ordered me to give you this food

> These were used in the ceremonies in the temple, the purpose of which was to bridge the gap between an unholy people and a Holy God.

> The goal was to stamp out the Hebrew culture and indoctrinate them in the their own.

and drink. If you don't eat this food, you will begin to look weak and sick. You will look worse than other young men your age. The king will see this, and he will become angry with me. He might cut off my head. And it would be your fault."

11 Then Daniel talked to the guard who had been put in charge of Daniel, Hananiah, Mishael, and Azariah by Ashpenaz. 12 He said, "Please give us this test for ten days: **Don't give us anything but vegetables to eat and water to drink.** 13 Then after ten days, compare us with the other young men who eat the king's food. See for yourself who looks healthier, and then decide how you want to treat us, your servants."

14 So the guard agreed to test Daniel, Hananiah, Mishael, and Azariah for ten days. 15 After ten days, Daniel and his friends looked healthier than all the young men who ate the king's food. 16 So the guard continued to take away the king's special food and wine and to give only vegetables to Daniel, Hananiah, Mishael, and Azariah.

17 God gave these four young men the wisdom and ability to learn many different kinds of writing and science. Daniel could also understand all kinds of visions and dreams.

18 At the end of the three years of training, Ashpenaz brought all the young men to King Nebuchadnezzar. 19 The king talked to them and found that none of the young men were as good as Daniel, Hananiah, Mishael, and Azariah. So these four young men became the king's servants. 20 Every time the king asked them about something important, they showed great wisdom and understanding. The king found they were ten times better than all the magicians and wise men in his kingdom. 21 So Daniel served the king until the first year that Cyrus was king.

The Idol of Gold and the Hot Furnace

3:1 King Nebuchadnezzar had a gold idol made that was **60 cubits high and 6 cubits wide.** Then he set the idol up on the plain of Dura in the province of Babylon. 2 Then he called the satraps, prefects, governors, advisors, treasurers, judges, rulers, and all the other officials in his kingdom to come together. He wanted all of them to come to the dedication ceremony for the idol.

4 Then the man who makes announcements for the king spoke in a loud voice, "All you people from many nations and language groups, listen to me. This is what you are commanded to do: 5 You must bow down as soon as you hear the sound of all the musical instruments. When you hear the horns, flutes, lyres, sambucas, harps, bagpipes, and all the other musical instruments, you must worship the gold idol. King Nebuchadnezzar has set this idol up. 6 Whoever does not bow down and worship this gold idol will immediately be thrown into a very hot furnace."

7 So as soon as they heard the sound of the horns, flutes, lyres, sambucas, bagpipes, and all the other musical instruments, they bowed down and worshiped the gold idol. All the peoples, nations, and different language groups there worshiped the gold idol

Who would've known that this is actually a healthy diet.

About 90 feet high and 9 feet wide.

that King Nebuchadnezzar had set up.

8 Then some of the Chaldeans came up to the king and began speaking against the people from Judah. 9 They said, "King, may you live forever! 10 King, you gave a command. You said that everyone who hears the sound of the horns, flutes, lyres, sambucas, harps, bagpipes, and all the other musical instruments must bow down and worship the gold idol. 11 And you also said that whoever does not bow down and worship the gold idol will be thrown into a very hot furnace. 12 There are some Judeans who you made important officials in the province of Babylon that ignored your order, King. Their names are Shadrach, Meshach, and Abednego. **They don't worship your gods, and they didn't bow down to worship the gold idol you set up.**"

13 Nebuchadnezzar became very angry. He called for Shadrach, Meshach, and Abednego. So they were brought to him. 14 And Nebuchadnezzar said to them, "Shadrach, Meshach, and Abednego, is it true that you don't worship my gods? And is it true that you didn't bow down and worship the gold idol I have set up? 15 Now when you hear the sound of the horns, flutes, lyres, sambucas, harps, bagpipes, and all the other musical instruments, you must bow down and worship the gold idol. If you are ready to worship the idol I have made, that is good. But if you don't worship it, you will be thrown very quickly into the hot furnace. Then no god will be able to save you from my power!"

16 Shadrach, Meshach, and Abednego answered the king, "Nebuchadnezzar, we don't need to explain these things to you. 17 If you throw us into the hot furnace, the God we serve can save us. And if he wants to, he can save us from your power. 18 But even if God does not save us, we want you to know, King, that **we refuse to serve your gods.** We will not worship the gold idol you have set up."

19 Then Nebuchadnezzar became very angry with Shadrach, Meshach, and Abednego. He gave an order for the oven to be heated seven times hotter than it usually was. 20 Then he commanded some of the strongest soldiers in his army to tie up Shadrach, Meshach, and Abednego. He told the soldiers to throw them into the hot furnace.

21 So Shadrach, Meshach, and Abednego were tied up and thrown into the hot furnace. They were wearing their robes, pants, cloth caps, and other clothes. 22 The king was very angry when he gave the command, so the soldiers quickly made the furnace very hot. The fire was so hot that the flames killed the strong soldiers. They were killed when they went close to the fire to throw in Shadrach, Meshach, and Abednego. 23 Shadrach, Meshach, and Abednego fell into the fire. They were tied up very tightly.

24 Then King Nebuchadnezzar jumped to his feet. He was very surprised and he asked his advisors, "We tied only three men, and we threw only three men into the fire. Is that right?"

His advisors said, "Yes, King."

25 The king said, "Look! I see four men walking around in the fire. They are not tied up and they are not burned. **The fourth man**

Young men boldly resisting the godless culture around them.

When have you refused to serve the culture around you?

Many believe the

> 4th man was Jesus - the one who stands with us in our trials and suffering.

looks like an angel."

26 Then Nebuchadnezzar went to the opening of the hot furnace. He shouted, "Shadrach, Meshach, and Abednego, come out! Servants of the Most High God, come here!"

So Shadrach, Meshach, and Abednego came out of the fire. 27 When they came out, the satraps, prefects, governors, and royal advisors crowded around them. They could see that the fire had not burned Shadrach, Meshach, and Abednego. Their bodies were not burned at all. Their hair was not burned, and their robes were not burned. They didn't even smell as if they had been near fire.

28 Then Nebuchadnezzar said, "Praise the God of Shadrach, Meshach, and Abednego. Their God has sent his angel and saved his servants from the fire! These three men trusted their God and refused to obey my command. They were willing to die instead of serving or worshiping any other god.

Daniel and the Lions

6:1 Darius thought it would be a good idea to choose 120 satraps to rule throughout his kingdom. 2 He chose three men to rule over the 120 satraps. Daniel was one of the three supervisors. The king put these men in this position to keep anyone from cheating him. 3 Daniel proved himself to be a better supervisor than any of the others. He did this by his good character and great ability. The king was so impressed with Daniel that he planned to make him ruler over the whole kingdom. 4 But when the other supervisors and the satraps heard about this, they were very jealous. They tried to find reasons to accuse Daniel. So they watched what Daniel did as he went about doing the business of the government. But they could not find anything wrong with him, so they could not accuse him of doing anything wrong. Daniel was a man people could trust. He did not cheat the king, and he worked very hard.

5 Finally, they said, "We will never find any reason to accuse Daniel of doing something wrong. So we must find something to complain about that is connected to the law of his God."

6 So the two supervisors and the satraps went as a group to the king. They said, "King Darius, live forever! 7 The supervisors, prefects, satraps, advisors, and governors have all agreed on something. We think that the king should make this law and that everyone must obey it: For the next 30 days, whoever prays to any god or man except you, King, will be thrown into the lions' den. 8 Now, King, make the law and sign the paper it is written on so that it cannot be changed, because the laws of the Medes and Persians cannot be canceled or changed." 9 So King Darius made the law and signed it.

10 **Daniel always prayed to God three times every day.** Three times every day, he bowed down on his knees to pray and praise God. Even though Daniel heard about the new law, he still went to his house to pray. He went up to the upper room of his house and opened the windows that faced toward Jerusalem. **Then Daniel**

> Daniel had a habit of praying 3 times a day.

bowed down on his knees and prayed just as he always had done.

11 Then the supervisors and satraps went as a group and found Daniel praying and asking God for help. 12 So they went to the king and talked to him about the law he had made. They said, "King Darius, you signed a law that says, for the next 30 days anyone who prays to any god or man except you, the king, would be thrown into the lions' den. You did sign that law, didn't you?"

The king answered, "Yes, I signed that law, and the laws of the Medes and Persians cannot be canceled or changed."

13 Then they said to the king, "That man Daniel is not paying any attention to you. He is one of the captives from Judah, and he is not paying attention to the law you signed. Daniel still prays to his God three times every day."

14 The king became very sad and upset when he heard this. He decided to save Daniel. He worked until sunset trying to think of a way to save him. 15 Then the men went as a group to the king and said to him, "Remember, King, that the law of the Medes and Persians says that no law or command signed by the king can ever be canceled or changed."

16 So King Darius gave the order. They brought Daniel and threw him into the lions' den. The king said to Daniel, "May the God you serve save you!" 17 A big rock was brought and put over the opening of the lions' den. Then the king used his ring and put his seal on the rock. He also used the rings of his officials and put their seals on the rock. This showed that no one could move that rock and bring Daniel out of the lion's den. 18 Then King Darius went back to his house. He did not eat that night. He did not want anyone to come and entertain him. He could not sleep all night.

19 The next morning, King Darius got up just as it was getting light and ran to the lions' den. 20 He was very worried. When he got to the lions' den, he called to Daniel. He said, "Daniel, servant of the living God, has your God been able to save you from the lions?"

21 Daniel answered, "King, live forever! 22 My God sent his angel to save me. The angel closed the lions' mouths. The lions have not hurt me because my God knows I am innocent. I never did anything wrong to you, King."

23 King Darius was very happy. He told his servants to lift Daniel out of the lions' den. And when Daniel was lifted out of the den, they did not find any injury on his body. The lions did not hurt Daniel because he trusted in his God.

24 Then the king gave a command to bring the men who had accused Daniel to the lions' den. The men and their wives and children were thrown into the lions' den. The lions grabbed them before they hit the floor. The lions ate their bodies and then chewed on their bones. 25 Then King Darius wrote this letter to all the people from other nations and language groups all around the world:

> Good habits help us stick with the things that are really important to us even when the culture around us is pushing the opposite direction.
> What God-connecting habits do you have in your life?

Greetings:

26 I am making a new law. This law is for people in every part of my kingdom. All of you must fear and respect the God of Daniel.

Daniel's God is the living God; he lives forever. His kingdom will never be destroyed. His rule will never end. 27 God helps and saves people. He does amazing miracles in heaven and on earth. He saved Daniel from the lions.

The End Times

12:1 "Daniel, at that time the great prince Michael will stand up. Michael is in charge of your people. There will be a time of much trouble, the worst time since nations have been on earth. But Daniel, at that time every one of your people whose name is found written in the book of life will be saved. 2 There are many who are dead and buried. Some of them will wake up and live forever, but others will wake up to shame and disgrace forever. 3 The wise people will shine as bright as the sky. Those who teach others to live right will shine like stars forever and ever.

4 "But you, Daniel, keep this message a secret. You must close the book and keep this secret until the time of the end. Many people will go here and there looking for true knowledge, and the true knowledge will increase."

5 Then I, Daniel, noticed two other men. One man was standing on my side of the river, and the other was standing on the other side. 6 The man who was dressed in linen was standing over the water in the river. One of the two men said to him, "How long will it be before these amazing things come true?"

7 The man dressed in linen and standing over the water lifted his right and left hands toward heaven. And I heard him make a promise using the name of God who lives forever. He said, "It will be for three and one-half years. The power of the holy people will be broken, and then all these things will finally come true."

8 I heard the answer, but I really didn't understand. So I asked, "Sir, what will happen after all this comes true?"

9 He answered, "Go on about your life Daniel. The message is hidden. It will be a secret until the time of the end. 10 Many people will be made pure—they will make themselves clean. But evil people will continue to be evil. And those wicked people will not understand these things, but the wise people will understand them.

11 "The daily sacrifice will be stopped. There will be 1290 days from that time until the time that the terrible thing that destroys is set up. 12 The one who waits for and comes to the end of the 1335 days will be very happy.

13 "As for you, Daniel, go and live your life until the end. You will get your rest. At the end you will rise from death and receive your share of the promise."

Is this your God as well?

the book of Hosea

Category: The 12 Minor Prophets
Author: Hosea
Theme: Unfaithfulness
Location & Date: Israel, the northern kingdom; 755-715 B.C.
Version of Bible: Easy-to-Read Version (ERV)
Summary: The prophet Hosea lived in the time just before the fall of the northern kingdom of Israel and his message focused on the people of that land. God commanded Hosea to live a lifestyle that mirrored the Lord's relationship with his wayward people. As such, God ordered Hosea to marry an adulterous wife. The relationship between the two symbolized the relationship between God and his people, including their exile and eventual restoration.

The Lord God's Message Through Hosea

Hosea 1:1 This is the LORD's message that came to Hosea son of Beeri during the time that Uzziah, Jotham, Ahaz, and Hezekiah were kings of Judah, and Jeroboam son of Joash was king of Israel.

2 This was the LORD's first message to Hosea. The LORD said, "Go, marry a prostitute who has had children as a result of her prostitution. Do this because the people in this country have acted like prostitutes—they have been unfaithful to the LORD."

The Birth of Jezreel

3 So Hosea married Gomer daughter of Diblaim. She became pregnant and gave birth to a son for Hosea.

The Birth of Lo-Ruhamah

6 Then Gomer became pregnant again and gave birth to a daughter. The LORD said to Hosea, "Name her **Lo-Ruhamah**, because I will not show mercy to the nation of Israel anymore, nor will I forgive them. 7 But I will show mercy to the nation of Judah. I will save them, but I will not use bows or swords or war horses and soldiers to save them. I will save them by my own power."

The name means "not pitied."

The Birth of Lo-Ammi

8 After Gomer had finished nursing Lo-Ruhamah, she became pregnant again and gave birth to a son. 9 Then the Lord said, "Name him **Lo-Ammi**, because you are not my people, and I am not your God."

The name means "not my people."

The Lord Speaks to the Nation of Israel

10 "In the future the number of the people of Israel will be like the sand of the sea, which you cannot measure or count. In the same place that God told them, 'You are not my people,' he will call them 'children of the Living God.'

11 "Then the people of Judah and the people of Israel will be gathered together. They will choose one ruler for themselves, and their nation will be too large for the land. Jezreel's day will be great!

2:1 "Then you will say to your brothers, 'You are my people,' and you will say to your sisters, 'He has shown mercy to you.'"

2 "Argue with your mother. Argue with her because she is no longer my wife, and I am no longer her husband! Tell her to stop being like a prostitute. Tell her to take away her lovers from between her breasts. 3 If she refuses to stop her adultery, I will strip her naked and leave her like the day she was born. I will take away her people, and she will be like an empty, dry desert. I will kill her with thirst. 4 I will have no pity on her children because they are the children of prostitution. 5 Their mother has acted like a prostitute. She should be ashamed of what she did. She said, 'I will go to my lovers, who give me food and water, wool and linen, wine and olive oil.'

6 "So I, the Lord, will block Israel's road with thorns, and I will build a wall. Then she will not be able to find her path. 7 She will run after her lovers, but she will not be able to catch up with them. She will look for her lovers, but she will not be able to find them. Then she will say, 'I will go back to my husband. Life was better for me when I was with him. Life was better then than it is now.'

8 "Israel didn't know that I, the Lord, was the one who gave her grain, wine, and oil. I kept giving her more and more silver and gold, but she used this silver and gold to make statues of Baal. 9 So I will return and take back my grain at the time it is ready to be harvested. I will take back my wine at the time the grapes are ready. I will take back my wool and linen. I gave those things to her so that she could cover her naked body. 10 Now I will strip her. She will be naked, so all her lovers can see her. No one will be able to save her from my power. 11 I will take away all her fun. I will stop her festivals, her New Moon celebrations, and her days of rest. I will stop all her special feasts. 12 I will destroy her vines and fig trees. She said, 'My lovers gave these things to me.' But I will change her gardens—they will become like a wild forest. Wild animals will come and eat from those plants.

13 "Israel served false gods, so I will punish her. She burned incense to those false gods. She dressed up - she put on her jewelry and nose ring. Then she went to her lovers and forgot me." This is what the LORD has said.

14 "So I, the Lord, will speak romantic words to her. I will lead her into the desert and speak tender words. 15 There I will give her vineyards. I will give her Achor Valley as a doorway of hope. Then she will answer as she did when she came out of the land of Egypt." 16 This is what the LORD says.

"At that time you will call me 'My husband.' You will not call me 'My **Baal**.' 17 I will take the names of those false gods out of her mouth. Then people will not use those names again.

18 "At that time I will make an agreement for the Israelites with the animals of the field, the birds of the sky, and the crawling things on the ground. I will break the bow, the sword, and the weapons of war in that land. I will make the land safe, so the people of Israel can lie down in peace. 19 And I will make you my bride forever. I will make you my bride with goodness and justice and with love and mercy. 20 I will make you my faithful bride. Then you will really know the LORD. 21 And at that time I will answer." This is what the LORD says.

"I will speak to the skies, and they will give rain to the earth. 22 The earth will produce grain, wine, and oil, and they will meet Jezreel's needs. 23 I will sow her many seeds on her land. To Lo-Ruhamah, I will show mercy. To Lo-Ammi, I will say, 'You are my people.' And they will say to me, 'You are our God.'"

> The god of the native people of the land of Canaan.

Hosea Buys Gomer Back From Slavery

3:1 Then the LORD said to me again, "Gomer has many lovers, but you must continue loving her. Do this because it is an example of the LORD's love for Israel. He continues to love them, but they continue to turn to other gods, and they love to eat those raisin cakes."

2 So I bought Gomer back for 6 ounces of silver and 9 bushels of barley. 3 Then I told her, "You must stay at home with me for many days. You will not be like a prostitute. You will not have sexual relations with another man. I will be your husband."

4 In the same way the people of Israel will continue many days without a king or a leader. They will be without a sacrifice or a memorial stone. They will be without an ephod or a household god. 5 After this, the people of Israel will come back and look for the LORD their God and for David their king. In the last days they will come to honor the LORD and his goodness.

Israel Has Forgotten the Lord

11:1 The Lord said, "**I loved Israel when he was a child, and I called my son out of Egypt.** 2 But the more I called the Israelites, the more they left me. The Israelites gave sacrifices to the false gods and burned incense to the idols.

3 "But I was the one who taught Ephraim to walk. I took the Israelites in my arms. I healed them, but they don't know that. 4 I led them with ropes, but they were ropes of love. I was like a person who set them free. I bent down and fed them.

> Israel was originally called out of slavery in Egypt. Interestingly the family of Jesus was also called out of Egypt when Jesus was just a boy.

the book of **Joel**

Category: *The 12 Minor Prophets*
Author: *Joel*
Theme: *The day of the Lord*
Location & Date: *Judah, the southern kingdom; 835-796 B.C.*
Version of Bible: *Easy-to-Read Version (ERV)*
Summary: *The prophet Joel saw the recent ravaging of the lands of Judah as signs of the horrible and destructive day of the Lord—the end of the world as we know it.*

Locusts Will Destroy the Crops

Joel 1:1 Joel son of Pethuel received this message from the Lord: 2 Leaders, listen to this message! Listen to me, all you people who live in the land. Has anything like this ever happened in your life? Did anything like this happen during your fathers' lifetime? 3 You will tell these things to your children, and your children will tell their children, and your grandchildren will tell the people of the next generation. 4 What the cutting locust has left, the swarming locust has eaten.

The People Cry

8 Cry like a young woman crying because the man she was ready to marry has died. 9 Priests, servants of the LORD, cry because there will be no more grain and drink offerings in the LORD's Temple. 10 The fields are ruined. Even the ground is crying because the grain is destroyed; the new wine is dried up, and the olive oil is gone. 11 Be sad, farmers! Cry loudly for the grapes, for the wheat, and for the barley, because the harvest in the field is ruined. 12 The vines have become dry, and the fig tree is dying. All the trees in the field—the pomegranate, the palm, and the apple—have withered. And happiness among the people has died.

{Joel then predicted that, as it happened with the locust, so too would an army advance against Jerusalem during the "day of the Lord."}

The Coming Day of the Lord

2:1 Blow the trumpet on Zion. Shout a warning on my holy mountain. Let all the people who live in the land shake with fear. The LORD's special day is coming; it is near. 2 It will be a dark, gloomy day. It will be a dark and cloudy day. At sunrise you will see the army spread over the mountains. It will be a great and powerful army. There has never been anything like it before, and there will never be anything like it again.

3 The army will destroy the land like a burning fire. In front of them the land will be like the Garden of Eden. Behind them the land will be like an empty desert. Nothing will escape them.

6 Before this army, people shake with fear. Their faces become pale from fear. 7 The soldiers run fast. They climb over the walls. Each soldier marches straight ahead. They don't move from their path.

10 Before them, earth and sky shake. The sun and the moon become dark, and the stars stop shining. 11 The LORD calls loudly to his army. His camp is very large. The army obeys his commands. His army is very powerful. The LORD's special day is a great and terrible day. No one can stop it.

The Land Will Be Made New Again

25 "I, the Lord, sent my army against you. The swarming locusts and the hopping locusts and the destroying locusts and the cutting locusts ate everything you had. But I will pay you back for those years of trouble. 26 Then you will have plenty to eat. You will be full. **You will praise the name of the LORD your God. He has done wonderful things for you...**

28 **"After this, I will pour out my Spirit on all kinds of people. Your sons and daughters will prophesy, your old men will have dreams, and your young men will see visions.** 29 In those days I will pour out my Spirit even on servants, both men and women. 30 I will work wonders in the sky and on the earth. There will be blood, fire, and thick smoke. 31 The sun will be changed into darkness, and the moon will be as red as blood. Then the great and fearful day of the Lord will come! 32 And everyone who trusts in the Lord will be saved.

Judah's Enemies Will Be Punished

3:1 "Yes, at that time I will bring back the people of Judah and Jerusalem from captivity. 2 I will also gather all the nations together. I will bring all these nations down into Jehoshaphat Valley. There I will judge them. Those nations scattered my people, Israel. They forced them to live in other nations, so I will punish those nations. They divided up my land.

Prepare for War

14 There are many, many people in the **Valley of Decision**. The LORD's special day is near in the Valley of Decision. 15 The sun and the moon will become dark. The stars will stop shining. 16 The LORD God will shout from Zion. He will shout from Jerusalem, and the sky and the earth will shake. But the LORD God will be a safe place for his people. He will be a place of safety for the people of Israel. 17 "Then you will know that I am the LORD your God... 18 "On that day the mountains will drip with sweet wine. The hills will flow with milk, and water will flow through all the empty rivers of Judah. A fountain will come from the LORD's Temple. It will give water to Acacia Valley.

How has this been true for you?

See Acts 2:17; pg. 298.

The Lord's special day is ultimately the day the world, as we know it, will come to an end. The days and years leading up to that day are called "the valley of decision" - to follow God or not.

the book of Amos

Category: *The 12 Minor Prophets*
Author: *Hosea*
Theme: *Judgment*
Location & Date: *Israel, the northern kingdom; 790 B.C.*
Version of Bible: *Easy-to-Read Version (ERV)*
Summary: The prophet Amos was a farmer from the southern kingdom of Judah. He lived in the time before the fall of the northern kingdom, Israel. Although he lived in the southern kingdom of Judah, the bulk of his message was directed at the Israelites in the north. Amos specifically focused his message on the elite of the Israelite society. He rebuked them for their pride, complacency, and for their oppression of the poor. For those sins, as well as for worshiping idols and ignoring the religious decrees, God promised to destroy Israel.

Punishment for Israel

Amos 2:6 This is what the LORD says: "I will definitely punish Israel for the many crimes they have done. They sold honest people for a little silver. They sold the poor for the price of a pair of sandals. 7 They pushed their faces into the ground and walked on them. They stopped listening to suffering people. Fathers and sons had sexual relations with the same woman. They ruined my holy name. 8 They took clothes from the poor, and then they sat on those clothes while worshiping at their altars. They loaned money to the poor, and then they took their clothes as a promise for payment. They made people pay fines and used the money to buy wine for themselves to drink in the temple of their god.

The Women Who Love Pleasure

4:1 Listen to me, you cows of Bashan on Samaria's mountain. You hurt the poor and crush those in need. You tell your husbands, "Bring us something to drink!"

2 The Lord GOD made a promise. He promised by his holiness that troubles will come to you. People will use hooks and take you away as prisoners. They will use fishhooks to take away your children.

12 "So, Israel, this is what I will do to you. You people of Israel, prepare to meet your God." 13 He is the one who made the mountains. He created the wind. He lets people know his thoughts. He changes the darkness into dawn. He walks over the mountains of the earth. His name is YAHWEH, LORD God All-Powerful.

Israel's Good Times Will Be Taken Away

6:1 Oh, look at the people enjoying life in Zion, and those on Mount Samaria who feel so safe. They are such important leaders of a most important nation. The "House of Israel" comes to you for advice.

3 You people are rushing toward the day of punishment. You bring near the rule of violence. 4 But now you lie on ivory beds and stretch out on your couches. You eat tender young lambs from the flock and young calves from the stable. 5 You play your harps, and like David, you practice on your musical instruments. 6 You drink wine in fancy cups. You use the best perfumes. And it doesn't even bother you that **Joseph's family** is being destroyed.

7 You people are stretched out on your couches now, but your good times will end. You will be taken away as prisoners to a foreign country, and you will be some of the first people taken. 8 The Lord GOD used his own name and made an oath. The LORD God All-Powerful said, "I hate what Jacob is proud of. I hate his strong towers. So I will let an enemy take the city and everything in it."

{While God was determined to punish His people, He is a merciful God and so promised to restore them in due time.}

God Promises to Restore the Kingdom

9:11 "**David's tent** has fallen, but at that time I will set it up again. I will fix its holes and repair its ruined parts. I will set it up as it was before.

13 The LORD says, "A time of great blessing is coming. Workers will still be harvesting when it is time to plow the fields again. They will still be trampling the grapes when it is time for a new crop. Sweet wine will drip from the mountains and pour from the hills. 14 I will bring my people, Israel, back from captivity. They will rebuild the ruined cities, and they will live in them. They will plant vineyards and drink the wine they produce. They will plant gardens and eat the crops they produce. 15 I will plant my people on their land, and never again will they be pulled up out of the land that I gave them."

This is what the LORD your God said.

Code name for the people of Israel.

Jesus is of "David's tent," and He ultimately will restore His people.

the book of Obadiah

Category: The 12 Minor Prophets
Author: Hosea
Theme: Pay back
Location & Date: Jerusalem, Edom; 850-840 B.C.
Version of Bible: Easy-to-Read Version (ERV)

Summary: In a time when the people of Judah were in need, the proud city of Edom turned its back on them, and for this inhospitality, the Lord promised to punish Edom. The events described in this book took place during the invasion of Judah by Babylon, during the time of the prophet Jeremiah. The people of Edom lived south of the Dead Sea and maintained strongholds high in the mountains. Because of this, they had a great sense of security. They thought they were untouchable. They were not expecting the wrath of God.

Edom Will Be Punished

Obadiah 1:1 This is the vision of Obadiah. This is what the Lord GOD says about Edom: We heard a report from the LORD. A messenger was sent to the nations. He said, "Let's go fight against Edom."

The Lord Speaks to Edom

2 "Edom, I will make you the smallest nation. Everyone will hate you very much. 3 Your pride has fooled you. You live in those caves high on the cliff. Your home is high in the hills. So you say to yourself, 'No one can bring me to the ground.'"

Edom Will Be Brought Low

4 This is what the LORD says: "Even though you fly high like the eagle and put your nest among the stars, I will bring you down from there."

{Up to this point, the people of Edom had a so-so relationship with the Judeans. When the Jews entered Edom during the time the book was written, they were met with outright hostility. Some were captured and returned back to their captors, and others were killed. In addition, the Edomites plundered Jewish cities and mocked the Jewish people. These actions were made all the more despicable by the fact that the Edomites, descendants of Esau, were cousins to the Judeans, the descendants of his brother Jacob.}

the book of Jonah

Category: *The 12 Minor Prophets*
Author: *Jonah*
Theme: *God's grace to those who don't deserve it*
Location & Date: *Nineveh; 780-750 B.C.*
Version of Bible: *Easy-to-Read Version (ERV)*
Summary: *The book of Jonah is unique among the prophetic books in that it is composed entirely of narrative rather than prophetic oracle. It recounts the story of the prophet Jonah and his struggle to deliver the Lord's message of hope to a foreign nation.*

God Calls and Jonah Runs

Jonah 1:1 The LORD spoke to Jonah son of Amittai: 2 "Nineveh is a big city. I have heard about the many evil things the people are doing there. So go there and tell them to stop doing such evil things."

3 But Jonah tried to run away from the LORD. He went to Joppa and found a boat that was going to the faraway city of Tarshish. Jonah paid money for the trip and went on the boat. He wanted to travel with the people on this boat to Tarshish and run away from the LORD.

The Great Storm

4 But the LORD brought a great storm on the sea. The wind made the sea very rough. The storm was very strong, and the boat was ready to break apart. 5 The men wanted to make the boat lighter to stop it from sinking, so they began throwing the cargo into the sea. The sailors were very afraid. Each man began praying to his god.

Jonah had gone down into the boat to lie down, and he went to sleep. 6 The captain of the boat saw Jonah and said, "Wake up! Why are you sleeping? Pray to your god! Maybe your god will hear your prayer and save us!"

What Caused This Storm?

7 Then the men said to each other, "We should throw lots to find out why this is happening to us."

So the men threw lots. The lots showed that the troubles came to them because of Jonah. 8 Then the men said to Jonah, "It is your fault that this terrible thing is happening to us. Tell us, what have you done? What is your job? Where do you come from?

What is your country? Who are your people?"

9 Jonah said to them, "I am a Hebrew. I worship the LORD, the God of heaven, who made the land and the sea."

10 Jonah told the men he was running away from the LORD. The men became very afraid when they learned this. They asked Jonah, "What terrible thing did you do against your God?"

11 The wind and the waves of the sea were becoming stronger and stronger. So the men said to Jonah, "What should we do to save ourselves? What should we do to you to make the sea calm?"

12 Jonah said to the men, "I know I did wrong—that is why the storm came on the sea. So throw me into the sea, and the sea will become calm."

13 Instead, the men tried to row the ship back to the shore, but they couldn't do it. The wind and the waves of the sea were too strong—and they were becoming stronger and stronger.

Jonah's Punishment

14 So the men cried to the LORD, "LORD, please don't say we are guilty of killing an innocent man. Please don't make us die for killing him. We know you are the LORD, and you will do whatever you want."

15 So the men threw Jonah into the sea. The storm stopped, and the sea became calm. 16 When the men saw this, they began to fear and respect the LORD. They offered a sacrifice and made special promises to the LORD.

17 When Jonah fell into the sea, the LORD chose a very big fish to swallow Jonah. He was in the stomach of the fish for **three days and three nights**.

Jesus made reference to this verse as he predicted his death and how many days He would be in the grave.

Jonah's Prayer

2:1 While Jonah was in the stomach of the fish, he prayed to the LORD his God. He said, 2 "I was in very bad trouble. I called to the LORD for help, and he answered me. I was deep in the grave. I cried to you, and you heard my voice. 3 "You threw me into the sea. Your powerful waves splashed over me. I went down, down into the deep sea. The water was all around me. 4 Then I thought, 'Now I must go where you cannot see me,' but I continued looking to your holy Temple for help.

5 **"The seawater closed over me. The water covered my mouth, and I could not breathe.** I went down, down into the deep sea. Seaweed wrapped around my head. 6 I was at the bottom of the sea, the place where the mountains begin. I thought I was locked in this prison forever, but the LORD my God took me out of my grave. God, you gave me life again!

This is what sin does - it traps you, closes in on you, and squeezes the life out of you.

7 "My soul gave up all hope, but then I remembered the LORD. I prayed to you, and you heard my prayers in your holy Temple.

8 "Some people worship useless idols, but those statues nev-

er help them. 9 I will give sacrifices to you, and I will praise and thank you. I will make special promises to you, and I will do what I promise."

Salvation Only Comes from the LORD!

10 Then the LORD spoke to the fish, and it vomited Jonah out of its stomach onto the dry land.

God Calls and Jonah Obeys

3:1 Then the LORD spoke to Jonah again and said, 2 "Go to that big city Nineveh, and say what I tell you."

3 So Jonah obeyed the LORD and went to Nineveh. It was a very large city. A person had to walk for three days to travel through it.

4 Jonah went to the center of the city and began speaking to the people. He said, "After 40 days, Nineveh will be destroyed!"

5 The people of Nineveh believed God. They decided to stop eating for a time to think about their sins. They put on special clothes to show they were sorry. All the people in the city did this, from the most important to the least important.

6 When the king of Nineveh heard about this, he left his throne, removed his robe, put on special clothes to show that he was sorry, and sat in ashes. 7 The king wrote a special message and sent it throughout the city:

A command from the king and his great rulers: For a short time no person or animal should eat anything. No herd or flock will be allowed in the fields. Nothing living in Nineveh will eat or drink water. 8 But every person and every animal must be covered with a special cloth to show they are sad. People must cry loudly to God. Everyone must change their life and stop doing bad things. 9 Who knows? Maybe God will stop being angry and change his mind, and we will not be punished.

10 God saw what the people did. He saw that they stopped doing evil. So God changed his mind and did not do what he planned. He did not punish the people.

God's Mercy Makes Jonah Angry

4:1 Jonah was not happy that God saved the city. Jonah became angry. 2 He complained to the LORD and said, "LORD, I knew this would happen! I was in my own country, and you told me to come here. At that time **I knew that you would forgive the people** of this evil city, so I decided to run away to Tarshish. I knew that you are a kind God. I knew that you show mercy and don't want to punish people. I knew that you are kind, and if these people stopped sinning, you would change your plans to destroy them. 3 So now, LORD, just kill me. It is better for me to die than to live."

4 Then the LORD said, "Do you think it is right for you to be angry?"

5 Jonah went out of the city to a place near the city on the east side. He made a shelter for himself and sat there in the shade,

> Sometimes God's salvation in our lives looks more like trouble. But in the end it is what we need.

> Jonah was unhappy because his suspicions turned out to be true: that God was too gracious, not only to Israel but also to foreign peoples such as those in Nineveh - and to us.

waiting to see what would happen to the city.

The Gourd Plant and the Worm

6 The LORD made a gourd plant grow quickly over Jonah. This made a cool place for Jonah to sit and helped him to be more comfortable. He was very happy because of this plant.

7 The next morning, God sent a worm to eat part of the plant. The worm began eating the plant, and the plant died.

8 After the sun was high in the sky, God caused a hot east wind to blow. The sun became very hot on Jonah's head, and he became very weak. He asked God to let him die. He said, "It is better for me to die than to live."

9 But God said to Jonah, "Do you think it is right for you to be angry just because this plant died?"

Jonah answered, "Yes, it is right for me to be angry! I am angry enough to die!"

10 And the LORD said, "You did nothing for that plant. You did not make it grow. It grew up in the night, and the next day it died. And now you are sad about it. 11 If you can get upset over a plant, surely I can feel sorry for a big city like Nineveh. There are many people and animals in that city. There are more than 120,000 people there who did not know they were doing wrong."

{God spared the city of Nineveh in Jonah's time, but the story doesn't end here. The fate of Nineveh is revisited during the time of the prophet Nahum, as recounted in the book of Nahum.}

the book of Micah

Category: The 12 Minor Prophets
Author: Micah
Theme: God's grace to those who don't deserve it
Location & Date: Samaria and Jerusalem; 735-710 B.C.
Version of Bible: Easy-to-Read Version (ERV)
Summary: The prophet Micah was a contemporary with Isaiah before the fall of Israel and Judah. He predicted the fall of both and indeed lived to see them invaded. While Micah's purpose was to point out the people's sins leading them to Gods judgment and wrath, he also tried to focus on the positive. Micah spoke against those who used their wealth and power to cheat the poor through extortion and fraud.

The Leaders of Israel Are to Blame

Micah 3:9 Leaders of Jacob and rulers of Israel, listen to me! You hate the right way of living! If something is straight, then you make it crooked! 10 You build Zion by murdering people. You build Jerusalem by cheating people! 11 The judges in Jerusalem accept bribes to help them decide who wins in court. The priests in Jerusalem must be paid before they will teach the people. People must pay the prophets before they will look into the future. Then those leaders expect the LORD to help them. They say, "The LORD lives here with us, so nothing bad will happen to us."

{Micah also spoke out against the corrupt political and religious leaders of the day. Despite their sin, they were deluded into a false sense of security, believing that their actions did not offend the Lord.}

The Evil Plans of People

2:1 Trouble will come to those who make plans to sin. They lie on their beds making their evil plans. Then when the morning light comes, they do what they planned, because they have the power to do what they want. 2 They want fields, so they take them. They want houses, so they take them. They cheat a man and take his house and his land.

{The common folk also violated the covenant with God by worshiping idols.}

People Will Depend on God

5:12 You will no longer try to do magic. You will have no more fortunetellers. 13 I will destroy your statues of false gods. I will pull down your memorial stones. You will not worship what your hands have made. 14 I will destroy the Asherah poles and your false gods. 15 Some nations will not listen to me, but I will show my anger and get my revenge."

1:5 This will happen because of Jacob's sin, because of the sins of the nation of Israel.

Samaria, the Cause of Sin

6 So I will change Samaria into a pile of rocks in the field, a place ready for planting grapes. I will push Samaria's stones down into the valley, leaving nothing but the foundations. 7 All her idols will be broken to pieces. And the offerings to her idols will be burned. I will destroy all her statues of false gods, because she got them as pay for being a prostitute. So those things will be taken away to be used again for paying prostitutes.

The Leaders of Israel Are to Blame

3:12 Leaders, because of you, Zion will be destroyed. It will become a plowed field. Jerusalem will become a pile of rocks. Temple Mount will be an empty hill overgrown with bushes.

{God also promised redemption and restoration. He would not abandon the people with whom He had made His covenant, but would restore them to even greater heights than they had previously attained. Micah predicted that the Lord would make His people righteous again and that He would establish His temple on a mountain where "it will be exalted above the hills, and peoples will stream to it" and that "He will teach us his ways, so that we may walk in his paths." (Micah 4:1,2).}

Praise for the Lord

7:18 There is no God like you. You take away people's guilt. God will forgive his people who survive. He will not stay angry with them forever, because he enjoys being kind. 19 He will come back and comfort us again. He will throw all our sins into the deep sea. 20 God, please be true to Jacob. Be kind and loyal to Abraham, as you promised our ancestors long ago.

{Micah predicted that a great king would emerge from a small town in Judah called Bethlehem—We know that king as Jesus.}

The Messiah to Be Born in Bethlehem

5:2 But you, **Bethlehem** Ephrathah, are the smallest town in Judah. Your family is almost too small to count, but the "**Ruler of Israel**" will come from you to rule for me. His beginnings are from ancient times, from long, long ago. 3 The Lord will let his people be defeated until the woman gives birth to her child, the promised king. Then the rest of his brothers will come back to join the people of Israel. 4 He will begin to rule Israel in the power of the LORD. Like a shepherd, he will lead his people in the wonderful name of the LORD his God. And they will live in safety because then his greatness will be known all over the world.

Jesus would one day be the one born in Bethlehem and become, not just the ruler of Israel, but the ruler of all.

the book of Nahum

Category: *The 12 Minor Prophets*
Author: *Nahum*
Theme: *Justice*
Location & Date: *Jerusalem and Nineveh; 690-640 B.C.*
Version of Bible: *Easy-to-Read Version (ERV)*

Summary: *Nahum was written shortly before the fall of the city of Nineveh. Years before, Jonah was tasked by God to warn Nineveh that their sinful lifestyle was leading them to destruction. At the last minute the people of Nineveh made an effort toward reform and were spared. In the time of Nahum, they are back to their old ways. Nineveh was, at this time, the capital of the Assyrian empire which had overrun the Northern Tribes of Israel and now posed a threat to Judah. The Assyrians were known for their wickedness, brutality and pride. Nahum was thus commissioned to warn them of God's wrath.*

The Lord Is Angry at Nineveh

Nahum 1:3 The LORD is patient, but he is also very powerful! **The LORD will punish the guilty; he will not let them go free.** He will use whirlwinds and storms to show his power. People walk on the dusty ground, but he walks on the clouds.

5 The Lord will come, and the mountains will shake and the hills will melt away. He will come, and the earth will shake with fear. The earth and everyone on it will shake with fear.

14 King of Assyria, the LORD gave this command about you: "You will not have any descendants to wear your name. I will destroy your carved idols and metal statues that are in the temple of your gods. I am preparing your grave, because your end is coming soon!"

15 Judah, look! There, coming over the mountains, is a messenger bringing good news! He says there is peace. Judah, celebrate your special festivals and do what you promised. Those worthless troublemakers will not come through and attack you again. They have all been destroyed.

3:19 Nineveh, you have been hurt badly, and nothing can heal your wound. Everyone who hears the news of your destruction claps their hands. They are all happy, because they all felt the pain you caused again and again.

{Nahum forcefully testified to God's power and anger against the city. Nineveh was completely wiped off the face of the earth.}

I do not have to worry about "paying back" people that do me wrong. God is just. He will take care of it.

the book of Habakkuk

Category: The 12 Minor Prophets
Author: Habakkuk
Theme: Hope when God seems silent
Location & Date: Jerusalem and Nineveh; 690-640 B.C.
Version of Bible: Easy-to-Read Version (ERV)
Summary: A little known prophet during the time of Jeremiah, Habakkuk questioned God's purpose in letting His chosen people face destruction.

Habakkuk Complains to God

Habakkuk 1:1 This is the message that was given to Habakkuk the prophet. 2 LORD, I continue to ask for help. When will you listen to me? I cried to you about the violence, but you did nothing! 3 People are stealing things and hurting others. They are arguing and fighting. Why do you make me look at these terrible things?

God Answers Habakkuk

2:2 The LORD answered me, "Write down what I show you. Write it clearly on a sign so that the message will be easy to read. 3 This message is about a special time in the future. This message is about the end, and it will come true. Just be patient and wait for it. That time will come; it will not be late."

20 But the LORD is in his holy temple, so the whole earth should be silent in his presence and show him respect.

Habakkuk's Prayer

3:1 The prayer of Habakkuk the prophet. 2 LORD, I have heard the news about you. I am amazed, LORD, at the powerful things you did in the past. Now I pray that you will do great things in our time. Please make these things happen in our own days. But in your anger, remember to show mercy to us.

Always Rejoice in the Lord

17 Figs might not grow on the fig trees, and grapes might not grow on the vines. Olives might not grow on the olive trees, and food might not grow in the fields. There might not be any sheep in the pens or cattle in the barns. 18 **But I will still be glad in the LORD and rejoice in God my Savior.** 19 The Lord GOD gives me my strength. He helps me run fast like a deer. He leads me safely on the mountains. To the music director. On my stringed instruments.

It is easy to praise God in the good times; harder to trust Him in the bad.

the book of Zephaniah

Category: *The 12 Minor Prophets*
Author: *Zephaniah*
Theme: *Justice and mercy*
Location & Date: *Jerusalem; 635-625 B.C.*
Version of Bible: *Easy-to-Read Version (ERV)*
Summary: *Zephaniah, a contemporary of Jeremiah, expanded God's judgment to the entire world. But he speaks of hope as well.*

The Lord's Day for Judging the People

Zephaniah 1:2 The LORD says, "I will destroy everything on earth. 3 ... I will destroy the evil people and everything that makes them sin. I will remove all people from the earth." This is what the LORD said.

15 The Lord will show his anger at that time. It will be a time of terrible troubles and a time of destruction. It will be a time of darkness—a black, cloudy, and stormy day. 16 It will be like a time of war when people hear horns and trumpets in the defense towers and protected cities.

17 The Lord said, "I will make life very hard on the people. They will walk around like the blind who don't know where they are going. That will happen because they sinned against the LORD. Their blood will be spilled on the ground. Their dead bodies will lie like dung on the ground. 18 Their gold and silver will not help them! At that time the Lord will become very upset and angry. The LORD will destroy the whole world! He will completely destroy everyone one earth!"

A Happy Song

3:14 Jerusalem, sing and be happy! Israel, shout for joy! Jerusalem, be happy and have fun! 15 The LORD stopped your punishment. He destroyed your enemies' strong towers. **King of Israel, the LORD is with you.** You don't need to worry about anything bad happening. 16 At that time Jerusalem will be told, "Be strong, don't be afraid! 17 **The LORD your God is with you**. He is like a powerful soldier. He will save you. He will show how much he loves you and how happy he is with you. He will laugh and be happy about you.

20 At that time I will lead you back home. I will bring your people back together. I will cause people everywhere to honor and praise you. You will see me bring back all the blessings you once had." This is what the Lord said.

Sounds like Jesus.

the book of Haggai

Category: The 12 Minor Prophets
Author: Haggai
Theme: Rebuilding the Temple and the people of God
Location & Date: Judah; 520 B.C.
Version of Bible: Easy-to-Read Version (ERV)

Summary: The Babylonian invasion of Jerusalem during the time of Jeremiah had left the temple of the Lord in ruin. After they were defeated, many Jews were deported to Babylon. About 50 years later, the Persians conquered the conquerors: the Babylonians were at the mercy of King Cyrus, and so too were the Jewish political prisoners. The king respected the Jewish religion, however, and allowed them to return to Jerusalem to rebuild the temple. After arriving they quickly set to work laying the foundations of what was to be the house of the Lord. They rejoiced at the semi-completion of the temple after two years of hard labor. But the neighboring peoples became suspicious of this newly restored Jewish nation and they convinced the Persians to put a halt to the construction—for fear that a taste of independence, symbolized by the construction of the temple, would inspire rebellion amongst the Jews.

The project remained suspended for 18 years until the prophet Haggai, spurred on by the Lord, took it up again. This came about during a time of trouble for the Jews in the area, who were plagued by a poor harvest that year.

It Is Time to Build the Temple

Haggai 1:3 Again Haggai received a message from the LORD. Haggai spoke this message: 4 "You people think the right time has come for you to live in nice houses. You live in houses with beautiful wooden paneling on the walls, but the Lord's house is still in ruins. 5 Now the LORD All-Powerful says, 'Think about what is happening. 6 You have planted many seeds, but you have gathered only a few crops. You have food to eat, but not enough to get full. You have something to drink, but not enough to get drunk. You have some clothes to wear, but not enough to keep warm. You earn a little money, but you don't know where it all goes. It's as though there is a hole in your pocket!'"

7 The LORD All-Powerful said, "Think about what you are doing. 8 Go up to the mountains, get the wood, and build the Temple. Then I will be pleased with the Temple, and I will be honored." This is what the LORD said.

10 That is why the sky holds back its dew and why the earth holds back its crops.

11 "I gave the command for the land and the mountains to be dry. The grain, the new wine, the olive oil, and everything the earth produces will be ruined. All the people and all the animals will become weak."

{The Lord was incensed because for 18 years (since construction was halted), His people tended to their own needs, while neglecting His house. Equipped with the knowledge of the Lord's will, Haggai was in a position to better the lot of the Jews by righting this wrong. However, by himself, he lacked the means. For that reason, he solicited the help of Zerubbabel who was the Governor of Judah. God granted him success.}

Work Begins on the New Temple

12 The LORD God had sent Haggai to speak to Zerubbabel son of Shealtiel and to the high priest, Joshua son of Jehozadak. So these men and all the people listened to the voice of the LORD their God and to the words of Haggai the prophet. And the people showed their fear and respect for the LORD their God.

13 Then Haggai, the LORD's messenger, delivered this message to the people: "The LORD says, 'I am with you!'"

14 Zerubbabel son of Shealtiel was the governor of Judah. Joshua son of Jehozadak was the high priest. The LORD made them and the rest of the people excited about **working on the Temple of their God,** the LORD All-Powerful. 15 So they began this work on the 24th day of the sixth month in the second year Darius was the king.

The Lord Encourages the People

2:6 This is what the LORD All-Powerful said, 'In just a little while, I will once again shake things up. I will shake heaven and earth, and I will shake the sea and the dry land. 7 I will shake up the nations, and they will come to you with wealth from every nation. And then I will fill this Temple with glory.' That is what the LORD All-Powerful said! 8 'All their silver really belongs to me! And all the gold is mine!' This is what the LORD All-Powerful said. 9 And the LORD All-Powerful said, 'This last Temple will be more beautiful than the first one, and I will bring peace to this place.' Remember, this is what the LORD All-Powerful said."

{Darius the Great was king of Persia and he was a great patron of the religions of his empire. When opposition arose again against the Jewish efforts, Darius supported the Jews. And so, with the inspiration of Haggai from the Lord, the enthusiasm of Zerubbabel and the Jewish people, and the backing of King Darius, the temple was completed and dedicated four years after Haggai began preaching.}

The people of Israel returned from exile and began rebuilding the temple... But soon they quit - for 18 years. The temple was finally rebuilt under the prophet Haggai; the temple was the symbol of God living among his people.

Later Jesus became the living temple - the living presence of God.

the book of Zechariah

Category: The 12 Minor Prophets
Author: Zechariah
Theme: Hope of restoration
Location & Date: Jerusalem; 520-480 B.C.
Version of Bible: Easy-to-Read Version (ERV)
Summary: Zechariah, a contemporary of Haggai, encouraged the return of the Jews from exile in Babylon.

The Lord Wants His People to Return

Zechariah 1:1 Zechariah son of Berekiah received a message from the LORD. This was in the eighth month of the second year that Darius was king in Persia. (Zechariah was the son of Berekiah, who was the son of Iddo the prophet.) This is that message:

2 The LORD became very angry with your ancestors. 3 So you must tell the people what the LORD All-Powerful says, "Come back to me, says the LORD All-Powerful, and I will come back to you." This is what the LORD All-Powerful said.

4 "Don't be like your ancestors. In the past the prophets spoke to them and said, 'The LORD All-Powerful wants you to change your evil way of living. Stop doing evil things!' But your ancestors did not listen to me." This is what the LORD said.

5 "Your ancestors are gone, and those prophets did not live forever. 6 The prophets were my servants. I used them to tell your ancestors about my laws and teachings. Your ancestors finally learned their lesson and said, 'The LORD All-Powerful did what he said he would do. He punished us for the way we lived and for all the evil things we did.' So they came back to God."

Measuring Jerusalem

2:1 Then I looked up and saw a man holding a rope for measuring things. 2 I asked him, "Where are you going?"

He said to me, "I am going to measure Jerusalem, to see how wide and how long it is."

3 Then the angel who was speaking to me left, and another angel went out to talk to him. 4 He said to him, "Run and tell that young man this: 'Jerusalem will be a city without walls, because there will be too many people and animals living there.' 5 The LORD says, 'I will be a wall of fire around her, to protect her, and to bring glory to that city, I will live there.'"

God Calls His People Home

The LORD says, 6 "Hurry! Leave the land in the North in a hurry. Yes, it is true that I scattered your people in every direction. 7 You people from Zion now live in Babylon. Escape! Run away from that city!" 8 The Lord sent me to the nations that took away your wealth. He sent me to bring you honor. And this is what the LORD All-Powerful said: "If anyone even touches you, it is as if they did it to the pupil of my eye. 9 Watch and see how I will punish them: Their own slaves will become their masters and take all their wealth." Then you will know it was the LORD All-Powerful who sent me to tell you these things.

10 The LORD says, "Zion, be happy, because I am coming, and I will live in your city. 11 At that time people from many nations will come to me. They will become my people, and I will live in your city." Then you will know it was the LORD All-Powerful who sent me to tell you these things.

12 The LORD will again choose Jerusalem to be his special city. Judah will be his share of the holy land. 13 Everyone, be quiet! The LORD is coming out of his holy house.

The Four Chariots

6:1 Then I turned around. I looked up and saw four chariots going between two bronze mountains. 2 Red horses were pulling the first chariot. Black horses were pulling the second chariot. 3 White horses were pulling the third chariot, and horses with red spots were pulling the fourth chariot. 4 I asked the angel who was talking with me, "Sir, what does this mean?"

5 The angel said, "These are the four winds. They have just come from the Lord of the whole world. 6 The black horses will go north, the red horses will go east, the white horses will go west, and the horses with red spots will go south."

7 The red spotted horses were anxious to go look at their part of the earth, so the angel told them, "Go walk through the earth." So they went walking through their part of the earth.

8 Then he shouted at me and said, "Look, those horses that were going north finished their job in Babylon. They have calmed my spirit; I am not angry now."

The Future King

9:9 People of Zion, rejoice! People of Jerusalem, shout with joy! **Look, your king is coming to you!** He is the good king who won the victory, but he is humble. **He is riding on a donkey**, on a young donkey born from a work animal.

The Lord's Promises

10:1 Pray to the LORD for rain in the springtime. The LORD will send the lightning and the rain will fall, and he will make the plants grow in each person's field.

2 People use their little statues and magic to learn what will

Christians celebrate Jesus' fulfillment of this event on Palm Sunday. John 12:14,15; pg. 281.

happen in the future, but that is useless. They see visions and tell about their dreams, but it is nothing but worthless lies. So the people are like sheep wandering here and there crying for help, but there is no shepherd to lead them.

3 The Lord says, "I am very angry with the shepherds. I made them responsible for what happens to my sheep." (The people of Judah are his flock, and the LORD All-Powerful really does take care of his flock. He cares for them as a soldier cares for his beautiful war horse.)

4 "The cornerstone, the tent peg, the war bow, and the advancing soldiers will all come from Judah together. 5 They will defeat their enemy—it will be like soldiers marching through mud in the streets. They will fight, and since the LORD is with them, they will defeat even the enemy soldiers riding horses. 6 I will make Judah's family strong. I will help Joseph's family win the war. I will bring them back safely and comfort them. It will be as if I never left them. I am the LORD their God, and I will help them.

No More False Prophets

13:7 The LORD All-Powerful says, "Sword, wake up and strike the shepherd, my friend! Strike the shepherd, and the sheep will run away. And I will punish those little ones. 8 Two-thirds of the people in the land will be struck down and die," says the LORD, "but one-third will survive. 9 Then I will test those survivors by giving them many troubles. The troubles will be like the fire a person uses to prove silver is pure. I will test them the way a person tests gold. Then they will call to me for help, and I will answer them. I will say, 'You are my people.' And they will say, 'The LORD is my God.'"

The Day of Judgment

14:1 Look, the LORD has a special day of judgment coming, when the riches you have taken will be divided in your city.

9 And the LORD will be the King of the whole world. At that time all people will worship him as the only LORD with only one name.

20 At that time even the harnesses on the horses will have the label, HOLY TO THE LORD. And all the pots used in the LORD's Temple will be just as important as the bowls used at the altar. 21 In fact, every dish in Jerusalem and Judah will have the label, HOLY TO THE LORD ALL-POWERFUL. All the people offering sacrifices will come, take those dishes, and cook their special meals in them.

At that time there will not be any merchants buying and selling things in the Temple of the LORD All-Powerful.

the book of Malachi

Category: *The 12 Minor Prophets*
Author: *Malachi*
Theme: *Not taking God seriously*
Location & Date: *Jerusalem; 430 B.C.*
Version of Bible: *Easy-to-Read Version (ERV)*

Summary: *Through the efforts of the prophets Haggai and Zachariah as well as the governor Zerubbabel, the temple was finished. Approximately 50 years later, the Jewish community was given another boost by the influx of deported Jews led by the priest Ezra, who re-instituted many lost religious practices. About 15 years later, Nehemiah returned to Jerusalem to rebuild the city walls. Under his governorship, the city of Jerusalem saw many cultural and religious reforms. However, once Nehemiah returned to Persia, the Israelites fell back into their old sinful ways. It is during this time that Malachi is thought to have prophesied.*

Their sin this time was a bit of a departure from the sins of their ancestors. They had not renounced God, exactly, nor had they started worshiping idols—a frequent agitator of God's wrath in the Old Testament. It's not that the Israelites were turning their backs on God, but rather, that they were shrugging off His religious decrees. They developed a lax attitude toward religious practices. They were merely going through the motions. It is for this lackluster attitude that Malachi, and by extension, God, rebuked them.

One of the religious decrees that the people violated had to do with animal sacrifice. The system of sacrifice was put in place by God as a way for the people to atone for sins. Rather than being punished themselves, they offered sacrifices that took their place. Since this institution was so important for their relationship with God, it should not have been taken lightly. Yet the people did not treat the practice with reverence and the priests of the temple let them get away with it.

The People Don't Respect God

Malachi 1:8 You bring blind animals as sacrifices, and that is wrong. You bring sick and crippled animals for sacrifices, and that is wrong. Try giving those sick animals as a gift to your governor. Would he accept those sick animals? No, he would not accept them." This is what the LORD All-Powerful said.

10 "I wish one of you would close the Temple doors to stop the lighting of useless fires on my altar. I am not pleased with you. I will not accept your gifts." This is what the LORD All-Powerful said.

13 You smell the food and refuse to eat it. You say it is bad. Then you bring sick, crippled, and hurt animals to me. You try to give

sick animals to me as sacrifices, but I will not accept them." This is what the LORD All-Powerful said.

{Another longstanding religious practice the Jewish people ignored was tithing. In Leviticus, it was written that the people were to give 10 percent of their income to the Lord. Tithing was the means through which the temple and all other religious institutions were maintained, but the people were complacent and skimped on their offerings.}

Stealing From God

3:8 "People should not steal things from God, but you stole things from me."

"You say, 'What did we steal from you?'

"You should have given me one-tenth of your things. You should have given me special gifts. 9 In this way your whole nation has stolen things from me, so bad things are happening to you."

10 The LORD All-Powerful says, "Try this test. Bring one-tenth of your things to me. Put them in the treasury. Bring food to my house. Test me! If you do these things, I will surely bless you. Good things will come to you like rain falling from the sky. You will have more than enough of everything. 11 I will not let pests destroy your crops. All your grapevines will produce grapes." This is what the LORD All-Powerful said.

{The effect of this reached far beyond the temples and the priests because those institutions were designed ultimately to serve the people's religious needs. In this way, the people were cheating themselves.

Malachi also spoke out against Jewish men who were marrying foreign women who worshiped idols, as well as adulterers, employers who cheated their employees, and those who oppressed the poor and foreigners. The Lord promised judgment for these sins, but he also promised good things for those who were faithful to him.}

3:1 The LORD All-Powerful says, "I am sending my messenger to prepare the way for me. Then suddenly, the Lord you are looking for will come to his temple. Yes, the messenger you are waiting for, the one who will tell about my agreement, is really coming!

2 "No one can prepare for that time or stand against him when he comes. He will be like a burning fire. He will be like the strong soap people use to make things clean. 3 He will make the Levites clean. He will make them pure, like silver is made pure with fire! He will make them pure like gold and silver. Then they will bring gifts to the LORD, and they will do things the right way. 4 Then the LORD will accept the gifts from Judah and Jerusalem. It will be as it was in the past—as the time long ago.

4:1 "That time of judgment is coming. It will be like a hot furnace. All the proud people will be punished. All the evil people will burn like straw. At that time they will be like a bush burning in the fire, and there will not be a branch or root left." This is what the

---

Margin note: This was called the "tithe" and was kind of like a 10% flat tax to support, not only the priests and the Temple, but also the government (Israel was a theocracy - where religion and the civil government were one and the same).

LORD All-Powerful said.

2 "But, for my followers, goodness will shine on you like the rising sun. And it will bring healing power like the sun's rays. You will be free and happy, like calves freed from their stalls. 3 Then you will walk on the evil people - they will be like ashes under your feet. I will make this happen at the time of judgment." This is what the LORD All-Powerful said.

5 "Look, I will send Elijah the prophet to you. He will come before that great and terrible time of judgment from the Lord. 6 Elijah will help the parents become close to their children, and he will help the children become close to their parents. This must happen, or I will come and completely destroy your country.

Part Two:
The New Testament

the books of **Matthew, Mark, Luke & John**

Category: The 4 Gospels
Authors: Matthew, Mark, Luke, John
Theme: Story of Jesus
Location & Date: Israel; A.D. 60-90
Version of Bible: Multiple Versions

Summary: Matthew told the story of Jesus from a Jewish perspective (with many quotes from the Old Testament); Mark told the story emphasizing Jesus as the mighty miracle worker; Luke told the story in an orderly way emphasizing Jesus as the teacher and friend of sinners; John told the story with images: Jesus is the Word, the light, the door, the good shepherd, the vine, the way, the truth and the life. All four told the one story. For ease of reading, the Sampler Bible presents the four gospels (Matthew, Mark, Luke, and John) as one seamless story.

Matthew's contribution will be from the New Revised Standard Version (NRSV). Mark, the New Living Translation (NLT). Luke, the New American Standard Bible (NASB). John, the New International-al Version (NIV).

Note: The 4 gospels are 4 different books, but we'll be looking at them as one.

1. The Coming of Jesus: His Ministry Begins

John 1:1 **In the beginning** was the Word, and the Word was with God, and the Word was God. 2 He was with God in the beginning. 14 The **Word became flesh** and made his **dwelling** among us. We have seen his glory, the glory of the one and only Son, who came from the Father, full of grace and truth.

In the beginning God created ... Genesis 1:1

Jesus is the Word. He is God. He became a human being. He lived among us.

Birth of John the Baptist Foretold

Luke 1:5 In the days of Herod, king of Judea, there was a priest named Zacharias, of the division of Abijah; and he had a wife from the daughters of Aaron, and her name was Elizabeth. 6 They were both righteous in the sight of God, walking blamelessly in all the commandments and requirements of the Lord. 7 But they had no child, because Elizabeth was **barren**, and they were both advanced in years.

8 Now it happened that while he was performing his priestly service before God in the appointed order of his division, 9 according to the custom of the priestly office, he was chosen by lot to enter the temple of the Lord and burn incense. 10 And the whole multitude of the people were in prayer outside at the hour of the incense offering. 11 And an angel of the Lord appeared to

Like Sarah, Rebekah, and Hannah and the mother of Samson in the Old Testament.

> Elijah, the great prophet in the Old Testament, never died and so many thought he would come back to earth one day and usher in some great era.
>
> Like Abraham and Sarah.

him, standing to the right of the altar of incense. 12 Zacharias was troubled when he saw the angel, and fear gripped him. 13 But the angel said to him, "Do not be afraid, Zacharias, for your petition has been heard, and your wife Elizabeth will bear you a son, and you will give him the name John. 14 You will have joy and gladness, and many will rejoice at his birth. 15 For he will be great in the sight of the Lord; and he will drink no wine or liquor, and he will be filled with the Holy Spirit while yet in his mother's womb. 16 And he will turn many of the sons of Israel back to the Lord their God. 17 It is he who will go as a forerunner before Him in the spirit and power of **Elijah**, to turn the hearts of the fathers back to the children, and the disobedient to the attitude of the righteous, so as to make ready a people prepared for the Lord."

18 Zacharias said to the angel, "How will I know this for certain? For I am an **old man** and my wife is **advanced in years**."

19 The angel answered and said to him, "I am Gabriel, who stands in the presence of God, and I have been sent to speak to you and to bring you this good news. 20 And behold, you shall be silent and unable to speak until the day when these things take place, because you did not believe my words, which will be fulfilled in their proper time."

21 The people were waiting for Zacharias, and were wondering at his delay in the temple. 22 But when he came out, he was unable to speak to them; and they realized that he had seen a vision in the temple; and he kept making signs to them, and remained mute. 23 When the days of his priestly service were ended, he went back home.

24 After these days Elizabeth his wife became pregnant, and she kept herself in seclusion for five months, saying, 25 "This is the way the Lord has dealt with me in the days when He looked with favor upon me, to take away my disgrace among men."

Jesus' Birth Foretold

26 Now in the sixth month the angel Gabriel was sent from God to a city in Galilee called Nazareth, 27 to a virgin engaged to a man whose name was Joseph, of the descendants of David; and the virgin's name was Mary. 28 And coming in, he said to her, "Greetings, favored one! The Lord is with you."

29 But she was very perplexed at this statement, and kept pondering what kind of salutation this was. 30 The angel said to her, "Do not be afraid, Mary; for you have found favor with God. 31 And behold, you will conceive in your womb and bear a son, and you shall name Him Jesus. 32 He will be great and will be called the Son of the Most High; and the Lord God will give Him the throne of His father David; 33 and He will reign over the house of Jacob forever, and His kingdom will have no end."

34 Mary said to the angel, "How can this be, since **I am a virgin**?"

35 The angel answered and said to her, "The Holy Spirit will come upon you, and the power of the Most High will overshadow you; and for that reason the holy Child shall be called the Son of

> The virgin birth was predicted hundreds of years before. What

God. 36 And behold, even your relative Elizabeth has also conceived a son in her old age; and she who was called barren is now in her sixth month. 37 For nothing will be **impossible** with God."

38 And Mary said, **"Behold, the bondslave of the Lord; may it be done to me according to your word."** And the angel departed from her.

Mary Visits Elizabeth

39 Now at this time Mary arose and went in a hurry to the hill country, to a city of Judah, 40 and entered the house of Zacharias and greeted Elizabeth. 41 When Elizabeth heard Mary's greeting, the baby leaped in her womb; and Elizabeth was filled with the Holy Spirit. 42 And she cried out with a loud voice and said, "Blessed are you among women, and blessed is the fruit of your womb! 43 And how has it happened to me, that the mother of my Lord would come to me? 44 For behold, when the sound of your greeting reached my ears, the baby leaped in my womb for joy. 45 And blessed is she who believed that there would be a fulfillment of what had been spoken to her by the Lord."

The Magnificat

46 And Mary said: "My soul exalts the Lord, 47 And my spirit has rejoiced in God my Savior. 48 "For He has had regard for the humble state of His bondslave; For behold, from this time on all generations will count me blessed. 49 **"For the Mighty One has done great things for me**; And holy is His name. 50 "and His mercy is upon generation after generation toward those who fear Him.

The Birth of Jesus the Messiah

Matthew 1:18 Now the birth of Jesus the Messiah took place in this way. When his mother Mary had been engaged to Joseph, but before they lived together, **she was found to be with child from the Holy Spirit**. 19 Her husband Joseph, being a righteous man and unwilling to expose her to public disgrace, planned to dismiss her quietly. 20 But just when he had resolved to do this, an angel of the Lord appeared to him in a dream and said, "Joseph, son of David, do not be afraid to take Mary as your wife, for the child conceived in her is from the Holy Spirit. 21 She will bear a son, and you are to name him Jesus, for he will save his people from their sins." 22 All this took place to fulfill what had been spoken by the Lord through the prophet:

23 "Look, the **virgin shall conceive** and bear a son, and they shall name him Emmanuel," which means, "God is with us." 24 When Joseph awoke from sleep, he did as the angel of the Lord commanded him; he took her as his wife, 25 but had no marital relations with her until she had borne a son; and he named him Jesus.

Jesus' Birth in Bethlehem

Luke 2:1 Now in those days a decree went out from Caesar Augustus, that a census be taken of all the inhabited earth. 2 This was the first census taken while Quirinius was governor of Syria. 3 And everyone was on his way to register for the census, each to

---

impossible things do you face today?

Are you ready to pray these words?

How has God, the Mighty One, done great things for you in your life?

Imagine trying to explain this to your parents.

See Isaiah 7:14 pg. 195.

his own city. 4 Joseph also went up from Galilee, from the city of Nazareth, to Judea, to the city of David which is called Bethlehem, because he was of the house and family of David, 5 in order to register along with Mary, who was engaged to him, and was with child. 6 While they were there, the days were completed for her to give birth. 7 And she gave birth to her firstborn son; and she wrapped Him in cloths, and laid Him in a manger, because there was **no room** for them in the inn.

8 In the same region there were some **shepherds** staying out in the fields and keeping watch over their flock by night. 9 And an angel of the Lord suddenly stood before them, and the glory of the Lord shone around them; and they were terribly frightened. 10 But the angel said to them, "Do not be afraid; for behold, I bring you good news of great joy which will be for all the people; 11 for today in the city of David there has been born for you a Savior, who is Christ the Lord. 12 This will be a sign for you: you will find a baby wrapped in cloths and lying in a manger." 13 And suddenly there appeared with the angel a multitude of the heavenly host praising God and saying, 14 "Glory to God in the highest, And on earth **peace** among men with whom He is pleased." 15 When the angels had gone away from them into heaven, the shepherds began saying to one another, "Let us go straight to Bethlehem then, and see this thing that has happened which the Lord has made known to us." 16 So they came in a hurry and found their way to Mary and Joseph, and the baby as He lay in the manger. 17 When they had seen this, they made known the statement which had been told them about this Child. 18 And all who heard it wondered at the things which were told them by the shepherds. 19 But Mary treasured all these things, pondering them in her heart. 20 The shepherds went back, glorifying and praising God for all that they had heard and seen, just as had been told them.

Jesus Presented at the Temple

21 And when eight days had passed, before His **circumcision**, His name was then called Jesus, the name given by the angel before He was conceived in the womb.

22 And when the days for their purification according to the law of Moses were completed, they brought Him up to Jerusalem to present Him to the Lord 23 (as it is written in the Law of the Lord, "every firstborn male that opens the womb shall be called holy to the Lord"), 24 and to offer a sacrifice according to what was said in the Law of the Lord, **"A pair of turtledoves or two young pigeons."**

25 And there was a man in Jerusalem whose name was Simeon; and this man was righteous and devout, looking for the consolation of Israel; and the Holy Spirit was upon him. 26 And it had been revealed to him by the Holy Spirit that he would not see death before he had seen the Lord's Christ. 27 And he came in the Spirit into the temple; and when the parents brought in the child Jesus, to carry out for Him the custom of the Law, 28 then he took Him into his arms, and blessed God, and said,

---

Margin notes:

How are you making room for Jesus in your life?

Shepherds were often the poor, the young, and the marginalized. Why do you think they were the first to hear of Jesus' birth?

See Isaiah 9:6, pg. 195.

The sign of being dedicated to God.

This was the offering of the poor.

29 "Now Lord, You are releasing Your bond-servant to depart in peace, According to Your word; 30 For my eyes have seen Your salvation, 31 Which You have prepared in the presence of all peoples, 32 A light of revelation to the **gentiles**, And the glory of Your people Israel."

Non-Jews

33 And His father and mother were amazed at the things which were being said about Him. 34 And Simeon blessed them and said to Mary His mother, "Behold, this Child is appointed for the fall and rise of many in Israel, and for a sign to be opposed—35 and **a sword will pierce even your own soul**—to the end that thoughts from many hearts may be revealed."

Mary would one day watch her son die on a cross.

36 And there was a prophetess, Anna the daughter of Phanuel, of the tribe of Asher. She was advanced in years and had lived with her husband seven years after her marriage, 37 and then as a widow to the age of eighty-four. She never left the temple, serving night and day with fastings and prayers. 38 At that very moment she came up and began giving thanks to God, and continued to speak of Him to all those who were looking for the redemption of Jerusalem.

Return to Nazareth

39 When they had performed everything according to the Law of the Lord, they returned to Galilee, to their own city of Nazareth. 40 The Child continued to grow and become strong, increasing in wisdom; and the grace of God was upon Him.

The Visit of the Wise Men

Matthew 2:1 In the time of King Herod, after Jesus was born in Bethlehem of Judea, **wise men** from the East came to Jerusalem, 2 asking, "Where is the child who has been born king of the Jews? For we observed his star at its rising, and have come to pay him homage." 3 When King Herod heard this, he was frightened, and all Jerusalem with him; 4 and calling together all the chief priests and scribes of the people, he inquired of them where the Messiah was to be born. 5 They told him, "In **Bethlehem** of Judea; for so it has been written by the prophet:

They didn't know the truth, but they were looking for it. How have you been looking for the truth?

Predicted by the prophet Micah.

7 Then Herod secretly called for the wise men and learned from them the exact time when the star had appeared. 8 Then he sent them to Bethlehem, saying, "Go and search diligently for the child; and when you have found him, bring me word so that I may also go and pay him homage." 9 When they had heard the king, they set out; and there, ahead of them, went the star that they had seen at its rising, until it stopped over the place where the child was. 10 When they saw that the star had stopped, they were overwhelmed with joy. 11 On entering the house, they saw the child with Mary his mother; and they knelt down and paid him homage. Then, opening their treasure chests, they offered him gifts of **gold, frankincense,** and **myrrh.** 12 And having been warned in a dream not to return to Herod, they left for their own country by another road.

Gold: Jesus as King. Frankincense: Jesus as Priest. Myrrh: Jesus' burial.

The 4 Gospels

John the Baptist Prepares the Way

Mark 1:1 This is the Good News about Jesus the Messiah, the Son of God. It began 2 just as the prophet Isaiah had written: "Look, I am sending my messenger ahead of you, and he will prepare your way. 3 He is a voice shouting in the wilderness, 'Prepare the way for the LORD's coming! Clear the road for him!'

4 This messenger was John the Baptist. He was in the wilderness and preached that people should be baptized to show that they had repented of their sins and turned to God to be forgiven. 5 All of Judea, including all the people of Jerusalem, went out to see and hear John. And when they confessed their sins, he baptized them in the Jordan River. 6 His clothes were woven from coarse camel hair, and he wore a leather belt around his waist. For food he ate locusts and wild honey. 7 John announced: "Someone is coming soon who is greater than I am—so much greater that I'm not even worthy to stoop down like a slave and untie the straps of his sandals. 8 I baptize you with water, but he will baptize you with the Holy Spirit!"

John Testifies About Jesus

John 1:29 The next day John saw Jesus coming toward him and said, "Look, the **Lamb of God**, who takes away the sin of the world!

The Baptism and Temptation of Jesus

Mark 1:10 As Jesus came up out of the water, he saw the heavens splitting apart and the Holy Spirit descending on him like a dove. 11 And a voice from heaven said, **"You are my dearly loved Son, and you bring me great joy."**

Genealogy of Jesus

Luke 3:23 When He began His ministry, Jesus Himself was about thirty years of age, being, as was supposed, the son of Joseph, the son of Eli,

Mark 1:12 The Spirit then compelled Jesus to go into the wilderness, 13 where he was tempted by Satan for **forty days**. He was out among the wild animals, and angels took care of him.

14 Later on, after John was arrested, Jesus went into Galilee, where he preached God's Good News. 15 "The time promised by God has come at last!" he announced. "The Kingdom of God is near! Repent of your sins and believe the Good News!"

The First Disciples

16 One day as Jesus was walking along the shore of the Sea of Galilee, he saw Simon and his brother Andrew throwing a net into the water, for they fished for a living. 17 Jesus called out to them, "Come, follow me, and I will show you how to fish for people!" 18 And they left their nets at once and followed him.

19 A little farther up the shore Jesus saw Zebedee's sons,

Margin notes:

The lamb was used as a sacrifice at the first Passover, making it possible for the people of Israel to be freed from their bondage to Egypt (see Exodus 12, pg 55).

Have you ever heard anyone say these words to you?

The people of Israel wandered in the desert for 40 years before they entered the Promised Land - Exodus 14:34; pg. 78.

James and John, in a boat repairing their nets. 20 He called them at once, and they also **followed** him, leaving their father, Zebedee, in the boat with the hired men.

> What or who are you following?

Call of Levi (Matthew)

Luke 5:27 After that He went out and noticed a **tax collector** named Levi sitting in the tax booth, and He said to him, "Follow Me." 28 And he left everything behind, and got up and began to follow Him.

> A self-employed IRS man of the 1st century.

29 And Levi gave a **big reception for Him** in his house; and there was a great crowd of tax collectors and other people who were reclining at the table with them. 30 The Pharisees and their scribes began grumbling at His disciples, saying, "Why do you eat and drink with the tax collectors and sinners?" 31 And Jesus answered and said to them, "**It is not those who are well who need a physician, but those who are sick.** 32 I have not come to call the righteous but sinners to repentance."

> Who in your life needs to be introduced to Jesus?
>
> Good point!

Jesus Chooses the Twelve Apostles

Mark 3:13 Afterward Jesus went up on a mountain and called out the ones he wanted to go with him. And they came to him. 14 Then **he appointed twelve** of them and called them his apostles. They were to accompany him, and he would send them out to preach, 15 giving them authority to cast out demons. 16 These are the twelve he chose: Simon (whom he named Peter), 17 James and John (the sons of Zebedee, but Jesus nicknamed them "Sons of Thunder"), 18 Andrew, Philip, Bartholomew, Matthew, Thomas, James (son of Alphaeus), Thaddaeus, Simon (the zealot), 19 Judas Iscariot (who later betrayed him).

> Just like the 12 tribes of Israel.

2. The Teaching Ministry of Jesus: Event Based

Jesus Teaches Nicodemus

John 3:1 Now there was a **Pharisee**, a man named Nicodemus who was a member of the Jewish ruling council. 2 He came to Jesus at night and said, "Rabbi, we know that you are a teacher who has come from God. For no one could perform the signs you are doing if God were not with him."

> A religious lawyer.

3 Jesus replied, "Very truly I tell you, no one can see the kingdom of God unless they are born again."

4 "How can someone be born when they are old?" Nicodemus asked. "Surely they cannot enter a second time into their mother's womb to be born!"

5 Jesus answered, "Very truly I tell you, no one can enter the kingdom of God unless they are born of water and the Spirit. 6 Flesh gives birth to flesh, but the Spirit gives birth to spirit. 7 You should not be surprised at my saying, 'You must be born again.'

8 The wind blows wherever it pleases. You hear its sound, but you cannot tell where it comes from or where it is going. So it is with everyone born of the Spirit.

9 "How can this be?" Nicodemus asked.

10 "You are Israel's teacher," said Jesus, "and do you not understand these things? 11 Very truly I tell you, we speak of what we know, and we testify to what we have seen, but still you people do not accept our testimony. 12 I have spoken to you of earthly things and you do not believe; how then will you believe if I speak of heavenly things? 13 No one has ever gone into heaven except the one who came from heaven—the Son of Man. 14 Just as Moses lifted up the **snake in the wilderness**, so the Son of Man must be lifted up, 15 that everyone who believes may have eternal life in him."

[margin: See Numbers 21.]

16 **For God so loved the world that he gave his one and only Son, that whoever believes in him shall not perish but have eternal life.** 17 For God did not send his Son into the world to condemn the world, but to save the world through him. 18 Whoever believes in him is not condemned, but whoever does not believe stands condemned already because they have not believed in the name of God's one and only Son. 19 This is the verdict: Light has come into the world, but people loved darkness instead of light because their deeds were evil. 20 Everyone who does evil hates the light, and will not come into the light for fear that their deeds will be exposed. 21 But whoever lives by the truth comes into the light, so that it may be seen plainly that what they have done has been done in the sight of God.

[margin: Here it is, the most famous verse in the Bible. Do you believe?]

John Testifies Again About Jesus

22 After this, Jesus and his disciples went out into the Judean countryside, where he spent some time with them, and baptized. 23 Now John also was baptizing at Aenon near Salim, because there was plenty of water, and people were coming and being baptized. 24 (This was before John was put in prison.) 25 An argument developed between some of John's disciples and a certain Jew over the matter of ceremonial washing. 26 They came to John and said to him, "Rabbi, that man who was with you on the other side of the Jordan—the one you testified about—look, he is baptizing, and everyone is going to him."

27 To this John replied, "A person can receive only what is given them from heaven. 28 You yourselves can testify that I said, 'I am not the Messiah but am sent ahead of him.' 29 The bride belongs to the bridegroom. The friend who attends the bridegroom waits and listens for him, and is full of joy when he hears the bridegroom's voice. That joy is mine, and it is now complete. 30 He must become greater; I must become less."

31 The one who comes from above is above all; the one who is from the earth belongs to the earth, and speaks as one from the earth. The one who comes from heaven is above all. 32 He testifies to what he has seen and heard, but no one accepts his testimony. 33 Whoever has accepted it has certified that God is

truthful. 34 For the one whom God has sent speaks the words of God, for God gives the Spirit without limit. 35 The Father loves the Son and has placed everything in his hands. 36 Whoever believes in the Son has eternal life, but whoever rejects the Son will not see life, for God's wrath remains on them.

Jesus Talks with a Samaritan Woman

John 4:5 So he came to a town in Samaria called Sychar, near the plot of ground Jacob had given to his son Joseph. 6 Jacob's well was there, and Jesus, tired as he was from the journey, sat down by the well. It was about noon. 7 When a Samaritan woman came to draw water, Jesus said to her, "Will you give me a drink?" 8 (His disciples had gone into the town to buy food.) 9 The Samaritan woman said to him, "You are a Jew and I am a Samaritan woman. How can you ask me for a drink?" (For Jews do not associate with Samaritans.)

10 Jesus answered her, "If you knew the gift of God and who it is that asks you for a drink, you would have asked him and he would have given you living water."

11 "Sir," the woman said, "you have nothing to draw with and the well is deep. Where can you get this living water? 12 Are you greater than our father Jacob, who gave us the well and drank from it himself, as did also his sons and his livestock?"

13 Jesus answered, "Everyone who drinks this water will be thirsty again, 14 but whoever drinks the water I give them will never thirst. Indeed, the water I give them will become in them a spring of water welling up to eternal life."

15 The woman said to him, "Sir, give me this water so that I won't get thirsty and have to keep coming here to draw water."

16 He told her, "Go, call your husband and come back."

17 "I have no husband," she replied.

Jesus said to her, "You are right when you say you have no husband. 18 The fact is, you have had five husbands, and the man you now have is not your husband. What you have just said is quite true."

19 "Sir," the woman said, "I can see that you are a prophet. 20 Our ancestors worshiped on this mountain, but you Jews claim that the place where we must worship is in Jerusalem."

21 "Woman," Jesus replied, "believe me, a time is coming when you will worship the Father neither on this mountain nor in Jerusalem. 22 You Samaritans worship what you do not know; we worship what we do know, for salvation is from the Jews. 23 Yet a time is coming and has now come when the true worshipers will worship the Father in the Spirit and in truth, for they are the kind of worshipers the Father seeks. 24 God is spirit, and his worshipers must worship in the Spirit and in truth."

25 The woman said, "I know that Messiah" (called Christ) "is coming. When he comes, he will explain everything to us."

26 Then Jesus declared, "I, the one speaking to you - I am he."

The Disciples Rejoin Jesus

27 Just then his disciples returned and were surprised to find him talking with a woman. But no one asked, "What do you want?" or "Why are you talking with her?"

28 Then, leaving her water jar, the woman went back to the town and said to the people, 29 "Come, see a man who told me everything I ever did. Could this be the Messiah?" 30 They came out of the town and made their way toward him.

31 Meanwhile his disciples urged him, "Rabbi, eat something."

32 But he said to them, "I have food to eat that you know nothing about."

33 Then his disciples said to each other, "Could someone have brought him food?"

34 "My food," said Jesus, "is to do the will of him who sent me and to finish his work. 35 Don't you have a saying, 'It's still four months until harvest'? I tell you, open your eyes and look at the fields! They are ripe for harvest. 36 Even now the one who reaps draws a wage and harvests a crop for eternal life, so that the sower and the reaper may be glad together. 37 Thus the saying 'One sows and another reaps' is true. 38 I sent you to reap what you have not worked for. Others have done the hard work, and you have reaped the benefits of their labor."

Many Samaritans Believe

39 Many of the Samaritans from that town believed in him because of the woman's testimony, "He told me everything I ever did." 40 So when the Samaritans came to him, they urged him to stay with them, and he stayed two days. 41 And because of his words many more became believers.

42 They said to the woman, "We no longer believe just because of what you said; now we have **heard for ourselves**, and we know that this man really is the Savior of the world."

Jesus Rejected at Nazareth

Luke 4:16 And He came to Nazareth, where He had been brought up; and as was His custom, He entered the synagogue on the Sabbath, and stood up to read. 17 And the book of the prophet Isaiah was handed to Him. And He opened the book and found the place where it was written,

18 "The Spirit of the Lord is upon me, because He anointed me to preach the gospel to the poor. He has sent me to proclaim release to the captives, and **recovery of sight to the blind**, to set free those who are oppressed, 19 to proclaim the favorable year of the Lord."

20 And He closed the book, gave it back to the attendant and sat down; and the eyes of all in the synagogue were fixed on Him.

It would seem people need to experience Jesus in some way before they recognize Him as the Savior.

See Isaiah 61:1; pg. 199.

21 And He began to say to them, "Today this Scripture has been fulfilled in your hearing." 22 And all were speaking well of Him, and wondering at the gracious words which were falling from His lips; and they were saying, "Is this not Joseph's son?" 23 And He said to them, "No doubt you will quote this proverb to Me, 'Physician, heal yourself! **Whatever we heard was done at Capernaum, do here in your hometown as well.'**" 24 And He said, "Truly I say to you, no prophet is welcome in his hometown. 25 But I say to you in truth, there were many widows in Israel in the days of Elijah, when the sky was shut up for three years and six months, when a great famine came over all the land; 26 and yet Elijah was sent to none of them, but only to **Zarephath**, in the land of Sidon, to a woman who was a widow. 27 And there were many lepers in Israel in the time of Elisha the prophet; and none of them was cleansed, but only **Naaman the Syrian**." 28 And all the people in the synagogue were filled with rage as they heard these things; 29 and they got up and drove Him out of the city, and led Him to the brow of the hill on which their city had been built, in order to throw Him down the cliff. 30 But passing through their midst, He went His way.

[margin: Jesus had healed many in Capernaum and were disappointed that He didn't do the same in his hometown.

Both non-Jews]

Luke 7:36 Now one of the Pharisees was requesting Him to dine with him, and He entered the Pharisee's house and reclined at the table. 37 And there was a woman in the city who was a sinner; and when she learned that He was reclining at the table in the Pharisee's house, she brought an alabaster vial of perfume, 38 and standing behind Him at His feet, weeping, she began to wet His feet with her tears, and kept wiping them with the hair of her head, and kissing His feet and anointing them with the perfume. 39 Now when the Pharisee who had invited Him saw this, he said to himself, "If this man were a prophet He would know who and what sort of person this woman is who is touching Him, that she is a sinner."

Parable of Two Debtors

40 And **Jesus answered him**, "Simon, I have something to say to you." And he replied, "Say it, Teacher." 41 "A moneylender had two debtors: one owed five hundred denarii, and the other fifty. 42 When they were unable to repay, he graciously forgave them both. So which of them will love him more?" 43 Simon answered and said, "I suppose the one whom he forgave more." And He said to him, "You have judged correctly." 44 Turning toward the woman, He said to Simon, "Do you see this woman? I entered your house; you gave Me no water for My feet, but she has wet My feet with her tears and wiped them with her hair. 45 You gave Me no kiss; but she, since the time I came in, has not ceased to kiss My feet. 46 You did not anoint My head with oil, but she anointed My feet with perfume. 47 For this reason I say to you, her sins, which are many, have been forgiven, for she loved much; but he who is forgiven little, loves little." 48 Then He said to her, "Your sins have been forgiven." 49 Those who were reclining at the table with Him began to say to themselves, "Who is this man who even forgives sins?" 50 And He said to the woman, "Your faith has saved you; go in peace."

[margin: Jesus answered him thus proving to Simon that he was indeed a prophet.]

The 4 Gospels

The Harvest Is Great, the Laborers Few

Matthew 9:35 Then Jesus went about all the cities and villages, teaching in their synagogues, and proclaiming the good news of the kingdom, and curing every disease and every sickness. 36 When he saw the crowds, he had compassion for them, because they were harassed and helpless, like **sheep without a shepherd**. 37 Then he said to his disciples, "The harvest is plentiful, but the laborers are few; 38 therefore ask the Lord of the harvest to send out laborers into his harvest."

> Do you ever feel like a sheep without a shepherd?

True Greatness

Matthew 18:1 At that time the disciples came to Jesus and asked, "Who is the greatest in the kingdom of heaven?" 2 He called a child, whom he put among them, 3 and said, "Truly I tell you, unless you change and become like children, you will never enter the kingdom of heaven. 4 Whoever becomes humble like this child is the greatest in the kingdom of heaven. 5 Whoever welcomes one such child in my name welcomes me.

Temptations to Sin

6 "If any of you put a stumbling block before one of these little ones who believe in me, it would be better for you if a great millstone were fastened around your neck and you were drowned in the depth of the sea.

The Rich Young Man

Matthew 19:16 Then someone came to him and said, "Teacher, what good deed must I do to have eternal life?" 17 And he said to him, "Why do you ask me about what is good? There is only one who is good. If you wish to enter into life, keep the commandments." 18 He said to him, "Which ones?" And Jesus said, "You shall not murder; You shall not commit adultery; You shall not steal; You shall not bear false witness; 19 Honor your father and mother; also, You shall love your neighbor as yourself." 20 The young man said to him, "I have kept all these; what do I still lack?" 21 Jesus said to him, "If you wish to be perfect, go, sell your possessions, and give the money to the poor, and you will have treasure in heaven; then come, follow me." 22 When the young man heard this word, he went away grieving, for he had many possessions.

23 Then Jesus said to his disciples, "Truly I tell you, it will be hard for a rich person to enter the kingdom of heaven. 24 Again I tell you, it is easier for a camel to go through the eye of a needle than for someone who is rich to enter the kingdom of God." 25 When the disciples heard this, they were greatly astounded and said, "Then who can be saved?" 26 But Jesus looked at them and said, "For mortals it is impossible, but for God all things are possible."

27 Then Peter said in reply, "Look, we have left everything and followed you. What then will we have?" 28 Jesus said to them, "Truly I tell you, at the renewal of all things, when the Son of Man is seated on the throne of his glory, you who have followed me

will also sit on twelve thrones, judging the twelve tribes of Israel. 29 And everyone who has left houses or brothers or sisters or father or mother or children or fields, for my name's sake, will receive a hundredfold, and will inherit eternal life. 30 But many who are first will be last, and the last will be first.

Woman Caught in Adultery

John 8:3 The teachers of the law and the Pharisees brought in a **woman caught in adultery.** They made her stand before the group 4 and said to Jesus, "Teacher, this woman was **caught in the act** of adultery. 5 In the Law Moses commanded us to stone such women. Now what do you say?" 6 They were using this question as a trap, in order to have a basis for accusing him.

But Jesus bent down and started to **write** on the ground with his finger. 7 When they kept on questioning him, he straightened up and said to them, "Let any one of you who is without sin be the first to throw a stone at her." 8 Again he stooped down and wrote on the ground.

9 At this, those who heard began to go away one at a time, the older ones first, until only Jesus was left, with the woman still standing there. 10 Jesus straightened up and asked her, "Woman, where are they? **Has no one condemned you?**"

11 "No one, sir," she said.

"Then neither do I condemn you," Jesus declared. "Go now and leave your life of sin."

Where was the guilty man? The men must've been looking and watching.

What do you think Jesus wrote?

Don't throw stones if you live in a glass house.

The Teaching Ministry of Jesus: His Sayings

Jesus Sermon on the Mount (Beatitudes)

Matthew 5:1 When Jesus saw the crowds, he went up the mountain; and after he sat down, his disciples came to him. 2 Then he began to speak, and taught them, saying:

3 "Blessed are the poor in spirit, for theirs is the kingdom of heaven 4 "Blessed are those who mourn, for they will be comforted. 5 "Blessed are the meek, for they will inherit the earth. 6 "Blessed are those who hunger and thirst for righteousness, for they will be filled. 7 "Blessed are the merciful, for they will receive mercy. 8 "Blessed are the pure in heart, for they will see God. 9 "Blessed are the peacemakers, for they will be called children of God. 10 "Blessed are those who are persecuted for righteousness' sake, for theirs is the kingdom of heaven. 11 "Blessed are you when people revile you and persecute you and utter all kinds of evil against you falsely on my account. 12 Rejoice and be glad, for your reward is great in heaven, for in the same way they persecuted the prophets who were before you.

Salt and Light

13 "You are the salt of the earth; but if salt has lost its taste, how

can its saltiness be restored? It is no longer good for anything, but is thrown out and trampled under foot.

14 "You are the light of the world. A city built on a hill cannot be hid. 15 No one after lighting a lamp puts it under the bushel basket, but on the lampstand, and it gives light to all in the house. 16 In the same way, let your light shine before others, so that they may see your good works and give glory to your Father in heaven.

The Law and the Prophets

17 "Do not think that I have come to abolish the law or the prophets; I have come not to abolish but to fulfill. 18 For truly I tell you, until heaven and earth pass away, not one letter, not one stroke of a letter, will pass from the law until all is accomplished. 19 Therefore, whoever breaks one of the least of these commandments, and teaches others to do the same, will be called least in the kingdom of heaven; but whoever does them and teaches them will be called great in the kingdom of heaven. 20 For I tell you, unless your righteousness exceeds that of the **scribes** and **Pharisees**, you will never enter the kingdom of heaven.

These were the most religious people of the day.

Concerning Anger

21 "You have heard that it was said to those of ancient times, 'You shall not murder'; and 'whoever murders shall be liable to judgment.' 22 But I say to you that if you are **angry** with a brother or sister, you will be liable to judgment; and if you insult a brother or sister, you will be liable to the council; and if you say, 'You fool,' you will be liable to the hell of fire. 23 So when you are offering your gift at the altar, if you remember that your brother or sister has something against you, 24 leave your gift there before the altar and go; first be reconciled to your brother or sister, and then come and offer your gift. 25 Come to terms quickly with your accuser while you are on the way to court with him, or your accuser may hand you over to the judge, and the judge to the guard, and you will be thrown into prison. 26 Truly I tell you, you will never get out until you have paid the last penny.

So many struggle with anger issues. Do you?

Concerning Adultery

27 "You have heard that it was said, 'You shall not commit adultery.' 28 But I say to you that everyone who **looks** at a woman with lust has already committed adultery with her in his heart. 29 If your right eye causes you to sin, tear it out and throw it away; it is better for you to lose one of your members than for your whole body to be thrown into hell. 30 And if your right hand causes you to sin, cut it off and throw it away; it is better for you to lose one of your members than for your whole body to go into hell.

So easy to do with the internet.

Concerning Divorce

31 "It was also said, 'Whoever divorces his wife, let him give her a certificate of divorce.' 32 But I say to you that anyone who divorces his wife, except on the ground of unchastity, causes her to commit adultery; and whoever marries a divorced woman com-

mits adultery.

Concerning Oaths

33 "Again, you have heard that it was said to those of ancient times, 'You shall not swear falsely, but carry out the vows you have made to the Lord.' 34 But I say to you, Do not swear at all, either by heaven, for it is the throne of God, 35 or by the earth, for it is his footstool, or by Jerusalem, for it is the city of the great King. 36 And do not swear by your head, for you cannot make one hair white or black. 37 Let your word be 'Yes, Yes' or 'No, No'; anything more than this comes from the evil one.

Concerning Retaliation

38 "You have heard that it was said, 'An eye for an eye and a tooth for a tooth.' 39 But I say to you, Do not resist an evildoer. But if anyone strikes you on the right cheek, turn the other also; 40 and if anyone wants to sue you and take your coat, give your cloak as well; 41 and if anyone forces you to go one mile, go also the second mile. 42 Give to everyone who begs from you, and do not refuse anyone who wants to borrow from you.

Love for Enemies

43 "You have heard that it was said, 'You shall love your neighbor and hate your enemy.' 44 But I say to you, **Love your enemies** and pray for those who persecute you, 45 so that you may be children of your Father in heaven; for he makes his sun rise on the evil and on the good, and sends rain on the righteous and on the unrighteous. 46 For if you love those who love you, what reward do you have? Do not even the tax collectors do the same? 47 And if you greet only your brothers and sisters, what more are you doing than others? Do not even the Gentiles do the same? 48 **Be perfect**, therefore, as your heavenly Father is perfect.

Really? How hard is this to do?

Another tough word.

Concerning Almsgiving

Matthew 6:1 "Beware of practicing your piety before others in order to be seen by them; for then you have no reward from your Father in heaven.

2 "So whenever you give **alms**, do not sound a trumpet before you, as the hypocrites do in the synagogues and in the streets, so that they may be praised by others. Truly I tell you, they have received their reward. 3 But when you give alms, do not let your left hand know what your right hand is doing, 4 so that your alms may be done in secret; and your Father who sees in secret will reward you.

Gifts for the poor.

Concerning Prayer

5 "And whenever you pray, do not be like the hypocrites; for they love to stand and pray in the synagogues and at the street corners, so that they may be seen by others. Truly I tell you, they have received their reward. 6 But whenever you pray, go into your room and shut the door and pray to your Father who is in secret;

and your Father who sees in secret will reward you.

7 "When you are praying, do not heap up empty phrases as the Gentiles do; for they think that they will be heard because of their many words. 8 Do not be like them, for your Father knows what you need before you ask him.

9 "Pray then in this way:

Our Father in heaven, hallowed be your name. 10 Your kingdom come. Your will be done, on earth as it is in heaven. 11 Give us this day our daily bread. 12 And forgive us our debts, as we also have forgiven our debtors. 13 And do not bring us to the time of trial, but rescue us from the evil one.

14 For if you forgive others their trespasses, your heavenly Father will also forgive you; 15 but if you do not forgive others, neither will your Father forgive your trespasses.

[margin note: This is the Lord's Prayer.]

Concerning Fasting

16 "And whenever you fast, do not look dismal, like the hypocrites, for they disfigure their faces so as to show others that they are fasting. Truly I tell you, they have received their reward. 17 But when you fast, put oil on your head and wash your face, 18 so that your fasting may be seen not by others but by your Father who is in secret; and your Father who sees in secret will reward you.

Concerning Treasures

19 "Do not store up for yourselves treasures on earth, where moth and rust consume and where thieves break in and steal; 20 but store up for yourselves treasures in heaven, where neither moth nor rust consumes and where thieves do not break in and steal. 21 For where your **treasure** is, there your heart will be also.

[margin note: But you can serve God with your wealth.]

The Sound Eye

22 "The eye is the lamp of the body. So, if your eye is healthy, your whole body will be full of light; 23 but if your eye is unhealthy, your whole body will be full of darkness. If then the light in you is darkness, how great is the darkness!

Serving Two Masters

24 "No one can serve two masters; for a slave will either hate the one and love the other, or be devoted to the one and despise the other. You cannot serve God and wealth.

Do Not Worry

25 "Therefore I tell you, do not worry about your life, what you will eat or what you will drink, or about your body, what you will wear. Is not life more than food, and the body more than clothing? 26 Look at the birds of the air; they neither sow nor reap nor gather into barns, and yet your heavenly Father feeds them. Are you not of more value than they? 27 And can any of you by worrying add a single hour to your span of life? 28 And why do you worry about

clothing? Consider the lilies of the field, how they grow; they neither toil nor spin, 29 yet I tell you, even Solomon in all his glory was not clothed like one of these. 30 But if God so clothes the grass of the field, which is alive today and tomorrow is thrown into the oven, will he not much more clothe you—you of little faith? 31 Therefore do not worry, saying, 'What will we eat?' or 'What will we drink?' or 'What will we wear?' 32 For it is the Gentiles who strive for all these things; and indeed your heavenly Father knows that you need all these things. 33 But strive first for the kingdom of God and his righteousness, and all these things will be given to you as well.

34 "So **do not worry about tomorrow**, for tomorrow will bring worries of its own. Today's trouble is enough for today.

> What are you worrying about these days?

Judging Others

Matthew 7:1 "Do not judge, so that you may not be judged. 2 For with the judgment you make you will be judged, and the measure you give will be the measure you get. 3 Why do you see the **speck** in your neighbor's eye, but do not notice the log in your own eye? 4 Or how can you say to your neighbor, 'Let me take the speck out of your eye,' while the log is in your own eye? 5 You hypocrite, first take the log out of your own eye, and then you will see clearly to take the speck out of your neighbor's eye.

> Makes sense. Why don't we do it this way?

Profaning the Holy

6 "Do not give what is holy to dogs; and do not throw your pearls before swine, or they will trample them under foot and turn and maul you.

Ask, Search, Knock

7 "**Ask**, and it will be given you; **search**, and you will find; **knock**, and the door will be opened for you. 8 For everyone who asks receives, and everyone who searches finds, and for everyone who knocks, the door will be opened. 9 Is there anyone among you who, if your child asks for bread, will give a stone? 10 Or if the child asks for a fish, will give a snake? 11 If you then, who are evil, know how to give good gifts to your children, how much more will your Father in heaven give good things to those who ask him!

> For what are you asking, seeking, and knocking on the door for?

The Golden Rule

12 "**In everything do to others as you would have them do to you**; for this is the law and the prophets.

> I bet you have heard this one before.

The Narrow Gate

13 "Enter through the narrow gate; for the gate is **wide** and the road is **easy** that leads to destruction, and there are many who take it. 14 For the gate is narrow and the road is hard that leads to life, and there are few who find it.

> It is easy to just do as everyone around you does.

A Tree and Its Fruit

15 "Beware of false prophets, who come to you in sheep's

The 4 Gospels

What kind of fruit are you bearing?

clothing but inwardly are ravenous wolves. 16 You will know them by their fruits. Are grapes gathered from thorns, or figs from thistles? 17 In the same way, every good tree bears good fruit, but the bad tree bears bad fruit. 18 A good tree cannot bear bad fruit, nor can a bad tree bear good fruit. 19 Every tree that does not bear good fruit is cut down and thrown into the fire. 20 Thus **you will know them by their fruits.**

Concerning Self-Deception

Very sobering!

21 "Not everyone who says to me, 'Lord, Lord,' will enter the kingdom of heaven, but only the one who does the will of my Father in heaven. 22 On that day many will say to me, 'Lord, Lord, did we not prophesy in your name, and cast out demons in your name, and do many deeds of power in your name?' 23 Then I will declare to them, '**I never knew you**; go away from me, you evildoers.'

Hearers and Doers

28 Now when Jesus had finished saying these things, the crowds were astounded at his teaching, 29 for he taught them as one having authority, and not as their scribes.

Teaching Ministry: The 7 "I am" Sayings of Jesus

1. "I am the Bread of Life."

The bread from heaven (manna as it was called) fell from the sky miraculously to feed the people of Israel in the desert Exodus (Exodus 16:14,15; pg. 59).

John 6:32 Jesus said to them, "Very truly I tell you, it is not **Moses** who has given you the **bread from heaven**, but it is my Father who gives you the true bread from heaven. 33 For the bread of God is the bread that comes down from heaven and gives life to the world."

34 "Sir," they said, "always give us this bread."

35 Then Jesus declared, "I am the bread of life. Whoever comes to me will never go hungry, and whoever believes in me will never be thirsty. 36 But as I told you, you have seen me and still you do not believe.

41 At this the Jews there began to grumble about him because he said, "I am the bread that came down from heaven." 42 They said, "Is this not Jesus, the son of Joseph, whose father and mother we know? How can he now say, 'I came down from heaven'?"

43 "Stop grumbling among yourselves," Jesus answered. 44 "No one can come to me unless the Father who sent me draws them, and I will raise them up at the last day. 45 It is written in the Prophets: 'They will all be taught by God.' Everyone who has heard the Father and learned from him comes to me. 46 No one has seen the Father except the one who is from God; only he has seen the Father. 47 Very truly I tell you, the one who believes has eternal life. 48 I am the bread of life. 49 Your ancestors ate the manna in the wilderness, yet they died. 50 But here is the bread

that comes down from heaven, which anyone may eat and not die. 51 I am the living bread that came down from heaven. Whoever eats this bread will live forever. This bread is my flesh, which I will give for the life of the world."

52 Then the Jews began to argue sharply among themselves, "How can this man give us his flesh to eat?"

53 Jesus said to them, "Very truly I tell you, unless you eat the flesh of the Son of Man and drink his blood, you have no life in you. 54 Whoever eats my flesh and drinks my blood has eternal life, and I will raise them up at the last day. 55 For my flesh is real food and my blood is real drink. 56 Whoever eats my flesh and drinks my blood remains in me, and I in them. 57 Just as the living Father sent me and I live because of the Father, so the one who feeds on me will live because of me. 58 This is the bread that came down from heaven. Your ancestors ate manna and died, but whoever feeds on this bread will live forever." 59 He said this while teaching in the synagogue in Capernaum.

Many Disciples Desert Jesus

60 On hearing it, many of his disciples said, "This is a hard teaching. Who can accept it?"

61 Aware that his disciples were grumbling about this, Jesus said to them, "Does this offend you? 62 Then what if you see the Son of Man ascend to where he was before! 63 The Spirit gives life; the flesh counts for nothing. The words I have spoken to you—they are full of the Spirit and life. 64 Yet there are some of you who do not believe." For Jesus had known from the beginning which of them did not believe and who would betray him. 65 He went on to say, "This is why I told you that no one can come to me unless the Father has enabled them."

66 From this time many of his disciples turned back and no longer followed him.

67 "You do not want to leave too, do you?" Jesus asked the Twelve.

68 **Simon Peter answered him, "Lord, to whom shall we go?** You have the words of eternal life. 69 We have come to believe and to know that you are the Holy One of God."

2. "I am the Light of the World."

Dispute Over Jesus' Testimony

John 8:12 When Jesus spoke again to the people, he said, "I am the light of the world. Whoever follows me will never walk in darkness, but will have the light of life."

Jesus Heals a Man Born Blind

John 9:1 As he went along, he saw a man blind from birth. 2 His disciples asked him, "Rabbi, who sinned, this man or his parents, that he was born blind?"

Good question. If you are not going to follow Jesus, who are you going to follow?

3 "Neither this man nor his parents sinned," said Jesus, "but this happened so that the works of God might be displayed in him. 4 As long as it is day, we must do the works of him who sent me. Night is coming, when no one can work. 5 While I am in the world, I am the light of the world."

John 12:44 Then Jesus cried out, "Whoever believes in me does not believe in me only, but in the one who sent me. 45 The one who looks at me is seeing the one who sent me. 46 I have come into the world as a light, so that no one who believes in me should stay in darkness."

3. "I am the Door."

The Good Shepherd and His Sheep

John 10:1 "Very truly I tell you Pharisees, anyone who does not enter the sheep pen by the gate, but climbs in by some other way, is a thief and a robber. 2 The one who enters by the gate is the shepherd of the sheep. 3 The gatekeeper opens the gate for him, and the sheep listen to his voice. He calls his own sheep by name and leads them out. 4 When he has brought out all his own, he goes on ahead of them, and his sheep follow him because they know his voice. 5 But they will never follow a stranger; in fact, they will run away from him because they do not recognize a stranger's voice." 6 Jesus used this figure of speech, but the Pharisees did not understand what he was telling them.

7 Therefore Jesus said again, "Very truly I tell you, I am the gate for the sheep. 8 All who have come before me are thieves and robbers, but the sheep have not listened to them. 9 I am the gate; whoever enters through me will be saved. They will come in and go out, and find pasture. 10 The thief comes only to steal and kill and destroy; I have come that they may have life, and have it to the full."

4. "I am the Good Shepherd."

See Psalms 23, pg. 108.

John 10:11 "I am the good shepherd. The good shepherd lays down his life for **the sheep**. 12 The hired hand is not the shepherd and does not own the sheep. So when he sees the wolf coming, he abandons the sheep and runs away. Then the wolf attacks the flock and scatters it. 13 The man runs away because he is a hired hand and cares nothing for the sheep.

On the cross.

14 "I am the good shepherd; I know my sheep and my sheep know me—15 just as the Father knows me and I know the Father—and **I lay down my life** for the sheep. 16 I have other sheep that are not of this sheep pen. I must bring them also. They too will listen to my voice, and there shall be one flock and one shepherd. 17 The reason my Father loves me is that I lay down my life—only to take it up again. 18 No one takes it from me, but I lay it down of my own accord. I have authority to lay it down and authority to take it up again. This command I received from my Father."

5. "I am the Resurrection and the Life."

{Lazarus, a friend of Jesus, had died and was in the grave for four days when Jesus came on the scene and talked with Martha, the sister of Lazarus.}

John 11:21 "Lord," Martha said to Jesus, "if you had been here, my brother would not have died. 22 But I know that even now God will give you whatever you ask."

23 Jesus said to her, "Your brother will rise again."

24 Martha answered, "I know he will rise again in the resurrection at the last day."

25 Jesus said to her, "I am the resurrection and the life. The one who believes in me will live, even though they die; 26 and whoever lives by believing in me will never die. **Do you believe this?**"

How about you? Do you believe this?

27 "Yes, Lord," she replied, "I believe that you are the Messiah, the Son of God, who is to come into the world."

Jesus Raises Lazarus From the Dead

38 Jesus, once more deeply moved, came to the tomb. It was a cave with a stone laid across the entrance. 39 "Take away the stone," he said.

"But, Lord," said Martha, the sister of the dead man, "by this time there is a bad odor, for he has been there four days."

40 Then Jesus said, "Did I not tell you that if you believe, you will see the glory of God?"

41 So they took away the stone. Then Jesus looked up and said, "Father, I thank you that you have heard me. 42 I knew that you always hear me, but I said this for the benefit of the people standing here, that they may believe that you sent me."

43 When he had said this, Jesus called in a loud voice, "Lazarus, come out!" 44 The dead man came out, his hands and feet wrapped with strips of linen, and a cloth around his face.

Jesus said to them, "Take off the grave clothes and let him go."

6. "I am the Way and the Truth and the Life."

Jesus Comforts His Disciples

John 14:1 "Do not let your hearts be troubled. You believe in God; believe also in me. 2 My Father's **house** has many rooms; if that were not so, would I have told you that I am going there to prepare a place for you? 3 And if I go and prepare a place for you, I will come back and take you to be with me that you also may be where I am. 4 You know the way to the place where I am going."

Heaven

Jesus the Way to the Father

5 Thomas said to him, "Lord, we don't know where you are going, so how can we know the way?"

6 Jesus answered, "**I am the way** and the truth and the life. No

If you are not following the way of Jesus, what way are you following?

one comes to the Father except through me. 7 If you really know me, you will know my Father as well. From now on, you do know him and have seen him."

7. "I am the Vine."

John 15:1 "I am the true vine, and my Father is the gardener. 2 He cuts off every branch in me that bears no fruit, while every branch that does bear fruit he **prunes** so that it will be even more fruitful.

How has God been pruning you lately?

4 Remain in me, as I also remain in you. No branch can bear fruit by itself; it must remain in the vine. Neither can you bear fruit unless you remain in me.

5 "I am the vine; you are the branches. If you remain in me and I in you, you will bear much fruit; apart from me you can do nothing. 6 If you do not remain in me, you are like a branch that is thrown away and withers; such branches are picked up, thrown into the fire and burned. 7 If you remain in me and my words remain in you, ask whatever you wish, and it will be done for you. 8 This is to my Father's glory, **that you bear much fruit**, showing yourselves to be my disciples.

What kind of fruit are you bearing?

9 "As the Father has loved me, so have I loved you. Now remain in my love. 10 If you keep my commands, you will remain in my love, just as I have kept my Father's commands and remain in his love. 11 I have told you this so **that my joy may be in you** and that your joy may be complete. 12 My command is this: Love each other as I have loved you. 13 Greater love has no one than this: to lay down one's life for one's friends. 14 You are my friends if you do what I command. 15 I no longer call you servants, because a servant does not know his master's business. Instead, I have called you friends, for everything that I learned from my Father I have made known to you. 16 You did not choose me, but I chose you and appointed you so that you might go and bear fruit—fruit that will last—and so that whatever you ask in my name the Father will give you.

This is God's desire for you - JOY!

The Teaching Ministry of Jesus: Other Sayings

Luke 11:33 "No one, after lighting a lamp, puts it away in a cellar nor under a basket, but on the lampstand, so that those who enter may see the light. 34 The eye is the lamp of your body; when your eye is clear, your whole body also is full of light; but when it is bad, your body also is full of darkness. 35 Then watch out that the light in you is not darkness. 36 If therefore your whole body is full of light, with no dark part in it, it will be wholly illumined, as when the lamp illumines you with its rays."

Woes upon the Pharisees

37 Now when He had spoken, a Pharisee asked Him to have lunch with him; and He went in, and reclined at the table. 38 When the Pharisee saw it, he was surprised that He had not first ceremo-

nially washed before the meal. 39 But the Lord said to him, "Now you Pharisees clean the outside of the cup and of the platter; but inside of you, you are full of robbery and wickedness. 40 You foolish ones, did not He who made the outside make the inside also? 41 But give that which is within as charity, and then all things are clean for you.

42 "But woe to you Pharisees! For you pay tithe of mint and rue and every kind of garden herb, and yet disregard justice and the love of God; but these are the things you should have done without neglecting the others. 43 Woe to you Pharisees! For you love the chief seats in the synagogues and the respectful greetings in the market places.

God Knows and Cares

Luke 12:4 "I say to you, My friends, do not be afraid of those who kill the body and after that have no more that they can do. 5 But I will warn you whom to fear: fear the One who, after He has killed, has authority to cast into hell; yes, I tell you, fear Him! 6 Are not five sparrows sold for two cents? Yet not one of them is **forgotten** before God. 7 Indeed, the very hairs of your head are all numbered. Do not fear; you are more valuable than many sparrows.

8 "And I say to you, everyone who confesses Me before men, the Son of Man will confess him also before the angels of God; 9 but he who denies Me before men will be denied before the angels of God. 10 And everyone who speaks a word against the Son of Man, it will be forgiven him; but he who blasphemes against the Holy Spirit, it will not be forgiven him. 11 When they bring you before the synagogues and the rulers and the authorities, do not worry about how or what you are to speak in your defense, or what you are to say; 12 for the Holy Spirit will teach you in that very hour what you ought to say."

Covetousness Denounced

Luke 12:22 And He said to His disciples, "For this reason I say to you, do not **worry** about your life, as to what you will eat; nor for your body, as to what you will put on. 23 For life is more than food, and the body more than clothing. 24 Consider the ravens, for they neither sow nor reap; they have no storeroom nor barn, and yet God feeds them; how much more valuable you are than the birds! 25 **And which of you by worrying can add a single hour to his life's span?** 26 If then you cannot do even a very little thing, why do you worry about other matters? 27 Consider the lilies, how they grow: they neither toil nor spin; but I tell you, not even Solomon in all his glory clothed himself like one of these. 28 But if God so clothes the grass in the field, which is alive today and tomorrow is thrown into the furnace, how much more will He clothe you? You men of little faith! 29 And do not seek what you will eat and what you will drink, and do not keep worrying. 30 For all these things the nations of the world eagerly seek; but your Father knows that you need these things. 31 But seek His kingdom, and these things will be added to you. 32 Do not be afraid, little flock, for your Father has chosen gladly to give you the kingdom.

Perhaps you at times have felt forgotten, ignored, and all alone. You never are.

Meditation is going over the same thought over and over. Worry is negative meditation.

Something to think about.

33 "Sell your possessions and give to charity; make yourselves money belts which do not wear out, an unfailing treasure in heaven, where no thief comes near nor moth destroys. 34 For where your treasure is, there your heart will be also.

Reproving Another Who Sins

Matthew 18:15 **"If another member of the church sins against you, go and point out the fault when the two of you are alone.** If the member listens to you, you have regained that one. 16 But if you are not listened to, take one or two others along with you, so that every word may be confirmed by the evidence of two or three witnesses. 17 If the member refuses to listen to them, tell it to the church; and if the offender refuses to listen even to the church, let such a one be to you as a Gentile and a tax collector.

> *What we often do instead is share our hurt with someone else who then passes the story to someone else, and on it on it goes.*

The Teaching Ministry of Jesus: The Parables

The Parable of the Sower

Matthew 13:1 ... Jesus went out of the house and sat beside the sea. 2 Such great crowds gathered around him that he got into a boat and sat there, while the whole crowd stood on the beach. 3 And he told them many things in parables, saying: "Listen! A sower went out to sow. 4 And as he sowed, some seeds fell on the **path**, and the birds came and ate them up. 5 Other seeds fell on **rocky ground**, where they did not have much soil, and they sprang up quickly, since they had no depth of soil. 6 But when the sun rose, they were scorched; and since they had no root, they withered away. 7 Other seeds fell among **thorns**, and the thorns grew up and choked them. 8 Other seeds fell on **good soil** and brought forth grain, some a hundredfold, some sixty, some thirty. 9 Let anyone with ears listen!"

> *Which of the 4 soils can you relate to?*

The Parable of the Sower Explained

18 "Hear then the parable of the sower. 19 When anyone hears the word of the kingdom and does not understand it, the evil one comes and snatches away what is sown in the heart; this is what was sown on the **path**. 20 As for what was sown on **rocky ground**, this is the one who hears the word and immediately receives it with joy; 21 yet such a person has no root, but endures only for a while, and when trouble or persecution arises on account of the word, that person immediately falls away. 22 As for what was sown among **thorns**, this is the one who hears the word, but the cares of the world and the lure of wealth choke the word, and it yields nothing. 23 But as for what was sown on **good soil**, this is the one who hears the word and understands it, who indeed bears fruit and yields, in one case a hundredfold, in another sixty, and in another thirty."

The Parable of Weeds Among the Wheat

24 He put before them another parable: "The kingdom of heav-

en may be compared to someone who sowed good seed in his field; 25 but while everybody was asleep, an enemy came and sowed weeds among the wheat, and then went away. 26 So when the plants came up and bore grain, then the weeds appeared as well. 27 And the slaves of the householder came and said to him, 'Master, did you not sow good seed in your field? Where, then, did these weeds come from?' 28 He answered, 'An enemy has done this.' The slaves said to him, 'Then do you want us to go and gather them?' 29 But he replied, 'No; for in gathering the weeds you would uproot the wheat along with them. 30 Let both of them grow together until the harvest; and at harvest time I will tell the reapers, Collect the weeds first and bind them in bundles to be burned, but gather the wheat into my barn.'"

The Parable of the Mustard Seed

31 He put before them another parable: "The kingdom of heaven is like a mustard seed that someone took and sowed in his field; 32 it is the smallest of all the seeds, but when it has grown it is the greatest of shrubs and becomes a tree, so that the birds of the air come and make nests in its branches."

The Parable of the Yeast

33 He told them another parable: "The kingdom of heaven is like yeast that a woman took and mixed in with three measures of flour until all of it was leavened."

The Use of Parables

34 Jesus told the crowds all these things in parables; without a parable he told them nothing. 35 This was to fulfill what had been spoken through the prophet:

"I will open my mouth to speak in parables; I will proclaim what has been hidden from the foundation of the world."

Jesus Explains the Parable of the Weeds

36 Then he left the crowds and went into the house. And his disciples approached him, saying, "Explain to us the parable of the weeds of the field." 37 He answered, "The one who sows the good seed is the Son of Man; 38 the field is the world, and the good seed are the children of the kingdom; the weeds are the children of the evil one, 39 and the enemy who sowed them is the devil; the harvest is the end of the age, and the reapers are angels. 40 Just as the weeds are collected and burned up with fire, so will it be at the end of the age. 41 The Son of Man will send his angels, and they will collect out of his kingdom all causes of sin and all evildoers, 42 and they will throw them into the furnace of fire, where there will be weeping and gnashing of teeth. 43 Then the righteous will shine like the sun in the kingdom of their Father. Let anyone with ears listen!

Three Parables

44 "The kingdom of heaven is like treasure hidden in a field,

which someone found and hid; then in his joy he goes and sells all that he has and buys that field.

45 "Again, the kingdom of heaven is like a merchant in **search** of fine pearls; 46 on finding one pearl of great value, he went and sold all that he had and bought it.

47 "Again, the kingdom of heaven is like a net that was thrown into the sea and caught fish of every kind; 48 when it was full, they drew it ashore, sat down, and put the good into baskets but threw out the bad. 49 So it will be at the end of the age. The angels will come out and separate the evil from the righteous 50 and throw them into the furnace of fire, where there will be weeping and gnashing of teeth.

The Parable of the Good Samaritan

Luke 10:25 And a lawyer stood up and put Him to the test, saying, "Teacher, what shall I do to inherit eternal life?" 26 And He said to him, "What is written in **the Law**? How does it read to you?" 27 And he answered, "you shall love the lord your god with all your heart, and with all your soul, and with all your strength, and with all your mind; and your neighbor as yourself." 28 And He said to him, "You have answered correctly; do this and you will live." 29 But wishing to justify himself, he said to Jesus, "And **who is my neighbor?**"

30 Jesus replied and said, "A man was going down from Jerusalem to Jericho, and fell among robbers, and they stripped him and beat him, and went away leaving him half dead. 31 And by chance a **priest** was going down on that road, and when he saw him, he passed by on the other side. 32 Likewise a **Levite** also, when he came to the place and saw him, passed by on the other side. 33 But a **Samaritan**, who was on a journey, came upon him; and when he saw him, he felt compassion, 34 and came to him and bandaged up his wounds, pouring oil and wine on them; and he put him on his own beast, and brought him to an inn and took care of him. 35 On the next day he took out two denarii and gave them to the innkeeper and said, 'Take care of him; and whatever more you spend, when I return I will repay you.' 36 Which of these three do you think proved to be a neighbor to the man who fell into the robbers' hands?" 37 And he said, "The one who showed mercy toward him." Then Jesus said to him, "Go and do the same."

The Parable of the Rich Fool

Luke 12:16 And He told them a parable, saying, "The land of a rich man was very productive. 17 And he began reasoning to himself, saying, 'What shall I do, since I have no place to store my crops?' 18 Then he said, 'This is what I will do: I will tear down my barns and build larger ones, and there I will store all my grain and my goods. 19 And I will say to my soul, "Soul, you have many goods laid up for many years to come; take your ease, eat, drink and be merry."' 20 But God said to him, 'You fool! This very night your soul is required of you; and now who will own what you have prepared?' 21 So is the man who stores up **treasure for himself**, and

---

Finding the truth is worth the effort of looking.

The word "Law" often stands for the Ten Commandments.

Good question.

A priest would be declared "unclean" if he touched blood.
A Levite was a religious official.
Samaritans were looked down upon by the average Jewish person in those days.

Where are you laying up your treasures?

is not rich toward God."

Parable of the Fig Tree

Luke 13:6 And He began telling this parable: "A man had a fig tree which had been planted in his vineyard; and he came looking for fruit on it and did not find any. 7 And he said to the vineyard-keeper, 'Behold, for three years I have come looking for fruit on this fig tree without finding any. Cut it down! Why does it even use up the ground?' 8 And he answered and said to him, 'Let it alone, sir, for this year too, until I dig around it and **put in fertilizer**; 9 and if it bears fruit next year, fine; but if not, cut it down.'"

A metaphor for God's patience with us.

The Parable of the Great Banquet

Luke 14:15 When one of those who were reclining at the table with Him heard this, he said to Him, "Blessed is everyone who will eat bread in the kingdom of God!"

The Parable of the Dinner

16 But He said to him, "A man was giving a big dinner, and he invited many; 17 and at the dinner hour he sent his slave to say to those who had been invited, 'Come; for everything is ready now.' 18 But they all alike began to make **excuses**. The first one said to him, 'I have bought a piece of land and I need to go out and look at it; please consider me excused.' 19 Another one said, 'I have bought five yoke of oxen, and I am going to try them out; please consider me excused.' 20 Another one said, 'I have married a wife, and for that reason I cannot come.' 21 And the slave came back and reported this to his master. Then the head of the household became angry and said to his slave, 'Go out at once into the streets and lanes of the city and bring in here the poor and crippled and blind and lame.' 22 And the slave said, 'Master, what you commanded has been done, and still there is room.' 23 And the master said to the slave, 'Go out into the highways and along the hedges, and compel them to come in, so that my house may be filled. 24 For I tell you, none of those men who were invited shall taste of my dinner.'"

In other words... We are too busy for God and His Kingdom. What are your best excuses for not getting involved?

The Lost Sheep

Luke 15:1 Now all the tax collectors and the sinners were coming near Him to listen to Him. 2 Both the Pharisees and the scribes began to grumble, saying, "This man receives sinners and eats with them."

3 So He told them this parable, saying, 4 "What man among you, if he has a hundred sheep and has lost one of them, does not leave the ninety-nine in the open pasture and go after the one which is lost until he finds it? 5 When he has found it, he lays it on his shoulders, rejoicing. 6 And when he comes home, he calls together his friends and his neighbors, saying to them, 'Rejoice with me, for I have found my sheep which was lost!' 7 I tell you that in the same way, there will be more joy in heaven over one sinner who repents than over ninety-nine righteous persons who

need no repentance.

The Lost Coin

8 "Or what woman, if she has ten silver coins and loses one coin, does not light a lamp and sweep the house and search carefully until she finds it? 9 When she has found it, she calls together her friends and neighbors, saying, 'Rejoice with me, for I have found the coin which I had lost!' 10 In the same way, I tell you, there is joy in the presence of the angels of God over one sinner who repents."

The Prodigal Son

11 And He said, "A man had two sons. 12 The younger of them said to his father, 'Father, give me the share of the estate that falls to me.' So he divided his wealth between them. 13 And not many days later, the younger son gathered everything together and went on a journey into a distant country, and there he squandered his estate with loose living. 14 Now when he had spent everything, a severe famine occurred in that country, and he began to be impoverished. 15 So he went and hired himself out to one of the citizens of that country, and he sent him into his fields to feed **swine**. 16 And he would have gladly filled his stomach with the pods that the swine were eating, and no one was giving anything to him. 17 **But when he came to his senses**, he said, 'How many of my father's hired men have more than enough bread, but I am dying here with hunger! 18 I will get up and go to my father, and will say to him, "Father, I have sinned against heaven, and in your sight; 19 I am no longer worthy to be called your son; make me as one of your hired men."' 20 So he got up and came to his father. **But while he was still a long way off, his father saw him and felt compassion for him, and ran and embraced him and kissed him.** 21 And the son said to him, 'Father, I have sinned against heaven and in your sight; **I am no longer worthy to be called your son.**' 22 But the father said to his slaves, 'Quickly bring out the best robe and put it on him, and put a ring on his hand and sandals on his feet; 23 and bring the fattened calf, kill it, and let us eat and celebrate; 24 for this son of mine was dead and has come to life again; he was lost and has been found.' And they began to celebrate.

25 "Now his older son was in the field, and when he came and approached the house, he heard music and dancing. 26 And he summoned one of the servants and began inquiring what these things could be. 27 And he said to him, 'Your brother has come, and your father has killed the fattened calf because he has received him back safe and sound.' 28 But he became angry and was not willing to go in; and his father came out and began pleading with him. 29 But he answered and said to his father, 'Look! For so many years I have been serving you and I have never neglected a command of yours; and yet you have never given me a young goat, so that I might celebrate with my friends; 30 but when this son of yours came, who has devoured your wealth with prostitutes, you killed the fattened calf for him.' 31 And he said to him, **'Son, you have always been with me, and all that is mine is yours.** 32 But

---

Margin notes:

For the Jews swine or pigs were unclean animals.

What was his motive? Sorrow or hunger?

His father accepted him back before the son even said he was sorry.

Notice the son didn't say, "Make me one of your hired servants." He didn't say it because he had already been accepted back as a son.

In other words: "I love you as much as your younger brother." Jesus was inviting the we had to celebrate and rejoice, for this brother of yours was dead and has begun to live, and was lost and has been found.'"

Story of the Rich Man and Lazarus

Luke 16:19 "Now there was a rich man, and he habitually dressed in purple and fine linen, joyously living in splendor every day. 20 And a poor man named Lazarus was laid at his gate, covered with sores, 21 and longing to be fed with the crumbs which were falling from the rich man's table; besides, even the dogs were coming and licking his sores. 22 Now the poor man died and was carried away by the angels to Abraham's bosom; and the rich man also died and was buried. 23 In Hades he lifted up his eyes, being in torment, and *saw Abraham far away and Lazarus in his bosom. 24 And he cried out and said, 'Father Abraham, have mercy on me, and send Lazarus so that he may dip the tip of his finger in water and cool off my tongue, for I am in agony in this flame.' 25 But Abraham said, 'Child, remember that during your life you received your good things, and likewise Lazarus bad things; but now he is being comforted here, and you are in agony. 26 And besides all this, between us and you there is a great chasm fixed, so that those who wish to come over from here to you will not be able, and that none may cross over from there to us.' 27 And he said, 'Then I beg you, father, that you send him to my father's house— 28 for I have five brothers—in order that he may warn them, so that they will not also come to this place of torment.' 29 But Abraham *said, 'They have Moses and the Prophets; let them hear them.' 30 But he said, 'No, father Abraham, but if someone goes to them from the dead, they will repent!' 31 But he said to him, '**If they do not listen to Moses and the Prophets, they will not be persuaded even if someone rises from the dead.**'"

The Parable of the Pharisee and the Tax Collector

Luke 18:9 And He also told this parable to some people who trusted in themselves that they were righteous, and viewed others with contempt: 10 "Two men went up into the temple to pray, one a Pharisee and the other a tax collector. 11 The Pharisee stood and was praying this to himself: 'God, I thank You that I am not like other people: swindlers, unjust, adulterers, or even like this tax collector. 12 I fast twice a week; I pay tithes of all that I get.' 13 But the tax collector, standing some distance away, was even unwilling to lift up his eyes to heaven, but was beating his breast, saying, 'God, be merciful to me, the sinner!' 14 I tell you, this man went to his house justified rather than the other; for everyone who exalts himself will be humbled, but he who humbles himself will be exalted."

The Parable of the Ten Bridesmaids

Matthew 25:1 "Then the kingdom of heaven will be like this. Ten bridesmaids took their lamps and went to meet the bridegroom. 2 Five of them were foolish, and five were wise. 3 When the foolish took their lamps, they took no oil with them; 4 but the wise took flasks of oil with their lamps. 5 As the bridegroom was

---

scribes and Pharisees mentioned in Luke 15:1 to the party.

How could this be true?

You might be saying to yourself: "I thank God I am humble like the tax collector - not like this Pharisee." But then you would be out-phariseeing the pharisee.

delayed, all of them became drowsy and slept. 6 But at midnight there was a shout, 'Look! Here is the bridegroom! Come out to meet him.' 7 Then all those bridesmaids got up and trimmed their lamps. 8 The foolish said to the wise, 'Give us some of your oil, for our lamps are going out.' 9 But the wise replied, 'No! There will not be enough for you and for us; you had better go to the dealers and buy some for yourselves.' 10 And while they went to buy it, the bridegroom came, and those who were ready went with him into the wedding banquet; and the door was shut. 11 Later the other bridesmaids came also, saying, 'Lord, lord, open to us.' 12 But he replied, 'Truly I tell you, I do not know you.' 13 Keep awake therefore, for you know neither the day nor the hour.

The Parable of the Talents

14 "For it is as if a man, going on a journey, summoned his slaves and entrusted his property to them; 15 to one he gave five talents, to another two, to another one, to each according to his ability. Then he went away. 16 The one who had received the five talents went off at once and traded with them, and made five more talents. 17 In the same way, the one who had the two talents made two more talents. 18 But the one who had received the one talent went off and dug a hole in the ground and hid his master's money. 19 After a long time the master of those slaves came and settled accounts with them. 20 Then the one who had received the five talents came forward, bringing five more talents, saying, 'Master, you handed over to me five talents; see, I have made five more talents.' 21 His master said to him, 'Well done, good and trustworthy slave; you have been trustworthy in a few things, I will put you in charge of many things; enter into the joy of your master.' 22 And the one with the two talents also came forward, saying, 'Master, you handed over to me two talents; see, I have made two more talents.' 23 His master said to him, 'Well done, good and trustworthy slave; you have been trustworthy in a few things, I will put you in charge of many things; enter into the joy of your master.' 24 Then the one who had received the one talent also came forward, saying, 'Master, I knew that you were a harsh man, reaping where you did not sow, and gathering where you did not scatter seed; 25 so **I was afraid, and I went and hid your talent** in the ground. Here you have what is yours.' 26 But his master replied, 'You wicked and lazy slave! You knew, did you, that I reap where I did not sow, and gather where I did not scatter? 27 Then you ought to have invested my money with the bankers, and on my return I would have received what was my own with interest. 28 So take the talent from him, and give it to the one with the ten talents. 29 For to all those who have, more will be given, and they will have an abundance; but from those who have nothing, even what they have will be taken away. 30 As for this worthless slave, throw him into the outer darkness, where there will be weeping and gnashing of teeth.'

How are you hiding the talents that you have been given?

The Judgment of the Nations

31 "When the Son of Man comes in his glory, and all the angels with him, then he will sit on the throne of his glory. 32 All the nations will be gathered before him, and he will separate people one from another as a shepherd separates the sheep from the goats, 33 and he will put the sheep at his right hand and the goats at the left. 34 Then the king will say to those at his right hand, 'Come, you that are blessed by my Father, inherit the kingdom prepared for you from the foundation of the world; 35 for I was hungry and you gave me food, I was thirsty and you gave me something to drink, I was a stranger and you welcomed me, 36 I was naked and you gave me clothing, I was sick and you took care of me, I was in prison and you visited me.' 37 Then the righteous will answer him, 'Lord, when was it that we saw you hungry and gave you food, or thirsty and gave you something to drink? 38 And when was it that we saw you a stranger and welcomed you, or naked and gave you clothing? 39 And when was it that we saw you sick or in prison and visited you?' 40 And the king will answer them, 'Truly I tell you, just as you did it to one of the least of these who are members of my family, you did it to me.' 41 Then he will say to those at his left hand, 'You that are accursed, depart from me into the eternal fire prepared for the devil and his angels; 42 for I was hungry and you gave me no food, I was thirsty and you gave me nothing to drink, 43 I was a stranger and you did not welcome me, naked and you did not give me clothing, sick and in prison and you did not visit me.' 44 Then they also will answer, 'Lord, when was it that we saw you hungry or thirsty or a stranger or naked or sick or in prison, and did not take care of you?' 45 Then he will answer them, 'Truly I tell you, just as you did not do it to one of the least of these, you did not do it to me.' 46 And these will go away into eternal punishment, but the righteous into eternal life."

3. The Miracles of Jesus

Water to Wine

John 2:1 On the third day a wedding took place at Cana in Galilee. Jesus' mother was there, 2 and Jesus and his disciples had also been invited to the wedding. 3 When the wine was gone, Jesus' mother said to him, "They have no more wine."

4 "Woman, why do you involve me?" Jesus replied. "My hour has not yet come."

5 His mother said to the servants, "Do whatever he tells you."

6 Nearby stood six stone water jars, the kind used by the Jews for ceremonial washing, each holding from twenty to thirty gallons.

7 Jesus said to the servants, "Fill the jars with water"; so they filled them to the brim.

8 Then he told them, "Now draw some out and take it to the master of the banquet."

They did so, 9 and the master of the banquet tasted the water that had been turned into wine. He did not realize where it had come from, though the servants who had drawn the water knew. Then he called the bridegroom aside 10 and said, "Everyone brings out the choice wine first and then the cheaper wine after the guests have had too much to drink; but you have saved the best till now."

11 What Jesus did here in Cana of Galilee was the first of the signs through which he revealed his glory; and his disciples believed in him.

Heals Leper

Mark 1:40 A man with leprosy came and knelt in front of Jesus, begging to be healed. "If you are willing, you can heal me and make me clean," he said.

41 Moved with compassion, Jesus reached out and **touched** him. "I am willing," he said. "Be healed!" 42 Instantly the leprosy disappeared, and the man was healed.

> Jesus touched the man, a leper, an untouchable, before he healed him as if to say, "I love you, I accept you as you are."

The Healing at the Pool

John 5:2 Now there is in Jerusalem near the Sheep Gate a pool, which in Aramaic is called Bethesda and which is surrounded by five covered colonnades. 3 Here a great number of disabled people used to lie—the blind, the lame, the paralyzed. 5 One who was there had been an invalid for thirty-eight years. 6 When Jesus saw him lying there and learned that he had been in this condition for a long time, he asked him, "Do you want to get well?"

7 "Sir," the invalid replied, "I have no one to help me into the pool when the water is stirred. While I am trying to get in, someone else goes down ahead of me."

8 Then Jesus said to him, "Get up! Pick up your mat and walk." 9 At once the man was cured; he picked up his mat and walked.

The day on which this took place was a Sabbath, 10 and so the Jewish leaders said to the man who had been healed, "It is the Sabbath; the law forbids you to carry your mat."

11 But he replied, "The man who made me well said to me, 'Pick up your mat and walk.'"

12 So they asked him, "Who is this fellow who told you to pick it up and walk?"

13 The man who was healed had no idea who it was, for Jesus had slipped away into the crowd that was there.

Jesus Heals a Centurion's Servant

Luke 7:1 ... He went to Capernaum.

2 And a centurion's slave, who was highly regarded by him, was sick and about to die. 3 When he heard about Jesus, he sent some Jewish elders asking Him to come and save the life of his slave. 4 When they came to Jesus, they earnestly implored Him, saying,

"He is worthy for You to grant this to him; 5 for he loves our nation and it was he who built us our synagogue." 6 Now Jesus started on His way with them; and when He was not far from the house, the centurion sent friends, saying to Him, "Lord, do not trouble Yourself further, for I am not worthy for You to come under my roof; 7 for this reason I did not even consider myself worthy to come to You, but just say the word, and my servant will be healed. 8 For I also am a man placed under authority, with soldiers under me; and I say to this one, 'Go!' and he goes, and to another, 'Come!' and he comes, and to my slave, 'Do this!' and he does it." 9 Now when Jesus heard this, He marveled at him, and turned and said to the crowd that was following Him, "I say to you, not even in Israel have I found such great faith." 10 When those who had been sent returned to the house, they found the slave in good health.

The Pigs

Matthew 8:28 When he came to ... the country of the Gadarenes, two demoniacs coming out of the tombs met him. They were so fierce that no one could pass that way. 29 Suddenly they shouted, "What have you to do with us, Son of God? Have you come here to torment us before the time?" 30 Now a large herd of swine was feeding at some distance from them. 31 The demons begged him, "If you cast us out, send us into the herd of swine." 32 And he said to them, "Go!" So they came out and entered the swine; and suddenly, **the whole herd rushed down the steep bank into the sea and perished in the water**. 33 The swineherds ran off, and on going into the town, they told the whole story about what had happened to the demoniacs. 34 Then the whole town came out to meet Jesus; and when they saw him, they begged him to leave their neighborhood.

The goal of all evil in your life is to destroy you and all you love.

Jesus Heals in Response to Faith

21 Jesus got into the boat again and went back to the other side of the lake, where a large crowd gathered around him on the shore. 22 Then a leader of the local synagogue, whose name was Jairus, arrived. When he saw Jesus, he fell at his feet, 23 pleading fervently with him. "My little daughter is dying," he said. "Please come and lay your hands on her; heal her so she can live."

24 Jesus went with him, and all the people followed, crowding around him. 25 A woman in the crowd had suffered for twelve years with constant bleeding. 26 She had suffered a great deal from many doctors, and over the years she had spent everything she had to pay them, but she had gotten no better. In fact, she had gotten worse. 27 She had heard about Jesus, so she came up behind him through the crowd and touched his robe. 28 For she thought to herself, "If I can just touch his robe, I will be healed." 29 Immediately the bleeding stopped, and she could feel in her body that she had been healed of her terrible condition.

30 Jesus realized at once that healing power had gone out from him, so he turned around in the crowd and asked, "Who touched my robe?"

31 His disciples said to him, "Look at this crowd pressing

around you. How can you ask, 'Who touched me?'"

32 But he kept on looking around to see who had done it. 33 Then the frightened woman, trembling at the realization of what had happened to her, came and fell to her knees in front of him and told him what she had done. 34 And he said to her, "Daughter, your faith has made you well. Go in peace. Your suffering is over."

While he was still speaking to her, messengers arrived from the home of Jairus, the leader of the synagogue. They told him, "Your daughter is dead. There's no use troubling the Teacher now."

36 But Jesus overheard them and said to Jairus, **"Don't be afraid. Just have faith."**

> *Not always easy to do.*

37 Then Jesus stopped the crowd and wouldn't let anyone go with him except Peter, James, and John (the brother of James). 38 When they came to the home of the synagogue leader, Jesus saw much commotion and weeping and wailing. 39 He went inside and asked, "Why all this commotion and weeping? The child isn't dead; she's only asleep."

40 The crowd laughed at him. But he made them all leave, and he took the girl's father and mother and his three disciples into the room where the girl was lying. 41 Holding her hand, he said to her, "Talitha koum," which means "Little girl, get up!" 42 And the girl, who was twelve years old, immediately stood up and walked around! They were overwhelmed and totally amazed. 43 Jesus gave them strict orders not to tell anyone what had happened, and then he told them to give her something to eat.

Feeding of the 5,000

{Jesus withdrew to Bethsaida but the crowds followed Him.}

Luke 9:11 He began speaking to them about the kingdom of God and curing those who had need of healing. He began speaking to them about the kingdom of God and curing those who had need of healing.

> *The people in Jesus' day would have remembered that Elisha, the prophet, who lived hundreds of years before, did this same miracle - multiplying loaves of bread to feed 100 in this same region of Israel. See 2 Kings 4:42, 43; pg. 133.*

12 Now the day was ending, and the twelve came and said to Him, "Send the crowd away, that they may go into the surrounding villages and countryside and find lodging and get something to eat; for here we are in a desolate place." 13 But He said to them, "You give them something to eat!" And they said, "We have no more than five loaves and two fish, unless perhaps we go and buy food for all these people." 14 (For there were about five thousand men.) And He said to His disciples, "Have them sit down to eat in groups of about fifty each." 15 They did so, and had them all sit down. 16 Then He took the five loaves and the two fish, and looking up to heaven, He blessed them, and broke them, and kept giving them to the disciples to set before the people. 17 And they all ate and were satisfied; and the broken pieces which they had left over were picked up, twelve baskets full.

Jesus Walks on the Water

Matthew 14:22 ... he made the disciples get into the boat and go on ahead to the other side, while he dismissed the crowds. 23 And after he had dismissed the crowds, he went up the mountain by himself to pray. When evening came, he was there alone, but by this time the boat, battered by the waves, was far from the land, for the wind was against them. 25 And early in the morning he came walking toward them on the sea. 26 But when the disciples saw him walking on the sea, they were terrified, saying, "It is a ghost!" And they cried out in fear. 27 But immediately Jesus spoke to them and said, "Take heart, it is I; do not be afraid."

28 Peter answered him, "Lord, if it is you, command me to come to you on the water." 29 He said, "Come." So Peter got out of the boat, started walking on the water, and came toward Jesus. 30 But **when he noticed the strong wind, he became frightened, and beginning to sink, he cried out, "Lord, save me!"** 31 Jesus immediately reached out his hand and caught him, saying to him, "You of little faith, why did you doubt?" 32 When they got into the boat, the wind ceased. 33 And those in the boat worshiped him, saying, "Truly you are the Son of God."

Lesson: "keep your eyes of Jesus, not the storm" or "stay in the boat."

Blind Man at Bethsaida

Mark 8:22 When they arrived at Bethsaida, some people brought a blind man to Jesus, and they begged him to touch the man and heal him. 23 Jesus took the blind man by the hand and led him out of the village. Then, spitting on the man's eyes, he laid his hands on him and asked, "Can you see anything now?"

24 The man looked around. "Yes," he said, "I see people, but I can't see them very clearly. They look like trees walking around."

25 Then Jesus placed his hands on the man's eyes again, and his eyes were opened. His sight was completely restored, and he could see everything clearly.

Boy with Evil Spirit

Mark 9:17 One of the men in the crowd spoke up and said, "Teacher, I brought my son so you could heal him. He is possessed by an evil spirit that won't let him talk. 18 And whenever this spirit seizes him, it throws him violently to the ground. Then he foams at the mouth and grinds his teeth and becomes rigid. So I asked your disciples to cast out the evil spirit, but they couldn't do it."

19 Jesus said to them, "You faithless people! How long must I be with you? How long must I put up with you? Bring the boy to me."

20 So they brought the boy. But when the evil spirit saw Jesus, it threw the child into a violent convulsion, and he fell to the ground, writhing and foaming at the mouth.

21 "How long has this been happening?" Jesus asked the boy's father.

He replied, "Since he was a little boy. 22 The spirit often throws

> Doubt is sometimes evidence of faith. You have to believe something before you can doubt it.

him into the fire or into water, trying to kill him. Have mercy on us and help us, if you can."

23 "What do you mean, 'If I can'?" Jesus asked. "Anything is possible if a person believes."

24 The father instantly cried out, "**I do believe, but help me overcome my unbelief!**"

25 When Jesus saw that the crowd of onlookers was growing, he rebuked the evil spirit. "Listen, you spirit that makes this boy unable to hear and speak," he said. "I command you to come out of this child and never enter him again!"

26 Then the spirit screamed and threw the boy into another violent convulsion and left him. The boy appeared to be dead. A murmur ran through the crowd as people said, "He's dead." 27 But Jesus took him by the hand and helped him to his feet, and he stood up.

28 Afterward, when Jesus was alone in the house with his disciples, they asked him, "Why couldn't we cast out that evil spirit?"

29 Jesus replied, "This kind can be cast out only by prayer."

4. The Plot to Kill Jesus

{Jesus raised his friend Lazarus from the dead. The common people were thrilled; the religious leaders were fearful.}

The Plot to Kill Jesus

John 11:45 Therefore many of the Jews who had come to visit Mary, and had seen what Jesus did, believed in him. 46 But some of them went to the Pharisees and told them what Jesus had done. 47 Then the chief priests and the Pharisees called a meeting of the Sanhedrin.

"What are we accomplishing?" they asked. "Here is this man performing many signs. 48 If we let him go on like this, everyone will believe in him, and then the Romans will come and take away both our temple and our nation."

49 Then one of them, named Caiaphas, who was high priest that year, spoke up, "You know nothing at all! 50 You do not realize that it is better for you that one man die for the people than that the whole nation perish."

51 He did not say this on his own, but as high priest that year he prophesied that Jesus would die for the Jewish nation, 52 and not only for that nation but also for the scattered children of God, to bring them together and make them one. 53 So from that day on they plotted to take his life.

54 Therefore Jesus no longer moved about publicly among the people of Judea. Instead he withdrew to a region near the wilderness, to a village called Ephraim, where he stayed with his disciples.

55 When it was almost time for the Jewish **Passover**, many went up from the country to Jerusalem for their ceremonial cleansing before the Passover. 56 They kept looking for Jesus, and as they stood in the temple courts they asked one another, "What do you think? Isn't he coming to the festival at all?" 57 But the chief priests and the Pharisees had given orders that anyone who found out where Jesus was should report it so that they might arrest him.

See Exodus 12, pg. 55.

Jesus Anointed at Bethany

John 12:1 Six days before the Passover, Jesus came to Bethany, where Lazarus lived, whom Jesus had raised from the dead. 2 Here a dinner was given in Jesus' honor. Martha served, while Lazarus was among those reclining at the table with him. 3 Then Mary took about a pint of pure nard, an expensive perfume; she poured it on Jesus' feet and wiped his feet with her hair. And the house was filled with the fragrance of the perfume.

4 But one of his disciples, Judas Iscariot, who was later to betray him, objected, 5 "Why wasn't this perfume sold and the money given to the poor? It was worth a year's wages." 6 He did not say this because he cared about the poor but because he was a thief; as keeper of the money bag, he used to help himself to what was put into it.

7 "Leave her alone," Jesus replied. "It was intended that she should save this perfume for the day of my burial. 8 You will always have the poor among you, but you will not always have me."

9 Meanwhile a large crowd of Jews found out that Jesus was there and came, not only because of him but also to see Lazarus, whom he had raised from the dead. 10 So the chief priests made plans to kill Lazarus as well, 11 for on account of him many of the Jews were going over to Jesus and believing in him.

Jesus Comes to Jerusalem as King

12 The next day the great crowd that had come for the festival heard that Jesus was on his way to Jerusalem. 13 They took palm branches and went out to meet him, shouting,

"Hosanna!"

"Blessed is he who comes in the name of the Lord!"

"Blessed is the king of Israel!"

14 Jesus found a young donkey and sat on it, as it is written: 15 **"Do not be afraid, Daughter Zion; see, your king is coming, seated on a donkey's colt."**

See Zechariah 9:9, pg. 239.

Luke 19:39 Some of the Pharisees in the crowd said to Him, "Teacher, rebuke Your disciples." 40 But Jesus answered, "I tell you, if these become silent, the stones will cry out!"

41 When He approached Jerusalem, He saw the city and wept over it, 42 saying, "If you had known in this day, even you, the things which make for peace! But now they have been hidden from your eyes. 43 For the days will come upon you when your

enemies will throw up a barricade against you, and surround you and hem you in on every side, 44 and they will level you to the ground and your children within you, and they will not leave in you one stone upon another, because you did not recognize the time of your visitation."

Traders Driven from the Temple

45 Jesus entered the temple and began to drive out those who were selling, 46 saying to them, "It is written, 'and my house shall be a house of prayer,' but you have made it a robbers' den."

47 And He was teaching daily in the temple; but the chief priests and the scribes and the leading men among the people were trying to destroy Him, 48 and they could not find anything that they might do, for all the people were hanging on to every word He said.

Jesus Anointed at Bethany

Mark 14:1 It was now two days before Passover and the Festival of Unleavened Bread. The leading priests and the teachers of religious law were still looking for an opportunity to capture Jesus secretly and kill him. 2 "But not during the Passover celebration," they agreed, "or the people may riot."

Judas Agrees to Betray Jesus

10 Then Judas Iscariot, one of the twelve disciples, went to the leading priests to arrange to betray Jesus to them. 11 They were delighted when they heard why he had come, and they promised to give him money. So he began looking for an opportunity to betray Jesus.

The Last Supper

12 On the first day of the Festival of Unleavened Bread, when the Passover lamb is sacrificed, Jesus' disciples asked him, "Where do you want us to go to prepare the Passover meal for you?"

13 So Jesus sent two of them into Jerusalem with these instructions: "As you go into the city, a man carrying a pitcher of water will meet you. Follow him. 14 At the house he enters, say to the owner, 'The Teacher asks: Where is the guest room where I can eat the Passover meal with my disciples?' 15 He will take you upstairs to a large room that is already set up. That is where you should prepare our meal." 16 So the two disciples went into the city and found everything just as Jesus had said, and they prepared the Passover meal there.

17 In the evening Jesus arrived with the twelve disciples.

Jesus Washes His Disciples' Feet

John 13:1 It was just before the Passover Festival. Jesus knew that the hour had come for him to leave this world and go to the Father. Having loved his own who were in the world, he loved them to the end.

2 The evening meal was in progress, and the devil had already prompted Judas, the son of Simon Iscariot, to betray Jesus. 3 Jesus knew that the Father had put all things under his power, and that he had come from God and was returning to God; 4 so he got up from the meal, took off his outer clothing, and wrapped a towel around his waist. 5 After that, he poured water into a basin and began to wash his disciples' feet, drying them with the towel that was wrapped around him.

6 He came to Simon Peter, who said to him, "Lord, are you going to wash my feet?"

7 Jesus replied, "You do not realize now what I am doing, but later you will understand."

8 "No," said Peter, "you shall never wash my feet."

Jesus answered, "Unless I wash you, you have no part with me."

9 "Then, Lord," Simon Peter replied, "not just my feet but my hands and my head as well!"

10 Jesus answered, "Those who have had a bath need only to wash their feet; their whole body is clean. And you are clean, though not every one of you." 11 For he knew who was going to betray him, and that was why he said not every one was clean.

12 When he had finished washing their feet, he put on his clothes and returned to his place. "Do you understand what I have done for you?" he asked them. 13 "You call me 'Teacher' and 'Lord,' and rightly so, for that is what I am. 14 Now that I, your Lord and Teacher, have washed your feet, you also should wash one another's feet. 15 I have set you an example that you should do as I have done for you. 16 Very truly I tell you, no servant is greater than his master, nor is a messenger greater than the one who sent him. 17 Now that you know these things, you will be blessed if you do them.

Mark 14:18 As they were at the table eating, Jesus said, "I tell you the truth, one of you eating with me here will betray me."

19 Greatly distressed, each one asked in turn, "Am I the one?"

20 He replied, "It is one of you twelve who is eating from this bowl with me. 21 For the Son of Man must die, as the Scriptures declared long ago. But how terrible it will be for the one who betrays him. It would be far better for that man if he had never been born!"

22 As they were eating, Jesus took some bread and blessed it. Then he broke it in pieces and gave it to the disciples, saying, "Take it, for this is my body."

23 And he took a cup of wine and gave thanks to God for it. He gave it to them, and they all drank from it. 24 And he said to them, "This is my blood, which confirms the covenant between God and his people. It is poured out as a sacrifice for many. 25 I tell you the truth, I will not drink wine again until the day I drink it new in the Kingdom of God."

Your Sorrow Will Turn into Joy

John 16:16 Jesus went on to say, "In a little while you will see me no more, and then after a little while you will see me."

17 At this, some of his disciples said to one another, "What does he mean by saying, 'In a little while you will see me no more, and then after a little while you will see me,' and 'Because I am going to the Father'?" 18 They kept asking, "What does he mean by 'a little while'? We don't understand what he is saying."

See Habakkuk 3:17, pg. 234.

19 Jesus saw that they wanted to ask him about this, so he said to them, "Are you asking one another what I meant when I said, 'In a little while you will see me no more, and then after a little while you will see me'? 20 Very truly I tell you, you will weep and mourn while the world rejoices. **You will grieve, but your grief will turn to joy.** 21 A woman giving birth to a child has pain because her time has come; but when her baby is born she forgets the anguish because of her joy that a child is born into the world. 22 So with you: Now is your time of grief, but I will see you again and you will rejoice, and no one will take away your joy.

Mark 14:26 Then they sang a hymn and went out to the Mount of Olives.

Jesus Predicts Peter's Denial

27 On the way, Jesus told them, "All of you will desert me. For the Scriptures say,

'God will strike the Shepherd, and the sheep will be scattered.'

28 But after I am raised from the dead, I will go ahead of you to Galilee and meet you there."

29 Peter said to him, "Even if everyone else deserts you, I never will."

30 Jesus replied, "I tell you the truth, Peter—this very night, before the rooster crows twice, you will deny three times that you even know me."

31 "No!" Peter declared emphatically. "Even if I have to die with you, I will never deny you!" And all the others vowed the same.

Jesus Prays in Gethsemane

32 They went to the olive grove called Gethsemane, and Jesus said, "Sit here while I go and pray." 33 He took Peter, James, and John with him, and he became deeply troubled and distressed. 34 He told them, "My soul is crushed with grief to the point of death. Stay here and keep watch with me."

A good way to pray for all of us.

35 He went on a little farther and fell to the ground. He prayed that, if it were possible, the awful hour awaiting him might pass him by. 36 "Abba, Father," he cried out, "everything is possible for you. Please take this cup of suffering away from me. Yet **I want your will to be done, not mine.**"

37 Then he returned and found the disciples asleep. He said to Peter, "Simon, are you asleep? Couldn't you watch with me even

one hour? 38 Keep watch and pray, so that you will not give in to temptation. For the spirit is willing, but the body is weak."

39 Then Jesus left them again and prayed the same prayer as before. 40 When he returned to them again, he found them sleeping, for they couldn't keep their eyes open. And they didn't know what to say.

41 When he returned to them the third time, he said, "Go ahead and sleep. Have your rest. But no—the time has come. The Son of Man is betrayed into the hands of sinners. 42 Up, let's be going. Look, my betrayer is here!"

Jesus Is Betrayed and Arrested

43 And immediately, even as Jesus said this, Judas, one of the twelve disciples, arrived with a crowd of men armed with swords and clubs. They had been sent by the leading priests, the teachers of religious law, and the elders. 44 The traitor, Judas, had given them a prearranged signal: "You will know which one to arrest when I greet him with a kiss. Then you can take him away under guard." 45 As soon as they arrived, Judas walked up to Jesus. "Rabbi!" he exclaimed, and gave him the kiss.

46 Then the others grabbed Jesus and arrested him. 47 But one of the men with Jesus pulled out his sword and struck the high priest's slave, slashing off his ear.

48 Jesus asked them, "Am I some dangerous revolutionary, that you come with swords and clubs to arrest me? 49 Why didn't you arrest me in the Temple? I was there among you teaching every day. But these things are happening to fulfill what the Scriptures say about me."

50 Then all his disciples deserted him and ran away. 51 One young man following behind was clothed only in a long linen shirt. When the mob tried to grab him, 52 he slipped out of his shirt and ran away naked.

Jesus Before the Council

53 They took Jesus to the high priest's home where the leading priests, the elders, and the teachers of religious law had gathered. 54 Meanwhile, Peter followed him at a distance and went right into the high priest's courtyard. There he sat with the guards, warming himself by the fire.

55 Inside, the leading priests and the entire high council were trying to find evidence against Jesus, so they could put him to death. But they couldn't find any. 56 Many false witnesses spoke against him, but they contradicted each other. 57 Finally, some men stood up and gave this false testimony: 58 "We heard him say, 'I will destroy this Temple made with human hands, and in three days I will build another, made without human hands.'" 59 But even then they didn't get their stories straight!

60 Then the high priest stood up before the others and asked Jesus, "Well, aren't you going to answer these charges? What do

See Isaiah 53:7, pg. 198.

you have to say for yourself?" 61 But **Jesus was silent** and made no reply. Then the high priest asked him, "Are you the Messiah, the Son of the Blessed One?"

62 Jesus said, "I AM. And you will see the Son of Man seated in the place of power at God's right hand and coming on the clouds of heaven."

63 Then the high priest tore his clothing to show his horror and said, "Why do we need other witnesses? 64 You have all heard his blasphemy. What is your verdict?"

"Guilty!" they all cried. "He deserves to die!"

65 Then some of them began to spit at him, and they blindfolded him and beat him with their fists. "Prophesy to us," they jeered. And the guards slapped him as they took him away.

Peter Denies Jesus

66 Meanwhile, Peter was in the courtyard below. One of the servant girls who worked for the high priest came by 67 and noticed Peter warming himself at the fire. She looked at him closely and said, "You were one of those with Jesus of Nazareth."

68 But Peter denied it. "I don't know what you're talking about," he said, and he went out into the entryway. Just then, a rooster crowed.

69 When the servant girl saw him standing there, she began telling the others, "This man is definitely one of them!" 70 But Peter denied it again.

A little later some of the other bystanders confronted Peter and said, "You must be one of them, because you are a Galilean."

71 Peter swore, "A curse on me if I'm lying—I don't know this man you're talking about!" 72 And immediately the rooster crowed the second time.

Suddenly, Jesus' words flashed through Peter's mind: "Before the rooster crows twice, you will deny three times that you even know me." And he broke down and wept.

Jesus Brought Before Pilate

Matthew 27:1 When morning came, all the chief priests and the elders of the people conferred together against Jesus in order to bring about his death. 2 They bound him, led him away, and handed him over to Pilate the governor.

The Suicide of Judas

3 When Judas, his betrayer, saw that Jesus was condemned, he repented and brought back the thirty pieces of silver to the chief priests and the elders. 4 He said, "I have sinned by betraying innocent blood." But they said, "What is that to us? See to it yourself." 5 Throwing down the pieces of silver in the temple, he departed; and he went and hanged himself. 6 But the chief priests, taking the pieces of silver, said, "It is not lawful to put them into the

treasury, since they are blood money." 7 After conferring together, they used them to buy the potter's field as a place to bury foreigners. 8 For this reason that field has been called the Field of Blood to this day. 9 Then was fulfilled what had been spoken through the prophet Jeremiah, "And they took the **thirty pieces of silver**, the price of the one on whom a price had been set, on whom some of the people of Israel had set a price, 10 and they gave them for the **potter's field**, as the Lord commanded me."

> This was predicted by the prophet Zechariah hundreds of years before.

Pilate Questions Jesus

11 Now Jesus stood before the governor; and the governor asked him, "Are you the King of the Jews?" Jesus said, "You say so." 12 But when he was accused by the chief priests and elders, he did not answer. 13 Then Pilate said to him, "Do you not hear how many accusations they make against you?" 14 But he gave him no answer, not even to a single charge, so that the governor was greatly amazed.

Jesus Before Herod

Luke 23:8 Now Herod was very glad when he saw Jesus; for he had wanted to see Him for a long time, because he had been hearing about Him and was hoping to see some sign performed by Him. 9 And he questioned Him at some length; but He answered him nothing. 10 And the chief priests and the scribes were standing there, accusing Him vehemently. 11 And Herod with his soldiers, after treating Him with contempt and mocking Him, dressed Him in a gorgeous robe and sent Him back to Pilate. 12 Now Herod and Pilate became friends with one another that very day; for before they had been enemies with each other.

Pilate Seeks Jesus' Release

13 Pilate summoned the chief priests and the rulers and the people, 14 and said to them, "You brought this man to me as one who incites the people to rebellion, and behold, having examined Him before you, I have found no guilt in this man regarding the charges which you make against Him. 15 No, nor has Herod, for he sent Him back to us; and behold, nothing deserving death has been done by Him. 16 Therefore I will punish Him and release Him." 17 [Now he was obliged to release to them at the feast one prisoner.]

18 But they cried out all together, saying, "Away with this man, and release for us Barabbas!" 19 (He was one who had been thrown into prison for an insurrection made in the city, and for murder.) 20 Pilate, wanting to release Jesus, addressed them again, 21 but they kept on calling out, saying, "Crucify, crucify Him!" 22 And he said to them the third time, "Why, what evil has this man done? I have found in Him no guilt demanding death; therefore I will punish Him and release Him." 23 But they were insistent, with loud voices asking that He be crucified. And their voices began to prevail. 24 And Pilate pronounced sentence that their demand be granted. 25 And he released the man they were asking for who had been thrown into prison for insurrection and

murder, but he delivered Jesus to their will.

Jesus Sentenced to Be Crucified

John 19:1 Then Pilate took Jesus and had him flogged. 2 The soldiers twisted together a crown of thorns and put it on his head. They clothed him in a purple robe 3 and went up to him again and again, saying, "Hail, king of the Jews!" And they slapped him in the face.

4 Once more Pilate came out and said to the Jews gathered there, "Look, I am bringing him out to you to let you know that I find no basis for a charge against him." 5 When Jesus came out wearing the crown of thorns and the purple robe, Pilate said to them, "Here is the man!"

6 As soon as the chief priests and their officials saw him, they shouted, "Crucify! Crucify!"

But Pilate answered, "You take him and crucify him. As for me, I find no basis for a charge against him."

7 The Jewish leaders insisted, "We have a law, and according to that law he must die, because he claimed to be the Son of God."

8 When Pilate heard this, he was even more afraid, 9 and he went back inside the palace. "Where do you come from?" he asked Jesus, but Jesus gave him no answer. 10 "Do you refuse to speak to me?" Pilate said. "Don't you realize I have power either to free you or to crucify you?"

11 Jesus answered, "You would have no power over me if it were not given to you from above. Therefore the one who handed me over to you is guilty of a greater sin."

12 From then on, Pilate tried to set Jesus free, but the Jewish leaders kept shouting, "If you let this man go, you are no friend of Caesar. Anyone who claims to be a king opposes Caesar."

13 When Pilate heard this, he brought Jesus out and sat down on the judge's seat at a place known as the Stone Pavement (which in Aramaic is Gabbatha). 14 It was the day of Preparation of the Passover; it was about noon.

"Here is your king," Pilate said to the Jews.

15 But they shouted, "Take him away! Take him away! Crucify him!"

"Shall I crucify your king?" Pilate asked.

"We have no king but Caesar," the chief priests answered.

16 Finally Pilate handed him over to them to be crucified.

5. The Death of Jesus

17 Carrying his own cross, he went out to the place of the Skull (which in Aramaic is called Golgotha).

Simon Bears the Cross

Luke 23:26 When they led Him away, they seized a man, Simon of Cyrene, coming in from the country, and placed on him the cross to carry behind Jesus.

27 And following Him was a large crowd of the people, and of women who were mourning and lamenting Him. 28 But Jesus turning to them said, "Daughters of Jerusalem, stop weeping for Me, but weep for yourselves and for your children. 29 For behold, the days are coming when they will say, 'Blessed are the barren, and the wombs that never bore, and the breasts that never nursed.' 30 Then they will begin to say to the mountains, 'fall on us,' and to the hills, 'cover us.' 31 For if they do these things when the tree is green, what will happen when it is dry?"

32 Two others also, who were criminals, were being led away to be put to death with Him.

The Crucifixion

33 When they came to the place called The Skull, there they crucified Him and the criminals, one on the right and the other on the left.

The 7 Words of the Cross

Word One ...

Luke 23:34 But Jesus was saying, "Father, forgive them; for they do not know what they are doing." And they cast lots, dividing up His garments among themselves. 35 And the people stood by, looking on. And even the rulers were sneering at Him, saying, "He saved others; let Him save Himself if this is the Christ of God, His Chosen One."

37 and saying, "If You are the King of the Jews, save Yourself!" 38 Now there was also an inscription above Him, "this is the king of the Jews."

Word Two ...

Luke 23:39 One of the criminals who were hanged there was hurling abuse at Him, saying, "Are You not the Christ? Save Yourself and us!" 40 But the other answered, and rebuking him said, "Do you not even fear God, since you are under the same sentence of condemnation? 41 And we indeed are suffering justly, for we are receiving what we deserve for our deeds; but this man has done nothing wrong." 42 And he was saying, "Jesus, remember me when You come in Your kingdom!" 43 And He said to him, "Truly I say to you, today you shall be with Me in Paradise."

Word Three ...

John 19:23 When the soldiers crucified Jesus, they took his clothes, dividing them into four shares, one for each of them, with the undergarment remaining. This garment was seamless, woven in one piece from top to bottom.

The 4 Gospels

Psalm 22

24 "Let's not tear it," they said to one another. "Let's decide by lot who will get it."

This happened that the **scripture** might be fulfilled that said,

"They divided my clothes among them and cast lots for my garment."

So this is what the soldiers did.

25 Near the cross of Jesus stood his mother, his mother's sister, Mary the wife of Clopas, and Mary Magdalene. 26 When Jesus saw his mother there, and the disciple whom he loved standing nearby, he said to her, "Woman, here is your son," 27 and to the disciple, "Here is your mother." From that time on, this disciple took her into his home.

Word Four ...

These words are from Psalm 22:1, pg. 107.

Mark 15:33 At noon, darkness fell across the whole land until three o'clock. 34 Then at three o'clock Jesus called out with a loud voice, "Eloi, Eloi, lema sabachthani?" which means "**My God, my God, why have you abandoned me?**"

Word Five ...

What scripture was fulfilled? Why a stalk of the hyssop plant? See Exodus 12, pg. 55.

John 19:28 Later, knowing that everything had now been finished, and so that **Scripture would be fulfilled**, Jesus said, "I am thirsty." 29 A jar of **wine** vinegar was there, so they soaked a sponge in it, put the sponge on a stalk of the **hyssop** plant, and **lifted** it to Jesus' lips.

Word Six ...

Jesus was not finished. His work on the cross was finished.

30 When he had received the drink, Jesus said, "It is **finished**."

Word Seven ...

Whose hands are you in?

Luke 23:46 And Jesus, crying out with a loud voice, said, "**Father, into your hands I commit my spirit.**" Having said this, He breathed His last.

The Story Continues ...

The curtain separated the Holy part of the temple from the Holy of Holies - the room reserved for God.

Matthew 27:51 At that moment the **curtain** of the temple was torn in two, from top to bottom. The earth shook, and the rocks were split. 52 The tombs also were opened, and many bodies of the saints who had fallen asleep were raised. 53 After his resurrection they came out of the tombs and entered the holy city and appeared to many. 54 Now when the centurion and those with him, who were keeping watch over Jesus, saw the earthquake and what took place, they were terrified and said, "Truly this man was God's Son!"

55 Many women were also there, looking on from a distance; they had followed Jesus from Galilee and had provided for him. 56 Among them were Mary Magdalene, and Mary the mother of James and Joseph, and the mother of the sons of Zebedee.

The Death of Jesus

John 19:31 Now it was the day of Preparation, and the next day was to be a special Sabbath. Because the Jewish leaders did not want the bodies left on the crosses during the Sabbath, they asked Pilate to have the legs broken and the bodies taken down. 32 The soldiers therefore came and broke the legs of the first man who had been crucified with Jesus, and then those of the other. 33 But when they came to Jesus and found that he was already dead, they did not break his legs. 34 Instead, one of the soldiers **pierced** Jesus' side with a spear, bringing a sudden flow of blood and water. 35 The man who saw it has given testimony, and his testimony is true. He knows that he tells the truth, and he testifies so that you also may believe. 36 These things happened so that the scripture would be fulfilled: "**Not one of his bones will be broken,**" 37 and, as another scripture says, "**They will look on the one they have pierced.**"

See Isaiah 53:7, pg. 198.

Exodus 12 regulations for the Passover lamb, pg. 55.

The Burial of Jesus

Mark 15:42 This all happened on Friday, the day of preparation, the day before the Sabbath. As evening approached, 43 Joseph of Arimathea took a risk and went to Pilate and asked for Jesus' body. (Joseph was an honored member of the high council, and he was waiting for the Kingdom of God to come.) 44 Pilate couldn't believe that Jesus was already dead, so he called for the Roman officer and asked if he had died yet. 45 The officer confirmed that Jesus was dead, so Pilate told Joseph he could have the body.

John 19:38 Later, Joseph of Arimathea asked Pilate for the body of Jesus. Now Joseph was a disciple of Jesus, but secretly because he feared the Jewish leaders. With Pilate's permission, he came and took the body away. 39 He was accompanied by Nicodemus, the man who earlier had visited Jesus at night. **Nicodemus** brought a mixture of myrrh and aloes, about seventy-five pounds. 40 Taking Jesus' body, the two of them wrapped it, with the spices, in strips of linen. This was in accordance with Jewish burial customs. 41 At the place where Jesus was crucified, there was a garden, and in the garden a new tomb, in which no one had ever been laid. 42 Because it was the Jewish day of Preparation and since the tomb was nearby, they laid Jesus there.

See John 3, pg. 251.

Luke 23:55 Now the women who had come with Him out of Galilee followed, and saw the tomb and how His body was laid. 56 Then they returned and prepared spices and perfumes.

And on the **Sabbath** they rested according to the commandment.

The Sabbath was a Saturday.

6. The Resurrection of Jesus

The Guard at the Tomb

Matthew 27:62 The next day, that is, after the day of Preparation, the chief priests and the Pharisees gathered before Pilate 63 and said, "Sir, we remember what that impostor said while he was still alive, 'After three days I will rise again.' 64 Therefore command the tomb to be made secure until the third day; otherwise his disciples may go and steal him away, and tell the people, 'He has been raised from the dead,' and the last deception would be worse than the first." 65 Pilate said to them, "You have a guard of soldiers; go, make it as secure as you can." 66 So they went with the guard and made the tomb secure by sealing the stone.

The Empty Tomb

Sunday

John 20:1 Early on the **first day of the week**, while it was still dark, Mary Magdalene went to the tomb and saw that the stone had been removed from the entrance. 2 So she came running to Simon Peter and the other disciple, the one Jesus loved, and said, "They have taken the Lord out of the tomb, and we don't know where they have put him!"

3 So Peter and the other disciple started for the tomb. 4 Both were running, but the other disciple outran Peter and reached the tomb first. 5 He bent over and looked in at the strips of linen lying there but did not go in. 6 Then Simon Peter came along behind him and went straight into the tomb. He saw the strips of linen lying there, 7 as well as the cloth that had been wrapped around Jesus' head. The cloth was still lying in its place, separate from the linen. 8 Finally the other disciple, who had reached the tomb first, also went inside. He saw and believed. 9 (They still did not understand from Scripture that Jesus had to rise from the dead.) 10 Then the disciples went back to where they were staying.

Jesus Appears to Mary Magdalene

11 Now Mary stood outside the tomb crying. As she wept, she bent over to look into the tomb 12 and saw two angels in white, seated where Jesus' body had been, one at the head and the other at the foot.

13 They asked her, "Woman, why are you crying?"

"They have taken my Lord away," she said, "and I don't know where they have put him." 14 At this, she turned around and saw Jesus standing there, but she did not realize that it was Jesus.

15 He asked her, "Woman, why are you crying? Who is it you are looking for?"

Thinking he was the gardener, she said, "Sir, if you have carried him away, tell me where you have put him, and I will get him."

16 Jesus said to her, "Mary."

She turned toward him and cried out in Aramaic, "Rabboni!" (which means "Teacher").

17 Jesus said, "Do not hold on to me, for I have not yet ascended to the Father. Go instead to my brothers and tell them, 'I am ascending to my Father and your Father, to my God and your God.'"

18 Mary Magdalene went to the disciples with the news: "I have seen the Lord!" And she told them that he had said these things to her.

The Report of the Guard

Matthew 28:11 While they were going, some of the guard went into the city and told the chief priests everything that had happened. 12 After the priests had assembled with the elders, they devised a plan to give a large sum of money to the soldiers, 13 telling them, "You must say, 'His disciples came by night and stole him away while we were asleep.' 14 If this comes to the governor's ears, we will satisfy him and keep you out of trouble." 15 So they took the money and did as they were directed. And this story is still told among the Jews to this day.

The Road to Emmaus

Luke 24:13 And behold, two of them (followers of Jesus) were going that very day to a village named Emmaus, which was about seven miles from Jerusalem. 14 And they were talking with each other about all these things which had taken place. 15 While they were talking and discussing, Jesus Himself approached and began traveling with them. 16 But their eyes were prevented from recognizing Him. 17 And He said to them, "What are these words that you are exchanging with one another as you are walking?" And they stood still, looking sad. 18 One of them, named Cleopas, answered and said to Him, "Are You the only one visiting Jerusalem and unaware of the things which have happened here in these days?" 19 And He said to them, "What things?" And they said to Him, "The things about Jesus the Nazarene, who was a prophet mighty in deed and word in the sight of God and all the people, 20 and how the chief priests and our rulers delivered Him to the sentence of death, and crucified Him. 21 But we were hoping that it was He who was going to redeem Israel. Indeed, besides all this, it is the third day since these things happened. 22 But also some women among us amazed us. When they were at the tomb early in the morning, 23 and did not find His body, they came, saying that they had also seen a vision of angels who said that He was alive. 24 Some of those who were with us went to the tomb and found it just exactly as the women also had said; but Him they did not see." 25 And He said to them, "O foolish men and slow of heart to believe in all that the prophets have spoken! 26 Was it not necessary for the Christ to suffer these things and to enter into His glory?" 27 Then beginning with **Moses and with all the prophets**, He explained to them the things concerning Himself in all the Scriptures.

This was a shortcut way of saying the whole Old Testament.

28 And they approached the village where they were going, and He acted as though He were going farther. 29 But they urged Him, saying, "Stay with us, for it is getting toward evening, and the day is now nearly over." So He went in to stay with them. 30 When He had reclined at the table with them, He took the bread and blessed it, and breaking it, He began giving it to them. 31 Then their eyes were opened and they recognized Him; and He vanished from their sight. 32 They said to one another, "Were not our hearts burning within us while He was speaking to us on the road, while He was explaining the Scriptures to us?" 33 And they got up that very hour and returned to Jerusalem, and found gathered together

the eleven and those who were with them, 34 saying, "The Lord has really risen and has appeared to Simon." 35 They began to relate their experiences on the road and how He was recognized by them in the breaking of the bread.

Jesus Appears to His Disciples

John 20:19 On the evening of that first day of the week, when the disciples were together, with the doors locked for fear of the Jewish leaders, Jesus came and stood among them and said, "Peace be with you!" 20 After he said this, he showed them his hands and side. The disciples were overjoyed when they saw the Lord.

21 Again Jesus said, "Peace be with you! As the Father has sent me, I am sending you." 22 And with that he breathed on them and said, "Receive the Holy Spirit. 23 If you forgive anyone's sins, their sins are forgiven; if you do not forgive them, they are not forgiven."

Jesus Appears to Thomas

24 Now Thomas (also known as Didymus), one of the Twelve, was not with the disciples when Jesus came. 25 So the other disciples told him, "We have seen the Lord!"

But he said to them, "Unless I see the nail marks in his hands and put my finger where the nails were, and put my hand into his side, I will not believe."

26 A week later his disciples were in the house again, and Thomas was with them. Though the doors were locked, Jesus came and stood among them and said, "Peace be with you!" 27 Then he said to Thomas, "Put your finger here; see my hands. Reach out your hand and put it into my side. Stop doubting and believe."

28 Thomas said to him, "My Lord and my God!"

29 Then Jesus told him, "Because you have seen me, you have believed; blessed are those who have not seen and yet have believed."

The Miraculous Catch of Fish

John 21:1 Afterward Jesus appeared again to his disciples, by the Sea of Galilee. It happened this way: 2 Simon Peter, Thomas (also known as Didymus), Nathanael from Cana in Galilee, the sons of Zebedee, and two other disciples were together. 3 "I'm going out to fish," Simon Peter told them, and they said, "We'll go with you." So they went out and got into the boat, but that night they caught nothing.

4 Early in the morning, Jesus stood on the shore, but the disciples did not realize that it was Jesus.

5 He called out to them, "Friends, haven't you any fish?"

"No," they answered.

6 He said, "Throw your net on the right side of the boat and you will find some." When they did, they were unable to haul the net in

because of the large number of **fish**.

7 Then the disciple whom Jesus loved said to Peter, "It is the Lord!" As soon as Simon Peter heard him say, "It is the Lord," he wrapped his outer garment around him (for he had taken it off) and jumped into the water. 8 The other disciples followed in the boat, towing the net full of fish, for they were not far from shore, about a hundred yards. 9 When they landed, they saw a fire of burning coals there with fish on it, and some bread.

10 Jesus said to them, "Bring some of the fish you have just caught." 11 So Simon Peter climbed back into the boat and dragged the net ashore. It was full of large fish, 153, but even with so many the net was not torn. 12 Jesus said to them, "Come and have breakfast." None of the disciples dared ask him, "Who are you?" They knew it was the Lord. 13 Jesus came, took the bread and gave it to them, and did the same with the fish. 14 This was now the third time Jesus appeared to his disciples after he was raised from the dead.

Jesus Reinstates Peter

15 When they had finished eating, Jesus said to Simon Peter, "Simon son of John, do you love me more than these?"

"Yes, Lord," he said, "you know that I love you."

Jesus said, "Feed my lambs."

16 Again Jesus said, "Simon son of John, do you love me?"

He answered, "Yes, Lord, you know that I love you."

Jesus said, "Take care of my sheep."

17 The third time he said to him, "Simon son of John, do you love me?"

Peter was **hurt** because Jesus asked him the third time, "Do you love me?" He said, "Lord, you know all things; you know that I love you."

Jesus said, "Feed my sheep. 18 Very truly I tell you, when you were younger you dressed yourself and went where you wanted; but when you are old you will stretch out your hands, and someone else will dress you and lead you where you do not want to go." 19 Jesus said this to indicate the kind of **death** by which Peter would glorify God. Then he said to him, "Follow me!"

20 Peter turned and saw that the disciple whom Jesus loved was following them. (This was the one who had leaned back against Jesus at the supper and had said, "Lord, who is going to betray you?") 21 When Peter saw him, he asked, "Lord, what about him?"

22 Jesus answered, "If I want him to remain alive until I return, what is that to you? You must follow me." 23 Because of this, the rumor spread among the believers that this disciple would not die. But Jesus did not say that he would not die; he only said, "If I want him to remain alive until I return, what is that to you?"

This fish story happened at the beginning of Jesus' ministry as well as here at the end.

Jesus' 3 questions hurt Peter because he had denied knowing Jesus 3 times.

According to church history, Peter was eventually crucified.

7. The Great Commission of Jesus

Matthew 28:16 Now the eleven disciples went to Galilee, to the mountain to which Jesus had directed them. 17 When they saw him, they worshiped him; but some doubted. 18 And Jesus came and said to them, "All authority in heaven and on earth has been given to me. 19 **Go** therefore and **make disciples** of all nations, **baptizing** them in the name of the Father and of the Son and of the Holy Spirit, 20 and **teaching** them to obey everything that I have commanded you. And remember, I am with you always, to the end of the age."

Simple: Go, make disciples - baptizing and teaching.

The Purpose of the Gospels

John 20:30 Jesus performed many other signs in the presence of his disciples, which are not recorded in this book. 31 But these are written that **you may believe** that Jesus is the Messiah, the Son of God, and that by believing you may have life in his name.

This is the purpose of the Bible.

Mark 16:19 When the Lord Jesus had finished talking with them, he was taken up into heaven and sat down in the place of honor at God's right hand. 20 And the disciples went everywhere and preached, and the Lord worked through them, confirming what they said by many miraculous signs.

the book of Acts

Category: The Book of Acts
Author: Luke
Theme: The church begins, grows, and expands
Location & Date: Middle East; A.D. 60-62
Version of Bible: New English Translation (NET)
Summary: The book of Acts is the story of how the Church got started and grew—first in Jerusalem (Chapters 1-7), then in Samaria (Chapters 8-12) and then to the ends of the earth (Chapters 13-28).

Jesus Ascends to Heaven

Acts 1:1 **I wrote the former account**, Theophilus, about all that Jesus began to do and teach 2 until the day he was taken up to heaven, after he had given orders by the Holy Spirit to the apostles he had chosen. 3 To the same apostles also, after his suffering, he presented himself alive with many convincing proofs. He was seen by them over a forty-day period and spoke about matters concerning the kingdom of God. 4 While he was with them, he declared, "Do not leave Jerusalem, but wait there for what my Father promised, which you heard about from me. 5 For John baptized with water, but you will be baptized with the Holy Spirit not many days from now."

The Ascension of Jesus

6 So when they had gathered together, they began to ask him, "Lord, is this the time when you are restoring the kingdom to Israel?" 7 He told them, "You are not permitted to know the times or periods that the Father has set by his own authority. 8 But you will receive power when the Holy Spirit has come upon you, and **you will be my witnesses in Jerusalem, and in all Judea and Samaria, and to the farthest parts of the earth.**" 9 After he had said this, while they were watching, he was lifted up and a cloud hid him from their sight. 10 As they were still staring into the sky while he was going, suddenly two men in white clothing stood near them 11 and said, "Men of Galilee, why do you stand here looking up into the sky? **This same Jesus who has been taken up from you into heaven will come back in the same way you saw him go into heaven.**"

12 Then they returned to Jerusalem from the mountain called the Mount of Olives (which is near Jerusalem, a Sabbath day's journey away). 13 When they had entered Jerusalem, they went to the upstairs room where they were staying. Peter and John, and James, and Andrew, Philip and Thomas, Bartholomew and

Luke (the author of the book of Luke) wrote the book of Acts. Theophilus is Greek for "friend of God." He must have been an important Gentile (non-Jew) who was interested in Christianity.

Here is the summary of the book of Acts.

Jesus will come back again. Christians call it the "second coming"- Jesus will come to judge the living and the dead.

Matthew, James son of Alphaeus and Simon the Zealot, and Judas son of James were there. 14 All these continued together in prayer with one mind, together with the women, along with Mary the mother of Jesus, and his brothers.

The Holy Spirit and the Day of Pentecost

2:1 Now when the day of **Pentecost** had come, they were all together in one place. 2 Suddenly a sound like a violent wind blowing came from heaven and filled the entire house where they were sitting. 3 And tongues spreading out like a fire appeared to them and came to rest on each one of them. 4 All of them were filled with the Holy Spirit, and they began to speak in other languages as the Spirit enabled them.

5 Now there were devout Jews from every nation under heaven residing in Jerusalem. 6 When this sound occurred, a crowd gathered and was in confusion, because each one heard them speaking in his own language. 7 Completely baffled, they said, "Aren't all these who are speaking Galileans? 8 And how is it that each one of us hears them in our own native language? 9 Parthians, Medes, Elamites, and residents of Mesopotamia, Judea and Cappadocia, Pontus and the province of Asia, 10 Phrygia and Pamphylia, Egypt and the parts of Libya near Cyrene, and visitors from Rome, 11 both Jews and proselytes, Cretans and Arabs—we hear them speaking in our own languages about the great deeds God has done!" 12 All were astounded and greatly confused, saying to one another, "What does this mean?" 13 But others jeered at the speakers, saying, "They are drunk on new wine!"

Peter's Address on the Day of Pentecost

14 But Peter stood up with the eleven, raised his voice, and addressed them: "You men of Judea and all you who live in Jerusalem, know this and listen carefully to what I say. 15 In spite of what you think, these men are not drunk, for it is only nine o'clock in the morning. 16 But this is what was spoken about through the **prophet Joel:**

17 'And in the last days it will be,' God says, 'that I will pour out my Spirit on all people, and your sons and your daughters will prophesy, and your young men will see visions, and your old men will dream dreams. 18 Even on my servants, both men and women, I will pour out my Spirit in those days, and they will prophesy. 19 And I will perform wonders in the sky above and miraculous signs on the earth below, blood and fire and clouds of smoke. 20 The sun will be changed to darkness and the moon to blood before the great and glorious day of the Lord comes. 21 **And then everyone who calls on the name of the Lord will be saved.**'

22 "Men of Israel, listen to these words: Jesus the Nazarene, a man clearly attested to you by God with powerful deeds, wonders, and miraculous signs that God performed among you through him, just as you yourselves know—23 this man, who was handed over by the predetermined plan and foreknowledge of God, you executed by nailing him to a cross at the hands of Gentiles. 24 But

---

Margin notes:

Pentecost (meaning 50) is the Greek name of the Hebrew festival "shovat" - meaning feast of weeks. See Lev. Jews from all over the world were in Jerusalem to celebrate this yearly harvest festival.

See Joel 2:28; pg. 223.

What do you need saving from?

God raised him up, having released him from the pains of death, because it was not possible for him to be held in its power.

32 This Jesus God raised up, and we are all witnesses of it. 33 So then, exalted to the right hand of God, and having received the promise of the Holy Spirit from the Father, he has poured out what you both see and hear.

36 Therefore let all the house of Israel know beyond a doubt that God has made this Jesus whom you crucified both Lord and Christ."

37 Now when they heard this, they were acutely distressed and said to Peter and the rest of the apostles, "What should we do, brothers?" 38 Peter said to them, "Repent, and each one of you be baptized in the name of Jesus Christ for the forgiveness of your sins, and you will receive the gift of the Holy Spirit. 39 For the promise is for you and your children, and for all who are far away, as many as the Lord our God will call to himself." 40 With many other words he testified and exhorted them saying, "Save yourselves from this perverse generation!" 41 So those who accepted his message were baptized, and that day about **three thousand people were added.**

The church grew from 70 people to 3,070 in one day.

The Believers Form a Community

42 They were devoting themselves to the apostles' **teaching** and to **fellowship**, to the **breaking of bread** and to **prayer**. 43 Reverential awe came over everyone, and many wonders and miraculous signs came about by the apostles. 44 All who believed were **together** and held everything in common, 45 and they began selling their property and possessions and distributing the proceeds to everyone, as anyone had need. 46 Every day they continued to gather **together** by common consent in the temple courts, breaking bread from **house to house**, **sharing** their food with **glad and humble hearts,** 47 **praising God** and having the good will of all the people. And the **Lord was adding to their number every day those who were being saved.**

This is what church is all about.

Peter and John Heal a Lame Man at the Temple

3:1 Now Peter and John were going up to the temple at the time for prayer, at three o'clock in the afternoon. 2 And a man lame from birth was being carried up, who was placed at the temple gate called "the Beautiful Gate" every day so he could beg for money from those going into the temple courts. 3 When he saw Peter and John about to go into the temple courts, he asked them for money. 4 Peter looked directly at him (as did John) and said, "Look at us!"

5 So the lame man paid attention to them, expecting to receive something from them. 6 But Peter said, "I have no silver or gold, but what I do have I give you. In the name of Jesus Christ the Nazarene, stand up and walk!" 7 Then Peter took hold of him by the right hand and raised him up, and at once the man's feet and ankles were made strong. 8 He jumped up, stood and began walking around, and he entered the temple courts with them, walking and

leaping and praising God. 9 All the people saw him walking and praising God, 10 and they recognized him as the man who used to sit and ask for donations at the Beautiful Gate of the temple, and they were filled with astonishment and amazement at what had happened to him.

Peter Addresses the Crowd

11 They all rushed out in amazement to Solomon's Colonnade, where the man was holding tightly to Peter and John. 12 When Peter saw this, he declared to the people, "Men of Israel, why are you amazed at this? Why do you stare at us as if we had made this man walk by our own power or piety? 13 The God of Abraham, Isaac, and Jacob, the God of our forefathers, has glorified his servant Jesus, whom you handed over and rejected in the presence of Pilate after he had decided to release him. 14 But you rejected the Holy and Righteous One and asked that a man who was a murderer be released to you. 15 You killed the Originator of life, whom God raised from the dead. To this fact we are witnesses! 16 And on the basis of faith in Jesus' name, his very name has made this man—whom you see and know—strong. The faith that is through Jesus has given him this complete health in the presence of you all.

17 And now, brothers, I know you acted in ignorance, as your rulers did too. 18 But the things God foretold long ago through all the prophets—that his Christ would suffer—he has fulfilled in this way. 19 Therefore repent and turn back so that your sins may be wiped out, 20 so that times of refreshing may come from the presence of the Lord, and so that he may send the Messiah appointed for you—that is, Jesus. 21 This one heaven must receive until the time all things are restored, which God declared from times long ago through his holy prophets. 22 Moses said, '**The Lord your God will raise up for you a prophet like me from among your brothers.** You must obey him in everything he tells you. 23 Every person who does not obey that prophet will be destroyed and thus removed from the people.'

Deuteronomy 18:15.

24 And all the prophets, from Samuel and those who followed him, have spoken about and announced these days. 25 You are the sons of the prophets and of the covenant that God made with your ancestors, saying to Abraham, '**And in your descendants all the nations of the earth will be blessed.**' 26 God raised up his servant and sent him first to you, to bless you by turning each one of you from your iniquities."

Genesis 12:3, pg. 19.

Peter and John Before the Council

4:1 While Peter and John were speaking to the people, the priests and the commander of the temple guard and the Sadducees came up to them, 2 angry because they were teaching the people and announcing in Jesus the resurrection of the dead. 3 So they seized them and put them in jail until the next day (for it was already evening). 4 But many of those who had listened to the message believed, and **the number of the men came to about five thousand.**

The church continued to grow at a rapid pace.

5 On the next day, their rulers, elders, and experts in the law came together in Jerusalem. 6 Annas the **high priest** was there, and Caiaphas, John, Alexander, and others who were members of the high priest's family. 7 After making Peter and John stand in their midst, they began to inquire, "By what power or by what name did you do this?"

8 Then Peter, filled with the Holy Spirit, replied, "Rulers of the people and elders, 9 if we are being examined today for a good deed done to a sick man—by what means this man was healed—10 let it be known to all of you and to all the people of Israel that by the name of Jesus Christ the Nazarene whom you crucified, whom God raised from the dead, this man stands before you healthy. 11 **This Jesus is the stone that was rejected by you, the builders, that has become the cornerstone**. 12 And there is salvation in no one else, for there is no other name under heaven given among people by which we must be saved."

13 When they saw the boldness of Peter and John, and discovered that they were uneducated and ordinary men, **they were amazed and recognized these men had been with Jesus**. 14 And because they saw the man who had been healed standing with them, they had nothing to say against this. 15 But when they had ordered them to go outside the council, they began to confer with one another, 16 saying, "What should we do with these men? For it is plain to all who live in Jerusalem that a notable miraculous sign has come about through them, and we cannot deny it. 17 But to keep this matter from spreading any further among the people, let us warn them to speak no more to anyone in this name."

18 And they called them in and ordered them not to speak or teach at all in the name of Jesus. 19 But Peter and John replied, "Whether it is right before God to obey you rather than God, you decide, 20 for **it is impossible for us not to speak about what we have seen and heard**."

21 After threatening them further, they released them, for they could not find how to punish them on account of the people, because they were all praising God for what had happened.

The Apostles Heal Many

5:12 Now many miraculous signs and wonders came about among the people through the hands of the apostles. By common consent they were all meeting together in Solomon's Portico. 13 None of the rest dared to join them, but the people held them in high honor. 14 **More and more believers in the Lord were added** to their number, crowds of both men and women. 15 Thus they even carried the sick out into the streets, and put them on cots and pallets, so that when Peter came by at least his shadow would fall on some of them. 16 A crowd of people from the towns around Jerusalem also came together, bringing the sick and those troubled by unclean spirits. They were all being healed.

Margin notes:

- The high priest held the highest position in the Jewish faith.
- Psalm 18:22.
- Spending time with Jesus will make a noticeable difference in your life.
- When people's lives are changed, they talk about it.
- The church continued to grow.

Further Trouble for the Apostles

17 Now the high priest rose up, and all those with him (that is, the religious party of the Sadducees), and they were filled with jealousy. 18 They laid hands on the apostles and put them in a public jail. 19 But during the night an angel of the Lord opened the doors of the prison, led them out, and said, 20 "Go and stand in the temple courts and proclaim to the people all the words of this life." 21 When they heard this, they entered the temple courts at daybreak and began teaching.

Now when the high priest and those who were with him arrived, they summoned the Sanhedrin—that is, the whole high council of the Israelites—and sent to the jail to have the apostles brought before them. 22 But the officers who came for them did not find them in the prison, so they returned and reported, 23 "We found the jail locked securely and the guards standing at the doors, but when we opened them, we found no one inside." 24 Now when the commander of the temple guard and the chief priests heard this report, they were greatly puzzled concerning it, wondering what this could be. 25 But someone came and reported to them, "Look! The men you put in prison are standing in the temple courts and teaching the people!" 26 Then the commander of the temple guard went with the officers and brought the apostles without the use of force (for they were afraid of being stoned by the people).

27 When they had brought them, they stood them before the council, and the high priest questioned them, 28 saying, "We gave you strict orders not to teach in this name. Look, you have filled Jerusalem with your teaching, and you intend to bring this man's blood on us!"

29 But Peter and the apostles replied, "We must obey God rather than people. 30 The God of our forefathers raised up Jesus, whom you seized and killed by hanging him on a tree. 31 God exalted him to his right hand as Leader and Savior, to give repentance to Israel and forgiveness of sins. 32 And we are witnesses of these events, and so is the Holy Spirit whom God has given to those who obey him."

33 Now when they heard this, they became furious and wanted to execute them. 34 But a Pharisee whose name was Gamaliel, a teacher of the law who was respected by all the people, stood up in the council and ordered the men to be put outside for a short time. 35 Then he said to the council, "Men of Israel, pay close attention to what you are about to do to these men. 36 For some time ago Theudas rose up, claiming to be somebody, and about four hundred men joined him. He was killed, and all who followed him were dispersed and nothing came of it. 37 After him Judas the Galilean arose in the days of the census, and incited people to follow him in revolt. He too was killed, and all who followed him were scattered. 38 So in this case I say to you, stay away from these men and leave them alone, because if this plan or this undertaking originates with people, it will come to nothing, 39 but if it is from God, you will not be able to stop them, or you may even be found fighting against God."

He convinced them, 40 and they summoned the apostles and had them beaten. Then they ordered them not to speak in the name of Jesus and released them. 41 So they left the council rejoicing because they had been considered worthy to suffer dishonor for the sake of the name. 42 And every day both in the temple courts and from **house to house**, they did not stop teaching and proclaiming the good news that Jesus was the Christ.

> For the first 300 years of Christianity there were no church buildings.

The Appointment of the First Seven Deacons

6:1 Now in those days, when the disciples were growing in number, a complaint arose on the part of the Greek-speaking Jews against the native Hebraic Jews, because their widows were being overlooked in the daily distribution of food. 2 So the twelve called the whole group of the disciples together and said, "It is not right for us to neglect the word of God to wait on tables. 3 But carefully select from among you, brothers, seven men who are well-attested, full of the Spirit and of wisdom, whom we may put in charge of this necessary task. 4 But we will devote ourselves to prayer and to the ministry of the word." 5 The proposal pleased the entire group, so they chose **Stephen**, a man full of faith and of the Holy Spirit, with **Philip**, Prochorus, Nicanor, Timon, Parmenas, and Nicolas, a Gentile convert to Judaism from Antioch. 6 They stood these men before the apostles, who prayed and placed their hands on them. 7 The word of God continued to spread, the number of disciples in Jerusalem increased greatly, and a large group of priests became obedient to the faith.

> It is interesting that these men were originally chosen to manage a food distribution program, but the next two stories are about Stephen preaching and Philip evangelizing, teaching and baptizing.

Stephen Is Arrested

8 Now Stephen, full of grace and power, was performing great wonders and miraculous signs among the people. 9 But some men from the Synagogue of the Freedmen (as it was called), both Cyrenians and Alexandrians, as well as some from Cilicia and the province of Asia, stood up and argued with Stephen. 10 Yet they were not able to resist the wisdom and the Spirit with which he spoke. 11 Then they secretly instigated some men to say, "We have heard this man speaking blasphemous words against Moses and God." 12 They incited the people, the elders, and the experts in the law; then they approached Stephen, seized him, and brought him before the council. 13 They brought forward false witnesses who said, "This man does not stop saying things against this holy place and the law. 14 For we have heard him saying that Jesus the Nazarene will destroy this place and change the customs that Moses handed down to us." 15 All who were sitting in the council looked intently at Stephen and saw his face was like the face of an angel.

Stephen Addresses the Council

7:1 Then the high priest said, "Are these things true?" 2 So he replied, "**Brothers and fathers, listen to me.** The God of glory appeared to our forefather Abraham when he was in Mesopotamia, before he settled in Haran, 3 and said to him, 'Go out from your country and from your relatives, and come to the land I will show you.'

> What follows is an incredible summary of Bible history.

4 Then he went out from the country of the Chaldeans and settled in Haran. After his father died, God made him move to this country where you now live. 5 He did not give any of it to him for an inheritance, not even a foot of ground, yet God promised to give it to him as his possession, and to his descendants after him, even though Abraham as yet had no child. 6 But God spoke as follows: 'Your descendants will be foreigners in a foreign country, whose citizens will enslave them and mistreat them for four hundred years. 7 But I will punish the nation they serve as slaves,' said God, 'and after these things they will come out of there and worship me in this place.' 8 Then God gave Abraham the covenant of circumcision, and so he became the father of Isaac and circumcised him when he was eight days old, and Isaac became the father of Jacob, and Jacob of the twelve patriarchs. 9 The patriarchs, because they were jealous of Joseph, sold him into Egypt. But God was with him, 10 and rescued him from all his troubles, and granted him favor and wisdom in the presence of Pharaoh, king of Egypt, who made him ruler over Egypt and over all his household. 11 Then a famine occurred throughout Egypt and Canaan, causing great suffering, and our ancestors could not find food. 12 So when Jacob heard that there was grain in Egypt, he sent our ancestors there the first time. 13 On their second visit Joseph made himself known to his brothers again, and Joseph's family became known to Pharaoh. 14 So Joseph sent a message and invited his father Jacob and all his relatives to come, seventy-five people in all. 15 So Jacob went down to Egypt and died there, along with our ancestors, 16 and their bones were later moved to Shechem and placed in the tomb that Abraham had bought for a certain sum of money from the sons of Hamor in Shechem.

17 "But as the time drew near for God to fulfill the promise he had declared to Abraham, the people increased greatly in number in Egypt, 18 until another king who did not know about Joseph ruled over Egypt. 19 This was the one who exploited our people and was cruel to our ancestors, forcing them to abandon their infants so they would die. 20 At that time Moses was born, and he was beautiful to God. For three months he was brought up in his father's house, 21 and when he had been abandoned, Pharaoh's daughter adopted him and brought him up as her own son. 22 So Moses was trained in all the wisdom of the Egyptians and was powerful in his words and deeds. 23 But when he was about forty years old, it entered his mind to visit his fellow countrymen the Israelites. 24 When he saw one of them being hurt unfairly, Moses came to his defense and avenged the person who was mistreated by striking down the Egyptian. 25 He thought his own people would understand that God was delivering them through him, but they did not understand. 26 The next day Moses saw two men fighting, and tried to make peace between them, saying, 'Men, you are brothers; why are you hurting one another?' 27 But the man who was unfairly hurting his neighbor pushed Moses aside, saying, 'Who made you a ruler and judge over us? 28 You don't want to kill me the way you killed the Egyptian yesterday, do you?' 29 When the man said this, Moses fled and became a foreigner in the land of Midian, where he became the father of two sons.

30 "After forty years had passed, an angel appeared to him in the desert of Mount Sinai, in the flame of a burning bush. 31 When Moses saw it, he was amazed at the sight, and when he approached to investigate, there came the voice of the Lord, 32 'I am the God of your forefathers, the God of Abraham, Isaac, and Jacob.' Moses began to tremble and did not dare to look more closely. 33 But the Lord said to him, 'Take the sandals off your feet, for the place where you are standing is holy ground. 34 I have certainly seen the suffering of my people who are in Egypt and have heard their groaning, and I have come down to rescue them. Now come, I will send you to Egypt.' 35 This same Moses they had rejected, saying, 'Who made you a ruler and judge?' God sent as both ruler and deliverer through the hand of the angel who appeared to him in the bush. 36 This man led them out, performing wonders and miraculous signs in the land of Egypt, at the Red Sea, and in the wilderness for forty years. 37 This is the Moses who said to the Israelites, 'God will raise up for you a prophet like me from among your brothers.' 38 This is the man who was in the congregation in the wilderness with the angel who spoke to him at Mount Sinai, and with our ancestors, and he received living oracles to give to you. 39 Our ancestors were unwilling to obey him, but pushed him aside and turned back to Egypt in their hearts, 40 saying to Aaron, 'Make us gods who will go in front of us, for this Moses, who led us out of the land of Egypt—we do not know what has happened to him!' 41 At that time they made an idol in the form of a calf, brought a sacrifice to the idol, and began rejoicing in the works of their hands. 42 But God turned away from them and gave them over to worship the host of heaven, as it is written in the book of the prophets: 'It was not to me that you offered slain animals and sacrifices forty years in the wilderness, was it, house of Israel? 43 But you took along the tabernacle of Moloch and the star of the god Rephan, the images you made to worship, but I will deport you beyond Babylon.' 44 Our ancestors had the tabernacle of testimony in the wilderness, just as God who spoke to Moses ordered him to make it according to the design he had seen. 45 Our ancestors received possession of it and brought it in with Joshua when they dispossessed the nations that God drove out before our ancestors, until the time of David. 46 He found favor with God and asked that he could find a dwelling place for the house of Jacob. 47 But Solomon built a house for him. 48 Yet the Most High does not live in houses made by human hands, as **the prophet says,**

49 'Heaven is my throne, and earth is the footstool for my feet. What kind of house will you build for me, says the Lord, or what is my resting place? 50 Did my hand not make all these things?'

51 "You stubborn people, with uncircumcised hearts and ears! You are always resisting the Holy Spirit, like your ancestors did! 52 Which of the prophets did your ancestors not persecute? They killed those who foretold long ago the coming of the Righteous One, whose betrayers and murderers you have now become! 53 You received the law by decrees given by angels, but you did not obey it."

I Kings 8:27.

The Book of Acts

Stephen Is Killed

54 When they heard these things, they became furious and ground their teeth at him. 55 But Stephen, full of the Holy Spirit, looked intently toward heaven and saw the glory of God, and Jesus standing at the right hand of God. 56 "Look!" he said. "I see the heavens opened, and the Son of Man standing at the right hand of God!" 57 But they covered their ears, shouting out with a loud voice, and rushed at him with one intent. 58 When they had driven him out of the city, they began to stone him, and the witnesses laid their cloaks at the feet of a young man named **Saul**. 59 They continued to stone Stephen while he prayed, "Lord Jesus, receive my spirit!" 60 Then he fell to his knees and cried out with a loud voice, "Lord, do not hold this sin against them!" When he had said this, he died.

8:1 And **Saul** agreed completely with killing him.

Much of the book of Acts is going to be about this man.

Saul Begins to Persecute the Church

Now on that day a great persecution began against the church in Jerusalem, and all except the apostles were forced to scatter throughout the regions of Judea and Samaria. 2 Some devout men buried Stephen and made loud lamentation over him. 3 But Saul was trying to destroy the church; entering one house after another, he dragged off both men and women and put them in prison.

Philip and the Ethiopian Eunuch

Philip was one of the 7 chosen to help the apostles (Acts 8:5).

26 Then an angel of the Lord said to **Philip**, "Get up and go south on the road that goes down from Jerusalem to Gaza." (This is a desert road.) 27 So he got up and went. There he met an Ethiopian eunuch, a court official of Candace, queen of the Ethiopians, who was in charge of all her treasury. He had come to Jerusalem to worship, 28 and was returning home, sitting in his chariot, reading the prophet Isaiah. 29 Then the Spirit said to Philip, "Go over and join this chariot." 30 So Philip ran up to it and heard the man reading Isaiah the prophet. He asked him, **"Do you understand what you're reading?"**

Good question. How about you?

31 The man replied, "How in the world can I, unless someone guides me?" So he invited Philip to come up and sit with him. 32 Now the **passage of scripture** the man was reading was this:

See Isaiah 53:7,8; pg. 198. Isaiah 53 talks about a messiah that would come and suffer for the sins, the guilt of his people: Jesus.

"He was led like a sheep to slaughter, and like a lamb before its shearer is silent, so he did not open his mouth. 33 In humiliation justice was taken from him. Who can describe his posterity? For his life was taken away from the earth."

34 Then the eunuch said to Philip, "Please tell me, who is the prophet saying this about—himself or someone else?" 35 So Philip started speaking, and beginning with this scripture proclaimed the good news about Jesus to him. 36 Now as they were going along the road, they came to some water, and the eunuch said, "Look, there is water! What is to stop me from being baptized?" 38 So he ordered the chariot to stop, and both Philip and the eunuch went down into the water, and Philip baptized him. 39 Now when they came up out of the water, the Spirit of the Lord snatched Philip away, and the eunuch did not see him any more, but went

on his way rejoicing. 40 Philip, however, found himself at Azotus, and as he passed through the area, he proclaimed the good news to all the towns until he came to Caesarea.

Saul's Conversion

9:1 Meanwhile Saul, still breathing out threats to murder the Lord's disciples, went to the high priest 2 and requested letters from him to the synagogues in Damascus, so that if he found any who belonged to the Way, either men or women, he could bring them as prisoners to Jerusalem. 3 As he was going along, approaching Damascus, suddenly a light from heaven flashed around him. 4 He fell to the ground and heard a voice saying to him, "Saul, Saul, why are you persecuting me?"

5 So he said, "Who are you, Lord?"

He replied, "I am Jesus whom you are persecuting! 6 But stand up and enter the city and you will be told what you must do."

7 (Now the men who were traveling with him stood there speechless, because they heard the voice but saw no one.) 8 So Saul got up from the ground, but although his eyes were open, he could see nothing. Leading him by the hand, his companions brought him into Damascus. 9 For **three days** he could not see, and he neither ate nor drank anything.

> Just as Jesus was 3 days in the grave.

10 Now there was a disciple in Damascus named Ananias. The Lord said to him in a vision, "Ananias," and he replied, "Here I am, Lord."

11 Then the Lord told him, "Get up and go to the street called 'Straight,' and at Judas' house look for a man from Tarsus named Saul. For he is praying, 12 and he has seen in a vision a man named Ananias come in and place his hands on him so that he may see again."

13 But Ananias replied, "Lord, I have heard from many people about this man, how much harm he has done to your saints in Jerusalem, 14 and here he has authority from the chief priests to imprison all who call on your name!"

15 But the Lord said to him, "Go, because **this man is my chosen instrument** to carry my name before Gentiles and kings and the people of Israel. 16 For I will show him how much he must suffer for the sake of my name."

17 So Ananias departed and entered the house, placed his hands on Saul and said, "Brother Saul, the Lord Jesus, who appeared to you on the road as you came here, has sent me so that you may see again and be filled with the Holy Spirit." 18 Immediately something like scales fell from his eyes, and he could see again. He got up and was baptized, 19 and after taking some food, his strength returned.

> God often chooses the most unlikely people for his purpose - maybe even someone like you.

Saul in Damascus and Jerusalem

For several days he was with the disciples in Damascus, 20 and immediately he began to proclaim Jesus in the **synagogues**, saying,

> A synagogue is a Jewish church.

"This man is the Son of God." 21 All who heard him were amazed and were saying, "Is this not the man who in Jerusalem was ravaging those who call on this name, and who had come here to bring them as prisoners to the chief priests?" 22 But Saul became more and more capable, and was causing consternation among the Jews who lived in Damascus by proving that Jesus is the Christ.

Saul's Escape from Damascus

23 Now after some days had passed, the Jews plotted together to kill him, 24 but Saul learned of their plot against him. They were also watching the city gates day and night so that they could kill him. 25 But his disciples took him at night and let him down through an opening in the wall by lowering him in a basket.

Saul Returns to Jerusalem

26 When he arrived in Jerusalem, he attempted to associate with the disciples, and they were all afraid of him, because they did not believe that he was a disciple. 27 But Barnabas took Saul, brought him to the apostles, and related to them how he had seen the Lord on the road, that the Lord had spoken to him, and how in Damascus he had spoken out boldly in the name of Jesus. 28 So he was staying with them, associating openly with them in Jerusalem, speaking out boldly in the name of the Lord. 29 He was speaking and debating with the Greek-speaking Jews, but they were trying to kill him. 30 When the brothers found out about this, they brought him down to Caesarea and sent him away to Tarsus.

31 Then the church throughout Judea, Galilee, and Samaria experienced peace and thus was strengthened. Living in the fear of the Lord and in the encouragement of the Holy Spirit, **the church increased in numbers.**

The church was by now thousands and thousands of believers.

Peter Visits Cornelius

10:1 Now there was a man in Caesarea named Cornelius, a centurion of what was known as the Italian Cohort. 2 He was a devout, God-fearing man, as was all his household; he did many acts of charity for the people and prayed to God regularly. 3 About three o'clock one afternoon he saw clearly in a vision an angel of God who came in and said to him, "Cornelius."

4 Staring at him and becoming greatly afraid, Cornelius replied, "What is it, Lord?"

The angel said to him, "Your prayers and your acts of charity have gone up as a memorial before God. 5 Now send men to Joppa and summon a man named Simon, who is called Peter. 6 This man is staying as a guest with a man named Simon, a tanner, whose house is by the sea."

7 When the angel who had spoken to him departed, Cornelius called two of his personal servants and a devout soldier from among those who served him, 8 and when he had explained everything to them, he sent them to Joppa.

9 About noon the next day, while they were on their way and

approaching the city, Peter went up on the roof to pray. 10 He became hungry and wanted to eat, but while they were preparing the meal, a trance came over him. 11 He saw heaven opened and an object something like a large sheet descending, being let down to earth by its four corners. 12 In it were all kinds of four-footed animals and reptiles of the earth and wild birds. 13 Then a voice said to him, "Get up, Peter; slaughter and eat!"

14 But Peter said, "Certainly not, Lord, for I have never eaten anything defiled and ritually unclean!" 15 The voice spoke to him again, a second time, "What God has made clean, you must not consider ritually unclean!" 16 This happened three times, and immediately the object was taken up into heaven.

17 Now while Peter was puzzling over what the vision he had seen could signify, the men sent by Cornelius had learned where Simon's house was and approached the gate. 18 They called out to ask if Simon, known as Peter, was staying there as a guest.

19 While Peter was still thinking seriously about the vision, the Spirit said to him, "Look! Three men are looking for you. 20 But get up, go down, and accompany them without hesitation, because I have sent them."

21 So Peter went down to the men and said, "Here I am, the person you're looking for. Why have you come?"

22 They said, "Cornelius the centurion, a righteous and God-fearing man, well spoken of by the whole Jewish nation, was directed by a holy angel to summon you to his house and to hear a message from you." 23 So Peter invited them in and entertained them as guests.

Peter at Cornelius's House

On the next day he got up and set out with them, and some of the brothers from Joppa accompanied him. 24 The following day he entered Caesarea. Now Cornelius was waiting anxiously for them and had called together his relatives and close friends. 25 So when Peter came in, Cornelius met him, fell at his feet, and worshiped him. 26 But Peter helped him up, saying, "Stand up. I too am a mere mortal."

27 Peter continued talking with him as he went in, and he found many people gathered together. 28 He said to them, "You know that it is unlawful for a Jew to associate with or visit a Gentile, yet God has shown me that I should call no person defiled or ritually unclean. 29 Therefore when you sent for me, I came without any objection. Now may I ask why you sent for me?"

30 Cornelius replied, "Four days ago at this very hour, at three o'clock in the afternoon, I was praying in my house, and **suddenly a man in shining clothing stood before me** 31 and said, 'Cornelius, your prayer has been heard and your acts of charity have been remembered before God. 32 Therefore send to Joppa and summon Simon, who is called Peter. This man is staying as a guest in the house of Simon the tanner, by the sea.' 33 Therefore I sent for you at once, and you were kind enough to come. So now we are

Interestingly many Muslims have become Christians because they had a vision of a man in dazzling clothes. Maybe this might happen to you as well.

all here in the presence of God to listen to everything the Lord has commanded you to say to us."

34 Then Peter started speaking: "I now truly understand that God does not show favoritism in dealing with people, 35 but in every nation the person who fears him and does what is right is welcomed before him. 36 You know the message he sent to the people of Israel, proclaiming the good news of peace through Jesus Christ (he is Lord of all)—37 you know what happened throughout Judea, beginning from Galilee after the baptism that John announced: 38 with respect to Jesus from Nazareth, that God anointed him with the Holy Spirit and with power. He went around doing good and healing all who were oppressed by the devil, because God was with him.

39 We are witnesses of all the things he did both in Judea and in Jerusalem. They killed him by hanging him on a tree, 40 but God raised him up on the third day and caused him to be seen, 41 not by all the people, but by us, the witnesses God had already chosen, who ate and drank with him after he rose from the dead. 42 He commanded us to preach to the people and to warn them that he is the one appointed by God as judge of the living and the dead. 43 About him all the prophets testify, that everyone who believes in him receives forgiveness of sins through his name."

The Gentiles Receive the Holy Spirit

44 While Peter was still speaking these words, the Holy Spirit fell on all those who heard the message. 45 The circumcised believers who had accompanied Peter were greatly astonished that the gift of the Holy Spirit had been poured out even on the Gentiles, 46 for they heard them speaking in tongues and praising God.

Then Peter said, 47 "No one can withhold the water for these people to be baptized, who have received the Holy Spirit just as we did, can he?" 48 So he gave orders to have them baptized in the name of Jesus Christ. Then they asked him to stay for several days.

Peter Explains His Actions

11:1 Soon the news reached the apostles and other believers in Judea that the Gentiles had received the word of God. 2 But when Peter arrived back in Jerusalem, the Jewish believers criticized him. 3 "You entered the home of Gentiles and even ate with them!" they said.

4 Then Peter told them exactly what had happened.

18 When the others heard this, they stopped objecting and began praising God. They said, "**We can see that God has also given the Gentiles the privilege of repenting of their sins and receiving eternal life.**"

James Is Killed and Peter Imprisoned

13:1 Now there were these prophets and teachers in the church at Antioch: **Barnabas**, Simeon called Niger, Lucius the Cyrenian, Manaen (a close friend of Herod the tetrarch from childhood) and

This was a big moment in the history of Christianity. Jesus is the savior for all people.

Barnabas means son of encouragement.

Saul.

2 While they were serving the Lord and fasting, the Holy Spirit said, "Set apart for me Barnabas and Saul for the work to which I have called them."

3 Then, after they had fasted and prayed and placed their hands on them, they sent them off.

Paul and Barnabas Preach in Cyprus

4 So Barnabas and Saul, sent out by the Holy Spirit, went down to Seleucia, and from there they sailed to Cyprus.

Paul Preaches in Antioch of Pisidia

13 Then Paul and his companions put out to sea from Paphos and came to Perga in Pamphylia, but John left them and returned to Jerusalem. 14 Moving on from Perga, they arrived at Pisidian Antioch, and on the Sabbath day they went into the synagogue and sat down. 15 After the reading from the law and the prophets, the leaders of the synagogue sent them a message, saying, "Brothers, if you have any message of exhortation for the people, speak it."

16 So Paul stood up, gestured with his hand and said, "Men of Israel, and you Gentiles who fear God, listen: 17 The God of this people Israel chose our ancestors and made the people great during their stay as foreigners in the country of Egypt, and with uplifted arm he led them out of it. 18 For a period of about forty years he put up with them in the wilderness. 19 After he had destroyed seven nations in the land of Canaan, he gave his people their land as an inheritance. 20 All this took about four hundred fifty years.

After this he gave them judges until the time of Samuel the prophet. 21 Then they asked for a king, and God gave them Saul son of Kish, a man from the tribe of Benjamin, who ruled forty years. 22 After removing him, God raised up David their king. He testified about him: 'I have found David the son of Jesse to be a man after my heart, who will accomplish everything I want him to do.'

23 From the descendants of this man God brought to Israel a Savior, Jesus, just as he promised. 24 Before Jesus arrived, John had proclaimed a baptism for repentance to all the people of Israel. 25 But while John was completing his mission, he said repeatedly, 'What do you think I am? I am not he. But look, one is coming after me. I am not worthy to untie the sandals on his feet!'

26 Brothers, descendants of Abraham's family, and those Gentiles among you who fear God, the message of this salvation has been sent to us. 27 For the people who live in Jerusalem and their rulers did not recognize him, and they fulfilled the sayings of the prophets that are read every Sabbath by condemning him. 28 Though they found no basis for a death sentence, they asked Pilate to have him executed. 29 When they had accomplished everything that was written about him, they took him down from the cross and placed him in a tomb. 30 But God raised him from

the dead, 31 and for many days he appeared to those who had accompanied him from Galilee to Jerusalem. These are now his witnesses to the people.

32 And we proclaim to you the good news about the promise to our ancestors, 33 that this promise God has fulfilled to us, their children, by raising Jesus, as also it is written in the second psalm, 'You are my Son; today I have fathered you.'

34 But regarding the fact that he has raised Jesus from the dead, never again to be in a state of decay, God has spoken in this way: 'I will give you the holy and trustworthy promises made to David.'

35 Therefore he also says in another psalm, 'You will not permit your Holy One to experience decay.'

36 For David, after he had served God's purpose in his own generation, died, was buried with his ancestors, and experienced decay, 37 but the one whom God raised up did not experience decay.

38 Therefore let it be known to you, brothers, that through this one forgiveness of sins is proclaimed to you, 39 and by this one everyone who believes is justified from everything from which the law of Moses could not justify you. 40 Watch out, then, that what is **spoken about by the prophets does** not happen to you:

[margin: Habakkuk 1:5]

41 'Look, you scoffers; be amazed and perish! For I am doing a work in your days, a work you would never believe, even if someone tells you.'"

42 As Paul and Barnabas were going out, the people were urging them to speak about these things on the next Sabbath. 43 When the meeting of the synagogue had broken up, many of the Jews and God-fearing proselytes followed Paul and Barnabas, who were speaking with them and were persuading them to continue in the grace of God.

44 On the next Sabbath almost the whole city assembled together to hear the word of the Lord. 45 But when the Jews saw the crowds, they were filled with jealousy, and they began to contradict what Paul was saying by reviling him.

46 Both Paul and Barnabas replied courageously, "It was necessary to speak the word of God to you first. Since you reject it and do not consider yourselves worthy of eternal life, we are turning to the Gentiles. 47 For this is what the Lord has commanded us: 'I have appointed you to be a light for the Gentiles, to bring salvation to the ends of the earth.'"

48 When the Gentiles heard this, they began to rejoice and praise the word of the Lord, and all who had been appointed for eternal life believed.

[margin: Often it is the people closest to you that reject change of]

49 So the word of the Lord was spreading through the entire region. 50 But the Jews incited the God-fearing women of high social standing and the prominent men of the city, stirred up persecution against Paul and Barnabas, and **threw them out of their**

region. 51 So after they shook the dust off their feet in protest against them, they went to Iconium. 52 And the disciples were filled with joy and with the Holy Spirit.

{The first missionary journey continued to Iconium, Lystra, and Derbe.}

Paul and Barnabas at Iconium

14:1 The same thing happened in Iconium when Paul and Barnabas went into the Jewish synagogue and spoke in such a way that a large group of both Jews and Greeks believed. 2 But the Jews who refused to believe stirred up the Gentiles and poisoned their minds against the brothers. 3 So they stayed there for a considerable time, speaking out courageously for the Lord, who testified to the message of his grace, granting miraculous signs and wonders to be performed through their hands. 4 But the population of the city was divided; some sided with the Jews, and some with the apostles. 5 When both the Gentiles and the Jews (together with their rulers) made an attempt to mistreat them and stone them, 6 Paul and Barnabas learned about it and fled to the Lycaonian cities of Lystra and Derbe and the surrounding region. 7 There they continued to proclaim the good news.

Paul and Barnabas at Lystra

8 In Lystra sat a man who could not use his feet, lame from birth, who had never walked. 9 This man was listening to Paul as he was speaking. When Paul stared intently at him and saw he had faith to be healed, 10 he said with a loud voice, "Stand upright on your feet." And the man leaped up and began walking.

11 So when the crowds saw what Paul had done, they shouted in the Lycaonian language, "The gods have come down to us in human form!" 12 They began to call Barnabas Zeus and Paul Hermes, because he was the chief speaker. 13 The priest of the temple of Zeus, located just outside the city, brought bulls and garlands to the city gates; he and the crowds wanted to offer sacrifices to them.

14 But when the apostles Barnabas and Paul heard about it, they tore their clothes and rushed out into the crowd, shouting, 15 "Men, why are you doing these things? We too are men, with human natures just like you! We are proclaiming the good news to you, so that you should turn from these worthless things to the living God, who made the heaven, the earth, the sea, and everything that is in them. 16 In past generations he allowed all the nations to go their own ways, 17 yet he did not leave himself without a witness by doing good, by giving you rain from heaven and fruitful seasons, satisfying you with food and your hearts with joy." 18 Even by saying these things, they scarcely persuaded the crowds not to offer sacrifice to them.

19 But Jews came from Antioch and Iconium, and after winning the crowds over, they stoned Paul and dragged him out of the city, presuming him to be dead. 20 But after the disciples had surrounded him, he got up and went back into the city. On the next

[margin note: any sort. When have you experienced this?]

day he left with Barnabas for Derbe.

Paul and Barnabas Return to Antioch in Syria

21 After they had proclaimed the good news in that city and made many disciples, they returned to Lystra, to Iconium, and to Antioch. 22 They strengthened the souls of the disciples and encouraged them to continue in the faith, saying, "We must enter the kingdom of God through many persecutions."

{Because of the success of Paul's first missionary journey, the believers needed to meet as a council in Jerusalem to decide what to do with all the new Gentile believers.}

The Jerusalem Council

15:1 Now some men came down from Judea and began to teach the brothers, "Unless you are circumcised according to the custom of Moses, you cannot be saved." 2 When Paul and Barnabas had a major argument and debate with them, the church appointed Paul and Barnabas and some others from among them to go up to meet with the apostles and elders in Jerusalem about this point of disagreement. 3 So they were sent on their way by the church, and as they passed through both Phoenicia and Samaria, they were relating at length the conversion of the Gentiles and bringing great joy to all the brothers. 4 When they arrived in Jerusalem, they were received by the church and the apostles and the elders, and they reported all the things God had done with them.

5 But some from the religious party of the **Pharisees** who had believed stood up and said, "It is necessary to circumcise the Gentiles and to order them to observe the law of Moses."

6 Both the apostles and the elders met together to deliberate about this matter. 7 After there had been much debate, Peter stood up and said to them, "Brothers, you know that some time ago God chose me to preach to the Gentiles so they would hear the message of the gospel and believe. 8 And God, who knows the heart, has testified to them by giving them the Holy Spirit just as he did to us, 9 and he made no distinction between them and us, cleansing their hearts by faith. 10 So now why are you putting God to the test by placing on the neck of the disciples a yoke that neither our ancestors nor we have been able to bear? 11 On the contrary, we believe that **we are saved through the grace of the Lord Jesus,** in the same way as they are."

12 The whole group kept quiet and listened to Barnabas and Paul while they explained all the miraculous signs and wonders God had done among the Gentiles through them. 13 After they stopped speaking, James replied, "Brothers, listen to me. 14 Simeon has explained how God first concerned himself to select from among the Gentiles a people for his name. 15 **The words of the prophets** agree with this, as it is written,

16 'After this I will return, and I will rebuild the fallen tent of David; I will rebuild its ruins and restore it, 17 so that the rest of humanity may seek the Lord, namely, all the Gentiles I have called

---

Jewish religious lawyers.

Are we saved by doing the law or by the grace of the Lord Jesus?

Amos 9:11; pg. 225.

to be my own,' says the Lord, who makes these things 18 known from long ago.

19 "Therefore I conclude that we should not cause extra difficulty for those among the Gentiles who are turning to God, 20 but that we should write them a letter telling them to abstain from things defiled by idols and from sexual immorality and from what has been strangled and from blood. 21 For Moses has had those who proclaim him in every town from ancient times, because he is read aloud in the synagogues every Sabbath."

22 Then the apostles and elders, with the whole church, decided to send men chosen from among them, Judas called Barsabbas and Silas, leaders among the brothers, to Antioch with Paul and Barnabas. 23 They sent this letter with them:

From the apostles and elders, your brothers, to the Gentile brothers and sisters in Antioch, Syria, and Cilicia, greetings! 24 Since we have heard that some have gone out from among us with no orders from us and have confused you, upsetting your minds by what they said, 25 we have unanimously decided to choose men to send to you along with our dear friends Barnabas and Paul, 26 who have risked their lives for the name of our Lord Jesus Christ. 27 Therefore we are sending Judas and Silas who will tell you these things themselves in person. 28 For it seemed best to the Holy Spirit and to us not to place any greater burden on you than these necessary rules: 29 that you abstain from meat that has been sacrificed to idols and from blood and from what has been strangled and from sexual immorality. If you keep yourselves from doing these things, you will do well. 'Farewell.'

30 So when they were dismissed, they went down to Antioch, and after gathering the entire group together, they delivered the letter. 31 When they read it aloud, the people rejoiced at its encouragement. 32 Both Judas and Silas, who were prophets themselves, encouraged and strengthened the brothers with a long speech. 33 After they had spent some time there, they were sent off in peace by the brothers to those who had sent them. 35 But Paul and Barnabas remained in Antioch, teaching and proclaiming (along with many others) the word of the Lord.

{Paul began his second missionary journey.}

Paul and Barnabas Part Company

36 After some days Paul said to Barnabas, "**Let's return and visit the brothers in every town where we proclaimed the word of the Lord to see how they are doing.**" 37 Barnabas wanted to bring John called Mark along with them too, 38 but Paul insisted that they should not take along this one who had left them in Pamphylia and had not accompanied them in the work. 39 They had a sharp disagreement, so that they parted company. Barnabas took along Mark and sailed away to Cyprus, 40 but Paul chose Silas and set out, commended to the grace of the Lord by the brothers and sisters. 41 He passed through Syria and Cilicia, strengthening the churches.

If you are new to the faith you need people like Paul and Barnabas in your life to 'see how you are doing.'

The Book of Acts

Notice the personal "we" this sentence begins with. Many scholars think this is where Luke, the author of the book of Acts, joins Paul in his journey.

Lydia of Philippi Believes in Jesus

16:11 **We put out to sea** from Troas and sailed a straight course to Samothrace, the next day to Neapolis, 12 and from there to Philippi, which is a leading city of that district of Macedonia, a Roman colony. We stayed in this city for some days.

13 On the Sabbath day we went outside the city gate to the side of the river, where we thought there would be a place of prayer, and we sat down and began to speak to the women who had assembled there. 14 A woman named Lydia, a dealer in purple cloth from the city of Thyatira, a God-fearing woman, listened to us. The Lord opened her heart to respond to what Paul was saying. 15 After she and her household were baptized, she urged us, "If you consider me to be a believer in the Lord, come and stay in my house." And she persuaded us.

Paul and Silas Are Thrown into Prison

16 Now as we were going to the place of prayer, a slave girl met us who had a spirit that enabled her to foretell the future by supernatural means. She brought her owners a great profit by fortune-telling. 17 She followed behind Paul and us and kept crying out, "These men are servants of the Most High God, who are proclaiming to you the way of salvation." 18 She continued to do this for many days. But Paul became greatly annoyed, and turned and said to the spirit, "I command you in the name of Jesus Christ to come out of her!" And it came out of her at once.

19 But when her owners saw their hope of profit was gone, they seized Paul and Silas and dragged them into the marketplace before the authorities. 20 When they had brought them before the magistrates, they said, "These men are throwing our city into confusion. They are Jews 21 and are advocating customs that are not lawful for us to accept or practice, since we are Romans."

22 The crowd joined the attack against them, and the magistrates tore the clothes off Paul and Silas and ordered them to be beaten with rods. 23 After they had beaten them severely, they threw them into prison and commanded the jailer to guard them securely. 24 Receiving such orders, he threw them in the inner cell and fastened their feet in the stocks.

25 About midnight Paul and Silas were praying and singing hymns to God, and the rest of the prisoners were listening to them. 26 Suddenly a great earthquake occurred, so that the foundations of the prison were shaken. Immediately all the doors flew open, and the bonds of all the prisoners came loose. 27 When the jailer woke up and saw the doors of the prison standing open, he drew his sword and was about to kill himself, because he assumed the prisoners had escaped. 28 But Paul called out loudly, "Do not harm yourself, for we are all here!"

At some point in your life you will ask this question. And here is the Bible's answer.

29 Calling for lights, the jailer rushed in and fell down trembling at the feet of Paul and Silas. 30 Then he brought them outside and asked, **"Sirs, what must I do to be saved?"**

31 They replied, **"Believe in the Lord Jesus and you will be saved,** you

and your household." 32 Then they spoke the word of the Lord to him, along with all those who were in his house. 33 At that hour of the night he took them and washed their wounds; then he and all his family were baptized right away. 34 The jailer brought them into his house and set food before them, and he rejoiced greatly that he had come to believe in God, together with his entire household.

35 At daybreak the magistrates sent their police officers, saying, "Release those men." 36 The jailer reported these words to Paul, saying, "The magistrates have sent orders to release you. So come out now and go in peace."

37 But Paul said to the police officers, "They had us beaten in public without a proper trial—even though we are Roman citizens—and they threw us in prison. And now they want to send us away secretly? Absolutely not! They themselves must come and escort us out!"

38 The police officers reported these words to the magistrates. They were frightened when they heard Paul and Silas were Roman citizens 39 and came and apologized to them. After they brought them out, they asked them repeatedly to leave the city. 40 When they came out of the prison, they entered Lydia's house, and when they saw the brothers, they encouraged them and then departed.

{They then went to Thessalonica where there was trouble, so they moved on to Berea.}

Paul and Silas at Berea

17:10 The brothers sent Paul and Silas off to Berea at once, during the night. When they arrived, they went to the Jewish synagogue. 11 These Jews were more open-minded than those in Thessalonica, for **they eagerly received the message, examining the scriptures carefully every day to see if these things were so.** 12 Therefore many of them believed, along with quite a few prominent Greek women and men.

13 But when the Jews from Thessalonica heard that Paul had also proclaimed the word of God in Berea, they came there too, inciting and disturbing the crowds. 14 Then the brothers sent Paul away to the coast at once, but Silas and Timothy remained in Berea. 15 Those who accompanied Paul escorted him as far as Athens, and after receiving an order for Silas and Timothy to come to him as soon as possible, they left.

Paul at Athens

16 While Paul was waiting for them in Athens, his spirit was greatly upset because he saw the city was full of idols. 17 So he was addressing the Jews and the God-fearing Gentiles in the synagogue, and in the marketplace every day those who happened to be there. 18 Also some of the **Epicurean and Stoic philosophers** were conversing with him, and some were asking, "What does this foolish babbler want to say?" Others said, "He seems to be a proclaimer of foreign gods." (They said this because he was proclaiming the good news about Jesus and the resurrection.) 19 So they

---

Don't ever just take the word of a preacher or teacher as the truth. Always check out what they say against what the Bible says.

Epicureanism = life is about your happiness and pleasure.
Stoicism = life is hard; deny the pain and just get on with it.

> Paul began his presentation from where they were. He then tried to build out from that. Why might this be an effective way to persuade people to your way of thinking?

took Paul and brought him to the Areopagus, saying, "May we know what this new teaching is that you are proclaiming? 20 For you are bringing some surprising things to our ears, so we want to know what they mean." 21 (All the Athenians and the foreigners who lived there used to spend their time in nothing else than telling or listening to something new.)

22 So Paul stood before the Areopagus and said, **"Men of Athens, I see that you are very religious in all respects.** 23 For as I went around and observed closely your objects of worship, I even found an altar with this inscription: 'To an unknown god.' Therefore what you worship without knowing it, this I proclaim to you.

24 The God who made the world and everything in it, who is Lord of heaven and earth, does not live in temples made by human hands, 25 nor is he served by human hands, as if he needed anything, because he himself gives life and breath and everything to everyone. 26 From one man he made every nation of the human race to inhabit the entire earth, determining their set times and the fixed limits of the places where they would live, 27 so that they would search for God and perhaps grope around for him and find him, though he is not far from each one of us. 28 For in him we live and move about and exist, as even some of your own poets have said, 'For we too are his offspring.'

29 So since we are God's offspring, we should not think the deity is like gold or silver or stone, an image made by human skill and imagination. 30 Therefore, although God has overlooked such times of ignorance, he now commands all people everywhere to repent, 31 because he has set a day on which he is going to judge the world in righteousness, by a man whom he designated, having provided proof to everyone by raising him from the dead."

32 Now when they heard about the resurrection from the dead, some began to scoff, but others said, "We will hear you again about this." 33 So Paul left the Areopagus.

Paul at Corinth

18:1 After this Paul departed from Athens and went to Corinth.

9 The Lord said to Paul by a vision in the night, "Do not be afraid, but speak and do not be silent, 10 because I am with you, and no one will assault you to harm you, because **I have many people in this city.**" 11 So he stayed there a year and six months, teaching the word of God among them.

{Then Paul briefly passed through Ephesus, then to Caesarea, and finally back to Antioch. After spending some time in Antioch, Paul left on his third missionary journey.}

Disciples of John the Baptist at Ephesus

19:1 While Apollos was in Corinth, Paul went through the inland regions and came to Ephesus.

8 So Paul entered the synagogue and spoke out fearlessly for three months, addressing and convincing them about the king-

> Two things about sharing your faith with others:
> 1. God is with you.
> 2. God has and is already working on the people you will share your faith with.

dom of God. 9 But when some were stubborn and refused to believe, reviling the Way before the congregation, he left them and took the disciples with him, addressing them every day in the lecture hall of Tyrannus. 10 This went on for two years, so that all who lived in the province of Asia, both Jews and Greeks, heard the word of the Lord.

11 God was performing extraordinary miracles by Paul's hands ... 20 In this way the word of the Lord continued to grow in power and to prevail.

21 Now after all these things had taken place, Paul resolved to go to Jerusalem, passing through Macedonia and Achaia. He said, "After I have been there, I must also see Rome." 22 So after sending two of his assistants, Timothy and Erastus, to Macedonia, he himself stayed on for a while in the province of Asia.

23 At that time a great disturbance took place concerning **the Way**. 24 For a man named Demetrius, a silversmith who made silver shrines of Artemis, brought a great deal of business to the craftsmen. 25 He gathered these together, along with the workmen in similar trades, and said, "Men, you know that our prosperity comes from this business. 26 And you see and hear that this Paul has persuaded and turned away a large crowd, not only in Ephesus but in practically all of the province of Asia, by saying that gods made by hands are not gods at all. 27 There is danger not only that this business of ours will come into disrepute, but also that the temple of the great goddess Artemis will be regarded as nothing, and she whom all the province of Asia and the world worship will suffer the loss of her greatness."

28 When they heard this they became enraged and began to shout, **"Great is Artemis of the Ephesians!"** 29 The city was filled with the uproar, and the crowd rushed to the theater together, dragging with them Gaius and Aristarchus, the Macedonians who were Paul's traveling companions. 30 But when Paul wanted to enter the public assembly, the disciples would not let him. 31 Even some of the provincial authorities who were his friends sent a message to him, urging him not to venture into the **theater**.

32 So then some were shouting one thing, some another, for the assembly was in confusion, and most of them did not know why they had met together. 33 Some of the crowd concluded it was about Alexander because the Jews had pushed him to the front. Alexander, gesturing with his hand, was wanting to make a defense before the public assembly. 34 But when they recognized that he was a Jew, they all shouted in unison, "Great is Artemis of the Ephesians!" for about two hours.

35 After the city secretary quieted the crowd, he said, "Men of Ephesus, what person is there who does not know that the city of the Ephesians is the keeper of the temple of the great Artemis and of her image that fell from heaven? 36 So because these facts are indisputable, you must keep quiet and not do anything reckless. 37 For you have brought these men here who are neither temple robbers nor blasphemers of our goddess. 38 If then Demetri-

---

Christians were called people of "the way." Christianity is not just a belief system, it is a way of life that affects all aspects of your life.

The temple of Artemis was one of the Wonders of the World at that time (All that remains is a single column).

You can still sit in this 5,000 seat amphitheater today.

us and the craftsmen who are with him have a complaint against someone, the courts are open and there are proconsuls; let them bring charges against one another there. 39 But if you want anything in addition, it will have to be settled in a legal assembly. 40 For we are in danger of being charged with rioting today, since there is no cause we can give to explain this disorderly gathering." 41 After he had said this, he dismissed the assembly.

Paul Travels Through Macedonia and Greece

20:1 After the disturbance had ended, Paul sent for the disciples, and after encouraging them and saying farewell, he left to go to Macedonia. 2 After he had gone through those regions and spoken many words of encouragement to the believers there, he came to Greece, 3 where he stayed for three months. Because the Jews had made a plot against him as he was intending to sail for Syria, he decided to return through Macedonia.

16 For Paul had decided to sail past Ephesus so as not to spend time in the province of Asia, for he was hurrying to arrive in Jerusalem, if possible, by the day of **Pentecost**. 17 From Miletus he sent a message to Ephesus, telling the elders of the church to come to him.

18 When they arrived, he said to them, "You yourselves know how I lived the whole time I was with you, from the first day I set foot in the province of Asia, 19 serving the Lord with all humility and with tears, and with the trials that happened to me because of the plots of the Jews. 20 You know that I did not hold back from proclaiming to you anything that would be helpful, and from teaching you publicly and from house to house, 21 testifying to both Jews and Greeks about repentance toward God and faith in our Lord Jesus.

22 And now, compelled by the Spirit, I am going to Jerusalem without knowing what will happen to me there, 23 except that the Holy Spirit warns me in town after town that imprisonment and persecutions are waiting for me. 24 But **I do not consider my life worth anything to myself, so that I may finish my task and the ministry that I received from the Lord Jesus, to testify to the good news of God's grace.**

25 "And now I know that none of you among whom I went around proclaiming the kingdom will see me again. 26 Therefore I declare to you today that I am innocent of the blood of you all. 27 For I did not hold back from announcing to you the whole purpose of God. 28 Watch out for yourselves and for all the flock of which the Holy Spirit has made you overseers, to shepherd the church of God that he obtained with the blood of his own Son. 29 I know that after I am gone fierce wolves will come in among you, not sparing the flock. 30 Even from among your own group men will arise, teaching perversions of the truth to draw the disciples away after them. 31 Therefore be alert, remembering that night and day for three years I did not stop warning each one of you with tears.

32 And now I entrust you to God and to the message of his

> *This is the 2nd of 2 harvest festivals giving thanks to the Lord (the first would have been 50 days earlier - hence the word "pente" meaning 50).*

> *This is a good verse for all of us.*

grace. This message is able to build you up and give you an inheritance among all those who are sanctified. 33 I have desired no one's silver or gold or clothing. 34 You yourselves know that these hands of mine provided for my needs and the needs of those who were with me. 35 By all these things, I have shown you that by working in this way we must help the weak, and remember the words of the Lord Jesus that he himself said, 'It is more blessed to give than to receive.'"

36 When he had said these things, he knelt down with them all and prayed. 37 They all began to **weep loudly, and hugged Paul and kissed him,** 38 especially saddened by what he had said, that they were not going to see him again. Then they accompanied him to the ship.

Paul's Journey to Jerusalem

21:17 When we arrived in Jerusalem, the brothers welcomed us gladly. 18 The next day Paul went in with us to see James, and all the elders were there. 19 When Paul had greeted them, he began to explain in detail what God had done among the Gentiles through his ministry.

20 When they heard this, they praised God. Then they said to him, "You see, brother, how many thousands of Jews there are who have believed, and they are all ardent observers of the law. 21 They have been informed about you—that you teach all the Jews now living among the Gentiles to abandon Moses, telling them not to circumcise their children or live according to our customs. 22 What then should we do? They will no doubt hear that you have come. 23 So do what we tell you: We have four men who have taken a vow; 24 take them and purify yourself along with them and pay their expenses, so that they may have their heads shaved. Then everyone will know there is nothing in what they have been told about you, but that you yourself live in conformity with the law. 25 But regarding the Gentiles who have believed, we have written a letter, having decided that they should avoid meat that has been sacrificed to idols and blood and what has been strangled and sexual immorality."

26 Then Paul took the men the next day, and after he had purified himself along with them, he went to the temple and gave notice of the completion of the days of purification, when the sacrifice would be offered for each of them.

Paul Arrested

27 When the seven days were almost over, the Jews from the province of Asia who had seen him in the temple area stirred up the whole crowd and seized him, 28 shouting, "Men of Israel, help! This is the man who teaches everyone everywhere against our people, our law, and this sanctuary! Furthermore he has brought Greeks into the inner courts of the temple and made this holy place ritually unclean!" 29 (For they had seen Trophimus the Ephesian in the city with him previously, and they assumed Paul had brought him into the inner temple courts.) 30 The whole city was

Saying good-bye to people you love often involves tears. When have you experienced this?

stirred up, and the people rushed together. They seized Paul and dragged him out of the temple courts, and immediately the doors were shut. 31 While they were trying to kill him, a report was sent up to the commanding officer of the cohort that all Jerusalem was in confusion. 32 He immediately took soldiers and centurions and ran down to the crowd. When they saw the commanding officer and the soldiers, they stopped beating Paul. 33 Then the commanding officer came up and arrested him and ordered him to be tied up with two chains; he then asked who he was and what he had done. 34 But some in the crowd shouted one thing, and others something else, and when the commanding officer was unable to find out the truth because of the disturbance, he ordered Paul to be brought into the barracks. 35 When he came to the steps, Paul had to be carried by the soldiers because of the violence of the mob, 36 for a crowd of people followed them, screaming, "Away with him!"

Paul Speaks to the Crowd

37 As Paul was about to be brought into the barracks, he said to the commanding officer, "May I say something to you?" The officer replied, "Do you know Greek? 38 Then you're not that Egyptian who started a rebellion and led the four thousand men of the 'Assassins' into the wilderness some time ago?" 39 Paul answered, "I am a Jew from Tarsus in Cilicia, a citizen of an important city. Please allow me to speak to the people." 40 When the commanding officer had given him permission, Paul stood on the steps and gestured to the people with his hand. When they had become silent, he addressed them in Aramaic,

22:1 "Brothers and fathers, listen to my defense that I now make to you." 2 (When they heard that he was addressing them in Aramaic, they became even quieter.) Then Paul said, 3 "I am a Jew, born in Tarsus in Cilicia, but brought up in this city, educated with strictness under **Gamaliel** according to the law of our ancestors, and was zealous for God just as all of you are today. 4 I persecuted this Way even to the point of death, tying up both men and women and putting them in prison, 5 as both the high priest and the whole council of elders can testify about me. From them I also received letters to the brothers in Damascus, and I was on my way to make arrests there and bring the prisoners to Jerusalem to be punished. 6 As I was en route and near Damascus, about noon a very bright light from heaven suddenly flashed around me. 7 Then I fell to the ground and heard a voice saying to me, 'Saul, Saul, why are you persecuting me?' 8 I answered, 'Who are you, Lord?' He said to me, 'I am Jesus the Nazarene, whom you are persecuting.' 9 Those who were with me saw the light, but did not understand the voice of the one who was speaking to me. 10 So I asked, 'What should I do, Lord?' The Lord said to me, 'Get up and go to Damascus; there you will be told about everything that you have been designated to do.' 11 Since I could not see because of the brilliance of that light, I came to Damascus led by the hand of those who were with me. 12 A man named Ananias, a devout man according to the law, well spoken of by all the Jews who live there,

Paul was educated in the Jewish law under one of the most respected lawyers in the Jewish religion. Isn't it interesting that in some way God was already preparing Paul to be a great leader long before Paul became a Christian?

13 came to me and stood beside me and said to me, 'Brother Saul, regain your sight!' And at that very moment I looked up and saw him. 14 Then he said, 'The God of our ancestors has already chosen you to know his will, to see the Righteous One, and to hear a command from his mouth, 15 because you will be his witness to all people of what you have seen and heard. 16 And now what are you waiting for? Get up, be baptized, and have your sins washed away, calling on his name.' 17 When I returned to Jerusalem and was praying in the temple, I fell into a trance 18 and saw the Lord saying to me, 'Hurry and get out of Jerusalem quickly, because they will not accept your testimony about me.' 19 I replied, 'Lord, they themselves know that I imprisoned and beat those in the various synagogues who believed in you. 20 And when the blood of your witness Stephen was shed, I myself was standing nearby, approving, and guarding the cloaks of those who were killing him.' 21 Then he said to me, 'Go, because I will send you far away to the Gentiles.'"

The Roman Commander Questions Paul

22 **The crowd was listening to him until he said this.** Then they raised their voices and shouted, "Away with this man from the earth! For he should not be allowed to live!"

23 While they were screaming and throwing off their cloaks and tossing dust in the air, 24 the commanding officer ordered Paul to be brought back into the barracks. He told them to interrogate Paul by beating him with a lash so that he could find out the reason the crowd was shouting at Paul in this way. 25 When they had stretched him out for the lash, Paul said to the centurion standing nearby, "Is it legal for you to lash a man who is a Roman citizen without a proper trial?" 26 When the centurion heard this, he went to the commanding officer and reported it, saying, "What are you about to do? For this man is a Roman citizen." 27 So the commanding officer came and asked Paul, "Tell me, are you a Roman citizen?" He replied, "Yes." 28 The commanding officer answered, "I acquired this citizenship with a large sum of money." "But I was even born a citizen," Paul replied. 29 Then those who were about to interrogate him stayed away from him, and the commanding officer was frightened when he realized that Paul was a Roman citizen and that he had had him tied up.

Paul Before the Sanhedrin

30 The next day, because the commanding officer wanted to know the true reason Paul was being accused by the Jews, he released him and ordered the chief priests and the whole council to assemble. He then brought Paul down and had him stand before them.

23:1 Paul looked directly at the council and said, "Brothers, I have lived my life with a clear conscience before God to this day." 2 At that the high priest Ananias ordered those standing near Paul to strike him on the mouth. 3 Then Paul said to him, "God is going to strike you, you whitewashed wall! Do you sit there judging me according to the law, and in violation of the law you order me to

> The Jews did not think their religion was for the Gentiles - non-Jews.

be struck?" 4 Those standing near him said, "Do you dare insult God's high priest?" 5 Paul replied, "I did not realize, brothers, that he was the high priest, for it is written, 'You must not speak evil about a ruler of your people.'"

6 Then when Paul noticed that part of them were Sadducees and the others Pharisees, he shouted out in the council, "Brothers, I am a Pharisee, a son of Pharisees. I am on trial concerning the hope of the resurrection of the dead!" 7 When he said this, an argument began between the Pharisees and the Sadducees, and the assembly was divided. 8 (For the Sadducees say there is no resurrection, or angel, or spirit, but the Pharisees acknowledge them all.) 9 There was a great commotion, and some experts in the law from the party of the Pharisees stood up and protested strongly, "We find nothing wrong with this man. What if a spirit or an angel has spoken to him?" 10 When the argument became so great the commanding officer feared that they would tear Paul to pieces, he ordered the detachment to go down, take him away from them by force, and bring him into the barracks.

11 The following night the Lord stood near Paul and said, "Have courage, for just as you have testified about me in Jerusalem, so you must also testify in Rome."

The Plot to Kill Paul

12 When morning came, the Jews formed a conspiracy and bound themselves with an oath not to eat or drink anything until they had killed Paul. 13 There were more than forty of them who formed this conspiracy. 14 They went to the chief priests and the elders and said, "We have bound ourselves with a solemn oath not to partake of anything until we have killed Paul. 15 So now you and the council request the commanding officer to bring him down to you, as if you were going to determine his case by conducting a more thorough inquiry. We are ready to kill him before he comes near this place."

16 But when the son of Paul's sister heard about the ambush, he came and entered the barracks and told Paul. 17 Paul called one of the centurions and said, "Take this young man to the commanding officer, for he has something to report to him." 18 So the centurion took him and brought him to the commanding officer and said, "The prisoner Paul called me and asked me to bring this young man to you because he has something to tell you." 19 The commanding officer took him by the hand, withdrew privately, and asked, "What is it that you want to report to me?" 20 He replied, "The Jews have agreed to ask you to bring Paul down to the council tomorrow, as if they were going to inquire more thoroughly about him. 21 So do not let them persuade you to do this, because more than forty of them are lying in ambush for him. They have bound themselves with an oath not to eat or drink anything until they have killed him, and now they are ready, waiting for you to agree to their request." 22 Then the commanding officer sent the young man away, directing him, "Tell no one that you have reported these things to me." 23 Then he summoned two of the centurions and said, "Make ready two hundred soldiers to go to

Caesarea along with seventy horsemen and two hundred spearmen by nine o'clock tonight, 24 and provide mounts for Paul to ride so that he may be brought safely to Felix the governor."

The Accusations Against Paul

{Paul made his case before Felix the governor but was kept under guard for two years.}

24:27 After two years had passed, Porcius Festus succeeded Felix, and because he wanted to do the Jews a favor, Felix left Paul in prison.

25:7 When he (Festus) arrived, the Jews who had come down from Jerusalem stood around him, bringing many serious charges that they were not able to prove. 8 Paul said in his defense, "I have committed no offense against the Jewish law or against the temple or against Caesar." 9 But Festus, wanting to do the Jews a favor, asked Paul, "Are you willing to go up to Jerusalem and be tried before me there on these charges?" 10 Paul replied, "I am standing before Caesar's judgment seat, where I should be tried. I have done nothing wrong to the Jews, as you also know very well. 11 If then I am in the wrong and have done anything that deserves death, I am not trying to escape dying, but if not one of their charges against me is true, no one can hand me over to them. **I appeal to Caesar!**" 12 Then, after conferring with his council, Festus replied, "You have appealed to Caesar; to Caesar you will go!"

Festus Asks King Agrippa for Advice

13 After several days had passed, King Agrippa and Bernice arrived at Caesarea to pay their respects to Festus. 14 While they were staying there many days, Festus explained Paul's case to the king to get his opinion, saying, "There is a man left here as a prisoner by Felix. 15 When I was in Jerusalem, the chief priests and the elders of the Jews informed me about him, asking for a sentence of condemnation against him. 16 I answered them that it was not the custom of the Romans to hand over anyone before the accused had met his accusers face to face and had been given an opportunity to make a defense against the accusation. 17 So after they came back here with me, I did not postpone the case, but the next day I sat on the judgment seat and ordered the man to be brought. 18 When his accusers stood up, they did not charge him with any of the evil deeds I had suspected. 19 Rather they had several points of disagreement with him about their own religion and about a man named Jesus who was dead, whom Paul claimed to be alive. 20 Because I was at a loss how I could investigate these matters, I asked if he were willing to go to Jerusalem and be tried there on these charges. 21 But when Paul appealed to be kept in custody for the decision of His Majesty the Emperor, I ordered him to be kept under guard until I could send him to Caesar." 22 Agrippa said to Festus, "I would also like to hear the man myself." "Tomorrow," he replied, "you will hear him."

> As a Roman citizen, Paul had the right to make his case before Caesar.

Paul Before King Agrippa and Bernice

23 So the next day Agrippa and Bernice came with great pomp and entered the audience hall, along with the senior military officers and the prominent men of the city. When Festus gave the order, Paul was brought in. 24 Then Festus said, "King Agrippa, and all you who are present here with us, you see this man about whom the entire Jewish populace petitioned me both in Jerusalem and here, shouting loudly that he ought not to live any longer. 25 But I found that he had done nothing that deserved death, and when he appealed to His Majesty the Emperor, I decided to send him. 26 But I have nothing definite to write to my lord about him. Therefore I have brought him before you all, and especially before you, King Agrippa, so that after this preliminary hearing I may have something to write. 27 For it seems unreasonable to me to send a prisoner without clearly indicating the charges against him."

26:1 So Agrippa said to Paul, "You have permission to speak for yourself." Then Paul held out his hand and began his defense:

2 "Regarding all the things I have been accused of by the Jews, King Agrippa, I consider myself fortunate that I am about to make my defense before you today, 3 because you are especially familiar with all the customs and controversial issues of the Jews. Therefore I ask you to listen to me patiently. 4 Now all the Jews know the way I lived from my youth, spending my life from the beginning among my own people and in Jerusalem. 5 They know, because they have known me from time past, if they are willing to testify, that according to the strictest party of our religion, I lived as a Pharisee. 6 And now I stand here on trial because of my hope in the promise made by God to our ancestors, 7 a promise that our twelve tribes hope to attain as they earnestly serve God night and day. Concerning this hope the Jews are accusing me, Your Majesty! 8 Why do you people think it is unbelievable that God raises the dead? 9 Of course, I myself was convinced that it was necessary to do many things hostile to the name of Jesus the Nazarene. 10 And that is what I did in Jerusalem: Not only did I lock up many of the saints in prisons by the authority I received from the chief priests, but I also cast my vote against them when they were sentenced to death. 11 I punished them often in all the synagogues and tried to force them to blaspheme. Because I was so furiously enraged at them, I went to persecute them even in foreign cities.

12 "While doing this very thing, as I was going to Damascus with authority and complete power from the chief priests, 13 about noon along the road, Your Majesty, **I saw a light from heaven, brighter than the sun, shining everywhere around me** and those traveling with me. 14 When we had all fallen to the ground, I heard a voice saying to me in Aramaic, 'Saul, Saul, why are you persecuting me? You are hurting yourself by kicking against the goads.' 15 So I said, 'Who are you, Lord?' And the Lord replied, 'I am Jesus whom you are persecuting. 16 But get up and stand on your feet, for I have appeared to you for this reason, to designate you in advance as a servant and witness to the things you have seen and to the things

---

Notice how Paul kept telling the same story over and over - the story of how Jesus made a difference in his life. How has Jesus made a difference in your life?

in which I will appear to you. 17 I will rescue you from your own people and from the Gentiles, to whom I am sending you 18 to open their eyes so that they turn from darkness to light and from the power of Satan to God, so that they may receive forgiveness of sins and a share among those who are sanctified by faith in me.'

19 "Therefore, King Agrippa, I was not disobedient to the heavenly vision, 20 but I declared to those in Damascus first, and then to those in Jerusalem and in all Judea, and to the Gentiles, that they should repent and turn to God, performing deeds consistent with repentance. 21 For this reason the Jews, after they seized me while I was in the temple courts, were trying to kill me. 22 I have experienced help from God to this day, and so I stand testifying to both small and great, saying nothing except what the prophets and Moses said was going to happen: 23 that the Christ was to suffer and be the first to rise from the dead, to proclaim light both to our people and to the Gentiles."

24 As Paul was saying these things in his defense, Festus exclaimed loudly, "You have lost your mind, Paul! Your great learning is driving you insane!" 25 But Paul replied, "I have not lost my mind, most excellent Festus, but am speaking true and rational words. 26 For the king knows about these things, and I am speaking freely to him, because I cannot believe that any of these things has escaped his notice, for this was not done in a corner. 27 Do you believe the prophets, King Agrippa? I know that you believe." 28 Agrippa said to Paul, "In such a short time are you persuading me to become a Christian?" 29 Paul replied, "I pray to God that whether in a short or a long time not only you but also all those who are listening to me today could become such as I am, except for these chains."

30 So the king got up, and with him the governor and Bernice and those sitting with them, 31 and as they were leaving they said to one another, "This man is not doing anything deserving death or imprisonment." 32 Agrippa said to Festus, "This man could have been released if he had not appealed to Caesar."

Paul and Company Sail for Rome

{Paul and several other prisoners set sail for Italy, encountering headwinds and slow going. Paul warned the crew of trouble ahead.}

27:10 "Men, I can see the voyage is going to end in disaster and great loss not only of the cargo and the ship, but also of our lives." 11 But the centurion was more convinced by the captain and the ship's owner than by what Paul said. 12 Because the harbor was not suitable to spend the winter in, the majority decided to put out to sea from there. They hoped that somehow they could reach Phoenix, a harbor of Crete facing southwest and northwest, and spend the winter there. 13 When a gentle south wind sprang up, they thought they could carry out their purpose, so they weighed anchor and sailed close along the coast of Crete. 14 Not long after this, a hurricane-force wind called the northeaster blew down from the island. 15 When the ship was caught in it and could not head into the wind, we gave way to it and were driven along. 16 As we ran under the lee of a small island called Cauda, we were able with difficulty to get the ship's boat under control. 17 After the crew had hoisted it aboard, they used supports to undergird the ship. Fearing they would run aground on the Syrtis, they lowered the sea anchor, thus letting themselves be driven along. 18 The next day, because we were violently battered by the storm, they began throwing the cargo overboard, 19 and on the third day they threw the ship's gear overboard with their own hands. 20 When neither sun nor stars appeared for many days and a violent storm continued to batter us, we finally abandoned all hope of being saved.

21 Since many of them had no desire to eat, Paul stood up among them and said, "Men, you should have listened to me and not put out to sea from Crete, thus avoiding this damage and loss. 22 And now I advise you to keep up your courage, for there will be no loss of life among you, but only the ship will be lost. 23 For last night an angel of the God to whom I belong and whom I serve came to me 24 and said, 'Do not be afraid, Paul! You must stand before Caesar, and God has graciously granted you the safety of all who are sailing with you.' 25 Therefore keep up your courage, men, for I have faith in God that it will be just as I have been told. 26 But we must run aground on some island."

27 When the fourteenth night had come, while we were being driven across the Adriatic Sea, about midnight the sailors suspected they were approaching some land. 28 They took soundings and found the water was twenty fathoms deep; when they had sailed a little farther they took soundings again and found it was fifteen fathoms deep. 29 Because they were afraid that we would run aground on the rocky coast, they threw out four anchors from the stern and wished for day to appear. 30 Then when the sailors tried to escape from the ship and were lowering the ship's boat into the sea, pretending that they were going to put out anchors from the bow, 31 Paul said to the centurion and the soldiers, "Unless these men stay with the ship, you cannot be saved." 32 Then the soldiers cut the ropes of the ship's boat and let it drift away.

33 As day was about to dawn, Paul urged them all to take some food, saying, "Today is the fourteenth day you have been in suspense and have gone without food; you have eaten nothing. 34 Therefore I urge you to take some food, for this is important for your survival. For not one of you will lose a hair from his head." 35 After he said this, Paul took bread and gave thanks to God in front of them all, broke it, and began to eat. 36 So all of them were encouraged and took food themselves. 37 (We were in all two hundred seventy-six persons on the ship.) 38 When they had eaten enough to be satisfied, they lightened the ship by throwing the wheat into the sea.

Paul Is Shipwrecked

39 When day came, they did not recognize the land, but they noticed a bay with a beach, where they decided to run the ship aground if they could. 40 So they slipped the anchors and left

them in the sea, at the same time loosening the linkage that bound the steering oars together. Then they hoisted the foresail to the wind and steered toward the beach. 41 But they encountered a patch of crosscurrents and ran the ship aground; the bow stuck fast and could not be moved, but the stern was being broken up by the force of the waves. 42 Now the soldiers' plan was to kill the prisoners so that none of them would escape by swimming away. 43 But the centurion, wanting to save Paul's life, prevented them from carrying out their plan. He ordered those who could swim to jump overboard first and get to land, 44 and the rest were to follow, some on planks and some on pieces of the ship. And in this way all were brought safely to land.

Paul on the Island of Malta

28:1 After we had safely reached shore, we learned that the island was called Malta. 2 The local inhabitants showed us extraordinary kindness, for they built a fire and welcomed us all because it had started to rain and was cold. 3 When Paul had gathered a bundle of brushwood and was putting it on the fire, a viper came out because of the heat and fastened itself on his hand. 4 When the local people saw the creature hanging from Paul's hand, they said to one another, "No doubt this man is a murderer! Although he has escaped from the sea, Justice herself has not allowed him to live!" 5 However, Paul shook the creature off into the fire and suffered no harm. 6 But they were expecting that he was going to swell up or suddenly drop dead. So after they had waited a long time and had seen nothing unusual happen to him, they changed their minds and said he was a god.

7 Now in the region around that place were fields belonging to the chief official of the island, named Publius, who welcomed us and entertained us hospitably as guests for three days. 8 The father of Publius lay sick in bed, suffering from fever and dysentery. Paul went in to see him and after praying, placed his hands on him and healed him. 9 After this had happened, many of the people on the island who were sick also came and were healed. 10 They also bestowed many honors, and when we were preparing to sail, they gave us all the supplies we needed.

Paul Finally Reaches Rome

11 After three months we put out to sea in an Alexandrian ship that had wintered at the island and had the "Heavenly Twins" as its figurehead. 12 We put in at Syracuse and stayed there three days. 13 From there we cast off and arrived at Rhegium, and after one day a south wind sprang up and on the second day we came to Puteoli. 14 There we found some brothers and were invited to stay with them seven days. And in this way we came to Rome. 15 The brothers from there, when they heard about us, came as far as the Forum of Appius and Three Taverns to meet us. When he saw them, Paul thanked God and took courage. 16 When we entered Rome, Paul was allowed to live by himself, with the soldier who was guarding him.

Paul Addresses the Jewish Community in Rome

17 After three days Paul called the local Jewish leaders together. When they had assembled, he said to them, "Brothers, although I had done nothing against our people or the customs of our ancestors, from Jerusalem I was handed over as a prisoner to the Romans. 18 When they had heard my case, they wanted to release me, because there was no basis for a death sentence against me. 19 But when the Jews objected, I was forced to appeal to Caesar—not that I had some charge to bring against my own people. 20 So for this reason I have asked to see you and speak with you, for I am bound with this chain because of the hope of Israel." 21 They replied, "We have received no letters from Judea about you, nor have any of the brothers come from there and reported or said anything bad about you. 22 But we would like to hear from you what you think, for regarding this sect we know that people everywhere speak against it."

23 They set a day to meet with him, and they came to him where he was staying in even greater numbers. From morning until evening he explained things to them, testifying about the kingdom of God and trying to convince them about Jesus from both the law of Moses and the prophets. 24 Some were convinced by what he said, but others refused to believe. 25 So they began to leave, unable to agree among themselves, after Paul made one last statement: "The Holy Spirit spoke rightly to your ancestors through the **prophet Isaiah** 26 when he said,

Isaiah 6:9.

'Go to this people and say, "You will keep on hearing, but will never understand, and you will keep on looking, but will never perceive. 27 For the heart of this people has become dull, and their ears are hard of hearing, and they have closed their eyes, so that they would not see with their eyes and hear with their ears and understand with their heart and turn, and I would heal them."' 28 "Therefore be advised that this salvation from God has been sent to the Gentiles; they will listen!"

30 Paul lived there two whole years in his own rented quarters and welcomed all who came to him, 31 proclaiming the kingdom of God and teaching about the Lord Jesus Christ with complete boldness and without restriction.

the book of Romans

Category: The Letters
Author: Paul
Theme: The basics of Christianity
Location & Date: Corinth to Rome; A.D. 56-57
Version of Bible: New Living Translation (NLT)
Summary: On his third missionary journey Paul stopped in Corinth, Greece and wrote a letter to the churches in Rome. In this letter Paul explains how sin and law come together in the gospel (good news). He explains how law cannot save because every human being is a sinner. The grace of God through the death and resurrection of Jesus is the only path of salvation. Once saved, God's love and the power of the Holy Spirit enables and inspires us to live for Him (the Law). Some Christians summarize Romans in 3 words: Sin, Salvation, Service.

Greetings from Paul

Romans 1:1 This letter is from Paul, a slave of Christ Jesus, chosen by God to be an apostle and sent out to preach his Good News. 7 I am writing to all of you in Rome who are loved by God and are called to be his own holy people. May God our Father and the Lord Jesus Christ give you grace and peace.

God's Good News

8 Let me say first that I thank my God through Jesus Christ for all of you, because your faith in him is being talked about all over the world. 9 God knows how often I pray for you. Day and night I bring you and your needs in prayer to God, whom I serve with all my heart by spreading the Good News about his Son.

10 One of the things I always pray for is the opportunity, God willing, to come at last to see you. 11 For I long to visit you so I can bring you some spiritual gift that will help you grow strong in the Lord. 12 When we get together, **I want to encourage you in your faith, but I also want to be encouraged by yours**. 15 So I am eager to come to you in Rome, too, to preach the Good News.

16 For I am not ashamed of this Good News about Christ. It is the power of God at work, saving everyone who believes—the Jew first and also the Gentile. 17 This Good News tells us how God makes us right in his sight. This is accomplished from start to finish by faith. As the Scriptures say, "It is through faith that a righteous person has life."

This is the essence of the Christian life.

God's Anger at Sin

18 But God shows his anger from heaven against all sinful, wicked people who suppress the truth by their wickedness. 19 They know the truth about God because he has made it obvious to them. 20 For ever since the world was created, people have seen the earth and sky. Through everything God made, they can clearly see his invisible qualities—his eternal power and divine nature. So they have no excuse for not knowing God.

God's Judgment of Sin

2:2 You may think you can condemn such people, but you are just as bad, and you have no excuse! When you say they are wicked and should be punished, you are condemning yourself, for you who judge others do these very same things... 9 ...all people, whether Jews or Gentiles, are under the power of sin. 10 As the Scriptures say,

"No one is righteous—not even one. 11 No one is truly wise; no one is seeking God. 12 All have turned away; all have become useless. No one does good, not a single one."

Christ Took Our Punishment

21 But now God has shown us a way to be made right with him without keeping the requirements of the law, as was promised in the writings of Moses and the prophets long ago. 22 We are made right with God by placing our faith in Jesus Christ. And this is true for everyone who believes, no matter who we are.

This is the heart of what people sometimes refer to as "the gospel."

23 For everyone has sinned; we all fall short of God's glorious standard. 24 Yet God, with undeserved kindness, declares that we are righteous. He did this through Christ Jesus when he freed us from the penalty for our sins.

28 So we are made right with God through faith and not by obeying the law.

We are saved by faith. But faith then helps us fulfill the law.

29 After all, is God the God of the Jews only? Isn't he also the God of the Gentiles? Of course he is. 30 There is only one God, and he makes people right with himself only by faith, whether they are Jews or Gentiles. 31 **Well then, if we emphasize faith, does this mean that we can forget about the law? Of course not! In fact, only when we have faith do we truly fulfill the law.**

Faith Brings Joy

5:1 Therefore, since we have been made right in God's sight by faith, we have peace with God because of what Jesus Christ our Lord has done for us. 2 Because of our faith, Christ has brought us into this place of undeserved privilege where we now stand, and we confidently and joyfully look forward to sharing God's glory.

This is sometimes easier to believe years after the problem and/or trial.

3 **We can rejoice, too, when we run into problems and trials**, for we know that they help us develop endurance. 4 And endurance develops strength of character, and character strengthens our confident hope of salvation. 5 And this hope will not lead to disap-

pointment. For we know how dearly God loves us, because he has given us the Holy Spirit to fill our hearts with his love.

6 When we were utterly helpless, Christ came at just the right time and died for us sinners. 7 Now, most people would not be willing to die for an upright person, though someone might perhaps be willing to die for a person who is especially good. 8 **But God showed his great love for us by sending Christ to die for us while we were still sinners.**

> You don't have to live up to some standard before God will love you.

Adam and Christ Contrasted

12 **When Adam sinned, sin entered the world. Adam's sin brought death, so death spread to everyone, for everyone sinned.** 13 Yes, people sinned even before the law was given. But it was not counted as sin because there was not yet any law to break. 14 Still, everyone died - from the time of Adam to the time of Moses - even those who did not disobey an explicit commandment of God, as Adam did. Now Adam is a symbol, a representation of Christ, who was yet to come. 15 But there is a great difference between Adam's sin and God's gracious gift. For the sin of this one man, Adam, brought death to many. But even greater is God's wonderful grace and his gift of forgiveness to many through this other man, Jesus Christ.

> This is hard to figure out. Somehow everyone sinned when Adam sinned.

18 **Yes**, Adam's one sin brings condemnation for everyone, but Christ's one act of righteousness brings a right relationship with God and new life for everyone. 19 Because one person disobeyed God, many became sinners. But because one other person obeyed God, many will be made righteous.

> Paul says it again.

20 God's law was given so that all people could see how sinful they were. But as people sinned more and more, God's wonderful grace became more abundant. 21 So just as sin ruled over all people and brought them to death, now God's wonderful grace rules instead, giving us right standing with God and resulting in eternal life through Jesus Christ our Lord.

Sin's Power Is Broken

6:1 **Well then, should we keep on sinning so that God can show us more and more of his wonderful grace?** 2 Of course not! Since we have died to sin, how can we continue to live in it? 3 Or have you forgotten that when we were joined with Christ Jesus in baptism, we joined him in his death? 4 For we died and were buried with Christ by baptism. And just as Christ was raised from the dead by the glorious power of the Father, now we also may live new lives.

> Seems like an obvious question. Maybe you have been thinking it for sometime.

5 Since we have been united with him in his death, we will also be raised to life as he was. 6 We know that our old sinful selves were crucified with Christ so that sin might lose its power in our lives. **We are no longer slaves to sin.** 7 For when we died with Christ we were **set free** from the power of sin. 8 And since we died with Christ, we know we will also live with him. 9 We are sure of this because Christ was raised from the dead, and he will never die again. Death no longer has any power over him. 10 When he died, he died once to break the power of sin. But now that he lives, he

> Faith saves us. It also frees us from the slavery of sin.

lives for the glory of God. 11 So you also should consider yourselves to be dead to the power of sin and alive to God through Christ Jesus.

12 Do not let sin control the way you live; do not give in to sinful desires. 13 Do not let any part of your body become an instrument of evil to serve sin. Instead, give yourselves completely to God, for you were dead, but now you have new life. So use your whole body as an instrument to do what is right for the glory of God. 14 Sin is no longer your master, for you no longer live under the requirements of the law. Instead, you live under the freedom of God's grace.

> *Another obvious question.*

15 Well then, since God's grace has set us free from the law, does that mean we can go on sinning? Of course not! 16 Don't you realize that you become the slave of whatever you choose to obey? You can be a slave to sin, which leads to death, or you can choose to obey God, which leads to righteous living. 17 Thank God! Once you were slaves of sin, but now you wholeheartedly obey this teaching we have given you. 18 **Now you are free from your slavery to sin, and you have become slaves to righteous living.**

> *Freedom is choosing what or to whom you wish to be enslaved. The options: Slave to self and the Devil, or slave to God. Your choice.*

19 Because of the weakness of your human nature, I am using the illustration of slavery to help you understand all this. Previously, you let yourselves be slaves to impurity and lawlessness, which led ever deeper into sin. Now you must give yourselves to be slaves to righteous living so that you will become holy.

20 When you were slaves to sin, you were free from the obligation to do right. 21 And what was the result? You are now ashamed of the things you used to do, things that end in eternal doom. 22 But now you are free from the power of sin and have become slaves of God. Now you do those things that lead to holiness and result in eternal life. 23 **For the wages of sin is death, but the free gift of God is eternal life through Christ Jesus our Lord.**

> *A good verse to memorize!*

Struggling with Sin

> *Paul gets personal.*

7:14 So the trouble is not with the law, for it is spiritual and good. **The trouble is with me, for I am all too human,** a slave to sin. 15 I don't really understand myself, for I want to do what is right, but I don't do it. Instead, I do what I hate. 16 But if I know that what I am doing is wrong, this shows that I agree that the law is good. 17 So I am not the one doing wrong; it is sin living in me that does it.

> *Can you relate?*

18 And I know that nothing good lives in me, that is, in my sinful nature. I want to do what is right, but I can't. 19 **I want to do what is good, but I don't. I don't want to do what is wrong, but I do it anyway.** 20 But if I do what I don't want to do, I am not really the one doing wrong; it is sin living in me that does it.

21 I have discovered this principle of life—that when I want to do what is right, I inevitably do what is wrong. 22 I love God's law with all my heart. 23 But there is another power within me that is at war with my mind. This power makes me a slave to the sin that is still within me. 24 Oh, what a miserable person I am! Who will free me from this life that is dominated by sin and death? 25 Thank

God! The answer is in Jesus Christ our Lord. So you see how it is: In my mind I really want to obey God's law, but because of my sinful nature I am a slave to sin.

Life in the Spirit

8:1 So now there is no condemnation for those who belong to Christ Jesus. 2 And because you belong to him, the power of the life-giving Spirit has freed you from the power of sin that leads to death.

5 Those who are dominated by the sinful nature think about sinful things, but those who are controlled by the Holy Spirit think about things that please the Spirit. 6 So letting your sinful nature control your mind leads to death. But letting the Spirit control your mind leads to life and peace. 7 For the sinful nature is always hostile to God. It never did obey God's laws, and it never will. 8 That's why those who are still under the control of their sinful nature can never please God.

9 But you are not controlled by your sinful nature. You are controlled by the Spirit if you have the Spirit of God living in you. (And remember that those who do not have the Spirit of Christ living in them do not belong to him at all.) 10 And Christ lives within you, so even though your body will die because of sin, the Spirit gives you life because you have been made right with God. 11 The Spirit of God, who raised Jesus from the dead, lives in you. And just as God raised Christ Jesus from the dead, he will give life to your mortal bodies by this same Spirit living within you.

12 **Therefore, dear brothers and sisters, you have no obligation to do what your sinful nature urges you to do.** 13 For if you live by its dictates, you will die. But if through the power of the Spirit you put to death the deeds of your sinful nature, you will live. 14 For all who are led by the Spirit of God are children of God.

15 So you have not received a spirit that makes you fearful slaves. Instead, you received God's Spirit when he adopted you as his own children. Now we call him, "Abba, Father." 16 For his Spirit joins with our spirit to affirm that we are God's children. 17 And since we are his children, we are his heirs. In fact, together with Christ we are heirs of God's glory. But if we are to share his glory, we must also share his suffering.

The Future Glory

18 Yet what we suffer now is nothing compared to the glory he will reveal to us later. 19 For all creation is waiting eagerly for that future day when God will reveal who his children really are. 20 Against its will, all creation was subjected to God's curse. But with eager hope, 21 the creation looks forward to the day when it will join God's children in glorious freedom from death and decay. 22 For we know that all creation has been groaning as in the pains of childbirth right up to the present time. 23 And we believers also groan, even though we have the Holy Spirit within us as a foretaste of future glory, for we long for our bodies to be released from sin and suffering. We, too, wait with eager hope for the day when God

---

Though the sinful nature in us is calling us toward selfishness, greed, and insecurity, we are not obligated to follow this call. There is another way - to follow the Spirit that God puts in us.

will give us our full rights as his adopted children, including the new bodies he has promised us. 24 We were given this hope when we were saved. (If we already have something, we don't need to hope for it. 25 But if we look forward to something we don't yet have, we must wait patiently and confidently.)

26 **And the Holy Spirit helps us in our weakness.** For example, we don't know what God wants us to pray for. But the Holy Spirit prays for us with groanings that cannot be expressed in words. 27 And the Father who knows all hearts knows what the Spirit is saying, for the Spirit pleads for us believers in harmony with God's own will. 28 **And we know that God causes everything to work together for the good of those who love God and are called according to his purpose for them.** 29 For God knew his people in advance, and he chose them to become like his Son, so that his Son would be the firstborn among many brothers and sisters. 30 And having chosen them, he called them to come to him. And having called them, he gave them right standing with himself. And having given them right standing, he gave them his glory.

Nothing Can Separate Us from God's Love

31 What shall we say about such wonderful things as these? If God is for us, who can ever be against us? 32 Since he did not spare even his own Son but gave him up for us all, won't he also give us everything else? 33 Who dares accuse us whom God has chosen for his own? No one—for God himself has given us right standing with himself. 34 Who then will condemn us? No one—for Christ Jesus died for us and was raised to life for us, and he is sitting in the place of honor at God's right hand, pleading for us.

35 **Can anything ever separate us from Christ's love? Does it mean he no longer loves us if we have trouble or calamity, or are persecuted, or hungry, or destitute, or in danger, or threatened with death?** 36 (As the Scriptures say, "For your sake we are killed every day; we are being slaughtered like sheep.") 37 No, despite all these things, overwhelming victory is ours through Christ, who loved us.

38 **And I am convinced that nothing can ever separate us from God's love.** Neither death nor life, neither angels nor demons, neither our fears for today nor our worries about tomorrow—not even the powers of hell can separate us from God's love. 39 No power in the sky above or in the earth below—indeed, nothing in all creation will ever be able to separate us from the love of God that is revealed in Christ Jesus our Lord.

{Paul was dealing with the anguish he had over the fact that the Israelites, God's people, rejected faith and the Gentiles (non-Israelites) found it.}

Israel's Unbelief

9:30 What does all this mean? Even though the Gentiles were not trying to follow God's standards, they were made right with God. And it was by faith that this took place. 31 But the people of Israel, who tried so hard to get right with God by keeping the law, never succeeded. 32 **Why not? Because they were trying to get right**

You are not in this alone.

When you are going through tough times, this is one of the most comforting and hard to understand verses in the Bible.

These are exactly the tough questions people have when trouble comes near.

Ultimate security.

This is the heart of it. It is interesting

with God by keeping the law instead of by trusting in him.

10:1 Dear brothers and sisters, the longing of my heart and my prayer to God is for the people of Israel to be saved.

God's Mercy on Israel

11:1 I ask, then, has God rejected his own people, the nation of Israel? Of course not! I myself am an Israelite, a descendant of Abraham and a member of the tribe of Benjamin.

2 No, God has not rejected his own people, whom he chose from the very beginning. **Do you realize what the Scriptures say about this?** Elijah the prophet complained to God about the people of Israel and said, 3 "LORD, they have killed your prophets and torn down your altars. I am the only one left, and now they are trying to kill me, too."

4 And do you remember God's reply? He said, "No, I have 7,000 others who have never bowed down to Baal!"

5 It is the same today, for a few of the people of Israel have remained faithful because of God's grace—his undeserved kindness in choosing them. 6 And since it is through God's kindness, then it is not by their good works. For in that case, God's grace would not be what it really is—free and undeserved.

11 Did God's people stumble and fall beyond recovery? Of course not! They were disobedient, so God made salvation available to the Gentiles. But he wanted his own people to become jealous and claim it for themselves. 12 Now if the Gentiles were enriched because the people of Israel turned down God's offer of salvation, think how much greater a blessing the world will share when they finally accept it.

13 I am saying all this especially for you Gentiles. God has appointed me as the apostle to the Gentiles. I stress this, 14 for I want somehow to make the people of Israel jealous of what you Gentiles have, so I might save some of them. 15 For since their rejection meant that God offered salvation to the rest of the world, their acceptance will be even more wonderful. It will be life for those who were dead! 16 And since Abraham and the other patriarchs were holy, their descendants will also be holy—just as the entire batch of dough is holy because the portion given as an offering is holy. For if the roots of the tree are holy, the branches will be, too.

17 But some of these branches from Abraham's tree—some of the people of Israel—have been broken off. And you Gentiles, who were branches from a wild olive tree, have been grafted in. So now you also receive the blessing God has promised Abraham and his children, sharing in the rich nourishment from the root of God's special olive tree. 18 But you must not brag about being grafted in to replace the branches that were broken off. You are just a branch, not the root.

19 "Well," you may say, "those branches were broken off to make room for me." 20 Yes, but remember—those branches were

[margin note: that people today are still trying to live "good lives" in the hope that God will love them and give them eternal life.

See I Kings 19; pg. 127.]

Good point.

This is the hope for God's people Israel.

Who are your heroes? Who are you following? God has a plan for you life. Seek it out.

When you become a Christian, God gives you a present-a gift that will enable you to be of great value to the community of believers.

broken off because they didn't believe in Christ, and you are there because you do believe. So don't think highly of yourself, but fear what could happen. 21 **For if God did not spare the original branches, he won't spare you either.**

22 Notice how God is both kind and severe. He is severe toward those who disobeyed, but kind to you if you continue to trust in his kindness. But if you stop trusting, you also will be cut off. 23 And if the people of Israel turn from their unbelief, they will be grafted in again, for God has the power to graft them back into the tree. 24 You, by nature, were a branch cut from a wild olive tree. **So if God was willing to do something contrary to nature by grafting you into his cultivated tree, he will be far more eager to graft the original branches back into the tree where they belong.**

God's Mercy Is for Everyone

25 I want you to understand this mystery, dear brothers and sisters, so that you will not feel proud about yourselves. Some of the people of Israel have hard hearts, but this will last only until the full number of Gentiles comes to Christ.

{Paul was dealing with our sin and then the mystery of salvation. He moved on to how we can live for God with the power of our salvation.}

A Living Sacrifice to God

12:1 And so, dear brothers and sisters, I plead with you to give your bodies to God because of all he has done for you. Let them be a living and holy sacrifice—the kind he will find acceptable. This is truly the way to worship him. 2 **Don't copy the behavior and customs of this world, but let God transform you into a new person by changing the way you think.** Then you will learn to know God's will for you, which is good and pleasing and perfect.

3 Because of the privilege and authority God has given me, I give each of you this warning: Don't think you are better than you really are. Be honest in your evaluation of yourselves, measuring yourselves by the faith God has given us. 4 Just as our bodies have many parts and each part has a special function, 5 so it is with Christ's body. We are many parts of one body, and we all belong to each other.

6 **In his grace, God has given us different gifts for doing certain things well.** So if God has given you the ability to prophesy, speak out with as much faith as God has given you. 7 If your gift is serving others, serve them well. If you are a teacher, teach well. 8 If your gift is to encourage others, be encouraging. If it is giving, give generously. If God has given you leadership ability, take the responsibility seriously. And if you have a gift for showing kindness to others, do it gladly.

9 Don't just pretend to love others. Really love them. Hate what is wrong. Hold tightly to what is good. 10 Love each other with genuine affection, and take delight in honoring each other. 11 Never be lazy, but work hard and serve the Lord enthusiasti-

cally. 12 Rejoice in our confident hope. Be patient in trouble, and keep on praying. 13 When God's people are in need, be ready to help them. Always be eager to practice hospitality.

14 Bless those who persecute you. Don't curse them; pray that God will bless them. 15 Be happy with those who are happy, and weep with those who weep. 16 Live in harmony with each other. Don't be too proud to enjoy the company of ordinary people. And don't think you know it all!

17 Never pay back evil with more evil. Do things in such a way that everyone can see you are honorable. 18 Do all that you can to live in peace with everyone.

19 Dear friends, never take revenge. Leave that to the righteous anger of God. For the Scriptures say, "I will take revenge; I will pay them back," says the LORD.

21 Don't let evil conquer you, but conquer evil by doing good.

The Danger of Criticism

14:1 Accept other believers who are weak in faith, and don't argue with them about what they think is right or wrong.

8 If we live, it's to honor the Lord. And if we die, it's to honor the Lord. So whether we live or die, we belong to the Lord. 9 Christ died and rose again for this very purpose—to be Lord both of the living and of the dead.

10 So why do you condemn another believer? Why do you look down on another believer? Remember, we will all stand before the judgment seat of God. 11 For the Scriptures say, "'As surely as I live,' says the LORD, 'every knee will bend to me, and every tongue will confess and give praise to God.'"

12 Yes, each of us will give a personal account to God. 13 So let's stop condemning each other. Decide instead to live in such a way that you will not cause another believer to stumble and fall.

19 So then, let us aim for harmony in the church and try to build each other up.

Good advice.

Living to Please Others

15:1 We who are strong must be considerate of those who are sensitive about things... We must not just please ourselves. 2 We should help others do what is right and build them up in the Lord. 3 For even Christ didn't live to please himself. As the Scriptures say, "The insults of those who insult you, O God, have fallen on me." 4 Such things were written in the Scriptures long ago to teach us. And the Scriptures give us hope and encouragement as we wait patiently for God's promises to be fulfilled.

This is what a worship service is all about.

5 May God, who gives this patience and encouragement, help you live in complete harmony with each other, as is fitting for followers of Christ Jesus. 6 **Then all of you can join together with one voice, giving praise and glory to God, the Father of our Lord Jesus Christ.**

7 Therefore, **accept each other** just as **Christ has accepted you** so

The key to all your relationships.

that God will be given glory.

13 I pray that God, the source of hope, will fill you completely with joy and peace because you trust in him. Then you will overflow with confident hope through the power of the Holy Spirit.

Paul's Reason for Writing

14 I am fully convinced, my dear brothers and sisters, that you are full of goodness. You know these things so well you can teach each other all about them. 15 Even so, I have been bold enough to write about some of these points, knowing that all you need is this reminder. For by God's grace, 16 I am a special messenger from Christ Jesus to you Gentiles. I bring you the Good News so that I might present you as an acceptable offering to God, made holy by the Holy Spirit. 17 So I have reason to be enthusiastic about all Christ Jesus has done through me in my service to God. 18 Yet I dare not boast about anything except what Christ has done through me, bringing the Gentiles to God by my message and by the way I worked among them. 19 They were convinced by the power of miraculous signs and wonders and by the power of God's Spirit. In this way, I have fully presented the Good News of Christ from Jerusalem all the way to Illyricum.

20 My ambition has always been to preach the Good News where the name of Christ has never been heard, rather than where a church has already been started by someone else.

Paul's Final Instructions

16:17 And now I make one more appeal, my dear brothers and sisters. Watch out for people who cause divisions and upset people's faith by teaching things contrary to what you have been taught. Stay away from them. 18 Such people are not serving Christ our Lord; they are serving their own personal interests. By smooth talk and glowing words they deceive innocent people. 19 But everyone knows that you are obedient to the Lord. This makes me very happy. I want you to be wise in doing right and to stay innocent of any wrong. 20 The God of peace will soon crush Satan under your feet. May the grace of our Lord Jesus be with you.

the books of 1 & 2 Corinthians

Category: *The Letters*
Author: *Paul*
Theme: *Encouragement and challenge for the church*
Location & Date: *Ephesus and Philippi; A.D. 55*
Version of Bible: *Contemporary English Version (CEV)*
Summary: *While Paul was teaching in Ephesus, Turkey, he received word that the church he planted three years before in Corinth, Greece was full of divisions, immorality, and misunderstandings. He wrote a first letter, 1 Corinthians, in an attempt to set them straight. While in Philippi, he heard that the Corinthians accepted his first letter well, so Paul wrote a second letter expressing his joy.*

1 Corinthians 1:1 From Paul, chosen by God to be an apostle of Christ Jesus, and from Sosthenes, who is also a follower. 2 To God's church in Corinth. Christ Jesus chose you to be his very own people, and you worship in his name, as we and all others do who call him Lord.

3 My prayer is that God our Father and the Lord Jesus Christ will be kind to you and will bless you with peace!

4 I never stop thanking my God for being kind enough to give you Christ Jesus, 5 who helps you speak and understand so well. 6 Now you are certain that everything we told you about our Lord Christ Jesus is true. 7 You are not missing out on any blessings, as you wait for him to return. 8 And until the day Christ does return, he will keep you completely innocent. 9 God can be trusted, and he chose you to be partners with his Son, our Lord Jesus Christ.

Christ Is God's Power and Wisdom

18 The message about the cross doesn't make any sense to lost people. But for those of us who are being saved, it is God's power at work. 19 As God says in the Scriptures,

"I will destroy the wisdom of all who claim to be wise. I will confuse those who think they know so much."

20 What happened to those wise people? What happened to those experts in the Scriptures? What happened to the ones who think they have all the answers? Didn't God show that the wisdom of this world is foolish? 21 God was wise and decided not to let the people of this world use their wisdom to learn about him.

Instead, God chose to save only those who believe the foolish message we preach. 22 Jews ask for miracles, and Greeks want something that sounds wise. 23 But we preach that Christ was nailed to a cross. Most Jews have problems with this, and most Gentiles think it is foolish. 24 Our message is God's power and wisdom for the Jews and the Greeks that he has chosen. 25 Even when God is foolish, he is wiser than everyone else, and even when God is weak, he is stronger than everyone else.

26 My dear friends, remember what you were when God chose you. The people of this world didn't think that many of you were wise. Only a few of you were in places of power, and not many of you came from important families. 27 But God chose the foolish things of this world to put the wise to shame. He chose the weak things of this world to put the powerful to shame.

28 What the world thinks is worthless, useless, and nothing at all is what God has used to destroy what the world considers important. 29 God did all this to keep anyone from bragging to him. 30 You are God's children. He sent Christ Jesus to save us and to make us wise, acceptable, and holy. 31 So if you want to brag, do what the Scriptures say and brag about the Lord.

Working Together for God

3:1 My friends, you are acting like the people of this world. That's why I could not speak to you as spiritual people. You are like babies as far as your faith in Christ is concerned. 2 So I had to treat you like babies and feed you milk. You could not take solid food, and you still cannot, 3 because you are not yet spiritual. You are jealous and argue with each other. This proves that you are not spiritual and that you are acting like the people of this world.

4 Some of you say that you follow me, and others claim to follow Apollos. Isn't that how ordinary people behave? 5 Apollos and I are merely servants who helped you to have faith. It was the Lord who made it all happen. 6 I planted the seeds, Apollos watered them, but God made them sprout and grow. 7 **What matters isn't those who planted or watered, but God who made the plants grow**. 8 The one who plants is just as important as the one who waters. And each one will be paid for what they do. 9 Apollos and I work together for God, and you are God's garden and God's building.

Don't make the mistake of making your spiritual mentor more than he or she is.

Only One Foundation

10 God was kind and let me become an expert builder. I laid a foundation on which others have built. But we must each be careful how we build, 11 because Christ is the only foundation. 12-13 Whatever we build on that foundation will be tested by fire on the day of judgment. Then everyone will find out if we have used gold, silver, and precious stones, or wood, hay, and straw. 14 We will be rewarded if our building is left standing. 15 But if it is destroyed by the fire, we will lose everything. Yet we ourselves will be saved, like someone escaping from flames.

16 All of you surely know that you are God's temple and that his Spirit lives in you. 17 Together you are God's holy temple, and God will destroy anyone who destroys his temple.

18 Don't fool yourselves! If any of you think you are wise in the things of this world, you will have to become foolish before you can be truly wise. 19 This is because God considers the wisdom of this world to be foolish. It is just as the Scriptures say, "God catches the wise when they try to outsmart him." 20 The Scriptures also say, "The Lord knows that the plans made by wise people are useless." 21-22 So stop bragging about what anyone has done. Paul and Apollos and Peter all belong to you. In fact, everything is yours, including the world, life, death, the present, and the future. Everything belongs to you, 23 and you belong to Christ, and Christ belongs to God.

Taking Each Other to Court

6:1 When one of you has a complaint against another, do you take your complaint to a court of sinners? Or do you take it to God's people?

7 When one of you takes another to court, all of you lose. It would be better to let yourselves be cheated and robbed. 8 But instead, you cheat and rob other followers.

15 **Don't you know that your bodies are part of the body of Christ?** Is it right for me to join part of the body of Christ to a prostitute? No, it isn't! 16 Don't you know that a man who does that becomes part of her body? The Scriptures say, "The two of them will be like one person." 17 But anyone who is joined to the Lord is one in spirit with him.

18 Don't be immoral in matters of sex. That is a sin against your own body in a way that no other sin is. 19 **You surely know that your body is a temple where the Holy Spirit lives.** The Spirit is in you and is a gift from God. You are no longer your own. 20 God paid a great price for you. So use your body to honor God.

> Sex is not just a recreational sport. It is a deeply spiritual activity that unites 2 people in a mysterious and holy way.

Questions About Marriage

7:3 **Husbands and wives should be fair with each other about having sex.** 4 A wife belongs to her husband instead of to herself, and a husband belongs to his wife instead of to himself. 5 So don't refuse sex to each other, unless you agree not to have sex for a little while, in order to spend time in prayer. Then Satan won't be able to tempt you because of your lack of self-control.

> Fair is when you try to do more for the other person than they do for you.

Rules for the Lord's Supper

11:17 Your worship services do you more harm than good. I am certainly not going to praise you for this. 18 I am told that you can't get along with each other when you worship, and I am sure that some of what I have heard is true. 19 You are bound to argue with each other, but it is easy to see which of you have God's approval.

20 **When you meet together, you don't really celebrate the Lord's Supper.** 21 You even start eating before everyone gets to the meeting, and some of you go hungry, while others get drunk. 22 Don't you have homes where you can eat and drink? Do you hate God's church? Do you want to embarrass people who don't have any-

> The Corinthians were celebrating God's love for them in the ceremony

of the Lord's Supper (our vertical relationship). But there were divisions between different factions in the church (the horizontal). Communion is celebrating both the vertical and the horizontal.

thing? **What can I say to you?** I certainly cannot praise you.

The Lord's Supper

23 I have already told you what the Lord Jesus did on the night he was betrayed. And it came from the Lord himself. He took some bread in his hands. 24 Then after he had given thanks, he broke it and said, "This is my body, which is given for you. Eat this and remember me." 25 After the meal, Jesus took a cup of wine in his hands and said, "This is my blood, and with it God makes his new agreement with you. Drink this and remember me." 26 The Lord meant that when you eat this bread and drink from this cup, you tell about his death until he comes.

27 But if you eat the bread and drink the wine in a way that isn't worthy of the Lord, you sin against his body and blood. 28 That's why you must examine the way you eat and drink. 29 If you fail to understand that you are the body of the Lord, you will condemn yourselves by the way you eat and drink.

Spiritual Gifts

12:1 My friends, you asked me about spiritual gifts. 4 There are different kinds of spiritual gifts, but they all come from the same Spirit. 5 There are different ways to serve the same Lord, 6 and we can each do different things. Yet the same God works in all of us and helps us in everything we do.

Paul again talks about how each Christian is given a special gift that is to be used to serve others. See Romans 12.

7 **The Spirit has given each of us a special way of serving others.** 8 Some of us can speak with wisdom, while others can speak with knowledge, but these gifts come from the same Spirit. 9 To others the Spirit has given great faith or the power to heal the sick 10 or the power to work mighty miracles. Some of us are prophets, and some of us recognize when God's Spirit is present. Others can speak different kinds of languages, and still others can tell what these languages mean. 11 But it is the Spirit who does all this and decides which gifts to give to each of us.

One Body with Many Parts

12 The body of Christ has many different parts, just as any other body does. 13 Some of us are Jews, and others are Gentiles. Some of us are slaves, and others are free. But God's Spirit baptized each of us and made us part of the body of Christ. Now we each drink from that same Spirit.

14 Our bodies don't have just one part. They have many parts. 15 Suppose a foot says, "I'm not a hand, and so I'm not part of the body." Wouldn't the foot still belong to the body? 16 Or suppose an ear says, "I'm not an eye, and so I'm not part of the body." Wouldn't the ear still belong to the body? 17 If our bodies were only an eye, we couldn't hear a thing. And if they were only an ear, we couldn't smell a thing. 18 But God has put all parts of our body together in the way that he decided is best.

19 A body isn't really a body, unless there is more than one part. 20 It takes many parts to make a single body. 21 That's why the

eyes cannot say they don't need the hands. That's also why the head cannot say it doesn't need the feet. 22 In fact, we cannot get along without the parts of the body that seem to be the weakest. 23 We take special care to dress up some parts of our bodies. We are modest about our personal parts, 24 but we don't have to be modest about other parts.

God put our bodies together in such a way that even the parts that seem the least important are valuable. 25 He did this to make all parts of the body work together smoothly, with each part caring about the others. 26 If one part of our body hurts, we hurt all over. If one part of our body is honored, the whole body will be happy.

27 **Together you are the body of Christ. Each one of you is part of his body.** 28 First, God chose some people to be apostles and prophets and teachers for the church. But he also chose some to work miracles or heal the sick or help others or be leaders or speak different kinds of languages. 29 Not everyone is an apostle. Not everyone is a prophet. Not everyone is a teacher. Not everyone can work miracles. 30 Not everyone can heal the sick. Not everyone can speak different kinds of languages. Not everyone can tell what these languages mean. 31 I want you to desire the best gifts. So I will show you a much better way.

Love

13:1 What if I could speak all languages of humans and of angels? If I did not love others, I would be nothing more than a noisy gong or a clanging cymbal. 2 What if I could prophesy and understand all secrets and all knowledge? And what if I had faith that moved mountains? I would be nothing, unless I loved others. 3 What if I gave away all that I owned and let myself be burned alive? I would gain nothing, unless I loved others.

4 **Love is kind and patient, never jealous, boastful, proud, or** 5 **rude. Love isn't selfish or quick tempered. It doesn't keep a record of wrongs that others do.** 6 **Love rejoices in the truth, but not in evil.** 7 **Love is always supportive, loyal, hopeful, and trusting.**

8 **Love never fails!** Everyone who prophesies will stop, and unknown languages will no longer be spoken. All that we know will be forgotten. 9 We don't know everything, and our prophecies are not complete. 10 But what is perfect will someday appear, and what isn't perfect will then disappear. 11 When we were children, we thought and reasoned as children do. But when we grew up, we quit our childish ways. 12 Now all we can see of God is like a cloudy picture in a mirror. Later we will see him face to face. We don't know everything, but then we will, just as God completely understands us.

13 For now there are faith, hope, and love. But of these three, the greatest is love.

Christ Was Raised to Life

15:1 My friends, I want you to remember the message that I preached and that you believed and trusted. 2 You will be saved

---

You may not feel important, talented, or needed. But if you have accepted Jesus as your Lord and Savior then you are part of His body - the church. And you have gifts that the body needs.

Love is more than what you like.

by this message, if you hold firmly to it. But if you don't, your faith was all for nothing.

3 I told you the most important part of the message exactly as it was told to me. That part is:

Christ died for our sins, as the Scriptures say. 4 He was buried, and three days later he was raised to life, as the Scriptures say. 5 Christ appeared to Peter, then to the twelve. 6 **After this, he appeared to more than five hundred other followers. Most of them are still alive**, but some have died. 7 He also appeared to James, and then to all of the apostles. 8 Finally, he appeared to me, even though I am like someone who was born at the wrong time.

9 I am the least important of all the apostles. In fact, I caused so much trouble for God's church that I don't even deserve to be called an apostle. 10 But God was kind! He made me what I am, and his wonderful kindness wasn't wasted. I worked much harder than any of the other apostles, although it was really God's kindness at work and not me. 11 But it doesn't matter if I preached or if they preached. All of you believed the message just the same.

> *Paul is saying, "Don't take my word for it. There are many people out there who can testify to this."*

God's People Will Be Raised to Life

12 If we preach that Christ was raised from death, how can some of you say that the dead will not be raised to life? 13 If they won't be raised to life, Christ himself wasn't raised to life. 14 And if Christ wasn't raised to life, our message is worthless, and so is your faith. 15 If the dead won't be raised to life, we have told lies about God by saying that he raised Christ to life, when he really did not.

16 So **if the dead won't be raised to life**, Christ wasn't raised to life. 17 Unless Christ was raised to life, your faith is useless, and you are still living in your sins. 18 And those people who died after putting their faith in him are completely lost. 19 If our hope in Christ is good only for this life, we are worse off than anyone else.

> *If, when we die, that's it, then don't waste your time with Christianity. Actually, if there is no life after death it really doesn't matter what you believe or do with your life. Nothing will really matter.*

20 But Christ has been raised to life! And he makes us certain that others will also be raised to life. 21 Just as we will die because of Adam, we will be raised to life because of Christ. 22 Adam brought death to all of us, and Christ will bring life to all of us. 23 But we must each wait our turn. Christ was the first to be raised to life, and his people will be raised to life when he returns. 24 Then after Christ has destroyed all powers and forces, the end will come, and he will give the kingdom to God the Father.

25 Christ will rule until he puts all his enemies under his power, 26 and the last enemy he destroys will be death.

32 If the dead are not raised to life, "Let's eat and drink. Tomorrow we die."

What Our Bodies Will Be Like

35 Some of you have asked, "How will the dead be raised to life? What kind of bodies will they have?" 36 Don't be foolish. A seed must die before it can sprout from the ground. 37 Wheat

seeds and all other seeds look different from the sprouts that come up. 38 This is because God gives everything the kind of body he wants it to have.

42 That's how it will be when our bodies are raised to life. These bodies will die, but the bodies that are raised will live forever. 43 These ugly and weak bodies will become beautiful and strong. 44 As surely as there are physical bodies, there are spiritual bodies. And our physical bodies will be changed into spiritual bodies.

50 My friends, I want you to know that our bodies of flesh and blood will decay. This means that they cannot share in God's kingdom, which lasts forever. 51 I will explain a mystery to you. Not every one of us will die, but we will all be changed. 52 It will happen suddenly, quicker than the blink of an eye. At the sound of the last trumpet the dead will be raised. We will all be changed, so that we will never die again. 53 Our dead and decaying bodies will be changed into bodies that won't die or decay. 54 The bodies we now have are weak and can die. But they will be changed into bodies that are eternal. Then the Scriptures will come true,

"Death has lost the battle! 55 Where is its victory? Where is its sting?"

56 Sin is what gives death its sting, and the Law is the power behind sin. 57 But thank God for letting our Lord Jesus Christ give us the victory!

58 My dear friends, stand firm and don't be shaken. Always keep busy working for the Lord. You know that everything you do for him is worthwhile.

2 Corinthians

2 Corinthians 1:1 From Paul, chosen by God to be an apostle of Jesus Christ, and from Timothy, who is also a follower. To God's church in Corinth and to all of God's people in Achaia.

2 I pray that God our Father and the Lord Jesus Christ will be kind to you and will bless you with peace!

Paul Gives Thanks

3 Praise God, the Father of our Lord Jesus Christ! The Father is a merciful God, who always gives us comfort. 4 He comforts us when we are in trouble, so that we can share that same comfort with others in trouble.

2:1 I have decided not to make my next visit with you so painful. 2 If I make you feel bad, who would be left to cheer me up, except the people I had made to feel bad? 3 The reason I want to be happy is to make you happy. I wrote as I did because I didn't want to visit you and be made to feel bad, when you should make me feel happy. 4 At the time I wrote, I was suffering terribly. My eyes were full of tears, and my heart was broken. But I didn't want to make you feel bad. I only wanted to let you know how much I cared for you.

In his first letter, Paul had some hard things to say to the church in Corinth. They took his words to heart. Paul's second letter was written to encourage the church.

Forgiveness

12 When I went to Troas to preach the good news about Christ, I found that the Lord had already prepared the way. 13 But I was worried when I didn't find my friend Titus there. So I left the other followers and went on to Macedonia.

14 I am grateful that God always makes it possible for Christ to lead us to victory. God also helps us spread the knowledge about Christ everywhere, and this knowledge is like the smell of perfume. 15-16 In fact, God thinks of us as a perfume that brings Christ to everyone. For people who are being saved, this perfume has a sweet smell and leads them to a better life. But for people who are lost, it has a bad smell and leads them to a horrible death.

No one really has what it takes to do this work. 17 A lot of people try to get rich from preaching God's message. But we are God's sincere messengers, and by the power of Christ we speak our message with God as our witness.

God's New Agreement

> See Exodus 34:29-35; pg. 84.

3:7 The Law of Moses brought only the promise of death, even though it was carved on stones and given in a wonderful way. Still the **Law made Moses' face shine** so brightly that the people of Israel could not look at it, even though it was a fading glory. 8 So won't the agreement that the Spirit brings to us be even more wonderful? 9 If something that brings the death sentence is glorious, won't something that makes us acceptable to God be even more glorious? 10 In fact, the new agreement is so wonderful that the Law is no longer glorious at all. 11 The Law was given with a glory that faded away. But the glory of the new agreement is much greater, because it will never fade away.

> Paul said that the law was given and that it was a great, glorious gift. But, ultimately we cannot live the law perfectly, so it doesn't, in the end, save us. The new agreement is the promise of Jesus. He fulfills the law for us. The glory of Jesus in us is even brighter than the law.

12 This wonderful hope makes us feel like speaking freely. 13 We are not like Moses. His face was shining, but he covered it to keep the people of Israel from seeing the brightness fade away. 14 The people were stubborn, and something still keeps them from seeing the truth when the Law is read. Only Christ can take away the covering that keeps them from seeing.

15 When the Law of Moses is read, they have their minds covered over 16 with a covering that is removed only for those who turn to the Lord. 17 The Lord and the Spirit are one and the same, and the Lord's Spirit sets us free. 18 So our faces are not covered. They show the bright glory of the Lord, as the Lord's Spirit makes us more and more like our glorious Lord.

{Next Paul wrote of his mission and how nothing could stop him because of the power of Christ in him.}

Treasure in Clay Jars

4:1 God has been kind enough to trust us with this work. That's why we never give up. 2 We don't do shameful things that must be kept secret. And we don't try to fool anyone or twist God's message around. God is our witness that we speak only the truth, so others will be sure that we can be trusted.

5 We are not preaching about ourselves. Our message is that Jesus Christ is Lord. He also sent us to be your servants. 6 The Scriptures say, "God commanded light to shine in the dark." Now God is shining in our hearts to let you know that his glory is seen in Jesus Christ.

7 **We are like clay jars in which this treasure is stored.** The real power comes from God and not from us. 8 We often suffer, but we are never crushed. Even when we don't know what to do, we never give up. 9 **In times of trouble, God is with us, and when we are knocked down, we get up again.** 10-11 We face death every day because of Jesus. Our bodies show what his death was like, so that his life can also be seen in us. 12 This means that death is working in us, but life is working in you.

14 We know that God raised the Lord Jesus to life. And just as God raised Jesus, he will also raise us to life. Then he will bring us into his presence together with you. 15 All of this has been done for you, so that more and more people will know how kind God is and will praise and honor him.

Faith in the Lord

16 **We never give up.** Our bodies are gradually dying, but we ourselves are being made stronger each day. 17 These little troubles are getting us ready for an eternal glory that will make all our troubles seem like nothing. 18 Things that are seen don't last forever, but things that are not seen are eternal. That's why we keep our minds on the things that cannot be seen.

Immoral Followers

5:1 Our bodies are like tents that we live in here on earth. But when these tents are destroyed, we know that God will give each of us a place to live. These homes will not be buildings that someone has made, but they are in heaven and will last forever. 2 While we are here on earth, we sigh because we want to live in that heavenly home. 3 We want to put it on like clothes and not be naked.

4 These tents we now live in are like a heavy burden, and we groan. But we don't do this just because we want to leave these bodies that will die. It is because we want to change them for bodies that will never die. 5 God is the one who makes all of this possible. He has given us his Spirit to make us certain that he will do it. 6 So always be cheerful!

As long as we are in these bodies, we are away from the Lord. 7 But we live by faith, not by what we see.

Bringing People to God

16 We are careful not to judge people by what they seem to be, though we once judged Christ in that way. 17 Anyone who belongs to Christ is a new person. The past is forgotten, and everything is new. 18 God has done it all! He sent Christ to make peace between himself and us, and he has given us the work of making

---

Fragile, weak, insecure.

As a Christian you may experience trouble, grief, setbacks, and frustration but you will ultimately win the battle - because God is with you.

What are you thinking of giving up on these days?

The Letters

Through Christ you can be reconciled to God. Why not share the possibility of reconciliation with others?

peace between himself and others.

19 **What we mean is that God was in Christ, offering peace and forgiveness to the people of this world. And he has given us the work of sharing his message about peace.** 20 We were sent to speak for Christ, and God is begging you to listen to our message. We speak for Christ and sincerely ask you to make peace with God. 21 Christ never sinned! But God treated him as a sinner, so that Christ could make us acceptable to God.

The Church Makes Paul Happy

7:2 Make a place for us in your hearts! We haven't mistreated or hurt anyone. We haven't cheated anyone. 3 I am not saying this to be hard on you. But, as I have said before, you will always be in our thoughts, whether we live or die. 4 I trust you completely. **I am always proud of you, and I am greatly encouraged.** In all my trouble I am still very happy.

Maybe you long to hear words like these.

5 After we came to Macedonia, we didn't have any chance to rest. We were faced with all kinds of problems. We were troubled by enemies and troubled by fears. 6 But God cheers up people in need, and that is what he did when he sent Titus to us. 7 Of course, we were glad to see Titus, but what really made us glad is the way you cheered him up. He told how sorry you were and how concerned you were about me. And this made me even happier.

Paul is talking about what we now call the book of I Corinthians.

8 I don't feel bad anymore, even though **my letter hurt your feelings.** I did feel bad at first, but I don't now. I know that the letter hurt you for a while. 9 Now I am happy, but not because I hurt your feelings. It is because God used your hurt feelings to make you turn back to him, and none of you were harmed by us. 10 When God makes you feel sorry enough to turn to him and be saved, you don't have anything to feel bad about. But when this world makes you feel sorry, it can cause your death.

{Next Paul wrote about money.}

The Money for God's People

9:6 Remember this saying, "A few seeds make a small harvest, but a lot of seeds make a big harvest."

7 Each of you must make up your own mind about how much to give. But don't feel sorry that you must give and don't feel that you are forced to give. God loves people who love to give. 8 God can bless you with everything you need, and you will always have more than enough to do all kinds of good things for others. 9 The Scriptures say, "God freely gives his gifts to the poor, and always does right."

10 God gives seed to farmers and provides everyone with food. He will increase what you have, so that you can give even more to those in need. 11 You will be blessed in every way, and you will be able to keep on being generous. Then many people will thank God when we deliver your gift.

12 What you are doing is much more than a service that sup-

plies God's people with what they need. It is something that will make many others thank God. 13 The way in which you have proved yourselves by this service will bring honor and praise to God. You believed the message about Christ, and you obeyed it by sharing generously with God's people and with everyone else. 14 Now they are praying for you and want to see you, because God used you to bless them so very much. 15 Thank God for his gift that is too wonderful for words!

Paul's Sufferings for Christ

{Some thought less of Paul as a leader because he was not one of the original 12 Disciples of Jesus, therefore Paul felt the need to defend his ministry.}

11:22 Are **they** Hebrews? So am I. Are they Jews? So am I. Are they from the family of Abraham? Well, so am I. 23 Are they servants of Christ? I am a fool to talk this way, but I serve him better than they do. I have worked harder and have been put in jail more times. I have been beaten with whips more and have been in danger of death more often.

24 Five times the Jews gave me thirty-nine lashes with a whip. 25 Three times the Romans beat me with a big stick, and once my enemies stoned me. I have been shipwrecked three times, and I even had to spend a night and a day in the sea. 26 During my many travels, I have been in danger from rivers, robbers, my own people, and foreigners. My life has been in danger in cities, in deserts, at sea, and with people who only pretended to be the Lord's followers.

27 I have worked and struggled and spent many sleepless nights. I have gone hungry and thirsty and often had nothing to eat. I have been cold from not having enough clothes to keep me warm. 28 Besides everything else, each day I am burdened down, worrying about all the churches. 29 When others are weak, I am weak too. When others are tricked into sin, I get angry. 30 If I have to brag, I will brag about how weak I am.

{Paul had some kind of affliction that he often prayed would be removed. We don't know what it was. Some think it was his eyesight.}

12:8 Three times I begged the Lord to make this suffering go away. 9 But he replied, "My kindness is all you need. My power is strongest when you are weak." So if Christ keeps giving me his power, I will gladly brag about how weak I am. 10 Yes, I am glad to be weak or insulted or mistreated or to have troubles and sufferings, if it is for Christ. Because when I am weak, I am strong.

Margin notes:

The original 12 disciples of Jesus.

What suffering in you life have you wanted God to take away? How has that suffering enabled you to do God's work?

the book of Galatians

Category: *The Letters*

Author: *Paul*

Theme: *Saved by grace, not law*

Location & Date: *Antioch; A.D. 49*

Version of Bible: *Expanded Bible (EXB)*

Summary: Paul wrote this letter to the church he planted in Galatia on his first missionary journey. He wrote to correct the notion that a person can be saved by doing the law. The law is God's will for our lives but we cannot earn our salvation by doing it. We fail too often. So, whether Jew or Greek, we must be saved by faith in Jesus who paid the price of our sin on the cross.

Galatians 1:1 From Paul, an apostle [messenger]. I was not chosen to be an apostle by human beings, nor was I sent from human beings [not from men/humans or by a man/human authority]. I was made an apostle [but] through Jesus Christ and God the Father who raised Jesus from the dead. 2 This letter is also from all those of God's family [the brothers (and sisters)] who are with me.

To the churches in Galatia [a Roman province in present-day central Turkey; Paul started churches in Galatia on his first missionary journey (Acts 13-14)]:

3 Grace and peace to you from God our Father and the Lord Jesus Christ, 4 who gave himself for our sins to free [rescue; deliver] us from this evil world we live in [present evil age], as God the Father planned [willed; desired]. 5 The glory belongs to God [to whom be glory] forever and ever. Amen.

Paul's Authority Is from God

11 Brothers and sisters, I want you to know that the Good News [Gospel] I preached to you was not made up by human beings. 12 I did not get it from humans [a human source; man], nor did anyone teach it to me, but Jesus Christ showed it to me [by a revelation of/from/about Jesus Christ; Acts 9].

Paul Shows that Peter Was Wrong

2:15 We were not born as Gentile "sinners," but as Jews. 16 Yet we know that a person is made right with God [justified; declared righteous] not by following [the works of] the law, but by trusting in [faith in; or the faithfulness of] Jesus Christ. So we, too, have put our faith in Christ Jesus, that we might be made right with God [justified; declared righteous] because we trusted in [through faith in; or because of the faithfulness of] Christ. It is not because we followed [by the works of] the law, because no one [human being; flesh] can be made right with God [justified; declared righteous] by following [the works of] the law.

17 We Jews came to Christ, trying to be made right with God, and it became clear that we are sinners, too [or But if we ourselves, also, by seeking to be justified in Christ, were found to be sinners…]. Does this mean that Christ encourages [is a servant/minister of] sin? No [Absolutely not; May it never be]! 18 But I would really be wrong [or prove myself to be a lawbreaker/sinner] to begin teaching again those things that I gave up [if I rebuild those things I tore down; dependence on the law for salvation]. 19 It was the law that put me to death [or Trying to keep the law condemned me to death; For through the law I died to the law], and I died to the law so that I can now live for God [no longer depending on the law for salvation, Paul now depends on God's grace]. 20 I was put to death on the cross [have been crucified] with Christ, and I do not live anymore—it is Christ who lives in me. I still live in my body [flesh], but I live by faith in [or because of the faithfulness of] the Son of God who loved me and gave himself to save me [for me; on my behalf]. 21 By saying these things I am not going against [do not set aside/nullify] God's grace. Just the opposite [For…], if the law could make us right with God, then Christ's death would be useless [in vain; for nothing].

Blessing Comes Through Faith

3:1 You [O] foolish [stupid] Galatians! Who has tricked [or cast a spell on; bewitched] you? You were told very clearly about the death of Jesus Christ on the cross [Before your eyes Jesus Christ was publicly portrayed/announced as crucified]. 2 Tell me this one thing: How did you receive the Holy Spirit? Did you receive the Spirit by following [the works of] the law? No, you received the Spirit […or] because you heard the Good News and believed it [by believing what you heard]. 3 Are you so foolish [How can you be so stupid]? You began your life in Christ by [by; or through] the Spirit. Now are you trying to make it complete [finish; or be perfected] by your own power [human effort; the flesh]? 4 Were all your experiences wasted [or Have you suffered so much for nothing]? I hope not [or Surely it was not for nothing; —if indeed for nothing]! 5 Does God give you the Spirit and work miracles among you because you follow [by the works of] the law? No, he does these things […or] because you heard the Good News and believed it [by your believing what you heard; v. 2].

6 The Scriptures say the same thing about Abraham [Just as (it says)]: "Abraham believed God, and God accepted Abraham's faith, and that faith made him right with God [it (Abraham's faith) was credited to him as righteousness; Gen. 15:6; Rom. 4]." 7 So you should know that the true children of Abraham are those who have faith. 8 The Scriptures, telling what would happen in the future, said [Scripture foresaw; Scripture is personified as foreseeing and speaking] that God would make the Gentiles right [justify the Gentiles] through their faith. This Good News was told [Gospel

was proclaimed] to Abraham beforehand, as the Scripture says: "All nations will be blessed through you [Gen. 12:3; 18:18]." 9 So all who believe as Abraham believed [rely on faith; have faith; are of faith] are blessed just as Abraham was [with faithful Abraham; or with Abraham, the man of faith]. 10 But [For] those who depend on following [the works of] the law to make them right are under a curse, because the Scriptures say, "Anyone [All; Everyone] will be cursed who does not always obey what [keep doing everything that] is written in the Book of the Law [Deut. 27:26]." 11 Now it is clear that no one can be made right with [justified/declared righteous before] God by the law, because the Scriptures say, "Those who are right with God will live by faith [The righteous will live by faith; or Those made righteous by faith will live; Gen. 15:6; Hab. 2:4]." 12 The law is not based on faith. It says [Rather; On the contrary], "A person who obeys [does; practices] these things will live because of [gain life by/in] them [Lev. 18:5]." 13 Christ took away [redeemed us from; bought our freedom from] the curse the law put on us [of the law]. He changed places with us and put himself under that curse [...by becoming a curse for us]. [For; Because] It is written in the Scriptures, "Anyone whose body is displayed [who is hung] on a tree is cursed [Deut. 21:23; Can executed man's body was hung on a stake or tree for humiliation and warning; Paul here applies it to Christ's crucifixion as the curse/judgment for our sin]." 14 Christ did this so that God's blessing promised to Abraham [Gen. 12:2–3] might come through Jesus Christ to the Gentiles. Jesus died so that by our believing [...so that by faith] we could receive the Spirit that God promised.

The Purpose of the Law of Moses

26 [For] You are all children of God through faith in Christ Jesus [or In Christ Jesus you are all children/sons of God through faith]. 27 [For] All of you who were baptized into Christ have clothed yourselves with Christ. 28 **In Christ, there is no difference** between Jew and Greek [neither Jew nor Greek], slave and free person, male and female. You are all the same [or united; one] in Christ Jesus. 29 You [If you...] belong to Christ, so you are Abraham's descendants [seed]. You will inherit all of God's blessings because of the promise God made to Abraham [...heirs according to the promise].

Keep Your Freedom

5:1 Christ set us free so that we could live in freedom [to a place of freedom; or by means of freedom; 4:31]. So stand strong. Do not change and go back into the slavery of the law [submit/be fastened to a yoke of slavery]. 2 Listen, I Paul tell you that if you go back to the law by being [let yourself be] circumcised, Christ does you no good. 3 Again, I warn every man: If you allow yourselves to be circumcised, you must follow [are obligated to obey] all the law. 4 If you try to be made right with God [justified] through the law, your life with Christ is over [you are alienated/separated/severed from Christ]—you have left [fallen away from] God's grace. 5 For by the Spirit and through faith we wait eagerly for a right relationship with God [righteousness]—the object of our

---

Your value is not based on your race, gender, or social standing. Your value is based on God's love for you - a love that was willing to pay the life of His son - Jesus, on the cross for you.

hope. 6 When we are [For] in Christ Jesus, it is not important if we are circumcised or not [neither circumcision nor uncircumcision accomplishes anything]. The important thing is faith—the kind of faith that works through love.

The Spirit and Human Nature

16 So I tell you: Live [Walk] by following [guided by; in the power of; by] the Spirit. Then you will not do what your sinful self [sinful nature; flesh] wants [desires; craves]. 17 Our sinful self [sinful nature; flesh] wants [desires] what is against the Spirit, and the Spirit wants [desires] what is against our sinful self [sinful nature; flesh]. [For] The two are against [opposed to; or hostile toward] each other, so you cannot do just what you please [want]. 18 But if the Spirit is leading you, you are not under the law.

19 The wrong things the sinful self does [works of the flesh/sinful nature] are clear [evident; obvious]: being sexually unfaithful [sexual immorality], not being pure [impurity], taking part in sexual sins [depravity; promiscuity], 20 worshiping gods [idolatry], doing witchcraft [sorcery], hating [hostility; antagonism], making trouble [discord; strife], being jealous, being angry [rage], being selfish [rivalries], making people angry with each other [dissensions], causing divisions among people [factions], 21 feeling envy, being drunk, having wild and wasteful parties [carousings; orgies], and doing other things like these. I warn you now as I warned you before: Those who do these things will not inherit God's kingdom. 22 But the Spirit produces the fruit of [fruit of the Spirit is] love, joy, peace, patience, kindness, goodness, faithfulness [or faith], 23 gentleness, self-control. There is no law that says these things are wrong [or No law can oppose such things]. 24 Those who belong to Christ Jesus have crucified their own sinful selves [the sinful nature; the flesh]. They have given up their old selfish feelings and the evil things they wanted to do [its passions and desires]. 25 We [If/Since we...] get our new life from the Spirit [live by the Spirit], so we should follow [be guided by; walk in step with] the Spirit. 26 We must not be proud [conceited] or make trouble with [provoke] each other or be jealous [envious] of each other.

Help Each Other

6:1 Brothers and sisters, if someone in your group [a person] does something wrong [or is overcome by some transgression/sin; or is discovered/caught in some transgression/sin], you who are spiritual should go to that person and gently help make him right again [restore him gently/with a gentle spirit]. But be careful, because you might [or so that you won't] be tempted to sin, too. 2 By **helping each other with your troubles** [bearing each other's burdens], you truly obey [accomplish; fulfill] the law of Christ. 3 If anyone thinks he is important [something] when he really is not, he is only fooling [deceiving; deluding] himself. 4 Each person should judge [examine; test] his own actions [or achievements; work] and not compare himself with others. Then he can be proud for what he himself has done. 5 Each person must be responsible for himself [will carry their own load].

Life is really not that complicated, is it. Who can you help today?

6 Anyone who is learning the teaching of God [being instructed in the word] should share all the good things he has with his teacher.

Life Is like Planting a Field

7 Do not be fooled [deceived; mistaken]: You cannot cheat [mock; make a fool of] God. **People harvest only what they plant** [reap what they sow]. 8 If they plant to satisfy [or in the field of; into; to] their sinful selves [sinful nature; flesh], their sinful selves will bring them ruin [they will reap destruction from the flesh]. But if they plant to please [or in the field of; into; to] the Spirit, they will receive [reap; harvest] eternal life from the Spirit. 9 We must not become tired [or discouraged] of doing good. We will receive our harvest of eternal life at the right [or in due] time if we do not give up. 10 [Therefore; So then] When we have the opportunity to help [do good to] anyone, we should do it. But we should give special attention [especially] to those who are in the family [household] of believers [faith].

Paul Ends His Letter

11 See what large letters I use to write this myself [with my own hand; added to authenticate the letter; the rest had likely been dictated]. 12 Some people are trying to force you to be circumcised so the Jews will accept them [or to impress others by external standards; to make a good showing in the flesh]. They do this only to avoid persecution for the cross of Christ [the Gospel message of Christ's sacrificial death on the cross]. 13 [For] Those who are circumcised do not obey the law themselves, but they want you to be circumcised so they can brag [boast] about what they forced you to do [in your flesh]. 14 I hope I will never [May it never be that I] brag [boast] about anything except the cross of our Lord Jesus Christ. Through that cross [or Through Jesus Christ; ...through which/whom] the world has been crucified to me and I have been crucified to the world. 15 It is not important [makes no difference; is nothing] if a man is circumcised or uncircumcised. The important thing is being the new people God has made [a new creation; 2 Cor. 5:17]. 16 Peace and mercy to those who follow [walk/live by] this rule—and to all of God's people [the Israel of God; either: (1) Jewish Christians or (2) the church as the "new Israel"].

This is one of the most practical, profound statements you will find in the Bible. If you plant seeds of anger, discord, and gossip, don't be surprised when you reap hurt, pain, and brokenness.

the book of Ephesians

Category: The Letters
Author: Paul
Theme: Encouragement from prison
Location & Date: A Roman Prison; A.D. 60-62
Version of Bible: New International Version (NIV)
Summary: Paul was in a prison cell in Rome. He was awaiting his trial before Caesar. While in prison he wrote a letter to a church he spent three years with in Ephesus, the city that contained one of the wonders of the ancient world: the temple of Artemus. This must have been an incredibly encouraging letter to the people of Ephesus and it still is for readers today. Enjoy!

Ephesians 1:1 Paul, an apostle of Christ Jesus by the will of God, To God's holy people in Ephesus, the faithful in Christ Jesus: 2 Grace and peace to you from God our Father and the Lord Jesus Christ.

Praise for Spiritual Blessings in Christ

3 Praise be to the God and Father of our Lord Jesus Christ, who has blessed us in the heavenly realms with every spiritual blessing in Christ. 4 For **he chose us in him before the creation of the world** to be holy and blameless in his sight. In love 5 he predestined us for adoption to sonship through Jesus Christ, in accordance with his pleasure and will—6 to the praise of his glorious grace, which he has freely given us in the One he loves. 7 In him we have redemption through his blood, the forgiveness of sins, in accordance with the riches of God's grace 8 that he lavished on us. With all wisdom and understanding, 9 he made known to us the mystery of his will according to his good pleasure, which he purposed in Christ, 10 to be put into effect when the times reach their fulfillment—to bring unity to all things in heaven and on earth under Christ.

11 In him we were also chosen, having been predestined according to the plan of him who works out everything in conformity with the purpose of his will, 12 in order that we, who were the first to put our hope in Christ, might be for the praise of his glory. 13 And you also were included in Christ when you heard the message of truth, the gospel of your salvation. When you believed, you were marked in him with a seal, the promised Holy Spirit, 14 who is a deposit guaranteeing our inheritance until the redemption of those who are God's possession—to the praise of his glory.

God, in His grace, had His eye on you before you were even born.

Thanksgiving and Prayer

15 For this reason, ever since I heard about your faith in the Lord Jesus and your love for all God's people, 16 I have not stopped giving thanks for you, remembering you in my prayers. 17 I keep asking that the God of our Lord Jesus Christ, the glorious Father, may give you the Spirit of wisdom and revelation, so that you may know him better. 18 I pray that the eyes of your heart may be enlightened in order that you may know the hope to which he has called you, the riches of his glorious inheritance in his holy people, 19 and his incomparably great power for us who believe. That power is the same as the mighty strength 20 he exerted when he raised Christ from the dead and seated him at his right hand in the heavenly realms, 21 far above all rule and authority, power and dominion, and every name that is invoked, not only in the present age but also in the one to come. 22 And God placed all things under his feet and appointed him to be head over everything for the church, 23 which is his body, the fullness of him who fills everything in every way.

Made Alive in Christ

2:1 As for you, you were dead in your transgressions and sins, 2 in which you used to live when you followed the ways of this world and of the ruler of the kingdom of the air, the spirit who is now at work in those who are disobedient. 3 All of us also lived among them at one time, gratifying the cravings of our flesh and following its desires and thoughts. Like the rest, we were by nature deserving of wrath. 4 But because of his great love for us, God, who is rich in mercy, 5 **made us alive with Christ even when we were dead in transgressions**—it is by grace you have been saved. 6 And God raised us up with Christ and seated us with him in the heavenly realms in Christ Jesus, 7 in order that in the coming ages he might show the incomparable riches of his grace, expressed in his kindness to us in Christ Jesus. 8 **For it is by grace you have been saved, through faith—and this is not from yourselves, it is the gift of God—9 not by works, so that no one can boast.** 10 For we are God's **handiwork**, created in Christ Jesus to do good works, which God prepared in advance for us to do.

Jew and Gentile Reconciled Through Christ

11 Therefore, remember that formerly you who are Gentiles by birth and called "uncircumcised" by those who call themselves "the circumcision" (which is done in the body by human hands) —12 remember that at that time you were separate from Christ, **excluded from citizenship in Israel and foreigners to the covenants of the promise**, without hope and without God in the world. 13 But now in Christ Jesus you who once were far away have been brought near by the blood of Christ.

14 For he himself is our peace, who has made the two groups one and has destroyed the barrier, the **dividing wall of hostility**, 15 by setting aside in his flesh the law with its commands and regulations. His purpose was to create in himself one new humanity out of the two, thus making peace, 16 and in one body to reconcile

---

A dead person cannot even "want" to be alive.

Grace is by faith, not by your good works. In fact the good works you do are also part of God's grace to you.

Christianity is for everyone.

There were divisions between Jewish and Gentile Christians in Ephesus.

both of them to God through the cross, by which he put to death their hostility. 17 He came and preached peace to you who were far away and peace to those who were near. 18 For through him we both have access to the Father by one Spirit.

19 Consequently, you are no longer foreigners and strangers, but fellow citizens with God's people and also members of his household, 20 built on the foundation of the apostles and prophets, with Christ Jesus himself as the chief cornerstone. 21 In him the whole building is joined together and rises to become a holy temple in the Lord. 22 And in him you too are being built together to become a dwelling in which God lives by his Spirit.

A Prayer for the Ephesians

3:16 I pray that out of his glorious riches he may strengthen you with power through his Spirit in your inner being, 17 so that Christ may dwell in your hearts through faith. And I pray that you, being rooted and established in love, 18 may have power, together with all the Lord's holy people, to grasp how wide and long and high and deep is the love of Christ, 19 and to know this love that surpasses knowledge—that you may be filled to the measure of all the fullness of God.

20 Now **to him who is able to do immeasurably more than all we ask or imagine, according to his power that is at work within us,** 21 to him be glory in the church and in Christ Jesus throughout all generations, for ever and ever! Amen.

Unity and Maturity in the Body of Christ

4:1 As a prisoner for the Lord, then, I urge you to live a life worthy of the calling you have received. 2 Be completely humble and gentle; be patient, bearing with one another in love. 3 Make every effort to keep the unity of the Spirit through the bond of peace. 4 There is one body and one Spirit, just as you were called to one hope when you were called; 5 one Lord, one faith, one baptism; 6 one God and Father of all, who is over all and through all and in all.

7 But to each one of us grace has been given as Christ apportioned it. 11 So Christ himself gave the apostles, the prophets, the evangelists, the pastors and teachers, 12 to equip his people for works of service, so that the body of Christ may be built up 13 until we all reach unity in the faith and in the knowledge of the Son of God and become mature, attaining to the whole measure of the fullness of Christ.

14 Then we will no longer be infants, tossed back and forth by the waves, and blown here and there by every wind of teaching and by the cunning and craftiness of people in their deceitful scheming. 15 Instead, speaking the truth in love, we will grow to become in every respect the mature body of him who is the head, that is, Christ. 16 **From him the whole body, joined and held together by every supporting ligament, grows and builds itself up in love, as each part does its work.**

What would you attempt if you knew you couldn't fail? Whatever you can imagine, God is able to do more than that.

This is the church. This is true community.

Instructions for Christian Living

17 So I tell you this, and insist on it in the Lord, that you must no longer live as the Gentiles do, in the futility of their thinking. 18 They are darkened in their understanding and separated from the life of God because of the ignorance that is in them due to the hardening of their hearts. 19 Having lost all sensitivity, they have given themselves over to sensuality so as to indulge in every kind of impurity, and they are full of greed.

20 That, however, is not the way of life you learned 21 when you heard about Christ and were taught in him in accordance with the truth that is in Jesus. 22 **You were taught, with regard to your former way of life, to put off your old self, which is being corrupted by its deceitful desires; 23 to be made new in the attitude of your minds; 24 and to put on the new self, created to be like God in true righteousness and holiness.**

25 Therefore each of you must put off falsehood and speak truthfully to your neighbor, for we are all members of one body. 26 "In your anger do not sin": **Do not let the sun go down while you are still angry, 27 and do not give the devil a foothold.** 28 Anyone who has been stealing must steal no longer, but must work, doing something useful with their own hands, that they may have something to share with those in need.

29 **Do not let any unwholesome talk come out of your mouths, but only what is helpful for building others up** according to their needs, that it may benefit those who listen. 30 And do not grieve the Holy Spirit of God, with whom you were sealed for the day of redemption. 31 Get rid of all bitterness, rage and anger, brawling and slander, along with every form of malice. 32 Be kind and compassionate to one another, forgiving each other, just as in Christ God forgave you.

5:1 Follow God's example, therefore, as dearly loved children 2 and walk in the way of love, just as Christ loved us and gave himself up for us as a fragrant offering and sacrifice to God.

15 Be very careful, then, how you live—not as unwise but as wise, 16 making the most of every opportunity, because the days are evil. 17 Therefore do not be foolish, but understand what the Lord's will is. 18 Do not get drunk on wine, which leads to debauchery. Instead, be filled with the Spirit, 19 speaking to one another with psalms, hymns, and songs from the Spirit. Sing and make music from your heart to the Lord, 20 always giving thanks to God the Father for everything, in the name of our Lord Jesus Christ.

Instructions for Christian Households

21 **Submit to one another out of reverence for Christ.**

22 Wives, submit yourselves to your own husbands as you do to the Lord. 23 For the husband is the head of the wife as Christ is the head of the church, his body, of which he is the Savior. 24 Now as the church submits to Christ, so also wives should submit to their husbands in everything.

Margin notes:

What old way do you need to put off?

What anger issues have you been holding on to lately?

If you don't have anything good to say about someone, maybe you should just be quiet.

Keep this heading in mind as you read Paul's thoughts on marriage.

25 Husbands, love your wives, just as Christ loved the church and gave himself up for her 26 to make her holy, cleansing her by the washing with water through the word, 27 and to present her to himself as a radiant church, without stain or wrinkle or any other blemish, but holy and blameless. 28 In this same way, husbands ought to love their wives as their own bodies. He who loves his wife loves himself. 29 After all, no one ever hated their own body, but they feed and care for their body, just as Christ does the church—30 for we are members of his body. 31 "For this reason a man will leave his father and mother and be united to his wife, and the two will become one flesh." 32 This is a profound mystery—but I am talking about Christ and the church. 33 However, **each one of you also must love his wife as he loves himself, and the wife must respect her husband.**

Men want respect; women want love. How are they the same? How are they different?

6:1 Children, obey your parents in the Lord, for this is right. 2 "Honor your father and mother"—which is the first commandment with a promise—3 "so that it may go well with you and that you may enjoy long life on the earth."

4 Fathers, do not exasperate your children; instead, bring them up in the training and instruction of the Lord.

The Armor of God

10 Finally, be strong in the Lord and in his mighty power. 11 Put on the full armor of God, so that you can take your stand against the devil's schemes. 12 **For our struggle is not against flesh and blood, but against the rulers, against the authorities, against the powers of this dark world and against the spiritual forces of evil in the heavenly realms.** 13 Therefore put on the full armor of God, so that when the day of evil comes, you may be able to stand your ground, and after you have done everything, to stand. 14 Stand firm then, with the belt of truth buckled around your waist, with the breastplate of righteousness in place, 15 and with your feet fitted with the readiness that comes from the gospel of peace. 16 In addition to all this, take up the shield of faith, with which you can extinguish all the flaming arrows of the evil one. 17 Take the helmet of salvation and the sword of the Spirit, which is the word of God.

Sometimes the battle in life is not what we see, but what we don't see.

18 And pray in the Spirit on all occasions with all kinds of prayers and requests. With this in mind, be alert and always keep on praying for all the Lord's people. 19 Pray also for me, that whenever I speak, words may be given me so that I will fearlessly make known the mystery of the gospel, 20 for which I am an ambassador in chains. Pray that I may declare it fearlessly, as I should.

the book of Philippians

Category: The Letters
Author: Paul
Theme: Pressing on
Location & Date: Prison; A.D. 62
Version of Bible: New Revised Standard Version (NRSV)
Summary: With this letter, Paul thanked the churches at Philippi (in present day Turkey) for their support and encouraged them to be humble like Jesus, to be like stars in a dark world, and to press on in the Christian life with the enthusiasm of one seeking a prize.

Philippians 1:1 Paul and Timothy, servants of Christ Jesus, To all the saints in Christ Jesus who are in Philippi, with the bishops and deacons: 2 Grace to you and peace from God our Father and the Lord Jesus Christ.

Paul's Prayer for the Philippians

3 I thank my God every time I remember you, 4 constantly praying with joy in every one of my prayers for all of you, 5 because of your sharing in the gospel from the first day until now. 6 **I am confident of this, that the one who began a good work among you will bring it to completion by the day of Jesus Christ.** 7 It is right for me to think this way about all of you, because you hold me in your heart, for all of you share in God's grace with me, both in my imprisonment and in the defense and confirmation of the gospel. 8 For God is my witness, how I long for all of you with the compassion of Christ Jesus. 9 And this is my prayer, that your love may overflow more and more with knowledge and full insight 10 to help you to determine what is best, so that in the day of Christ you may be pure and blameless, 11 having produced the harvest of righteousness that comes through Jesus Christ for the glory and praise of God.

Paul's Present Circumstances

12 I want you to know, beloved, that **what has happened to me** has actually helped to spread the gospel, 13 so that it has become known throughout the whole imperial guard and to everyone else that my imprisonment is for Christ; 14 and most of the brothers and sisters, having been made confident in the Lord by my imprisonment, dare to speak the word with greater boldness and without fear.

18 What does it matter? Just this, that Christ is proclaimed in every way, whether out of false motives or true; and in that I rejoice.

You may not be all you could be yet but God will not stop working on you and through you until you are what He wants you to be.

Paul wrote this letter from prison.

Yes, and I will continue to rejoice, 19 for I know that through your prayers and the help of the Spirit of Jesus Christ this will turn out for my deliverance. 20 **It is my eager expectation and hope that I will not be put to shame in any way, but that by my speaking with all boldness, Christ will be exalted now as always in my body, whether by life or by death.** 21 For to me, living is Christ and dying is gain. 22 If I am to live in the flesh, that means fruitful labor for me; and I do not know which I prefer. 23 I am hard pressed between the two: my desire is to depart and be with Christ, for that is far better.

What you are living for is often seen in what you would be willing to die for.

Imitating Christ's Humility

2:1 If there is any encouragement in Christ, any consolation from love, any sharing in the Spirit, any compassion and sympathy, 2 make my joy complete: be of the same mind, having the same love, being in full accord and of one mind. 3 Do nothing from selfish ambition or conceit, but in humility regard others as better than yourselves. 4 **Let each of you look not to your own interests, but to the interests of others.** 5 **Let the same mind be in you that was in Christ Jesus**, 6 who, though he was in the form of God, did not regard equality with God as something to be exploited, 7 but emptied himself, taking the form of a slave, being born in human likeness. And being found in human form, 8 he humbled himself and became obedient to the point of death—even death on a cross. 9 Therefore God also highly exalted him and gave him the name that is above every name, 10 so that at the name of Jesus every knee should bend, in heaven and on earth and under the earth, 11 and every tongue should confess that Jesus Christ is Lord, to the glory of God the Father.

This is the example of Jesus.

Shining as Lights in the World

12 Therefore, my beloved, just as you have always obeyed me, not only in my presence, but much more now in my absence, work out your own salvation with fear and trembling; 13 for it is God who is at work in you, enabling you both to will and to work for his good pleasure.

14 **Do all things without murmuring and arguing, 15 so that you may be blameless and innocent, children of God without blemish in the midst of a crooked and perverse generation, in which you shine like stars in the world.** 16 It is by your holding fast to the word of life that I can boast on the day of Christ that I did not run in vain or labor in vain. 17 But even if I am being poured out as a libation over the sacrifice and the offering of your faith, I am glad and rejoice with all of you—18 and in the same way you also must be glad and rejoice with me.

Do you want to shine like a star? Stop murmuring and arguing.

3:7 Yet whatever gains I had, these I have come to regard as loss because of Christ. 8 More than that, I regard everything as loss because of the surpassing value of knowing Christ Jesus my Lord. For his sake I have suffered the loss of all things, and I regard them as rubbish, in order that I may gain Christ 9 and be found in him, not having a righteousness of my own that comes from the law, but one that comes through faith in Christ, the righteousness from God based on faith. 10 I want to know Christ and the power of his resurrection and the sharing of his sufferings by becoming like him in his death, 11 if somehow I may attain the resurrection from the dead.

Pressing Toward the Goal

12 Not that I have already obtained this or have already reached the goal; but I press on to make it my own, because Christ Jesus has made me his own. 13 Beloved, I do not consider that I have made it my own; but this one thing I do: **forgetting what lies behind and straining forward to what lies ahead, 14 I press on toward the goal for the prize of the heavenly call of God in Christ Jesus.**

17 Brothers and sisters, join in imitating me, and observe those who live according to the example you have in us. 18 For many live as enemies of the cross of Christ; I have often told you of them, and now I tell you even with tears. 19 Their end is destruction; their god is the belly; and their glory is in their shame; their minds are set on earthly things. 20 But our citizenship is in heaven, and it is from there that we are expecting a Savior, the Lord Jesus Christ. 21 He will transform the body of our humiliation that it may be conformed to the body of his glory, by the power that also enables him to make all things subject to himself.

4:1 Therefore, my brothers and sisters, whom I love and long for, my joy and crown, stand firm in the Lord in this way, my beloved.

Exhortations

4 Rejoice in the Lord always; again I will say, Rejoice. 5 Let your gentleness be known to everyone. The Lord is near. 6 **Do not worry about anything, but in everything by prayer and supplication with thanksgiving let your requests be made known to God.** 7 And the peace of God, which surpasses all understanding, will guard your hearts and your minds in Christ Jesus.

8 Finally, beloved, whatever is true, whatever is honorable, whatever is just, whatever is pure, whatever is pleasing, whatever is commendable, if there is any excellence and if there is anything worthy of praise, **think about these things**. 9 Keep on doing the things that you have learned and received and heard and seen in me, and the God of peace will be with you.

Acknowledgment of the Philippians' Gift

10 I rejoice in the Lord greatly that now at last you have revived your concern for me; indeed, you were concerned for me, but had no opportunity to show it. 11 Not that I am referring to being in need; for I have learned to be content with whatever I have. 12 I know what it is to have little, and I know what it is to have plenty. In any and all circumstances I have learned the secret of being well-fed and of going hungry, of having plenty and of being in need. 13 **I can do all things through him who strengthens me.** 14 In any case, it was kind of you to share my distress.

15 You Philippians indeed know that in the early days of the gospel, when I left Macedonia, no church shared with me in the

---

What prize compels you to get out of bed in the morning? What motivates you to strain forward? What goal are you pressing on toward?

You can worry or pray. Which is it going to be?

Whatever you think about, that is going to control your attitude toward life.

Life is not about what you can do. It is about what God can do through you.

matter of giving and receiving, except you alone. 16 For even when I was in Thessalonica, you sent me help for my needs more than once. 17 Not that I seek the gift, but I seek the profit that accumulates to your account. 18 I have been paid in full and have more than enough; I am fully satisfied, now that I have received from Epaphroditus the gifts you sent, a fragrant offering, a sacrifice acceptable and pleasing to God. 19 And my God will fully satisfy every need of yours according to his riches in glory in Christ Jesus. 20 To our God and Father be glory forever and ever. Amen.

the book of Colossians

Category: *The Letters*
Author: *Paul*
Theme: *The importance of Christ*
Location & Date: *Prison; A.D. 60-61*
Version of Bible: *New Revised Standard Version (NRSV)*
Summary: *A man that Paul converted in the city of Ephesus came to visit Paul in Rome. He had planted a church in Colossae, but his church was struggling with false teachers. Paul wrote this letter to set them straight. It is good for us as well.*

Colossians 1:1 Paul, an apostle of Christ Jesus by the will of God, and Timothy our brother, 2 To the saints and faithful brothers and sisters in Christ in Colossae: Grace to you and peace from God our Father.

Paul Thanks God for the Colossians

3 In our prayers for you we always thank God, the Father of our Lord Jesus Christ, 4 for we have heard of your faith in Christ Jesus and of the love that you have for all the saints, 5 because of the hope laid up for you in heaven. You have heard of this hope before in the word of the truth, the gospel 6 that has come to you. Just as it is bearing fruit and growing in the whole world, so it has been bearing fruit among yourselves from the day you heard it and truly comprehended the grace of God.

{Paul then went on to talk about Jesus.}

The Supremacy of Christ

15 He is the image of the invisible God, the firstborn of all creation; 16 for in him all things in heaven and on earth were created, things visible and invisible, whether thrones or dominions or rulers or powers—all things have been created through him and for him. 17 He himself is before all things, and in him all things hold together. 18 He is the head of the body, the church; he is the beginning, the firstborn from the dead, so that he might come to have first place in everything. 19 For in him all the fullness of God was pleased to dwell, 20 and through him God was pleased to reconcile to himself all things, whether on earth or in heaven, by making peace through the blood of his cross.

21 And you who were once estranged and hostile in mind, doing evil deeds, 22 he has now reconciled in his fleshly body through death, so as to present you holy and blameless and irreproachable

before him - 23 provided that you continue securely established and steadfast in the faith, without shifting from the hope promised by the gospel that you heard, which has been proclaimed to every creature under heaven. I, Paul, became a servant of this gospel.

2:1 For I want you to know how much I am struggling for you, and for those in Laodicea, and for all who have not seen me face to face. 2 I want their hearts to be encouraged and united in love, so that they may have all the riches of assured understanding and have the knowledge of God's mystery, that is, Christ himself, 3 in whom are hidden all the treasures of wisdom and knowledge.

Fullness of Life in Christ

6 As you therefore have received Christ Jesus the Lord, continue to live your lives in him, 7 rooted and built up in him and established in the faith, just as you were taught, abounding in thanksgiving.

8 See to it that no one takes you captive through philosophy and empty deceit, according to human tradition, according to the elemental spirits of the universe, and not according to Christ. 9 For in him the whole fullness of deity dwells bodily, 10 and you have come to fullness in him, who is the head of every ruler and authority. 11 In him also you were circumcised with a spiritual circumcision, by putting off the body of the flesh in the circumcision of Christ; 12 when you were **buried with him in baptism**, you were also raised with him through faith in the power of God, who raised him from the dead. 13 And when you were dead in trespasses and the uncircumcision of your flesh, God made you alive together with him, when he forgave us all our trespasses, 14 erasing the record that stood against us with its legal demands. He set this aside, nailing it to the cross. 15 He disarmed the rulers and authorities and made a public example of them, triumphing over them in it.

The New Life in Christ

3:1 So if you have been raised with Christ, seek the things that are above, where Christ is, seated at the right hand of God. 2 Set your minds on things that are above, not on things that are on earth, 3 for you have died, and your life is hidden with Christ in God. 4 When Christ who is your life is revealed, then you also will be revealed with him in glory.

5 Put to death, therefore, whatever in you is earthly: fornication, impurity, passion, evil desire, and greed (which is idolatry). 6 On account of these the wrath of God is coming on those who are disobedient. 7 These are the ways you also once followed, when you were living that life. 8 But now you must get rid of all such things—anger, wrath, malice, slander, and abusive language from your mouth. 9 Do not lie to one another, seeing that you have stripped off the old self with its practices 10 and have clothed yourselves with the new self, which is being renewed in knowledge according to the image of its creator. 11 **In that renewal there is no longer Greek and Jew, circumcised and uncircumcised, barbarian, Scythian, slave and free; but Christ is all and in all!**

When a person is baptized in water it is as if they die to their old self when they go down in the water and as if they are raised to a new life when the come up.

Your identity, the thing that defines you, is found in Christ. Once you become a christian you can go anywhere in the world and there will be a group of people the will treat you like a brother or sister.

12 As God's chosen ones, holy and beloved, clothe yourselves with compassion, kindness, humility, meekness, and patience. 13 Bear with one another and, if anyone has a complaint against another, forgive each other; just as the Lord has forgiven you, so you also must forgive. 14 Above all, clothe yourselves with love, which binds everything together in perfect harmony. 15 And let the peace of Christ rule in your hearts, to which indeed you were called in the one body. And be thankful. 16 Let the word of Christ dwell in you richly; teach and admonish one another in all wisdom; and with gratitude in your hearts sing psalms, hymns, and spiritual songs to God. 17 And whatever you do, in word or deed, do everything in the name of the Lord Jesus, giving thanks to God the Father through him.

Further Instructions

4:2 Devote yourselves to prayer, keeping alert in it with thanksgiving. 5 Conduct yourselves wisely toward outsiders, making the most of the time. 6 Let your speech always be gracious, seasoned with salt, so that you may know how you ought to answer everyone.

the books of 1 & 2 Thessalonians

Category: *The Letters*
Author: *Paul*
Theme: *The hope of heaven*
Location & Date: *Corinth; A.D. 51*
Version of Bible: *Holman Christian Standard Bible (HCSB)*
Summary: *The response to Paul's message among the Gentiles (non-Jews) in the city of Thessalonica (Greece) caused some Jews to turn the whole city against Paul. Even under the cover of darkness, he barely escaped. Later he got a report from Timothy on how the church was doing and it is in response to this report that we now have the letters to the Thessalonians. In these letters Paul gives encouragement and specific teaching on the second coming of Jesus.*

Greeting

1 Thessalonians 1:1 Paul, Silvanus, and Timothy: To the church of the Thessalonians in God the Father and the Lord Jesus Christ. Grace to you and peace.

Thanksgiving

2 **We always thank God for all of you, remembering you constantly in our prayers.** 3 We recall, in the presence of our God and Father, your work of faith, labor of love, and endurance of hope in our Lord Jesus Christ, 4 knowing your election, brothers loved by God. 5 For our gospel did not come to you in word only, but also in power, in the Holy Spirit, and with much assurance. You know what kind of men we were among you for your benefit, 6 and you became imitators of us and of the Lord when, in spite of severe persecution, you welcomed the message with joy from the Holy Spirit. 7 As a result, you became an example to all the believers in Macedonia and Achaia. 8 For the Lord's message rang out from you, not only in Macedonia and Achaia, but in every place that your faith in God has gone out. Therefore, we don't need to say anything, 9 for they themselves report what kind of reception we had from you: how you turned to God from idols to serve the living and true God 10 and to wait for His Son from heaven, whom He raised from the dead—Jesus, who rescues us from the coming wrath.

It is good to have people in your life that are praying for you.

Paul's Conduct

2:7 Although we could have been a burden as Christ's apostles, instead we were gentle among you, as a nursing mother nurtures her own children. 8 We cared so much for you that we were

The Letters

You cannot share the gospel, the good news of Jesus, without sharing your life.

pleased to **share with you not only the gospel of God but also our own lives,** because you had become dear to us. 9 For you remember our labor and hardship, brothers. Working night and day so that we would not burden any of you, we preached God's gospel to you. 10 You are witnesses, and so is God, of how devoutly, righteously, and blamelessly we conducted ourselves with you believers. 11 As you know, like a father with his own children, 12 we encouraged, comforted, and implored each one of you to walk worthy of God, who calls you into His own kingdom and glory. 13 This is why we constantly thank God, because when you received the message about God that you heard from us, you welcomed it not as a human message, but as it truly is, the message of God, which also works effectively in you believers. 19 **For who is our hope or joy or crown of boasting in the presence of our Lord Jess at His coming? Is it not you? 20 For you are our glory and joy!**

Glory is not in what you do, but in whom you help connect to God.

Loving and Working

4:11 Seek to lead a quiet life, to mind your own business, and to work with your own hands, as we commanded you, 12 so that you may walk properly in the presence of outsiders and not be dependent on anyone.

The Comfort of Christ's Coming

13 We do not want you to be uninformed, brothers, concerning those who are asleep, so that you will not grieve like the rest, who have no hope. 14 Since we believe that Jesus died and rose again, in the same way God will bring with Him those who have fallen asleep through Jesus. 15 For we say this to you by a revelation from the Lord: We who are still alive at the Lord's coming will certainly have no advantage over those who have fallen asleep. 16 **For the Lord Himself will descend from heaven with a shout, with the archangel's voice, and with the trumpet of God, and the dead in Christ will rise first. 17 Then we who are still alive will be caught up together with them** in the clouds to meet the Lord in the air and so we will always be with the Lord. 18 Therefore encourage one another with these words.

Jesus is coming again. When he does the dead will be raised and we will join them to meet Christ as He comes.

Exhortations and Blessings

5:12 Now we ask you, brothers, to give recognition to those who labor among you and lead you in the Lord and admonish you, 13 and to regard them very highly in love because of their work. Be at peace among yourselves. 14 And we exhort you, brothers: warn those who are irresponsible, comfort the discouraged, help the weak, be patient with everyone. 15 See to it that no one repays evil for evil to anyone, but always pursue what is good for one another and for all.

16 **Rejoice always! 17 Pray constantly. 18 Give thanks in everything**, for this is God's will for you in Christ Jesus. 19 Don't stifle the Spirit. 20 Don't despise prophecies, 21 but test all things. Hold on to what is good. 22 Stay away from every kind of evil.

Today, consciously try to do these 3 things. See the difference it makes in your outlook.

23 Now may the God of peace Himself sanctify you completely. And may your spirit, soul, and body be kept sound and blameless

for the coming of our Lord Jesus Christ. 24 He who calls you is faithful, who also will do it.

God's Judgment and Glory

2 Thessalonians 1:3 We must always thank God for you, brothers. This is right, since your faith is flourishing and the love each one of you has for one another is increasing. 4 Therefore, we ourselves boast about you among God's churches—about your endurance and faith in all the persecutions and afflictions you endure.

11 And in view of this, we always pray for you that our God will consider you worthy of His calling, and will, by His power, fulfill every desire for goodness and the work of faith, 12 so that the name of our Lord Jesus will be glorified by you, and you by Him, according to the grace of our God and the Lord Jesus Christ.

Stand Firm

2:13 But we must always thank God for you, brothers loved by the Lord, because from the beginning God has chosen you for salvation through sanctification by the Spirit and through belief in the truth. 14 He called you to this through our gospel, so that you might obtain the glory of our Lord Jesus Christ. 15 Therefore, brothers, stand firm and hold to the traditions you were taught, either by our message or by our letter.

16 **May our Lord Jesus Christ Himself and God our Father, who has loved us and given us eternal encouragement and good hope by grace, 17 encourage your hearts and strengthen you in every good work and word.**

> This is a great blessing. Who can you share this blessing with?

Warning Against Irresponsible Behavior

3:6 Now we command you, brothers, in the name of our Lord Jesus Christ, to keep away from every brother who walks irresponsibly and not according to the tradition received from us. 7 For you yourselves know how you must imitate us: We were not irresponsible among you; 8 we did not eat anyone's food free of charge; instead, we labored and struggled, working night and day, so that we would not be a burden to any of you. 9 It is not that we don't have the right to support, but we did it to make ourselves an example to you so that you would imitate us. 10 In fact, when we were with you, this is what we commanded you: **"If anyone isn't willing to work, he should not eat."** 11 For we hear that there are some among you who walk irresponsibly, not working at all, but interfering with the work of others. 12 Now we command and exhort such people by the Lord Jesus Christ that quietly working, they may eat their own food. 13 Brothers, do not grow weary in doing good.

> Christians care about others, but sometimes the form your care should take is letting someone suffer for their bad choices.

the books of 1 & 2 Timothy

Category: *The Letters*
Author: *Paul*
Theme: *The passing of the baton*
Location & Date: *Macedonia, Philippi; A.D. 64*
Version of Bible: *Holman Christian Standard Bible (HCSB)*
Summary: Timothy, who was a companion missionary with Paul for 15 years, was now the pastor of the church in Ephesus. Paul's first letter to Timothy was filled with practical pastoral advise. In the second letter, Paul, knowing that he was coming to the end of his life, wanted to pass the baton to Timothy who was like a son to him. Listen to the love and concern in these letters.

Instructions on Prayer

1 Timothy 2:1 First of all, then, I urge that petitions, prayers, intercessions, and thanksgivings be made for everyone, 2 for kings and all those who are in authority, so that we may lead a tranquil and quiet life in all godliness and dignity. 3 This is good, and it pleases God our Savior, 4 who wants everyone to be saved and to come to the knowledge of the truth.

When Christians use the word "gospel," this is what they are talking about.

5 For there is one God and **one mediator between God and humanity, Christ Jesus,** Himself human, 6 who gave Himself—a ransom for all, a testimony at the proper time.

Qualifications of Church Leaders

A leader in the church.

3:1 This saying is trustworthy: "If anyone aspires to be an **overseer**, he desires a noble work." 2 An overseer, therefore, must be above reproach, the husband of one wife, self-controlled, sensible, respectable, hospitable, an able teacher, 3 not addicted to wine, not a bully but gentle, not quarrelsome, not greedy—4 one who manages his own household competently, having his children under control with all dignity. 5 **(If anyone does not know how to manage his own household, how will he take care of God's church?)** 6 He must not be a new convert, or he might become conceited and fall into the condemnation of the Devil. 7 Furthermore, he must have a good reputation among outsiders, so that he does not fall into disgrace and the Devil's trap.

Leadership in your own family is preparation of leadership in the church.

Deacons were leaders helping the overseers or elders.

8 **Deacons**, likewise, should be worthy of respect, not hypocritical, not drinking a lot of wine, not greedy for money, 9 holding the mystery of the faith with a clear conscience. 10 And they must also be tested first; if they prove blameless, then they can serve as deacons. 11 Wives, too, must be worthy of respect, not slan-

derers, self-controlled, faithful in everything. 12 Deacons must be husbands of one wife, managing their children and their own households competently. 13 For those who have served well as deacons acquire a good standing for themselves, and great boldness in the faith that is in Christ Jesus.

A Good Servant of Jesus Christ

4:7 But have nothing to do with irreverent and silly myths. Rather, train yourself in godliness, 8 for the training of the body has a limited benefit, but godliness is beneficial in every way, since it holds promise for the present life and also for the life to come.

Instructions for Ministry

11 Command and teach these things. 12 Let no one despise your youth; instead, you should be an example to the believers in speech, in conduct, in love, in faith, in purity. 13 Until I come, give your attention to public reading, exhortation, and teaching. 14 Do not neglect the gift that is in you; it was given to you through prophecy, with the laying on of hands by the council of elders. 15 Practice these things; be committed to them, so that your progress may be evident to all. 16 **Pay close attention to your life and your teaching**; persevere in these things, for by doing this you will save both yourself and your hearers.

False Doctrine and Human Greed

6:6 But godliness with contentment is a great gain. 7 For we brought nothing into the world, and we can take nothing out. 8 **But if we have food and clothing, we will be content with these**.

9 But those who want to be rich fall into temptation, a trap, and many foolish and harmful desires, which plunge people into ruin and destruction. 10 For the love of money is a root of all kinds of evil, and by craving it, some have wandered away from the faith and pierced themselves with many pains.

Fight the Good Fight

11 But you, man of God, run from these things, and pursue righteousness, godliness, faith, love, endurance, and gentleness.

12 Fight the good fight for the faith; take hold of eternal life that you were called to and have made a good confession about in the presence of many witnesses.

Instructions to the Rich

17 Instruct those who are rich in the present age not to be arrogant or to set their hope on the uncertainty of wealth, but on God, who richly provides us with all things to enjoy. 18 Instruct them to do what is good, to be rich in good works, to be generous, willing to share, 19 storing up for themselves a good reserve for the age to come, so that they may take hold of life that is real.

In the church, you must live out in your own life what you teach.

Why is it easy to believe that you would be happy if you just had a little bit more?

Guard the Heritage

20 Timothy, guard what has been entrusted to you, avoiding irreverent, empty speech and contradictions from the "knowledge" that falsely bears that name. 21 By professing it, some people have deviated from the faith.

Thanksgiving

2 Timothy 1:3 I thank God, whom I serve with a clear conscience as my ancestors did, when I constantly remember you in my prayers night and day. 4 Remembering your tears, I long to see you so that I may be filled with joy, 5 clearly recalling your sincere **faith that first lived in your grandmother Lois, then in your mother Eunice, and that I am convinced is in you also.**

6 Therefore, I remind you to keep ablaze the gift of God that is in you through the laying on of my hands. 7 For God has not given us a spirit of fearfulness, but one of power, love, and sound judgment.

> Christianity flows best down family lines. How did Christianity come into your household?

Not Ashamed of the Gospel

8 So don't be ashamed of the testimony about our Lord, or of me His prisoner. Instead, share in suffering for the gospel, relying on the power of God.

9 He has saved us and called us with a holy calling, not according to our works, but according to His own purpose and grace, which was given to us in Christ Jesus before time began.

10 This has now been made evident through the appearing of our Savior Christ Jesus, who has abolished death and has brought life and immortality to light through the gospel.

11 For this gospel I was appointed a herald, apostle, and teacher, 12 and that is why I suffer these things. But I am not ashamed, because I know the One I have believed in and am persuaded that He is able to guard what has been entrusted to me until that day.

Be Loyal to the Faith

13 Hold on to the pattern of sound teaching that you have heard from me, in the faith and love that are in Christ Jesus. 14 Guard, through the Holy Spirit who lives in us, that good thing entrusted to you. 15 This you know: **All those in Asia have turned away from me**, including Phygelus and Hermogenes.

Be Strong in Grace

2:1 You, therefore, my son, be strong in the grace that is in Christ Jesus. 2 And what you have heard from me in the presence of many witnesses, commit to faithful men who will be able to teach others also.

3 Share in suffering as a good soldier of Christ Jesus. 11 This saying is trustworthy: For if we have died with Him, we will also live with Him; 12 if we endure, we will also reign with Him; if we deny Him, He will also deny us; 13 if we are faithless, He remains

> Paul was at the end of his life - his execution was close. But the most painful thing he endured was the betrayal of his former friends.

faithful, for He cannot deny Himself.

An Approved Worker

14 Remind them of these things, charging them before God not to fight about words; this is in no way profitable and leads to the ruin of the hearers.

Difficult Times Ahead

3:1 But know this: Difficult times will come in the last days. 2 For people will be lovers of self, lovers of money, boastful, proud, blasphemers, disobedient to parents, ungrateful, unholy, 3 unloving, irreconcilable, slanderers, without self-control, brutal, without love for what is good, 4 traitors, reckless, conceited, lovers of pleasure rather than lovers of God, 5 holding to the form of godliness but denying its power. **Avoid these people!**

> Good advice.

Struggles in the Christian Life

14 But as for you, continue in what you have learned and firmly believed. You know those who taught you, 15 and you know that from childhood you have known the sacred Scriptures, which are able to give you wisdom for salvation through faith in Christ Jesus. 16 **All Scripture is inspired by God and is profitable** for teaching, for rebuking, for correcting, for training in righteousness, 17 so that the man of God may be complete, equipped for every good work.

> Because the Word is from God it is profitable - it will do a great deal of good in your life.

Fulfill Your Ministry

4:1 I solemnly charge you before God and Christ Jesus, who is going to judge the living and the dead, and because of His appearing and His kingdom: 2 Proclaim the message; persist in it whether convenient or not; rebuke, correct, and encourage with great patience and teaching. 3 For the time will come when they will not tolerate sound doctrine, but according to their own desires, will multiply teachers for themselves because they have an itch to hear something new. 4 They will turn away from hearing the truth and will turn aside to myths. 5 But as for you, be serious about everything, endure hardship, do the work of an evangelist, fulfill your ministry.

6 For I am already being poured out as a drink offering, and **the time for my departure is close.** 7 **I have fought the good fight, I have finished the race, I have kept the faith.** 8 There is reserved for me in the future the crown of righteousness, which the Lord, the righteous Judge, will give me on that day, and not only to me, but to all those who have loved His appearing.

> Ever wonder what others might write on your tombstone? These words of Paul would be good words to include.

the book of **Titus**

Category: *The Letters*
Author: *Paul*
Theme: *Hang in there disciple*
Location & Date: *Macedonia; A.D. 62-64*
Version of Bible: *New International Version (NIV)*
Summary: *Titus was a companion of Paul on his second and third missionary journeys. They both planted a church on the island of Crete, and Titus stayed on as the pastor. He was young and was being opposed by ungodly men. Paul wrote to encourage him and the new believers in this struggling church.*

Titus 1:1 Paul, a servant of God and an apostle of Jesus Christ to further the faith of God's elect and their knowledge of the truth that leads to godliness—2 in the hope of eternal life, which God, who does not lie, promised before the beginning of time, 3 and which now at his appointed season he has brought to light through the preaching entrusted to me by the command of God our Savior,

4 To Titus, my true son in our common faith: Grace and peace from God the Father and Christ Jesus our Savior.

Appointing Elders Who Love What Is Good

5 The reason I left you in Crete was that you might put in order what was left unfinished and appoint **elders** in every town, as I directed you. 6 An elder must be blameless, faithful to his wife, a man whose children believe and are not open to the charge of being wild and disobedient. 7 Since an overseer manages God's household, he must be blameless—not overbearing, not quick-tempered, not given to drunkenness, not violent, not pursuing dishonest gain. 8 Rather, he must be hospitable, one who loves what is good, who is self-controlled, upright, holy and disciplined. 9 He must hold firmly to the trustworthy message as it has been taught, so that he can encourage others by sound doctrine and refute those who oppose it.

> *Elders were leaders in a church.*

Doing Good for the Sake of the Gospel

2:1 You, however, must teach what is appropriate to sound doctrine. 2 Teach the older men to be temperate, worthy of respect, self-controlled, and sound in faith, in love and in endurance.

3 Likewise, teach the older women to be reverent in the way they live, not to be slanderers or addicted to much wine, but to teach what is good. 4 Then they can urge the younger women

to love their husbands and children, 5 to be self-controlled and pure, to be busy at home, to be kind, and to be subject to their husbands, so that no one will malign the word of God.

6 Similarly, encourage the young men to be self-controlled. 7 In everything set them an example by doing what is good. In your teaching show integrity, seriousness 8 and soundness of speech that cannot be condemned, so that those who oppose you may be ashamed because they have nothing bad to say about us.

Saved in Order to Do Good

3:1 Remind the people to be subject to rulers and authorities, to be obedient, to be ready to do whatever is good, 2 to slander no one, to be peaceable and considerate, and always to be gentle toward everyone.

9 But avoid foolish controversies and genealogies and arguments and quarrels about the law, because these are unprofitable and useless. 10 Warn a divisive person once, and then warn them a second time. After that, have nothing to do with them.

15 Everyone with me sends you greetings. Greet those who love us in the faith. Grace be with you all.

the book of Philemon

Category: *The Letters*
Author: *Philemon*
Theme: *How to win friends and influence people*
Location & Date: *Prison; A.D. 60-62*
Version of Bible: *Expanded Bible (EXB)*
Summary: *Paul was in prison. While in prison he converted a man named Onesimus. It turns out that Onesimus was a runaway slave from Ephesus where Paul had planted a church years before. Not only that, Onesimus was a slave of one of the church members—Philemon. Paul wrote this letter to ask that Philemon forgive Onesimus for running away. Paul also, very subtly and respectfully, conveyed his desire to keep Onesimus as his helper (Onesimus means helper). This is a great case study on how to deal with a tricky situation.*

How to win friends and influence people.

Step 1: Express genuine care for the other person.

[1] Express the fact that we are all on the same team.
[2] Give thanks for them.
[3] Pray for them.
[4] Express something positive that they have done.

Philemon 1:1 From Paul, a prisoner of Christ Jesus, and from Timothy, our brother. To Philemon, our dear friend [brother] and worker with us [coworker]; 2 to Apphia [perhaps Philemon's wife], our sister; to Archippus [possibly Philemon's son], a worker with us [our fellow soldier]; and to the church that meets in your home: 3 **Grace and peace to you from God our Father and the Lord Jesus Christ**.[1]

Philemon's Love and Faith

4 I always **thank**[2] my God when I mention [remember] you in my **prayers**[3], 5 because **I hear about the love you have for**[4] all God's holy people [the saints] and the faith you have in the Lord Jesus.

6 I pray that the faith you share [the sharing/fellowship of your faith] may make you [enable/empower you to] understand every blessing we have in Christ. 7 **I have great joy and comfort, my brother, because the love you have shown to God's people**[4] [the saints] has refreshed them [their hearts; their inward parts; the seat of emotions].

Accept Onesimus as a Brother

Step 2: Make your humble request or suggestion.

[5] Appeal to a higher motive.

8 So, in Christ, I could be bold and order you to do what is right [required; proper; your duty].

9 **But because I love you, I am pleading**[5] with [appealing to; urging; encouraging] you instead. I, Paul, an old man now and also a prisoner [in Rome, about AD 60; Acts 28:16–31; Phil. 1:7] for Christ Jesus, 10 am pleading with [appealing to; urging; encouraging] you for my child Onesimus, who became my child [whom I begat/

fathered; Paul evidently led Onesimus to Christ in Rome] while I was in prison. **11 In the past he was useless [unprofitable; worthless] to you, but now he has become useful [helpful; valuable] for both you and me**[6] [a play on words, since Onesimus means "useful" or "helpful"].

12 I am sending him back to you, and with him **I am sending my own heart**[7] [or he is my very heart].

13 **I wanted to keep him with me**[8] so that in your place [or on your behalf] he might help [serve] me while I am in prison for the Good News [Gospel].

14 But I did not want to do anything without asking you first[9] [your consent] so that any good you do for me will be because you want to do it, not because I forced you [out of compulsion].

15 [For] **Maybe Onesimus was separated from you for a short time so you could have him back forever-16 no longer as a slave, but better than a slave, as a loved brother.**[10]

I love him very much, but you will love him even more [...especially to me, but more so to you], both as a person [or in the natural realm; in the flesh] and as a believer in the Lord [or in the spiritual realm; in the Lord].

17 **So if you consider me your partner, welcome [receive; accept] Onesimus as you would welcome [receive; accept] me.**[11] 18 If he has done anything wrong to [defrauded; harmed] you or if he owes you anything, charge that to me. 19 I, Paul, am writing this with my own hand [contrary to his usual practice of using a scribe, or amanuensis; Rom. 16:22]. **I will pay it back, and I will say nothing about what [make no mention that] you owe me for your own life**[12] [very self; Paul had evidently led Philemon to Christ]. 20 So [Yes], my brother, I ask that you do this for me [for this benefit/favor from you] in the Lord: Refresh my heart in Christ. 21 **I write this letter, knowing [confident of your obedience/compliance, knowing] that you will do what I ask you and even more.**[13]

22 One more thing—**prepare a room [guest room] for me**[14] in which to stay, because I hope God will answer your prayers and I will be able to come [restored; granted] to you.

---

[6] Appeal to a mutual benefit.

[7] Share your heart.

[8] Express what you prefer ...

[9] But in the end leave the decision to them.

[10] See the potential good in the problem.

Step 3:

[11] Close the deal.

[12] Offer to help but also remind them of what they owe you.

[13] Expect the best.

[14] End on your relationship.

the book of Hebrews

Category: The 12 Minor Prophets
Author: Possibly Paul or some unknown author
Theme: All the past was about Jesus
Location & Date: Middle East; A.D. 67-69
Version of Bible: New American Standard Bible (NASB)
Summary: The book of Hebrews was written to try and convince people of Jewish background that all the rituals, laws, and sacrifices were ultimately about Jesus.

God's Final Word in His Son

Hebrews 1:1 God, after He spoke long ago to the fathers in the prophets in many portions and in many ways, 2 in these last days has spoken to us in **His Son**, whom He appointed heir of all things, through whom also He made the world.

This is Jesus.

2:14 Therefore, since the children share in flesh and blood, He Himself likewise also **partook of the same**, that through death He might render powerless him who had the power of death, that is, the devil, 15 and might free those who through fear of death were subject to slavery all their lives.

Jesus became a human being.

17 Therefore, He had to be made like His brethren in all things, so that He might become a merciful and faithful high priest in things pertaining to God, to make **propitiation** for the sins of the people. 18 **For since He Himself was tempted in that which He has suffered, He is able to come to the aid of those who are tempted.**

A payment.

Because Jesus was one of us He understands what we go through.

The Peril of Unbelief

4:14 For we have become partakers of Christ, if we hold fast the beginning of our assurance firm until the end, 15 while it is said, "Today if you hear his voice, do not harden your hearts, as when they provoked me."

16 For who provoked Him when they had heard? Indeed, did not all those who came out of Egypt led by Moses?

A New and Living Way

10:19 Therefore, brethren, **since we have confidence to enter the holy place by the blood of Jesus, 20 by a new and living way which He inaugurated for us through the veil, that is, His flesh,** 21 and since we have a great priest over the house of God, 22 let us draw near with a sincere heart in full assurance of faith, having our hearts sprinkled clean from an evil conscience and our bodies washed

Once a year a priest was allowed to go through a veil into the Holy Place- only with

with pure water. 23 Let us hold fast the confession of our hope without wavering, for He who promised is faithful; 24 and let us consider how to stimulate one another to love and good deeds, 25 not forsaking our own assembling together, as is the habit of some, but encouraging one another; and all the more as you see the day drawing near.

Christ or Judgment

35 Therefore, do not throw away your confidence, which has a great reward. 36 For you have need of endurance, so that when you have done the will of God, you may receive what was promised.

37 For yet in a very little while, he who is coming will come, and will not delay 38 but my righteous one shall live by faith; and if he shrinks back, my soul has no pleasure in him.

39 But we are not of those who shrink back to destruction, but of those who have faith to the preserving of the soul.

The Triumphs of Faith

11:1 Now faith is the assurance of things hoped for, the conviction of things not seen. 2 For by it the men of old gained approval.

3 By faith we understand that the worlds were prepared by the word of God, so that what is seen was not made out of things which are visible.

7 By faith Noah, being warned by God about things not yet seen, in reverence prepared an ark for the salvation of his household, by which he condemned the world, and became an heir of the righteousness which is according to faith.

8 By faith Abraham, when he was called, obeyed by going out to a place which he was to receive for an inheritance; and he went out, not knowing where he was going. 9 By faith he lived as an alien in the land of promise, as in a foreign land, dwelling in tents with Isaac and Jacob, fellow heirs of the same promise; 10 for he was looking for the city which has foundations, whose architect and builder is God. 11 By faith even Sarah herself received ability to conceive, even beyond the proper time of life, since she considered Him faithful who had promised. 12 Therefore there was born even of one man, and him as good as dead at that, as many descendants as the stars of heaven in number, and innumerable as the sand which is by the seashore.

13 All these died in faith, without receiving the promises, but having seen them and having welcomed them from a distance, and having confessed that they were strangers and exiles on the earth. 14 For those who say such things make it clear that they are seeking a country of their own. 15 And indeed if they had been thinking of that country from which they went out, they would have had opportunity to return. 16 But as it is, they desire a better country, that is, a heavenly one. Therefore God is not ashamed to be called their God; for He has prepared a city for them.

17 By faith Abraham, when he was tested, offered up Isaac,

---

the blood of a sacrifice. When Jesus died that veil mysteriously ripped from top to bottom. Jesus' blood makes it possible for us to enter the Holy Place of God's presence.

Faith is not sight. Faith is the willingness to move forward without every assurance and without all the answers. Paul here retells some of Bible history to show how faith is what motivated many of well-known Bible characters.

and he who had received the promises was offering up his only begotten son; 18 it was he to whom it was said, "in Isaac your decendants shall be called." 19 He considered that God is able to raise people even from the dead, from which he also received him back as a type. 20 By faith Isaac blessed Jacob and Esau, even regarding things to come. 21 By faith Jacob, as he was dying, blessed each of the sons of Joseph, and worshiped, leaning on the top of his staff. 22 By faith Joseph, when he was dying, made mention of the exodus of the sons of Israel, and gave orders concerning his bones.

23 By faith Moses, when he was born, was hidden for three months by his parents, because they saw he was a beautiful child; and they were not afraid of the king's edict. 24 By faith Moses, when he had grown up, refused to be called the son of Pharaoh's daughter, 25 choosing rather to endure ill-treatment with the people of God than to enjoy the passing pleasures of sin, 26 considering the reproach of Christ greater riches than the treasures of Egypt; for he was looking to the reward. 27 By faith he left Egypt, not fearing the wrath of the king; for he endured, as seeing Him who is unseen. 28 By faith he kept the Passover and the sprinkling of the blood, so that he who destroyed the firstborn would not touch them. 29 By faith they passed through the Red Sea as though they were passing through dry land; and the Egyptians, when they attempted it, were drowned.

30 By faith the walls of Jericho fell down after they had been encircled for seven days. 31 By faith Rahab the harlot did not perish along with those who were disobedient, after she had welcomed the spies in peace.

32 And what more shall I say? For time will fail me if I tell of Gideon, Barak, Samson, Jephthah, of David and Samuel and the prophets, 33 who by faith conquered kingdoms, performed acts of righteousness, obtained promises, shut the mouths of lions, 34 quenched the power of fire, escaped the edge of the sword, from weakness were made strong, became mighty in war, put foreign armies to flight. 35 Women received back their dead by resurrection; and others were tortured, not accepting their release, so that they might obtain a better resurrection; 36 and others experienced mockings and scourgings, yes, also chains and imprisonment. 37 They were stoned, they were sawn in two, they were tempted, they were put to death with the sword; they went about in sheepskins, in goatskins, being destitute, afflicted, ill-treated 38 (men of whom the world was not worthy), wandering in deserts and mountains and caves and holes in the ground.

39 **And all these, having gained approval through their faith, did not receive what was promised,** 40 because God had provided something better for us, so that apart from us they would not be made perfect.

Jesus, the Example

12:1 Therefore, since **we have so great a cloud of witnesses surrounding us**, let us also lay aside every encumbrance and the sin

---

All these Bible characters had faith but they never saw the object of their faith fulfilled in their lifetime. The object of faith is yet to come.

When you

which so easily entangles us, and let us run with endurance the race that is set before us, 2 fixing our eyes on Jesus, the author and perfecter of faith, who for the joy set before Him endured the cross, despising the shame, and has sat down at the right hand of the throne of God.

3 For consider Him who has endured such hostility by sinners against Himself, so that you will not grow weary and lose heart.

A Father's Discipline

7 It is for discipline that you endure; God deals with you as with sons; for what son is there whom his father does not discipline? 8 But if you are without discipline, of which all have become partakers, then you are illegitimate children and not sons.

15 See to it that no one comes short of the grace of God; that no root of bitterness springing up causes trouble, and by it many be defiled.

The Changeless Christ

13:1 Let love of the brethren continue. 2 **Do not neglect to show hospitality to strangers, for by this some have entertained angels without knowing it.** 3 Remember the prisoners, as though in prison with them, and those who are ill-treated, since you yourselves also are in the body. 4 Marriage is to be held in honor among all, and the marriage bed is to be undefiled; for fornicators and adulterers God will judge. 5 Make sure that your character is free from the love of money, being content with what you have; for He Himself has said, "I will never desert you, nor will I ever forsake you," 6 so that we confidently say,

"The Lord is my helper, I will not be afraid. What will man do to me?

7 Remember those who led you, who spoke the word of God to you; and considering the result of their conduct, **imitate their faith**. 8 Jesus Christ is the same yesterday and today and forever.

God-pleasing Sacrifices

15 Through Him then, let us continually offer up a sacrifice of praise to God, that is, the fruit of lips that give thanks to His name. 16 And do not neglect doing good and sharing, for with such sacrifices God is pleased.

18 Pray for us, for we are sure that we have a good conscience, desiring to conduct ourselves honorably in all things. 19 And I urge you all the more to do this, so that I may be restored to you the sooner.

20 Now the God of peace, who brought up from the dead the great Shepherd of the sheep through the blood of the eternal covenant, even Jesus our Lord, 21 equip you in every good thing to do His will, working in us that which is pleasing in His sight, through Jesus Christ, to whom be the glory forever and ever. Amen.

---

feel alone, discouraged, like quitting, try to imagine the crowd of those who have gone before you cheering you on.

This is a sobering thought, isn't it?

What mentors and leaders do you have in your life?

the book of James

Category: The Letters
Author: James
Theme: Faith in action
Location & Date: Jerusalem; A.D. 44-49
Version of Bible: New Revised Standard Version (NRSV)
Summary: James, Jesus' brother and the leader of the Jerusalem church, wrote this letter to encourage and challenge his scattered flock and to assure them that Christianity makes a practical change in one's life.

James 1:1 James, a servant of God and of the Lord Jesus Christ, To the twelve tribes in the Dispersion: Greetings.

Faith and Wisdom

2 **My brothers and sisters, whenever you face trials of any kind, consider it nothing but joy, 3 because you know that the testing of your faith produces endurance; 4 and let endurance have its full effect, so that you may be mature and complete, lacking in nothing.**

5 If any of you is lacking in wisdom, ask God, who gives to all generously and ungrudgingly, and it will be given you. 6 But ask in faith, never doubting, for the one who doubts is like a wave of the sea, driven and tossed by the wind; 7, 8 for the doubter, being double-minded and unstable in every way, must not expect to receive anything from the Lord.

Trial and Temptation

12 Blessed is anyone who endures temptation. Such a one has stood the test and will receive the crown of life that the Lord has promised to those who love him.

Hearing and Doing the Word

19 You must understand this, my beloved: **let everyone be quick to listen, slow to speak, slow to anger**; 20 for your anger does not produce God's righteousness. 21 Therefore rid yourselves of all sordidness and rank growth of wickedness, and welcome with meekness the implanted word that has the power to save your souls.

22 But be doers of the word, and not merely hearers who deceive themselves. 23 For if any are hearers of the word and not doers, they are like those who look at themselves in a mirror; 24 for they look at themselves and, on going away, immediately forget what they were like. 25 But those who look into the perfect law,

---

When in have you grown the most in your life - good times or bad times?

You want to get along with people? Simple. Write this verse on a card and put it in your pocket for 21 days. See what happens.

the law of liberty, and persevere, being not hearers who forget but doers who act—they will be blessed in their doing.

Faith Without Works Is Dead

2:14 What good is it, my brothers and sisters, if you say you have faith but do not have works? Can faith save you? 15 If a brother or sister is naked and lacks daily food, 16 and one of you says to them, "Go in peace; keep warm and eat your fill," and yet you do not supply their bodily needs, what is the good of that? 17 So faith by itself, if it has no works, is dead.

18 But someone will say, "You have faith and I have works." Show me your faith apart from your works, and I by my works will show you my faith. 19 You believe that God is one; you do well. Even the demons believe—and shudder. 20 Do you want to be shown, you senseless person, that faith apart from works is barren?

Taming the Tongue

3:9 With it we bless the Lord and Father, and with it we curse those who are made in the likeness of God. 10 From the same **mouth** come blessing and cursing. My brothers and sisters, this ought not to be so.

Gossip, talking negatively about someone behind their back, is probably the most destructive of all human behaviors.

Friendship with the World

4:1 Those conflicts and disputes among you, where do they come from? 2 ... you covet something and cannot obtain it; so you engage in disputes and conflicts. You do not have, because you do not ask. 3 You ask and do not receive, because you ask wrongly, in order to spend what you get on your pleasures.

Boasting about Tomorrow

13 Come now, you who say, "Today or tomorrow we will go to such and such a town and spend a year there, doing business and making money." 14 Yet you do not even know what tomorrow will bring. **What is your life?** For you are a mist that appears for a little while and then vanishes. 15 Instead you ought to say, "If the Lord wishes, we will live and do this or that."

A good question to contemplate.

The Prayer of Faith

5:13 Are any among you suffering? They should pray. Are any cheerful? They should sing songs of praise. 14 Are any among you sick? They should call for the elders of the church and have them pray over them, anointing them with oil in the name of the Lord. 15 The prayer of faith will save the sick, and the Lord will raise them up; and anyone who has committed sins will be forgiven. 16 Therefore confess your sins to one another, and pray for one another, so that you may be healed. **The prayer of the righteous is powerful and effective.**

Prayer connects us to each other and God - who is the most powerful force in the universe.

the books of 1 & 2 Peter

Category: *The Letters*
Author: *Peter*
Theme: *Christian, hang in there*
Location & Date: *A prison in Rome; A.D. 64-65*
Version of Bible: *Easy-to-Read Version (ERV)*
Summary: Peter wrote these letters to all the churches in Asia Minor who were facing persecution for their faith. This was around the time when Emperor Nero burned Rome to the ground and then blamed it on Christians. Peter encouraged church members to live an obedient lifestyle as a witness to the hostile environment around them.

1 Peter 1:1 Greetings from Peter, an apostle of Jesus Christ To God's chosen people who are away from their homes—people scattered all over the areas of Pontus, Galatia, Cappadocia, Asia, and Bithynia. 2 God planned long ago to choose you and to make you his holy people, which is the Spirit's work. God wanted you to obey him and to be made clean by the blood sacrifice of Jesus Christ. I pray that you will enjoy more and more of God's grace and peace.

A Living Hope

3 Praise be to the God and Father of our Lord Jesus Christ. God has great mercy, and because of his mercy he gave us a new life. **This new life brings us a living hope through Jesus Christ's resurrection from death.** 4 Now we wait to receive the blessings God has for his children. These blessings are kept for you in heaven. They cannot be ruined or be destroyed or lose their beauty.

5 God's power protects you through your faith, and it keeps you safe until your salvation comes. That salvation is ready to be given to you at the end of time. 6 I know the thought of that is exciting, even if you must suffer through different kinds of troubles for a short time now. 7 These troubles test your faith and prove that it is pure. And such faith is worth more than gold. Gold can be proved to be pure by fire, but gold will ruin. When your faith is proven to be pure, the result will be praise and glory and honor when Jesus Christ comes.

8 You have not seen Christ, but still you love him. You can't see him now, but you believe in him. You are filled with a wonderful and heavenly joy that cannot be explained. 9 Your faith has a goal, and you are reaching that goal—your salvation.

The resurrection of Jesus gives us hope of our own resurrection.

The Living Stone and the Holy Nation

2:1 So then, stop doing anything to hurt others. Don't lie anymore, and stop trying to fool people. Don't be jealous or say bad things about others. 2 Like newborn babies hungry for milk, you should want the pure teaching that feeds your spirit. With it you can grow up and be saved. 3 You have already tasted the goodness of the Lord.

4 The Lord Jesus is the living stone. The people of the world decided that they did not want this stone. But he is the one God chose as one of great value. So come to him. 5 You also are like living stones, and God is using you to build a spiritual house. You are to serve God in this house as holy priests, offering him spiritual sacrifices that he will accept because of Jesus Christ. 6 The Scriptures say,

"Look, I have chosen a cornerstone of great value, and I put that stone in Zion. Anyone who trusts in him will never be disappointed."

[Isaiah 28:16.]

7 So, that stone brings honor for you who believe. But for those who don't believe he is "the stone that the builders refused to accept, which became the most important stone." 8 For them he is also "a stone that makes people stumble, a rock that makes people fall."

People stumble because they don't obey what God says. This is what God planned to happen to those people.

9 But you are his chosen people, the King's priests. You are a holy nation, people who belong to God. He chose you to tell about the wonderful things he has done. He brought you out of the darkness of sin into his wonderful light.

10 In the past you were not a special people, but now you are God's people. Once you had not received mercy, but now God has given you his mercy.

Suffering for Doing Right

3:8 So all of you should live together in peace. Try to understand each other. Love each other like brothers and sisters. Be kind and humble. 9 Don't do wrong to anyone to pay them back for doing wrong to you. Or don't insult anyone to pay them back for insulting you. But ask God to bless them. Do this because you yourselves were chosen to receive a blessing. 10 The Scriptures say,

"If you want to enjoy true life and have only good days, then avoid saying anything hurtful, and never let a lie come out of your mouth. 11 Stop doing what is wrong, and do good. Look for peace, and do all you can to help people live peacefully. 12 The Lord watches over those who do what is right, and he listens to their prayers. But he is against those who do evil."

13 If you are always trying to do good, no one can really harm you. 14 But you may suffer for doing right. If that happens, you have God's blessing. "Don't be afraid of the people who make you suffer; don't be worried." 15 But keep the Lord Christ holy

[Notice it says "if you want to enjoy life." Your own happiness depends, in part, on not being negative to others.]

The Christian faith something a person joins of their own free will. You don't have to sell it. All you need to do is share why Christianity works for you and leave people to their own decision.

in your hearts. **Always be ready to answer everyone who asks you to explain about the hope you have. 16 But answer them in a gentle way with respect.** Keep your conscience clear. Then people will see the good way you live as followers of Christ, and those who say bad things about you will be ashamed of what they said.

Suffering as a Follower of Christ

4:12 My friends, don't be surprised at the painful things that you are now suffering, which are testing your faith. Don't think that something strange is happening to you. 13 But you should be happy that you are sharing in Christ's sufferings. You will be happy and full of joy when Christ shows his glory. 14 When people say bad things to you because you follow Christ, consider it a blessing. When that happens, it shows that God's Spirit, the Spirit of glory, is with you.

The Flock of God

5:1 Now I have something to say to the elders in your group. I am also an elder. I myself have seen Christ's sufferings. And I will share in the glory that will be shown to us. I beg you to 2 take care of the group of people you are responsible for. They are God's flock. Watch over that flock because you want to, not because you are forced to do it. That is how God wants it. Do it because you are happy to serve, not because you want money. 3 Don't be like a ruler over those you are responsible for. But be good examples to them. 4 Then when Christ the Ruling Shepherd comes, you will get a crown—one that will be glorious and never lose its beauty.

5 Young people, I have something to say to you too. You should accept the authority of the elders. You should all have a humble attitude in dealing with each other.

"God is against the proud, but he is kind to the humble."

What worries are dragging you down lately?

6 So be humble under God's powerful hand. Then he will lift you up when the right time comes. **7 Give all your worries to him, because he cares for you.**

8 Control yourselves and be careful! The devil is your enemy, and he goes around like a roaring lion looking for someone to attack and eat. 9 Refuse to follow the devil. Stand strong in your faith. You know that your brothers and sisters all over the world are having the same sufferings that you have.

10 Yes, you will suffer for a short time. But after that, God will make everything right. He will make you strong. He will support you and keep you from falling. He is the God who gives all grace. He chose you to share in his glory in Christ. That glory will continue forever. 11 All power is his forever. Amen.

God Has Given Us Everything We Need

2 Peter 1:3 Jesus has the power of God. And his power has given us everything we need to live a life devoted to God. We have these things because we know him. Jesus chose us by his glory and goodness, 4 through which he also gave us the very great

and rich gifts that he promised us. With these gifts you can share in being like God. And so you will escape the ruin that comes to people in the world because of the evil things they want.

5 Because you have these blessings, do all you can to add to your life these things: to your faith add goodness; to your goodness add knowledge; 6 to your knowledge add self-control; to your self-control add patience; to your patience add devotion to God; 7 to your devotion add kindness toward your brothers and sisters in Christ, and to this kindness add love. 8 If all these things are in you and growing, you will never fail to be useful to God. You will produce the kind of fruit that should come from your knowledge of our Lord Jesus Christ. 9 But those who don't grow in these blessings are blind. They cannot see clearly what they have. They have forgotten that they were cleansed from their past sins.

10 My brothers and sisters, God called you and chose you to be his. Do your best to live in a way that shows you really are God's called and chosen people. If you do all this, you will never fall. 11 And you will be given a very great welcome into the kingdom of our Lord and Savior Jesus Christ, a kingdom that never ends.

Jesus Will Come Again

3:1 My friends, this is the second letter I have written to you. I wrote both letters to you to help your honest minds remember something.

3 It is important for you to understand what will happen in the last days. People will laugh at you. They will live following the evil they want to do. 4 They will say, "Jesus promised to come again. Where is he? Our fathers have died, but the world continues the way it has been since it was made."

8 But don't forget this one thing, dear friends: To the Lord a day is like a thousand years, and a thousand years is like a day. 9 The Lord is not being slow in doing what he promised—the way some people understand slowness. But **God is being patient with you. He doesn't want anyone to be lost.** He wants everyone to change their ways and stop sinning.

10 But the day when the Lord comes again will surprise everyone like the coming of a thief. The sky will disappear with a loud noise. Everything in the sky will be destroyed with fire. And the earth and everything in it will be burned up.

14 Dear friends, we are waiting for this to happen. So try as hard as you can to be without sin and without fault. Try to be at peace with God.

18 But grow in the grace and knowledge of our Lord and Savior Jesus Christ. Glory be to him, now and forever! Amen.

Jesus' second coming is only delayed because there are people God still wants reached with His love.

the books of 1, 2 & 3 John

Category: *The Letters*
Author: *John*
Theme: *Love, God, and the Church*
Location & Date: *Ephesus; A.D. 90*
Version of Bible: *New Living Translation (NLT)*

Summary: *At the time John wrote these letters, he was the only one of the 12 disciples that was still alive. He had walked with Jesus, heard His words firsthand, and witnessed His miracles. Now John wanted to encourage all the churches to love each other with the love that he had experienced from Jesus Himself.*

> John is talking about Jesus.

1 John 1:1 We proclaim to you **the one who existed from the beginning**, whom we have heard and seen. We saw him with our own eyes and touched him with our own hands. He is the Word of life. 2 This one who is life itself was revealed to us, and we have seen him. And now we testify and proclaim to you that he is the one who is eternal life. He was with the Father, and then he was revealed to us. 3 We proclaim to you what we ourselves have actually seen and heard so that you may have fellowship with us. And our fellowship is with the Father and with his Son, Jesus Christ. 4 We are writing these things so that you may fully share our joy.

Living in the Light

5 This is the message we heard from Jesus and now declare to you: God is light, and there is no darkness in him at all. 6 So we are lying if we say we have fellowship with God but go on living in spiritual darkness; we are not practicing the truth. 7 But if we are living in the light, as God is in the light, then we have fellowship with each other, and the blood of Jesus, his Son, cleanses us from all sin.

8 If we claim we have no sin, we are only fooling ourselves and not living in the truth. 9 But if we confess our sins to him, he is faithful and just to forgive us our sins and to cleanse us from all wickedness. 10 If we claim we have not sinned, we are calling God a liar and showing that his word has no place in our hearts.

> The word "atone" means to "pay for."

2:1 My dear children, I am writing this to you so that you will not sin. But if anyone does sin, we have an advocate who pleads our case before the Father. He is Jesus Christ, the one who is truly righteous. 2 He himself is the sacrifice that **atones** for our sins— and not only our sins but the sins of all the world.

A New Commandment

9 If anyone claims, "I am living in the light," but hates a Christian brother or sister, that person is still living in darkness. 10 Anyone who loves another brother or sister is living in the light and does not cause others to stumble. 11 But anyone who hates another brother or sister is still living and walking in darkness. Such a person does not know the way to go, having been blinded by the darkness.

3:1 See how very much our Father loves us, for he calls us his children, and that is what we are! But the people who belong to this world don't recognize that we are God's children because they don't know him.

Love One Another

11 This is the message you have heard from the beginning: **We should love one another.**

16 We know what real love is because Jesus gave up his life for us. So we also ought to give up our lives for our brothers and sisters. 17 If someone has enough money to live well and sees a brother or sister in need but shows no compassion—how can God's love be in that person?

18 **Dear children, let's not merely say that we love each other; let us show the truth by our actions.**

The Christian message seems simple enough.

Words vs. action.

Loving One Another

4:7 Dear friends, let us continue to love one another, for love comes from God. Anyone who loves is a child of God and knows God. 8 But anyone who does not love does not know God, for God is love.

9 God showed how much he loved us by sending his one and only Son into the world so that we might have eternal life through him. 10 **This is real love—not that we loved God, but that he loved us and sent his Son as a sacrifice to take away our sins.**

11 Dear friends, since God loved us that much, we surely ought to love each other. 12 No one has ever seen God. But if we love each other, God lives in us, and his love is brought to full expression in us.

13 And God has given us his Spirit as proof that we live in him and he in us.

5:13 I have written this to you who believe in the name of the Son of God, so that you may know you have eternal life.

God's love for us empowers us to love others.

Live in the Truth

2 John 1:4 How happy I was to meet some of your children and find them living according to the truth, just as the Father commanded.

5 I am writing to remind you, dear friends, that we should love one another. This is not a new commandment, but one we have

had from the beginning. 6 Love means doing what God has commanded us, and he has commanded us to love one another, just as you heard from the beginning.

Greetings

3 John 1:1 This letter is from John, the elder. I am writing to Gaius, my dear friend, whom I love in the truth.

2 Dear friend, I hope all is well with you and that you are as healthy in body as you are strong in spirit. 3 Some of the traveling teachers recently returned and made me very happy by telling me about your faithfulness and that you are living according to the truth. 4 I could have no greater joy than to hear that my children are following the truth.

Caring for the Lord's Workers

5 Dear friend, you are being faithful to God when you care for the traveling teachers who pass through, even though they are strangers to you. 6 They have told the church here of your loving friendship. Please continue providing for such teachers in a manner that pleases God. 7 For they are traveling for the Lord, and they accept nothing from people who are not believers. 8 So we ourselves should support them so that we can be their partners as they teach the truth.

9 I wrote to the church about this, but Diotrephes, who loves to be the leader, refuses to have anything to do with us. 10 When I come, I will report some of the things he is doing and the evil accusations he is making against us. Not only does he refuse to welcome the traveling teachers, he also tells others not to help them. And when they do help, he puts them out of the church.

11 Dear friend, don't let this bad example influence you. Follow only what is good. Remember that those who do good prove that they are God's children, and those who do evil prove that they do not know God.

12 Everyone speaks highly of Demetrius, as does the truth itself. We ourselves can say the same for him, and you know we speak the truth.

Conclusion

13 I have much more to say to you, but I don't want to write it with pen and ink. 14 For I hope to see you soon, and then we will talk face to face.

the book of Jude

Category: The Letters
Author: Jude
Theme: Hanging in there together
Location & Date: Jerusalem; A.D. 68-69
Version of Bible: New Living Translation (NLT)
Summary: Jude was a brother to Jesus. He wrote this letter to warn the believers to guard against those in the church who were causing divisions.

Jude 1:1 This letter is from Jude, a slave of Jesus Christ and a brother of James. I am writing to all who have been called by God the Father, who loves you and keeps you safe in the care of Jesus Christ. 2 May God give you more and more mercy, peace, and love.

A Call to Remain Faithful

17 But you, my dear friends, must remember what the apostles of our Lord Jesus Christ said. 18 They told you that in the last times there would be scoffers whose purpose in life is to satisfy their ungodly desires. 19 These people are the ones who are creating divisions among you. They follow their natural instincts because they do not have God's Spirit in them.

20 But you, dear friends, must build each other up in your most holy faith, pray in the power of the Holy Spirit, 21 and await the mercy of our Lord Jesus Christ, who will bring you eternal life. In this way, you will keep yourselves safe in God's love.

22 And you must show mercy to those whose faith is wavering. 23 Rescue others by snatching them from the flames of judgment. Show mercy to still others, but do so with great caution, hating the sins that contaminate their lives.

A Prayer of Praise

24 **Now all glory to God, who is able to keep you from falling away and will bring you with great joy into his glorious presence without a single fault. 25 All glory to him who alone is God, our Savior through Jesus Christ our Lord. All glory, majesty, power, and authority are his before all time, and in the present, and beyond all time! Amen.**

If you are not sure what words you might use to give God praise, just pray these words.

the book of Revelation

Category: *The Book of Revelation*
Author: *John*
Theme: *Jesus, the past, the present, and the future*
Location & Date: *Island of Patmos; A.D. 94-96*
Version of Bible: *Expanded Bible (EXB)*
Summary: *John, the last remaining disciple of the 12, was banished to the island of Patmos (off the coast near Ephesus in the Mediterranean Sea) where he received a vision from God about the present and the future. Jesus revealed himself to John as a shepherd who cares for His sheep, as a righteous judge who will punish the wicked, and a victorious king who will establish His kingdom forever.*

John Tells About This Book

Revelation 1:1 This is the revelation of Jesus Christ [about Jesus Christ; or given by Jesus Christ; the author could be intentionally ambiguous], which God gave to him, to show his servants what must soon [quickly] happen. And Jesus sent his angel to show it [make it known] to his servant John, 2 who has told [witnessed; testified to] everything he has seen. It is the word of God; it is the message [witness; testimony] from Jesus Christ. 3 Blessed [Happy] is the one who reads the words of God's message [the prophecy], and blessed [happy] are the people who hear this message and do [keep; obey] what is written in it [the context envisioned is a leader reading to a congregation]. The time is near when all of this will happen [For the time is near].

Jesus' Message to the Churches

You can still visit the ruins of these churches today.

4 From John. **To the seven churches in Asia** [the Roman province of Asia, today part of western Turkey]:

Grace and peace to you from the One who is and [the One who] was and [the One who] is coming [these three descriptions function like titles for God; Ex. 3:14-15], and from the seven spirits [referring either to angels or to the "sevenfold Spirit"—the Holy Spirit portrayed in his perfection (the number seven indicating completeness)] before his throne, 5 and from Jesus Christ. Jesus is the faithful witness [or the faithful one, the witness], the first among those raised from [firstborn of/from among] the dead. He is the ruler of the kings of the earth.

He is the One [To him] who loves us, who made us free from our sins with the blood of his death [by his blood]. 6 He made us to be a kingdom of priests [or kingdom and priests; or kingdom, that is, priests; Ex. 19:6] who serve God his Father [his God and Father]. To Jesus Christ [him] be glory and power [dominion] forever and ever! Amen.

7 Look [Behold], Jesus is coming with the clouds [Dan. 7:13–14], and everyone [every eye] will see him, even those who stabbed [pierced] him [a reference to the crucifixion; Zech. 12:10]. And all peoples [people groups; tribes] of the earth will cry loudly [wail; mourn] because of him. Yes, this will happen [So it shall be; Yes]! Amen.

8 The Lord God says, "I am the **Alpha and the Omega** [the first and last letters of the Greek alphabet; 21:6; 22:13]. I am the One who is and [the One who] was and [the One who] is coming [see 1:4]. I am the Almighty [All-powerful]."

9 I, John, am your brother. All of us share [your brother and partner] with Jesus [or in Jesus; referring to salvation as joining oneself to Christ] in suffering [persecution], in the kingdom, and in patience to continue [perseverance]. I was on the island of **Patmos** [a small island in the Aegean Sea near Asia Minor, present-day Turkey], because I had preached [of] the word of God and the message [witness; testimony] about Jesus. 10 On the Lord's day [probably a reference to the first day of the week, Sunday, when Christians met for worship] I was in the Spirit [or spirit; a state of deep spiritual communion with God], and I heard a loud voice behind me that sounded like a trumpet [trumpet blasts often precede a divine appearance or speech; Ex. 19:16, 19]. 11 The voice said, "Write what you see in a book [scroll] and send it to the seven churches: to Ephesus, Smyrna, Pergamum, Thyatira, Sardis, Philadelphia, and Laodicea [locations in western Asia Minor, present-day Turkey]."

{John then wrote encouragement, challenges, and warnings to these churches. Below is a sample of what he wrote to the last Church—Laodicea.}

To the Church in Laodicea

3:14 "Write this to the angel [or messenger; see 1:20] of the church in Laodicea [a city in Phrygia, a mountainous province of western Asia]:

"The Amen [Hebrew for "so be it"; here referring to Jesus], the faithful and true witness, the ruler of all God has made [1:5; Prov. 8:30–31; the resurrected Jesus], says this [these things]: 15 I know what you do [your works], that you are not hot or cold. I wish that you were hot or cold [both positive images, alluding to cold refreshing mountain streams and healing hot springs near Laodicea]! 16 But because you are lukewarm—**neither hot, nor cold**—I am ready to spit [vomit] you out of my mouth. 17 [For] You say, 'I am rich, and I have become wealthy and do not need anything.' But you do not know that you are really miserable [wretched], pitiful, poor, blind, and naked. 18 I advise you to buy from me gold made pure in [refined by] fire so you can be truly rich. Buy from me white clothes [indicating purity] so you can be clothed and so you can

---

Alpha is the first letter and Omega is the last letter of the Greek alphabet.

You can still visit this island today.

Maybe your life - family, work, relationship to God, marriage - is not great but it is not bad either. Lukewarm is not a good place to be.

The Book of Revelation

cover your shameful nakedness. Buy from me medicine [salve; ointment] to put on your eyes so you can truly see.

19 "I correct [rebuke] and punish [discipline] those whom I love. So be eager to do right [zealous; earnest], and change your hearts and lives [repent]. 20 Here I am [Look; Behold]! I stand at the door and knock. If you [anyone] hear my voice and open the door, I will come in and eat with you, and you will eat with me.

> The Greek word here is "nike" just like the sports company. So when you see the "swoosh" logo think of the ultimate victory that Jesus has won for us.

21 "Those who win the **victory** [overcome; conquer] will sit with me on my throne in the same way that I won the victory [overcame; conquered; over death, by his resurrection] and sat down with my Father on his throne. 22 Everyone who has ears should listen to [hear; obey] what the Spirit says to the churches."

{The rest of the book is about the end times.}

John Sees Heaven

4:1 After the vision of these things I looked, and [look; behold] there before me was an open door in heaven. And the same [first] voice that spoke to me before, that sounded like a trumpet [1:8], said, "Come up here, and I will show you what must happen after this."

9 [Whenever] These living creatures give glory, honor, and thanks to the One who sits on the throne, who lives forever and ever. 10 Then the twenty-four elders bow down before the One who sits on the throne, and they worship him who lives forever and ever. They put their crowns down [cast/lay their crowns; 4:4] before the throne and say:

11 "You are worthy, our Lord and God, to receive glory and honor and power [strength], because you made all things. Everything existed and was made, because you wanted it [by your will]."

{John's vision of the future took him to a pivotal moment in the past—the birth of Jesus—the story behind the story.}

The Woman and the Dragon

> This story is an expanded version of what we read in Genesis (See Genesis 3:15, pg. 12). The woman represents Eve and then ultimately Mary (the mother of Jesus). The red dragon is the Devil. His goal was and

12:1 And then a great wonder [sign; portent; symbolic descriptions of heavenly/spiritual realities] appeared in heaven: A woman was clothed with the sun, and the moon was under her feet [indicating authority or victory; Gen. 37:9], and a crown [a reward of victory] of twelve stars was on her head [representing the twelve tribes of Israel; the woman is a symbol of the persecuted people of God]. 2 She was pregnant [in the womb] and cried out with [labor] pain, because she was about to give birth [to the Messiah]. 3 Then another wonder [sign; portent; 12:1] appeared in heaven: There was a giant red dragon with seven heads [reminiscent of the many-headed Leviathan representing evil and chaos, here representing Satan; Ps. 74:14; Is. 27:1; Dan. 7:1–9] and seven crowns [diadems; royal crowns] on each head. He [or It; the Greek masculine pronoun can refer to a person or thing] also had ten horns [symbols of strength and power; Dan. 7:7–8, 20, 24]. 4 His tail swept a third of the stars out of the sky [or heaven] and threw [cast; hurled; Dan. 8:10] them down to the earth [representing an early victory against God's people; 12:1]. He stood in front of the woman who was ready to give birth so he could eat [devour] her baby [child; Jesus the Messiah] as soon as it was born. 5 Then the woman gave birth to a son [a son, a male child,] who will rule [or shepherd] all the nations with an iron rod [sceptre; 19:15; Ps. 2:9]. And her child was taken up [or snatched away; probably a symbolic reference to the resurrection, where Satan's victory was thwarted] to God and to his throne. 6 The woman ran away [fled] into the desert [wilderness] to a place God prepared for her where she would be taken care of [nourished; fed] for one thousand two hundred sixty days [equal to three and one-half years; see 11:3].

{John described a time before the creation the book of Genesis—a prequel to Genesis.}

7 **Then there was a war in heaven.** Michael [an archangel and protector of God's people; Dan. 10:13, 21; 12:1; Jude 9] and his angels fought against the dragon, and the dragon and his angels fought back. 8 But the dragon was not strong enough, and he and his angels lost their place in heaven. 9 The giant [great] dragon was thrown down [cast; hurled] out of heaven. (He is that old snake [ancient serpent] called the devil or Satan [Gen. 3:1, 15], who tricks [deceives; leads astray] the whole world.) The dragon with his angels was thrown down [cast; hurled] to the earth.

10 Then I heard a loud voice in heaven saying:

"The salvation and the power and the kingdom of our God and the authority [power] of his Christ [Messiah; Anointed One] have now come [Dan. 7:14].

[For] The accuser [the name Satan means "Accuser" in Hebrew; Job 1:6–12; 2:1–6; Zech. 3:1–2] of our brothers and sisters, who accused them day and night before our God, has been thrown [cast; hurled] down.

11 And our brothers and sisters defeated [conquered] him by the blood of the Lamb's death [Lamb; by means of Christ's sacrificial death] and by the message they preached [word of their witness/testimony].

[And] **They did not love their lives so much that they were afraid of [avoided] death.**

12 So rejoice, you heavens and all who live there! But it will be terrible for [woe to] the earth and the sea, because the devil has come down to you! He is filled with anger [wrath], because he knows he does not have much time [has little time]."

13 When the dragon saw he had been thrown [cast; hurled] down to the earth, he hunted for [pursued; or persecuted] the woman who had given birth to the son [boy; male]. 14 But the woman was given the two wings of a great eagle [or vulture; Ex. 19:4; Deut. 32:10-11; Is. 40:31] so she could fly to the place prepared for her in the desert [wilderness]. There she would be taken care of [nourished; fed] for three and one-half years [a time, times, and half a time; 11:2, 3; 13:5; Dan. 7:25; 12:7], away from the snake [serpent; God will spiritually nourish his people though they

---

is to stop God's plan of salvation through Jesus.

This helps explains where the Devil came from originally before he shows up in Genesis 3 to tempt Adam and Eve into sin.

John is honoring the Christians that were put to death because of their faith in Jesus.

are persecuted]. 15 Then the snake [serpent] poured [spewed; threw] water out of its mouth like a river toward [after] the woman so the flood would carry [sweep] her away [overwhelming water signifies overwhelming trouble; Ps. 18:4; 69:2]. 16 But the earth helped [rescued] the woman by opening its mouth and swallowing the river that came [spewed; was thrown] from the mouth of the dragon. 17 **Then the dragon was very angry [furious; full of wrath] at the woman, and he went off to make war against all her other children** [the rest of her seed/offspring]—those who obey God's commands and who have the message Jesus taught [or hold fast to their testimony about Jesus].

{There was victory over the dragon, the beast, the one called Satan.}

> This is the battle that we human beings have been fighting throughout all human history.

The Rider on the White Horse

19:11 Then I saw heaven opened, and there before me was a white horse. **The rider [Jesus] on the horse is called Faithful and True, and he is right when [with justice/righteousness] he judges and makes war** [Ps. 96:13; 98:9]. 12 His eyes are like burning [blazing; flames of] fire [Dan. 10:6], and on his head are many crowns [diadems; royal crowns; contrast 12:3; 13:1]. He has a name written on him, which no one but himself knows. 13 He is dressed in a robe [garment] dipped in blood [indicating judgment; Is. 63:1-3], and his name is the Word of God [John 1:1]. 14 The armies of heaven, dressed in fine linen, white and clean [pure], were following him on white horses. 15 Out of the rider's mouth comes a sharp sword [1:16] that he will use to defeat [strike down] the nations [Is. 11:4], and he will rule [or shepherd] them with a rod [staff; scepter] of iron [Ps. 2:9]. He will crush out [tread; stomp] the wine in the winepress of the terrible anger [furious wrath] of God the Almighty [All-powerful; 19:13; Is. 63:1–6]. 16 On his robe and on his upper leg was written this name: KING OF KINGS AND LORD OF LORDS [17:14; Deut. 10:17; Dan. 2:47].

> Most people view Jesus as a kind, loving, forgiving, encouraging friend. Jesus is all of that. But he is also a judge, a king, a Lord, and one not afraid to use the sword.

The Thousand Years

20:1 I saw an angel coming down from heaven. He had the key to the bottomless pit [Abyss; 9:1] and a large [great] chain in his hand. 2 The angel grabbed [seized] the dragon, that old snake [ancient serpent] who is the devil and Satan [12:9; Gen. 3:15], and tied him up [bound him; Mark 3:27] **for a thousand years.** 3 Then he threw him into the bottomless pit [Abyss], closed [or locked] it, and locked it [sealed it; or placed a seal on it] over him. The angel did this so he could not trick [deceive; lead astray] the people of the earth [nations] anymore until the thousand years were ended [finished; completed]. After a thousand years [these things] he must be set free for a short time.

7 When the thousand years are over, Satan will be set free from his prison. 8 Then he will go out to trick [deceive; lead astray] the nations in all [the four corners of] the earth—Gog and Magog—to gather them for battle [Ezek. 38-39]. There are so many people [In number] they will be like sand on the seashore [or the sand of the sea]. 9 And Satan's army [they] marched across [the breadth of;

> Some think we are living in the 1,000 years now. Some believe it will begin when Jesus comes back again. And others think it will just happen at some point before Jesus comes back. What do you think?

or the broad plain of] the earth and gathered around [surrounded] the camp of God's people [the saints] and the city God loves. But fire came down from heaven and burned them up [consumed/devoured them; 13:13; 1 Kin. 18:38; 2 Kin. 1:10, 12]. 10 And Satan [the Devil], who tricked them [deceived them; led them astray], was thrown into the lake of burning sulfur [fire and sulfur] with the beast and the false prophet. There they will be punished [tormented; tortured] day and night forever and ever.

People of the World Are Judged

11 Then I saw a great white throne and the One who was sitting on it. Earth and sky [heaven] ran away [fled] from him [his presence/face] and disappeared [no place was found for them]. 12 And I saw the dead, great and small, standing before the throne. Then books [scrolls] were opened, and [another book/scroll, which is] the book [scroll] of life was opened [3:5; Dan. 12:1–2]. The dead were judged by what they had done, which was written [recorded] in the books [scrolls]. 13 The sea gave up the dead who were in it, and Death and Hades [the realm of the dead, also known as Sheol; 6:8] gave up the dead who were in them. Each person was judged by what he had done. 14 And Death and Hades were thrown into the lake of fire. The lake of fire is the second death. 15 **And anyone whose name was not found written in the book [scroll] of life was thrown into the lake of fire.**

The New Jerusalem

21:1 Then I saw a new heaven and a new earth [Is. 65:17; 66:22; 2 Pet. 3:13]. [For] The first heaven and the first earth had disappeared [passed away], and there was no sea anymore [the sea represents chaos and evil, so its absence indicates peace and security]. 2 And I saw the holy city, the new Jerusalem [the believers' eternal dwelling place; 3:12], coming down out of heaven from God. It was prepared like a bride dressed [adorned] for her husband [19:7, 9]. 3 And I heard a loud voice from the throne, saying, "[Look; Behold] Now God's presence [dwelling; tabernacle] is with people, and he will live [dwell; tabernacle; John 1:14] with them, and they will be his people [Ex. 29:45; Jer. 31:33; Ezek. 37:27]. God himself will be with them and will be their God. 4 **He will wipe away every tear from their eyes [7:17; Is. 25:8], and there will be no more death [Is. 25:8; 1 Cor. 15:54], sadness [mourning], crying, or pain, because all the old ways [the old order; the first things] are gone.**"

5 The One who was sitting on the throne [Jesus] said, "Look! I am making everything new!" Then he said, "Write this, because these words are true and can be trusted [faithful/reliable and true]."

6 The One on the throne said to me, "It is finished [done; accomplished]. I am the Alpha and the Omega [the first and last letters of the Greek alphabet; 1:8], the Beginning and the End. I will give free water [freely] from the spring of the water of life to anyone who is thirsty [Is. 55:1; John 7:37]. 7 Those who win the **victory** [conquer] will receive [inherit] this [these things; God's promise], and I will be their God, and they will be my children [21:3; 2 Sam. 7:14].

If you become a Christian and Christianity turns out to be false, what do you lose? Nothing! If you become a Christian and Christianity turns out to be true, what do you gain? Everything!

So many tears in life. So much sadness and pain. All of it will be gone. All will be made new.

"Nike"

The Book of Revelation

We first heard of the tree of life at the very beginning of the Bible. Because of sin, we human beings were banned from it. But now it brings us life.

22:1 Then the angel showed me the river of the water of life [or living water]. It was shining [bright; clear] like crystal and was flowing from the throne of God and of the Lamb 2 down the middle of the street [main street; square] of the city [Gen. 2:10; Ezek. 47:1-12]. **The tree of life** was on each side of the river [Gen. 2:9; heaven is like Eden, only better]. It produces fruit twelve times a year, once each month [or twelve kinds of fruit, producing fruit each month]. The leaves of the tree are for the healing of all the nations. 3 Nothing that God judges guilty will be in that city [Nothing accursed will be there; or There will no longer be any curse; Gen. 3:16-19; Zech. 14:11]. The throne of God and of the Lamb will be there, and God's servants will worship [serve] him. 4 They will see his face, and his name will be written on their foreheads [denoting ownership; 3:12; 7:3; contrast 13:16; Ex. 28:36-38]. 5 There will never be night again. They will not need the light of a lamp or the light of the sun, because the Lord God will give them light. And they will rule as kings [reign] forever and ever.